14.99

C

RICHARD BUCKLE founded the magazine *Ballet* in 1939, and edited it, with a six-year gap during World War II, until 1953. From 1948 to 1955 he was ballet critic of the *Observer* and from 1959 to 1975 of the *Sunday Times*. His new and imaginative methods of display for the exhibition 'Diaghilev' (Edinburgh Festival and London, 1954–5) led to commissions to design twenty more. These included 'Epstein' (Edinburgh, 1971), 'Shakespeare' (Stratford-upon-Avon, 1964), a Theme Pavilion for Expo '67, Montreal and 'Cecil Beaton Portraits' (National Portrait Gallery, 1968).

Richard Buckle's cataloguing of the Diaghilev scenery and wardrobe, which had been many years in storage and were to be sold by Sotheby's, led indirectly to the amalgamation of several collections which became the Theatre Museum, a department of the Victoria and Albert Museum, opened in the former flower market of Covent Garden in 1987.

Diaghilev

RICHARD BUCKLE

WEIDENFELD · LONDON

First published in Weidenfeld paperback in 1993
by Weidenfeld & Nicolson,
a division of the Orion Publishing Group,
Orion House, 5 Upper St Martin's Lane,
London WC2H 9EA

Copyright © 1979 by Richard Buckle

A catalogue record for this book is
available from the British Library.

ISBN 0 297 81377 3

Printed in Great Britain by
Butler & Tanner Ltd,
Frome and London

·

To John Taras,
first and dearest
of my American friends

Contents

CONTENTS

Illustrations

Acknowledgements

THREE PEOPLE in particular have made this book possible: Boris Kochno, Parmenia Ekstrom and John Taras. The way in which they helped will be told below.

The idea for the book was Lord Weidenfeld's: on 24 September 1975 he rushed at me during a party in the Crush Bar at the Royal Opera House (where Diaghilev had given his last party on 15 July 1929) and asked me to write another book for him. The subject of Diaghilev was proposed when he and John Curtis lunched with me on 3 November; on the eighth, in Paris, I met Boris Kochno at an exhibition of Jean Hugo's theatre designs and got his blessing on the projected book; and George Weidenfeld and I came to an agreement on the telephone on 18 November. It was Mr Curtis who steered me with kindness and imagination through the checkered campaign of the book's progress, which was not unopposed. It must be said, however, that Nigel Gosling had for years, on and off, been urging me to undertake the long-dreaded task of writing Diaghilev's life; and a letter from Lincoln Kirstein proposing that I should do this crossed with my letter to him announcing that I had begun.

M. Kochno could be counted on, along with Diaghilev's other surviving collaborators in the 1920s, some of whom were my friends, to help with the final period. I had already covered the years 1909–14 in some detail in my *Nijinsky*. (This was a mixed blessing.) With the years of war and those just after, Leonide Massine had helped me before and would help me again. When Lifar wrote his life of Diaghilev (published in 1940), he had the help of Diaghilev's cousin Pavel Georgievitch Koribut-Kubitovitch, and of other relations who supplied information about Diaghilev's early years. Likewise, Haskell, in his biography (1935), had enjoyed the collaboration of Walter Nuvel, who, with a gap during the war years, was close to Diaghilev from 1890 till 1929. Of course, I drew on their valuable information.

ACKNOWLEDGEMENTS

I set about studying Diaghilev's magazine *Mir Iskusstva, The World of Art*, which he edited from 1899 to 1904. As I knew no Russian, I was fortunate in being able to enlist the help of Olive Stevens, to whom I had been introduced by letter by Joan Lawson a few years before. Travelling up and down from Devonshire, Mrs Stevens worked in the Reading Room of the Victoria and Albert Museum, analysing the contents of *The World of Art*, number by number, and translating Diaghilev's articles for me. In the Reading Room of the British Library, Bloomsbury (the British Museum), I studied an even more complete set. I could read the names of artists in Russian characters, and I listed and pondered over every illustration on every page. Much of what I wrote about the artists whose work Diaghilev reproduced, or who provided decorations for *The World of Art*, was later cut, because it was out of proportion to the scale of this book.

While Olive Stevens, who was partly Russian, earned my deep gratitude for making this study of the magazine possible, two other Russian-born friends later gave their time and knowledge unstintedly to bolster up my ignorance. Mrs Stevens's speciality was literature: that of Larissa Haskell was art, and Igor Vinogradoff was versed not only in literature, but in history and genealogy. Mrs Haskell, who had studied under Grabar at the Leningrad Academy, translated passages from his memoirs and from other books, and put me right about many questions of art history. Mr Vinogradoff's research into Diaghilev's family background produced results which I thought threw a new light on his character; he also criticized the typescript of my early chapters and helped me to make them more exact over social and historical details. These three friends were tireless in correspondence. A fourth student of Russian history and literature, Edward Morgan, whom I met through Mme Galina von Meck, grand-niece of Tchaikovsky, not only lent me books, but translated long passages from Princess Tenishev's *Memoirs* and from the letters of Bakst.

Of Diaghilev's friends who had helped me with *Nijinsky*, and whose information is also incorporated in this book, I will mention first those who have died since that help was given. Memories of Tamara Karsavina's beauty, intelligence and goodness will echo for ever in theatres where ballet is performed. Bronislava Nijinska, the choreographer of *Les Noces* and of that epitome of the 1920s, *Les Biches*, was a woman of sinewy soul to whom I felt very close when I got to know her at the end of her life. Of whom more than of Grigoriev could Diaghilev have said 'Thou good and faithful servant!'? His wife, Lubov Tchernicheva, did not long survive him. My warmhearted friend Lydia Sokolova always seemed to me to have acquired, during her many years with Diaghilev, a curious distinction of mind, for the daily dedication of a dancer's work breeds its own aristocracy. At the memorial service for Stanislas Idzikovsky, whose classes I had first watched in the 1930s, the coda from the Blue Bird *pas de deux* was played. It was Romola

Nijinsky's romantic life of her husband which first 'turned me on' to ballet in 1933. I never met Igor Stravinsky, whose genius Diaghilev revealed, but he used to answer questions and send messages to me through his devoted Boswell, Robert Craft, and he cheered me with occasional words of approval or encouragement. The support afforded to Diaghilev by Juliet Duff, who talked to me so often about him, is recorded more fully in this book than in *Nijinsky*, since it was given at the end of Diaghilev's life: even so, I had no room to quote more than a fraction of the letters she wrote him about fund-raising in 1928 and 1929, which survive at Lincoln Center.

Lady Keynes (Lydia Lopukhova) and Dame Marie Rambert, who helped so generously with the earlier book and who are quoted in the present one, are happily still with us.

Among those friends of Diaghilev who gave me information and helped in the early stages of the present book were Anton Dolin, who answered many questions, and whose first autobiography proved valuable, and Sacheverell Sitwell, who for a long time wrote to me almost every week.

In February 1977 I went to Paris to see Boris Kochno. He read and criticized my early chapters (which were too long), and gave me many notes for the later ones.

At the end of April 1977 I went to New York. This was a turning-point in the story of my book. I had been suffering from various disabilities, physical and mental, but the hospitality of John Taras, and the welcome given me by George Balanchine, who seemed glad to talk about the old days, changed the aspect of everything. Mme Felia Dubrovska and Mme Alexandra Danilova poured out information. On the insistence of Rudolf Nureyev, who got me invited to a party of Mr André Harley's, I interviewed Mme Vera Nemtchinova after midnight. Mme Tamara Geva, whom I had not met before, was kind enough to answer questions, too.

Mrs Stravinsky and Robert Craft, whom I had never met, although we had been corresponding for ten years, received me three times. Again, I regularly outstayed my welcome. (I went to lunch one Sunday and left after seven.) I told them that my great-aunt and godmother used to say of a caller who would not leave that he had 'brought his sitting-breeches'.

Now I must speak of the two great New York collections which have enriched this book. I had done research for *Nijinsky* in the Dance Collection of the New York Public Library in the Library and Museum of Performing Arts at Lincoln Center, so I was familiar with the extraordinary hoard of Astruc papers. Another miscellany of letters, telegrams and bills, given to the Library by Lincoln Kirstein, was new to me. It was odd and exciting to find, preserved in a museum, letters to Diaghilev from old friends or acquaintances of my own such as Lady Juliet Duff, Lady Diana Cooper, Lady Cunard, Lady Aberconway, Mr Anton Dolin, Sir Sacheverell Sitwell and Constant Lambert! There was also the correspondence with Lord

Rothermere's underlings, and evidence of Diaghilev's incessant money troubles. Miss Genevieve Oswald and her assistants made me very welcome as I scribbled away, copying documents.

I had no idea of the extent of Parmenia Ekstrom's collection of Diaghilev papers until she received me at her home, which also houses the Stravinsky–Diaghilev Foundation, on East 85th Street. 'Là tout n'est qu'ordre et beauté,/Luxe, calme et volupté' – but one must add 'travail', which, as we get older, is our chief source of 'volupté'. On the first day I arrived at 10.30 a.m. When the countless files of telegrams, bills and accounts were revealed, and Mrs Ekstrom asked me 'Where do you wish to start?', I did not know how to reply. I began copying bills at random. That day I left my hostess – exhausted, but still patient – at 3.15. I returned five times – to copy hundreds of telegrams received, and drafts of telegrams sent (the latter written either in Diaghilev's or Kochno's hands), dating from 1914 to 1929. As I copied away, Mrs Ekstrom sat talking informatively on the sofa beside me, and we became friends. Sometimes she gave me lunch. I am a great believer in the importance of dates, being sure that an exact chronology of Diaghilev's movements and decisions (which the telegrams in the Stravinsky–Diaghilev Foundation helped to provide) must precede an analysis of his states of mind. It will be readily understood why Mrs Ekstrom's continued generosity, which made me postpone my departure from New York, and John Taras's prolonged hospitality – together with the help Boris Kochno gave me in Paris – were the chief foundations of this book.

Back in England, I retired to Wiltshire and wrote the chapters of the book dealing with the 1920s. I next wrote the 1914–21 'Massine period'; I rewrote the early chapters; and I rewrote passages of the whole book several times. In fact, I have only been back to London half-a-dozen times, never for as long as a week, since my return from America; for I gave up my flat (after twenty years) in the autumn of 1977.

For the first year and a half of my work David Dougill typed what I had written. As his duties with the *Sunday Times* took more and more of his time, Margaret Power, who had helped me with *Nijinsky*, began to type for me instead. This was the last of many selfless tasks she undertook during a life of enthusiasm for ballet, for she died in October 1977. My country neighbour, Jane Harriss, to whom I had been introduced by James Stern, took over. It was she who helped me organize and re-organize the many 'final' versions. On 30 January 1978, Charles Murland delivered the bulky typescript of my book to Boris Kochno, who, by the time I arrived in Paris on 7 February, had read it and filled many pages with notes. In the following five days we spent many hours together. During this short week in Paris Serge Lifar was kind enough to come to my hotel and talk for two hours; and Henri Sauguet welcomed me. Igor Markevitch changed all his plans to travel from the South of France and devote an evening to telling me much that had never previously been revealed about Diaghilev, and which I prized highly as an enrichment of my book's final chapter.

The Kochno collection of Diaghilev papers had been sold to the Bibliothèque Nationale in 1975: they were now in order and available for study at the Musée de l'Opéra. Although many letters had been quoted by Kochno in his invaluable book *Diaghilev and the Ballets Russes*, the riches of the unfamiliar material amazed me. I spent a day copying letters, and, through the kindness of Martine Kahane, with whom I had long been in correspondence, remained alone, working under the huge chandeliers of the library long after the Museum was closed to the public. Because there was so much that I had not time to copy, David Dougill prolonged a visit to Paris ten days later in order to spend two and a half days copying more papers.

M. Kochno reread the new version of my last chapter and sent me more notes. M. Markevitch also read it and offered comments.

The 'finished' book was much too long to be a practical proposition in the 1970s. After I had cut twenty thousand words, Nigel Gosling courageously agreed to read through it and cut another fifty thousand. Compiling the Notes took months, partly because I had forgotten what some of my sources were, partly because many of the xeroxes of old foreign newspapers were lost or stolen during my move from London, partly because I tried to inject into the Notes some of the facts that had been cut from the text.

The fairest method of thanking those who helped me in so many different ways is to name them at random: some who may have thought they did little in fact contributed much. Robert Craft continued to answer questions about Stravinsky's correspondence. The late Naum Gabo, on his last visit to London, talked at length to me about his collaboration with Diaghilev, and Mrs Gabo sent me his comments on the notes I made of our conversation. It was Baron Tassilo von Watzdorf who had told me Gabo was in London. Sir Sacheverell Sitwell's many letters were not only full of information but a steady encouragement in times of despair. Mr Lincoln Kirstein, as ever, provided unexpected facts and recommended books (such as Morand's *Journal*) which I might have overlooked. (I think he later lost faith in my ability to carry the work through, after being told by Mr Gottlieb of Knopf that there was 'nothing about Diaghilev' in it!) Lord Harewood did detailed research into Wagner productions which Diaghilev might have seen or did see at different times of his life – 1890, 1912 and 1929; he also lent me books. Mr Peter Heyworth kept turning up facts about Diaghilev's relations with Hindemith and Weill. Mr Jochen Voigt translated some passages of German in the correspondence of Hindemith which I did not understand. Prince George Galitzine lent me the memoirs of Prince Serge Wolkonsky. (The pages concerning Diaghilev have been torn out of the British Museum copy.) Mr Cecil Lewis, editor of Charles Rickett's precious *Self*

Portrait, wrote me two helpful letters from Corfu. While I was having a thigh operation in the Salisbury General Infirmary, the ladies who administer the St John Ambulance and Red Cross lending library produced the Russian memoirs of Meriel Buchanan, containing a photograph of the Persian Quadrille at Countess Kleinmichel's ball in January 1914, which was described by Nekludov. When I was lunching one day with Mr and Mrs Alexander Schouvaloff, their aunt, Princess Peter Lieven, rang up another Countess Kleinmichel and got her opinion for me on Diaghilev's social position in St Petersburg society. Dr Wendy Baron answered my questions about Diaghilev's lunches and dinners with Ethel Sands in a letter. Mr Michael de Cossart wrote me a long letter about Princesse Edmond de Polignac. Mr E. Mollo received me and allowed me to study his *Dictionary of the Chevaliers Gardes*, translating the entry on Diaghilev's father. Mr Rudolf Nureyev, as related, overcame my reluctance to question Mme Nemtchinova in the small hours of the morning. Mme René Mayer invited me to meet M. Pierre Souvtchinsky, who gave me the idea that Diaghilev's efficacy and part of his importance came from his having had a foot in every camp. Lord St Just lent me – and Lady St Just brought across Wiltshire to me – the theatrical scrapbook and diary which the former Lady St Just (née Florence Henderson) kept when she was young. Mr Rollo Myers talked to me about Satie, Poulenc and his own visit to Monte Carlo in January 1924. Signor Vittorio Rieti wrote me two amusing and informative letters. Sir Cecil Beaton allowed me to quote the account of his meeting with Diaghilev in 1926, and gave me steady encouragement. Dr Brian Blackwood, who had been my musical adviser on *Nijinsky*, spent a day playing unfamiliar scores to me in the Library of the Senate House, London University, and listened with me to tapes at the British Institute of Recorded Sound; he also supplied information and criticized my descriptions of music. Mr John O'Brien and Mr David Leonard of Dance Books helped me to trace recordings or tapes of little-known Diaghilev scores, and made presents to me of several records. M. Jean Hugo answered many questions about French society in the 1920s and was helpful over niceties of translation from the French. Dame Alicia Markova, who has so clear a memory for detail, spent an afternoon reminiscing and answering questions. Dame Ninette de Valois could not believe that there was 'anything else to say' about Diaghilev: but she still contributed information and an anecdote. Sir Harold Acton, whose *Memoirs of an Aesthete* I quote, wrote me two letters about Diaghilev's last supper in England. When I no longer had a London flat and needed to do research, I stayed with friends (which I found I liked much better than having a flat of my own): those who kindly let me 'use their houses as an hotel' were Lady Harewood, Lady Daubeny and Miss Astrid Zydower. Mme Irina Baronova invited me to Switzerland and showed me where Diaghilev reassembled his company in 1915. Mr Douglas Cooper gave me his opinion about the Impressionist paintings Diaghilev exhibited in Russia. Miss Dorothy Dickson gave me her reminiscences of Diaghilev over lunch. Mr Peter Williams lent me his copy of Polunin's book. Mr Danny Arensky exerted himself on my behalf. Miss Mary Clarke sent me the copy of a letter the Soviet ballet historian Yuri Slonimsky had written years ago to Ivor Guest about the mention of Diaghilev's grandfather in Leskov's novel, thus giving me a clue which was followed up by Mr Igor Vinogradoff and Mrs Haskell. Mr Leslie Katz gave me information about vanished buildings in New York. Mr Ronald Crichton answered a number of musical queries. M. Hughes Gall, Secrétaire Général of the Théâtre National de l'Opéra, courteously facilitated my studies in several ways. Just as Mlle Martine Kahane and her colleague Mlle Marie-José Kerhoas sent me details of programmes of the Diaghilev Ballet at the Paris Opéra, so did Mme Nadia Lacoste and Mme Huguette Combouilhaud of the Société des Bains de Mer send me details of performances at Monte Carlo. Mr Bengt Häger, Director of the Dansmuseet, Stockholm, supplied me with details of Diaghilev's Spanish tours, which no one in Spain knew anything about, although Señor Carbajal of the Spanish Embassy, London (who thought Diaghilev was a dancer), kindly gave me the addresses of the principal libraries in Madrid. (Copies of Madrid newspapers came from the Newspaper Library, British Library, Colindale.) The staffs of the Newspaper Library, Colindale, the British Library, Bloomsbury, and the Library of the Victoria and Albert Museum were consistently helpful. Dr M. A. Baird of the Music Library, Senate House, London University, helped me with research. The staff of the Central Reference Library, St Martin's Street, London, and of the Music Library, Westminster Public Library, Buckingham Palace Road, came to my rescue when I was in difficulties. Miss Alex MacCormick edited and Mr Michael Graham-Dixon copy-edited my typescript, querying many inconsistencies and making it ready for the printer. To all these I express my warmest gratitude.

ILLUSTRATIONS

ELEVEN OF MY PHOTOGRAPHIC illustrations come from the Musée de l'Opéra, Paris: I thank Mlle Kahane, Director of the Museum, for showing them to me and the Bibliothèque Nationale for allowing me to reproduce them. Mr Anton Dolin generously gave me two snapshots. Mrs Stravinsky was kind enough to have copied for me two photographs which I saw framed together and standing on her table. One, the picture of Diaghilev, her husband, Kochno and Lifar at the Savoy, was by herself; the other, of Nijinsky – an image so striking that Cecil Beaton could not take his eyes off it for one whole evening – was by Igor Stravinsky. These were expeditiously copied for me by no less a photographer than Gjon Mili. The drawing of

ACKNOWLEDGEMENTS

Karsavina by Viktor Stretti came from the autograph albums of Princess
Mary Windisch-Graetz, who very kindly allowed me to have it copied. Cecil
Beaton's drawing of Diaghilev (after a photograph by Kochno) was a Christ-
mas present. I thank him for allowing me to reproduce that and his caricature
of Lopukhova, which first appeared in *Vogue*. I am grateful, too, to *The
Tatler* and to Mr Einar Nerman for allowing me to reproduce his caricatures.
Mr Robert Fraser generously supplied prints from Baron de Meyer's originals of Lady Ripon and Lady Juliet Duff, formerly in Sir Cecil Beaton's
collection. M. Markevitch kindly sent me photographs of his portrait by
Bérard and of the caricature of Diaghilev by Cocteau which I used on the
jacket. Sources of all other illustrations are gratefully acknowledged in the
list of illustrations. Whilst we have made every effort to give due acknowledg-
ment, we shall be happy to correct any omissions in a future edition.

Spelling of Russian Names

RUSSIAN SPELLING is phonetic, and I have tried to be logical in my transliterations, but 'Benua' would look odd, if not unrecognizable, so I have not been consistent. Every Russian to whom I have shown my manuscript has changed many names, and the next Russian has changed half of them back again. The British Library catalogue has its own system and writes 'Dyagilef', which is phonetic but odd after all these years. Diaghilev always wrote his name with a 'w', as if it were German. He persistently simplified and misspelt his dancers' names in the West. 'Lopokova' does *not* give the right idea of 'Lopukhova' or (as the French might prefer) 'Lopoukhova'. Nor is 'Nijinsky' as good as 'Nizhinsky', for it gives an Englishman the option of saying, wrongly, 'Nidjinsky': but 'Nijinsky' is now so widely accepted that I have stuck to it and written, for instance, 'Derjavin' to match. Incidentally, the great dancer's name was often printed 'Nijinski' in Europe and America. I have not attempted to indicate the unaccountable Russian variations in accenting names. Most people (but not the French) know that it is correct to say 'Karsávina'. Why then should 'Sokolóva' be correct? 'Lariónov' but 'Gontcharóva'. 'Koróvin' but 'Golovín'. 'Tchernicheva' is pronounced 'Tchernishóva', though never so written. I have avoided writing 'Semyónov' for 'Semenov' or 'Syérov' for 'Serov'. I have tried to avoid the ambiguous 'c', and written 's' in 'Shabelska' although she was usually written 'Chabelska', and have written 'Tchaikovsky' and 'Tchekhov' to make the pronunciation clear. Yet, here again I have been inconsistent, for I should have written 'Shalyápin' or 'Shaliapin', but shirked it. I wanted to be consistent in omitting the unnecessary final 'e' in 'Fokin', 'Massin', 'Balanchin' and 'Mordkin', which made life easier for the French, who might have been tempted to rhyme 'Massin' with '*bassin*': but I was persuaded to revert to the accepted spelling. Vladimir Polunin, the scene-painter, however, never wrote his name with an 'e', which gives me the excuse to leave it off not only his, but the great names of Apraxin and Galitzin. Mr Igor Vinogradoff – whose name Diaghilev would have written 'Winogradow' and I should have standardized as 'Vinogradov' – advised me to change 's' to 'z' wherever it made the pronunciation clearer, as in 'Ziloti' and 'Bezobrazov'. My friend Mr Alexander Schouvaloff, Director of the Theatre Museum, writes his name in this mixture of German, French and English styles, but he will forgive me, I hope, for spelling his noble forbears 'Shuvalov'. The British Library would write 'Shuvalof'. I should like to have written the name of my dear friend Boris Kochno as 'Kokhno', but the former spelling is now famous throughout the world and even Diaghilev, when not writing in Russian, wrote 'Kochno'.

R.B.

PART I

Early Years

The Fortress of St Peter and St Paul, St Petersburg. Drawing by Eugene Lancerey for *The World of Art*.

CHAPTER 1

1872–90

Childhood in St Petersburg – Schooldays in Perm –
Meeting with Benois – First Journey abroad with
Filosofov

'HE DOTH BESTRIDE the narrow world like a Colossus.' In borrowing
the complaint of Cassius against Caesar to begin this chronicle
of Diaghilev's campaigns in Gaul and elsewhere, I do so to
emphasize less his huge stature than the width of his stride. His range and
his scope were tremendous. He bridged the chasm of the Russian Revolution. The youth who had kissed the hand of Glinka's sister, known Tchaikovsky and Mussorgsky, and studied under Rimsky-Korsakov, lived to
commission the first ballets of Prokofiev. The man who had visited Tolstoy,
and offered Tchekhov the editorship of his magazine, was discussing projects
at the end of his life with Mayakovsky.

Diaghilev, who had worked in the same theatre as the old choreographer
Marius Petipa, born in 1818, lived, in a comparatively short life of fifty-seven
years, to commission the first masterpieces of Balanchine, who is still pouring out incomparable ballets in 1978.

One of the characters in Leskov's *Anecdotes of Archiepiscopal Life* is a
Bishop Neofit of Perm (a provincial capital near the Ural Mountains), who
is based on a real person of that name. The Bishop obtains large sums of
money for the Church from a local landowner, who holds the state monopoly
for vodka. Although Leskov calls him Mr N (the equivalent of 'Mr X' in
English), this man in real life was Pavel Dmitrievitch Diaghilev, grandfather
of Sergei Pavlovitch Diaghilev, the subject of this book.[1] 'Mr N. [was] a
very rich and extremely devout man, the comforts of whose life were based
on transactions in vodka.... The piety of Mr N. was so great that people
close to this worthy man, incapable of understanding his disposition, considered it a mania requiring medical attention.'[2]

A third of the Russian state's revenue was believed to come from the tax
on vodka[3] – that is, from making the peasants drunk. If, in middle age, Pavel
Dmitrievitch Diaghilev craved to atone for his ill-gotten gains by building

3

churches, his grandson's shame at this commerce would drive him to excel in the world's eyes, to earn a nobility which was not his by ancient right. Pavel Dmitievitch was a parvenu, a self-made man, and although the artistic labours of Sergei Pavlovitch became an end in themselves it seems to me likely that what first spurred him on was the knowledge that in St Petersburg and at Court he was nobody, a distiller's grandson.

The lives of the obscure are seldom recorded in detail, but the following bare facts, ignored by Diaghilev's previous biographers, speak for themselves. The first of his family to leave a trace was his great-great-grandfather Vassili Dmitrievitch Diaghilev, whose wife's name is unknown, but who was a *Conseiller titulaire*, ninth in the table of fourteen ranks in the Civil Service, in 1799. His son Dmitri Vassilievitch, born in 1771, was an *Assesseur de collège* (eighth rank in the table) in 1804. At this time the eighth rank conferred hereditary 'nobility': later in the century the law was changed and it became more difficult to be 'noble', or, as we should say, a gentleman. Vassili owned only four serfs and no land, but his wife, also the child of an *Assesseur de collège*, though of a family without history, must have been some kind of heiress (that is, without brothers), for how else can we account for the amazing elevation of their son? Pavel Dmitrievitch, Diaghilev's grandfather (1803–83), was admitted to the exclusive regiment of the Chevaliers Gardes, in which he became a major in 1839. To have 'broken into' this close-knit corps he must have served with outstanding distinction in some regiment of the line, possibly in the Persian War of 1826–8, in the Turkish War of 1827–9, or in suppressing the Polish insurrection of 1831. He was awarded the Cross of St Vladimir (which would have made him automatically 'noble' if he were not so already) in 1842, and in 1847 became *Conseiller de collège* (sixth rank). He married Anna Ivanovna, daughter of Admiral Ivan Savvovitch Sulmenev (of a family first recorded in 1620), and owned forty-eight serfs and six thousand hectares in the government of Perm.[4] It is clear that he obtained the state monopoly for vodka in the province. Perm was so remote that it was not numbered among those governments established with elected bodies of nobles, marshals of the nobility, and magistrates, by the Empress Catherine in 1785. Many landowners became comparatively impoverished after the Emancipation of the Serfs in 1861, and were obliged to sell off land to the newly swollen merchant class or to shrewd self-improved peasants (as did Prince Stefan Oblonsky in Tolstoy's *Anna Karenina* and Mme Ranevskaya in Tchekhov's *Cherry Orchard*), but the new Diaghilev fortune was evidently maintained at a high level by the vodka distillery. In fact, Pavel Dmitrievitch Diaghilev disliked the idea of possessing serfs and himself decided to employ only paid labour. It followed that when the Emperor Alexander II formed a committee to free the serfs, he was appointed to represent Perm province at its sessions in the capital.[5]

Leskov's narrator tells how when the Bishop came on a visit to N. he was greeted in the church by a choir bursting into a religious chant. He was delighted with this and got talking to the young people, of whom two brothers turned out to be students, while another wore cavalry uniform. They admitted to being only a family choir – they normally lived in St Petersburg and were spending the summer with their father. The boys and their sisters begged the Bishop to come to dinner. The Bishop then shocked N. by asking them to sing some non-religious music; and they sang extracts from operas – Glinka's *A Life for the Tsar* and *Ruslan and Ludmila*, Gounod's *Faust* and Meyerbeer's *Le Prophète*.[6]

Pavel Dmitrievitch had eight children – four sons and four daughters. The eldest, Anna Pavlovna (1837–1912), married Vladimir Dmitrievitch Filosofov, *Conseiller privé actuel* (second rank), whose ancient family was descended from St Vladimir. Anna became an ardent liberal, reformer, social worker and fighter for the rights of women – a true 'woman of the sixties', just as her father had been a 'man of the sixties', eager to right ancient wrongs. This movement of Liberalism in the sixties, incidentally, was associated with a group of painters called *Peredvijniki* (Vagrants, Peripatetics) because of their travelling exhibitions. Rebelling against the aloofness of the academic painting of that time they aspired to a more human art, understandable to simple people; their pictures told stories and would 'point a moral to adorn the tale.' After the assassination of Alexander II in 1881, his heir returned to the extreme conservatism of Nicolas I: Alexander III detested Anna Filosofov and all that she stood for, and even exiled her for a while.[7]

The youngest of the Diaghilev sons was Pavel Pavlovitch (1849–1914), the cavalry cadet of the improvised choir who had sung to the Bishop in Leskov's story. He went into the Chevaliers Gardes like his father, and ended as a General ADC.[8] He loved music and had a good voice.[9] While Sergei Pavlovitch Diaghilev, his only child by his first wife, inherited the originality of his grandfather and his aunt, along with Anna's liberal principles and her persistence in striking out a line of her own, it was from the soldier father that he got his love of music.

Shortly after Pavel Pavlovitch was commissioned in the Chevaliers Gardes, he married Evgenia Nicolaevna Essipov, of an old noble family from Novgorod, first mentioned in 1435.[10] In 1872, when he was twenty-five, he was posted for one year to the Selistchev Barracks, situated in the beautiful estate of Grusino, a former property of Count Araksheyev, the favourite of the Emperor Paul and Minister of Alexander I, which had become Crown property. This lay on the banks of the River Volkhov in the province of Novgorod. Evgenia was pregnant, and, shortly before the time came for her delivery, Pavel's second sister, Maria Pavlovna Koribut-Kubitovitch, who was seven years older than him and who had been widowed only two months before, came to be with her sister-in-law. Jenia had a hard labour, and, when her boy was delivered, it was realized that this was due to the size of his head. So, like many soldiers' sons, Sergei Pavlovitch Diaghilev was born far from home. A few days after his birth on 17 March, his mother died in the arms of his Aunt Maria. Pavel Pavlovitch was inconsolable.[11]

Sergei's youngest aunt, who had recently left the Smolny Institute in St Petersburg (an imperially subsidized boarding school for girls of gentle birth), remembered her mother's grief, the business of buying mourning clothes, their arrival from St Petersburg at the Barracks, where Jenia was laid out on a table, the little boy crying in the next room, the procession with a number of officers who followed the coffin to the river, and the journey by steamer to Kuzmino for the funeral. Nanny Dunia, who had been nurse to Jenia, became nurse to little Sergei and remained with him till her death. She had been born a domestic serf in the Essipov family and only served them and the Diaghilevs all her life.

It was decided that the Koribut-Kubitovitch children, who had lost their father, and Sergei, who had lost his mother, should join forces under the former children's mother, Maria; and when, shortly afterwards, Pavel Pavlovitch was gazetted Squadron Commander in the Chevaliers Gardes, they all moved to St Petersburg and took possession of a fine flat in the barracks at Shpalernaya Street. Sergei's cousin Pavel Georgievitch Koribut-Kubitovitch (Pavka), who was six and a half years older than him, remembered 'how, sometime in spring they brought us the fair-haired, dark eyed Serioja [diminutive of Sergei], and how I began to look him over as he lay in the arms of his magnificent, red-haired wet-nurse, while Nanny Dunia, in the typical white pleated cap worn by all nurses of good family in those days, stood beside'.[12]

Mstislav Dobujinsky has described how the wet-nurse in a noble family was the most spectacular person to be seen in the streets of St Petersburg:

> She had a kind of 'parade uniform', a pseudo-peasant costume, theatrically designed, and this was worn right up to the war of 1914. One often saw a fat, red-cheeked wet-nurse in a brocade blouse and cape, hung with beads, and in a pink head-dress if she was nursing a girl, a blue one if it was a boy, walking beside her fashionably dressed mistress. In the summer the wet-nurses used to wear coloured sarafans with lots of small gold or glass buttons and muslin balloon sleeves.[13]

The gorgeous wet-nurses are familiar to us in the West from the ballet *Petrushka*.

In 1874 Pavel Pavlovitch married again, taking as his wife Elena Valerianovna Panaev. Sergei and his cousins all loved her, and Sergei always spoke of her as the best woman in the world.[14] The Panaevs, like the Diaghilevs, were a musical family, and Elena's sister Alexandra

6

Valerianovna Kartsov, whose mother-in-law was a Tchaikovsky, was a famous soprano.[15] She had been a pupil of Pauline Viardot (whom Turgenev loved), the sister of Malibran (hymned by Musset); and her father had built a private opera house. In the course of time Elena had two sons, Valentine and Yuri. She kept open house and was at home on Thursdays, but she did not aspire to a smart or worldly salon. People who loved music came to the house and sometimes complete operas were performed. Pavel Diaghilev himself knew the whole of Glinka's *Ruslan and Ludmila* by heart. Elena recorded that 'even the smallest boys whistle a Schumann quintet or Beethoven symphony as they stroll about....' Dmitri Filosofov, the cousin who was nearest to Sergei in age, recalled:

Among these boys, Serioja's passion for music was especially marked. Greedily he absorbed everything that he heard, and was deeply affected by it. He had a really enthusiastic cult for Tchaikovsky, many of whose songs had long been familiar to him through hearing them sung by his step-aunt.... Tchaikovsky himself highly esteemed the manner in which she rendered his songs.... All his life, Diaghilev remembered how, as a child, he had visited 'Uncle Petia' [Tchaikovsky] in Klin, and it was always a pleasure to him to recall his connection with Tchaikovsky....[16]

Diaghilev also met Mussorgsky in childhood, and related how his aunt used to say to her servants, 'Tomorrow I'm going to sing. Don't forget to send for Mussorgsky.' This unfortunate composer was sometimes reduced to earning a pittance as an accompanist; but, as Diaghilev noted, 'naturally it was never his own music he was asked to play'.[17]

So Sergei Pavlovitch's earliest boyhood was passed in that fantastic northern capital and he grew to know the sights and sounds of the city. In winter the house-porters scraped the ice from the pavements, or these would be temporarily roped off while they cleared the snow off the roofs, and it would fall with a subdued thud. In spring the double windows which sealed up the rooms throughout the winter were removed so that the house could be aired. The cracking ice in the drain pipes made an alarming noise which startled the passers-by; and great chunks of ice floated down the Neva, splitting in two as they struck the piers of a bridge. The sound of ice floes brushing against each other was like the unwrapping of a parcel done up in silver paper. Other typical sounds were the ringing of tram bells, the jingling of little bells on the troikas, church bells, the roar of the draymen's iron sledges, and military music. In summer the noise increased: only on the elegant Nevsky Prospekt, on the Embankment, or on the Bolshaya Morskaya were there wooden blocks to deaden the sound. But in summer the gentry left the city for their country houses, and roads were mended, plasterers went about singing cheerfully, servants sat on benches outside the houses, cracking sunflower seeds or playing the harmonica.[18]

All this time the old Pavel Dmitrievitch Diaghilev was living alone, except

7

for one unmarried son, in his town house at Perm. The eldest son ran the nearby estate of Bikbarda, where the family would assemble in the summer. Pavel Pavlovitch had amassed a heap of debts in the capital and his father undertook to pay these if his youngest son left the smart Chevaliers Gardes.[19] To leave the Chevaliers Gardes or the Gardes à Cheval and go on the General List meant quicker promotion, for, in the intimate corps of the Household Cavalry, each of whose regiments had four squadrons commanded by a colonel, one could remain a captain into old age. (The rank of major was abolished in Guards regiments in the mid-nineteenth century.) Pavel Pavlovitch would end up as a Lieutenant-General and ADC to the Emperor. In the meantime he was fortunate in being able to take over command of the garrison at his home town of Perm. Thus he could satisfy his father without giving up his army career. The ten-year-old Sergei was therefore to enter the Perm Gymnasium instead of going to school in St Petersburg. Perm is believed to be the boring provincial town of Tchekhov's *Three Sisters*.[20]

As the crow flies, Perm is nearly a thousand miles from St Petersburg; but in 1882 the necessarily circuitous journey was a great deal longer than that. Pavel Koribut-Kubitovitch describes what the journey entailed.

In those days neither Perm nor Kazan was on the railway line and one had to alight at Nijni-Novgorod, then travel down the Volga on a Lubimov steamer for four days, and at Kazan branch into the Kama River. To the children, the whole journey was a delightful, exciting adventure. All his life Diaghilev remembered the lovely banks of these rivers, their hills, their forests, their vast plains and pastures, the old villages, the small provincial towns and the ancient cities of Nijni-Novgorod and Kazan.[21]

In the provincial capital of Perm – which was only separated from Siberia by the Ural Mountains – the Diaghilevs were like a royal family. Their big house was in the main thoroughfare, Great Siberian Street. The ballroom windows looked on to a side street. We have pictures of this room with its parquet floor, its ornate grand piano, its chandelier (presumably one of several), its *capitonné* corner-seat in the Second Empire style, and its set of rather more *art nouveau* chairs upholstered in cut velvet. In another photograph of the dining-room we observe the very up-to-date (in the 1880s) bentwood chairs, with their cane seats – probably from Vienna – the embroidered white cloth on the table, and, over it, an ornate brass paraffin lamp with a glass shade. A footman stands at attention by one of the doors. Diaghilev's cousin writes that sixty could dine in this room, but in the picture the table, with its numerous cut-glass decanters of red and white wine or vodka and its bottles of liqueur standing in silver coasters, is only laid for sixteen. Probably it could be extended; or perhaps this is only a smaller dining-room which the family used when they were not entertaining.[22]

8

To the grandfather [continued Koribut-Kubitovitch], it was a great delight to see the huge house fill and become alive ... a new life began for him, cheerful and gay; with plenty of music, books and conversation. Cards were never seen in the Diaghilev house, no one ever played whist or preference, but art and literature were always welcome. Barely a year was out before the house had become the centre of the town's artistic activities. To be admitted to the house was considered an honour to which all the neighbours aspired. Little by little a musical circle was formed, its nucleus being Serioja's father and stepmother, who both sang beautifully, and Uncle Vanya, who, from childhood, had studied under the best St Petersburg teachers, and was an excellent executant on both the piano and 'cello. Two or three times a year a charity concert would be given by this circle in the Assembly Rooms of the Nobility. Soon, a small amateur orchestra organized itself, again conducted by Uncle Vanya, and during rehearsals in the big drawing-room, Serioja would be permitted to sit up till ten.... Aunt Elena, Sergei's stepmother, read aloud beautifully, and once or twice a week there would be a literary evening.

On the dining-room walls, and in grandfather's huge study, hung large old prints of works by Rembrandt, Raphael, etc., and the book case contained magnificent illustrated works devoted to famous collections.... These Sergei was allowed to handle in his grandfather's presence....[23]

Pavel Dmitrievitch died in 1883, when Sergei was eleven. Sergei's eldest uncle, as we have said, ran the estate at Bikbarda; and summers were spent there. So the boy who had already had the experience of a St Petersburg which had changed little since the days of Anna Karenina, would now live *la vie de château* which we know from the plays of Tchekhov. When all old Pavel's sons and daughters were present with their families, they would number nearly fifty.

Our veranda [wrote Elena Diaghilev] ... was just a plain Russian wooden veranda, with pillars and a roof, that stretched along the whole southern wing of the one-storied timber house, and even beyond, seeing that it ended with a big loggia, which projected past the corner of the house and ran out over the garden gate, and alongside the road bordering a ravine. Beyond this hollow were the distillery, the village and a forest that seemed to stretch illimitable as the sea. Here on this loggia, we would generally sit to take tea, as we watched the sun slowly setting.... In summer, part of the loggia would be used for meals, and could easily accommodate some fifty people. On the balcony itself, near the loggia, numbers of sofas and old shiny chintz-covered stools were arranged, while the wall at the back was almost completely obliterated by a living screen of plants and creepers.[24]

One of Diaghilev's school-fellows, Vassiliev, left a description of school life in Perm and of his fellow-pupil, who always seemed a cut above the other boys.

Our gymnasium in those days was an old-fashioned, provincial institution, with somewhat patriarchal customs and observances.... Classes often began late, the teachers would arrive at times not too sober or with obvious hangovers, having done themselves well the night before, and order and cleanliness, in the austere and sombre old building, were mainly conspicuous by their absence. . . .

Serioja Diaghilev . . . was a tall, bulky boy for his age, with an unusually big head and expressive face. His education and development were well beyond average, and far in advance of his class. He knew things of which we, his schoolmates, had no notion, such as Russian and foreign literature, the theatre and music. French and German he also spoke fluently, and could play the piano. Externally, too, he was very different. There was an elegance, a refinement, even a stateliness in his carriage. He was a perfect 'little gentleman' in comparison with us. Serioja Diaghilev had a funny attractive manner, which seemed to go with him, and to be part and parcel of that elegance of his.

. . . He would arrive in class totally unprepared, and immediately set to work to mug up his lesson, with the help of the best pupils. No one ever refused to help him, and when his turn came to be 'called', there would always be lots of zealous prompting, while during written lessons numbers of helpful notes would be passed to him. Owing to this help and his own dexterity, plus a natural resourcefulness, he generally emerged from critical situations completely victorious. One must add that the teachers assisted him in every possible way. Most of them frequented the Diaghilev house, and enjoyed the attentions and hospitality of its amiable and enlightened hosts.[25]

Meanwhile, Sergei's cousin Dmitri Filosofov ('Dima'), with whom he corresponded, was at the May School in St Petersburg. Compared with the St Petersburg Lycée, whose boarders wore black, red and gold, with cocked hats, this was a middle-class gymnasium, although there was an intersprinkling of boys from old families. The Filosofovs had a long pedigree, but they were country gentry, with no aspirations to mingle in Court circles. Dima was a tall, pale, thoughtful youth, considered handsome. He had a romantic friendship with Konstantin Somov ('Kostia'), who drew women's profiles on his exercise books, and who also came from an ancient family. Another classmate was Alexandre Benois ('Shura'), whom Dima mocked for his shapeless clothes and dirty nails. Shura, who was acquiring an interest in all the arts, had French and German blood on his father's side, Venetian on his mother's. His father, an architect, had built the Imperial Stables at Peterhof; and his maternal grandfather, Cavos, also an architect, had built the Bolshoi and Mariinsky Theatres in St Petersburg and the Bolshoi in Moscow. Yet another classmate was Walter Nuvel ('Valetchka'), small, dapper and witty, who smoked cigars to seem grown-up, read voraciously, loved the theatre, was an addict of Italian opera, and played the piano with facility. Kostia left school early to enter the Academy of Fine Arts; Dima, because his health was poor, was sent to the French Riviera. Shura and Valetchka neglected their scholastic work for their artistic hobbies and were obliged to stay on an extra year at school. It was only shortly after they had passed out in 1890 that they resumed their acquaintance with Dima and Kostia and that the four friends formed themselves into a group to improve their knowledge of the arts. A German company had given *Der Ring des Nibelungen*, with the Mariinsky orchestra under the German conductor Karl Muck, during Lent, 1889, and they were all mad about Wagner. Benois went to stay at the Filosofovs' country house and was much impressed by the colourful way of life of this family, who, up to 1861, had owned many serfs.[26]

Shortly before Benois and Nuvel passed their final examinations in the spring of 1890, a new friend was recruited to join their *cénacle*, a Jewish art student called Leon Rosenberg, later to become famous under his grandfather's name of Bakst. Benois, who first met him at the house of his eldest brother Albert, a painter, wrote:

On entering Albert's upstairs studio one day in March 1890 I came upon a young man I did not know. Albert introduced his new acquaintance to me as a gifted artist.... Mr Rosenberg's exterior was in no way remarkable. The rather regular features were spoilt by his short sighted eyes, his bright red hair and a thin moustache which straggled over his curved lips. His shy and at the same time ingratiating manner seemed to me, if not off-putting, at least unpleasing....

Our friendly feelings for 'Levushka' Rosenberg were mixed with some pity. He told Valetchka Nuvel and me how hard his life was. He had been left without any means of subsistence after the sudden death of his father ... Levushka had been obliged to find the means to keep not only himself but also his mother, his grandmother, two sisters and a very young brother. Moreover, he did not want to leave the Academy of Arts, which he attended as an external student....[27]

In 1890 the Nuvel family moved to a flat over that of the Filosofovs at 12 Galernaia Street. Before leaving for the country, Dima asked Valetchka Nuvel to look after his cousin Sergei Diaghilev, who would be passing through St Petersburg on the way to stay with the Filosofovs. When Diaghilev arrived, Valetchka let Shura Benois know, and the latter, 'dying with curiosity', jumped into a cab and went to take a look at him.

There was not the faintest likeness between the slight, pale Dima and his cousin, who impressed us rather by his fresh and healthy appearance. He had red cheeks and dazzling white teeth which formed two even rows between his scarlet lips. When he laughed the whole 'inside' of his jaws seemed to be flung wide open. Serioja laughed like a child, often, and on any pretext. He was obviously highly excited at finding himself in the capital and at meeting the closest friends of a cousin with whom he had corresponded assiduously for some years.... He seemed to us a 'good fellow', a lusty provincial, perhaps not very intelligent, rather primitive, but on the whole quite likeable. If at the time Valetchka and I immediately decided to accept him as a member of our group, it was solely because of his relationship with Dima. Being the same age as his cousin, Serioja was two years younger than I and one year younger than Valetchka. However, our impressions were very fleeting: after a few days' stay in Petersburg to put some affairs of his in order, Serioja left for the country.[28]

An incident which took place shortly after Benois' first meeting with Diaghilev made an impression on the former that he never forgot and convinced him once and for all that the soldier's son was by nature a *fighter*. They had gone to visit Valetchka Nuvel at his mother's house near St Petersburg. Finding that he was out for a walk, they set off to find him. It was a very hot day and they soon got tired and lay down on the grass to rest. Lying on his back, gazing at a cloudless sky, Shura decided to put Serioja through an artistic catechism to see how well he fitted in with the beliefs and enthusiasms of the group of old school friends. He must have been too persistent and caught out the young provincial in questions he could not answer, for he was startled to find Diaghilev on top of him, laughing uproariously and punching him with his fists. Such behaviour was unheard of by such a mother's boy as Benois: he was terrified, particularly as he realized Diaghilev was much stronger than he was.[29] Benois had cause to remember this scene, which struck him as symbolic, for in later years Diaghilev was often 'on top of him'.

Diaghilev went to join his cousin Dima at the Filosofov estate of Bogdanovskoye, beyond Pskov, about two hundred miles to the south-west. Dima and he were about to make their first journey abroad together.[30]

Diaghilev adored Pushkin, and the poet's family property was only a few miles from that of the Filosofovs. He knew the eldest son of the poet, who spent his summers at Mikhailovskoye; and, in fact, the father of his uncle Filosofov had married a sister of the wife of Grigori Pushkin, the poet's second son.

Diaghilev's route took him past Sviatogorsk, the Holy Mountains, where Pushkin was buried on a hill opposite the monastery. 'To sit there for a moment at sunset,' wrote Diaghilev, 'on a bench near the tomb, gave me a feeling of calm which lasted throughout the year. I was filled with love and humility in that sacred place. I always picked a few leaves from the trees near the grave and went away thinking "Till next year".'[31]

Sergei's uncle by marriage, Vladimir Dmitrievitch Filosofov, liked to tell the story of how, as a boy, he was sitting on the window-sill of his father's study when suddenly Pushkin came in. 'My uncle,' wrote Diaghilev, 'hid behind the curtain and spied on the unsuspecting poet. Pushkin went up to a big looking-glass and on the thick layer of dust with which it was covered wrote some lines of French verse.'[32]

Either the proximity of Pushkin's home and grave, or the charm of the Filosofov's country house in summer, or the excitement of going abroad, cast a spell on the cousins, and, when Sergei and Dmitri set off, they were in love with each other.[33] They travelled to Berlin, Paris, Venice – where of course they were photographed in a gondola – Rome, Florence and Vienna – where they heard *Lohengrin*. We can imagine that each city impressed Diaghilev more than the last. Indeed, this first Grand Tour, though brief, must have had on him the effect of several thunderbolts. Paris, the capital of elegance and sophistication, would always in future years be the city he set out to captivate with his newest and most daring experiments in ballet; Florence he would always think of as the sacred shrine of the most exalted art; Venice he loved so much as a city, apart from its treasures of painting, that it would become to this future nomad and exile the nearest he ever found to a 'home' – and, indeed, it would be his eternal resting place. Wagner's music filled him with a sense of glory; *Tristan* would be one of the last operas he ever heard, and he proclaimed its splendour on his death-bed.

Sergei Pavlovitch was, however, to be celebrated chiefly for his promotion of ballet; and earlier that year a girl who would play an important part in his life graduated from the Imperial Ballet School in St Petersburg.

Behind the Alexandrinsky Theatre, which faced the Nevsky Prospekt across gardens, there stretched Rossi's Theatre Street, nobly symmetrical, with its arcading and columns, painted pinkish-ochre and white. One side held ministries and the Lord Chamberlain's office: the other housed the Imperial drama and ballet schools. After ten years' training, the ballet students – those who had not been weeded out – graduated and joined the corps de ballet of the Mariinsky Theatre, where they had already grown used to taking part in crowd scenes: it was a mile away. The graduation performances in the school's little theatre took place shortly before the Imperial theatres closed for the three months' summer recess, and were usually attended by members of the Imperial family. At that of 1890 (which was held on 23 March), Matilda Kchessinskaya, a Polish girl, possibly of noble descent, whose father was a character-dancer and whose brother and sister had preceded her at the school, passed out with honours. The graduation performance, at which she danced in a *pas de deux* from *La Fille mal gardée*, had been attended by the Emperor Alexander, the Empress, the Emperor's four brothers, of whom the eldest was the Grand Duke Vladimir, married to the Grand Duchess Marie Pavlovna (a Princess of Mecklenburg-Schwerin), and the Tsarevitch Nicolas. Kchessinskaya was very small, pretty, vivacious and self-confident. Her personality made its impression, for when the Royalties came to join the young dancers at supper, the Tsar demanded in his powerful voice, 'Where is Kchessinskaya?' The headmistress, rather shaken, led her forward, and as she curtseyed, he held out his hand and said, 'Be the glory and adornment of our ballet.' At supper he insisted that she should sit next to him, with the Tsarevitch on her other side. A very ordinary plain glass stood by every place, and young Nicolas, to open the conversation, said, 'I am sure you don't use glasses like that at home.' Matilda fell in love with him 'on the spot'; and they spent the whole evening together.[34] She became a member of the Imperial Ballet on 1 June.

During the summer the army went into camp for manœuvres near Krasnoye Selo, south-west of the capital, and selected artists of the Imperial

Ballet performed in a wooden theatre in the village. Kchessinskaya danced there during that summer of 1890, and the Tsarevitch came to visit her every evening. She did not know whether he loved her or not, for they were never alone together. Shortly afterwards he went on a journey round the world.[35]

1890–8

The University – Education, mostly Musical –
Tchaikovsky's last Works – Kchessinskaya and the
Tsarevitch – Ambitions

I N SEPTEMBER RUSSIAN LANDOWNERS returned to Moscow or St Petersburg from their country estates or from their travels abroad; the Imperial
Theatres reopened; the University term began. Diaghilev, who stayed
at the Filosofovs' flat and shared a room with Dima,[1] embarked on his study
of the law without enthusiasm. He had no intention of becoming a lawyer:
but a degree in law was the passport to a minor post in the Civil Service,
which would in the normal course of events be found for him. (Mussorgsky,
for instance, had worked in the Engineering Department of the Ministry
of Communications, Tchaikovsky in the Ministry of Justice.) Russian university courses and lectures were bleakly standardized – they still are. To
pass an examination, it was necessary to learn a number of facts by heart.
Little initiative or imagination was demanded of professor or pupil.[2] Igor
Grabar, later a friend of Diaghilev's and a celebrated painter, was one year
older than Sergei Pavlovitch and studied under the same professors. He
wrote that, if it had not been for three teachers of special character and talent,
'it would have been waste of time to go to lectures and one could have spent
one's time better in a library'.[3]

The only alternatives to entering one of the innumerable departments of
the Civil Service were the army, to a lesser extent the navy (a smaller force),
or the Foreign Service. Certainly neither the army nor the navy attracted
Diaghilev.

To be born noble did not give automatic access to the Court, for just
as there were people or families of foreign descent, such as Baron (later
Count) Friedericx, the Minister of the Court, descended from a Finnish
banker, or the Baltic Benckendorffs, Pahlens, and Lievens, who held high
positions or belonged to the inner Court circle, so there were innumerable
members of the oldest families in Russia who were obliged to earn a living
as ill-paid minor functionaries in the Civil Service. It is true that an old

name made it easier for these to obtain a place. The higher aristocracy – Vorontzovs, Volkonskys, Bariatinskys, Apraxins, Shuvalovs, Orlov-Davidovs, Galitzins and so on, were infinitely removed from such provincial families as that of Diaghilev, although he numbered some distinguished names, such as Khitrovo and Rumiantsev, among his maternal ancestors, and made much of his probably fictitious descent through a Rumiantsev from Peter the Great.[4]

It seems to me that it was Diaghilev's minimal nobility on the side of his self-made paternal grandfather, the distiller, that coloured his whole thinking as a young man and gave him an incentive to excel.

He had been a little prince in distant Perm, but he was quick to realize that he was of no consequence in St Petersburg and must start again from scratch. He contrived to look exceptionally elegant, even in his student's uniform. He annoyed his new friends by his 'society manners', and by the fact that he felt obliged to make calls, leave cards and write his name in the books of distinguished people. Benois and Nuvel were repelled by his ingratiating manner when he bowed to illustrious acquaintances in the stalls at the theatre or went the round of boxes on the lower tiers. This made Benois' family and all the Filosofov relations 'furious with him'.[5] His reputation as a fop stuck to him even after he had proved his worth in the world.

It may have occurred to Diaghilev that his only way to achieve distinction lay through the arts: luckily it was in the arts that he was most interested. He might become a great singer or a great composer. He began to take lessons in singing from the baritone Cotogni and in composition under Sokolov and Rimsky-Korsakov.[6] For these musical lessons he neglected his studies in law. Grabar never remembered seeing him at a lecture.[7]

The group of friends all loved Tchaikovsky, though for different reasons – and in Perm Sergei had never seen a ballet – and they were enthusiastic about Rimsky-Korsakov: but Diaghilev knew much more about Mussorgsky's music than they did. 'We had heard a lot about Mussorgsky,' wrote Benois, 'but at that period it was not so easy to get to know his music ... Serioja ... actually *knew* Mussorgsky's music and not only his songs but even the piano score of *Boris Godunov*.' It must be borne in mind that Mussorgsky's chronicle operas, *Boris Godunov* and *Khovanshchina*, were aimed at a popular audience, like Shakespeare's chronicle plays; and that his musical 'realism' (comparable with, but so unlike, Wagner's or even Puccini's) derived partly from the liberal and Slavophil ideals of the 1860s and was allied to the 'realist' art of the *Peredvijniki*, the Vagrants, whose pictures not only told stories but appealed to the basic emotions, pity, horror, love, religion or patriotism.

Musical life in St Petersburg centred round the Conservatoire, round the Hall of Nobles, which held several thousand people and where the principal concerts were given, and round the Mariinsky Theatre. (The Alexandrinsky Theatre was devoted to drama and the Maly to French plays.)

The Conservatoire had been founded by Anton Rubinstein, pianist and composer, in 1862. (The Moscow Conservatoire was founded by his brother Nicolas four years later.) It sprang out of a series of musical soirées held by the intelligent Grand Duchess Elena, sister-in-law of Nicolas I, at her huge Mikhailovsky Palace.[8] The Bolshoi (Grand) Theatre, built by Benois' grandfather, facing the Mariinsky, was pulled down to make way for the Conservatoire's new building. While Rubinstein, its first Director, ruled it, it was run on extremely traditional, that is, European, lines. He hated Russian music – even that of Tchaikovsky, whom he recommended as Professor of Composition in Moscow. Although Rimsky-Korsakov later taught in the Conservatoire, its principles were on the whole anathema to Balakirev and his followers, Borodin, Mussorgsky and Cui, who, with Rimsky, constituted the group known as 'Mogushaya Kutshka': the Mighty Handful, or 'The Five'.

During 1889, the year before his matriculation, Diaghilev had been present at Rubinstein's last concert in the Hall of Nobles in St Petersburg. Loving and revering links with the past as he did, he was overwhelmed by the performance of this virtuoso, who, as a child prodigy, had played in Paris before Chopin and Liszt. Diaghilev wrote,

Rubinstein mounted the platform at the exact hour the concert was due to begin. Six thousand people greeted him with a burst of applause.... Rubinstein took no notice of this ovation, and as if deaf to it sat down at the piano and began to play. It was a sublime recital – particularly the *Etudes Symphoniques* of Schumann.... He played the whole programme straight through without any pauses; and at the end of the recital he rose and made with both hands a gesture of rejection towards the piano as if saying 'All over'. Without bowing to the audience he crossed the platform, put on his cloak and went away. I find it impossible to describe how he played that evening. Nobody since has ever rivalled his power or the genius of his strongly accented rhythms.[9]

During the winter of 1890 Diaghilev was thrilled to meet Ludmila Shestakov, the sister of Glinka, 'father of Russian music'.

She must have been about eighty-five [he wrote], and exactly like her portrait by Repin. She was like some dried-up Madonna surrounded by a swarm of worshippers – particularly the Rimsky-Korsakov family. Kissing her hand was like revering a relic of Glinka. In spite of her age she often appeared at symphonic concerts in the Hall of Nobles, especially those of Russian music which were called the Beliaev Concerts after the name of the music publisher. Mme Shestakov usually sat in the so-called Korsakov box, which was between two columns on the left of the hall, and she was always accompanied by members of the Korsakov family. She never applauded and seldom opened her mouth....

Near the entrance one used to see, surrounded by his followers, Balakirev, whom we honoured as a pupil of Glinka; and in the very middle of the hall the two gigantic Stassov brothers, like a pair of moss-grown oaks. It was said that Dmitri Stassov had played à quatre mains with Glinka. His brother Vladimir, that passionate critic [and propagandist for Russian music], never stayed in one place for a moment. He ranged about the hall getting in everyone's way....

Tchaikovsky did not often come to the concerts, but I did occasionally see him and talk to him. This young-looking but completely white-haired angel of a man was the idol of musical St Petersburg at that time. He was one of several composers who conducted their own works at the Beliaev Concerts, and like all of them he did it very badly. He used to get exasperated and his left hand fiddled feverishly with his heavy gold watch-chain. At rehearsals he maintained no discipline and got all mixed up.[10]

Diaghilev may have been present at the dress rehearsal or the first performance of Tchaikovsky's ballet *The Sleeping Beauty* on 15 January 1890. Bakst was certainly at the dress rehearsal, and Benois attended the second or third performance. When Diaghilev put on his production of the ballet in London in 1921 Bakst wrote an essay in the programme:

The ardently expected dress rehearsal of Tchaikovsky's *The Sleeping Beauty* fell upon a murky and cold November [sic] afternoon. But when one is very young, what matters the weather? Especially with a complimentary ticket in my pocket from my old and venerable friend, the chief stage-manager of the Imperial Opera.
Before entering the auditorium, already swarming with people, custom ordained a visit to the stage-manager's room, where he – a veritable pasha, with his Methusalem-like white beard and a Persian cap upon his head – smoked and drank his perpetual glass of tea in this club, wherein gathered the stars of the opera and the ballet. Everybody loved to gossip in this vast apartment.... At the end of the sumptuous, Persian-carpeted room, through the crowd of dancers in daintily puffed-out skirts, I saw in outline two central figures, and from the respectful distance kept by the artists, I gathered that they were personages of importance. One of them – tall, slightly bent, with an aquiline nose, and a smile at once affable and sly, wore the Star of Vladimir Order on the left breast of the blue uniform he wore as director of the Imperial theatres.... The other gentleman was shorter. His hair and beard were white, his complexion very pink, his manner shyly amiable. He appeared very nervous, but was making a visible effort to control himself. Who is it? I sought to catch the eye of my old friend, who at last saw me (I was then far from tall), hemmed in among the frothy mass of fluttering ballet-skirts.
'Levushka ... come here and let me introduce you to our glory and pride, Piotr Ilyitch Tchaikovsky.' Blushing with emotion in my tight uniform as a student of the School of Fine Arts, but wearing white gloves – so smart, I thought – with my carroty, close-cropped hair, I must have looked funny. Boldly escaping from my pleasant prison, without hesitating, I stepped forward and held out my hand to the famous musician. 'Here he is,' continued the old *régisseur*, 'this youngster adores the theatre and is already painting scenic designs. The other day, whilst telling some friends at tea about your *Sleeping Beauty*, he improvised scenery in his own way. Where is it now?' And he sought in vain in the drawer of his desk.

'I like the music of *The Sleeping Beauty*,' I exclaimed in a voice strangled with emotion, amidst the general stupefaction, which was quickly followed by a mad outburst of laughter. 'Ah! You already know my ballet?' laughingly said Tchaikovsky with surprise, and looking enquiringly at the patriarchal beard of the stage manager.

Unforgettable matinée! I lived in a magic dream for three hours, intoxicated with fairies and princesses, splendid palaces flowing with gold, in the enchantment of the old tale. My whole being was as if swayed in cadence to the rhythms, the radiant flow of refreshing and beautiful melodies, which were already friends.

But what a home-coming! What a cruel ending to the enchantment! Outside, a darkness grown murkier after all this bedazzling; snow, stinging horribly; an icy wind from the Neva; vain efforts to find a droshky (too expensive near the theatre), and, at last, home: the lamp with its depressingly commonplace petrol, suspended too high. Ah! What a contrast with the Mariinsky Theatre, all decorated in blue velvet, filled with brightly clad officers of the Guard, with ladies in evening dress, bejewelled and radiant, with a heterogeneous and perfumed crowd, in which a more solemn note was struck by the red coats and white stockings of the Court, so bedizened with Imperial eagles.

That evening, I believe, my vocation was determined.[11]

The vocation of Bakst may have been determined by his first glimpse of *The Sleeping Beauty* – and, incidentally, the Director of the Imperial Theatres whom he describes as wearing the Order of Vladimir, I.A.Vzevolojsky, had himself designed the costumes – but Benois' admiration for the ballet may have had a more far-reaching effect, if not on Bakst, on Diaghilev, and turned the thoughts of Sergei towards this art of ballet, which, in the late 1880s and early 1890s, because of the banality of the Court spectacles, serious artists and musicians were prone to despise. Benois, who had loved certain ballets, such as *Coppelia*, when he was younger and had been overwhelmed by the dramatic power of the Italian ballerina Zucchi, had since been disillusioned by the apparent decline of the art. He could not believe that Tchaikovsky might rival Delibes, and his brother Leonty had told him that *The Sleeping Beauty* had been coldly received at the dress rehearsal. The Emperor, it appeared, had even snubbed Tchaikovsky.

It was a matinée during the Christmas holidays [wrote Benois] which gave Dima Filosofov and me the opportunity of seeing [a performance].... I simply did not dare believe what was growing in the very depths of my heart....

After this I did not miss a single performance.... Moreover, I tried to listen to Tchaikovsky wherever possible – at public concerts and at home when Serioja Diaghilev and Valetchka Nuvel played duets of his suites and symphonies, more or less successfully. When they were joined by Serioja's cousin Kolia Diaghilev, who played the 'cello tolerably well, they would play the trio, of which we were particularly fond at that time. My delight in *The Sleeping Beauty* led me to appreciate and become fond of the whole of *Eugene Onegin*, which I used to look upon with some mistrust....[12]

Alexander Borodin, dying in 1887, had left his *Prince Igor* unfinished. Rimsky-Korsakov completed the work and Glazunov, who had often heard the composer playing its overture on the piano, orchestrated this. On 4 November 1890, at the Mariinsky Theatre, *Prince Igor* had its first performance. So, during Diaghilev's first term at the University, he heard the barbaric choruses accompanying the Polovtsian dances with which he and the choreographer Michel Fokine – still only twelve years old and a junior pupil at the Imperial Ballet School – would overwhelm Parisian audiences twenty-one years later.

In the same blue and gold interior of the glorious Mariinsky Theatre the friends were present, only a fortnight after *Prince Igor*, on 19 December at the first performance of Tchaikovsky's opera *The Queen of Spades*. It was over ten years since the production of *Eugene Onegin*, which had become the most popular Russian work in the repertory. Diaghilev and Filosofov were seated in the front stalls, Nuvel and Benois a little further back. Benois' uncle Mikhail Cavos was in the front row next to the brothers Stassov.[13]

The Tchaikovsky cult was at that time only at its beginning [wrote Benois] – [and] an atmosphere of hostility pervaded the first night of *The Queen of Spades*. The audience applauded their favourite singers but there was no stormy ovation for the composer.... During the scene in the 'Bed-chamber of the Countess' I even quarrelled with Valetchka. It seemed to me that he did not 'react sufficiently' to it. Moreover, he failed to understand the meaning of the scene with the 'toadies' choir' and muttered irritably: 'This is quite foolish.' [It] seemed to me to be a particularly clever device. Nothing leads up better to the horror of the following scene [of Hermann surprising the Countess to her death] than this little song with its caressing, servile and rather dance-like rhythm in which, nevertheless, a certain funeral note can be distinguished. I must point out in justice to Valetchka ... that after the scene of the Countess's death he abandoned his contemptuous attitude and shared my delight to the full.[14]

What St Petersburg society really enjoyed was French or Italian opera, sung by stars of international celebrity. The Australian, Melba, who, following her début as Gilda in Brussels three years before, had woken up, like Byron after the publication of *Childe Harold*, to find herself famous, and had gone on to triumph in Paris, London, Milan, and other Italian cities, came to sing at the Mariinsky in February 1891, for the Emperor Alexander wanted to hear her in Gounod's *Roméo et Juliette*. Jean de Reszke was her Roméo. Diaghilev wrote,

Neither Jean de Reszke nor Van Dyck [the first Werther in Massenet's opera] had much of a voice, nor were they always absolutely in tune. Still, I must admit that de Reszke was magnificent in *Roméo et Juliette* and *Tristan*. Seldom since have I witnessed simpler or more expressive acting or a more stylish manner. Edouard de Reszke had a big, full bass voice and a noble way of singing: women adored him. The de Reszkes were preceded by their reputation as social figures, men who kept racing stables in Warsaw and Paris. We knew that Lady de Grey had started – or rather revived – the opera seasons at Covent Garden for them, and that during these seasons, which were the most brilliant in the world, Jean de Reszke vied with the great Tamagno himself and often supplanted him in the favour of the snob public.[15]

It is remarkable that Diaghilev at twenty had already heard the name of Lady de Grey, who, as Lady Ripon (after the death of her father-in-law in 1909), would be responsible for the Russian Ballet coming to London in 1911, and who was to become Sergei's greatest English supporter and friend. Since Melba will hardly recur in this chronicle it is worth quoting here what she wrote in her memoirs about this remarkable woman, Gwladys de Grey. Melba's first appearance at Covent Garden, where, in 1889, Albani reigned supreme, had aroused little enthusiasm, but, back in Paris, she received a letter from Lady de Grey, offering to arrange for her to return under better circumstances and to sing Juliette, adding that the Princess of Wales (Alexandra) had been 'deeply impressed' by her singing. So Melba went back to London and on 15 June 1889 sang in the first English performance of *Roméo et Juliette* with Jean de Reszke, and with Edouard as the Friar. A packed house, uproarious reception, wonderful notices: all due to Lady de Grey, who also gave a party for Melba and arranged for her to sing to Queen Victoria and the German Empress at Windsor.[16]

During the winter of 1891, the great Tamagno, who had been the first to sing Verdi's *Otello* (at La Scala, Milan, 1887), came to sing it at a private opera house in Moscow. (He was painted by Valentin Serov during this visit.) Four performances of *Otello* were also scheduled at the Mariinsky in St Petersburg, and at the Tsar's request Tamagno was summoned to sing in one of them, replacing the popular Nicolai Figner and performing opposite the latter's Italian wife Medea Figner. 'He was not on form,' Diaghilev recalled,

and the acoustics of the Mariinsky did not suit his phenomenal voice. On top of this, Napravnik the conductor did not allow him to repeat his famous opening phrase ['*Esultate! L'orgoglio musulmano sepolto e in mar!*'] and Tamagno who had come back on stage with this intention was obliged to beat a retreat to the wings. Yet there were people who had travelled all the way from Moscow by express train to hear this phrase, and returned home immediately after hearing it. During this performance there was a comic incident. Since *Otello* was already in the repertory it had not been thought necessary to rehearse it with Tamagno. When the time came for him to cry '*Fuggite!*' the chorus were so overcome with terror by the sound of his colossal voice that they fled from the stage and had to be driven back on again by the *régisseur*.[17]

During Diaghilev's second winter at the University Massenet came to St Petersburg for the production of his lush and perfumed *Esclarmonde*, with the beautiful American soprano Sybil Sanderson, whom he loved. In *Esclarmonde*, Diaghilev noted, she sang the famous top G, 'which is supposed to be the highest note the human voice can reach.' Diaghilev made friends with Massenet, and two years later was present at the first night of his *Thaïs* at the Paris Opéra.[18]

Another romantic incident took place at the *répétition générale* of *Esclarmonde*. The Tsarevitch had returned from his tour round the world, which was followed by a visit to his Danish relations. He had not seen Matilda Kchessinskaya for over a year. But 'on January 4th, 1892,' she wrote,

> fortune granted us a fleeting encounter. The Emperor and the Tsarevitch were sitting in the front row, while the Empress and the Grand Duchesses were in the Imperial box in the middle of the Grand Tier. I was also in the Grand Tier. Leaving my box in the interval, I went downstairs, and ran into the Tsarevitch, who was on his way up, going to the Imperial box. He could hardly stop, for we were surrounded by too many people: but I was overwhelmed by the mere fact of having been able to come so near him.

Soon after this the Tsarevitch took a house for the ballerina, 18 English Prospekt, and they enjoyed a two-year idyll. The only shadow across their flower-strewn path was the possibility of the Prince's engagement to Princess Alix of Hessen-Darmstadt.[19]

Relationships between members of the Imperial family or the aristocracy and dancers of the Imperial theatres were common before the Revolution and continued after it. Kchessinskaya's new house had been built by the Grand Duke Konstantin Nicolaievitch for the dancer Kuznetsova. Prince Vladimir Dolgorukov, brother of the Emperor Alexander II's beautiful morganatic second wife, created Princess Yurievska, had a son, Mikhail Alexandrov, by the dancer Alexandrova: Mikhail himself became a dancer. (Kchessinskaya found him 'a most exhilarating companion', and he was probably the man who in later years introduced Nijinsky to Prince Lvov, who introduced him to Diaghilev.) The Grand Duke Nicolas Nicolaievitch the elder loved the dancer Tchislova, by whom he had two sons called Nicolaiev, who went into the Horse Grenadiers, and two daughters, one of whom, a great beauty, married Prince Cantacuzene. Count Andrei Shuvalov married the dancer Vera Legat. When Pavel Gerdt, the most celebrated male dancer in St Petersburg at the end of the nineteenth century, was baptized in the Orthodox faith – his father had been a German pinmaker – Count Pavel Andreievitch Shuvalov stood godfather to him. Prince Nikita Trubetskoy married the ballerina Lubov Egorova.[20] This mixing of aristocratic and lower-class blood often produced children of distinguished appearance and manners, who themselves became dancers. At least two of Diaghilev's ballerinas in later days, noted for their chic and charm, were illegitimate, one being Pavlova.

Tchaikovsky's last opera, *Yolanta*, was first performed at the Mariinsky Theatre on 6 December 1892, in a programme with the ballet *Casse-noisette*. The Emperor and the entire Court were present; and when the baritone sang his aria 'Who can compare with my Mathilda?' Diaghilev heard people making jokes about the relationship between Matilda Kchessinskaya and the Tsarevitch. After *Yolanta* Tchaikovsky wrote only his Sixth Symphony, the 'Pathétique'. Diaghilev was present when he conducted its first performance on 28 October 1893.

The work had been passionately awaited. At the rehearsal opinions were greatly divided.... The concert's success was naturally overwhelming and no one dreamed that within a week Tchaikovsky would be dead. That evening the composer conducted in his usual nervous way. I heard afterwards that he had overlooked numerous mistakes in the scoring. Napravnik, who conducted the symphony two weeks later, had by that time corrected these errors; and he wept throughout the performance.[21]

Diaghilev continued:

During the week following the first playing of the symphony, *Novoe Vremya*, the daily paper, published, among a lot of other short news items, the announcement that Tchaikovsky was ill, and that the illness was taking its course. Then suddenly I saw a sentence inserted at the foot of this announcement: 'Piotr Ilyitch Tchaikovsky died yesterday.' I could not believe my eyes. I felt I had only just left Tchaikovsky, having met him several evenings before at the Alexandrinsky Theatre, in the box of K.A.Varlamov [the actor]. Then I remembered that we had spoken of death, and Tchaikovsky had said: 'You know, I find it hard to believe that that old bogeyman will come for me one day too!'

In despair I rushed out of the house, and although I realized Tchaikovsky had died of cholera I made straight for Malaya Morskaya, where he lived. The doors were wide open and there was no one to be seen. The place was upside down. In the entrance hall the score of the Sixth Symphony lay open on a table, and I noticed on a sofa the camel-hair skull-cap which Tchaikovsky wore all the time. I heard voices from another room, and on entering I saw Piotr Ilyitch in a black morning coat stretched on a sofa. Rimsky-Korsakov and the singer Nicolai Figner were arranging a table to put him on. We lifted the body of Tchaikovsky, myself holding the feet, and laid it on the table. The three of us were alone in the flat, for after Tchaikovsky's death the whole household had fled. Piotr Ilyitch looked little different from when he was alive, and as young as ever. I went off to buy flowers. For the whole of that first day my wreath was the only one lying at his feet.

A lot of people assembled to hear the prayers for the dead, among them Vsevolojsky, Director of the Imperial Theatres, and Napravnik. Everyone kept his mouth covered with a handkerchief and spat constantly into it, which was what we were advised to do to avoid catching cholera.

An immense crowd flocked to Tchaikovsky's funeral; and although it was broad daylight, the street lamps were lit all the way along the processional route. The coffin was borne past the Mariinsky Theatre to the Cathedral of Kazan. We expected the Emperor to attend, but only the Grand Duke Konstantin Konstantinovitch came: he was then President of the Imperial Society of Music and of the Academy of Sciences. I followed the hearse together with Rimsky-Korsakov, who said to me, 'Here's a man gone in good time. Look at Gounod – he so long outlived his fame that no one noticed his death.' Gounod had died earlier that year.

Various myths soon sprang up around the death of Tchaikovsky. Some said he caught cholera by drinking a glass of tap water at the Restaurant Leiner. Certainly, we used to see Piotr Ilyitch eating there almost every day, but nobody at that time drank unbottled water, and it seemed inconceivable to us that Tchaikovsky should have done so.

Others invented the legend of Tchaikovsky's suicide, alleging that he poisoned himself for love of a certain member of his family [his nephew Vladimir Davidov], to whom he had dedicated one of his principal works [the 'Pathétique']. These people claimed that if Tchaikovsky had really died of cholera his flat would have been put out of bounds; and that the cholera epidemic was over (he was, in fact, one of the last to die of it). I myself place little credence in these stories. I knew all of Tchaikovsky's circle, and was a close friend of the person who was alleged to have caused his death; and I think there is no evidence to support the theory of suicide....[22]

Benois had a highly developed pedagogic instinct, and part of his fondness for Diaghilev was due to the fact that in these early years he regarded him as a pupil. Although Sergei had a respectable baritone voice and could play the piano not badly, the group of friends found his musical preferences somewhat naïve. 'Even when, moved by our example,' wrote Benois, 'Serioja began to appreciate Wagner, he remained indifferent to those things which particularly delighted us: the prelude to *Die Walküre* or the Forest Murmurs in *Siegfried*. On the other hand he liked the last great Monologue of Lohengrin, Walther's song in *Die Meistersinger*, and so on. These predilections and especially an enthusiasm for Verdi and Massenet, brought accusations of bad taste.' At first Diaghilev submitted tamely to the rebukes and teasing of his 'elders', but, Benois noticed, 'he later began to snap back at us and even shout at his critics, of whom Valetchka was the most violent and persistent.... Our example directed him to a more intellectual, less sensuous attitude towards music: on our side we profited from his natural intuition – and he steadily matured and gained in insight – and by the professionalism of musicianship.'

In the world of painting and sculpture Diaghilev was still groping his way, and he listened to Benois and Bakst without answering back. But, Benois wrote, 'We were not prepared for the surprise he sprang on us. In a series of leaps he moved from complete ignorance and indifference to a keen and even passionate interest. He suddenly acquired competence in questions which demanded a high degree of specialization.'[23] Diaghilev's 'leap' was a reaction against the realism of the *Peredvijniki*, who had progressed from being rebels in the 1860s to being universally accepted painters in the 1890s; they had even invaded and taken over the Academy. Diaghilev had begun to appreciate a bolder style of painting for painting's sake: he was making his way *via* Scotland, Scandinavia and Germany towards the Impressionism of Paris, the most vital movement of the late nineteenth century.

Benois had begun in 1891 to send watercolours to the Annual Watercolour Exhibition held at the Academy of Arts and Sciences, and in 1892 he sold six.[24] The Emperor and members of his family would usually appear for a private visit on the day before the *vernissage*. Shura was thrilled to observe the Tsar at close quarters. 'I came to the exhibition of 1891 in my student's uniform and this may have made a bad impression on the Tsar, who took a poor view of students as possible revolutionaries. But he shook my hand with his own huge one with great friendliness and murmured a few encouraging words.' Liberal-minded people had never forgiven this conservative ruler for not signing the constitution which lay ready on his father's desk on the day he was murdered. But, wrote Benois,

the manners of the Imperial couple... enhanced the liking I had for our Tsar.... With his colossal stature, his voice and particularly the expression in his penetrating eyes, Alexander III inspired a feeling of awe, even terror.... Sometimes he would start joking.... [He had] a loud, resounding laugh.... I was fascinated by the Tsaritsa [sister of the Princess of Wales]. Her tiny stature, her lisp, her faulty Russian accent, enhanced her fascination. All these little flaws together with her shyness were inexpressibly moving – perhaps not regal enough, but they helped to win one's heart.... The Tsarevitch produced a less favourable impression. His appearance was not inspiring.... He was obviously bored, had no interest in pictures nor in the dull people who wanted to sell them....[25]

The Tsarevitch's affair with Matilda Kchessinskaya coincided with her early successes on the Imperial stage. The Italian Carlotta Brianza, the first Aurora in *The Sleeping Beauty*, had retired, after enjoying the usual 'benefit performance' in December 1891. After this Kchessinskaya reigned supreme. She was what is called a *terre-à-terre* dancer, without much *élévation*, but quick in movement, dazzling in her *pirouettes* and bubbling over with smiles and charm. A distinguished dancer of a younger generation told me that 'she had a bad figure and bad legs, was never on full point, but was still an extraordinary and wonderful dancer.'[26]

After taking his degree in Law, Diaghilev left the University, and in February 1894 set off with Dima on one of the latter's visits to the South of France, stopping on the way in Paris for the first night of Massenet's *Thaïs* (16 March). 'On the evening before this great occasion,' wrote Diaghilev, 'Massenet took me back to his flat, and as we went in he said in his usual affected manner "Now I'm going to show you something Russian." He led me into a darkened room, where a night-light was burning before a big ikon of the Blessed Virgin. "In everyday life," he said, "*she* is the one I revere. On the stage I worship her whom you will see tomorrow." '[27] This was Sanderson, of course.

Dima and Sergei arrived in Nice at carnival time. Pavel Koribut-Kubitovitch was there, and was surprised, one day as he was wandering among the merrymaking crowds, to find himself belaboured by two masked revellers: these turned out to be his cousins. Leaving Filosofov at the Château Valrose to enjoy the sea air, Sergei and Pavel travelled together to Genoa, Milan, Venice, Bologna and Florence, combing the antique shops on the way.[28]

In the following month, April 1894, the engagement of the Tsarevitch to Princess Alix of Hesse was announced, and he ceased to visit Kchessinskaya. She wrote asking if she might continue calling him *tu* and whether she could 'come to him in case of necessity'. He replied, 'Whatever happens to my life, my days spent with you will ever remain the happiest memories of my youth.' Perhaps he took care to write 'my days', rather than 'my nights'. He told her that she could always apply to him when she was in trouble and that he would back her up. He kept his word. 'I saw quite clearly,' the ballerina recorded in later years, 'that the Tsarevitch did not have the qualities needed to be a ruler....'[29]

Benois got married that summer. His wife Atia suffered from poor health, and they went south for their honeymoon. Alexandre had already been in Germany, but now, in a state of rapture, crossed the Alps for the first time. On his very first day in Milan, 20 October, as he surveyed the pinnacled Duomo, he heard news-vendors announcing '*la morte del Tsar*'.[30]

The Emperor Alexander had been ill for several weeks and chronic nephritis had been diagnosed, but it seemed incredible that this big, burly man should die in his fiftieth year. On the morrow of the accession of Nicolas II, Princess Alix, who had only just arrived in Russia, was converted to the Orthodox religion and became Grand Duchess Alexandra Feodorovna. A week after the funeral their wedding took place in the Winter Palace.

Benois and his wife returned from their *voyage de noces* by Christmas 1894. They had visited Florence and Venice, and Benois had laid the foundations of the scholarship which would earn him in time the curatorship of the Hermitage. The friends gathered regularly in Benois' study at the family flat, and heated discussions on art would take place before they joined his father and sister and her family for tea in the dining-room. They also met at this time the novelist and poet Merejkovsky, whose *Julian the Apostate* was being serialized in a literary magazine. Merejkovsky had novel theories on religion, and organized conferences between philosophers and the more enlightened clergy. His blonde, beautiful wife, the poet Zinaida Hippius, whom Benois thought a *femme fatale* with 'a permanent Gioconda smile' and endless affectations, formed an intense friendship with Dima Filosofov. The friends were also pleased to get to know Repine, one of the most celebrated painters in Russia, and to attend his parties at the Academy of Arts, where, as Director of Studies, he had a flat.[31]

Diaghilev had continued his tuition under Rimsky-Korsakov and he invited his friends to hear one of his compositions. He had written to the words of Pushkin a new Fountain Scene (in the Polish act of *Boris Godunov*), which, though derivative from Mussorgsky, contained certain passages of broad melody in the Italian style to which he was so addicted. He himself sang the part of the false Dmitri, while his step-aunt Alexandra Valerianovna (Panaev) Kartsov sang Marina. The result, Benois and Nuvel agreed, was disastrous. It was this fiasco, and the fact that Rimsky-Korsakov told Diaghilev – probably about this time – that he had no talent for composition, which made him renounce his ambition to be a composer. Singing too he gave up.[32] Years later, when Boris Kochno asked him what kind of voice he had had, he replied, 'Very big and very ugly.'[33] But Diaghilev's musical studies had not been wasted.

He had moved out of his aunt Filosofov's flat and taken one of his own at 45 Liteiny Prospekt, which he shared for a time with a friend, Mikhail Andreyev, who had been at the University with him.[34] Here he was looked after by Dunia, his old nanny, and by a somewhat unconventional manservant (he wore a moustache),[35] Vassili Zuikov, who would remain devoted to him for the rest of his life. It was said that Vassili had been charged with raping a girl under age and that Diaghilev had somehow brought about his acquittal.[36]

The former palace of the Grand Duchess Elena, the Mikhailovsky, one of Rossi's handsomest and most enormous buildings, was being turned into a Museum of Russian Art, and Benois asked for a job there. His eldest brother Albert, however, was engaged instead; and Albert found Alexandre temporary employment in sorting out and cataloguing the vast collection of Princess Tenishev, which was going to form part of the museum.[37] Maria Klavdievna Tenishev was the wife of a millionaire, who had a monopoly of all the passenger steamers on the rivers of Russia.[38] She had a passion for reviving old Russian craftsmanship, and bought pictures indiscriminately.

In the summer of 1895 Diaghilev set out on the most extensive of his Grand Tours. He spent six weeks abroad. On coming of age, he had inherited sixty thousand roubles, which had been in trust for him since the death of his mother, and he was determined to buy some distinguished pictures and furniture for his new flat.[39] When abroad, it was easy for him to appear a rather more important personage than at home. While his best friends laughed at him for having 'Serge de Diaghilew' printed on his visiting cards,[40] French, Germans and Italians, seeing him staying at the best hotels, wearing well-cut clothes, a top-hat and (out of affectation) an eye-glass, regarded him as a real Russian nobleman *en voyage*. In fact, his mother's money lasted him about three years,[41] but the impressive exterior and grand manner which became second nature to him served him in good stead for the rest of his life. In Paris, Holland and Germany he bought several pictures: the head of a girl by Puvis de Chavannes, some sketches by Dagnan-Bouveret, sketches for portraits of Bismarck and Böcklin by Lenbach, two drawings by Menzel, some drawings by Liebermann – the most Impressionistic of the Germans – watercolours by Hans Bartels and Hans Hermann, and a large painting by Ludwig Dill. He acquired a fine Renaissance table and a set of Jacobean chairs. In June he wrote jokingly to Benois from Antwerp, where he had no doubt gone to see the work and home of Rubens, saying that he appointed him 'curator of the Diaghilev Museum'. He called on such celebrities as Gounod, Saint-Saëns, Zola, Puvis de Chavannes and Böcklin, and brought back signed photographs of them, arriving in St Petersburg wearing smart new clothes and smelling of the latest fashionable scent.[42]

That autumn Shura and Atia Benois, whose first child, a daughter, had been born in August, were delighted to find a flat in Glinka Street, just opposite Shura's old home. It was here that Diaghilev astonished Benois by showing him his first attempts at art criticism: reports on current exhibitions, published in *Novosti*. 'They were written with fervour,' Benois commented, 'and some with sarcasm and ruthlessness that bore witness to his age – he was only twenty-four. From then on he needed no help from me. ...'[43]

The new Emperor's coronation was to be in Moscow in May 1896. Kchessinskaya found that she had not been chosen to take part in the gala performance at the Bolshoi Theatre. Legnani, the Italian ballerina, would be appearing in a new ballet, with music by Drigo, called *La Perle*.

Seized with the deepest despair I ran to the Grand Duke Vladimir Alexandrovitch, Alexander III's favourite brother and the Tsar's eldest uncle, who had always shown me friendship and kindness.... The result was swift and decisive. The Administration of the Imperial Theatres received orders to allow me to participate in the Coronation gala.... I was filled with happiness to see Niki intervene thus on my behalf.... Drigo had to compose additional music, and Petipa arranged a *pas de deux* specially for me in which I danced a Yellow Pearl. (There were already white, black and pink pearls in the ballet.)[44]

This was the first of many successful appeals, for which 'blackmail' is perhaps too strong a word. From the windows of her hotel Kchessinskaya watched the coronation procession.

Troops lined the whole route.... Besides detachments from the various cavalry regiments of the Guard, there were representatives of the Asian tribes from the Russian Empire in their national dress. There were delegations of Cossacks, members of the high nobility led by the Marshal of the Nobles of the Moscow district, all on horseback followed by the Court orchestra and the Imperial Hunt in their rich uniforms, headed by His Majesty's Master of the Horse and Master of the Hounds.... Finally the Tsar appeared, riding a white horse, whose horseshoes had silver nails. He was followed by the Imperial Family and by foreign princes. Behind the latter came the Empress Marie Feodorovna and the Grand Duchess Olga Alexandrovna in a gold carriage with a crown above it, drawn by eight white horses. Two small pages sat on the traces. In the gold carriage which followed, the Tsarina Alexandra Feodorovna sat alone. Behind her, in other gold carriages, came the Grand Duchesses. The weather was magnificent....[45]

It was announced that Coronation cups in great number would be distributed to the populace in Khodynka Meadow outside the city. The crowds were so vast that stands collapsed, the people panicked and stampeded, and many were killed. The Tsar was criticized for attending a ball at the French Embassy on the night of this disaster; but he visited all the wounded in hospital.

Leon Bakst and Benois' nephew, Eugene Lancerey – Jenia – were already living in Paris when the Benois arrived to buy pictures for Princess Tenishev and took a flat in the Latin Quarter, so there was a happy group of friends to go sight-seeing, visit the Louvre, attend performances at the Opéra, the Opéra Comique, the Comédie Française and the Odéon together. 'However,' Benois recorded, 'we entirely disapproved of the French ballet.'

[It was] passing through a period of shameful degeneration particularly evident to us devotees of our wonderful Petersburg ballet.... In Paris ballet was regarded as a mere appendage to the opera and there were hardly any male dancers – they had been replaced by hordes of females. This was supposed to be at the insistence of the notorious *abonnés de l'Opéra*, who consisted mostly of very elegant grey-haired old gentlemen ... who occupied the first rows of seats and who retired whenever they wished, in their top-hats and with their canes, through a special passage to the stage to chat ... with their ballet beauties (who frequently were no beauties at all).[46]

Besides revelling in the riches of the Louvre, Benois began to appreciate the art of the Impressionists, whose work in those days, when there were almost no commercial galleries, could only be seen chez Durand Ruel, who had been exhibiting them since 1874. It was at the gallery of this go-ahead dealer that Benois realized that Monet was a great painter.[47] He was back in St Petersburg at the end of the year, for Princess Tenishev planned to exhibit her Russian collection at the Society for the Encouragement of the Arts, and he was to arrange it. There were many clashes between them, as he urged her to exclude a number of works which in his eyes fell beneath a certain standard.[48]

In January 1897 Diaghilev organized *his* first exhibition of German and British watercolours in the newly founded Stieglitz Museum, which was near where he lived. Works of Hermann, Bartels and Liebermann were hung alongside those of Lavery, Austen-Brown, Guthrie, Paterson and others of the Glasgow school, who had felt the influence of Impressionism before their English contemporaries.[49]

Between April and August 1897 the Tsar received four state visits, and the staff of the Imperial Theatres were kept busy planning gala performances. That for the Emperor Franz Joseph took place at the Mariinsky; that for the King of Siam at Peterhof, the beautiful palace which surveys the Gulf of Finland through a curtain of fountains; that for the Emperor Wilhelm on an island on the upper lake at Peterhof; that for President Félix Faure in the Peterhof theatre. The outdoor performance for the German Emperor, as described by Kchessinskaya, sounds exceptionally fairylike.

Stands for the spectators had been arranged all round on the island itself, while the stage had been raised on piles above the water; the orchestra played in an enormous iron stand below the level of the lake. The stage only had side scenery and wings: the magnificent view of the distant hills of Babigon served as a backcloth. Not far from the stage was a little island, decorated with rocks and a grotto, in which I hid myself at the beginning of the performance. The programme for this gala was the one-act ballet *Thétis et Pélée*, arranged by Petipa to music of Delibes and Minkus. The guest arrived in little boats. The whole scene was bathed in electric light and the ensemble had a truly fairylike appearance. The ballet started with the opening of the grotto in which I was hidden: I then stepped on to a mirror, which began to slide towards the stage. This gave the audience the impression that I was walking on the water. The spectacle ended with the lighting up of the pavilions and far-off hills beyond the stage.[50]

Meanwhile, the Benois family were spending their summer in Brittany and Diaghilev was listening to Wagner at Bayreuth. Here he had a serious talk with Prince Vladimir Argutinsky-Dolgorukov, a delightful man, who was a diplomat and a collector of beautiful objects.[51] The group of friends had long been planning a revolution in the arts in Russia, and the idea of a magazine in which to voice their opinions was forming in their minds. By now Diaghilev, the most energetic among them, was ready to assume leadership and be its editor. One inspiration for the magazine was the English *Studio*: perhaps *The Yellow Book* and *The Savoy* also played a part.

That autumn Benois, who had been joined by Kostia Somov in Paris, received from Diaghilev the following letter:

I am full of projects – each more grandiose than the last. At present I am planning a magazine which would embrace all our artistic life – drawings and paintings would be shown in the illustrations. The articles would be outspoken and, finally, it would be linked with the new brand of industrial art which is developing in Moscow and in Finland. In short, I see the future through a magnifying glass. But for all this I need help, and, obviously, to whom should I turn if not to you? For I count on you as I do on myself. The least I shall expect from you is five articles a year. Kostia has already promised to help with the cover and the posters.[52]

When Benois returned to St Petersburg in January 1898, to help arrange the Imperial collections of Russian art in the Mikhailovsky Palace, he was in time to see the opening of Diaghilev's second exhibition, held, like his previous one, in the big, two-storeyed hall of the Stieglitz Museum.[53]

The motto of Diaghilev and his friends was 'Art for Art's sake'. Like Oscar Wilde, and unlike the slavophil and politically committed *Peredvijniki*, they believed there was no morality in art. It is true that Diaghilev and Benois greatly admired Repine, who was ranged with the Vagrants, now in power at the Academy, for the quality of his paint: but even Repine painted pictures of *Dnieper Cossacks writing a Letter to the Tsar*, and of *Ivan the Terrible clasping his Dying Son in his Arms*; and his picture of the murdered Alexander II had been called *They could not wait* (for a Constitution). Because of their admiration of painting for paint's sake Diaghilev's group were labelled 'Decadents'.

Benois described the opening of the exhibition.

This time the hall seemed particularly festive, thanks to an extravagant abundance of hothouse plants and flowers which Serioja had placed everywhere, regardless of cost. A certain section of the advanced intelligentsia of the capital was displeased at the pomp – unprecedented at any exhibition – with which the opening took place. It was attended by almost the entire Imperial family, with the Tsar and both Tsarinas at its head. At their entrance into the hall an orchestra in the gallery struck up. Their attitude was one of calm routine semi-attention to which Imperial personages are brought up: they hardly ever express approval or disapproval. Only the Grand Duke Vladimir Alexandrovitch amazed all his exalted relatives by buying a watercolour – and one of Somov's at that! It is still a mystery whether this freak of Vladimir Alexandrovitch's was an act of bravado ... or whether this lovely thing, which showed a grove of trimmed trees, really pleased him.[54]

Sergei's talents and drive had thus brought him, at the age of twenty-seven, to the attention of the Imperial family; he had been presented to the Tsar, autocrat of all the Russias, the fountain of all honours. 'Foremost among his dreams,' wrote Benois, 'was one of receiving a title which would give him the right to be present at Court functions.'[55] (Benois' translator should have written 'appointment' for 'title'. Nicolas II gave very few titles.)[56] Although Diaghilev's birth did not entitle him to be received at Court, as a man of special distinction he might aspire to a personal invitation from the Emperor to a Court ball.[57] Lieutenant-General Mossolov, who in 1900 became Head of the Court Chancellery and chief Assistant of Count Friedericx, Minister of the Court, has described how 'the sons of personages admitted to Court balls could not be invited with their fathers; they had to merit the favour through their own position'. Mossolov describes vividly the ceremony which attended these receptions at the most sumptuous Court and in the most fantastic palace in the world.

Only one ball a year was organized in the Nicolas Room, which could hold 3,000 guests. In order to attend this ball it was necessary to belong to one of the first four 'classes' (of the fourteen classes into which Russian officers and officials are

31

divided); all the foreign diplomats and their wives were also invited, the senior officers of the regiments of the Guard (with their wives and daughters), certain young officers recognized by their chiefs as dancers, and finally persons invited individually by Their Majesties....

A practised eye could distinguish the men or women who did not belong to real 'society': their clothes might, for instance, be too new.... There was also the way of wearing a uniform or a ball dress, and that indefinable something that gives to the well-born the air of being 'at home everywhere'.

The time for arrival was about 8.30.... Everybody knew his proper entrance to the Palace. . . . The scene was fairylike. January. Intense cold. The whole of the three blocks of the winter Palace inundated with light. Braziers burning round the immense Alexander Column. Carriages arriving in an unbroken line. Open sledges bringing those officers who did not fear the cold; the horses' harness covered with blue netting.... Feminine silhouettes were to be seen hurrying feverishly across the few steps that separated the arriving carriages from the entrance.... Furs – heavens!... sable, silver fox, arctic fox. No shawls over the heads, because of the diadems of the married ladies and the flowers worn by the girls.... The guests went up the grand staircases of white marble on the soft velvety carpets. White and scarlet uniforms; spreadeagle helmets in gold and silver; countless epaulettes; the marvellous national costumes of the Hungarian guests ... the *beshmets* of the Caucasian nobles; white dolmans embroidered with previous beaver fur; finally, the Court uniforms, heavy with gold embroidery and completed by short breeches and white silk stockings.... All the ladies wore 'Court' dresses, cut very low, with the shoulders bare, and with a long train....

The long procession moved on between two lines of Cossacks of the Guard in scarlet uniforms, and Court 'Arabs', gigantic turbaned negroes. They were 'Arabs' only by tradition; actually they were Christian Abyssinians. The Masters of Ceremonies, grave and gracious, moved about quietly everywhere, to assist the flow of arrivals.... Each had his baton, a sort of long ebony wand surmounted by an ivory ball and a two-headed eagle with a bow of bright blue ribbon (the St Andrew's knot)....

The great moment was approaching. Their Majesties were coming, in full procession of state, from the Malachite Room. The orchestra plunged into a polonaise. The Masters of Ceremonies gave three taps with their wands; the Arabs opened the doors of the room. Everyone turned toward the procession....[58]

However insignificant in appearance or personality the Sovereign might be, he was surrounded by a godlike aura.

Such were the sights Diaghilev hoped to enjoy: such was the ceremony of a court to which he yearned to belong. Yet he had already begun to arouse hostility. On the one hand, he was accused by the serious younger artists he admired of trying to make his exhibition too smart; on the other, his choice of painters was mocked by the conservative members of society. The press notices were poor. An old general paid several visits and always burst out laughing in front of the same picture. Somebody made a row at the ticket office and asked for his money back. Even Benois' family thought Shura's

The Winter Palace, St Petersburg. Drawing by Mstislav Dobujinsky.

admiration for the advanced painters was a kind of pose.[59] That Diaghilev had by now 'settled down' into a homosexual way of life was another mark against him on the social register.

However, while Benois returned to Paris, Diaghilev set about planning his magazine. He already had ideas about whom he should get to back it.

PART II

The Magazine and the Exhibitions

CHAPTER 3

1898–1900

Early Years of *The World of Art* – The International
Exhibition

DIAGHILEV HAD BEEN BORN with a silver spoon in his mouth: but
the leisurely days were over. From the year he launched his magazine he was committed to battle for all that he thought new, imaginative and of true quality in the arts. He may have thought in 1898 that he
was on the crest of a wave, but in fact nothing would ever be easy for him
again. He would make enemies, subsidies would be withdrawn, supporters
would die: immense struggles lay ahead.

In spring 1898 Diaghilev travelled to Berlin, London and Paris. There
was no such thing as fine printing in Russia at this time and block-making
was primitive. Many of the plates for the magazine would have to be
engraved outside Russia: for this he had to make arrangements.[1] In the
course of this journey Diaghilev was also borrowing pictures for the International Exhibition he planned to hold in St Petersburg in the following
year.

Diaghilev had met Aubrey Beardsley in Dieppe during the previous summer,[2] and Beardsley had died in March: now, in May, Diaghilev sought
out the exiled Oscar Wilde in Paris. 'The Ballad of Reading Gaol' had been
published in February, in an edition of four hundred copies; and Wilde
complained that his rather disreputable publisher, Leonard Smithers, was
'so fond of "suppressed books" that he suppresses his own'. About 4 May
he wrote to Smithers: 'Have you a copy of Aubrey's drawing of Mlle de
Maupin? [This was, apart from posters, Beardsley's only colour print, of
which over a hundred reproductions were made.] There is a young Russian
here, who is a great amateur of Aubrey's art, who would love to have one.
He is a great collector, and rich. So you might send him a copy and name
a price, and also deal with him for drawings by Aubrey. His name is Serge
de Diaghilew, Hotel St James, Rue St Honoré, Paris....'[3] We can imagine
that Diaghilev was delighted to take Wilde out to dinner; that it was a very

good dinner; and that, hard up as Wilde was, he exerted himself to be amusing. (In a letter written shortly afterwards he describes a dinner at which he thought he had been 'rather wonderful'.)[4] When Oscar Wilde walked down the Grands Boulevards with Diaghilev, prostitutes stood on their chairs outside the cafés to see him arm-in-arm with a handsome young man who wore a white streak in his hair, and they shouted abuse.[5]

In answer to a letter from Benois expressing some doubts about the necessity for – or proposed nature of – the magazine, Diaghilev fired, on 2 June, the following fusillade:

When you build a house, God knows how many masons, carpenters and painters surround you.... You can be sure only of one thing – that the frontage of the house will be good because you believe in the friendship and talent of the architect. But the opposite occurs. When, covered in dust and soot, you come out from under the scaffolding and the timber, your architect tells you that he cannot build the house and in general questions the necessity for building it! Only then are you struck by all the loathesomeness of the bricks and the stink of the wall-paper and the glue, the inefficiency of the work etc. This is what your letter did to me. . . . Just as I cannot and would not know how to beg my parents to love me, in the same way I cannot ask you for your sympathy and help.... I have no time to give you a good shaking, I have no time to try and break your neck. This is all. . . .[6]

The two backers Diaghilev had in mind were Princess Tenishev and Savva Mamontov, the railway magnate; and it was during the summer of 1898 that he went to see Mamontov at Abramtsevo, near Moscow, visiting museums and artists in the old capital on the way.

Diaghilev had been to Moscow before, but, with the prospect of the magazine ahead of him, he must have taken his visit of 1898 more seriously than previous trips to hear music or to see the sights. He had to inform himself, keep an eye open for material for the magazine, miss nothing and waste no time. He made a thorough study of the famous Tretiakov collection. For thirty years Pavel Tretiakov, the Moscow merchant, had backed the *Peredvijniki* (Vagrants) and bought their paintings, as well as earlier works of Russian art. Viktor Vasnetsov had designed a fantastic building in the old Russian style to house this collection, which in 1892 Tretiakov gave, together with his brother's collection of French painting, to the city of Moscow. Even if Diaghilev viewed with distaste the majority of Tretiakov's collection, he fell temporarily under the spell of Vasnetsov, who, in paint as well as architecture, had a cult for medieval Russia, and who had close ties with Mamontov and Abramtsevo, which was Diaghilev's next port of call. Three of Tretiakov's daughters married three of Diaghilev's friends – namely, Dr Sergei Botkine, another collector, Alexander Ziloti, a musician, conductor and founder of a series of concerts, and Leon Bakst. Tretiakov died in the winter of 1898. Diaghilev's business call on Mamontov to raise money would also turn out to be – whether he realized it at the time or only some months later – a pilgrimage to the source of the modern movement in Russia. Mamontov himself may be regarded as a bridge between the socially conscious Vagrants – as well as the Arts and Crafts movement with which they were allied – and the 'modern' Moscow painters who were Russia's equivalent of the French Impressionists.

In 1872, the year of Diaghilev's birth, Mamontov, who had trained as a singer, and his wife Elizabeth, who was interested in reviving the liturgy of the Orthodox Church, were in Rome. Here they met the young art historian Prakhov, the popular Vagrant sculptor Antokolsky and a Moscow landscape painter named Polenov. The friends conferred on matters of art and social reform: in true Vagrant spirit they wanted to improve the lot of the Russian peasant. The Mamontovs had bought the Abramtsevo estate two years before, and were determined to continue the tradition of a former owner, Aksakov, who had entertained the liberal-minded writers of the 1840s, including Gogol. (Gogol had written part of his *Dead Souls* there.) Already, following a cholera epidemic, a hospital had been built on the estate. The Mamontovs brought their friends back from Rome to form the nucleus of an artistic colony. In 1874, in Paris, they picked up Polenov's friend, Ilya Repine, as well as the widow of Alexander Serov, composer of the opera *Judith*, and her nine-year-year-old son, Valentin. All these were made welcome to live in or near Abramtsevo. They were joined in 1879 by the brothers Viktor and Appollinary Vasnetsov.

From 1840, when it was founded, the Moscow Art College had stressed the importance of working from nature – *sur le motif*. In this it differed entirely from the St Petersburg Academy, founded by the Empress Elizabeth I in 1758 and organized by Catherine the Great. This split can be seen throughout the whole course of the modern movement in Russian painting. Polenov was appointed Professor at the Moscow school in 1882 and had soon introduced to Abramtsevo his most gifted pupils, Isaac Levitan, a Jew, destined to become Russia's leading landscape painter, and Konstantin Korovine, the first Russian to be influenced (after a period of study in Paris in 1885) by the French Impressionists. The boy Serov, who, through his German grandmother on his father's side, had Jewish blood, worked under Repine and developed into a portrait painter of genius; and he brought his friend, Mikhail Vrubel, who was ten years his senior and had studied at the St Petersburg Academy under Tchistiakov (the mentor of several talented artists), into the Abramtsevo circle.

A small church in the medieval Novgorod style was built on the Abramtsevo estate to designs of Appollinary Vasnetsov. Polenov, his sister Elena Polenov, who designed and executed embroideries, Mamontov's cousin, the painter Maria Yakuntchikova, Repine, and Viktor Vasnetsov, who laid a floor, all helped to adorn it. Thus began a revival of medieval architecture and ikon painting. Next, a museum of peasant art was founded which led to a new interest in carving and embroidery in a traditional style; so that a school grew up which can be compared to the workshops of William Morris, though the latter, deriving from a cosmopolitan medieval tradition, produced more sophisticated designs. (The ornate wooden building of the Abramtsevo museum looks like the cross between a Swiss chalet and a Siamese temple.) Finally, the evening reading sessions of the Mamontov circle and their amateur play-acting led to regular performances on a small scale in Mamontov's Moscow house, with décors and costumes by Viktor Vasnetsov, Serov, Levitan and Korovine. In 1897 Mamontov took over Solodovnikov's private theatre and launched an opera company, which opened with Rimsky-Korsakov's *Sadko*.

That Diaghilev and Filosofov, who accompanied him on his excursion, were deeply impressed by the achievements of Mamontov and his hive of artists is evident from the contents of early numbers of the new magazine.[7]

Two other great Moscow merchant collectors, Sergei Shchukin and Ivan Morosov, whose French paintings now enrich the Hermitage in Leningrad and the Pushkin Museum of Fine Arts in Moscow, may be mentioned here. Shchukin, who was to lend Diaghilev two Forains for the 1899 exhibition, had just bought his first Monet. To quote Mr John Richardson:

Subsequently he bought six Renoirs and eight great Cézannes.... By 1910 fourteen Gauguins hung on the walls of his dining-room.... By 1914 he owned fifty major paintings of Picasso.... Shchukin paid his first visit to Matisse in about 1906, and soon became the artist's most important patron.... The younger by twenty years ... Morosov was nevertheless the more conventional.... He had the sense to trust the excellent ... eye of Shchukin.... Serov was with him when he bought Van Gogh's 'Round of Prisoners' (after Doré).... But it was above all the 'Nabi' painters that appealed to Morosov....[8]

Roughly speaking, we may say that as the pioneer collector Shchukin began to buy Impressionist and Post-Impressionist paintings, so did Diaghilev begin to reproduce them in his magazine.

If, in the eighteenth century, it had been the Imperial family and a few great noblemen who patronized foreign artists and architects and fostered the earliest secular painters in Russia, in the nineteenth century it was the new class of merchant princes who were permanently to enrich the country by their enlightened taste.

Princess Tenishev had a flat adjoining her big house in St Petersburg where she could indulge in artistic activities out of her husband's sight. It was in this 'conspiratorial apartment' that Diaghilev came to discuss the magazine with her. 'The idea was delightful to me,' she wrote, 'because I had long dreamt of a similar undertaking, realizing that without a critical, artistic magazine there could be no contact in our country between artists and society. This was all the more true because the still influential Vagrants were on the wrong track and were an obstacle in the way of the improvement of public taste, which lagged behind that of Western Europe. . . .[9]

Diaghilev brought Mamontov to see the Princess. She respected Mamontov for his taste, and welcomed him as an investor, publisher and collaborator. But when she approached her husband for money, she ran into trouble.

'Believe me,' he said, 'they want you for your money. What are your artistic talents, abilities and taste to them? You live in a dream world. . . . What is it to Mamontov? Today he pokes his nose into one thing, tomorrow it will be something else – and you know what spurs him on! And I guarantee that you are of no more interest to Diaghilev than last year's snow. All he wants is money.' I was very unhappy when I heard this. But at that time Diaghilev sang like a nightingale. . . . My husband gradually gave way. . . . He received Diaghilev and Mamontov and a contract was signed. We spent 12,500 roubles in the first year on the establishment of *The World of Art.*[10]

Diaghilev and Princess Tenishev were in Paris during the autumn of 1898, not only planning the magazine, but borrowing paintings for next year's International Exhibition. 'We visited all the collectors,' wrote the Princess. 'We went to the studios of Boldini, and Whistler, and, thanks to my position, artists and collectors entrusted their masterpieces to me. Besnard gave us his full-length portrait of Réjane on stage. I also succeeded in getting one collector to lend us five or six Degas, and I sent all these things home wrapped up in my dresses. . . .'[11]

At first, Princess Tenishev's 'conspiratorial flat' was the centre of the new enterprise. Here Diaghilev brought Serov, Benois, Bakst, Golovine, Korovine, Levitan, Andreas Zorn, Filosofov and 'the tiny untalented Nuvel', as she called him, to meet her. Vrubel she knew already. 'After business discussions there were singing, cards, jokes and laughter. Tea, nuts and sweets were provided, and time passed in a flash; everything was so delightful and in those days we were all friendly and united.' At first, even some of the Vagrants were enthusiastic about the magazine. 'Repine was in raptures. . . . [Viktor] Vasnetsov was so favourably disposed that he promised a photograph of his *Bogatyri*, which had only just been revealed and had not been reproduced anywhere before, besides photographs of other works.'[12] These painters were soon to receive a nasty shock.

Leaflets were distributed to advertise the magazine, which was to be called *Mir Iskusstva* (*The World of Art*). From 1 January 1899 this would appear fortnightly—that is, there would be twenty-four issues a year. (In fact, it usually came out in double numbers: Vol. I, Nos 1 and 2, were issued together on 10 November 1898, ahead of the announced date, though dated January 1899.) There would be sections on art and on arts and crafts, and there would be a 'Chronicle'. This would cover events in the art world not only of Russia but of the West, with reviews of art exhibitions, new books on the arts and concerts. The price would be ten roubles a year (about £1 at that time) for St Petersburg residents, twelve roubles outside the capital and fourteen roubles abroad.[13]

The first thing that strikes one about *The World of Art* is its large format, 13 × 10 inches. The cover of the first double number was coarse hand-made paper of a light buff colour, bearing at the head a wide decorative strip and at the left foot a little square 'seal' containing two fish. These ornaments by Korovine were in grey-blue, grey-green, grey-pink and gold. The title, in bold, fanciful type, crosses the middle of the page. Inside, several kinds of paper were used: a thickish, shiny 'art paper' (inferior by today's standards) for most of the magazine, with a thinner, rather shoddy, shiny paper for the chronicle of *actualités*. In the sets in the British Museum and Victoria and Albert Museum the 'Chronicles' of current events in these early numbers are all bound in together at the end of a volume (which covered six months). This may have been the custom with Russian subscribers who had their numbers bound at the end of a year, or it may be an attempt at consistency, because in subsequent years illustrations and text were, in fact, often kept separate. There is a more sensitive paper for a few pages of reproductions in gravure. Then, on inserted sheets of thick buff paper, which had to be 'tipped in', there were stuck two decorative 'panels' by Korovine and one of a rather feeble flower by Mamontov himself. These were the only polychrome illustrations. Bakst's bold eagle (which at first sight looks like a woodcut, but is not), printed in greenish gold, serves as a decoration on the otherwise blank page following the title page.[14] It was also used as a letter-heading on the magazine's writing-paper. Most of the black-and-white illustrations in half-tone have nothing to do with the articles they adorn. (The 'Chronicle' pages are not illustrated.) For instance, Diaghilev's opening essay, a kind of manifesto, is broken up by reproductions of the depressing paintings of shaggy old Russian types by Viktor Vasnetsov, including his *Bogatyri*. This famous picture of three legendary warriors on horseback, of which Princess Tenishev was so proud, had taken fifteen years to paint, and was on show in the Tretiakov collection. Repine's portrait of Vasnetsov was also reproduced.

Diaghilev's 'manifesto' was a defence against the charge of 'decadence'. As a motto at the head of his article he placed a saying of Michelangelo: 'He who follows another will never overtake him.' Then, quoting Dostoievsky – he was determined to relate literature to the fine arts – he wrote, 'Ideas fly through the air, but they are conditioned by laws which we cannot understand. Ideas are infectious, and an idea which might be thought the prerogative of a highly cultured person can suddenly alight in the mind of a simple, carefree being and take possession of him.' Diaghilev thought that his own generation, greatly misunderstood by their elders, were so infused by certain ideas which they held in common that the new movement in the arts had a unity which had been lacking earlier in the nineteenth century, when classicism vied with romanticism and when artistic and social problems were confused. Baudelaire had been accused of decadence, Dickens had attacked Millais' *Holy Family* and Ruskin had vilified Whistler's *Fireworks*. Diaghilev's generation were united in admiration of Baudelaire, Böcklin and Balzac – the last being so superior to the theatrical Hugo; they had been reproached for admiring the Pre-Raphaelites and for worshipping Puvis de Chavannes. Their enemies, who were the real decadents, could be divided into three groups: (1) the academicians – these were the *classical* decadents; (2) the sentimentalists who sighed over Mendelssohn's *Songs Without Words*, considered Dumas serious reading and admired mass-produced Madonnas from Germany – these were the *romantic* decadents; (3) a new group who 'dragged peasant rags and shoes on to canvas or into literature, when this had been done far better fifty years before by Millet and Balzac – these were the *realist* decadents.[15]

In another article, called 'The Eternal Struggle', Diaghilev preached the gospel of art for art's sake, recalled Zola's rebuking Proudhon for writing that the purpose of art was to improve mankind, and rejected the theories of the great Tolstoy. 'It is possible to get the most immoral impression from reading the edifying story of Potiphar's wife, while Titian's *Danaë* or the novels of Flaubert can give rise to purely artistic ecstasy. Of course art created solely for immoral purposes is not art, and will not have its place in history, but it seems to me that it was not for Titian and Fragonard to bother about the effect their creations would have on schoolgirls and juvenile soldiers several centuries later.'[16] Diaghilev gave evidence of wide reading, which is surprising, since Benois thought his knowledge of literature – even of the classics – was superficial.

This number also contained an article by Dmitri Filosofov on Puvis de Chavannes, who had just died, a piece by Merejkovsky, an account of an exhibition at Helsingfors by Diaghilev, book reviews, announcements of lectures and of the *World of Art* International Exhibition to be held at the Stieglitz Museum in February 1899.

Benois received the first number in Paris, and disliked both its size and the 'pretentious nudity' of the cover. 'The ill-fashioned, purely amateurish attempts to produce something new in the sphere of decorative art were even less to my liking.' By this he evidently meant the coloured panels by Korovine on their wide mounts, and the reproductions of artifacts from Abramtsevo. (Benois would always be basically anti-Moscow.) He hated the work of Vasnetsov, 'so-called founder of a new school of Russian church and national painting', and he thought that the proliferation of Vasnetsovs and the too literary nature of the first number must be the result of it having been largely put together by Filosofov.[17]

If Benois was disgusted by the predominance of Viktor Vasnetsov, that artist himself disliked the way the magazine had turned out. Repine too went

43

into opposition. In order to mollify Vasnetsov, Princess Tenishev tried to buy a series of his designs for Mamontov's production of *The Snow Maiden*, but he would not sell them to her, knowing she was only trying to sway him in favour of *The World of Art*. Repine grudgingly lent only one portrait to the International Exhibition, instead of the three he had promised.[18]

There was one contribution which particularly scandalized St Petersburg: this was an unsigned note in the 'Chronicle' about an exhibition of the paintings of Klever and Vereshchagin which was to be sent to England.[19] Vereshchagin, a Vagrant, was one of the few internationally known Russian painters, enormously successful and, in Slavophil circles, sacrosanct. The note, which was, in fact, written by Alfred Nurok, read: 'Unhappy England is threatened with an exhibition of pictures by the Russian painters, Yu. Klever and V. Vereshchagin. How can [the reputation of] Russian art and the English public be protected from this dreadful shock?' Princess Tenishev was indignant at the tone of this paragraph, scared by the scandal and furious with Diaghilev at having allowed it.[20] But Diaghilev, I think, was already beginning to enjoy scandals, which he found made good publicity.

Benois' father died on 23 December 1898, and he returned to St Petersburg. All the friends attended the funeral. On the day following, Shura went to visit Diaghilev and saw the flat in Liteiny Prospekt for the first time since it had become an editorial office. Dima Filosofov, who had undertaken all the 'dirty work', to leave Diaghilev free to exercise his flair as a creative editor, showed Shura how things were done. He explained how they dealt with the printing and proof-reading and how the special photographs were prepared. They were all retouched by hand by Bakst.[21] The next day, however, Shura was shocked to learn that an article on genre painting he had written had been rejected. Genre painting too often told a story, and that would not do. 'The magazine was to be a champion of "pure art", and it regarded as its enemies the by then officially recognized *Peredvijniki*, to whom the reformed Academy of Arts had been delivered, with the well-known and typical genre painter Vladimir Makovsky at its head.'[22]

On 22 January 1899 the International Exhibition, held, like the two previous shows organized by Diaghilev, at the Stieglitz Museum, opened its doors. Princess Tenishev and Diaghilev were there to welcome several members of the Imperial family; and the Grand Duke Boris Vladimirovitch bought a Bakst. It was a really remarkable collection. Apart from the Russian painters, who included Bakst, Benois, Korovine, Golovine, Lancerey, Levitan, Maliavin, Maliutin, Nesterov, the Polenovs, Repine, Serov, Somov, Appollinary Vasnetsov and Yakuntchikova, there were works by Finnish artists, by the Swede Zorn, by the Norwegian Thaulow, by the Germans Bartels, Böcklin, Dill, Lenbach and Liebermann, by Belgians, by the American Whistler (though under the banner of England), by the Italian Boldini, by the British Brangwyn, Conder, Patterson and Thomas. Then, perhaps most interesting of all, the French artists Diaghilev exhibited were as different as Puvis de Chavannes, Moreau (who had died in the previous year), Dagnan-Bouveret, Carrière, Forain, Blanche, La Touche, Degas, Monet and Renoir. There was glass by Tiffany (United States) and Lalique (France), as well as artifacts from Russia's Abramtsevo workshops. Diaghilev's energy in organizing this exhibition at the same time as he was founding his magazine strikes one as prodigious.

One of the two Renoirs, painted as long before as 1874, was *La Loge* (*The Opera Box*), now in the Courtauld Institute, London. Degas was represented by his *Return from the Races, Jockeys* and *Woman ironing*. Monet contributed a *Sunny Day* and a *Winter Landscape*.

It is interesting that one of Lenbach's two paintings should have been his portrait of Bismarck, of which Diaghilev owned a sketch; that among the Jacques-Emile Blanche portraits were those of Thaulow and Beardsley; that Georges La Touche contributed a portrait of Puvis de Chavannes; that Boldini should have shown his portrait of Whistler, Repine his portrait of Prince Sergei Volkonsky (of whom we shall hear more later), Serov his pastel of the sculptor Prince Paul Trubetskoy, and Bakst his pastel of Benois, reading in a leather armchair, with the little picture of the Empress Elizabeth Petrovna on the chimney-piece behind him.[23] Apart from being 'decadent', Diaghilev was historically minded, and 'subject matter' evidently did interest him, after all.

Princess Tenishev remembered the Emperor's visit to the International Exhibition as a comic occasion.

One morning I was sitting at lunch when they telephoned from the Palace that the Emperor would visit the exhibition after luncheon. I immediately ordered the carriage, and realizing that I would not be able to change I decided to go as I was. As my carriage approached the Winter Palace I saw the Emperor's sledge drawing up at the entrance. He came out, sat down in the sledge and set off. I told the coachman to keep up with him, and managed to arrive at the same time, threw off my furs and met the Emperor at the doors of the Stieglitz Museum. Nobody had known where Diaghilev was to be found or where he was lunching, so that neither he nor the artists he wanted to present to His Majesty were there, and I received the Emperor alone. Only Korovine, who had been presented to the Grand Duchess Elizaveta Fedorovna that morning, and who had by chance dropped in to the exhibition to meet a woman friend, was there and in a frock coat. In the hall he bumped into Diaghilev, who had been found at last, and who had rushed round, beating his head, without having had time to change. As he was not wearing a dress coat he could not be presented to the Emperor, and he was in a dreadful state. Seeing Korovine, he asked him to exchange clothes, which they did behind an exhibition stand. But Korovine was a couple of heads shorter than Diaghilev and very thin, while Diaghilev was a stout, thick-set man. With an incredible effort he got into Korovine's coat and appeared before the Emperor. As I presented him I caught sight of his sleeve, which hardly covered his wrist, his protruding cuffs, his restricted back and apoplectic face – he could hardly breathe. I didn't know where to look or what to say, and Diaghilev fought to suppress his laughter as he tried to give serious answers and explanations. We were afraid to catch each other's eyes.... The Emperor was very complimentary and said goodbye in a most charming way.[24]

Diaghilev's recollection of the Emperor's manner was less favourable. 'Although he listened to what was said, he spoke very little, and was not easy.' Once, looking at a portrait sketch by Somov [it cannot have been at the 1899 exhibition, at which Somov only showed landscapes], he asked 'Why didn't Somov finish this picture?' and Diaghilev was obliged to give the answer, 'Because he thought the head alone was enough.'[25]

The World of Art reported the occasion tersely. 'On 13 February the Tsar visited the exhibition at the Stieglitz Museum with the Grand Duke Alexei Alexandrovitch and Princess Eugénie of Oldenburg. He arrived at 2.35 and left at 4.10.'[26]

On 20 February – to mention an episode in contrast to this tranquil artistic occasion – there was a demonstration by students of the University (on Vassilievsky Island), and a number of them were beaten up by Cossacks.

The most striking feature of the February 1899 number of *The World of Art* (Nos 3 and 4 being issued together) was the series of Levitsky's 'Smolnianki' (girls of the Smolny Institute), which hung at Peterhof and were reproduced by permission of the Emperor. Levitsky was Russia's outstanding portrait painter in the eighteenth century.

Although the early numbers of *The World of Art* were somewhat confused and ill-organized, certain themes were stated which would recur for years. These included Beardsley, the Russian arts and crafts movement emerging from Mamontov's Abramtsevo workshops and from the Tenishev estate at Talashkino, and Russia's past from the sixteenth century to the Romantic period, with special emphasis on the eighteenth century. Finnish and Scandinavian painting was another theme, and if these boldly blocked-in pictures of snowbound landscapes, in which peasants go about their unchanging business, seem dull to us today, we must remember what a release their simplicity must have represented to the younger Russians after the high moral tone and carefully researched detail of the Vagrants.

On the Tsar's prompting, Kchessinskaya was living under the protection of Grand Duke Sergei Mikhailovitch. On 13 February 1900, a few days after the benefit performance to celebrate her tenth year on the stage, she gave a dinner party to which the two elder sons of the Grand Duke Vladimir Alexandrovitch, Cyril and Boris, whom she knew, brought their youngest brother Andrei, whom she had not met. Once again, as with the Tsarevitch, it was *le coup de foudre*. Matilda and Andrei began to see more of each other.[27] It must have been about this time that Prince Constantine Radziwill said to her, 'Madame, vous devez être fière d'avoir deux grands ducs à vos pieds!' To which she replied, 'Quoi d'étonnant? N'ai-je pas deux pieds?'[28]

During Lent 1899, when the Mariinsky was closed, Savva Mamontov, who, as we have seen, ran Solodovnikov's theatre in Moscow, apart from all his other activities, paid a second visit with his opera company to St Petersburg. They had performed a year before in the theatre hall of the Conservatoire, giving Rimsky-Korsakov's *Sadko*, with Vrubel's wife, Nadejda Ivanovna Zabela, as the Princess, Rimsky's *May Night* and *The Snow Maiden*, Mussorgsky's *Khovanshchina*, Gluck's *Orfeo* and Tchaikovsky's *Maid of Orleans*. This year they gave Rimsky-Korsakov's *The Maid of Pskov*, which Diaghilev was later to rename *Ivan the Terrible*, his *Sadko* and *Mozart and Salieri* and Mussorgsky's *Boris Godunov* with Chaliapine. This was the beginning of the great basso's fame. There were poor houses, but Mamontov paid up.[29]

In Vol. I, No. 10 of *The World of Art*, Diaghilev reprinted a letter Repine had written to *Novoe Vremya*. In this Repine attacked *The World of Art* for stating that certain pictures in the Alexander III Museum of Russian Art (Mikhailovsky Palace) were 'shameful objects discreditable to the nation's art' and should be removed.[30] Repine also complained of the criticism by Igor Grabar and of the magazine's high-handed attitude towards the Academy of Art and the Russian Museum. He censured some of the Finns, and called Benois, Somov and Maliutin 'half-educated'. Diaghilev's reply, prefaced by a quotation from Repine himself – 'I have not the presumption to prophesy anything. I only have the courage to look every manifestation straight in the eye without covering it up with a vine-leaf' – was an attempt to charge Repine with inconsistency,[31] and to answer his points one by one. This quibbling is only of significance in that it reveals the august Professor of the Academy, one of the greatest names in Russian painting at the time, being confronted by an almost unknown young man. Diaghilev conceded his admiration for Repine's work by reproducing several of his portraits, including those of Tolstoy (seated at his desk), Vladimir Stassov (the defender of the Five) and Rimsky-Korsakov, and a drawing of Serov as a youth. Repine would return to the attack in 1900, and Diaghilev would again reply.

Igor Grabar, to whom Repine referred, and who had been at the University with Diaghilev, was now not only a talented painter who exhibited in the *World of Art* group's exhibitions, but a regular contributor of critical articles to the magazine. He had studied in St Petersburg and Munich, and would survive the Revolution to become Director of the Tretiakov Gallery and of various institutes and academies, and the grand old man of Russian art. The delightful Impressionist of *September Snow* (1903, Tretiakov Gallery) would later paint Lenin and the young Prokofiev.

A contributor to the second and third numbers of *The World of Art* had been Prince Sergei Mikhailovitch Volkonsky. This intelligent man came on both sides of his family – for his mother was a Volkonsky too – from one of the greatest houses in Russia, but it is extraordinary to consider that his father, Prince Mikhail, had been born in exile in Siberia, for the grandfather of Sergei Mikhailovitch had been a 'Decembrist'. Sergei Mikhailovitch Volkonsky admired Diaghilev, and at a time when the latter and his magazine were being derided in the press, Volkonsky 'esteemed him as a thorough connoisseur of art in all its branches'.[32] He was himself a good pianist and a good amateur actor. He was also homosexual. In July 1899 Volkonsky was appointed Director of the Imperial Theatres in place of Ivan Alexandrovitch Vsevolojsky, who became Director of the Hermitage instead. Volkonsky was extremely reluctant to take on this arduous post, for he disliked the bustle of social life: however, to give pleasure to his father, he accepted. The appointment caused surprise in St Petersburg, as it was unheard of that the Director should be only thirty-nine years old. His was a much envied position, for he would have constant access to the Imperial presence, an honour which even Ministers could only obtain through application to the Minister of the Court. Volkonsky was far from thinking this a blessing, because, as he wrote, 'You are pulled about from morning to night; there are constant alterations, constant grievances and misunderstandings.... Even after the performance there is business.... The Director is obliged to be in the theatre whenever the Emperor or Empress is there. For this reason one's evenings are never free; it is necessary to wait and see if they intend to go to the theatre....'[33]

Risking the disapproval of his colleagues, Prince Sergei attached Diaghilev to the staff of the theatre directorate 'as a functionary for special missions'. Diaghilev thought his fortune was made. He would be the power behind the throne, and with the aid of his artist friends he would launch the Imperial Theatres on a new golden age. One day he might even succeed Volkonsky! Dmitri Filosofov was given a job on the board of the Alexandrinsky Theatre, so he would be in a position to influence the choice of the dramatic repertory. Bursting with the news, the two cousins hurried down to a country villa where Benois and his family were spending the summer. Diaghilev told Benois that Volkonsky was expecting him to call in order to hear of an offer he had to make him. Shura observed that, from then on, Sergei 'adopted a dictatorial manner, so that Serov and I were obliged to put him in his place from time to time, although we were sincerely pleased by the appointment'.[34] Benois was working on a history of Russian art.

The year 1899 was the centenary of Pushkin's birth. This was celebrated throughout Russia, and Vol. II, Nos 13–14 of *The World of Art* carried articles by Vassili Rozanov and Minsky relating to the poet. In No. 15 there was a scathing comment on an interview given to *Novoe Vremya* by Baron Heekkeren-d'Anthès, son of the man who killed Pushkin in a duel. In the double number Vol. II, Nos 16–17, reviewing the centenary edition of Push-kin's works, illustrated by some of the outstanding Russian artists of the day, including Repine, Somov, Viktor Vasnetsov and Maliutin, Diaghilev queried the desirability of illustrating a literary work and proposed that if this were done at all it was more important for the artist to express himself and his own views of the work in question, rather than try to 'illustrate' those of the writer.

Diaghilev's annual visit to Pushkin's grave, on his way to stay with the Filosofov family at Bogdanovskoye, was more eventful than in previous years.

Soon after I arrived at Sviatogorsk station I was told that when they were putting Pushkin's tomb in order there had been a slight landslide of the sandy soil and that the coffin had become visible. I rushed to the tomb and found that ... I could, in fact, see a corner of the coffin. Putting my arm around it, I kissed it piously. I even tore off a fragment of what seemed once to have been a trimming of gold lace, and this I preserved religiously in my St Petersburg flat.[35]

The Pushkin centenary numbers, Vol. II, Nos 13–14, were adorned by works of early nineteenth-century Russian painters and engravers. Other specialities of the second volume, which covered the second half of 1899, were: British eighteenth-century portraits; Whistler; Vrubel; Dagnan-Bouveret; the late Elena Polenov's decorative work, embroideries and illustra-tions to children's books; Somov; Korovine; Millet; and Golovine. The wide selection of the paintings of Korovine included eleven panels depicting life in the extreme north – the fruit of a journey in 1894 – which had been shown at an exhibition organized by Mamontov in Nijni-Novgorod in 1896. Korovine's decorative style of painting, flat and linear, was utterly different from the flamboyant impasto of his 'easel paintings'. The Golovine illustra-tions were of his furniture and interiors.

Mikhail Vrubel (1866–1910), who was born in Omsk, Siberia, and studied under Tchistiakov at the St Petersburg Academy, was the most original artist of the Mamontov circle and the one from whom Diaghilev most confidently expected a series of masterpieces. Like his friends Levitan and the younger Serov, he died comparatively young – he was almost blind and mentally disturbed – but he left less work behind him than the other two. When he was still a student, he had been selected by Professor Prakhov to help with the restoration of frescoes in the church of St Cyril in Kiev, for which he also painted four ikons. He was profoundly influenced by Byzantine art. In 1889, his designs for new wall-paintings in St Vladimir's Cathedral in Kiev having been rejected, he arrived in Moscow, met Mamontov, joined the Abramtsevo group and designed many artifacts which were executed in their workshops. An image which obsessed him was the Demon of Ler-montov's poem, 'a spirit which unites in itself the male and female, a spirit not so much evil as suffering and vulnerable, yet withal powerful and noble'. This brooding, muscular Titan, with the huge, tragic eyes and blossoming mouth of Rossetti's Elizabeth Siddall, was depicted observing the behaviour of human beings, meditating in solitude among mountains, and finally downcast 'like Lucifer, Never to rise again'. The thick slabs of paint with which Vrubel painted his Demon and other subjects were perhaps intended to impart to his pictures the strength of mosaic. Though carefully calculated, they give a feeling of frenzy, like those of Van Gogh at the end of his life. When he makes use of a similar technique in a watercolour, such as the *Lily* in the Russian Museum, we seem to be observing an explosion in close-up. Another technique used in watercolour (for instance, in the *Oriental Tale*, 1886) is Pointillism (without the science); so that we are presented with a Gustave Moreau subject as Seurat might have painted it. To risk another odious comparison in order to pay tribute to the variety of this prophetic genius, an oil sketch of Portofino (1894) in the Tretiakov Gallery might have been painted by Nicolas de Staël.

CHAPTER 4

1900–1902

Backers – Brief Employment by the Imperial Theatres – Flight

DIAGHILEV'S FORTUNES were destined to be entangled for over a decade with those of Kchessinskaya. Now that he was a member of the staff of the Imperial Theatres, knowing how powerful she was, with all her Grand Ducal friends, he took care to make up to her, and they got on very well together. They were exactly the same age. 'Curiously enough,' she wrote,

I have always been successful with men in whom I expected least of all to awake admiration! And yet there was nothing boyish about me.... I liked him from the first.... [He] had a rich head of hair with a greying lock in front, which earned him the nickname 'Chinchilla'. When he entered the Administration's box while I was dancing the waltz in *Esmeralda* my stage companions began to hum under their breath:

> 'I've just heard
> That Chinchilla is in his box,
> And I'm terribly afraid
> To make a mistake.'

Diaghilev nearly always accompanied me home after the performance.[1]

Through Kchessinskaya, Diaghilev naturally saw a great deal of the Grand Duke Sergei Mikhailovitch, and Benois thought this familiarity with an Imperial Highness went to his head.[2]

Leon Bakst had a brother, Isaiah Rosenberg, who had recently been employed as a journalist on the *Petersburg Gazette*, 'where', Benois thought, 'his pert and slightly scandalous articles fitted perfectly into the generally vulgar tone of the paper.' Diaghilev's acquaintance with the staff and artists of the Mariinsky naturally gave him access to inside information, and he used to discuss the latest theatre gossip at meetings with his friends. It was found that these secrets of state began to appear in Isaiah's column. After one especially obvious leak, Diaghilev and Filosofov had a row with Bakst, and, when he protested, Sergei kicked him forcibly out of the flat. The far from bellicose Levushka was forgiven and forgave in no time at all, and the scene was forgotten – but not by Kostia Somov. The display of physical violence revolted him and it may have served as a pretext for this gentle, well-brought-up creature, whose father was curator of the Hermitage, to break with the ruthless parvenu, whose leadership he had perhaps resented all along. He never entered Diaghilev's flat or spoke to him again. He did not, however, withdraw his collaboration from *The World of Art*.[3]

Such an impression had the early numbers of *The World of Art* made as examples of book production that, when Volkonsky employed Diaghilev, the staff of the Imperial Theatres thought it inevitable that the latter would be asked to edit the *Theatres Annual*. This rather dull publication recorded performances at the three subsidized theatres in St Petersburg and the two in Moscow, and provided lists of the companies and pictures of the principal singers, dancers and actors. For years past it had been edited by one Molt-chanov, husband of the actress Savina, who now forestalled his dismissal by resigning.[4] Diaghilev was immediately appointed in his place: he set about his task with a will, determined to transform the dowdy year-book into something comparable with *The World of Art*.

The Imperial Ballet was ruled by the French-born Marius Petipa, who for nearly fifty years had been its choreographer. Engaged as principal dancer by the Imperial Ballet in 1847, he invented the first of many ballets for the company ten years later. He, who had danced in Paris with Carlotta Grisi, the original Giselle, formed a link between that remote age of the Romantic ballet and the new generation of young dancers who were to make 'Russian' ballet celebrated throughout the Western world. The time has come to speak of these young dancers, whom Diaghilev would later present in the West. Michel Fokine, handsome, intelligent and idealistic, had passed out of the Imperial Theatre Ballet School and made his début in 1898, at the time when Diaghilev was planning the first numbers of his magazine. Anna Pavlova, in her last year, and Tamara Karsavina, in her fourth year, were then still pupils in the School; and Vaslav Nijinsky joined it that September. Although the boys lived and worked in quarters over those of the girls in Theatre Street, they were kept strictly apart, and were not supposed even to address each other when they came together for classes in 'double work' or in lessons in ballroom dancing; so that at the end of 1899 neither had Fokine and Nijinsky met each other – for eight years is a big gap – nor had they met the girls. Pavlova, the illegitimate daughter of a Jewish businessman and a poor laundress (married off to a soldier), had known extreme hardship and would follow the course which had become traditional – in the Russian ballet as well as the French – of attaching herself to a series of rich protectors. Botkine once remarked to Diaghilev that she had seven lovers, one for each day of the week.[5] Karsavina, whose father was a dancer and whose mother was of gentle birth, was never promiscuous, although her dark, lustrous beauty won her innumerable admirers.[6] She was unusually intelligent and observant, as subsequent quotation from her memoirs will reveal.

'Through Diaghilev,' wrote Prince Volkonsky, 'I was able to obtain the assistance of many artists for the staging of new productions. Appollinary Vasnetsov made the designs for the scenery and costumes of *Sadko*. They were beautiful and new.'[7]

Wagner's *Tristan und Isolde* had been first produced at the Mariinsky on 25 March 1898; and the article Diaghilev somewhat belatedly wrote about it showed how knowledgeable he already was about Wagner productions throughout Europe. Usually *Tannhäuser* and *Lohengrin* were the only Wagner operas given in Russia, so new productions of *Die Walküre* in Moscow and *Tristan* in St Petersburg were welcome. He referred to good performances of Wagner in Paris, Belgium and Sweden, and thought highly of the Paris productions of *Die Walküre*, *Lohengrin* and *Die Meistersinger*. Those in Milan and Bayreuth were inferior, but Bayreuth was improving.[8]

During the autumn of 1899 there was an economic slump in Russia, and the great Mamontov was one of several businessmen to face bankruptcy and ruin. Pending the result of investigations, he was put under house arrest; and he consoled himself by working at his sculpture. His opera company did not, however, cease to function: it changed its name (to the Association of Russian Private Opera). There could be no more subsidy from him, and Princess Tenishev had turned cool. She found herself not only blamed by the world at large for Diaghilev's 'excesses', but increasingly ignored by Diaghilev, who went his own way.[9] *The World of Art* was therefore threatened with extinction after only one year. Diaghilev had to rack his brains. There was a rallying-round of friends. Ilya Ostroukhov, a Moscow businessman, and Dr Sergei Botkine put up money to keep the magazine going for another year – or at least for a time.[10] The whole question of subsidy for *The World of Art* is mysterious, and had better be dealt with here once and for all. The information about Ostroukhov and Botkine was given to Arnold Haskell in the 1930s by Nuvel, who, at the time of Diaghilev's death in 1929, was his closest – or certainly oldest – friend. But the Tsar also subsidized the journal for three years at least. Haskell, informed by Nuvel, who may not have been *strictly* accurate, wrote that

later, when funds got low again, there took place an event of capital importance. . . . Serov received the commission to paint [posthumous] portraits of Alexander III in Danish uniform, which Nicolas II wished to present to the Danish regiment of which his father was colonel, . . . and of old Grand Duke Mikhail Nicolaievitch, the Tsar's great-uncle. These successes gained him the commission to paint the Emperor's own portrait. He told his friends of the sittings and of the simplicity and charm of the Emperor. They saw that he had the royal sympathy, and Diaghilev, greatly daring, suggested that he should invite the Emperor to subsidize *Mir Iskusstva*. This was done, and the sum of 10,000 roubles a year (£1,000) was guaranteed for a period of five years.... The portrait ... was given to the Empress and hung in her private apartment until the taking of the Winter Palace by the Bolsheviks, when it was wantonly destroyed.[11]

This portrait was exhibited at the *World of Art* exhibition in the Academy of the Arts in January 1901.

Dobujinsky, who only met Diaghilev in 1902, gives another version of this story:

Serov was painting his famous portrait of the Emperor (in a double-breasted jacket) and, talking to him casually during the sittings, told him about *The World of Art*, of its cultural significance and of its financial difficulties, and even of the misfortunes that had befallen Mamontov. To Serov's surprise the Tsar offered to subsidize the journal from his private purse for two years to the tune of 5,000 rubles. This gesture remained a secret from almost everybody, and Diaghilev ... would not allow anyone to discuss it. (I myself learned of the subsidy many years later.) This subsidy came to an end in 1904, when Russia was engaged in an unsuccessful war, revolution was approaching, and there could be no question of raising the matter.[12]

Even before 1904, though, it seems that Diaghilev returned shamelessly to the attack on Princess Tenishev. 'After a year or two,' she wrote, 'when Diaghilev was again in financial straits and again turned to me for help (I received a long letter from him and he came himself to Talashkino) I again helped financially and gave him 5,000 roubles.'[13] This visit and donation probably prompted Diaghilev's fulsome article on Maliutin's work at Talashkino, with many illustrations of the *izbas* (cottages), theatre and furniture he had designed there, which was published in March 1903.[14]

When the Tsar's subsidy stopped at the time of the Russian–Japanese War, Diaghilev again approached Princess Tenishev, who made it a condition of her help that her protégé Nicolas Roerich should replace Benois (by now an enemy) on the editorial board. Diaghilev did not mind including Roerich, but, at a time when he was touring Russia in search of unknown or forgotten portraits for his great Historical Portrait Exhibition, he could not dispense with Benois. When the Princess saw Benois' name on the list of contributors, she 'immediately put an announcement in the papers to the effect that [she] took no part in the journal and never would again'.[15]

At the end of his life Diaghilev wrote that he never had a penny from the Imperial purse for any of his ballet enterprises in the West.[16] This was no doubt true, but he might have added that he *did* receive official support for his production of the opera *Boris Godunov* in Paris in 1908, and the Tsar *had* helped with *The World of Art* – whether with ten thousand roubles for five years, as Nuvel told Haskell, or, which seems more probable, with five thousand roubles for two years, as Dobujinsky says he heard many years after the event. The Tsar must certainly have helped between 1900 or 1901 and 1904.

Serov painted two other portraits of Nicolas II. One, for the British regiment of the Scots Greys, of which the Emperor was Colonel, showed him in a scarlet tunic, with a bearskin held in the crook of his right arm.[17] The sittings for the other, which represented the Tsar in the uniform of a Caucasian regiment, were said by Nuvel to have been interrupted because the painter was rude to the Empress, who 'began criticizing the painting to the Emperor in English. Serov could not understand the language, and was deeply offended. Turning to the Empress, he offered his palette and brushes, saying "If Your Majesty wishes to paint it herself – *voilà!*" She at once left the room and the sitting was continued in silence. It was the last.'[18]

Serov held advanced liberal opinions, and, after the massacre of 'Bloody Sunday' in January 1905, he made some anti-monarchical caricatures, including one which portrayed Nicolas, tennis-racket under arm, pinning medals on the breasts of soldiers lined up in front of rows of dead civilians, who were laid out like game after a shoot.[19] On Serov's death in 1911, however, the Tsar was asked to give a pension to his widow, and this was not refused.[20]

The magazine now bore the inscription, 'Editor-publisher S.P. Diaghilev.' All the half-tone illustrations in the January 1900 volume were by Serov.

The second exhibition of *The World of Art* (but Diaghilev's fourth) was opened at the Stieglitz Museum on 29 January 1900. Grand Duke George Mikhailovitch, Director of the Alexander III Museum, came to the opening and bought Serov's *Children* for his museum.[21] On 3 February the Emperor, the Empress and other members of the Imperial family were greeted by Diaghilev and several of the painters.

Diaghilev had hitherto exercised dictatorial powers in choosing works for *World of Art* exhibitions. His artist friends now demanded 'a constitution'. It was perhaps a sign of the times. On 24 February 1900 a meeting took place at Diaghilev's flat. Among those present were: Bakst; Benois; Appollinary Vasnetsov; Levitan; Ivan Bilibine, the expert on North Russian peasant art, who made many decorative pen-and-ink decorations for the magazine; Lancerey, Benois' nephew, whose black-and-white adornments were even more regularly called for; Maliavin, who about this time painted a full-length portrait of Diaghilev in a top-hat and dark overcoat; Nesterov, whose much-collected paintings of sanctimonious boy saints, processing nuns and praying peasants it is hard to admire;[22] the grotesque sculptor, A. Ober; and the maker of delightful topographical woodcuts, Alexandra Ostroumova. It was agreed that, in addition to Diaghilev, two members were to be elected annually to form a selection committee – for 1901 these would be Benois and Serov. Exhibitors were to be divided into three categories: permanent members, including, besides those present, Vrubel, Golovine, Korovine, Maliutin, Mikhail Mamontov (nephew of Savva), Prince Trubetskoy, the sculptor, and Yakuntchikova; specially invited guest painters chosen by the organizers; and other outside artists approved by seven members of the group.[23]

New artists whose work was illustrated in the magazine in the first half of 1900 were Alexandra Ostroumova, Nicolas Roerich, the St Petersburg enthusiast for medieval Russia, as Appollinary Vasnetsov was the Moscow one, and the English painter William Nicholson, who (with James Pryde, under the collective name of 'Beggarstaff Brothers') had evolved a new, bold style of book illustration and poster design. Whistler's etchings were also given a good showing. There was an article on Beardsley by D.S. MacColl, with thirteen illustrations. Diaghilev had written to MacColl as early as September 1898, explaining that Conder had suggested he should contribute an article, and that he himself had known Beardsley at Dieppe. 'The dimensions of our magazine do not allow the article to be too long, not above the quantity of 35,000 letters [5,000–6,000 words?]. The price . . . is 12 pounds at our redaction. . . .' As Haskell pointed out in his life of Diaghilev (1935), 'the very drawing on the letter heading [the eagle], signed L. Bakst, is a tribute to Beardsley.'[24]

In June 1900 Diaghilev and Benois visited the Paris International Exhibition, at which the Russian Empire displayed an enormous range of exhibits, from agriculture and electricity to education and art. Most of the works of 'fine' art, such as Serov's paintings and the sculptures of Paul Trubetskoy, were housed in part of the Grand Palais; while the *village russe*, with Korovine's and Golovine's fantastic pavilion in the old Russian style, 'looked slightly toy-like beside the Trocadéro towers'.[25] Diaghilev had the Trocadéro touched out in the photographs he reproduced in his magazine, so that the gabled, domed and turreted building appeared against a snowy sky.[26] This 'Kremlin' and its contents could be taken as an indirect triumph for *The World of Art*, the ultimate flowering of the Abramtsevo workshops, which Elena Polenov had not lived to see, a vindication of the fallen Mamontov. For his portrait of Grand Duke Pavel Alexandrovitch, Serov was awarded a gold medal by the Paris judges. Korovine and Maliavin were also honoured.[27]

That autumn Diaghilev moved to a new flat, No. 11, Fontanka. Perhaps he thought his magazine, his position in the Imperial Theatres and his growing fame entitled him to a more elegant background. The curving Fontanka canal, bordered by princely palaces, was more dignified, quieter and in every way more attractive than the wide, endless but commercial Liteinaya. He was now next to the house of Countess Panina, near to the famous Shuvalov palace and the 'Engineering Castle', which had been occupied by the School of Engineering since the Emperor Paul had been murdered there in 1801, and opposite the palace of Count Sheremetev,[28] one of the most illustrious nobles.

Sets of photographs of the Engineering Castle[29] and of Veliaminov's Toboggan Pavilion at the Imperial Palace of Oranienbaum,[30] which had appeared in recent numbers, bore witness to the increasing influence of Benois, with his passion for old architecture, on the magazine. The last number for 1900 was illustrated entirely by old master paintings from the Yusupov Palace on the Moika Canal.[31]

The year 1901 saw an improvement in the production of *The World of Art*, which now gave up the attempt to appear fortnightly. The half-tone illustrations on art paper and the text on heavy cream paper were now kept separate. The 'Chronicle' of current events was now printed on the same paper and in the same type as the long serials by Merejkovsky, Hippius, Rozanov and Minsky. One result of the separation of pictures from text was that Diaghilev found it necessary, more than before, to adorn and break up the solid pages of type with black-and-white illustrations in line. There had from the beginning been delightful decorations by Lancerey, Bakst, Somov or Bilibine, in rococo, classical, Beardsleyesque, medieval or Viking styles. Now the headpieces and tailpieces appeared more frequently and became more elaborate.

The first twenty-six pages of Vol. V, No. 1, constituted a memorial to Levitan, who had died in 1900. Of all painters he shows up least well in poor half-tone blocks on 1901 art paper. He is so unemphatic, and so much of his art depends on delicate gradations of tone, that he loses far more in reproduction than, say, the Spaniard Zuloaga – Diaghilev's latest enthusiasm, with whom Levitan shared the number – or the German Böcklin (who died on 16 January 1901), to whose gloomy mythological picnics part of Nos 2–3 was devoted, or the Impressionist Pissarro, who made his Russian début in that February–March number, or Vrubel, whose frescoes for St Cyril at Kiev as well as murals for Morozov's home in Moscow were published at the same time. The tribute to Levitan therefore misfired pictorially. Yet Diaghilev wrote very nicely of him, comparing his premature death with that of Beardsley. Levitan had

the freshness of a Turgenev morning, the scent of Tolstoy's hay harvest [*Anna Karenina*, Part III], and the sure strokes of Tchekhov.... It would be wrong to say that Levitan had been scorned in his lifetime: he had simply passed unnoticed.[32] In the West, too, Levitan had been comparatively unknown. In Russia landscapes are expected to depict typical 'Russian' features; and the dear, dull, tranquil landscape of Russia as observed by Levitan struck nobody as interesting.... His character was like his work. In his last years he accepted his approaching end without fear or regret. Only recently [three years before] I saw the dying Beardsley a few months before his death. When I compare these two men – the emaciated youth, feverishly, incessantly whispering of death, grasping at religion with animal desperation, overwhelmed by fear of the end, and the Russian, like a poet fading quietly away – the figure of Levitan appears to me exceptionally great and tender.[33]

The World of Art could not permanently sustain a controversial and provocative atmosphere at fever pitch, and if, as I suspect, Diaghilev was content, in the literary pages, when he was not attacking the Vagrants, the Academy and Russian Museum, to keep going long features by such distinguished figures as the novelist-poet-philosopher Merejkovsky, the art critic Rozanov or the music critic Laroche (whom Rimsky called 'the Russian Hanslick'; he died in October 1904) – whose names alone imparted distinction – their solid essays (some of which would later appear in book form) provided fine ploughed furrows of double-column type on which some bold bird from the imagination of Bakst or Lancerey could settle and catch the eye. For Vol. V, No. 4, he planned a novelty – a set of poems with illustrations, which would tax the fantasy and graphic powers of his collaborators to the utmost. Ten pages of poems by Merejkovsky would be adorned by Lancerey and Bilibine; four pages of Sologub's poems would be decorated by Benois; drawings by Lancerey and Bakst would illustrate respectively the verses of Hippius and Balmont; while Minsky would be interpreted by Lancerey. Of these artists in black-and-white Lancerey is the most versatile and the most sure: whether he is framing two reclining ladies in gigantic irises, engirdling a verse with tangled straps of pearls or evolving a miniature bouquet out of Crown Imperial and fish with bearded, plaintive human heads, his line, varying in thickness, is always effective, his imagination nicely bridled. Bilibine usually restricts himself to the lakes, mountains and birch-trees of the North Russian scene on which he was expert. Benois too is surest when he is most naturalistic: his free, calligraphic, Tiepolesque style of figure-drawing tends to freeze into a tight, inflexible child's story-book manner, partly comic, when he draws a little turbaned prince and three queens under a canopy. Bakst is the most audacious – and the most Beardsleyesque – in imagination, and, when one of his formal designs succeeds, it is even better than one of Lancerey's. Yet before this venturesome Vol. V, No. 4, could appear in April, events would take a turn to spoil Diaghilev's pleasure in it.

In the meantime the King of Siam's dancers appeared in St Petersburg and gave the young dancer Fokine some ideas which would be useful to him later. Bakst, in love with the mysterious Orient, made a painting of the Siamese in their pagoda-like head-dresses, stamping by torchlight.[34]

The third exhibition mounted by the *World of Art* group was devoted to Russian painters. As Baron Stieglitz no longer let out the big gallery in his Museum, Diaghilev had approached the Academy for the loan of one or more of their halls. The Academicians, tired of being attacked by *The*

World of Art, had opposed the application, but Repine and another painter supported Diaghilev, and their votes prevailed. 'When we substituted for the easels wooden frames covered with canvas [to form false walls],' wrote Diaghilev,

we were told they were dangerous and highly inflammable, and as a result found ourselves involved in endless correspondence, committee meetings, negotiations. Our honourable professors and academicians actually tried to strike terror into the hearts of the public through interviews 'that just happened to get' reported in the newspapers. Others, and some of the most venerable at that, went so far as to state that our adversaries would not even hesitate to set fire to the show.... When ... the exhibition was finally opened, all our art critics found nothing better to do than mock at our 'decadent' venture and declare that 'in boosting Zionglinsky we were forgetting Titian.'[35]

Photographs of the big hall of the exhibition and of the four smaller rooms into which another big hall was subdivided were reproduced in Vol. IV,

Illustration by Bakst of a poem by Balmont in *The World of Art*.

No. 4, and give us a clear idea of how Diaghilev arranged an exhibition. (The décor was attributed to Korovine and two other artists, but it is probable that Diaghilev laid down the main principles.) In the big hall the distracting Titian (or Raphael) murals on the north wall facing the windows were hidden by tall, plain curtains borrowed from the Mariinsky. Korovine's 'screen' of South Russian panels, which had been shown in Paris, towered at one end. Sculpture and pottery were shown down the middle. The smaller square rooms were contrived by carpenters from the Mariinsky out of hessian or coarse canvas stretched on (invisible) wooden frames, and had false ceilings to keep the height in proportion to their size. In these, Korovine's frieze-like decorative panels of North Russian scenes, done from sketches made on the spot in 1894 – seals, reindeer, villages on stilts and shipping in frozen harbours – hung high up to form a dado above the easel pictures. It was evidently a fashion in Russia at the time to hang pictures not flat on the wall, but at a sharp angle to it. (Matisse complained about this when he visited Shchukin in Moscow in 1911.) The rooms were furnished with chairs, ancient and modern; artistic textiles broke up, here and there, the lines of pictures; there were plants; and on a draped table in the first of the enfilade of small rooms – the one with the Tsar's portrait by Serov – there was a pot of hyacinths.

At three o'clock on February 3rd, 1901, the Tsar, accompanied by the Grand Duke of Hesse [his brother-in-law], visited the Third World of Art Exhibition and the Levitan [memorial] exhibition in the Academy of Arts. They were met by the President of the Academy, the Grand Duke Vladimir Alexandrovitch, and by the President of the Russian Museum, the Grand Duke George Mikhailovitch, and the Vice-President of the Academy, Count I. I. Tolstoy; by the Editor of the *World of Art*, S. P. Diaghilev, and the artists Nesterov, Benois, Braz, Purvit, Rushchitz, Lancerey, Ober and Ostroumova. The Imperial party spent an hour and a half at the exhibition, and the Tsar bought Benois' 'Lake in front of the Great Palace' [at Tsarskoye Selo]. The exhibition had been open since January 10th.[36]

This announcement appeared in the February number, Vol. V, No. 2, which must consequently have come out late in the month. (The catalogue of the exhibition and illustrations of its rooms and exhibits are in No. 4.) It was also announced that 'The 9–10 Annual of the Imperial Theatres has been published, together with the first literary supplement.'

Diaghilev's publication, which amazed St Petersburg and was said to have evoked favourable comment from the unimpressionable Emperor himself,[37] was ostensibly just another number in the annual series of records of performances at the five Imperial Theatres, but the facts, dates and photographs of performers, with appropriate backgrounds painted in by Bakst, were confined to one volume, while, in a splendid 'Supplement', the extravagant editor really let himself go. As in *The World of Art*, past and present were glorified alongside each other; and when, out of politeness, official portraits had

to be included, they were by the best artists Diaghilev could rope in. Benois
wrote about the architecture of the Alexandrinsky Theatre. The critic
Valerian Svetlov wrote about ancient choreography. The late Director,
Vsevolojsky (whose designs for *The Sleeping Beauty* and other works were reproduced), was portrayed by Serov, the retired Moltchanov by Bakst, César
Cui and the actor Gay (Gué) by Repine, Wagner by Lenbach and the
actress Savina by Braz. There were three delicate programme designs for
the Hermitage Theatre by Bakst and Somov; and a cover and tailpiece by
Bakst. The cost of producing this annual was thirty thousand roubles – that
is, over ten thousand roubles in excess of the sum allotted in the budget.

The February number[38] printed two reviews of the Moscow Arts
Theatre, which had brought a repertory to St Petersburg. After discussing
The Three Sisters, Pertsov summed up the new movement: 'Instead of a
great actor there has arisen the great ensemble.' The age of the stage-director
had dawned. Of *Uncle Vanya* (first performed in Moscow in 1899, now given
its first performance in St Petersburg, 19 February 1901), an anonymous
critic wrote, somewhat missing the point, that Tchekhov had been well
served by Stanislavsky and Nemirovitch-Danchenko, but that the theatre
should be a spectacle, a celebration, and not something grey, dreary and
provincial. 'The future belongs only to those who recognize in themselves
the birth of a new culture.' This smells of Nietzsche, so may have been by
Filosofov. Ibsen's *Dr Stockman* was also reviewed, by Gneditch.

Diaghilev and Benois had long esteemed Delibes as the greatest of ballet
composers, and his *Coppelia* was given regularly at the Mariinsky. Now
Shura had persuaded Serioja to put forward the idea of a production of the
composer's other famous ballet, *Sylvia*, on which the friends could all work
together. The suggestion was accepted by Volkonsky early in 1901 and he
gave a written order to the office manager that Diaghilev was to be in charge
of the production. 'This order ought to have been printed the next day in
the journal of instructions,' wrote the Prince. But Diaghilev had been making enemies by his arrogance. The same evening the Director was told by
two of his assistants that 'these instructions would cause such fermentations
that they could not answer for the work being done.' 'I gave in.... I told
Diaghilev that I was obliged to retract my promise.'[39]

Diaghilev was outraged. Although Volkonsky was perfectly willing to let
things go on as before, provided that Diaghilev – who was, after all, only
a minor official – surrendered the *nominal* direction of *Sylvia*, Sergei Pavlovitch wanted not only the satisfaction of planning and carrying through the
production, but the credit for it as well. He also felt he was in a strong position because of the success of his 'Supplement' to the Theatre Annual –
and he had already begun collecting material for the next one. He had yet
another string to his bow. Grand Duke Sergei Mikhailovitch, Kchessinskaya's elder protector, hated Volkonsky and aspired to take over his post

(the better to fulfil Kchessinskaya's wishes, no doubt). If he was successful, Diaghilev presumed that he himself would become the Grand Duke's right-hand man, do all the work and have his own way in the theatre. Diaghilev probably telephoned at once to Kchessinskaya, who may have urged him to take a stand. (She glosses over the end of Diaghilev's career at the Mariinsky in her memoirs, though not the end of Volkonsky's, which came soon after.)

What is certain is that Diaghilev returned to his flat, boiling with indignation, to break the news to his colleagues, who were working happily together on their sketches for *Sylvia*. Benois was to design Act I, Korovine Act II and Lancerey Act III. (It sounds a very bad arrangement.) Bakst was to devise all the costumes except one, which would be by Serov. The friends had already talked to the brothers Sergei and Nicolas Legat, who were to create the choreography and to dance; and Nuvel had played the score of *Sylvia* through to them on the piano. When Diaghilev announced that he intended to refuse to continue editing the *Annual*, Benois, Filosofov and Lancerey agreed to send in letters of resignation or protest. Korovine, who was afraid of losing his job at the theatre, abstained; and the older, wiser Serov remained silent throughout the tirades.[40]

Volkonsky did everything he could to heal the breach, even calling with Teliakovsky, his Moscow colleague, at the flat on the Fontanka, in an attempt to appease Diaghilev.[41] But by this time Diaghilev, possibly encouraged by Kchessinskaya, saw greater vistas opening before him, and decided to stand firm and risk his luck. Volkonsky ordered him to resign, and he refused.

The Grand Duke Sergei Mikhailovitch took the train to Tsarskoye Selo to talk to the Emperor. Under the impetus of his cousin's urging, the volatile sovereign is said to have declared, 'In Diaghilev's place I too would refuse to resign.' Diaghilev thought he had won and that Volkonsky would have to go. If, as it seems from evidence offered above, it was shortly before this time that Diaghilev had received his subsidy for the magazine from the Tsar through the good offices of Serov, he may have had further reason to delude himself that he was secure in Imperial favour.

Baron Friederickx, the Minister of the Court, was ill at the time, and his representative, General Rydjevsky, came to inform Prince Volkonsky that he had just had a conversation with the Emperor and gained permission for Diaghilev's discharge.

'It is a good thing,' he said, 'that you gave me copies of your letters to Diaghilev, I took them with me and showed them. The Emperor said "Well, in that case, have the order for dismissal published!" "Then," asked Volkonsky, "is the affair settled?" "How is it possible to answer for that! The order in the *Government Gazette* can only appear the day after tomorrow." [It was a Saturday.] "New instructions may be given tomorrow. Sergei Mikhailovitch may run in and ask for an alteration.... I mean to give orders that if a telephone call comes for me they are to answer that I am out...." '⁴²

Benois knew that the General disliked Diaghilev. 'On the Monday,' he wrote, 'when Serioja, who was still in bed, opened the *Government Gazette*, he read under the heading "Government Order": "S. P. Diaghilev is dismissed without pension according to point 3." He almost fainted. He was publicly disgraced, finished. Point 3 was applied only in extreme cases, as a penalty for an official's improper conduct – graft, theft and goodness knows what else. ...' It was the equivalent of being cashiered from the army. Diaghilev may have feared that people would think he was being penalized for his homosexuality.

'Serioja submitted to the inevitable.... His main wish was to conceal his feelings....'⁴³ It was the greatest blow to his ambitions that he had so far received. Who could guess at the time (except, perhaps, Diaghilev himself, who would soon be forming new resolutions) that this dismissal was a blow to the Russian theatre in general – and would prove a godsend to Western Europe? In more ways than one, this severe punishment for his arrogance was a blessing in disguise. Diaghilev learned his lesson and would never again behave so brashly. The young man whose self-assurance put everyone off was to become in the course of years a diplomat whose charm could move mountains.

The production of *The World of Art* had to go on. Yet it looks as if the disgrace and despondency of Diaghilev nearly tripped up the magazine in full career. No. 5 never appeared.⁴⁴ It was as if *The World of Art* missed a heart-beat. For Diaghilev had fled abroad to hide his face.

On 15 April 1901 Kchessinskaya was to dance in the ballet *Camargo*, in which the Italian guest artist Legnani had made her farewell benefit performance in January. This involved wearing a hooped skirt in the Louis XV style. Being short, she decided (quite rightly) that such a skirt would not suit her, and, although warned by Baron Kussov, the theatre manager, she appeared on stage in a *tutu*.⁴⁵ The next day there was published in the journal of the Directorate the announcement that 'The Director of the Imperial Theatres has imposed a fine [of so many roubles] on the ballerina Kchessinskaya for wilfully changing the costume prescribed for the ballet *Camargo*.' Let poor Volkonsky continue his story:

Two days later I was informed that the Minister [of the Court] begged me to come at once to him. I dressed and drove to Post Street.... 'I have a very unpleasant commission to execute. The Emperor wishes that the fine imposed on Kchessinskaya should be annulled.' 'Very well,' I answered, 'but do you know what is left for me to do after this?' 'Yes, I know; you are young, you take things too much to heart.... In half an hour I am going to Tsarskoe Selo; may I tell [the Emperor] that his orders have been executed?' 'Certainly.' At five o'clock [that evening] I was at the Minister's reception.... 'The Emperor will receive you on Monday....'

I was at the Tsarskoe Selo station by eight o'clock next morning ... the usual picture of elegant bustle – uniforms, three-cornered hats, white gloves, portfolios, couriers.... The Grand Duke Alexei was on the train.... I learned, I don't remember from whom, that, the day before, the Grand Duke Sergei Mikhailovitch had been the aide-de-camp on duty. It was not his turn, but the Grand Dukes had the right to change their day....

When I entered the Emperor's study I felt at once that whatever I might say would be to no purpose.... I talked for a long time, for at least ten minutes.... We were standing between the windows, to the right of me was a small cupboard, on which stood a clock; the wandering eyes often looked at the clock, while the fingers pulled at the moustache; it was twenty-five minutes to one, the lunch hour was approaching.... He did not ask a single question.... Only once he put in a word. I was saying that, when the Moscow ballerina, Roslavleva, came to Petersburg to dance in *The Corsair*, in which ballet there was an intercalated number, Kchessinskaya had asserted her rights to the music of that number; the leader of the ballet band, Drigo, and his assistants, had passed a whole night in the library searching for some other appropriate music. 'These are some of the difficulties caused by such a system of ballet monopoly,' I said. It was here he uttered his only word, when I mentioned the intercalated number in *The Corsair*, he asked 'Is not the music by Delibes?'

... I finished my monologue with the request to be relieved of my duties.... The tension on both sides was at once relieved.

'Yes, but how – It will be very difficult to replace you.'

'I am willing to wait, Sire, as long as you command.... I only beg you to take into consideration that the theatrical season is prepared during the summer, and, consequently, the sooner the new appointment is made the better it will be for the work, and the easier it will be for my successor.'

'Well, please wait till June.'

I also wanted to have my lunch. In one of the rooms of the palace the 'Marshal of the Court's table' awaited us. The Tsarskoe park was radiant with the brilliancy of a beautiful April day when I drove to the station in a Court calesh. . . .[46]

Prince Sergei Mikhailovitch Volkonsky was given the honorary appointment of Hofmeister. On 8 July 1901 Colonel Teliakovsky from Moscow took his place as Director of the Imperial Theatres. These appointments were reported in *The World of Art*, Vol. V, No. 6, which also contained reproductions of works by Sisley, Manet and Monet (including one of the Rouen Cathedral series).

Diaghilev's first notes from abroad were published in the same number. Early in May he had made straight for London. Whether or not this was the first time he had crossed the Channel is not clear. He could perhaps have borrowed British paintings for his exhibitions without doing so, and the prior knowledge of British artistic standards revealed in the report he sent home could have been acquired from magazines: but it is likely that he had been in London before, for he would surely have wanted to make his own selection of the paintings of Brangwyn or the Scottish artists he exhibited. For a young dandy, English tailoring must have been a strong attraction. In any case, to cross the Channel was a bitter ordeal. A fortune-teller had told him to expect death by water – he was childish enough to believe such prophecies – and to the end of his life he was haunted by the anticipation of a watery grave. In London Diaghilev found a loan exhibition of Spanish pictures at the Guildhall, which gave him the chance to see a number of paintings by Velazquez, El Greco, Zurbarán and Murillo from English private collections to which he might not otherwise have gained access. Queen Victoria's death had left its mark on the Royal Academy, where several paintings dealt with the ceremonies attendant upon her funeral, and Diaghilev noted that interest was particularly aroused by Benjamin Constant's state portrait of the Queen. He reported that by far the most distinguished works at Burlington House, 'where the artistic level had sunk so low in recent years', were Sargent's portraits. These included the *Two Daughters of Ascher Wertheimer*,[47] one of whom, Ena, would, as Mrs Mathias, be Diaghilev's friend in the 1920s, and the *Sitwell Family*, whose execution Osbert Sitwell (depicted in a sailor suit) later described so brilliantly in his autobiography. His younger brother, Sacheverell (playing on the floor with a toy), would be one of Diaghilev's closest friends in the last years of his life, as well as the author of his ballet *The Triumph of Neptune*. Although the future achievements of the young Sitwells were hidden from Diaghilev, he was quite certain of Sargent's genius, and admired his work again at the New Gallery in Regent Street. At the Academy he also liked a painting by the young Byam Shaw.[48]

Diaghilev arrived in Paris later in May, in time for the Salon at the Petit Palais. (He thought the flamboyant new Pont d'Alexandre III was hideous.)

The public is the same as ever [he wrote], sincerely full of good taste and respectful of tradition. They enjoy looking at the pictures, they all understand art and react sensitively to it – for not to do so would be to lack taste and understanding. Of course, even in the Salon there are some 'monstrosities' – with us they would be called decadent.... Everything else, though, is quite easy for the visitor to take in: well-drawn pictures, even in tone, which ask only to be hung in little bourgeois drawing-rooms the world over, with nothing startling about them to disturb their purchasers, who, over an excellent cigar after dinner, only want to observe a naughty black-eyed girl looking down on them from her frame, secure in the knowledge that they paid good money for her at the very latest and largest of Paris exhibitions....

All these little pictures at the Champs de Mars stretch out like ribbons throughout the halls: one feels it would even be possible to cut them into yard lengths. All the little pseudo-Whistlers, pseudo-Cazins and pseudo-Simons are so grey and so 'full of atmosphere' – landscape or portrait, they are all 'symphonies in grey and green'. And all those dour-faced Bretons either catching or eating fish! When I discussed the Salon with French painters, complaining of its insipidity, they were surprised. 'Is it so bad? It seems much the same as ever.' Now, that's the whole point – '*The same as ever*'![49]

Thus Diaghilev proclaimed in his twenty-eighth year the creed which was to guide him when his ballet company swept across the Western world, always on the crest of the latest wave. To him repetition was death. In art he would never grow old. In this he differed from his friend Benois, who increasingly accused the experimental artists of Moscow and Paris of trying to draw attention to themselves by showing off and shocking the bourgeois.

Diaghilev thought Besnard was the most interesting of the younger artists; indeed, rumours of his talent had already reached Russia, 'where little interest is taken in art, and modern art least of all'. He sent home for reproduction in the next number not only two Besnards but works by his recent favourites, Zuloaga and Anglada. Of the old favourites, Maurice Denis, seven pages of whose pictures appeared in Vol. VI, No. 7, *The World of Art* would reproduce an untypical but later famous painting (bought by André Gide), *Hommage à Cézanne*, an echo of Fantin-Latour's *Hommage à Delacroix*, which contained portraits not only of the artist, but also of Redon, Vuillard, Bonnard, Roussel, Sérusier and the dealer Vollard standing around Cézanne's still-life, *Le Compotier*, on an easel.

From Paris Diaghilev travelled to Darmstadt, where there was an artists' colony, designed by the *art nouveau* architect Olbrich. His criticism of this venture, of which he came out, on the whole, in favour, was that the tasteful, utilitarian style of the buildings made no allowance for the inclusion of real works of art. Dresden was the next place he visited, and he noted that all German towns were ambitious to hold big international exhibitions, which was an advantage, since this meant that there were at least a number of exhibition halls available. He liked the décor of the Dresden exhibition, with its not too big rooms, some colonnaded, and with a golden light coming from the skylights: but the pictures were the same as elsewhere, with works by Besnard, Blanche, Carrière, Zorn and Walter Crane apparently doing the rounds. At Berlin the Secessionists had a small exhibition – six rooms in a good quarter, though far from the centre: but their work showed a falling-off. Every new venture was good in its first year [the first exhibition of *Sezession* had been in 1882]: now 'secession' had no real meaning.[50]

In his hotel rooms in London, Paris, Darmstadt, Dresden and Berlin – and I think it likely that he visited Bayreuth and spent part of the summer of 1901 in Venice – and during his train journeys across Europe, Diaghilev had time to think. He had begun to reveal to a small circle of Russians the potential of the younger generation of artists, and with Benois he had begun to make his more intelligent fellow-countrymen a little conscious of their heritage from the early nineteenth, the eighteenth and seventeenth centuries and from medieval times – for in Russia the Middle Ages only ended with Peter the Great. But he saw nothing except artistic chaos under the present regime, and he longed to establish order. Works of art were scattered and too many bad ones – as in the Alexander III Museum – were shown alongside the good. He dreamed of collecting all the artistic wealth of Russia under one roof. He summed up his cogitations in an article. Museums were apt to get cluttered up with ugly and undesirable works. The Russian Museum (Alexander III) in St Petersburg was an accumulation of pictures and objects accepted indiscriminately as part of whole collections – the Russian rooms of the Hermitage, the Museum of the Academy of Arts, the Palace of Tsarskoe Selo, the collections of Prince Lobanov-Rostovsky (Foreign Minister, 1895–6) and Princess Tenishev. Assembled together, these collections presented no general plan. In the five years of its existence the Russian Museum had made no attempt to bring together a representative display of Russian art, as Tretiakov had privately contrived to do in Moscow. Yet Tretiakov had collected for forty years; since his death, his gallery had been run by a commission, and in the three years of its existence this commission had bought nothing but trivialities. The Russian Museum in St Petersburg only bought works by artists who had had their day. As for the Rumiantsev Museum, moved to Moscow by Alexander II, until the Tretiakov collection came into existence it had been the only museum of Russian and foreign painting in Moscow: now it had lost its point; and it was housed in an old, tumbledown building. Museums ought to reflect the history of their countries. Some of the vast Hermitage collections should be shown elsewhere, and exhibitions should be held in other Imperial palaces.[51]

Diaghilev was back in St Petersburg for a stay in November 1901. Igor Grabar, who had just returned home from Munich, came to the Fontanka flat. He had not yet met Diaghilev, although they had been at the University together, and although he had sent reports on art exhibitions to the magazine. He was hoping to earn a living by working for *The World of Art*.

Everyone was in the office. I came at exactly the right time, 5 o'clock, when they all used to be there. I had never seen Diaghilev before, but somehow I recognized him at once. He was seated behind a huge writing-desk, and as the butler announced me he got up and came to meet me, with both hands outstretched in a friendly way. He started to talk about my articles in *Niva*, in which I had been the first to appreciate the exhibitions of Finnish and West European painters, and which had on the whole had rather a hostile reception from the reactionary press. He showed me his rooms and his pictures, telling me how they were acquired.... He introduced me to Filosofov, Nuvel, Bakst and Rozanov.[52]

One of Teliakovsky's first acts as Director of the Imperial Theatres was to bring the Moscow choreographer Alexander Gorsky to St Petersburg. In January 1902 the latter's new version of *Don Quixote* was staged, with

Kchessinskaya in the role of Kitri, the Innkeeper's daughter, and décor by Korovine. It received a harsh review from Benois in the magazine:

> Gorsky's new vision was vitiated by the abhorrent lack of organization that is typical of amateur performances. His 'novelties' consisted of making the crowds on the stage bustle and move about fitfully and aimlessly. As regards the action, the dramatic possibilities and the dancers themselves were depressed to a uniformly commonplace level. *Don Quichotte* has never been an adornment to the Imperial Stage; now it has become something unworthy of it and almost disreputable.[53]

Although Teliakovsky had no intention of getting involved with Diaghilev, he was glad to employ the talents of Bakst and Benois, as will shortly be seen.[54] When his friends accepted commissions from the enemy theatre, Diaghilev was highly indignant and regarded them henceforth as turncoats and traitors. In future years he would use them when he needed them, but would discard them ruthlessly when he did not. It is likely that his high-handed behaviour, which was to cause many bitter partings and many tearful reconciliations in the future, had its first cause in the resentments of 1902, when Levushka and Shura took on work from the theatre which had rejected him.

Kchessinskaya was pregnant by the Grand Duke Andrei Vladimirovitch, which was rather embarrassing for her and for the Grand Duke Sergei, who had been her official protector for eight years. When she danced, in February 1902, in a special performance at the little Hermitage Theatre, she tried not to turn sideways for fear of revealing her condition to the Emperor, who sat very close in the *parterre*. Quarenghi's semicircular court theatre, with its pink marbled columns between white marble statues in niches, was joined to the great picture gallery by a bridge, inside which was a long anteroom in Chinese rococo style. (It was into the canal beneath this that Lisa threw herself in Tchaikovsky's *The Queen of Spades*. In Pushkin's story, of course, she married a rich official and lived happily ever after.)

It was at this time, probably because of her pregnancy, that Kchessinskaya gave up her role in *La Bayadère* to the young Anna Pavlova, whose ethereal features, delicately arched instep, unusual lightness and dramatic gifts were beginning to attract attention.[55]

Vol. VII, No. 1, of *The World of Art* is a good example of how Benois would have edited the magazine without Diaghilev's collaboration. It was devoted largely to the architecture of St Petersburg. There is something haphazard about Benois' choice and arrangement of the fifty pages of photographs. One feels Diaghilev would have done it better. For if you are going to include, say, several pictures of the Petropavlovsk Fortress, several of Rastrelli's Smolny Cathedral, several of Rinaldi's Marble Palace, and several of the statues in the Summer Garden, it would seem not only natural but more useful to group together illustrations of any one subject. This Benois

The arch at the entrance of New Holland, St Petersburg. Woodcut by Alexandra
Ostroumova, from *The World of Art*.

did not do. Between the photographs are sandwiched nine admirable woodcuts of St Petersburg by Ostroumova.

The black-and-white illustrations in line (as opposed to those in half-tone)
in *The World of Art*, whether fantastic ornaments or realistic views, had
been from the start of outstanding merit. Since the 1880s, when Japanese
prints had begun to be imported into Paris (and the Goncourt brothers had
collected them), their rapid, calligraphic style of drawing had aroused the
emulation of Western artists. Diaghilev's illustrators, although their style
was mainly rococo (Bilibine and the German T.T.Heine excepted – and

occasionally Lancerey, who had his Gothick side), had become aware of the Japanese either at first hand or through Beardsley. It therefore seemed apposite that when the editors of *The World of Art* decided to devote a large part of their February 1902 number (Vol. VII, No. 2) to the drawings of Hiroshige, Hokusai and other Japanese (incongruously adorning endless articles by Shestov on Nietzsche and Dostoievsky and by Merejkovsky on Tolstoy and Dostoievsky), there should follow nine pages of drawings by Beardsley and that Bakst should design a black-and-white title-page to an article by Rozanov on the Paestum temples – urns, foliage, water, woods and sunset, with a cupid lying dead or drunk on a terrace in the middle distance.

Diaghilev was settled again in his St Petersburg flat, and in the same February number he reviewed an exhibition of Russian Historical Portraits in Moscow. He considered it a dilettante affair, run by a few lady patronesses of the arts, who had made do with inadequate accommodation in the Academy of Sciences. There had been a big exhibition of Russian portraits in 1870, with 879 pictures. The Moscow show had 260 exhibits – he named the new 'discoveries': a few portraits by Antropov, Argunov, Levitsky and Borovikovsky. If the Russian Museum or the Historical Society could not produce annual exhibitions, a show of this nature should be more comprehensive. He thus anticipated his own great exhibition of 1905.[56]

CHAPTER 5

1902–5

Last Years of *The World of Art* – Isadora Duncan – Exhibition of Historical Portraits

T HE COLLAPSE OF THE CAMPANILE of St Mark's in Venice on 14 July 1902 may be said to have presaged the collapse of Diaghilev's magazine. Filosofov wrote an article discussing whether or not the tower should be rebuilt. He decided that, if anything old showed signs of tottering, it should be given a push.[1] This verdict, which smacked of Nietzsche's doctrine, revolted Benois, who wrote a stinging reply. The basic difference in outlook between Dima and Shura was a factor which contributed to the closing down of *The World of Art* in 1904. Besides this, all the original group of friends had developed interests outside the magazine. Filosofov and Merejkovsky had founded their own philosophical periodical, *The New Path*. Benois worked for 'The Treasures of Russian Art', a series of publications issued by the Society for the Encouragement of the Arts. Both he and Bakst – as well, of course, as Korovine and Golovine – were being employed in the Imperial Theatres. In 1902 Bakst designed *Hippolytus* for the Alexandrinsky, and Benois *Götterdämmerung* for the Mariinsky. Serov had his own life as a painter, and was in constant demand for portraits. Diaghilev had been collecting material for a book on Levitsky, and in 1903 began the immense task of assembling a representative exhibition of Russian portraits to be held in the capital in 1905. Another symptom of decay was the Moscow artists' 'Secession' – in 1902, when a new group, the Union of Russian Artists, was formed and a *World of Art* exhibition was held for the first time in Moscow, from 15 November till 1 January. (It came on to St Petersburg and was open there at the Society for the Encouragement of the Arts, 38 Bolshaya Morskaya, from 13 February till 26 March 1903.) Above all, there was Diaghilev's declining interest. It does become extremely wearisome to keep a monthly magazine going year after year.

In the time that remained, the latest theatrical productions – notably those of the Moscow Arts Theatre – would be recorded; there would be more successful essays in illustration; foreign painters, with an increasing emphasis on the great Impressionists and Post-Impressionists, would be introduced to the Russian public; and young Russian painters, including at least one of outstanding talent, would be brought forward.

A new arrival described the way Diaghilev and his friends worked. One day in the autumn of 1902, Grabar introduced the young Mstislav Dobujinsky to Benois, who liked his work, commissioned some decorative drawings for *The World of Art* and took him to see Diaghilev. Dobujinsky wrote:

Diaghilev's home was a typical St Petersburg gentleman's apartment, with big windows looking out on the Fontanka. His contributors used to gather there on Tuesdays, and I took to attending this meeting every week. There was always a large crowd and it was very lively. The old nurse, immortalized by Bakst in his picture of her and Diaghilev, with her wrinkled face and the mole in the middle of her forehead, presided at the samovar. Tea and biscuits were served on a table in the dining-room, and the presence of the nurse gave an air of unexpected cosiness to the proceedings. Everybody used to shake hands with her.... The journal itself was discussed very little. It used to be put together somewhere behind the scenes in a home-made sort of way. All the work was done by Diaghilev himself and Filosofov, and for a long time they did not even have a secretary, until a very modest student, Grishkovsky, made his appearance. Bakst also worked in a back room, doing the 'manual work' – retouching the photographs for the blocks, even doing his elaborate headings for the journal. Copies of the magazine were stored in a little room near the hall in the care of Diaghilev's valet, the swarthy Vassili Zuikov, who used to rush round St Petersburg on all sorts of editorial business.... The instigators of all the disputes and biting remarks were the little elegant Nuvel ... who was always breaking into infectious laughter, the bald Nurok ... an amusing cynic with the imperturbable face of a Mephistofeles, and the tall, thin Yaremich, with his sly, screwed-up eyes and his merciless, taunting wit.[2]

Dobujinsky did not feel at ease with Diaghilev, friendly as he was, and 'in spite of his charm, smile, soft handshake and the attention he paid when one spoke to him'. He noted Diaghilev's 'fine singer's voice', 'lisping accent' and 'manner of a *grand seigneur*'. Smart young men, brought up at the Imperial Corps des Pages (as Diaghilev had not been) allowed the last syllables of long words to fade out into inaudibility. At the same time, Dobujinsky noticed the childish aspect of Diaghilev's chubby face and soft lips, and a funny habit he had of rubbing his eyes with his fist. In the evenings Diaghilev would vanish to change his clothes. He did not encourage intimacy or drop in on his acquaintances except on business; and only at the house of Benois, which was a general meeting-place, did Dobujinsky see him once or twice.

Yet, the new collaborator wrote,

The wonderful thing about Diaghilev was that in spite of his manner of being the leader he went into every detail: nothing was too insignificant for him, he wanted to do everything himself.... I remember how once, in order to hurry me up with some work for a portrait exhibition, he arrived at my house at the back of beyond in the Ismailovsky Row, and, as I happened to be out, waited a whole hour, simply to assure himself of what I was doing and shame me for my dilatoriness. From the beginning of *The World of Art* Diaghilev was notoriously dictatorial, but this was accepted as perfectly natural, and everybody submitted willingly.... Serov and Benois were the only people Diaghilev turned to for advice. . . .³

Diaghilev ran into Tchekhov at the *World of Art* exhibition in Moscow and they began a serious conversation about art and religion, which was cut short. Back in St Petersburg, Diaghilev wrote to the playwright on 23 December 1902: 'At the art exhibition we were interrupted at the most interesting point: whether a serious religious movement is possible in Russia today. The question is, in other words, a "to be or not to be" of the whole of contemporary culture. I hope to see you again and continue where we left off.'⁴ Perhaps Diaghilev was less interested in the possibility of 'a serious religious movement' than in keeping in touch with a man he admired. Filosofov had reviewed *The Seagull*, which had been a failure on its first production at the Alexandrinsky in October 1896 and which was now a great success; and Diaghilev enclosed a copy of the November number.

Tchekhov replied:

30 December, 1902

Dear Sergei Pavlovitch

I have received *Mir Iskusstva* with the *Seagull* article and read the article. Thank you very much. When I finished the article I felt like writing a play, and I probably shall after January.

You write that we spoke about a serious religious movement in Russia. I can't say anything about Russia as a whole, but as for the intelligentsia it is so far only playing at religion, mostly because it has nothing better to do. It is safe to say that the educated section of our society has moved away from religion and is moving further and further away from it, whatever people may say and whatever philosophical and religious societies may be formed. I won't venture to say whether this is good or bad, but I will say that the religious movement you write about and all contemporary culture are something quite different, and there's no point in trying to derive the latter from the former. Present-day culture is the beginning of work in the name of a great future, work which will perhaps continue for tens of thousands of years with the result that finally, if only in the distant future, mankind will perceive the truth of the real God, that is, not make conjectures or search for Him in Dostoyevsky [this is perhaps a dig at Merejkovsky's articles in *The World of Art*], but perceive Him as clearly as they perceive that twice two is four. Present-day culture is the beginning of a work, while the religious movement we talked about is a vestige, the end or nearly the end of something that has had its day.... When you see Mr Filosofov please convey to him my deep gratitude. Happy New Year and all good wishes.

Your devoted
A. Tchekhov.⁵

It is unexpected to find Diaghilev and Tchekhov writing to each other about religion. Neither was, in the strict sense of the word, a believer. Diaghilev did not scorn certain observances, and his life of effort might be said to have been lived *as if* he believed. Tchekhov, it seems, believed in a future when it might be possible to believe. His words recall those of Olga at the end of *Three Sisters*: 'Our sufferings may mean happiness for the people who come after us. There'll be a time when peace and happiness reign in the world, and then we shall be remembered kindly and blessed....' Sonia's last speech in *Uncle Vanya* also comes to mind.

Now that he was back from self-imposed exile, Diaghilev turned his guns on the Mariinsky. In an article on the three ballets of Delibes he began by explaining that he had been abroad for a long while and had just set foot in the Mariinsky for the first time in eighteen months. '*Coppelia* is the most beautiful ballet in existence, a pearl which has no equal in the ballet repertory.' A superhuman effort was needed to take all the colour out of it, and he 'could not remain silent about the ill-fated evening' when he had seen again this most frequently performed of the ballets of Delibes. 'The décor was bedraggled, the costumes dirty and the dancers third-rate. Last year *Sylvia* failed through false economy [the sacking of Diaghilev?]. As for *La Source*, Delibes, a master of French classicism, has at last had the honour of being castrated by the civil servants in charge of St Petersburg's music and ballet.'[6]

When the Moscow Arts Theatre returned to St Petersburg in the winter of 1902–3, Diaghilev (or one of his colleagues) commented on a speech by Nemirovitch-Danchenko at the first-night supper party, in which he complained of the lack of new Russian plays. The reason that there were no good plays was that there was no Russian theatre worth writing for. 'Until the old conventional, realistic theatre disappears – and it is high time it did – no development in drama can be expected.' And what talented writer was going to write plays which were never put on, as was the case with Tchekhov?[7] This attack on Stanislavsky's extreme 'realism' – which the writer saw not as something new, but as a continuation of the old tradition – was followed up by an article called 'Unnecessary Truth', by the poet Brusov. Moscow was proud of its Arts Theatre, he wrote, which had been in existence for three years and which played to full houses when it came to St Petersburg. Why was it so successful? Was it the theatre of the future? No, it was the old theatre refurbished: it did what other theatres had tried to do, but did it more perfectly. But, along with the entire European theatre, it was on a false trail.

It strives for reality, for truth to life. There are real rooms and there is appropriate weather outside the windows. Chairs are placed naturally and when actors address each other they look at each other and turn their backs to the audience. But it is impossible, nevertheless, to portray life truthfully on the stage. The stage

74

itself imposes a convention. There is no real advance between putting up a sign inscribed 'Forest' and having forest scenery, as nothing more than the symbol of a forest can be achieved. No art-form can portray reality.[8]

Brusov was anticipating the experiments of Meyerhold, who was at that time a minor member of Stanislavsky's company. He was also on the same track as Gordon Craig.

Diaghilev was instinctively attracted to men of genius, and he was suddenly possessed by the idea of involving Tchekhov with the magazine, the literary side of which was in danger of becoming absurdly monotonous. Historians have found Merejkovsky's essays on Tolstoy and Dostoievsky in *The World of Art* of prime importance, but when Merejkovsky became preoccupied by *The New Path* in 1902, Minsky and Shestov stepped in to write for Diaghilev about Dostoievsky and Nietzsche in their turn, while Minsky contributed endless 'Philosophical Discussions' and Rozanov wrote about Merejkovsky and Gogol.[9] The thing became absurd. In 1903 Shestov was writing about Merejkovsky, Tolstoy and Dostoievsky to keep things going, while Rozanov prepared another article on Merejkovsky.[10] Diaghilev decided that these abstract speculations must be curbed, and he wrote to Tchekhov about it on 3 July 1903, proposing a reorganization of the magazine. There should, he suggested, be four editors: Tchekhov in charge of poetry and fiction; Merejkovsky in charge of literary criticism; Filosofov for theatre; Benois for the visual arts. This subdivision of power was, however, entirely dependent on Tchekhov's consent to co-operate.[11]

On 12 July 1903 Tchekhov replied from Yalta to Diaghilev's letter of invitation.

I've given your letter much thought, and even though your proposal or invitation is very tempting, I'm afraid that I won't be able to respond in the way you want me to, and that I should like to.

I cannot be an editor of *Mir Iskusstva* because it is impossible for me to live in St Petersburg; the journal won't move to Moscow for my sake, editing by mail and wire is impossible, and the journal will gain nothing by having me as a nominal editor only. That's point Number One. Point Number Two is that just as only one artist can paint a picture and only one orator can make a speech, so only one person can edit a journal. I'm no critic, of course, and would probably make a poor job of editing the critical section. What is more, how could I work under the same roof as Dmitri Merejkovsky? He is a resolute believer, a proselytizing one, whereas I squandered away my faith long ago and never fail to be puzzled by an intellectual who is also a believer. I respect Merejkovsky and value him as a person and writer, but if we ever do get the cart moving we shall end up pulling it in opposite directions.... I've always thought and am certain that there should only be one editor, and that *Mir Iskusstva* in particular should be edited by you alone....

Don't be angry with me, dear Sergei Pavlovitch, but it seems to me that if you continue editing the journal for another five years you'll come to agree with me....

I wish you all the best and firmly clasp your hand. The weather in Yalta is cool, or at least not hot, and I am flourishing.[12]

Diaghilev wrote back on 26 July, offering to put Tchekhov in charge of all editorial decisions and only to retain Merejkovsky as a regular contributor. Tchekhov still refused, and two more persuasive letters from Sergei Pavlovitch, who by now believed – or said he believed – that Tchekhov alone could save the journal, did not move him. The playwright died a year later.

Although he accepted their wages, Benois had been on bad terms with the Society for the Encouragement of the Arts almost since he began editing 'The Treasures of Russian Art', which they subsidized; and he could not restrain himself – or his friends – from attacking its committee in *The World of Art*. As early as January 1901 he had written of a French exhibition they had organized at their premises in Bolshoya Morskaya: 'In the contemporary section ... the best and most important French artists were absent – artists already acclaimed as classics – Monet, Sisley, Pissarro, Degas ... Guillaumin, Signac, Cézanne, Forain, Toulouse-Lautrec, Ibels and many others; while ... the so-called [after their dealer] Vollard group refused to participate – Bonnard, Vuillard, Roussel, Vallotton, Maurice Denis, the most interesting of the younger artists. ...' In autumn 1902 he was rebuked at another exhibition by Sabaneyev, one of the committee of the Society which employed him, and he lost his temper, 'holding the lapels of his frock-coat, shaking him and hissing abuse in his face'. The mild Benois was prone to these 'blind furies'. 'I naturally expected Sabaneyev to challenge me to a duel and lost no time in nominating Diaghilev and Filosofov as seconds.' There was no duel, but after receiving a letter of remonstrance from the committee, in February 1903, Benois resigned.[13]

Apart from his stage designs and his work as an art historian, Benois will be chiefly remembered as a recorder in watercolour of the architectural beauties of St Petersburg and its neighbouring country palaces. *The World of Art* published one fine set of illustrations to which he must have given himself heart and soul. In autumn 1903 the Neva flooded, and conditions in St Petersburg were similar to – but not nearly so serious as – those during the great flood of 1824, which prompted Pushkin to write his poem *The Bronze Horseman*. No doubt it was the 1903 inundation that gave Benois the idea of illustrating the famous poem; and in the first number for 1904[14] Diaghilev printed this work of his beloved poet with Benois' illustrations. The feature occupied thirty-six pages. The bold brush drawings, which resemble woodcuts, but without the woodcut's crisp edges, are printed sometimes in black alone, sometimes in black and one or two other flat colours, grey-green and buff. Benois' images of the flood – with despairing oarsmen, drowned men, dead cats and wreckage – of panicking crowds, of the Emperor, surrounded by his staff, watching the river from the Embankment of the Winter Palace, of the poor young student seated in his attic bedroom, of his battle with the waters to find his beloved's ruined cottage on the farther shore, of his madness and his haunting by the Bronze Horseman who rears at him even from the hump-backed bridge over the Fontanka on the Nevsky Prospekt, are extremely varied and powerful, not only enabling the artist to work in the sinister-Romantic Hoffmannesque mood which had always been and always would be dear to him, but to introduce in the background many of his favourite buildings: the Fortress, the Admiralty, the Stock Exchange and the old Bolshoi Theatre, built by his grandfather but since destroyed.

Although his other old friend, Somov, was no longer speaking to him, Diaghilev had devoted the first double number of 1903[15] to his work, with lavish frontispieces and title-pages in colour, gold and silver, with portraits of the artist and his parents. Other works are in Somov's fanciful eighteenth-century vein, like designs for the lids of superior chocolate boxes. How can one take seriously these nymphs, these *marquises*, these *bassins*, these negro pages, or the coyness with which the artist places, beneath a *chaise longue* whereon a Marie-Antoinette lady in a dressing-gown sips chocolate, a *pot de chambre*? Benois committed the same minimal enormities. And it must be added that these epicene travesties were in the air, for half the painters of the Paris Salon indulged in them. Yet Somov could draw and paint quite well, as his portrait of Ostroumova, among others, bears witness, and when he painted a scene from life (or, at least, a scene of real life recollected in the tranquillity of the studio), as in *Baigneuses*, a view from above of girls in summer dresses in the shade of trees on a steep slope above a pond where other naked girls are bathing, the result is delightful. That Diaghilev thought so too is proved by the fact that he singled out this landscape to reproduce *hors texte* on cream-coloured card, in gravure, with a plate-mark.

The black-and-white decorations by Bakst for *The World of Art* have been referred to: but it is odd – in view of the extraordinary fame and influence he attained ten years later in Western Europe as a stage-designer for Diaghilev – that few of his paintings were reproduced in the magazine. He was never allotted a whole number, or even a section of several pages. Although he contributed to all the *World of Art* exhibitions, he was evidently regarded mainly as an illustrator or as a maker of portrait drawings. Fine drawings by him of Maliavin, Rozanov and others were reproduced, but only four paintings appeared over the six years.[16] If Diaghilev – and perhaps Benois – did not consider that his individual genius found its best expression in oil paint, posterity would support this judgement. But there was one outstanding exception to the rule.

On 20 April 1904 Bakst began his famous portrait of Diaghilev. He painted him in his Fontanka flat, standing, three-quarter length, his hands in his trouser pockets, regarding the spectator with an insolent stare. His old nurse was seated in the background. Bakst wrote to his wife that everyone thought it better than Maliavin's portrait of Diaghilev as a young dandy in a top-hat, with a cane, which had been shown at the *World of Art* exhibition in Moscow in 1902. Throughout the first half of June Bakst was prevented from joining his family in the country because of work on the portrait. On 4 June he wrote, 'Today has been terrible. Diaghilev continually broke off posing and even tried to get round me to make him more handsome. I nearly hit him. That's the last time I shall let him interfere.' On 7 June he reported that Serov had been at Diaghilev's, that they had spent the whole day and lunched together, and Serov had drawn a caricature of him in his smock, working on the portrait. 'Serov couldn't stop looking at the portrait. He likes it. Hurray!' A few days later he had finished the head and part of the torso, and hoped to finish the whole thing in October or November, but work was interrupted as Diaghilev was leaving for Moscow.[17] In fact, the big portrait, with its all-over silvery-grey tones, in which the warm brown of a mahogany portfolio for prints strikes the only contrasting note of colour, was not resumed and completed until 1906; and it bears that date. It was a masterpiece, comparable to that of the far superior Serov, whose portrait of the actress Yermolova, standing with hands folded, like some godlike governess whose divine pupils have kept her waiting, was not reproduced in *The World of Art* either, though shown, like Bakst's *Diaghilev*, in the 1906 Paris exhibition. Yet Bakst would achieve, through the stage designs he made for Diaghilev, a wider world fame than Serov, to whom they both looked up, and who is still (in 1979) almost unknown outside Russia.

Serov was amply illustrated in *The World of Art* from 1899 till 1904. He and Vrubel were the greatest Russian painters of their day, as well as the two Diaghilev chiefly admired. A number at the end of 1903[18] was largely devoted to Vrubel, illustrating his superb *Demon seated*, sketches for the *Fallen Demon*, the portrait of his wife Zabela in a mauve Empire dress, a décor for Rimsky's *Tsar Saltan*, a glittering 'bejewelled' watercolour, called *Oriental Tale* (referred to above), of a Sultan in his harem surrounded by beauties, which may have influenced Bakst's décor for *Schéhérazade* in 1910, and some pottery busts fired in the Abramtsevo workshops. These last are of extreme interest. They are modelled with bold strokes accentuating the planes, comparable to the strokes of unworked paint with which the artist 'carved out' some of his paintings in oil. Most are of fairy-tale characters, such as Lel and Kupava, who appear in Rimsky's *Snow Maiden*, and Sadko from the opera of that name, but one is of the Demon.

In the middle of 1903[19] a new painter with claims to originality and greatness made his début in the pages of the magazine. Borissov-Musatov was born in 1870 in remote Saratov on the eastern Volga. He studied in Moscow, then in St Petersburg under Tchistiakov, and in Paris was influenced – as who was not, from Gauguin to Picasso? – by Puvis de Chavannes. Back in Saratov, he worked much in the abandoned grounds of Zubrilovka, an eighteenth-century country house, which, like Yakuntchikova's old home, Vedenskoye, haunts many of his later paintings. Against these backgrounds are posed his pensive heroines in a vague, simple 'fancy-dress' of the crino-line period, which seemed as necessary to the release of his imagination as the tight-bodiced, long-skirted dresses in which Augustus John, in art as in life, clothed his family. Dreaming among trees, staring up avenues or resting beneath the porch of their mansion, they seem to mourn a departed father or to be awaiting a lover who will never come. Musatov creates a twilit atmosphere of brooding, of suspended volition, like Gauguin's Polynesian women, but his colours are usually restricted to subdued blues, mauves and greens. More than any other artist he embodies the melan-choly of Verlaine, thus qualifying as Russia's principal Symbolist painter. Diaghilev only became aware of his work in 1902, and at once fell under his spell. Dobujinsky remembered meeting Musatov at 11 Fontanka, and described him as 'an unhealthy little man, hunchbacked, with a sharp little beard, dressed very carefully' and wearing a gold bracelet.[20] Borissov-Musatov died in 1905, aged thirty-five, and Diaghilev organized an exhibi-tion of his work in Moscow a year later.

When, early in 1904, Russia found herself at war with Japan, and Diaghi-lev had (as related above) to go the rounds in search of further subsidy, it was perhaps his enthusiasm for the work of Borissov-Musatov, his desire to give the recently deceased Maria Yakuntchikova a posthumous retrospec-tive showing in *The World of Art* and his wish to illustrate the increasingly amazing Shchukin collection of French paintings that gave him the incentive to keep his magazine alive. We know that Benois, doubtless on Diaghilev's instigation, had the Shchukin collection photographed,[21] though the maga-zine did not survive long enough to publish the results. Since Princess Teni-shev was making conditions and Mamontov was out of the running, it seems likely (though we have no proof) that Diaghilev applied to Shchukin for funds – for the simple reason that he would have been mad not to do so. Into the first number of the magazine for 1904, Vol. XI, No. 1, was inserted a slip of pink paper announcing that alternate numbers of *The World of Art* throughout the year would be edited by Diaghilev and Benois. That is to say, Nos 1, 3, 5 and 8–9 would be edited by Diaghilev, Nos 2, 4, 6, 7, 10 and 11 by Benois.[22]

The Benois-edited numbers of the magazine for 1904 – all but one – dealt with the riches of Russia's past, and could almost be considered a continua-tion of Shura's work for the Society for the Encouragement of the Arts. The exception was Vol. XII, No. 6, devoted to medieval miniatures. This number also contained an article by Benois on Frederick Watts, who had just died, and a review by Nurok of four concerts conducted by Vincent d'Indy at Pavlovsk. 'Our musical world can boast total ignorance of the deathless compositions of César Franck.' Nuvel made friends with d'Indy at this time.[23] Vol. XII, No. 2, was given over to the architecture, gardens, decorations and sculpture of Arkhangelskoe, the huge Yusupov (formerly Galitzin) villa near Moscow; Vol. XII, No. 4, illustrated an exhibition held in St Petersburg of treasures from Russian collections – sculptures, miniatures, Oriental and Sèvres porcelain, snuff-boxes and so on; Vol. XII, No. 7, was about the classical architecture of Moscow, some of which was already beginning to be 'ruined' or has disappeared since (this number contained obituaries of Lenbach, Vereshchagin and Riaboushkin, as well as a report on the Paris Salon by Alexander Shervashidze, a painter who would later paint scenery for Diaghilev). Vol. XII, No. 10, was on the treasures of the Patriarchate – crowns, pluvials, *manchettes*, copes, crosses and chalices; and, finally, Vol. XII, No. 11, was a remarkable record in words and photographs by Ivan Bilibine of seventeenth- and eighteenth-century wooden buildings, furniture, implements and peasant embroidery from northern Russia.

The contents of the five Diaghilev-edited numbers of the magazine for 1904 (one a double number) show him in his triple role as a patron of illustrators – for the Pushkin poem, with Benois' illustrations, was in the first of his numbers[24]; as a promoter of established and lesser-known Russian painters – No. 3 was entirely devoted to Maria Yakuntchikova and No. 5 carried not only reproductions of Yuon, Yaremitch, Rylov, Grabar, Maliavin, Vrubel, Benois, Pasternak (father of Boris, the poet and novelist), Maliutin, Korovine and Somov, but of Borissov-Musatov and Kandinsky (who had written an account of an exhibition in Munich in Vol. VII, Nos 5–6); and as a revealer to Russians of the best new painting in Western Europe.

If Diaghilev were to be judged solely as a propagandist for the Impressionists and the Post-Impressionists, his achievement is not to be despised. From the beginning of *The World of Art*, he had given a showing to Degas, Monet, Renoir, Pissarro and Sisley, either in the magazine or in exhibitions, or both. In Vol. XI, Nos 8–9, though we may think Diaghilev was over-generous in space to such temporary favourites as Anglada and Maurice Denis, he reproduced seven Gauguins – a year before the big Gauguin retrospective in 1905 – one Cézanne, one Lautrec, three Vuillards, two Bonnards, two works by the *pointilliste* Cross (Seurat was never reproduced in *The World of Art*, though mentioned in articles translated from Meyer-Gräfe), one Van Gogh and one Matisse. Only the collectors Shchukin and Ivan Morosov were comparable as pioneers of new movements in the cultural backwater of Russia. England was just as slow to appreciate the Impressionists, and even in France only Camondo began to form a collection as early as Shchukin in 1890.

In Vol. XII, No. 7, it was announced that Diaghilev's book on D.M. Levitsky had won the gold medal of the Imperial Academy of Science. It was less a critical appraisal than an attempt to list, verify and illustrate as many genuine surviving works of the master as possible. The extent to which Diaghilev was breaking fresh ground in writing about Russia's most accomplished pre-nineteenth-century painter (ikons apart) may be measured by the fact that in the fourth edition of Bryan's *Dictionary of Painters and Engravers*, published in 1915, Levitsky was not included. (Nor were Borovikovsky, Brullov, Ivanov, Kiprensky or Venezianov. In fact, the only Russians I can find in this edition – which I happen to have – are the Italian-born Feodor Bruni, President of the Academy in the mid-nineteenth century, and Vereshchagin, who is given over three columns.) Diaghilev's monograph was intended to be the first of a series on 'Russian Painting in the Eighteenth Century', but although Diaghilev worked on Borovikovsky, the only other essay to appear (in Vol. XI, No. 3, of the magazine) was on the two Shibanovs, who had hitherto been believed to be one person. (Diaghilev was the first to distinguish between the Academy student, A.P.Shibanov, who went abroad with a grant in 1785, and Mikhail Shibanov, a serf of Prince Potemkin, who painted the Empress Catherine in a fur hat.) Diaghilev's sole data on Levitsky had been Petrov's catalogue of an exhibition of six-teenth- to eighteenth-century portraits organized by the Society for the Encouragement of the Arts in 1870, which had been commemorated by an album of 440 photographs, and Rovinsky's *Dictionary* of engraved Russian portraits. In the autumn of 1901 Diaghilev had sent out six hundred letters to provincial governors and country gentry, with questionnaires, asking for evidence of works by Levitsky. He had received twenty-eight replies. From people he had written to privately he had received thirty-six replies. A letter to the press brought twenty replies.

Diaghilev had made a list of Levitsky portraits whose whereabouts were known, and another list of those which were merely known to have been painted. He faced certain problems. There were portraits which he did not consider authentic, including a series of twelve portraits of the Knights of St Vladimir at Gatchina. Yet it was known that Levitsky *had* painted the Knights of St Vladimir. There were also a few 'Levitskys' in the Hermitage which had been attributed to Borovikovsky, but which Diaghilev did not believe were by either painter, although all were by the same hand. Documents relative to the painter's life were included in the book, as well as a list of his appointments and his pedigree – his forbears were priests, but mentioned as early as 1680 in the Poltava district. Finally, there were sixty-four large photographic reproductions of Levitsky's portraits accepted by Diaghilev (besides a number of smaller reproductions at the back). Apart from those of the Empress Catherine and her two successors, among the most interesting personages represented were: Prince Alexander Nikolai-evitch Galitzin (1773–1844), Minister of Public Instruction in the 1820s; Gavrila Romanovitch Derjavin (1743–1816), the first great Russian poet;

Ekaterina Ivanovna Nelidova (1756–1839), mistress of the Emperor Paul and friend of the Empress Maria Feodorovna; Alexander Vassilievitch Khrapovitsky (1749–1801), secretary of Catherine the Great, author of memoirs; Glafira Ivanovna Alymova (1758–1826), daughter of Betsky, who had been the lover of the Empress Catherine's mother; and Nikolai Ivanovitch Novikov (1744–1818), freemason and apostle of 'Enlightenment', exiled by Catherine. Apart from his magazine and the *Theatre Annual*, Diaghilev's *Levitsky* was the only book he ever published.

Although the magazine came to an end in December 1904, Diaghilev's *World of Art* period would culminate a few months later in his most stupendous exhibition, that of Historical Portraits. Looked at in another way, this period could, however, be said to extend into 1906 and 1907, when Diaghilev exhibited Russian art in Paris, Berlin and Venice; in which case it would have filled out a decade.

The arrival in St Petersburg in December 1904 of a young American dancer heralded a new phase of activity in Diaghilev's life. Isadora Duncan had just captivated Germany by her dancing in a free style, without ballet skirt or shoes, to the music of great composers. She was not sure from day to day whether she was an ambassador from Ancient Greece or from Democratic America, but she found it odd, at this time of poverty, strikes and revolution, to be dancing in the way she did before the pampered aristocracy of St Petersburg.

How strange it must have been to those dilettantes of the gorgeous ballet, with its lavish decorations and scenery, to watch a young girl, clothed in a tunic of cobweb, appear and dance before a simple blue curtain to the music of Chopin! Yet even for the first dance there was a storm of applause. My soul that yearned and suffered the tragic notes of the Preludes; my soul that aspired and revolted to the thunder of the Polonaises ... awakened in that wealthy, spoilt and aristocratic audience a response of stirring applause. How curious![25]

Isadora's soul had not aspired or revolted in vain. Two immediate results of this recital were the conversion of the young dancer Michel Fokine to a more naturalistic form of dance, and the arrival of Kchessinskaya, covered in pearls, diamonds and sables, to offer her a box for the ballet and ask her to supper.[26] It would be because of Isadora's influence on Fokine, which turned him into a new kind of choreographer, that Diaghilev was steered, only four years later, once more and for life into the world of ballet.

Fokine was fed up with the current state of ballet at the Mariinsky. The technique of dancing had been brought to a height of perfection in Russia that had never been attained before. In St Petersburg there had always been a preoccupation with style, whereas Moscow admired bravura; and in recent years Italian guest artists and teachers had grafted a new strength on to the stylish tree of the Mariinsky school. But the ballets given were so trite, conventional and divorced from life. 'Fairies have been the ruin of ballet,' Benois had written in *The World of Art*.[27] And the music of most ballets, with their obligatory marches, waltzes, mazurkas and polonaises, was on the whole uninspiring. The ballets of Delibes, Tchaikovsky and perhaps Glazunov, whose *Raimonda* had been given in 1898, were exceptions. Isadora set Fokine's mind working.

Benois wrote an article on the American dancer in the new magazine *Slovo*. 'If my enthusiasm for the traditional ballet ... was not in the least diminished,' he remembered later,

I still recall the delight which the American barefoot dancer provoked in me. . . . She had not, in my opinion, charm as a woman. . . . There was much that jarred with me in her dances; sometimes they exhibited thoroughly English airs and graces and a sugary affectation. But on the whole, in her leaps, her runs and particularly in her pauses, her movements were full of a genuine awareness of beauty. . . . [She had] an inner sense of music. This gift dictated all her movements, even to the slightest movement of her hands.[28]

At a supper at Pavlova's flat Isadora sat between Bakst and Benois.[29] Bakst told her fortune – he was to make two drawings of her.[30] With Diaghilev she had a long talk about dancing. At a supper given for her at Cubat's restaurant after one of her performances, the painter Zionglinsky became infatuated with her and called her 'a devil of an angel'. She insisted on dancing, drunk as she was, fell over, had to be taken home to the Europa Hotel and then tried to seduce her escort.[31] But she had made her mark.

It was a time of food shortage, of widespread agitation and strikes. Even the dancers at the Mariinsky staged an abortive strike.[32] A strike at the Putilov engineering works on 15 January led to the organization of a number of protest marches on 22 January, later known as Bloody Sunday: these crossed the forbidden line into central St Petersburg and converged on the Winter Palace. One procession was led by the unbalanced priest Gapon (subsequently murdered as a double agent). The Emperor was, as usual, at Tsarskoe Selo, fourteen miles away. The troops, mostly Guards, who had been ordered out, could only shoot on the command of the police, and when shots were fired at eight points throughout the city, the crowds ran berserk and looted arms shops. At least a thousand lives were lost.

In the Nevsky Prospekt, near the Alexandrinsky Theatre, young Vaslav Nijinsky got caught up in the crowd, and was struck on the forehead by a Cossack's lead-weighted knout.[33] In the evening, when Benois, who had gone out of curiosity to see what was going on and was making his way back by a circuitous route to his home at Kammeny Island, he found his sleigh attacked by the passers-by. 'What do you think you are doing – running people over?'[34] The Grand Duke Vladimir, who, as Governor of St Petersburg, could hardly be held responsible for the Chief of Police losing his head or for the troops firing on civilians, was also President of the Academy of Arts. Serov wrote a letter of protest to the Academy's journal. This was not published and he resigned.[35] On 17 February Grand Duke Sergei Alexandrovitch, another of the Tsar's uncles and his brother-in-law (his beautiful wife was an elder sister of the Tsaritsa), was assassinated outside the Kremlin in Moscow.

The Exhibition of Historical Russian Portraits which Diaghilev had been planning was due to open in February 1905. He had advertised for information about old portraits, he had gone through the files of the Public Record Office and he had worked in libraries. Hundreds of letters had been written, not only to the heads of noble houses, but to minor members of those houses who might be alive or dead, and to whom certain portraits might have descended in the female line. Apart from finding lost treasures, the eager searcher acquired in the course of his work an exceptional knowledge of Russian genealogy; and Grabar relates how, when nobody could recognize 'some obscure portrait which came from a remote estate ... Diaghilev would tell us with his charming smile – "What funny people you are! Can't you see? The painter is Luders and the sitter is Prince Alexander Mikhailovitch Galitzin in his youth!"'[36] Of course, Diaghilev was already familiar with many known portraits in the various Imperial palaces, in the Winter Palace, in Tsarskoe Selo, in Pavlovsk, in Peterhof, Gatchina and Oranienbaum. During 1904 he had invited himself to houses in St Petersburg and Moscow where he had never been before, he raided country houses as far apart as Prince Galitzin's at Mariino in the government of Novgorod, as the Apraxin house at Olgovo or as Count Orlov-Davidov's at Otrada, both near Moscow, as Prince Lopukhin-Demidov's at Korsun in the government of Kiev, as the Boldirev house Voronzovka in the government of Tambov, and as the Voronzov Palace at Odessa.

Although the majority of pictures outside the Imperial collections came from the Government of Moscow, there were portraits from twenty different governments, as well as from Estonia. There was one Borovikovsky in Rome, there was a Brullov in Nice, there was a Levitsky in the National Library at Geneva.[37] Diaghilev had begun compiling lists and making files some years before – as his article on Russian museums in Vol. VI, No. 10, bears witness. (Then there had been his work on Levitsky and the two Shibanovs, which had led to many other discoveries and classifications, and he had already begun to sketch out the monograph on Borovikovsky, which was never to be published.) He forced his way into the houses of remote country gentlemen and rifled their attics. He discovered portraits they did not know they possessed. When they hesitated to lend their little-valued and forgotten ancestors (possibly because they would leave a blank space on the wall to show how the silk or wallpaper had faded), he played on their fears of revolution, telling them that in a time of strikes and troubles, when the peasants in some areas had been pillaging and burning their master's property, their portraits would be safer in the capital.[38] How tiring – all that smiling at strangers! But Sergei Pavlovitch was indefatigable, for he foresaw the titanic result of his labours. It must be said that, in spite of the disfavour with which he was regarded by most of the Imperial family, neither the Tsar, nor the Dowager Empress nor the Grand Duke Sergei Alexandrovitch withheld their pictures. Diaghilev stayed with Tolstoy at Yasnaya Polyana, but he was so nervous that when the great man asked him if he played chess, he said 'Yes', although he did not. He was soon found out and reprimanded.[39]

Through the Grand Duke Nicolas Mikhailovitch, the President of the exhibition committee, Diaghilev had been able to secure the Tauride (or Tavrichevsky) Palace to house his exhibition. This in itself was an achievement – one hesitates to call it a stroke of luck, for it may have involved the most skilful negotiation. Not only was the palace one of the finest and most spacious in the capital; it was the only one that stood empty. Catherine the Great had ordered it for Potemkin after his conquest of the Crimea (La Tauride), of which she created him Prince. The architect Starov had built it between 1783 and 1789 and it was one of the first Neoclassical buildings in Russia. Most of it was on one floor, though on a huge scale: one passed through the portico into a square entrance hall, thence into a domed octagon and through a double screen of columns (there were no doors in the principal apartments) into the Colonnade hall, 124 feet long by 56 feet wide, then, crossing this, entered the immense covered Winter Garden, which had a round temple in the middle.[40] In 1791, the year of his death, Potemkin entertained Catherine there with ballets and a dinner – at which only six hundred sat down, the rest being served under the colonnade, though all ate off gold and silver plate. For the first months of 1905 the famous building housed Diaghilev's Exhibition of Historical Russian Portraits, and, in these troubled times of war, famine and unrest, he presented his summary of Russia's Imperial past. In the light of history the occasion stands out as an amazingly dramatic opening to the last act of the Romanov tragedy. Had Thomas Hardy written a Russian *Dynasts*, he must certainly have chosen to use it for his opening scene.

Diaghilev was exhausted by his travels and by the effort of getting the nearly three thousand pictures hung, the halls decorated and the catalogue printed in time. He also had reason to be apprehensive that some political event would prevent the show from going on. Anna Filosofov wrote, 'The boys look very down in the mouth. Serioja is almost unrecognizable.'[41] Grand Duke Nicolas came to watch the hanging of pictures. He put his foot through a full-length portrait standing on the floor, but made no remark about it at the time. As he walked away, however, he pointed at the damaged work and said, 'To be restored.'[42]

It was not until May that Russia's Baltic Fleet, which had sailed round Africa, being fuelled by German colliers on the way, arrived in the Straits of Tsushima to be almost totally annihilated by the Japanese. Had this happened earlier, it is doubtful if the exhibition could have been allowed to open.

Open it did in February, and Benois, who, for fear of a general strike, had fled with his family to Paris as soon as his work of hanging was completed, described how he heard the ceremony had gone:

It followed the traditional pattern: the Tsar arrived, accompanied by members of his family, and walked slowly past the endless rows of his ancestors. Diaghilev, the Grand Duke Nicolas Mikhailovitch and General Dashkov provided explanations. At the end of this review, which lasted for about two hours, Nicolas II thanked his uncle, Diaghilev and Dashkov, but not by a single word did he reveal his personal attitude to all he had seen, although it was all so closely related to his person: everything in it spoke of the past of the Russian monarchy, of his predecessors on the throne and of their collaborators and associates. It was known that the Tsar was interested in history and it might have been expected that this magnificent spectacle would make some kind of impression on him. Perhaps his attitude was due to an emotional paralysis which rendered him inarticulate; or he might have seen in the faces of his ancestors bitter reproaches and terrible warnings of approaching disaster.[43]

The exhibition made a sensation in St Petersburg. No one who saw it ever forgot it. Bakst created the backgrounds. The sequence of rooms, explained in a leaflet – for the elegant, unillustrated little catalogue came out in several parts, published at intervals of a week or so – was as follows: 'Peter the Great – the first dark green Rotunda. Paul I – the dark red room on the left. Catherine II – the two next rooms on the left and a hall, all red. Levitsky room, on the right, in red. Elizabeth I, on the left, pale green. Alexander I, on the left enfilade, in pale blue. Nicolas I – on the right, dark blue. Alexander II in light coffee colour. The modern pictures in the last light grey rooms.'[44] Every monarch's full-length portrait was placed beneath a canopy, and surrounded by portraits of his ministers and court. Years later Diaghilev described to Osbert Sitwell the sinister atmosphere in the room dedicated to the Emperor Paul, who wore his crown on one side.[45] The sculpture shone in the Winter Garden, retrellised and planted by Bakst. 'There was something oppressive', wrote Benois, 'in the multi-coloured assembly of magnates in gold-embroidered coats, those dressed-up ladies, all this Necropolis, this *Vanitas vanitatum*, which doubled the pleasure of relaxing in the greenery among the white marble busts.'[46]

Sergei's aunt Filosofov wrote to his stepmother,

It is difficult to write in times of such great distress, and that is why you have not heard from me lately. But my thoughts are often with you, and I write now, because I have just undergone a complete spiritual metamorphosis – alas, temporary, no doubt – which has raised me to the skies. I have been to the exhibition in the Tauride Palace, and you cannot imagine – not the liveliest imagination could picture it – the superhuman grandeur of what I saw. I was transported into a world that seems infinitely nearer than our own.[47]

And she wrote again a month later, 'I keep going to Serioja's exhibition: it brings balm to my soul. It's something amazing.'[48]

Grabar was not the only one to recognize that Diaghilev had done art historians an inestimable service by bringing to light many Russian painters – as well as painters invited from abroad – whose work was almost unknown, although some of it was first-rate. 'New and tempting vistas for deeper investigation were thrown open.'[49]

A banquet was arranged in Diaghilev's honour in Moscow,[50] and the exhausted but triumphant man bestirred himself to compose a speech. It was the most unexpected speech – no polite and diffident rejection of praise, no conventional expression of thanks. He who had shown Russia for the first time a complete pageant of her past history, now chose to relate that past to the future. Ceded, for once, a platform from which, at this unique ceremonial moment, no one could push him off, Diaghilev addressed Russia.

There is no doubt that every tribute is a summing-up, and every summing-up is an ending. Far from me the thought that tonight's banquet is in any sense the end of the aims for which we have lived up to now. I think you will agree with me that thoughts of summing-up and ending come to one's mind more and more in these days. That is the question that struck me the whole time I was working. Don't you feel that this long gallery of portraits of big and small people that I brought to live in the beautiful halls of the Palais Tauride is only a grandiose summing-up of a brilliant, but, alas! dead period of our history? . . . I have earned the right to proclaim this loudly, because with the last breath of the summer breezes I ended my long travels across the immensity of Russia. It was just after those acquisitive expeditions that I became convinced that the time to sum up was before us. I saw that not only in the brilliant portraits of those ancestors, so far removed from us, but more vividly from their descendants, who were ending their lives. The end of a period is revealed here, in those gloomy dark palaces, frightening in their dead splendour, and inhabited today by charming mediocre people who could no longer stand the strain of bygone parades. Here are ending their lives not only people, but pages of history. . . .

We are witnesses of the greatest moment of summing-up in history, in the name of a new and unknown culture, which will be created by us, and which will also sweep us away. That is why, without fear or misgiving, I raise my glass to the ruined walls of the beautiful palaces, as well as to the new commandments of a new aesthetic. The only wish that I, an incorrigible sensualist, can express, is that the forthcoming struggle should not damage the amenities of life, and that the death should be as beautiful and as illuminating as the resurrection.

In the same month of February 1905 Sergei had a row with his cousin Dima, which ended their friendship. Nuvel said something which made Diaghilev suspect that Dima was trying to steal his current boy-friend, a

Polish student called Vicky. He rushed to Donon's restaurant, where he found Dima dining with Zinaida Hippius. He made a scene, the waiters came running to the private room, there was a scandal: Sergei and Dmitri, who had once been lovers, ceased to be friends.[51]

The triumph of Diaghilev's grandiose exhibition gave him the even more grandiose idea that it should be permanently installed in the Tauride Palace. Some – perhaps most – of the owners of the portraits might well be content to offer their pictures on loan for an indefinite period. But nothing came of this. The portraits were returned to their lenders. In the troubles of 1905 some were destroyed, and many others fell victim to the Revolution of 1917.[52]

Although the little books which comprised the exhibition's catalogue – now so rare and precious – had not been illustrated, the Grand Duke Nicolas Mikhailovitch sponsored, two years later, an immense folio of Russian portraits, in five volumes, which could not have been put together unless Diaghilev's exhibition had taken place, which served to illustrate it after the event, and which remains as a record of so much history which has gone up in smoke.[53]

In October 1905 the Tsar, under pressure, published a Manifesto establishing a new legislature consisting of two Chambers – the State Council and the Duma, or Parliament. Thus Russia was given the semblance of a Constitution. In a letter to her daughter, Diaghilev's progressive aunt Filosofov, Dima's mother, wrote, 'We are rejoicing. Yesterday we even had champagne. You would never guess who brought the manifesto.... Serioja, of all people. Wonderful.'[54] When the First Duma, a powerless body, met, it was in the Tavrichevsky Palace.

PART III

The Movement West

CHAPTER 6

1906–7

Exhibition of Russian Painting in Paris – Concerts of Russian Music – Rimsky-Korsakov's Last Journey abroad

SHORT OF BEING an outstanding painter himself like Serov, or a collector like Morosov or Shchukin, Diaghilev had done more than any other man had – or could – for the cause of modern painting in Russia. (We have seen how few the sculptors were.) He had also done more than any other man to reveal to Russians the neglected riches of Russia's past. Now, in 1905, he turned his eyes to the West. Pending a change in the nature of the government – and he had reason to hope that now a Constitution had been granted and the power of the Tsar (apparently) limited, a post such as Minister of the Arts must sooner or later be created for him – he would exercise his energies by showing the wonders of Russian painting and music in the West. He set about planning a vast exhibition of Russian painting and sculpture, old and new, in Paris. But, as a Parthian shot (though, of course, he could hardly guess that his work inside Russia was over), he organized a show of Borissov-Musatov in Moscow.

Diaghilev had a new lover, a good-looking, intelligent, well-brought-up young man called Alexis Mavrine. They spent the spring of 1906 travelling together in Italy and Greece.[1]

L'Exposition de l'Art Russe at the Salon d'Automne in 1906 was a summing-up of all Diaghilev's work in the past eight years. The best (available) pictures by the most distinguished living, or recently dead, Russian artists were there. The best that he could assemble of the past of Russia was there – ikons from the fifteenth to the seventeenth centuries, portraits and landscapes of the seventeenth, eighteenth and early nineteenth centuries. But a big gap loomed: Diaghilev could not bring himself to exhibit the *Peredvijniki* (except Repine), and both he and Benois felt obliged to mention this gap and to apologize for it in their introductions to the catalogue.

The significant fact, however, when we consider Diaghilev's character, is that to sum up his previous achievements was not enough. He showed *new* painters who had lately attracted his attention and who, having hardly been noticed or acclaimed in Moscow or Leningrad, must have been ecstatic to find themselves transported on a magic carpet to Paris. Diaghilev was, and would always be, restless in pursuit of the new. With the handsome Sergei Sudeikine Diaghilev had for a time a very close relationship.[2] Michel Larionov, a rebel from Moscow, worshipped Diaghilev to the end of his days.[3]

The format of the elegant catalogue was small – I feel Benois had a say in this. The covers, back and front, bore the design of a crowned, double-headed eagle enclosed in a wreath, which is recognizably taken from the embroidered hanging in a room of the Russian 'Kremlin' at the Paris International Exhibition of 1900.[4]

The 'credit titles' are headed by the name of the President, SAI Le Grand-Duc Vladimir. The *Présidents d'honneur* were Nelidov, Russian Ambassador to France, Comtesse Greffulhe and Dujardin-Beaumetz, *Sous-Secrétaire d'Etat aux Beaux-Arts*. The *Comité de Patronage* was headed by M. le Comte I. Tolstoy (*Président*).[5] The *Commissaire général* was Serge Diaghilev. The decoration of the rooms was by Bakst.

'This Exhibition,' wrote Diaghilev,

does not aim at presenting a complete and methodical perspective of Russian art throughout its evolution. Such a task might have proved impossibly difficult and of doubtful use. Many previously celebrated names have lost their lustre, some temporarily, others for ever. ... This is the explanation for the absence of certain artists who were for many years considered the only representatives of Russian art and who long gave a false picture of its true development and importance. The present exhibition gives a glimpse of our tradition as seen through modern eyes [that is, Diaghilev's].

Benois summarized the history of Russian art. Up to the end of the seventeenth century it had been purely religious. The successive schools of ikon painting were represented by twenty-six ikons in the exhibition.[6] When Russia began to be one of the community of civilized nations and Peter the Great imported artists from abroad, he also rewarded local talent: the first secular Russian painters, Ivan Nikitin and Matveiev, were represented respectively by three paintings and one painting in the exhibition. Elizabeth (who founded the Academy of Arts in St Petersburg in 1757) and Catherine II attracted many foreign artists, but these inspired a whole school of Russian portrait painters – Levitzky (twenty-two pictures in the Paris show), Borovikovsky (twenty pictures), Rokotov (seven pictures), Drogin (one picture), Miropolsky (none), and 'the unhappy [Mikhail] Shibanov [one picture], who remained throughout his life a serf of Potemkin'. At the same time, 'modest landscape painters' such as Simon Shchedrin the elder (two pictures), Feodor Alexeiev (four pictures), Bielsky (two pictures) and Mikhail Ivanov (one picture) aspired to rival Bellotto, Pannini and Hubert

Robert. The sculptors Feodor Shchedrin (two works), Feodor Shubin (eleven works), Mikhail Koslovsky (one work), Ivan Prokofiev (two works) and Martos (none) also flourished in the eighteenth century. (Benois also mentioned architects, but as they were not represented in the exhibition I have omitted them here.)

The early Neoclassical period, inspired by Rome, by Winckelmann and by David, was hardly represented, perhaps, Benois supposed, for reasons of size and transport: but the Romantics Orest Kiprensky (nine pictures), Vassili Tropinin (two pictures), Maxime Vorobiev (two pictures), Alexei Venezianov (fourteen pictures) and Silvester Shchedrin (six pictures) were all included in the show. Charles Brullov (twelve pictures), whose famous *Destruction of Pompeii* had toured Europe and had an effect on Russia as powerful as Géricault's *Radeau de la Méduse* in France, was an excellent portraitist who drew in the manner of Ingres and was Russia's most eminent Romantic painter. Feodor Bruni (four pictures) had painted frescoes which combined the mystic dreams of the German Nazarenes with the classical perfection of the Bolognese Mannerists.

The little anecdotal pictures of Paul Fedotov (one picture), exhibited in 1848, had given rise to a political and social movement. Ivan Kramskoy, the father of the Vagrants (one picture), and Ilya Repine (five pictures) were on show, but Perov, Vereshchagin and Surikov were not. Gay was in (two pictures), Viktor Vasnetsov was out, though his brother Appollinary was in (two pictures). Nesterov was out, but Roerich, Vasnetsov's other follower, was in (sixteen pictures).

Then came Benois' excuses. 'Since most of the key works of this period [of the Vagrants] are in museums, which, by their statutes, may not lend, and as others are well known abroad from Universal Exhibitions and through a multitude of publications, we have been obliged to resign ourselves to representing this period in a summary way....' The hint of a divergence of opinion with Diaghilev was combined with a dig at Princess Tenishev's craft centre. 'The curious, incoherent eccentricities of Maliutin [nine pictures], and a few ceramic objects, notable for their bizarre technique, represent in our exhibition this movement which may seem sympathetic in principle, but which is devoid of all practical utility.'

Lastly, Benois summarized the new movements.

The end of the nineteenth century saw a turning of Russian art towards pure aestheticism. Certain painters, Levitan, Serov, Korovine and Mlle Yakuntchikova, were content with a straightforward study of nature; others – and among them one of the greatest artists Russia has produced, the unhappy Vrubel (now blind and confined in a mental home) – aspired to a more ideal art, hoping to revive strange evocations of past periods, at the same time essaying violent contrasts of colour....

At this time we can discern, if not two separate schools, at least two very different tendencies in Russian painting. St Petersburg is represented by Konstantin Somov [thirty pictures, two book covers and a porcelain figure], one of the most enchanting of modern artists, Bakst [eighteen pictures, including many ballet projects], Dobujinsky [eight pictures], Lancerey [eight pictures] and the author of these lines [twenty-three pictures). Ours is sometimes a rather literary art, for we are in love with the refinements of days gone by, lost in dreams of the past and pledged to the cult of all that is intimate, precious and rare. The art of Moscow, which derives chiefly from the great decorator Vrubel [twenty-two pictures and seven pottery sculptures], is largely represented by Golovine [six ballet décors], Millioti [fourteen pictures between the two brothers], Sudeikine [seven pictures] and Paul Kuznetsov [nine pictures], and is at once more decorative and more purely painterly....

In this exhibition there is nothing to suggest the terrible crisis our country is passing through. And although the art of Russia is shown more or less comprehensively, this phenomenon must be due to a total schism between our artists and the rest of Russian society – or can it be that the current political movement is prompted by less disinterested ideals?...[7]

Diaghilev had the opulent idea of hanging ikons on gold cloth, which hardly showed them to advantage, and Benois disapproved of this.[8] For the sculpture court Bakst designed a trellised Winter Garden, as he had done at the Tauride Palace.

About this time Diaghilev met Gabriel Astruc, a French-Jewish music publisher, exceptionally go-ahead and receptive to new ideas in music, a popular, witty Parisian personality. He had that year founded La Société Musicale, with the intention of promoting new music, and had enlisted Comtesse Greffulhe as President. His office was on the first floor of an eighteenth-century pavilion which had once stood in the garden of a great house, but now found itself incongruously at the busy corner of the Boulevard des Italiens and Rue Louis-le-Grand, opposite the Restaurant Paillard, which Astruc frequented. This Pavillon de Hanovre was to become famous in the history of French music. Astruc was 'stout, with an Assyrian charm, and dressed with *boulevardier* elegance. In the season he wore a grey bowler or top-hat as if going to the races. His love of jewelry was manifest from the pearl tie-pin, the heavy rings on the plump little-fingers of each hand, the emerald cuff-links and the gold bracelet on his right wrist. His buttonhole invariably sported a crimson carnation until he was able to replace this with the long-coveted Légion d'honneur.'[9]

Comtesse Guy de Pourtalès introduced Diaghilev to Comtesse Greffulhe, who was President of the Société des Concerts Français, besides being one of the most powerful society hostesses, famed for her beauty and elegance. Born Caraman-Chimay,[10] she married the immensely rich banker Greffulhe, lived in the Rue d'Astorg and was the original of Proust's Princesse de Guermantes. The first impression Diaghilev made on her was a bad one: he was evidently too eager to please and appeared rather ill-bred.

I took him to be a sort of young snob or shady adventurer, with a remarkable conversational gift. At first I kept wondering what on earth he wanted.... Then suddenly he got up and began looking at my pictures, and, I must say, some of the things he said were extraordinarily interesting. I soon realized he was remarkably well-informed.... This made me begin to like him. But when he went to the piano and began playing things by Russian composers whom I had never even heard of, I began to understand him and why he had come. His playing was excellent, and the music was so fresh, so altogether wonderful and lovely, that when he explained he was intending to organize a Festival of Russian music in the coming year I immediately promised to do everything in my power to help make it successful.[11]

If Diaghilev had been a Vorontzov or a Galitzin it would have been natural for him to have got to know *le gratin*, the highest society of Paris, from his first visit in 1890. But he had had to make his way deviously, like Marcel Proust, infiltrating through the worlds of art and music. Although the husband of Mme Greffulhe was only a banker of Dutch descent – but descended from a bastard of King Louis xv – her position was unassailable. From the moment Diaghilev was accepted by her most doors would be open to him.

Diaghilev had made up his mind to present some concerts of Russian music in Paris in the following year. These would take place at the Opéra and Gabriel Astruc was to act as agent and intermediary. From the start, Diaghilev was determined not only to let the French hear some of the finest Russian music, but to employ the most illustrious singers, instrumentalists and conductors, and to persuade as many composers as possible to conduct their own works. This last resolve was a form of snobbery and a means of publicity, for he was well aware that most composers were imperfect conductors.[12] He knew that he would have no trouble with Glazunov and Rachmaninov, but Rimsky would be hard to dislodge from his daily routine. Then, there were worldly considerations. To ensure the maximum official support, it would be wise to enrol Alexander Taneyev, who, though an uninteresting composer (a pupil of Rimsky's), was head of the Imperial Chancery. To include one of Taneyev's symphonies in his programmes was the first compromise he accepted.[13] To play something of Liapunov, who was said to appeal to the French, and something of Scriabine, who was the latest superman but whose music Diaghilev did not like, were two others.

Nuvel had made friends with Vincent d'Indy when he came to conduct some concerts at the Vauxhall at Pavlovsk in the summer of 1904 – it was during these that Debussy's *L'Après-midi d'un faune* and *L'Apprenti sorcier* of Dukas had first been heard in Russia – and d'Indy had introduced him to Dukas.[14] Through them he had learnt that, although the French were enthusiastic about what they had heard of the music of the Five they could see nothing in Tchaikovsky, whose Russian-ness was less obvious,[15] and whom they found trivial and vulgar. Diaghilev's French advisers throughout the operation were Robert Brussel, the music critic of *Le Figaro*, whom he relied on for publicity, and M. D. Calvocoressi, whom he employed to assist him. Brussel was among those who disliked Tchaikovsky.

Although the early stages of Diaghilev's planning are hidden from us, it is not difficult to see how his mind worked. At first there were to be only four concerts. Apart from working out representative programmes, he was bound to present Chaliapine for the first time in Paris. The greatest Russian soprano was Felia Litvinne, already well known in Paris: she must be included. Smirnov, the incomparable tenor, must make his European début. The Moscow *chef d'orchestre*, Felix Blumenfeld, would conduct the operatic excerpts. Then, at the beginning of 1907 we can begin to follow Diaghilev's plans, because of the survival of a few documents among Astruc's papers. On 18 January Diaghilev was in Paris and wrote to Astruc from the Hôtel Scribe that Ysaye would play Glazunov's Violin Concerto for two thousand francs.[16] On 7 March, back in St Petersburg, Diaghilev cabled that the concerts were definitely to take place, but that Glazunov wanted to omit the Violin Concerto in favour of an orchestral work. Diaghilev hoped to be in Paris by the middle of March.[17] But whereas Brussel was in St Petersburg in mid-March, Diaghilev had gone to Moscow, probably to talk to Chaliapine, and Nuvel was cabling to Astruc that nearly all the contracts were signed.[18] All we know about the backing of the concerts (from Nuvel) is that ten thousand roubles – about a thousand pounds at the time – were contributed by a rich St Petersburg amateur of music, Gilse van der Pals.[19] 'Litvinne wants her name before Chaliapine's.'[20] On 30 March Diaghilev cabled to Astruc, 'Just decided definitely give five concerts. The first [on] evening 16 May originally intended for *répétition générale*. *Générale* now to be in afternoon same day. Brussel will provide details. Arrange with Opéra.'[21]

Diaghilev wrote:

> Rimsky-Korsakov was extremely reluctant to go to Paris for these concerts: he kept insisting that he had no desire to appear in a city 'where they abuse our beloved Tchaikovsky'. He often came to see me in the Hôtel de l'Europe in St Petersburg to discuss this question of whether to go or not, looming up before me in a huge fur-coat, his spectacles frosted over, already bursting with indignation, wagging a long admonitory finger in the air and railing against French music.[22]

In March or April Diaghilev wrote to Rimsky, 'I am not giving up hope of your collaboration in Paris. With all the infinite difficulties which this enterprise presents, I cannot work without thinking of support from my beloved teacher. This journey will not be tiring for you; we shall surround you with every possible care. We shall be completely at your service, and you will do us the greatest favour and help us as *no one* else can help.[23] Then, Diaghilev remembered, 'One day on coming in I found his visiting-card inscribed with the words "Well, if we must go we must – as the sparrow said when the cat carried him off." And go he did.'[24]

There was trouble with Litvinne, for on 14 April Diaghilev, still in St Petersburg, cabled 'Litvinne replaced throughout by Marianne Tcherkassky prima donna Imperial Opera. Rimsky will conduct in person "Christmas Eve" and "Mount Triglav".'[25] Diaghilev had probably waited till he had Rimsky's promise to come before breaking the news that Litvinne had refused. In fact, both Litvinne and Tcherkassky sang at the concerts. Diaghilev arrived in Paris from Berlin on the afternoon of 26 April. On the twenty-ninth he authorized Astruc to deal with the Théâtre Sarah Bernhardt for orchestral rehearsals at two hundred francs a day from nine till twelve, but hoped for better terms. For one or two chorus rehearsals a day he would pay the Salle des Agriculteurs fifty francs.[26]

The first concert at the Opéra on 16 May 1907 began with Rimsky conducting his *Christmas Eve*. Richard Strauss was sitting in Diaghilev's box, and leant over to say to him, 'Why do you let them play this circus music?'[27] Robert Brussel welcomed Rimsky in *Le Figaro*:

This first concert more than fulfilled the hopes of those who love Russian music. I have already remarked on the beauty of the programmes planned by M. de Diaghilev to give a picture of modern music in Russia; having heard his artists in Russia I had some idea of their quality; and I guessed at the warm reception which Paris would give them. All my expectations were surpassed.

I know what difficulties the organizers had in persuading M. Rimsky-Korsakov to come to Paris. His essential modesty makes him prefer peace and solitude to noisy acclamations.... 'You'll have no trouble in finding French conductors who will conduct my music much better than I do myself.' He did not understand that it was sentiment rather than curiosity on our part that made us long for him to come to Paris.... He must have realized from the excitement shown in the theatre when he appeared on the podium that the public's admiration for him as a musician was equalled, in certain quarters, by the veneration felt for his person....

Rimsky's *Christmas Eve* was followed by Tchaikovsky's Second Symphony. Brussel wrote that he had certain reservations about this work by Russia's most famous composer, but suppressed them in the interests of hospitality.[29] There followed the first act of Glinka's *Ruslan*, which Nikisch took so slowly that Diaghilev almost regretted having invited him.[30] In Prince Galitzky's aria from the first scene and his duet with Yaroslavna from the second scene of the first act of Borodin's *Prince Igor*, Chaliapine and Litvinne made so strong an impression, and the applause they drew was so continuous, that Nikisch, who had replaced Blumenfeld on the podium to conclude the concert by conducting Glinka's *Kamarinskaya*, was offended. Diaghilev wrote:

My first concert ended with an appalling scandal.... [The Prince Galitzky scene] was so extraordinarily successful that the applause went on and on and there

Chaliapine. Drawing by Sem, from *Le Figaro*, 1907.

seemed no limit to the number of times the excited public would recall Chaliapine. Nikisch got ready to begin conducting 'Kamarinskaya' which was to conclude the programme. Several times he raised his arms, ready to start, but the public, by now quite out of hand, refused to be silenced. Then, mortally offended, he threw down his baton and walked out of the orchestra pit. The audience was taken by surprise. Several people began to make their way out. Upstairs in the gallery the din continued, then, in a sudden hush, we heard a deep bass voice thundering out from the remotest heights of the house, in Russian, the words 'Ka-ma-rinska-ya! I screwed your mother.' Grand Duke Vladimir, who was sitting beside me in the box, got up and said to the Grand Duchess, 'Well, I think it's time we went home.'[31]

In a column headed 'Dans la salle' and signed C.D., *Le Figaro* catalogued the exceptionally brilliant audience. Not only were the Grand Duke Vladimir and his wife present, but also the Grand Duke Alexis (his next brother), the Grand Duke Paul (his youngest brother) and the Grand Duke Cyril (his eldest son). Next were listed Comtesse Greffulhe, Taneyev and 'M. Serge de Diaghilew, organizer of these concerts', Nelidov, the Russian Ambassador, and a great number of distinguished people, including Messager and Broussan, Co-directors of the Opéra, Zimin, Director of the Moscow opera, Jean de Reszke, Misia Edwards (who would become a close friend of Diaghilev in the following year) and Princess Tenishev.[32]

On the next day (when these reports appeared) Richard Strauss conducted his *Salomé* at the Châtelet, and Rimsky went to hear it. He confessed to Diaghilev that he had behaved badly. 'I called out to the singers to shut up.'[33] Diaghilev had taken him to Debussy's *Pelléas et Mélisande* at the Opéra Comique a few days before (probably on the eleventh.) As they left the theatre, Rimsky was evidently in a state of emotional stress, and he finally burst out in a tone of annoyance, 'Don't ever bring me to this sort of rubbish again. I may end by liking it.'[34]

Scriabine, who had been playing in the United States, arrived in Paris in time for the concerts with his mistress Tatiana Schlözer and only thirty francs in his pocket.[35] To a select company consisting of the Rimsky-Korsakov family, Diaghilev and some of the Russian musicians assembled in Paris, he played a piano reduction of his *Poème de l'extase*. Rimsky thought him 'half-mad', but at the Café de Paris, after a rehearsal, they agreed that certain musical keys could be associated with certain colours.[36] Scriabine aroused attention by walking about Paris without a hat: this was because he feared going bald. He was followed by a crowd of street boys chanting 'Le monsieur sans chapeau!'[37]

Arthur Nikisch must have recovered his temper, flattered, no doubt, by Diaghilev, in time to conduct Taneyev's Second Symphony and the suite from Rimsky's *Tsar Saltan* at the second concert on 19 May, and it appears that *Kamarinskaya*, of which he had been 'deprived' at the first concert, was tacked on to the end of the second, for Nikisch conducted all the works mentioned above 'de façon prestigieuse'. Zbrueva sang two songs from *The Snow Maiden*; and she, Smirnov or Petrenko joined Chaliapine in some extracts – Pimen's cell, the song of drunken Varlam and the whole of Act II – from Mussorgsky's *Boris Godunov*. Chaliapine sang the monk Pimen, the vagabond Varlam and the Tsar Boris; Smirnov sang the young monk Grigori, and Petrenko the Nurse. Brussel had feared that the scene of Boris' hallucination, which Chaliapine made so overpowering on the stage, might not survive concert performance, but, although the singer's gestures and poses went beyond the accepted limits of the concert platform, Brussel thought the scene could not have been more moving than it was that night.[38]

On Thursday 23 May the third concert took place. In about 1870 Gedenov, the Director of the Imperial Theatres, had commissioned the fantastic opera *Mlada* from four composers, Cui, Borodin, Mussorgsky and Rimsky-Korsakov, with ballet music by Minkus. The grand but crazy conception was never realized, and after Mussorgsky's death Rimsky put in order his Witches' Sabbath, known as *La Nuit sur le Mont Chauve*. Rimsky, however, later wrote *Mlada* on his own, and it was his *Nuit sur le Mont Trijlav* which opened this concert. Brussel applauded Diaghilev's idea. 'The former [Mussorgsky] work is stronger in colour, more daring; the second more thought-out and perhaps more musical.' This was followed by Scriabine's Concerto for piano and orchestra, a work in the composer's early manner, played by Joseph Hofmann and conducted by Nikisch (who had already made familiar to Paris one of Scriabine's symphonies and some piano pieces two years before). Then came Tchaikovsky's *Francesca da Rimini*. Brussel thought that, in spite of the symphonic poem's impassioned romanticism and Tchaikovsky's facility of invention, 'the Russian master had not completely proved his mastery'. Chaliapine sang two songs from Mussorgsky's *Songs and Dances of Death*, the 'Trepak' and 'La Chanson de la Mort', then, called back by 'des bravos enthousiastes', gave as an encore a melody of Glazunov, 'marvellously accompanied by M. Felix Blumenfeld'. Felia Litvinne ('greeted with transports of joy in these concerts where her presence was indispensable') next sang with Chaliapine the ecstatic duet from the fourth act of *Prince Igor*, then, alone, Yaroslavna's lament from the first act. Brussel thought no adjectives could do justice to the beauty of her voice.[39]

Scriabine's free tickets for the third concert had only arrived as he was leaving his lodgings, and the self-important little composer, who was not far from thinking he was God, made a scene with Diaghilev in the interval, exclaiming, 'But for a miracle they might have arrived after I left the house!' Diaghilev impatiently told him that he had better take charge of the distribution of tickets himself. 'Is it possible', said the composer, 'that you dare to address me in this fashion? Let me remind you that I am a chosen representative of Art itself – while you are merely privileged to gallivant about on its fringe!' Diaghilev was so taken aback by this insolence that, for once, words failed him. 'Is it possible that you, Alexander Nikolaievitch, that you ——'[40]

On the following day Rimsky returned to Russia without waiting for the last two concerts.[41]

On Sunday 26 May the fourth concert of Russian music took place at the Opéra. Glazunov's *Au Moyen Age*, very different in feeling and style from his *Stenka Razin* and his early quartets, which had been heard in Paris, provided further evidence of the composer of *Raimonda's* preoccupation with the Gothic period. Rachmaninov played his Second Piano Concerto and conducted his cantata *Le Printemps*, which Chaliapine sang with the chorus. Then came Balakirev's symphonic poem *Thamar*, with whose 'wild charm, awkward grace, and pungent local colour' its conductor, Chevillard, had already made Paris familiar (and which would one day be made into a ballet by Diaghilev). The fifth act of Mussorgsky's *Khovanshchina*, called by Brussel 'the crown of all his work' (which opera Diaghilev would present in Paris and London in 1913), was sung by Chaliapine (Dosifey), Zbrueva (Martha) and Smirnov (Andrei Khovansky).[42]

Robert Brussel thought that the last concert, which took place on Thursday 30 May, was in some ways the most remarkable of all. This was perhaps because he adored the submarine act from Rimsky's *Sadko*, with which it ended, and which was conducted by Blumenfeld. The long evening began with Scriabine's Second Symphony, conducted by Nikisch, went on with Liapunov's Piano Concerto, played by Joseph Hofmann, and included two arias from forgotten operas sung by Tcherkassky – Maria's Romance from Cui's *William Ratcliff* and the arioso from the first act of Tchaikovsky's *Sorceress* – as well as Liadov's *Baba Yaga* and Glazunov's *Poème Symphonique*, conducted by the composer.[43]

'When the concerts were over,' wrote Calvocoressi,

Diaghilev asked me what he owed me for my work (which I had been called upon to extend far beyond the limits originally foreseen). I named a sum, and he handed it to me. When I thanked him, he asked: 'You are satisfied?' I assented. 'Quite satisfied?' I assented again. 'Well, you are the only one. Oh! How sick I am of it all!' Then, suddenly: 'Now, look here: I want to do an opera festival next year. But this time, things will have to be on very different lines. Will you be my second-in-command?' I accepted, and then and there we started discussing plans....[44]

CHAPTER 7

1908

Boris Godunov with Chaliapine at the Paris Opéra – Grand Duke Vladimir

DIAGHILEV LOST NO TIME in laying the foundations of his next year's opera season in Paris. In April 1907 he wrote to Rimsky-Korsakov that he intended to put on the latter's *Sadko* and Mussorgsky's *Boris* at the Opéra.[1] As was to become usual with him, the question of *cuts* was uppermost in his mind. His powers of persuasion were not always effective with his obstinate old master, but through sheer power of endurance he sometimes got his way. On 2 May he wrote, 'Don't forget that I have to convince the Grand Duke Vladimir that our undertaking is useful from the national point of view; the Minister of Finance that it is profitable from the economic point of view; and even the Director of Theatres that it will be of benefit for the Imperial Theatres. And how many others! And how difficult this is!'[2] Rimsky-Korsakov did not give a damn for the French or for the Minister of Finance or for the Grand Duke Vladimir.

On 18 June Diaghilev wrote to Rimsky that he intended that *Sadko* should be sung in French by French singers, with Alvarez in the role of Sadko; and that *Boris* should be sung in Russian, with Chaliapine and Sobinov.[3] This lyric tenor had a voice of 'crystalline transparency and extraordinary flexibility', with 'that unique quality of eternal youth so characteristic of Melba's voice prior to 1910'.[4] In fact, he did not appear for Diaghilev until 1909.

On 24 June Diaghilev wrote, 'The Russians in this production [*Sadko*] must be the conductor, the stage-manager, scene-painter and costumer.'[5] On 30 July, laying it on a bit thick, he wrote,

Once the question has come up about this most complex and difficult affair, if you will, I even prefer to lay before you in writing my view of it, for at an interview your charm, your authority, in fact your 'divine' side so eclipse your 'human' side that I know I shall be quailing and shall not say half of what I think. To turn to *Sadko* – Lord, how hard it is! – I shall again be stoically severe and shall mention the portions of this work – along with *Ruslan and Ludmila* the best Russian fairy-tale opera – which I take the liberty of liking less. [A list of suggested changes.] You see, the question is not of cuts, but rather of remodelling.... *Frenchmen are absolutely incapable* of listening to an opera from 8 till 12. Even their own *Pelléas* they cannot forgive for its length, and soon after 11 they frankly flee from the theatre, and that produces a deadly impression.[6]

On 24 August he wrote,

How I need and crave to see you! How many tears and supplications I have prepared, how many bright and irrefutable arguments!... I shall hypnotize you with arguments that really 'the most rational thing' (your words) would be to leave Lubava [the wife of Sadko, who stays at home when he goes on his quest] in Russia, that the scene in her room [Scene 3] does not enhance the interest of the action; that in the market scene [Scene 4] her two phrases which interrupt the chorus on the ship might be sung by the women's section of the chorus; and that the finale of the entr'acte, after the Undersea Kingdom, should conclude as though purposely in A-flat major in order to make a perfectly natural transition to the D-flat major closing hymn, against the background of a stylized, beautiful bright landscape with the blazing cupolas of glorious Novgorod and broad over-flow of the river Volkhova....[7]

The draft of Rimsky's reply – which was also an answer to Diaghilev's letter of 2 May – remained in his files:

Obviously my moving letters cannot move you from your theatrico-political point of view. The firmness with which you cling on to it deserves a better fate. You said that without my advice you would not venture to undertake *Sadko*, but my advice has nothing whatever to do with it, as you have formed a firm plan of action prior to any advice from me, and, at that, a plan from which you do not intend to swerve. I assure you that I too have a theatrico-artistic point of view from which it is impossible to dislodge me. Once there are mixed up with this business the nationalism of the Grand Duke Vladimir and the calculations of the Minister of Finance, success becomes imperative at all costs. But for me there exists only the artistic interest. To the taste of the French I remain utterly indifferent. I should even prefer them to esteem me for what I am, without adapting myself to their customs and tastes, which are by no means law. I have had an orchestral score of *Sadko* sent to me, and having examined it I have come to the conclusion that everything in the work is legitimate, and only those cuts which are current at the Mariinsky Theatre can be sanctioned by me. Not only is the suppression of the last scene, or part of it, inadmissible, but also the elimination of Lubava is not to be thought of. If *Sadko* in its present form is difficult for the taste of the feeble French public who drop into the theatre for a while in their dress coats and take notice of the voice of a venal press and a hired claque, then it should not be given.[8]

Diaghilev next suggested the presentation of certain scenes from *Sadko* in their entirety, and said he would speak to Messager and Broussan, Directors of the Opéra, about this.[9] But it was not destined that *Sadko* should be given in Paris in 1908. Diaghilev decided to concentrate on *Boris Godunov*.

He was not the only man in Paris during that summer of 1907 to be having trouble with Rimsky-Korsakov, who, in this last year of his life, saw the first production of *The City of Kitej*, and completed the piano score of *Coq d'or* and orchestrated it. Albert Carré, Director of the Opéra Comique, had formed the plan of presenting *The Snow Maiden* in the following year. On 13 July 1907 he wrote to ask the composer if the part of the boy hero, Lel, which was always sung by a woman, could be given to a tenor, as the French disliked *travesti*. Rimsky refused to consider this.[10] Carré had written to Mamontov, asking for Vasnetsov's designs for *The Snow Maiden*, but in the end the décor was executed by a Frenchman.[11]

Once he had made the decision to proceed with *Boris Godunov*, Diaghilev had to face the daunting task of producing a version which was as near as possible to what the composer intended and at the same time acceptable to Paris. He would have liked to return to Mussorgsky's original version. Calvocoressi, who was writing a book on Mussorgsky, said to him, 'Of course you will do the genuine *Boris*, not the Rimsky-Korsakov arrangement?' But Diaghilev replied that 'this was out of the question. The soloists and the choir all knew their parts in the remodelled version, and would be not only unwilling but positively unable to learn the genuine text even if time could be found for study.' Calvocoressi realized that he was right, and that a singer who had studied one version would find it almost impossible to adjust himself to the other. 'Rimsky-Korsakov tampered with keys and time-signatures and harmonies and modulations, and even, though more seldom, with melodies. Diaghilev's argument was unanswerable.'[12]

After the first rejection of *Boris Godunov* by the Committee of the Imperial Theatres in February 1871, Mussorgsky wrote in the two Polish scenes with Dmitri (the Pretender) and Marina – doubtless to introduce a soprano role into an opera almost devoid of women, as well as a polonaise; and he rewrote the scene of Boris with his children. In 1872 he added the Revolution Scene in the Forest of Kromy, placing it at the very end, after the death of Boris. In October 1873 Gedenov, Director of the Imperial Theatres, accepted *Boris*, and it was first performed on 8 February 1874, but without the scene in Pimen's cell. It was given few performances. After Mussorgsky's death in February 1881 Rimsky decided to revise and re-orchestrate the whole work.[13] 'No need to waste words,' wrote Diaghilev, 'on this disastrous enterprise, which should never have been attempted.'[14] Rimsky's operation had the effect of civilizing and rounding off the corners of an uncouth, barbaric masterpiece – 'as if Rubens had repainted a Pieter Breughel,' wrote Gerald Abrahams.[15]

Although anxious to revert wherever possible to the authentic score, Diaghilev still needed Rimsky's help with certain cuts, joins, reorchestrations and even additions.

I was terrified of the opera's length and worried about the running order. My friends and I had endless discussions with Rimsky-Korsakov about transposing certain scenes. Among other questions we considered whether we could place the Coronation [Prologue, Scene 2] after Pimen's Cell, so as to separate the two crowd scenes and end the first act with the Coronation Scene – which was chronologically possible (I asked the advice of the historian N. P. Kondakov about this) and theatrically a great improvement. [Benois did not agree.] This first year in Paris I gave neither the Inn Scene [Act I, Scene 2, which contained the song of drunken Varlam sung by Chaliapine at Diaghilev's second concert of Russian music in the previous year] nor the scene in Marina's bedroom [Act III, Scene 1, the first of the two Polish scenes, which preceded the Fountain Scene], so afraid was I of dragging out the opera – which most people anyway said the French would never understand. I persuaded Rimsky-Korsakov to revise the Coronation Scene, which struck me as too short, and to complete and elaborate some of the *carillons*. [This the composer did on 20 November 1907.] He threw himself excitedly into this work....

I had been hearing *Boris* for nearly twenty years at the Mariinsky, but it was given as seldom as possible, not even every year, and it was the least popular opera in the repertory. Latterly, since Chaliapine had begun to sing it [following his launching by Mamontov] his scenes were the only ones ever greeted by applause.... Tchaikovsky's *Eugene Onegin* had always been the most popular opera in Russia [the most popular Russian opera, Diaghilev means], and when I was organizing my Paris season the Court urged me to present it before any other. When the Empress heard that I was putting on *Boris*, she asked me 'Couldn't you find anything more boring to give them?'[16]

When it proved impossible to borrow the Mariinsky production of *Boris*, Golovine's sets had to be copied. Benois designed the more European second Polish scene, during which Marina and the false Dmitri plight their troth beside a fountain, and the Revolution Scene in Kromy Forest was designed by Yuon. Bilibine, the authority on North Russia, was put in charge of the costumes (except those for the Polish scene); Steletzky helped him; and they worked under Golovine, who fitted their finds into the general picture.[17] Diaghilev wrote:

Wanting to have the costumes for *Boris* as splendid and authentic as possible, I had sent out a sort of expedition under the painter Bilibine, the well-known expert on old Russia, to search the northern provinces, particularly those of Arkhangelsk and Vologda. Bilibine went from village to village buying up from the peasants a mass of beautiful hand-woven sarafans, head-dresses and embroidery, which had been hoarded in chests for centuries. From the heap of material Bilibine brought back for me Golovine put together the costumes for the opera. Grand Duke Vladimir was so impressed with this treasure-trove that he made me exhibit it in the Hermitage Museum. Two famous Moscow firms wove special brocades for us according to Golovine's specifications. There was no end to the care and ingenuity which went into the production. Golovine was always changing and improving his designs. For the Coronation Scene alone he showed me four sketches, one after the other. . . . The Imperial Theatres gave us every possible help on this occasion. The chorus was lent by the Bolshoi Theatre, Moscow. Our singers were the best available, namely Chaliapine, Smirnov, Yujina, Zbrueva and Petrenko. [He might have added Kastorsky, Sharonov, Shuprinikov, Ermolenko, Tugarinova and Renin.] A team of stage mechanics came from Moscow under the leadership of K. F. Valz, the supreme technical wizard of his time. Our conductor was Felix M. Blumenfeld.[18]

In February 1908 Rimsky selected Nicolas Tcherepnine to conduct *The Snow Maiden* for the Opéra Comique.[19] In March Serov made a pencil drawing of Rimsky for Diaghilev.[20] That month the Russian censors got busy on *Le Coq d'or*, which the composer would not, consequently, hear performed in his lifetime.[21] On 21 April Grand Duke Vladimir wrote inviting Rimsky to attend the performances of *Boris* in Paris.[22] It was to open on 19 May. Diaghilev was in Paris at the end of April. Before his company arrived he had to woo the press. On 9 May *Le Gaulois* reported that the chorus had arrived from Moscow and that the sets (which were being painted in Paris by the Russian scene-painters) were ready to leave the studios. Costume rehearsals were about to begin. 'Chaliapine arrives tomorrow.'[23]

A curious and expectant public awaited us [wrote Diaghilev]. But we ran into incredible difficulties with the hidebound bureaucracy of the Opéra officials. We were told on arrival that it was out of the question to mount an opera as complicated as *Boris* in the short time allowed for; that the theatre's own repertory was more than filling the available rehearsal time; and that there was no possibility of rehearsing the singers on stage or of setting up such elaborate scenery. Whatever I asked for I received the same answer: 'Unheard of! Impossible!'

When at last we began to rehearse with the orchestra – and we were allowed only two or three orchestra rehearsals – the stage-hands set up such a din on stage that I had to have a twenty-franc gold piece ready in my hand to tip them when Chaliapine or another principal came on to sing. This was the only way to make them stop hammering and go off for a drink.[24]

Russians have a tendency to plot, of which the corollary is to believe oneself plotted against. In his memoirs Calvocoressi probably gives a fairer picture of the situation at the Paris Opéra than did Diaghilev in his (hitherto unpublished) notes.

Boris Godunov was prepared with incredible difficulties and under adverse circumstances. . . . The only time that the managers of the Opéra had granted us for rehearsals was the amount left free by the ordinary duties of the Opéra – which comprised four performances a week and rehearsals on certain other nights. And we also had to take into account the usual trades-union restrictions, and the fact that, under the terms of their agreement, the orchestral players were not obliged to rehearse in the day-time. By a deplorable coincidence, the month selected for our performances of *Boris Godunov* was also selected for the production of Rameau's *Hippolyte et Aricie*. In consequence the 'ordinary duties' of the Opéra took up far more time than usual, and the stage-carpenters and hands were very much overworked. Diaghilev and his technical staff came to Paris rather late.... The choir was even later, having temporarily lost, between Moscow and the Russian frontier, the guide in charge of the party and the tickets – an accident which gave rise to many frantic telegrams from and to Moscow, and from bewildered station-masters along the line.

Apart from the paucity of time available for rehearsals, there was the tiredness of the stage-hands to consider. The Opéra stage is a huge one with no single labour-saving appliance. Everything had to be done by hand and by sheer force of muscle. To raise or lower the back-cloth you did not press a button and let electricity do the rest: you sent fifteen men or so up to the flies (to which they climbed by means of rope ladders) and they manipulated the cloth almost as sailors would a sail. The job took nearly a quarter of an hour every time.... The men were working full time, and overtime, seven days a week. We waited in vain for them to tackle the settings of *Boris Godunov*. The tension grew, and rumours of an impending strike arose.... Being overwrought, we became suspicious and inclined to see foes and plots everywhere.[25]

Calvocoressi gave an example of how mistrust of the Opéra staff caused unnecessary extra work:

When we started preparing the setting for the Revolution scene – a clearing in a snow-clad forest, the trees being represented by painted canvas whose cut-out patterns had to be supported by netting – it turned out that the only available netting was black. 'Impossible!' Diaghilev declared. 'This will rob our setting of half the whiteness on which the effectiveness depends.'... So, after hastily consulting a trades directory, I jumped into a taxi and eventually obtained from a net factory the requisite amount of white netting.... Later on, however, the stage carpenter-in-chief of the Opéra assured me that black netting would not have affected the whiteness in the least....[26]

On 12 May Prince and Princesse Murat gave a soirée 'in honour of Mussorgsky'; Camille Bellaigue, the music critic of *Le Gaulois*, gave a talk on his music (which was reported in *Le Gaulois* next day), and Ermolenko and Smirnov (who were cast as Marina and the false Dmitri), as well as Kastorsky (the monk Pimen), sang.[27] On 14 May Chaliapine rehearsed the last act of *Boris* with the chorus and received an ovation from the company. Ermolenko and Smirnov ran through the love duet without costumes.[28]

At a rehearsal on Friday, 15 May, Pétrémand told Diaghilev that the sets would not fit the stage. 'Forty-eight hours before the *répétition générale* [on the Sunday],' wrote Benois, 'Pétrémand [the stage manager] announced that a mistake had occurred for which we were to blame – that the décor ... did not reach the floor, and that there was much repair work to be done which would take three or four days. Here Diaghilev showed his real self and saved the situation. He declared, quite calmly, that he was ready to produce the opera without décor. Pétrémand was so terrified of a scandal that the impossible was done. . . .' Yet that evening M. and Mme Benardaky, the Greek-Russian expatriates (whose daughter would inspire Proust's Gilberte), held a soirée at which Calvocoressi spoke about the score of *Boris* and several of Diaghilev's soloists sang passages from the opera. It is not clear whether it was that Friday that a nightmarish 'try-out' with extras took place. Benois described 'the huge stage of the Opéra, illuminated by only one candle, and crowding on to it a mass of two hundred filthy stinking people from the street, with false beards awry, and hastily pulled-on boyar fur coats and caps. No wonder that, surprised at their own appearance, these hungry casual "actors" decided to have some fun, and began to sing and dance, impervious to all calls to order. A catastrophe seemed inevitable and even our fearless Diaghilev took fright.'[29]

There was doubt as to whether the public dress rehearsal could take place on the Sunday night or not,[30] and whether the opening on Tuesday would have to be postponed.[31] Diaghilev summoned his friends, Sanin, the producer, Valz, the 'scenic wizard',[32] and all the Russian technicians, including Feodor Grigorievitch Zaika,[33] the stammering wig-maker and make-up man, whom Chaliapine 'trusted above everyone else'[34] and who always reminded Diaghilev of Hoffmann's Drosselmeyer,[35] to a supper at Larue. Benois thought Serioja 'must have been scared to have recourse to such a democratic method'. 'The most vociferous speaker was Valz,' wrote Diaghilev; but all 'worked themselves into a frenzy, declaring that postponement would mean the ruin of our enterprise.'[36] That evening Calvocoressi had spent the whole of the press rehearsal of *Hippolyte et Aricie* 'getting hold of one stage carpenter after another, questioning them and trying to find out how far we could rely on them'. He found them 'not ill-disposed, but worn-out with overwork'. Calvocoressi explained to Diaghilev and his friends, as they 'devoured duck in aspic', that if the *répétition générale* to an invited audience took place on Sunday evening, the men would have to spend the whole day rigging up the sets and all Sunday night changing them: this they were determined not to do. Sunday the seventeenth was to be their first day's rest for six weeks. On Monday all their time would be taken up with 'regular duties' – that is, the first performance of *Hippolyte*. On Tuesday they would 'start work at 7 a.m., carry on interruptedly and all would be ready for the performance at 8 p.m.'. It was agreed that Sunday's dress rehearsal would have to be abandoned. This was itself pretty disastrous. 'The seats for the 19th were nearly sold out, so there would be no possibility of accommodating that night the Press and the hundreds of influential people who had been invited for the 17th.' Diaghilev sent out to the press notice of the cancellation. The supper party broke up at three in the morning. The next thing to do was to stop the sale of tickets for the nineteenth.[37]

In the absence of all the stage staff except for the two head men, an

unofficial semi-dress rehearsal without scenery took place before a few
hundred privileged people on the Sunday evening. This was 'an amazing
affair,' according to Calvocoressi.

The settings and props were represented by extemporized landmarks: two
chairs for a door, another for a pillar, a crate for the Tsar's throne. .... All these
were put into place and moved about by a staff of stagehands consisting of Bakst,
Benois, Pétrémand and Loiseau [his lieutenant] (who had come in protest against
the defection of their men), Diaghilev, his secretary [Mavrine], his valet [Vassili]
and myself – all of us in our shirt-sleeves and very grimy. In the auditorium, a
hundred spectators or so could enjoy the sight of every one of our movements,
for there was nobody to raise or drop the curtain.
In this hideous setting the company rehearsed [a few of them] in splendid costumes. The situation was serious for them all: the settings to come were all new
and unknown to them, so that on Tuesday they would have to move among surroundings of which they had no experience.[38]

When Chaliapine was told that there would be no scenery and not all the
costumes for that Sunday's rehearsal, being 'all keyed up', as usual, he
exclaimed, 'As the scenery and costumes aren't ready, I'm not ready either.
I won't make myself up, I won't get dressed, I'll go through the rehearsal
in my everyday clothes.'[39] This he did.
This rehearsal, however, afforded an exceptional proof of the power of
Chaliapine's acting, recorded by himself. At the point where Boris tells the
young Tsarevitch about the kingdom which will one day be his, Chaliapine
was supposed to imagine that he saw something move in the ingle-nook of
the chimney-piece, and start up fearfully, gazing at a corner of the stage.
As he went through his usual routine, he became aware of an unusual
commotion.

I heard a strange sound in the auditorium that disturbed me. I looked askance
[that is, out of the corner of his eye] to see what was happening, and this is what
I saw: the spectators had risen to their feet, some of them were even standing on
their seats, and all were gazing towards that corner of the stage towards which I
myself was peering. They actually believed that I *had* seen something. . . . I was
singing in Russian; my words were incomprehensible to them, but from the
expression in my eyes, they were aware that I was afraid. . . .[40]

On the night of Monday, 18 May, according to Diaghilev,

We were all in a state of fever. I was staying at the Hôtel de Hollande, which
no longer exists, in the rue de la Paix. We all went late to bed. In the early hours
I heard a knock at my door.
'Who is it?'
'It is I, Chaliapine. Can I come in?'
'What's the matter, Feodor Ivanovitch?'
'Is there a settee in your room? I can't bear to be alone.'

So that giant spent the night in my room, sleeping fitfully, curled up on a tiny sofa.[41]

Then came the day of the first performance of Mussorgsky's opera in Western Europe.

The Opéra staff [wrote Diaghilev] threw open their doors to us with supercilious smiles, and we were able at last to unpack the thousands of costumes and the countless trunks of properties, to hang and light the seven huge sets and to rehearse for the first time the Coronation Scene and the Revolution Scene with the hundreds of supers necessary. We had to hang the backcloths to the exact inch in an unfamiliar theatre and fit together sections of scenery which none of us had ever yet seen assembled. When it was found that a batten had to be moved, I waved a 100-franc note in the face of the Opéra stage-hands. 'Oh well,' they said, 'If Monsieur looks at it that way ——'; and they grudgingly did what I asked.[42]

The excitement of seeing Golovine's décor and Bilibine's costumes coming to life under the lights of the Opéra must have been a consolation to Diaghilev and his friends and spurred them on to a final sprint.

Benois wrote, 'The coronation, the polonaise, the revolution were rehearsed three times in the afternoon under Diaghilev's supervision. The chief artists rehearsed their parts with the piano, the painter gave the last touch to banners and ikons, and thirty seamstresses sewed, mended and ironed, I dashed up and down like a madman (there were no lifts or telephones), Diaghilev was reading the proofs of the magnificent programme.'[43]

The polonaise was to be led by two artists from St Petersburg, Alexandra Vassilieva, a lady no longer young, who was the friend of the old balletomane Bezobrazov, one of Diaghilev's inner circle of advisers, and Mikhail Alexandrov, the son of Prince Dolgoruky (mentioned above), a handsome, dashing fellow. They had been chosen for their excellence in this Polish national dance, whose nuances were barely understood by Western dancers.

Diaghilev wrote,

One serious mistake in hanging our sets could have ruined the whole show. But luck was with us. The production was hung and lit a few moments before the performance began. I hardly had time to change before the curtain went up.

By the end of the first scene the public were beginning to enjoy themselves. Pimen's cell, with unseen choirs [of monks] singing in the wings, caused a sensation, and after the Coronation Scene our triumph began. I hardly saw this scene as I was in the wings supervising the entry of processions of supers.

During the second interval, when the stage-hands, thunderstruck by our success, saw me in my tail coat and white gloves moving on some hedges and placing benches for the Polish Scene, they ran to help me.

I had been refused water for the fountain – all available water, apparently, being reserved exclusively for the firemen. I believe this rule still applies at the Opéra [1928]. But the lack of water for the fountain did not diminish the success of the Polish Scene; nor did it prevent French ladies, infatuated with Smirnov, from beginning to trill 'O, povtori, povtori, Marina', pronouncing their guttural 'r's. The impression made on the public by Chaliapine's Mad Scene was really overwhelming, and the audience went wild. Even the Russian Court came to realize that this opera of Mussorgsky's was something more than a joke, and one heard people sobbing [in imitation of Chaliapine] 'Oh God, take pity on this poor sinner, Boris!'

In the Scene of Revolution [given by Diaghilev before the death scene of Boris], which I presented in deep snow, the episode of the Innocent, the passing of the impostor Dmitri, standing upright in his sledge, and the grand ensembles of the chorus, who brandished pitch-forks as they sang, impressed the public most favourably. The only set-back in the whole performance was the length of the last intermission, caused by the insistence of Valz, the technical director, on hanging some huge and enormously heavy chandeliers in the set representing the Great Hall (Granovitaya Palata) of the Kremlin. At this point the audience grew restive and began to stamp. But the scene of Boris' death, when the ascetic monks came on with tall candles and when Boris spoke his last words to his children, was a knock-out. The future of Russian opera in the West was assured.[44]

It was the Tsar's birthday. His uncle Grand Duke Paul, his first cousin Grand Duke Cyril and his first cousin once removed, Grand Duke Michael, who had come specially from Cannes, were present at the Opéra, besides President Faillières.[45]

Later that night, as Chaliapine strode beside Diaghilev along the *grands boulevards*, he kept exclaiming over and over again, 'We've done something tonight. I don't know what, but we've really done something!'[46] As the friends walked back to their hotels at dawn, Benois looked up at 'that other conqueror', Napoleon I, on top of the Colonne Vendôme. He and Koribut-Kubitovitch were staying at the Hôtel de l'Orient; and when the latter heard that Diaghilev's back room at the Hôtel de Hollande was within sight of Benois' window, he insisted, being drunk, on calling out across the back yards, until indignant Parisians appeared at their windows and the porter knocked on the door.[47]

In *Le Gaulois* Fourcaud acclaimed Chaliapine as singer and actor – indeed, he praised the whole company, including the chorus. The spectacle was beautiful, the whole production homogeneous. The score was the opposite of what was usually considered essential to lyric drama; and, in view of the episodic nature of the opera in chronicle form, he thought some cuts would do no harm. The admirable thing was the colour and pungency derived from a base of folk-song: every country should insist on popular folklore being taught in its musical conservatoires. The orchestration of Rimsky-Korsakov had perhaps softened certain intentionally harsh or bleak effects. There was hardly any development, and Mussorgsky had evidently brushed aside any lessons to be learnt from symphonic composition. However, the whole work carried conviction, and especially beautiful were the scenes of

Boris's lament in Act II, his entry into the assembly of boyars and his death, which imparted an almost physical shock to the spectators.[48]

Louis Schneider, critic of *Le Théâtre*, maintained that the opera should end with the Revolution Scene and the Innocent's song, for the People were the genuine protagonists of the work; and assumed that the death scene of Boris had been placed last to give the last word to Chaliapine. Apart from that, he had nothing but praise for the production, which was 'finer than anything we have seen before'.[49]

On 20 May (when Mary Garden sang *Thaïs* at the Opéra) the Opéra Comique held the *répétition générale* of Rimsky's *The Snow Maiden*.

Unwilling to be left out of what almost amounted to a Russian season in Paris, Kchessinskaya had arranged to appear as guest artist with the Opéra ballet. She danced in *Coppelia* on 23 May.

Diaghilev remembered: 'To show how dubious our whole undertaking had been considered in Russia I must admit that even the Grand Duke Vladimir Alexandrovitch, who was so fond of me, had not dared to come to Paris for our first performance. It was only when he was bombarded with telegrams announcing the triumph of *Boris* that he and the Grand Duchess made up their minds to take the Nord-Express, as it were, straight to the theatre.'[50]

Le Gaulois reported that, after the second act of *Boris* on Sunday 24 May, Grand Duke Vladimir and his Grand Duchess went on the stage to congratulate the company, who were recalled from the dressing-rooms by Diaghilev ('M. de Daiguilew'). His Imperial Highness spoke individually to every singer and studied their costumes.[51]

The Grand Duke was genuinely happy and proud [wrote Diaghilev] that this project which he had been almost the only one to encourage, which he had thrown himself into heart and soul, and which he had helped me to bring off, should have met with so outstanding a success. He was amazed at the high standard of our performance; and at a party he gave at his hotel, the Continental, for the whole company and stage staff he told them in the course of a little speech 'It isn't thanks to me or Diaghilev that *Boris* is such a success – it's all *your* doing. We only planned it: you made it come true.' The chorus misunderstood these words and thought the Grand Duke was dissatisfied with me.

Before he went back to St Petersburg the Grand Duke asked me 'Is it true that you are down 20,000 roubles? Tell me the truth and I'll ask the Emperor to make it up.' I told him it was not true. He smiled and said 'Perhaps you'd rather notify me in writing?' I insisted that there was not a word of truth in the story. Getting up and coming over to me, he raised his arm, made the sign of the cross and said 'May this blessing preserve you from all evil intrigues!' Then he embraced me.[52]

The supposition was that someone had been making mischief and exaggerating Diaghilev's losses. Even the authorities of the Opéra Comique,

whose *Snow Maiden* was considered very unequal, were jealous of Diaghilev's success.

Diaghilev wrote,

One day, going in to see the Grand Duke [Vladimir], I bumped into Carré, the
Director of the Opéra Comique, who was just leaving him. The Grand Duke told
me that Carré had come to complain about me. This was the reason.

For years Carré had been meaning to stage Rimsky's *Snegurotchka* [*The Snow
Maiden*], but put it off year after year. In March 1908, he wrote to me that he
still did not know whether he could put on the opera, or if he could, when.
Hearing that I was producing *Boris* at the Opéra he at once made up his mind
to produce *Snegurotchka* at the Opéra Comique. He summoned the composer
Tcherepnine to take charge of rehearsals and approached Princess Tenishev for
help with the costumes. In fact shortly after the *première* of *Boris*, Carré gave
Snegurotchka with Mme Carré in the principal role.

As we have seen, it was Rimsky-Korsakov who proposed Tcherepnine.
Carré applied to Mamontov for the old designs for the opera: he may
conceivably have asked the help of Princess Tenishev too. The *répétition
générale* of *The Snow Maiden* was on 20 May, the day after the *première*
of *Boris*.

For a number of reasons which it would be tedious to enumerate the opera was
not successful. On the day that I met him at the Grand Duke's, Carré, having
completely forgotten ever having written me the letter mentioned above, had
come to complain that my production of *Boris* had damaged his chances of success
with *Snegurotchka*, and that, as I had known of his intention to produce another
Russian opera at the same time, I had acted in bad faith. The Grand Duke was
very annoyed about the whole affair, which seemed to reflect on him, and ordered
me to sort the business out.

Without delay I went to see Briand, then Minister of Education, asking him
to act as arbiter in this dispute between Carré and myself. He appeared surprised,
but gave his consent. A few days later the arbitration took place. Carré began a
vehement denunciation of me, and Briand was obviously won over to his side.
Then, to cut the whole thing short, I produced my main evidence, Carré's letter.
Carré was extremely embarrassed. Briand asked me to leave them alone together.
Next day the Grand Duke received a letter of explanation from Briand with
Carré's apologies; and that was the end of the business.[53]

Diaghilev's legal training had at least taught him not to destroy documents
which might be used in evidence.

Boris Godunov brought Diaghilev together with a woman who was to
become his dearest friend. This was the half-Polish, half-Belgian Misia
Godebska, whose first husband had been Thadée Natanson, editor of *La
Revue Blanche*, and who in 1908 was married to the very rich but repulsive
Alfred Edwards, proprietor of *Le Matin*. She was an excellent pianist, and
her intelligence and devotion to the arts had won her the friendship of

Misia Natanson playing to a group including Vuillard, 1897. Woodcut by
Félix Vallotton.

Mallarmé, Lautrec, Renoir, Bonnard and Vuillard, the last four of whom
had painted her. (She had also been the subject of a woodcut by Félix
Vallotton, whose work Diaghilev had reproduced in *The World of Art*.)

   Her own life, if we are to believe her memoirs, dictated in old age when
she was blind, had been something of a fairy-tale, and her description of
the effect *Boris* had on her was perhaps too romantic to be exact. *Pelléas*
had been her first great love, she wrote (sweeping aside all the classics of
music): *Boris* was her second.

   For the first night I had invited a few friends to the big box between the
pillars. But in the middle of the first act I was so moved by the music that I made
my way to the gallery and remained there sitting on a step till the end.... The
stage streamed with gold. Chaliapine's voice rose powerful and magnificent above
Mussorgsky's overwhelming music.... I left the theatre stirred to the point of
realizing that something had been changed in my life. The music was with me
always.... I made incessant propaganda for this work and dragged to it all the
people I loved....

   It was shortly after the first night that, dining one evening at Prunier's with

Sert, I saw Diaghilev. Sert knew him, and introduced him to me. The fervour of my enthusiasm soon opened the doors of his heart for me. We remained until five in the morning, and found it intolerable to have to part. The next day he came to see me, and our friendship ended only with his death.[54]

We all know how a new work of art in the theatre, or the repertoire of a visiting company of actors, singers or dancers, can arouse in us a feeling of possessiveness second only to that felt by their creators and interpreters, so that not only do we attend every performance, dragging along potential converts, but we contrive to make friends with the artists, bind ourselves to them, and champion their cause for years to come. Misia's possessiveness and championship of Diaghilev's Russian seasons continued unabated for twenty years.

'It had been agreed with the Opéra management,' wrote Diaghilev, 'that in return for their putting the theatre and orchestra at our disposal the whole production of *Boris* should be [taken over by them free of charge and] included in their repertoire and sung in French. This revival never took place as they sold the entire production to the Metropolitan Opera, New York.'[55] Diaghilev erred, however, in stating in his notes that *Boris Godunov* was therefore given in the United States before being presented elsewhere in Europe. The opera was sung at La Scala, Milan, in 1909. The New York production, with Golovine's sets and costumes and the precious old garments which Bilibine had collected in the north of Russia, was performed in New York in 1913. (This was the year that Diaghilev revived the opera with new designs by Yuon, and gave Mussorgsky's *Khovanshchina* its first complete and first Western production, in Paris and London.) 'When all was over,' wrote Calvocoressi, 'a rain of rewards came from Russia. The managers of the Opéra were made Knights Commander of the Imperial order of St Anne, and I a Knight of the same order. Chaliapine received from the French Government the Cross of the Legion of Honour: Valz and Blumenfeld too; and I am glad to say that my faithful friends in need, Pétrémand and Loiseau, were not forgotten.'[56]

The last communication Diaghilev received from his old teacher Rimsky-Korsakov was a telegram to Paris after the opening of *Boris* to ask, 'How do my new bits sound?'[57] The composer died on 21 June 1908. Diaghilev judged that he had been on the verge of a new creative period; and that in *Coq d'or* he was much nearer to all that 'rubbish' – like Debussy's *Pélléas* – than he suspected.

He remained to the end of his days [wrote Diaghilev] that good-natured mixture of school-boy and schoolmaster which had always made us both laugh at him and love him. There was the story of him and the young Stravinsky [whom Diaghilev did not meet until a few months after Rimsky's death]. One day his pupil Stravinsky brought him a new composition to criticize. After reading through it Rimsky burst out 'This is disgusting, Sir. No, Sir, it is not permissible to write such nonsense until one is sixty.' He was in a bad mood all day; then, at dinner, he exclaimed to his wife 'What a herd of nonentities my pupils are! There's not one of them capable of producing a piece of rubbish such as Igor brought me this morning!'

It was in the country, on a stifling night of impending storm, that he breathed his last. Alas! What a ballet he might have written me! Stravinsky attended his funeral. Seeing him in tears, Rimsky-Korsakov's widow went up to him and said 'Don't cry, Igor. We still have Glazunov.' That was typical of her.[58]

PART IV

The Fokine-Nijinsky Period

CHAPTER 8

1908–9

Astruc – Fokine's Beginnings – Meeting with Nijinsky –
Planning the Châtelet Season – Insuperable Obstacles –
The First Russian Ballets in the West – Bankruptcy

R OBERT BRUSSEL IS OUR EVIDENCE that since as early as 1906 Diaghilev had contemplated bringing the Imperial Ballet to Paris.[1] Various
circumstances contributed to fortify him in this intention. Firstly,
the young Fokine had begun, under the influence of Isadora Duncan, to
evolve a new and more expressive form of choreography. Secondly, Benois
had collaborated with Fokine and produced a ballet which Diaghilev longed
to show in Paris. Thirdly, in Pavlova and Nijinsky the Imperial Ballet had
two dancers of genius whose art seemed to transcend anything that had
been achieved in ballet before.

In the autumn of 1908 Diaghilev began to plan an opera and ballet season,
for it had still not occurred to him that it would be feasible to present in the
West a season of ballet alone. To judge from accounts left behind by those
most concerned – or by their husbands or wives, who wrote their biographies
– he contrived that each person essential to the ballet side of his scheme
should think that he or she had personally persuaded him to embark on it.
Victor Dandré, a member of the City Council who became Pavlova's
manager and husband, wrote that he and Pavlova took advantage of a
discussion over luncheon to persuade Diaghilev to show Russian Ballet in
Paris.[2] Fokine recorded that during the summer of 1908, in Switzerland,
he received a letter from Benois telling him that he intended to persuade
Diaghilev to present *Le Pavillon d'Armide* and other Fokine ballets in Paris.[3]
Romola Nijinsky had no doubt that it was her husband Vaslav who persuaded Diaghilev to show the Ballet in the West.[4] Astruc is apt to rearrange
facts so as to make a good story, but I give verbatim his account of a
conversation with Diaghilev which took place on 2 June 1908. The subject
of ballet arose because he had been expressing admiration for the dancing
in the polonaise in *Boris*, which Alexandra Vassilieva had taught the French
corps de ballet, and led with Alexandrov.

'You seem so fond of dancing,' said Diaghilev. 'You ought to come to Petersburg to see our Imperial Ballet. You, in France, do not honour dancing any longer, and the art is incomplete as you show it today. You possess fine ballerinas, but you have no idea what a male dancer can be. Our male dancers are stars in Russia. Nothing can give you an idea how fine our Vaslav is – I believe nothing like him has been seen since Vestris.'

'Does he dance alone?'

'Yes, but sometimes with a partner who is almost his equal, la Pavlova. She is the greatest ballerina in the world, excelling both in classicism and character. She doesn't dance, she floats; of her it might be said, as was said of Taglioni, that she could walk over a cornfield without bending an ear.'

'But you must have great producers and *maîtres de ballet* to use all those fine talents.'

'We have. There is the old Cecchetti, master of us all, who carries the torch of classicism. Then there is a true genius, Michel Fokine, a descendant of the greatest *maîtres de ballet* of all time.'

'Fokine, Nijinsky and Pavlova *must* come to Paris next year.'

'But Paris will never come to see whole evenings of dancing.'[5]

Thus Astruc appears to take credit for the Russian Ballet coming west; and no doubt Diaghilev was very glad to give it to him. The remarkable fact is that a piece of paper survives, which illustrates how that conversation developed. It is a sheet of writing paper with the name and address of the Restaurant Paillard (opposite Astruc's office), where they were having supper. Astruc lists the proposed repertory: 'Le Pavillon d'Armide de Cherepnine avec la Pawlowa – dec et livret Benoist [sic] 2 actes. Sylvia – Leo Delibes. 3 tableaux.' But Sylvia is crossed out and 'Giselle ... 2 actes' replaces it. There is a list of possible patronesses, an estimate of the costs and takings, and a list of dancers, including Pavlova, Nijinsky and Fokine.[6]

Evidently Diaghilev, with his hard-learnt self-effacement, wished Astruc to be the one to broach with the Grand Duchess Vladimir (Marie Pavlovna), who was in Paris, the subject of bringing ballet to the West. Two days after the supper chez Paillard, Astruc spoke to the Grand Duchess at a party given by Princesse Edmond de Polignac, and she approved the plan.[7]

Diaghilev and Astruc signed a contract. Diaghilev accepted full financial responsibility for the Russian season of opera and ballet, while Astruc undertook the administration, the publicity and the sale of tickets, for which services Diaghilev persuaded him to accept half his usual commission, only $2\frac{1}{2}$ per cent.[8]

It is necessary to go back to 1905, the year of revolutions, strikes and the Russian defeat by the Japanese, in order to see how the various collaborators of Diaghilev's ballet company were drawn together, so that in the winter of 1908, after the conversation with Astruc and his first meeting with Nijinsky,

Diaghilev was able to plan a repertory and sign contracts for his 1909 Paris season.

Shortly after Isadora's first visit to St Petersburg, Fokine had been asked to arrange a ballet 'for the pupils' display at the end of term. Under the American's influence, he decided to do something Greek and went to the Public Library in search of subject-matter. The Director of the Library was none other than Vladimir Stassov, the staunch supporter of the Five composers; he was then in the last year of his life. He was impressed by the serious intentions of the young dancer and would-be choreographer, and took trouble to help him. They found the libretto of an old ballet Ivanov had arranged in 1896, *Acis and Galatea*, with music by Kadletz. Yet, in spite of the Greek subject, the Inspector of the Imperial Ballet School would not allow Fokine to abandon the traditional ballet style, with spectacular steps, turned-out movements and point shoes for the girls.

However [wrote Fokine], I still managed to produce the ballet not exactly as customary.... The groupings were unusual, asymmetrical; some performers were placed on different levels, on mounds, tree stubs, trees; others on the floor – thus avoiding the usual horizontal line grouping. The Dance of the Fauns seemed to be entirely new.... They performed no ballet steps and ... did some tumbling which was not in accordance with the classical school but corresponded very well with the mood of an animal dance.[9]

It was on this occasion that Fokine met the youth who was to be one of the two outstanding interpreters of his choreography. Noticing the soaring jump, he asked, 'What is your name?' 'Nijinsky,' was the reply; and *Acis* was the first of many Fokine ballets in which Nijinsky danced.[10] Fokine's other outstanding interpreter would be Tamara Karsavina, with whom he had had a romance a few years before. There had only been one obstacle to the marriage of this Byronic young man and the beautiful, thoughtful girl, who used to go for long walks and visit picture galleries together:[11] Tamara's mother, a former Smolny boarder, thought she could do better, and Tamara acquiesced.[12] So in 1905 Fokine married one of his pupils, Vera Antonova, a good-looking but rather dull girl, who was devoted to him; and in 1907 Karsavina married a nice man whom she did not love, Mukhin, who worked in the Ministry of Finance and played the violin.[13]

In February of the following year Fokine, at the request of Victor Dandré, undertook a whole evening of ballet for charity at the Mariinsky. For this he made a two-act ballet, *Eunice*, about the slave girl who loved Petronius, and another (to the music of Chopin, orchestrated by Glazunov) called *Chopiniana*. The score of the former work contained waltzes, which the choreographer knew to be quite out of keeping, and, although there was at that time no question of dancing barefoot on the Imperial stage, he tried, by omitting virtuoso steps such as *pirouettes*, *entrechats* and *battements*, and having toe-nails painted on the dancers' tights[14] (by Nijinsky's elder sister, Bronislava),[15] to be as ancient-Greek as possible. Kchessinskaya was Eunice, Pavel Gerdt – for many years the principal *danseur noble*, though now obliged to restrict himself to mime and stately partnering – played Petronius, and, as Akte, Pavlova performed a Dance of the Seven Veils. Nijinsky, too, had a small part. There was a dance with wine-skins, another with lighted torches, and an Egyptian *pas de trois* in which Vera Fokina and her companions darkened their bodies and made history by wearing clinging draperies instead of *tutus*.[16]

The other ballet given on that night of 23 February 1907, *Chopiniana*, was even more historic, for it contained the seeds of Fokine's *Les Sylphides*, although only one number, the waltz in C sharp minor, then danced by Pavlova and Mikhail Obukhov, survived in the latter version. The other numbers – a polonaise in Polish costumes, a nocturne in which Chopin was haunted by ghostly monks and consoled by a vision of his beloved, a mazurka in which the young bride of an old bridegroom eloped with her young lover, and a tarantella led by Vera Fokina – were very different. From the waltz – in which Pavlova wore a long white ballet skirt *à la* Taglioni designed for her by Bakst – Fokine banished all 'spectacular feats': yet, although he was 'totally unconcerned' about impressing the public, he enjoyed one of the greatest successes of his career.[17] He had created a new poetry of motion.

Fokine, in his *Memoirs*, is always anxious to protest that his ballets were created out of thin air, with no particular artists in mind. This can surely never be the case with any choreographer. The frail, unearthly quality of Pavlova, who was always being fed on cod-liver oil to build up her *embonpoint* to the degree considered essential in the early years of this century, must have suggested to him the ethereal quality of this waltz, which in turn dictated the eventual nature of his world-famous *Les Sylphides*.

A few years before this Benois had read a story of Théophile Gautier which gave him an idea for a ballet. He told this to his nephew by marriage, the composer Tcherepnine, who accordingly wrote some music. Early in 1907 Tcherepnine conducted a suite from the still unperformed ballet at a concert; Fokine liked the music and went to congratulate the composer. On 28 April 1907 he presented at a school performance, in costumes borrowed from the Mariinsky, a ballet arranged to Tcherepnine's suite, under the name of *Le Gobelins Animé* (*The Gobelins Tapestry which came to Life*). This was to all intents and purposes the middle act of the future ballet *Le Pavillon d'Armide*. There was a striking grotesque dance for jesters, led by Nijinsky's class-mate, the short, stocky George Rosaï. Krupensky, the Assistant Director of the Mariinsky, saw this *divertissement*, liked it and planned for the whole ballet, as devised by Benois and Tcherepnine, to be staged in the autumn.[18]

It was on the day after this school performance, a fortnight before Diaghilev's first concert of Russian music in Paris, that Nijinsky graduated from the school. His dancing made so great an impression that Kchessinskaya told him he must be her partner.[19] Although officially he had joined the company only as a member of the corps de ballet, he thus leapt from student to star.

That autumn, for the first time, Benois met Fokine, who came to the scene-painting studio. Fokine wrote,

I was gently and kindly greeted by a lively man with dark hair and a fresh pink face fringed with a thick beard.... A bunch of pencils – then as always – protruded from his pocket, signifying his immediate willingness to draw a costume, a bit of scenery or an architectural detail on any available piece of paper.... Until then I had had to make selections for my productions from ancient, shabby and worn scenery.... Benois took me up the scaffold right above the scenery. My head was spinning, both from the height and from joy. Under my feet the scenery was spread out: a marvellous pavilion for Armide. What a happy moment that was![20]

When Fokine invited Benois to a rehearsal, the latter was as overcome by his new experience as Fokine had been at the studio.

When I was taken into the rehearsal hall at the Theatre School I was almost dumbfounded. I had often been present at stage rehearsals and was acquainted with many dancers ... but the sight that now presented itself to my eyes was something entirely unexpected. The daylight, streaming through the tall windows on either side of the hall, seemed to make the sea of tarlatan dresses even more ethereal, transparent, foamy. These young women ... made no use whatsoever of cosmetics, and their youthful bodies and faces were radiant with health and vigour....
Fokine led me in and presented me to the company. My bow was answered by a mass curtsey performed by all the rules of Court etiquette.... The boys at the school stood in a separate group and they too wore their working dress and ballet shoes. When I passed them they bowed so deeply that I was embarrassed. A youth ... was standing with them. I would not have noticed him had not Fokine presented him to me as the artist for whom he had especially composed the part of Armide's slave, so as to give him a chance to display his remarkable talent.... I was rather surprised when I saw this wonder face to face. He was a short, rather thick-set little fellow with the most ordinary colourless face. He was more like a shop assistant than a fairy-tale hero. But this was – Nijinsky!...[21]

But difficulties lay ahead. Krupensky, for reasons which it is too late in the day to discover, turned against the new ballet. He began to treat Benois with condescension, and the sensitive painter 'saw red'. Kchessinskaya gave up her role of Armida. Gerdt tried to abandon his role of Vicomte René, saying he was too old; and he had to be dissuaded. Diaghilev came to watch a rehearsal at the Mariinsky, and, before half an hour was up, had been politely but firmly asked to leave by a police officer. Benois thought that after this humiliating incident Diaghilev must have sworn to wreak vengeance on the theatre which had rejected him – but he had surely done that in 1901. 'Certainly,' wrote Benois, 'he could not have invented a better way than to create his own world-famous theatre.'[22]

Pavlova undertook the role of Armida: but Krupensky allowed too few rehearsals, and the new ballet was postponed by a week. Even so, when it was performed on 25 November 1907, it followed the whole of *Le Lac des Cygnes* and only finished at one in the morning. When Pavlova, Gerdt, Nijinsky and the rest had taken their calls, Benois, Tcherepnine and Fokine were brought on the stage; and the painter, enjoying for the first time this 'vainglorious pleasure', was kissed by Pavlova, who clasped an armful of flowers.[23]

Diaghilev had taken no part in the planning of Benois' first ballet, but he was present to witness its success and to envisage other ballets in which composer, designer and choreographer would work together to achieve a new unity and expressiveness. Pavlova he had seen and admired for several years, but here in the same ballet was the marvellous youth Nijinsky! Diaghilev told Benois that '*Le Pavillon d'Armide* must be shown in Europe.'[24] This happened at the time he was preparing his production of *Boris Godunov*.

On 21 March 1908, a month before he set off for Paris, Diaghilev had another chance to appraise Fokine's versatility and the many-sided interpretive power of Nijinsky in two ballets performed at the Mariinsky. One was a ballet about Cleopatra, arranged by Fokine, called *Une Nuit d'Egypte*, in which Pavlova had a dramatic role as the deserted mistress of one of the queen's victims and Nijinsky danced a *pas de deux* with the ballerina Olga Preobrajenskaya. Here Fokine carried further his reform of ballet costume and his adherence to local colour and period style. The other ballet was the new version of *Chopiniana*. Only the C sharp minor waltz was retained from the earlier version, and the new dances were in the same style.[25] The new corps de ballet were dressed as Pavlova had been, in the manner of the old Romantic ballet. Fokine had abolished the short *tutu* from his works for ever. The white-clad sylphs, with hair drawn back and parted down the middle, were led by Pavlova, Preobrajenskaya and Karsavina, with Nijinsky, in a short black velvet tunic, as the dreaming poet, whose gestures and steps were designed less to display his prodigious technique, than to sustain a mood of nocturnal reverie. His was the only male role.

Nijinsky may have been insignificant-looking in private life, but he appeared fascinating enough on the stage, and it was natural that his remarkable performances during his first season at the Mariinsky should give him a kind of glamour, so that he attracted admirers who wanted to meet him, get to know him, perhaps make love to him. Some of these were men. Until his graduation and début on the stage, he had necessarily lived a sheltered life between the Imperial Ballet School, where he boarded, and the home where his valiant mother, separated from her dancer husband (who had started another family), struggled to keep things going. Eleanora Nijinsky's elder son, either through hereditary deficiency or as a result of a fall sustained in childhood, was feeble-minded and in a mental hospital. Her daughter Bronislava, two years older than Vaslav, with the same Tartar high cheek-bones and the same aerial jump, had preceded him on the Mariinsky stage. With Vaslav's precocious stardom, prospects looked bright for the family; they moved to a flat (over a shop) in Mokhovaya, off the Nevsky Prospekt;[26] and Vaslav began to supplement his salary, as was usual, by giving lessons in ballroom dancing to the children of rich merchant families. One of his class-mates, Anatol Burman, who later wrote a lurid and unreliable book about him, described how there was a man in the Imperial Ballet – he gave him a different name,[27] but this was Alexandrov, who led the polonaise in *Boris* in Paris – who specialized in introducing girl dancers to members of St Petersburg society. Being on his father's side of noble birth, though illegitimate, he was a link between the *beau monde* and the world of ballet. He may also have gone in for introducing male dancers to men, and, being handsome, was probably something of a whore himself. In Russian society affairs between men were not then considered as scandalous as they would have been in Paris and London.[28]

Alexandrov introduced Nijinsky to Prince Pavel Dmitrievitch Lvov. This man, tall, fair-haired and good-looking, was a patron of sportsmen as well as of dancers, and he became a good friend to the whole Nijinsky family. In fact, Bronislava maintained that, when she had a poisoned foot, he took her to a doctor who possibly saved her career.[29] Lvov helped the Nijinskys financially, and it was with him that Vaslav had his first homosexual affair.

How much of Nijinsky's famous *Diary*, written when he was on the verge of mental breakdown in 1918 (and erratically edited many years later), are we to accept? How are we to judge the proportion of truth to nonsense in this document, or to what extent it has been distorted? Did Nijinsky write – and, if so, was it true that – 'One day I met a Russian prince who intro-duced me to a Polish count.... This count bought me a piano: I did not love him. I loved the prince and not the count...'?[30] Bronislava Nijinska, who remembered Count Tishkevitch as being a family man of strict morals, told me that it was not he but Lvov who bought Nijinsky a piano.[31] At any rate, Lvov did not love Nijinsky so possessively that he kept him to himself. It was during the period of their intimacy that Nijinsky, who had flirted shyly with girls before, had his first physical experience with a woman. She was a tart, and Nijinsky was put off.

Then, in the autumn of 1908, when Diaghilev was back from his holiday in Venice, following the success of *Boris*, Lvov introduced Nijinsky to him.

According to Burman, this historic meeting took place at a supper chez Cubat after a performance at the Mariinsky.[32]

Of course, Nijinsky had heard of Diaghilev's achievements, and, of course, Diaghilev was aware of the outstanding talent of Nijinsky. Diaghilev was planning his 1909 season of mixed opera and ballet for Paris. He was beginning to sign contracts.[33] Nijinsky wrote in his 1918 *Diary*, 'Lvov introduced me to Diaghilev, who asked me to come to the Europa Hotel where he lived. I disliked him for his too self-assured voice, but went to seek my luck. I found my luck. I trembled like a leaf. I hated him, but pretended, because I knew that my mother and I would die of hunger otherwise. . . .'[34]

If Nijinsky really wrote these words, it is clear that his mental condition caused him to throw on this meeting with Diaghilev the coloured limelight of melodrama. It is as if he were suggesting the theme of a sensational film – of the hundred films planned between 1920 and 1979, but never realized – which people would want to make about him. Hollywood would obviously need to cast Diaghilev as the villain. The idea that Nijinsky might 'die of hunger' in 1908 was nonsense.

Diaghilev may have been attracted by the idea that the leading male dancer of his company-to-be – a dancer of genius – should also be his lover. He already had a boy-friend acting as his secretary, Alexis Mavrine, whom he had taken abroad (and who had helped move the improvized 'scenery' at the 'semi-official' rehearsal of *Boris* on 17 May). But Nijinsky! – might he not be as godlike in bed as on the stage? It appears that he was not.[35]

It was in a new flat Diaghilev had taken on the ground floor of a house in Zamiatin Pereulok (Passage), off Angliskaya (the English Quay) on the Neva, south-west of the Admiralty, that Diaghilev and his friends planned the repertory for the famous 1909 Paris season. In the drawing-room, with its grey-and-beige striped paper, hung the paintings Diaghilev had collected. In the slightly smaller dining-room, where the conspirators usually met round the long oval table covered by a cloth, tea and biscuits were served as ever, but Diaghilev's old nurse was dead, having not long survived her immortalization by Bakst; and Vassili Zuikov was the only servant.[36]

Fokine remembered Diaghilev by sight from the year 1900–1901.

I knew [he wrote] that there were always young men of privileged families in the administration [of the Imperial Theatres] who would rapidly bypass hundreds of office workers on the staff and be promoted to higher posts in the theatre organization. These were the clerks whom Gogol called by the derogatory but appropriate name of 'leeches'. No one ever knew just what the Official for Special Missions was supposed to do. . . . I do not recall ever speaking to him . . . until our meeting in 1908. . . . His personality charmed me right from our first conversation. . . . By this time . . . he was in my eyes certainly no longer just an official. We began immediately to discuss the programme. I learned with pleasure then that Diaghilev wished to present not only *Le Pavillon d'Armide* and *Les Sylphides*, but a whole repertoire of my ballets. The enterprise, it seemed, would immediately take on the customary elaborate Diaghilev proportions.... He asked me to think over some Russian themes. As we went over a list of the ballets which I had already created, Benois pointed out *Une Nuit d'Egypte*. This interested Diaghilev a good deal, but he considered the Arensky music very weak and felt that it would be impossible to present the ballet in Paris with such music.... I had to reconcile myself to Diaghilev's opinion.[37]

Benois, who, since the production of *Boris* in Paris, had worked with Fokine on a little ballet for a student's ball to the music of Clementi's sonatinas, was the link between Fokine and Diaghilev, while Fokine would be the link between Diaghilev and a new employee, Sergei Grigoriev, who was to serve Diaghilev as faithful *régisseur* and prop long after the latter had quarrelled with the choreographer and after his enthusiasm for the work of his old painter friend had waned.

I went to see Diaghilev in a great state of excitement [wrote Grigoriev]. Eight years had gone by since I had first seen him and heard his name.... I rang the bell of his flat with a certain trepidation.... Our interview was very brief. He said that Fokine had recommended me as a *régisseur*; that if I agreed he would pay me so much; and that my first duty would be to sign contracts with the artists. I agreed to the terms and he handed me the contracts.... He gave me a curious smile; his mouth alone smiled, the rest of his face remaining entirely serious.... Our meeting, his offer to me, and the coming visit to Paris, had completely changed my life. For the moment everything seemed interesting, eventful and full of meaning.[38]

When Grigoriev accompanied Fokine, a few days later, to a meeting of the 'artistic committee', he began to understand the composition of this group of friends.

The musical side was represented by Nuvel, who was less interested in ballet than in opera – which was still, of course, considered by Diaghilev as the staple diet of the Paris season; by Nicolas Tcherepnine, composer of *Le Pavillon d'Armide*; and up to a point by Benois, who had his own definite musical preferences. Benois, Bakst and Serov were the painters involved. If Borissov-Musatov had not died five years before and if Vrubel were not in a mental home – to die in 1910 – they would surely have been present. Korovine and Golovine paid occasional visits. The ballet specialists were the eminent critic Valerien Svetlov, with his white quiff, nicknamed 'Mr Parrot'[39] – a former protector of Pavlova and future husband of the dancer Vera Trefilova – and the great tea-drinker 'General' Bezobrazov, godfather to the ballet of St Petersburg. These balletomanes represented the right wing of the revolutionary movement.

Then there were two dear friends who had both been known to help socially and financially. They had in common a passion for old pictures, furniture and china: Dr Sergei Botkine, who lived in a beautiful house near the Tauride Palace, full of Peter the Great furniture; and Prince Argutinsky-Dolgorukov, whose rare objects were crammed into a small flat on Milionaya, near the Winter Palace.[40] Diaghilev's friend Alexis Mavrine was also present at these meetings. Grigoriev described him as 'modest and attractive'.[41]

When, with Fokine, Grigoriev attended the next meeting of the committee, Diaghilev announced certain decisions. To strengthen the score of *Une Nuit d'Egypte*, which he wanted to call *Cléopâtre*, he had found music of an Oriental type which would fit the various dance numbers in such a way that hardly a step need be changed. (Fokine seemed rather surprised by this in his *Memoirs* and claimed no credit for the choice, so it is, indeed, probable that Diaghilev alone selected the pieces.)[42] Arensky's overture would be replaced by that of Taneyev for his opera *Oresteia*. For the entrance of Cleopatra and the Dance of the Slave Girls there would be the weird 'Dream of Cleopatra', with the music of Pan's pipe, from Rimsky's *Mlada*. For the *pas de deux* of two Slaves with a scarf there was to be the 'Danse Orientale' from Glinka's *Ruslan*. A dance for two Bacchantes and two Fauns to the autumn music of Glazunov's *Seasons* would be inserted. The *divertissement* performed during the love-making of Cleopatra and Amoun was to end with the Dance of Persian Slave Girls from Mussorgsky's *Khovanshchina*. Finally, Diaghilev did not like the happy ending, when Amoun, having made love to and been poisoned by Cleopatra, was restored to life and to the embraces of his true love Ta-Hor. He was to remain dead and Ta-Hor must have a big dramatic scene of lamentation over his body. For this, Tcherepnine, to his astonishment, was asked to write new music.

Grigoriev wrote, 'We all sat silent, till at last Fokine spoke.'

'Well,' he said, 'with so many changes – it will be an entirely new ballet!' 'That does not matter,' said Diaghilev, 'what I want to know is whether you like the idea.' We all said yes, and he continued, 'As for you, Levushka [Bakst], you will have to paint us a lovely décor.' Levushka instantly began tracing the plan of the scene as he visualized it and describing it in his curious guttural accent. 'There will be a huge temple on the banks of the Nile. Columns; a sultry day; the scent of the East and a great many lovely women with beautiful bodies....' Diaghilev shook his head, as if at an incorrigible child.... Diaghilev asked us all to go into the next room, where he sat at the piano with Nuvel next to him and asked us to listen to the altered score. I did not know that Diaghilev could play the piano and watched him doing so. He played very well, biting his tongue the whole time, especially when he came to difficult bits. He would frequently stop and explain to Fokine the passages in the score that had been altered. Fokine sat holding the score and marking them. Nuvel laughed in his peculiar way, remarking that what we had just heard was just a mediocre *salade russe*. Diaghilev ... dismissed Nuvel's criticism almost without considering it.[43]

Diaghilev, however, knew that Nuvel was right; but even at this stage, four months before the Paris opening, he was chiefly interested in the operas he was going to present, namely Glinka's *Ruslan and Ludmila*, Borodin's *Prince Igor*, Mussorgsky's *Boris* and Rimsky-Korsakov's *The Maid of Pskov*;[44] and he thought of the ballets less as integrated works of art than as the means of showing off wonderful Russian dancers. *Cléopâtre* was not the only one of his ballets for 1909 which was unsatisfactory from a musical point of view. *Les Sylphides*, which was the name he had decided to give *Chopiniana*, was made up of heavenly Chopin pieces whose whole nature depended on their delicate rendering on the piano and which were coarsened by orchestration. Tcherepnine's score for *Armide* was charming, but derivative. Yet *Cléopâtre*, *Les Sylphides* and *Le Pavillon d'Armide* would each cause a tremendous sensation in Paris, and each in a different way. Diaghilev wished to astound at all costs and in this he was successful.

The odious notion of orchestrating Chopin had originated with Glazunov – for it was the score of a suite of his called *Chopiniana*, which Fokine had found in 1907, that gave the young choreographer his idea for the first version of the ballet. Then Fokine had asked Glazunov to orchestrate an additional number – the C sharp minor waltz, and this had been done. The second version of the ballet (made up, except for the waltz in C sharp minor, of new pieces) had been orchestrated by Maurice Keller.[45] Now, Diaghilev began tinkering.

On 6 February 1909 he attended one of the Ziloti concerts, so called after Alexander Ziloti, their founder, who, like Botkine and Bakst, had married a daughter of Pavel Tretiakov. That night he heard played two orchestral pieces by Igor Stravinsky, son of a *basso* in the Mariinsky opera company and a former pupil of Rimsky-Korsakov. Stravinsky's *Chant Funèbre* had been played on 1 January 1909 at Rimsky's memorial concert, at which Diaghilev must certainly have been present. The new works were Stravinsky's *Fantastic Scherzo* and *Feu d'artifice*. Unlike Glazunov, who commented on the latter, 'No talent, only dissonance',[46] Diaghilev was enthusiastic about it and went to introduce himself to the composer. They immediately became friends, and the first commission Diaghilev gave Stravinsky was to orchestrate Chopin's *Valse brillante* for the finale of *Les Sylphides*.

The keynote of the 1909 season was to be Chaliapine. It was understood that he and the other artists of the Imperial Theatres would be free to fulfil their Paris engagement after the Mariinsky and Bolshoi seasons ended. The scenery for the operas and for *Le Pavillon d'Armide* would be lent by the Imperial Theatres. That of *Cléopâtre* and *Les Sylphides* would be designed and built afresh. The Grand Duke Vladimir had obtained a subsidy of 100,000 roubles from the Emperor.[47]

When it came to casting the ballets, Fokine became difficult. He considered Kchessinskaya an old-fashioned type of dancer, unsuited to his new works, and would not have her in the Chopin ballet. Diaghilev thought she must be included at all costs, not only because of her fame and notoriety but because of her influence. Reluctantly, Fokine agreed to let her dance Armida, which she had backed out of doing in the first version of the ballet.[48] He himself would perform the hero Vicomte René, Gerdt would mime the old Marquis-magician, and Nijinsky would fill the role of Armida's Favourite Slave, which he had created at the Mariinsky. He would also be the Poet in *Les Sylphides*, with Pavlova, and Pavlova would be Ta-Hor in *Cléopâtre*. But who would mime Cleopatra?

Fokine and Bakst had been plotting secretly to put forward the claims of a beautiful young woman who came from a wealthy Jewish family, but aspired – much to their disapproval – to appear on the stage. Fokine had given her lessons and she had been on the point of performing Wilde's *Salomé*, ending her Dance of the Seven Veils in the nude, when this had been banned by the censor. Bezobrazov was against an amateur appearing in a professional company and 'went on grumbling for some time'. But Diaghilev scented the publicity value of the spectacular Ida Rubinstein.[49]

Diaghilev had already begun to sign contracts. Back from Moscow, where he engaged several dancers, he went to interview Karsavina. She was anxious not to be thought unsophisticated by this arbiter of elegance.

I sat waiting for Diaghilev [she wrote] in my small sitting-room. I had my own home now. 'The red plush of that suite – like a provincial hotel,' I thought, looking at my furniture. A piece of Dresden china, my first acquisition in the *bibelot* line, seemed alone capable of bearing witness to my taste. I moved it from the *étagère* to the piano. ... I moved it back again. Six o'clock; he should have come at five. My agitation grew.... I had almost given up hope when I saw his coupé stop at my door. Diaghilev would never drive in an open cab for fear of being infected with glanders.... A meeting for discussing various artistic questions had kept him so late. I had a first glimpse of the feverish activities that he called his life.... [He] was just back from Moscow.... Answering my questions about [the Moscow ballerina] Karalli [he said] 'It is certainly an unforgettable face; far, though, from perfection of features.... By the by, I will send you your contract signed tonight; or is it Monday today? – unlucky day. I will do it tomorrow,' ... A thought, like a small splinter, worried me. Only a secondary part is allotted me in Paris, and that mysterious forge [Diaghilev's flat] where creative minds worked a new armour of art, will it ever open to me?[50]

Diaghilev left for Paris to make what he believed to be final arrangements.[51] On the day of his return, 22 February 1909, the Grand Duke Vladimir Alexandrovitch died. This was a disaster. Diaghilev wrote:

The first funeral service for the Grand Duke took place on the night of his death. I was the earliest arrival at the Palace and slipped into the room where

Vladimir Alexandrovitch lay on a bier. As I stood beside him, weeping, I suddenly perceived the figure of a man appearing from the shadows. It was the Emperor. He came towards me, crossed himself, and, gazing thoughtfully at me, murmured, as if to himself, 'Yes, he was very fond of you.'[52]

Diaghilev was not so preoccupied with his own affairs that he could not put himself out to entertain a visitor from Paris. Maurice Denis, an old friend, whose work had been more reproduced in *The World of Art* than that of any other French painter, travelled to Moscow to see his 'Psyche' murals installed in Morosov's house, and visited St Petersburg both on the way there and on the way back. 'Golovine and Diaghilev obtained tickets for us at the Théâtre Marie,' he wrote in his journal. 'Golovine's décor for *Carmen* was dazzlingly vivid and so Spanish; ... Diaghilev says that Glinka's *Ruslan*, dating from about 1840, is the Gospel of Russian music, forestalling Wagner and sometimes going even further than he did.... Dinner with 'le beau Diaghilev' at Cubat's, then tea after the theatre at Benois'.'[53]

Matilda Kchessinskaya's relations with Diaghilev veered between hot and cold. Her longing to shine on the stage, which she had done so successfully for eighteen years, was equalled by her love of power and diamonds. She could be irresistible to those she wished to please and extremely helpful to younger dancers who did not directly challenge her supremacy. She was very kind, for instance, to Karsavina, who had nothing but good to say of her on stage or off.[54] Now, having learnt that Armida was to be her only role in Paris (and that she would share it with Karalli), she decided to use her authority to terminate the whole affair. 'I could not intercede on behalf of a project in which I was no longer taking part. I therefore asked that my requests for a subsidy should not be followed up. All Diaghilev's efforts to obtain that subsidy by other means failed.'[55] This was pompous nonsense, as it had not been she, but Diaghilev, who had asked the Grand Duke Vladimir for the subsidy in the first place. It is possible that Grand Duke Andrei, the father of her son, had been jealous of Diaghilev's influence with his late father; that he was even jealous of Diaghilev's former friendship with Kchessinskaya; and that he mistrusted the 'decadent' – that is, modern – tendencies which Diaghilev sponsored in the arts. Benois has left an explanation of what the unsuccessful 'other means' to obtain a subsidy were. Diaghilev had the promise of money from a Riga galosh-manufacturer, but this was dependent on the latter's receiving a patent of nobility. The widowed Grand Duchess Marie Pavlovna was supposed to have signed the recommendation for this – which was a quite normal reward for successful businessmen – but at the last moment decided not to.[56]

The Committee met in Zamiatin Pereulok. Diaghilev read them the letter from the Imperial Secretariat telling them that the subsidy had been cancelled.

Having read the letter to us [wrote Grigoriev], he put it in front of him, and, banging the table with his fist, said 'I am most indignant that the Emperor should act in such a way!' We all sat silent: there was nothing to be said. We all shared his indignation at such base intrigues in high places. Diaghilev was the first to break the silence. 'This alters our whole position,' he said. 'I shall have to think it over and find some way out. One thing is clear, though, we can no longer rely on help from above. And I should refuse it now, even if it were offered.' We said goodbye: and he asked us to come again in a few days. We were all greatly depressed. . . . I was very young; I did not know Diaghilev. . . .[57]

The measure of Diaghilev's own despair is evident from the fact that he communicated it to his collaborators. He did not like to appear snubbed or humbled. He could not have hidden his feelings from Nuvel and Benois, but he must have been utterly at a loss for the time being to reveal his disappointment to Fokine and Grigoriev. In later life he tended more and more to keep his financial troubles to himself.[58]

He went straight back to Paris and told Astruc that unless backers could be found at the French end the Russian season could not take place. He told him that he had a private subsidy of 50,000 francs in Russia[59] – which may or may not have been true at the time, although he must later have raised enough to pay for the scenery and costumes – but that he had no funds with which to hire the theatre or pay the artists, and no guarantee of any kind against failure. The dauntless Astruc rose to the occasion. He applied for help to several financiers, and secured the promise of 50,000 francs, which was only to be drawn upon if the average receipts of the season fell below 25,000 francs a performance.[60]

Back in St Petersburg, Diaghilev apparently told his friends merely that Comtesse Greffulhe and Mme Edwards[61] had come to his aid. When the committee assembled, according to Grigoriev,

Diaghilev arrived looking very spry and animated. . . . In view of the reduced budget, we should only be able to give one opera in its entirety, namely *Ivan the Terrible* [*The Maid of Pskov*], and only one act of each of the two others, *Ruslan and Ludmila* and *Prince Igor*. Each of these acts would be given on separate nights, and each followed by two ballets. . . . But since we had only three ballets decided on so far, we were still one short. What he had in mind to complete three programmes was a *grand divertissement*. We all welcomed this decision except Nuvel, who said that since we could not show the operas as intended and since the ballet would not really impress Paris sufficiently, it would be better to give up the whole season. Diaghilev got very angry with him at this and said he had signed too many contracts in Petersburg, Moscow and Paris itself. If Nuvel was not satisfied, perhaps he would raise enough backing for us to carry out the scheme as originally planned. This argument silenced Nuvel.[62]

Grigoriev does not mention *Boris Godunov*, but it is clear that at this stage

Diaghilev was still hoping that negotiations with the Opéra would enable him to include it in his repertoire.[63]

More blows were to fall. It seems extraordinary that the charming Kchessinskaya should have put the Grand Duke Andrei up to sending the following letter to his cousin the Emperor, warning him not to get mixed up in 'an unsavoury business which sullies the memory of dear Papa'.

As was to be expected [wrote the Grand Duke], your telegram wrought havoc in the whole Diaghilev business, and now in his attempt to save his beastly affair he is resorting to every subterfuge, from the vilest flatteries to absolute false-hoods. According to information given me, Boris, who will be in attendance on you tomorrow, has been got at on behalf of Diaghilev, and sympathizes with his grievances. He therefore means to ask you ... to allow him to continue to use the Hermitage for rehearsals, and to borrow the décor and costumes used in the Mariinsky theatre for the season in Paris. We very much hope you will not take the bait....[64]

The Emperor withdrew permission for Diaghilev to use the scenery and costumes of the operas and of *Le Pavillon d'Armide*. Diaghilev cabled Astruc on 12 March, asking him to find out if the Opéra would sell back to him last year's sets and costumes of *Boris*.[65] The answer was No: so, two days later, he telegraphed, 'If sale absolutely impossible try hiring.'[66] In the third week of March he resigned himself to the fact that *Boris* could not be included in the repertory.

The next blow was that permission to use the Hermitage Theatre for rehearsals, which had been obtained by Grand Duke Vladimir, was, as his youngest son had requested in the letter to the Tsar, withdrawn. Benois, who had painted the Polish scene for *Boris* there, and found it an inspiring place to work in, arrived on 2 April, full of anticipated enjoyment at the prospect of attending a rehearsal at the theatre he loved.

The artists were already in their dressing-rooms; the dressers, their arms full of foaming tulle skirts, were hurrying along the labyrinth of corridors.... But here I was suddenly accosted by Diaghilev's secretary, Mavrine, who imparted to me the astounding news that we were to collect all our belongings and leave the premises immediately.... Fortunately, half an hour later Mavrine had comforting news for us: our indefatigable leader had rushed all over the town to find some suitable rehearsing hall and had already something in view. Shortly after this came a telephone message inviting us all to a certain Catherine Hall on the Ekaterinsky Canal. I shall never forget that romantic exodus. Mavrine and I headed the procession in one cab; all our artists, dressers with their baskets and stage hands followed behind in others. The long procession stretched across the whole town. The day was dismal and dull but luckily dry. The atmosphere of adventure – almost of a picnic – seemed to soften our slight feeling of shame at having been 'turned out', and when we reached the little-known Catherine Hall we liked it so much that our spirits rose immediately.[67]

Grigoriev looked upon the rehearsal which took place that afternoon as 'the first, historic rehearsal of the Diaghilev Ballet'.[68] Indeed, we already think of this assembled company as 'The Diaghilev Ballet', although Diaghilev was still only allowed to present the Tsar's dancers during their vacation and would not have his own company till 1911. Pavlova and Ida Rubinstein were not present at this and subsequent rehearsals,[69] but all the other contracted St Petersburg artists were there, and, after Grigoriev had introduced them individually to Diaghilev, the latter made a little speech. The dancers clapped and swarmed round Diaghilev, eager to ask questions.[70]

That afternoon Fokine rehearsed the Polovtsian Dances from the second act of *Prince Igor* for the first time.[71] He had complained to Diaghilev that he knew nothing about the remote, extinct and barbaric tribe of the Polovtsi – he would have liked, as was his custom, to do some research in a museum – and was reluctant to undertake the arrangement. But 'You will do it perfectly, Mikhail Mikhailovitch,' Diaghilev told him. 'On other occasions,' wrote Fokine, 'I began to compose after I absorbed historical, ethnographical, musical and literary material. This time I came to rehearsals with Borodin's music under my arm. This comprised my total armament.'[72] He worked fast and had almost finished plotting out the mass groupings of the Polovtsian warriors, girls and boys and the Dance of the Captive Women at this first rehearsal. The company were so proud of him and were so full of hope and joy that they applauded their revolutionary choreographer.[73] The spirit that animated them at this time, whether they knew it or not, must have had something in common with student unrest and workers' rebellion. Change was in the air.

It was in the windowless auditorium of the Catherine Hall, where Diaghilev sometimes ordered meals to be brought in for the dancers and served from trestle tables,[74] that he was noticed to be friends with Nijinsky.[75]

The Théâtre du Châtelet, where the Russians were to perform, belonged to the City of Paris. It was a shabby old pile which specialized in melodrama. Children were taken there to see *The Adventures of Gavroche* or *Round the World in Eighty Days*. With a princely gesture, Diaghilev had asked Astruc to arrange for the redecoration of the whole theatre. Fontanes, the manager, had the proscenium arch and the six levels repainted, and the firm of Belsacq re-upholstered most of the seats. Walls, columns and floor were covered in red cloth. The boxes were draped with velvet. Nine rows of stalls were abolished to accommodate a larger orchestra.[76]

Where *was* the money coming from? Although presenting to the world a confident exterior, Diaghilev was inwardly faint with fear and doubt. Only one who has ventured on impossible gambles in the cause of art can sympathize with the solitude and depression which has to be undergone. But Diaghilev was proud – was he not descended on the wrong side of the blanket from Peter the Great? Well, he hoped he was. He did not show what he was going through: and that was half the battle. Benois described the 'happy atmosphere' in which he and the company worked.[77] Only when we read Diaghilev's surviving telegrams to Astruc can we trace the jittery graph of his heart's hesitations.

The Grand Duke Boris, on whom he had placed his hopes, did not dare to support him. Diaghilev felt at times that he had so many enemies that it was not safe for Astruc to associate his name with the publicity.[78] On 31 March, in reply to a cable from Astruc asking the size of the company, he telegraphed, 'A hundred walkers-on. Eighty singers. Seventy dancers. Thirty soloists.'[79] On 6 April, within a few hours of agreeing to the estimate of Fontanes and promising to send him an advance of five thousand francs the next day, he had decided that it would not be possible to give opera in Paris at all. He cabled, 'No opera this year. Bringing brilliant ballet company eighty strong, best soloists, 15 performances. Repertory can be enlarged if you think necessary to take series of bookings. We shall be able to give three ballets per programme. Have we the right to mount Adam's Giselle? Start big publicity....'[80] Astruc must have thought he was drunk; he refused to consider a season without opera. So the very next day Diaghilev asked whether it would be possible for Geraldine Farrar to sing Marguerite in Boito's *Mefistofele*.[81] This opera, though not Russian, would provide for Chaliapine the role in which he had made his name at La Scala in 1901. It was soon put out of mind.

Diaghilev began to suspect a hostile campaign in the French press, thought Astruc had not spent enough on publicity, grew abusive in his telegrams and authorized the spending of another three thousand francs. There was trouble in Russia over the author's rights of certain operas and Diaghilev pulled strings to have the question reviewed in the Duma and brought before the Imperial Council. And only on 27 April, when he decided to add two acts of Serov's opera *Judith* to the repertory, the orgy scene and the final hymn, with Litvinne, Chaliapine, Smirnov and Zbrueva, did the programme assume its final shape. On the twenty-eighth he informed Astruc that Emile Cooper as well as Nicolas Tcherepnine would be coming to conduct. A second telegram on the same day gave instructions for changes in the publicity circular. A third gave the insurance of *Judith*'s sets and costumes at fifteen thousand francs. The next day he cabled about the hire of a scene-painting studio; in a second cable he refused to allow Litvinne to take part in a concert arranged by a rival management; in a third he refused to consult 'a certain person' over the design of the poster.[82]

When the Mariinsky season ended on 1 May,[83] Pavlova was on tour: she would therefore join Diaghilev's company after the opening of the Paris season. Karsavina had to fulfil an engagement in Germany, so she did not travel with the company.[84] The rest of the dancers, under their 'General'

Bezobrazov, left St Petersburg on 2 May.[85] Like nearly all of his colleagues, Nijinsky, who had travelled all over Russia in his youth but had never been outside it before,[86] had a second-class ticket.[87] He was to receive 2,500 francs, as against Chaliapine's 55,000.

Diaghilev followed a day later. When Astruc met him at the Gare du Nord, he announced that he had arrived without a *sou* in his pockets, having spent all the Russian money on scenery and costumes. He said that he relied on Astruc to pay the company. The astonished Astruc replied that it would be dishonest and impossible for him to pay out money he had received in subscriptions and advance bookings, because, if the theatre caught fire or there was a strike, or if Chaliapine was ill, he would be obliged to refund it within twenty-four hours. 'In that case,' said Diaghilev, 'there can be no Russian season.'[88] Something had to be done, as he well knew: and, as usual, Astruc did it. Like the merchant of Venice – Antonio, not Shylock – he pledged his credit.

Most of the artists stayed in small hotels in the Boulevard St Michel, just across the river from the Châtelet.[89] Walking from his hotel to the theatre, Grigoriev could scarcely believe that his dream of seeing Paris had come true.[90]

If to most of the Russians Paris was synonymous with Paradise, to Karsavina, who arrived from Prague two days after the others had come from St Petersburg, 'Paris was a city of eternal pleasure, dissipation and sin.'

So exaggerated had been my ideas [she wrote] of its extreme elegance that in my heart of hearts I expected the streets to be like ballroom floors and to be peopled exclusively with smart ladies, walking along in a frou-frou of silk petticoats.... Above all I dreaded that I should be too provincial for Paris.... Soon after my arrival, I happened to pass down a back street. A little crowd of urchins interrupted their game to follow me. 'There it is,' I thought, 'They are laughing at me,' and I turned round to see if there were any witnesses of my humiliation. The grimacing urchins now raised a chorus, 'Elle est gentille parce-qu'elle est chic.' It was balm to me: Parisian *gamins* must have good taste, I thought.[91]

Karsavina stayed at the Hôtel Normandie in the rue de l'Echelle, off the Avenue de l'Opéra.[92] Diaghilev, Mavrine – and Nijinsky – were at the Hôtel de Hollande, in the rue de la Paix, nearby.[93]

Benois wrote, 'I was so infatuated with our Bohemian life that I preferred modest meals with our artists in the Quartier Latin.... Diaghilev's secretary Mavrine used to join us more and more often. He was extremely attracted by one of the most talented artists in the company....'

Three months before, when he was in Moscow with Diaghilev, Benois had been surprised one night, when the latter, during supper at the Metropole, had pointed out a woman leaning over the balcony of the upper floor

1 (*top*) Diaghilev listening to a concert by Wanda Landowska at the Hirschmann's house in Moscow, 7 March 1897. Pastel by Leonid Pasternak.

2 Alexandre Benois at home, St Petersburg, 1898. Pastel by Leon Bakst.

3 (*above*) Walter Nuvel, 1895.
Painting by Leon Bakst.

4 (*left*) Leon Bakst, c. 1890.
Watercolour by Valentin Serov.

5 (*opposite*) Diaghilev, 1902.
Painting by Philip Maliavine.

7 Vaslav Nijinsky in *Petrushka*, London, 1912. Photograph by Elliot and Fry.

6 (*opposite*) Nijinsky in a Monte Carlo hotel bedroom, probably 1913.
Photograph by Igor Stravinsky.

8 Anna Pavlova, St Petersburg, c. 1909.

9 Tamara Karsavina in *The Firebird*. Photograph by Bert.

10 (*above*) The
Marchioness of Ripon,
1911. Photograph by
Baron de Meyer.

11 Lady Juliet Duff in
fancy dress, c. 1914.
Photograph by Baron de
Meyer.

12 Tamara Karsavina. Drawing by Viktor Stretti. The original drawing was made before 1914, but the artist copied it into the owner's album in Prague in 1916.

as the *only* woman he could ever fall in love with. This was Olga Feodorova, sister of the more famous dancer Sophie. Benois did not take this seriously. (Karsavina and Misia would be among the other *only* women in Diaghilev's life.) But he was amused to see that the unique Olga was the woman now admired by Alexis Mavrine. 'Even before this happened,' wrote Benois, 'Diaghilev had quite openly deserted Mavrine, being more and more taken with Nijinsky.'[94]

From the time of their arrival, the Russians had just over a fortnight to rehearse. The building-up of Astruc's publicity campaign and a sense of mounting excitement aroused by the coming Russian season can be traced in the Paris newspapers, of which *Le Figaro*, for which Brussel wrote, was the most devoted. A preliminary announcement on Monday 3 May that *abonnés* could collect their tickets from the following Saturday[95] was followed by a lull. Sales of tickets were so good that on 10 May Astruc advertised extra performances.[96] On 11 May a picturesque article by Brussel appeared, describing a rehearsal:

We are at the Châtelet, in the feeble grey light of backstage. Scenery is being wheeled on, they are mending the stage, men are sawing and hammering. From far off one hears the little hammers of the upholsterers who are lining the auditorium with red cloth. In the midst of all this creaking wood and grinding metal, in this dim dusk without light or shade, there is still a brilliant focus – the Russian dancers.

The thin, highly-strung young man who looks like a fencing master in his cotton tunic is Michel Fokine, ballet-master and reformer of the Russian Ballet. This dark, slender girl with almond eyes and an ivory complexion, who evokes dreams of the gorgeous east, is Vera Karalli from Moscow. This blonde, so smart and supple in her movements, is Alexandra Baldina. That one in street clothes but with red boots, who is trying out a *Czardas* for *Le Festin* with Michel Mordkine, is Sophie Feodorova. This elusive, thoughtful beauty who seems wafted by infinite grace is Tamara Karsavina.... Among the men there is the extraordinary Nijinsky, a kind of modern Vestris, but whose dazzling technique is allied to a plastic feeling and a distinction of gesture which are certainly unequalled anywhere.

Fokine claps his hands, the talking stops, the dancers take up their positions. They are going to rehearse Tcherepnine's *Pavillon d'Armide*.... Fokine's sharp eye misses nothing. Watchful, stimulating, he restrains exaggerations, demonstrates, mimes, shows everyone his steps, darts from pianist to dancer and from dancer to pianist....

One by one, the dancers fade into the wings, and the stage is empty. Then they reappear, dressed for the street and talking, talking, talking. What are they talking about? About Paris, the big, terrifying, astounding and ravishing city! What have they seen so far? One has been to *Manon*, another has seen a famous monkey. One greedy girl has already been to some celebrated restaurants; another, more thoughtful, dreams of visiting Versailles.... All, as they talk, sketch out with their fingers the steps they will be dancing tomorrow.[97]

On Friday 14 May *Le Figaro* began a series of paragraphs on the dancers.[98] Benois noticed how Diaghilev was trying to attract publicity to Nijinsky, although Fokine and Mordkine were really the principal male dancers, and Bolm was the chief character dancer. 'My Paris friends used to say to me "Il paraît que vous avez parmi vos danseurs un prodige, un garçon formidable." Nobody asked anything about Pavlova, whose portraits were all over Paris, nor did anyone inquire in the same vein about Fokine.'[99] A delicate drawing of Pavlova by Serov, in charcoal and white chalk on grey-blue paper, had been enormously enlarged to become the first Russian ballet poster to appear on the walls of Paris.

It seemed impossible that everything should be ready in time. The opera company and the ballet company disputed for possession of the stage. 'Diaghilev arbitrated.' The vanquished side retired resentfully to a stifling studio under the roof – 'an atmosphere to breed salamanders in' was how Karsavina described it. There was no longer time to go out for meals. 'Our troupe remained at the theatre all day long,' wrote Karsavina. 'Diaghilev gave orders – roast fowls, pâtés, salads speedily arrived from a restaurant. Empty packing-cases made quite good tables. . . .'[100]

The Moscow orchestra arrived on 16 May, with little time left to work with the company before the *répétition générale* on the eighteenth.[101] On the very morning of that day another article, this time by Raoul Brevannes, was published in *Le Figaro*. We read about the forty thousand kilos of décors and properties, about the flock of sheep (French) with their shepherd (Russian), needed for *Le Pavillon d'Armide*. The orchestra was in full rehearsal, except for one oboist, who had got out at Smolensk, thinking it was Paris. Two hundred and fifty people were milling about the stage under the direction of the producer, Alexander Sanine. A carpenter's bench had become a buffet, with tea, coffee and *petits fours*. 'Near this an artist is sketching Karsavina from every angle. The gigantic Chaliapine and the delicate Nijinsky confront each other. Beyond them can be seen their chief-of-staff, Serge de Diaghilev, eager, subtle and courteous, who supports the whole enormous enterprise on his shoulders with weary fortitude.' Astruc, Calvocoressi, Nuvel, 'the propagandist of French music in Russia', Svetlov and 'certain elegant silhouettes from the banks of the Neva – old General X, Councillor Y, L'Adjutant-major Z . . . the 'daddies' of the ballet. . . . And tomorrow Paris will see, conjured up by magic, one of the finest spectacles with which it has ever been presented.'[102]

When the great night came, the transformation of the Châtelet into something as elegant as a hat-box from Reboux was one surprise. The composition of the audience was another. It was unusual to find representatives of so many worlds under one roof. The Russian Ambassador was a link between the official Republican circles of the Ministers of Finance, Education and Fine Arts and the Faubourg Saint-Germain, to which Comtesse

Greffulhe, Comtesse Adhéaume de Chevigné and Princesse Alexandre de Chimay belonged; and writers and composers such as Jean Richepin, George Cain, Léon and Lucien Daudet, Octave Mirbeau, Saint-Saëns, Lalo, Fauré and Ravel might not be out of place in the literary salons of Mme Madeleine Lemaire and Mme Bulteau, who were present: but there were also Rodin, Forain, Helleu, Blanche and the caricaturist Sem, besides the singers Litvinne, Farrar, Bréval, Cavalieri, Chaliapine and de Reszke, as well as the dressmakers Caron, Paquin and Doeillet, the actresses Cécile Sorel, Jane Marnac, Louise Balthy and Yvette Guilbert, the Directors of the Opéra, the Opéra Comique, the Comédie Française, the Metropolitan, New York, and the Boston Opera House.[103]

In addition, Astruc had had the novel idea of placing only pretty young women in the front row of the dress–circle. Blondes alternated with brunettes. These had been mainly recruited from among the actresses and dancers of the four subsidized theatres, but Isadora was also included. How they got on together without male company is not recorded, but the bower of beauty which they presented to the eye made such an impression that for ever afterwards *le balcon* (the dress–circle) was known as *la corbeille* (the flower basket). The front row of the upper circle was filled by dancers of the Opéra.[104]

With regard to *Le Pavillon d'Armide*, which opened the programme, Benois well knew that Paris had come to think of the rococo style as something sickly and sweet, in pastel colours, like (he pointed out) 'the production of *Manon* at the Opéra Comique'.[105] It suggested a Dresden shepherdess of the debased period or a tapestry screen with some faded pastoral.

Since its first version had been presented in St Petersburg, a quarter of an hour had been cut out of the ballet[106] and some numbers had been rearranged to form a new *pas de trois* for Karsavina, Baldina and Nijinsky.[107] Benois considered that he had greatly improved the sets and costumes, which had all been made anew. Although he insisted on the true rococo colours of Beauvais and of Sèvres porcelain, the apple-green, rose-pink, and turquoise blue, he had been worried before 'by the proximity of lilac, pink and yellow'. These defects he corrected.[108] The perspective of topiary in Armida's garden, leading to a baroque *tempietto* at the top of a splendid staircase, had previously been seen at an angle: it was now presented full-on, which enabled Valz to contrive 'two gigantic water pyramids'[109] (fed by the Seine) on either side. The *tempietto* was replaced by a larger, more distant palace. But this is all in the middle scene. The curtain has not risen on the first.

Silence falls – or what counts as silence in France – as Tcherepnine mounts his rostrum. Dark chords, played *pianissimo*, bring up the curtain on the dimly lit interior of a baroque pavilion. 'Tall windows with an ornate *oeil-de-boeuf* over each of them alternate with columns of polished marble, while the plaster modelling above the central niche of allegorical figures resting on clouds and supporting a sumptuous canopy adorned with feathers overhangs the magic Gobelins.'[110] In front of the latter stands a giant ormolu clock. with the figures of Time and Love, impersonated by dancers.

For all his devotion to the eighteenth century, Benois has read Hugo and Baudelaire, studied Géricault and Daumier, heard Berlioz and Debussy; he can no longer look through the unclouded spectacles of Voltaire. In this ballet, he was inspired by 'Omphale', a story by Hugo's friend, Théophile Gautier, and has imparted to his creation the mysterious atmosphere of the tales of E. T. A. Hoffmann.

When lanterns are seen through the windows of the pavilion, and lackeys open up the doors to admit the benighted Vicomte René in his caped over-coat, his tight buckskin breeches and lacquered boots, Parisians recognize that the action takes place at the beginning of their own Romantic period, in the time of Chateaubriand (another René), and that the bent old Marquis in his periwig, who conducts his young guest into the dusty pavilion, is a survivor from a former age. The expressive mime with which Bulgakov (the Marquis) points out to Mordkine (René) the representation in the Gobelins tapestry of his beautiful daughter, for whom three men took their lives, is something new to them.[111] (Benois thought Mordkine 'far too strong and vigorous for the part', lacking in 'poetical tenderness'.)[112] The host takes leave and René, by degrees, goes to bed in an alcove on the right. The coming to life of Time and Love (the clock) and the Dance of the Hours – twelve girls dressed as boys, who step forth at midnight to dance a clock-work *andantino* – are to give Mordkine time to change his clothes for the transformation scene. When René comes on in his dressing-gown, the Gobelins rolls up into its frame, revealing a group of living dancers, Armida surrounded by her courtiers, who form the same design. Karalli-Armida comes down from her frame, mourning the absent Rinaldo, then recognizes him in the astonished René. The latter's dressing-gown is whisked off down a trap and he stands in Louis XIV heroic 'Roman' costume, posing like a baroque statue.[113] The music swells, the architecture of the room flies away, and the sunlit garden scene is revealed.

It was in the landscapes of Fragonard and Hubert Robert that the rococo style verged on Romanticism, and it is these painters that Benois' natural arch of foliage, which frames the garden scene, recalls. But there is nothing in France quite like Benois' palace at the summit of the steps, circular behind its portico, like some Alp-girt fantasy of Juvara, rising above wavy woods and topped by the spire of Sakharov's Admiralty in St Petersburg. On the highest step at the back stands the old Marquis, in the guise of a Magician-king. As he waves his staff, the stage fills with dancers.

The *divertissement* performed in honour of the would-be Rinaldo, comprising a *valse noble*, an Oriental bacchanale and a comic number, is punctuated by processions crossing the stage and regroupings of the court to trumpet fanfares and solemn measures on the strings. The variety of these numbers is only less striking than the style with which they are performed. The Russians dance with such strength, grace and suppressed passion, that any comparison with the faded *coquetteries* of the Opéra is out of the question. Then comes the *pas de trois* of Karsavina, Baldina and Nijinsky, clad in orange, white, gold and silver. His costume, trimmed with festoons of silk, lace ruffles and ermine tails, is a simplified form of the male dancing costume of the eighteenth century, with a *tonnelet*, or wired skirt, over knee-breeches, and he wears a white silk turban with an ostrich feather. The conquest of Europe by Russian dancing and the reign of Diaghilev as Director of the Ballets Russes can be said to begin at the moment Nijinsky takes the stage with his two partners. The French who watch the trio rising and falling, beating and spinning, to a tune on the cor anglais, experience a new sensation. The temperature rises. When the dance ends, Nijinsky, instead of running after the two girls into the wings, decides on an impulse to jump off; and this is the first of many famous leaps which he times so cleverly that the public see him continually rising, but not beginning to come down.[114] A gasp from the whole audience[115] – followed by a volley of applause.[116]

Nijinsky comes on alone to dance his *variation*, and holds a pose, leaning forward with a faint smile, right arm directed towards an extended left toe.[117] His dance, to a commonplace, strongly marked tune, expresses nothing, yet he gives the impression, by the quality of 'aloofness' with which he performs difficult technical feats, that he is 'the hierophant of mysteries'.[118] A growing murmur in the audience alarms him, but at the end he is reassured by a thunder of cheering.[119] This is one of the moments Diaghilev has been waiting for. At the back of Misia's box, perhaps he feels that all the agony has been worth while.

Karsavina's tripping *allegro* forms a contrast: her dark, lustrous beauty seems the incarnation of Russia, and her mischievous smile wins all hearts. In one and a half minutes she has captivated Paris – a fortnight before the arrival of Pavlova.[120]

With the high-speed, grotesque Dance of the Buffoons, led by George Rosaï, Paris has its first experience of Russian character dancing. Fokine thinks this is the hardest dance he ever invented, and, indeed, the way the little men spin in a crouching position, crash to the ground and rise at once to catch at each other's feet in mid-air, is incredible.[121]

There follow Karalli's dance with the golden scarf, the waltz, the procession to mark Armida's union with René, the transformation back to the interior of the pavilion, the lovers' appearance in the frame of the Gobelins, the unrolling of the painted 'tapestry', the sun's rising with a clash of cymbals and bells, the dawn music, with the passing of the shepherd and his flock outside the windows – which enables Mordkine to change his clothes – the bustle of servants, the return of the old Marquis, René's realization that he is now the slave of the witch Armida, and his final swoon.

What more total contrast to *Le Pavillon d'Armide* than the third act of Borodin's *Prince Igor*? Roerich has designed an empty, desolate landscape, in which are pitched the beehive tents of the Polovtsi, and the smoke of their camp-fires rises against a tawny sky. The Parisian audience have the strange sensation of being transported to the ends of the earth. The act begins with dancing, continues with singing and concludes with both together. The passionate *cavatina* of Petrenko, as Khontchakovna, is followed by her duet with the tenor Smirnov, as Vladimir, Igor's son. Charonov, as Igor, laments his captivity. Then comes the bass Zaporojetz as the great Khan Khontchak[122] to engage with his noble prisoner in an heroic dialogue. When finally the Khan summons his tribesmen to entertain Igor, there surges on to the stage a horde 'ferocious of aspect, their faces smeared with soot and mud, their coats green and mottled red and ochre ... a lair of wild beasts rather than a camp of human beings'.[123] Then, after the languid dance of the captive women in their crimson and purple veils, there breaks out the frenzy of Fokine's Polovtsian dances, whose rhythms will excite half the world: the pounding charge of the warriors, led by Adolf Bolm, the frantic jigging of the boys, who strike their knees with wooden clappers, the dance of the spitfire girls, led by Sophie Feodorova – all this to the rising surge of the chorus, praising the Khan – to end, as Bolm, at the head of his warriors, charges at the audience, spins in the air and crashes to the ground, in a roaring crescendo.

Karsavina, in her costume for *Le Festin*, watches Bolm's 'unprecedented success' and sees from the wings the curtain rise and fall 'I don't know how many times'. Amid the crowds of breathless Polovtsian singers and dancers, she and Nijinsky are trying to practise and warm up, when 'the familiar barriers between the stage and the audience are broken. The side doors with their ingenious locks and stern notices – of no avail. The stage is so crowded with spectators that there is hardly room to move. To perform the usual rite of practising our steps and lifts before going on, Nijinsky and I have to dodge. Hundreds of eyes follow us about.... "He is a prodigy!" "C'est elle!"'[124]

Although Fokine's principles will not allow him to think that he has consented to something so old-fashioned as a *divertissement* being included in a programme supervised by himself, and he half pretends that *Le Festin*, with its traditional and modern choreography welded loosely into a whole, is a ballet,[125] this final work is really only an excuse for dancing, mostly to the most Russian of Russian music.

After the processional entry to the march from Rimsky's *Coq d'or* (now heard for the first time in public), and the Georgian *lesghinka* from Glinka's

Ruslan, adapted by Fokine from Petipa and danced by Vera Fokina with ten men, there follows the Blue Bird *pas de deux* from *The Sleeping Beauty*, disguised for some reason under the name 'L'Oiseau de feu'. This is danced by Karsavina and Nijinsky; and Petipa's arrangement gives an even more astonishing vision of classical virtuosity than did Fokine's for their numbers in *Le Pavillon d' Armide*. The traditional roles have been reversed. Karsavina is the bird, with a head-dress and skirt of orange and scarlet ostrich feathers, and Nijinsky, in a long gold tunic sewn with pearls and topaz, is her turbaned, capering prince. These are the first designs by Bakst to be seen in the West, and this is likewise the first fragment of the Tchaikovsky–Petipa masterpiece to be danced there. The company's courier will later describe the effect of this dance on the audience: '... when those two came on, good Lord! I have never seen such a public. You would have thought their seats were on fire.'[126] Karsavina balances and flutters, is raised on Nijinsky's shoulder and swept to the ground; Nijinsky goes through the repertory of brilliant steps, culminating in the *diagonale* of *cabrioles* and *brisés volés*. What are the thoughts of Fokine, who, though he upholds the classical school as the basis of theatrical dancing, despises virtuosity for its own sake? What does Isadora, who despises everything to do with the classical ballet, think? What do the Opéra dancers think? We can guess what Diaghilev is thinking.

Sophie Feodorova and Mordkine dance the Czardas from Glazunov's *Raimonda*; Olga Feodorova and Kremnev lead a gopak from Mussorgsky's *Fair at Sorotchinsk*; four couples dance the mazurka from Glinka's *A Life for the Tsar*; Rosaï scores again with his solo trepak to the Buffoons' Dance from *Casse-Noisette*; Karalli and Mordkine lead Petipa's Grand Pas Classique from *Raimonda*. All join in the finale to the last movement of Tchaikovsky's Second Symphony.

Once more the crowds flock back stage. Diaghilev edges his way through them, exclaiming, 'Where is she? I must embrace her.' Someone asks Nijinsky if it is easy to stay still in the air. Nijinsky, when he has understood the question, replies, 'No, no. Not difficult. You have to just go up and then pause a little up there.' Karsavina has cut herself on Nijinsky's jewelled tunic; her arm is bleeding. 'Somebody exquisitely dressed,' she will remember, 'staunched the blood trickling down my arm with a cobwebby handkerchief.'[127]

Next day, Wednesday, was fine and sunny. Critical notices had to wait until after the official *première*, but *Le Figaro* burst out, under the heading of 'Le Gala Russe', 'Quelle soirée, quelle salle, quelle assistance!'

Shall I ever find words to describe such a sight – from the panting, endless lines of motor-cars to the dazzle of diamonds reaching as far as the back row of the amphitheatre. Take the auditorium first: a magic hand has transformed it. These Russian gentlemen, accustomed to the grand gesture, have not hesitated to throw out six rows of stalls and all the folding seats. All this has the effect of making the huge hall of the Châtelet both larger and more intimate, with splendid hangings and velvet edged boxes. In fact, it is a new theatre.

Brevannes, the author of this piece, then took 126 lines to list some of the distinguished audience.[128] One name was not mentioned: that of an art student called Valentine Gross, who was never to miss a performance of the Russian Ballet for years, and who, from her seat in the gallery, began a series of 'automatic drawings' of Nijinsky and the other dancers in action, which constitute a precious documentation of those thousand and one nights.[129]

Thursday, 20 May, was Ascension Day and there was no performance. The notices appeared. In *Le Figaro* Brussel and his anonymous colleague, 'Un Monsieur de l'Orchestre', were allotted nearly three columns between them. Brussel noted that, apart from *Prince Igor*, it was not the music which made the evening so enjoyable. But he found that the Moscow orchestra, especially the brass, were excellent, and that the conductor, Cooper, was better still, bringing out all the character and passion of *Prince Igor*. He wrote of the Slav dancers' ability to live the music and of the integral part dancing plays in Russian life. He related Fokine to Petipa. He alluded to 'Mme Karsavina, whose subtle technique and marvellous sense of music are combined with expressive grace and poetic feeling, and whose success in [the Petipa *pas de deux*] *L'Oiseau de feu* stopped the show'. He praised Nijinsky's extraordinary technique.[130] The name of Vestris, Nijinsky's predecessor as 'God of the Dance', was much bandied by the other critics.[131] On Friday 21 May *Le Figaro* printed, across three columns, a drawing of Karsavina and Nijinsky in the Petipa *pas de deux*.[132]

In the next day or two there were two elopements which affected the history of the Russian Ballet. Karalli disappeared with the tenor Sobinov, and Mavrine ran off with Olga Feodorova. Sobinov was very good-looking, though already middle-aged – he was the most acclaimed Lensky in *Eugene Onegin* – but there is reason to believe that Karalli, the star from Moscow, was jealous of the success of Tamara Karsavina, of whom she had hardly heard before.[133] After all, one can have an affair with a tenor without breaking one's contract. The consequence was that Karsavina, whose beauty as well as her skill had made an enormous impression on Paris, became the company's star and danced the role of Armida on 25 May, six days before Pavlova arrived. Bolm was her René. Mavrine's disappearance with Olga Feodorova was more understandable, if perhaps just as impetuously romantic: for it was obviously awkward to continue as Diaghilev's confidential secretary while living with the 'one woman' who had ever attracted Diaghilev, and while Diaghilev had apparently found the love of his life in Nijinsky. This elopement, however, called forth Diaghilev's 'unbounded rage'.[134]

On Wednesday 26 May a letter from Astruc to the Editor was printed in *Le Figaro*:

You know what an enormous success the Russian season has been at the Châtelet and indeed you have often praised the artists and organizers in your columns. There is one man, whose modesty is excessive, but whose name I nevertheless wish to bring forward: I mean Serge de Diaghilev.

Let it be known, I beg you, that it was his brilliant initiative, his iron will and his remarkable understanding of the theatre which have made it possible for me to present the Paris public – and what a public – with these unique and unforgettable spectacles.

For a year he has laid the foundations of victory, marching forward, regardless of every obstacle, and I thank him for having associated me with one of the most beautiful phenomena ever to appear before the eyes of Paris.[135]

That night 'at nine o'clock sharp' the curtain rose on the first performance of *La Pskovitaine* (*The Maid of Pskov*, or *Ivan the Terrible*) to be heard outside Russia, and Chaliapine was seen by Paris in a second great role.

The Maid of Pskov was Rimsky's first opera, written in 1871, when the Five were at the peak of their enthusiasm to create a new Russian music. After a few initial performances at the Mariinsky in 1873, the opera had been twice revised; and the new version had its first performance only in 1898, when Mamontov staged it in Moscow, with Chaliapine. The composer had thought 'the highly talented Chaliapine's Tsar Ivan was a creation beyond compare'.[136] It was first produced (under Teliakovsky's directorate) at the Bolshoi Theatre in October 1901 and at the Mariinsky in October 1903.

The audience for the opera was as distinguished as that for the ballet, with the same representatives of every 'world', the same cascades of diamonds and the same (or a similar) *corbeille* of beautiful actresses and dancers, this time augmented by artists of the Russian Ballet, enjoying a night off. In spite of regulations, late arrivals pushed their way to their seats to the sound of sh'sh-ing.[137]

The great difference between Russian and French décors was noticed. 'While our designers strive for realism and *trompe l'oeil*, the Russian insist on "interpreting". They are Impressionists on a giant scale. Their skies are brushed in with sweeping broom-strokes, their clouds are made deliberately to look like heavy great dumplings, the pointed minarets of their palaces are splashed in without thought of detail or relief. These are huge sketches.'[138]

The entry of Chaliapine in the middle of Act II caused a sensation. 'Nothing could be more terrifying than the arrival on horseback, surrounded by his guards with raised sabres, amid a crowd of vanquished rebels, kneeling on the ground, of this ravaged, bilious Ivan, with his evil, suspicious eyes.

... In one instant we understand a whole reign, a whole epoch, a whole world.'[139]

The composer being dead, Brussel was able to write that it was impossible to compare Rimsky's talent with Mussorgsky's genius. At any rate, Diaghilev had done for the former what he had previously done for the latter – produced his work with care and piety. His choice of singers was praised: not only the extraordinary, unforgettable Chaliapine, but the Olga of Lipkovska, Petrenko's Nurse, Dumaev's Tutchka and the Tokmakov of Kastorsky.[140]

Even in St Petersburg, to hear Chaliapine had been a rare treat for Karsavina. 'Naturally,' she wrote, 'I was unwilling to miss a chance, and came often to hear him, now fortunate enough to get squeezed into the electrician's box, now standing in the wings. No matter how great the discomfort was, my admiration amounted to ecstasy before the divine artist.'[141]

With opera and ballet alternating, the singers and dancers had time to look around and enjoy themselves. Diaghilev took Nijinsky to the Louvre, and the new favourite, though insistent on his daily class, would be driven in the Bois by Bakst or Nuvel. After the performance Diaghilev usually entertained his committee of friends at Larue or Viel – Benois, Bakst, Roerich, Nuvel, Bezobrazov, Svetlov, Argutinsky – and Nijinsky began to appear at these gatherings, sitting silent while the older men planned new projects.[142] Among these was the ballet *Daphnis et Chloë*, on a scenario of Fokine, which Diaghilev commissioned from Maurice Ravel.[143] Apart from such functions as a party at the Quai d'Orsay, at which they performed Russian dances,[144] the company as a whole did not go out in society. Ida Rubinstein, Karsavina and Nijinsky were the only ones, besides Chaliapine, to do so. Robert de Montesquiou thought Rubinstein the most beautiful woman he had ever seen and carried her off to his Pavillon at Neuilly.[145] Everyone else was in love with Karsavina.[146]

Karsavina noticed that Diaghilev had become overnight a leader of the Paris homosexual set – 'and it rather went to his head'.[147] This set comprised, among others, Reynaldo Hahn, Lucien Daudet, Marcel Proust and the young Jean Cocteau. Because of Diaghilev's friendship with Nijinsky, and because the success of the ballet owed much to the new miracle of male dancing, there was something suspect about it.[148]

The décor and costume of Benois' ballet had been inspired by the tradition of Versailles, and Versailles rose like a mirage before the eyes of most Russian artists. They all wanted to go there. Karsavina wanted to go there and Dr Sergei Botkine took her, and it was in the Grove of Apollo that he taught her a lesson. Virtuous in spite of all her adorers, she had been worried about Diaghilev's homosexuality, which was something she had never known about before. Botkine said, 'It is a cruel misjudgement to give an ugly name to what is, after all, but a freak of nature'; and he gave her examples of homosexuals who had lived good lives. 'Botkine made me see that it was the quality of love that makes it beautiful, no matter who the object. The quality of Diaghilev's affections was single-hearted, true and deep, bury them as he would beneath his blasé mask.'[149]

Yet, in an electric atmosphere such as that which surrounded the Saison Russe, and in Paris, and in that sweet season between spring and summer, so conducive to love, a man's hovering affections may flit between two or three people, male or female, and the evening breeze may decide on whom they shall alight. Although Diaghilev was increasingly drawn towards the serious-minded Nijinsky – whose golden triumph had given him a glamour which made him more desirable than before, evoking the possibility of an ideal love which might give birth to masterpieces – he was also a little in love with Karsavina, whose intelligence appealed to him as well as her beauty. One sunny morning she was practising alone on the dark and empty stage when Diaghilev appeared and said, 'We are all living in the witchery of Armida's groves. The very air round the Russian season is intoxicated.'[150]

Eleonora Nijinsky had come to Paris to see her two children dance. Karsavina was touched to observe Vaslav go dutifully to kiss his mother and say 'Good-night'; and amused that Eleonora and Bronislava should leave quietly together while Vaslav went off to supper with Diaghilev.[151]

On 28 May a bold drawing of Chaliapine as Ivan appeared in *Le Figaro*: and on the same page the impending arrival of Pavlova was announced.[152]

The third Russian programme for 1909, which had its *répétition générale* on 2 June and its *première* on 4 June, comprised the first act of *Ruslan and Ludmila*, Fokine's ballet *Les Sylphides* and his *Cléopâtre*. If the operatic fragment was less startling than the act of *Prince Igor* which had been given previously, it had an incomparable cast of singers, and both ballets astonished the French; so that this programme was just as successful as the first. In fact, as Benois noted, *Cléopâtre* had the greatest single success of any work given that season – greater even than that of Chaliapine – and Diaghilev and Astruc began to give it even after the full-length *Maid of Pskov*.[153]

Ruslan and Ludmila, based by Glinka on an early fairy poem of Pushkin, was a difficult work to swallow for those slavophile French music-lovers who only savoured the strong Russian taste of Mussorgsky, Borodin and Rimsky-Korsakov. Just as they found nothing 'Russian' in Tchaikovsky, so they thought *Ruslan* reminiscent of Weber or purely Italian. It was an unequal opera, and Diaghilev had chosen to present, in the first act, the one with most unity. The French beheld, in Korovine's décor, a banquet held by Svietosar, Duke of Kiev, to welcome the suitors of his daughter Ludmila. Brussel thought Lipkovska sang ravishingly Ludmila's rather

insipid cantilena; praised the moving simplicity of the two tenor songs of
Bayan the bard; and thought particularly inspired the canon for four voices,
which, after the disappearance of Ludmila in a clap of thunder, 'rose
mysteriously out of the darkness to a calm murmur from the orchestra, a
meditation full of feeling which sprang directly from the tender gravity of
the musical thought'. Not for the first time praise was given to Avranek
(the chorus master), to the producer Sanine and to the conductor Cooper.[154]

Since Fokine's ballet had been renamed *Les Sylphides*, Diaghilev, who
could not leave a score alone, had ordered new orchestrations of Chopin's
piano pieces from Liadov, Glazunov, Taneyev and Sokolov, as well as
Stravinsky. Benois' Gothic ruin in a moonlit wood and his diaphanous white
dresses were in the spirit of the second act of *Giselle*, which Grisi had danced
in Paris nearly seventy years before. The painter had doubts about the get-
up he had designed for Nijinsky, with its black velvet *gilet*, floppy white
silk collar and sleeves, white tights and long curls: but, as so often happened,
Nijinsky's mysterious instinct told him how to wear the costume, so that it
became part of the choreography and seemed inevitable.[155]

At the *répétition générale* Svetlov noticed that 'the house was packed ...
and people were sitting on the steps of the balcony and in the aisles of the
stalls. Everyone was bursting with curiosity. When the curtain went up ...
the whole house gasped with admiration and surprise ... the dancers were
like blue pearls. . . .'[156]

Although the Chopin ballet was only a series of dances, it differed from the usual *divertissement* in that any show of virtuosity would have been out of place and broken the dream-like mood. Dance melted into dance and group into group, and all formal positions were removed from the *port de bras*, which became more windswept than geometrical. In spite of the absence of spectacular steps, the ballet was extremely hard to dance well, for strength and control were needed to hold poses and maintain a flow of movement.[157]

Between the rising of the curtain on the first group, in which Pavlova and Karsavina were seen leaning their heads on Nijinsky's shoulders, with Baldina and the corps reclining around them, and the dancers' resumption of this group at the end, the corps continually moved from one pattern to another, forming arches or festoons or clumps, standing, kneeling or reclining, hopping, dipping, curtseying and scooping the air with their arms, to frame the dances of the principals.

After the opening nocturne (Op. 32, No. 2), Karsavina performed her solo, the valse (Op. 70, No. 1), as Fokine thought, 'with rare romanticism',[158] leaping on to a tripping rhythm, running backwards, fluttering her arms, drifting, hand to lips, and making a spreading gesture, as if to part the curtains of the air. In her mazurka (Op. 33, No. 2), Pavlova appeared a creature too volatile to remain long in one place. Darting in and out, hopping, swooping, with trailing arms, she soon escaped to another part of the wood, and her companions waved to salute her transit. This first passing of Pavlova was to Paris a sensation as strange as first love to a boy, because, unlike the other wonderful Russians, she was not just a good-looking woman, but a transparent, weightless creature, all spirit, a fairy. To his slower mazurka (Op. 67, No. 3), Nijinsky crossed the stage diagonally in such languid jumps that he seemed to lie upon the breeze.[159] Then, as he knelt, brushing back a lock of hair with his left hand, he acknowledged with his right a distant summons and ran to answer it. The prelude previously played as the overture (Op. 28, No. 7), played again, was danced by Baldina, who sometimes leant forward with arms crossed on chest, or raised a hand to her lips, a pagan visionary awaiting her call. The *pas de deux* of Pavlova and Nijinsky, a valse (Op. 64, No. 2), was like the dance of a man with a butterfly. As he carried her on stage, lifted high in the air, it was as if she were flying off and he were trying to catch her. As she tripped ahead, he yearned. Lifting her, supporting her, turning her and kneeling to receive her on his shoulder was a kind of game. She ran backwards, as if drawn magnetically towards him, fluttered to and fro, paused and poised for a second, then flew off, with him after her, into the night. In the final 'Valse Brillante' (Op. 18, No. 1) the corps advanced and retired, the principals circled the stage, and the swinging music suddenly led back to the opening phrase as the first group was re-formed.

The erotic melodrama of *Cléopâtre*, a foretaste of Theda Bara in silent films, with its hotch-potch of music by six composers, sounds ridiculous to us today, but it bowled over the Paris audiences of 1909. The French saw their first Bakst décor, which was sensational. They heard weird music, they saw Pavlova, Karsavina, Fokine, Nijinsky and Feodorova all in the same ballet; and the cold, sadistic beauty of Ida Rubinstein gave them *un frisson nouveau*. Moreover, Fokine had arranged the production magnificently and created several incomparable dances.

Diaghilev had combined all these elements. We may think it no little achievement that he should even have presented Pavlova in a secondary role. Doubtless she was happy to show her dramatic side, after *Les Sylphides*. If Diaghilev was impervious to the ballet's absurdities, but only sure of its public appeal *at that moment of time* – and he grew heartily sick of it later – Benois, who had contributed several good ideas to the production, was not oblivious of them. Yet, as he wrote, '*Cléopâtre* brought the fullest houses.'[160] And the setting of Bakst, with its huge pink gods to left and right, framing a glimpse of the Nile between columns in the purple dusk, made so strong an impression that a new wave of exotic colouring, a new fashion in Oriental clothes and decoration, was launched from the moment the curtain rose.

A scene between Pavlova as Ta-Hor, one of the temple attendants, and Fokine as Amoun, a young nobleman out hunting, established their relationship. Heralded by a burst of triumphant music, the procession of Cleopatra advanced on to the stage. First the attendants opened a big sarcophagus to reveal a mummy-case, from which they lifted the bandaged body of the Queen. Her many-coloured veils were ritually unwound, then Rubinstein, with an imperious gesture, threw off the last to reveal her pale features, framed by a pale blue wig, bound with gold and jewels. (This entry was Benois' idea.)[161] Supporting herself with a hand on the head of her crouching slave, Nijinsky, she walked slowly to a couch and reclined, while fans began to wave. Amoun was captivated by the Queen, and after the Dance of the Temple Attendants, made his declaration – to be told that he might spend one night with her if he drank poison in the morning. Their lovemaking was hidden by the undulating draperies of Cleopatra's attendants; and the dancers of the *divertissment* conveyed in a variety of ways the languors and ecstasies of their bed. First Karsavina and Nijinsky, to the Turkish dance from *Ruslan*, performed a number with a scarf, which was flung billowing from side to side. There followed the Dance of the Jewish Women, led by Schollar. Glazunov's 'Autumn Bacchanale' was a wild number for two women pursued by satyrs. (The use of this music had been suggested by Benois, and he thought the dance Fokine had arranged was one of his finest inventions – 'a wonderful vision of the radiant beauty of the antique world'.)[162] Came the dawn, Fokine drained the poisoned cup, the Queen departed and Pavlova mourned frantically over the body of her dead lover.

A critic in *L'Intransigeant* deplored the fact that only one act each of *Prince Igor* and of *Ruslan* had been given by the Russians, and that they had had 'the Russian impudence' to orchestrate Chopin: but he wrote appreciatively of *Les Sylphides*, referring to Chalon's lithograph of Taglioni, and praised Rimsky's counter-chant of flutes and fifes which accompanied the sensational entry of Cleopatra. He had heard that Rubinstein acted tragedy in Russia (she certainly wanted to), and could well believe it from her noble attitudes. The Bacchanale was 'a dream of sensual bliss' ('un rêve de volupté').[163]

Felia Litvinne, who was a reigning queen of the Opéra, had sung Brunnhilde there on 2 June, and she sang *Judith* for Diaghilev, with Chaliapine, on 10 June. Thereafter, in all triple bills that included *Les Sylphides* and *Cléopâtre*, *Ruslan* was replaced by *Judith*, presumably because *Ruslan* had made little impact, and in order to show more of Chaliapine.

Karsavina thought that Pavlova had deliberately delayed her arrival until she knew how the Russian Ballet had been received in Paris:[164] once there, she remained till the end. But to be in at the beginning is half the battle, and Karsavina had stolen a march on her in the affection of the public. The season ended on Friday 18 June.

Shortly before the last night in Paris, Diaghilev, Nijinsky and Calvocoressi paid a lightning trip to London, to spy out the ground for a London season. Diaghilev had been offered an engagement 'in a big music-hall'. 'The Russian Ballet sandwiched between performing dogs and a fat lady playing a silver-plated trombone! Never! Never!' exclaimed Diaghilev, as they sat in the stalls. 'Nijinsky at his side nodded approval.' Calvocoressi added, 'After the war, however, the Russian Ballet was to appear on that very stage – but, I hasten to add, not thus sandwiched.' The music-hall must have been the Coliseum. 'Diaghilev decided to rent Drury Lane Theatre; and Collins, the lessee, met him readily. An agreement for the following year was arrived at, to come into force on the payment, within a fortnight, of a £500 earnest.'[165]

Diaghilev was hoping to have another Russian season at the Opéra in 1910, and, with this in mind, he readily agreed that his company should take part in a special gala performance at the 'Palais Garnier' on 19 June. The programme had been announced as two acts of *Boris* and the second act of *Giselle*,[166] but Nijinsky had never danced the principal role in *Giselle* before and the corps would have needed much rehearsal: this must have been why *Les Sylphides* and some numbers from *Le Festin* were substituted.[167] At a party after the gala – for which stalls and seats in boxes were sold at thirty francs each (the *abonnés* having the right to retain their seats at the normal price)[168] – Diaghilev made a speech, thanking the company, and a Minister bestowed the Palmes Académiques on Pavlova, Karsavina, Fokine, Nijinsky and Grigoriev.[169]

On the night of the Opéra gala, Nijinsky was suffering from a sore throat. He could not take part when *Les Sylphides* was danced at a party given by M. and Mme Ephrussi in the garden of their house in the Avenue du Bois on Sunday 20 June. Diaghilev had arranged that M. Ephrussi should pay Nijinsky a thousand francs and Karsavina five hundred. But, as stated, Nijinsky did not appear, and Astruc, who never stopped hinting to Karsavina in a pointed way that Mme Ephrussi was her 'fervent admirer', told her privately that the hostess wanted her to have a thousand francs too, which was an enormous sum for her in those days. (Dancers were always paid far more for dancing at parties than on the stage.)[170]

Dr Botkine examined Nijinsky, and diagnosed typhoid fever. Diaghilev took a small furnished flat, and, overcoming his terror of infection, looked after Vaslav himself.[171]

Diaghilev had been enjoying the triumph he had worked so hard to bring about. The success of the Russian season, his own pleasure in the performances and his love for Nijinsky had put all thoughts of money out of his mind. Yet, already on 15 June, the anxious Astruc had written to Diaghilev that takings so far were 405,000 francs (which made it possible to expect 500,000 or 510,000 by the end of the season in a few days' time), but that expenses would total 600,000. Astruc disclaimed all financial responsibility, but, as Diaghilev's sponsor in Paris, he felt a moral one, and asked how the bills were going to be paid.[172] When pressure from creditors had nearly prevented the Opéra gala from taking place, Astruc had again saved the situation.[173] Diaghilev told no one about the deficit: he may even have put off thinking about it. When, on 20 June, he gave Astruc a complete list of outstanding debts, it turned out that the sum to be found was 86,000 francs. One of the guarantors, who was under no obligation to hand over any money, since the average receipts per performance had exceeded 25,000 francs, generously paid up 10,000 francs: but Diaghilev's creditors were beginning to appeal to Astruc. Diaghilev was able (by borrowing, presumably) to pay off half his debt of 76,000 francs.[174]

It is not clear on what day the following account (shown opposite) was presented, but the relative costs are interesting.

Astruc seized Diaghilev's only tangible asset: the sets, costumes and properties of the Russian season. On these he secured a loan of 20,000 francs from Raoul Guinsbourg of the Société de Monaco, on the understanding that they would pass to the Casino Theatre at Monte Carlo if not redeemed by a certain date. An inventory was made of the 668 costumes and 12 decors (see opposite).[175]

Astruc also carried out a *saisie foraine*, an official seizure of Diaghilev's possessions at the Hôtel de Hollande, as Belsacq, the upholsterer, had already done. He then set about making Diaghilev bankrupt at the Tribunal de Commerce de la Seine. Astruc agreed to be paid last, after the other

Payments for 1909 season

Assistance public [a tax for the poor]	50,000
Authors' rights	25,000
Chaliapine	55,000
Other principal singers	100,000
Ballet soloists	40,000
Corps de ballet	60,000
Chorus	55,000
Orchestra	60,000
Châtelet rent	65,000
Stage staff, lighting	25,000
Publicity (Press and posters)	30,000
Direction, administration	15,000
Various tradesmen	10,000
TOTAL	590,000
Receipts	522,000
Deficit	68,000
Already repaid	30,000
Remaining deficit	38,000

creditors, and Diaghilev signed a bill undertaking to reimburse him his 15,000 francs within ninety days – that is to say, on 7 October.[176]

Karsavina had signed a contract to appear in music-hall at the London Coliseum. She had received many offers, including some from Australia and the United States, but had chosen England because she loved Dickens.[177]

Diaghilev could not find £500 as a down payment in earnest of his visit to Drury Lane, and so hopes of a London season in 1910 vanished.[178]

There was to be another gala at the Opéra on 26 June 1909 in aid of victims of an earthquake in Southern France. Pavlova stayed on in Paris to dance a Russian character dance with Mordkine. A rich programme included Chaliapine, Rousselière, Marguerite Carré, Smirnov, Lipkovska, Litvinne, Bréval and Cavalieri, the farandole from Bizet's *L'Arlésienne* danced by Kchessinskaya with the French corps de ballet, and the finale of *Faust* sung by the Opéra chorus.[179]

In the number of *La Vie Parisienne* for 3 July 1909, the writer of a column called 'On dit ... on dit ...' teased Kchessinskaya, whom he designated as 'Mlle Ktch ... ka,' for postponing her departure from Paris in order to dance for charity in the Opéra gala.

What a splendid character ... her goodness is infinite! ... It is true that most of us were unaware that she was here at all. We had even heard that she had done everything in her power to prevent the glorious Russian Ballet coming to Paris. ... A month before the troupe were due to leave Russia the whole enterprise nearly fell through. The Tsar withdrew his subsidy. The Ministry went back on its promise to lend sets and costumes. The Imperial Theatres refused the use of their stages for rehearsals. And all this havoc was the work of the dear good little Ktch ... ka, who had not been implored to lead the Russian expedition as its star. You have no idea what weight this young lady's *tutu* carries at court. And what an odd use of the word 'postponed' which she has had printed in all the unsuspecting newspapers! One would have thought that Mlle Ktch ... ka had taken part in the Châtelet season. The truth is that she came to Paris just to see the end of it – at her own expense. In ballet, it is fatal not to be in time![180]

Calvocoressi, without making a fuss about it, was 'particularly annoyed' with Diaghilev 'for having disregarded the repeated warnings' he had given him. How these warnings might have averted financial disaster is not clear.

I told him that I would never work for him again. We did not part bad friends: there was no reason to. But in my mind it was a parting for good and all. He thought so too. Not long before, he had said to me: 'You are a funny chap, Calvo. With some people one quarrels, and then makes it up again. But with you it is different.' 'It is,' I retorted. But this was not a quarrel. I simply was 'sick of it all' as he had been at the end of the 1907 season. And, as it happens, I did change my mind in that matter a few months later.[181]

While he was kept in Paris nursing Nijinsky and facing his financial problems, Diaghilev planned for the future. He had already commissioned *Daphnis et Chloë* from Ravel.[182] At Calvocoressi's suggestion he asked Gabriel Fauré for a ballet, but the latter was hard at work on his opera *Pénélope*, and put him off.[183] Next he got discussions going between Jean Cocteau and Reynaldo Hahn, which resulted in work being started on *Le Dieu bleu* in the following year. The critic Louis Laloy fancied himself as a librettist and proposed that he and his friend Debussy should work out a ballet together. Diaghilev was entirely in favour of this. It is wonderful to find Diaghilev, who was to all intents and purposes *bankrupt*, dreaming of great projects for the future.

Diaghilev, Nijinsky and Bakst spent some days at Carlsbad, where their hotel, the Villa Schöffler, stood on a hill amid pine forests next to the Russian church;[184] but Diaghilev had business in Paris in the second half of July, so Bakst took Nijinsky on to Venice without him.

On 19 July Diaghilev was writing to Astruc from the Hôtel de Hollande, asking for the return of all the musical scores.[185] During the next few days he had talks with Debussy without Laloy being present, which caused some indignation, but the ballet *Masques et Bergamasques*, which Debussy hoped to compose for him, never saw the light of day. Other collaborations between the two men would be more fruitful.[186]

On 6 August Diaghilev wrote to Astruc from the Hôtel de Hollande, asking for the return of Serov's original sketch for the Pavlova poster, which belonged to Dr Botkine.[187] After this he presumably left hot-foot for Venice. The friends stayed at the Grand Hôtel des Bains de Mer on the Lido.

Diaghilev and Bakst took Vaslav to the Accademia, the Scuola di San Rocco and the churches. D'Annunzio, Isadora and the flamboyant Marchesa Casati were in Venice to amuse them,[188] and Bakst painted a big oil sketch of Nijinsky, standing on the beach against the blue lagoon.[189]

Diaghilev and Nijinsky were in Paris again on 19 August,[190] on their way back to St Petersburg. The Mariinsky season would begin on 1 September, and Vaslav had to start practising. Because of his Paris debts, which were known about in the Russian capital, Diaghilev's return was not entirely triumphant.

He had made a serious mistake in concealing from Astruc his negotiations with the Opéra. He may have done this out of fear of a scene, or out of cunning, hoping to dispense with Astruc's services – which, indeed, if he continued to deal direct with Broussan and Messager, would have been possible, if unwise – but he had not allowed for the violence of Astruc's wrath or weighed the consequences of his revenge. Diaghilev was not only being ungrateful – for Astruc had made the 1909 season possible (even if he did seize the scenery and Diaghilev's luggage after it) – but short-sighted. For Astruc was planning a season of Italian opera, with Toscanini, Caruso and the Metropolitan Opera, at the Châtelet in the following June; and, if he were not to clash with the subscribers' days at the Opéra, he would have to give his performances on Tuesdays, Thursdays and Saturdays, which would be the days, naturally, when Diaghilev's troupe had the Opéra stage. This would be fierce competition; and Astruc set out to make it impossible for Diaghilev ever to bring artists of the Imperial Theatres to Paris again.

Astruc's first step was to try to detach Chaliapine. On 10 October 1909 he wrote to the singer, in reply to a terse telegram, that he expected fuller explanations of Chaliapine's plans than had been proffered, and he thought friendship alone would have prompted this.[191] Astruc next attacked Diaghilev through the Russian Court, and his report covered nearly eleven pages of foolscap and unfolded the story of his dealings with Diaghilev as related above. Astruc pointed out that he had secured a reduction of 50 per cent. for Diaghilev with the Société des Auteurs et Compositeurs Dramatiques de Paris, thus saving Diaghilev 25,000 francs, and that he himself had agreed to take the small percentage of $2\frac{1}{2}$ per cent. Accusing Diaghilev of fulfilling none of his undertakings, he observed that on every document Diaghilev had subscribed himself 'Attaché à la Chancellerie Personnelle de Sa Majesté l'Empereur de Russie'.[192]

Of course, Astruc was right to blame Diaghilev for incurring debts which he had no assurance of being able to pay. The only thing that can be said on Diaghilev's behalf is that, had he paused to consider at a given moment whether it was *right* or *wrong* to take a certain risk, there would have been no Russian season. Even the redecoration of the theatre was one means of *making sure* of success. Thus works of art are sometimes built on immoral foundations.

Astruc even inserted some scandal:

One morning when he was on the point of handing over a sum of 10,000 francs to Diaghilev's 'accredited representative' M. Astruc received a letter marked 'urgent and personal' which read as follows: 'Dear friend. Please do not on any account pay money to *any single one* of my secretaries *without a card from me for each payment* ...' M. Astruc, alarmed at this sudden indication of mistrust, asked for an explanation but failed to receive one. However, he heard a few days later that the confidential associate and *very intimate friend* who acted as accountant and who was trusted with delivery of monies had left Paris suddenly on the very evening the famous letter was sent – a fact which could lead to all kinds of suppositions.[193]

This reference is, of course, to the elopement of Mavrine, whom Astruc knew to have been Diaghilev's lover up to his replacement by Nijinsky. The impresario, who had not hesitated to urge Karsavina to encourage her fervent admirer Mme Ephrussi, was not above using Diaghilev's homosexuality as a weapon against him when business was at stake. And it is curious that Astruc, who was to collaborate so closely and so successfully with Diaghilev for several years to come, should have been responsible in the course of this winter 1909–10 for damaging his reputation at the Imperial Court once and for all. It was conceivable that although the Emperor distrusted Diaghilev, and although none of the Grand Dukes felt the same friendship for him as had the late Grand Duke Vladimir, and although since her husband's death the Grand Duchess Marie Pavlovna had been influenced against him, Diaghilev might still, as a result of the glory his Paris season had brought to Russia, have received subsidies from the Imperial purse. Astruc helped to make this impossible.

However, admirers of Diaghilev and of the Russian Ballet interceded. In the middle of December Diaghilev went to Paris, and through the good offices of the Comtesse de Béarn, Marquise de Ganay, Comtesse Adhéaume de Chevigné and Misia Edwards he and Astruc were brought together to discuss their differences. Sert and Robert Brussel were present at these meetings, and in a letter to Brussel dated 23 December Astruc summed up his conclusions.

Astruc agreed to change the days of his opera performances at the Châtelet, providing that (1) Diaghilev guaranteed him the collaboration of Chaliapine [in the Metroplitan Opera Season] for three performances of Boito's *Mefistofele* and three of *Il Barbiere di Siviglia* between 19 May and 25 June 1910; (2) the administration, box-office and publicity of the next Russian season were entrusted to Astruc, who would receive 5 per cent. of the gross takings of every performance, payable nightly, plus 25 per cent. of the total profits, if any; (3) Diaghilev paid him 24,711 francs still owing, plus costs and interest, that very day; (4) Messrs Astruc were to nominate the Paris representatives of the Paris season and Diaghilev was to pay them.[194]

So Diaghilev and Astruc were friends again: their collaboration was necessary for the Russian Ballet to fulfil its destiny.

Much seemed to depend on Chaliapine. On 5 January 1910 Astruc sent Robert Brussel to Russia to talk to him and to ensure his co-operation; and, knowing the Russian censor opened letters, he established a code for communicating with Brussel and his other contacts in St Petersburg. In this code Astruc gave himself the name *'Chrysale'*, which was that of the honest *bourgeois* in Molière's *Les Femmes Savantes*, Pavlova was *'Amour'*, Karsavina *'Raison'*, and Diaghilev was *'Chemineau'*, the French word for a tramp. Chaliapine, however, refused all offers.[195] He would not sing in Paris in 1910. This did not, however, prove fatal to Astruc's and Diaghilev's treaty of peace. Astruc was glad to show that his skill and resources were so great that he could make a success both of the Italian and Russian seasons, running concurrently.

There would, as it turned out, be no opera in the Russian season of 1910. That Diaghilev should stage a season of ballet alone was largely due to the fact that Chaliapine refused to come: without him, it was too risky to transport a large company of singers and several cumbersome opera productions. Nor would Diaghilev ever take a Russian orchestra abroad again.

CHAPTER 9

1910

Stravinsky's *Firebird*, a New Kind of Ballet – At the
Opéra without Opera – The Revelation of Bakst

URING THE WINTER of 1908–9 Diaghilev had merely confronted
the problem of raising money to subsidize his season in the West:
during the winter of 1909–10 he had not only to raise money for
the forthcoming season, but also to pay off the debts of the old. The bad
marks he had earned for his financial failure counted for more in Court
circles than the good marks for his artistic success. And *was* it such an artistic
success, the diehards may have asked themselves? The effete French could
be taken in by any decadent rubbish! Diaghilev saw enemies on every side.

It would have been easy to throw in the sponge and retire from the ring:
but Diaghilev had incentives to continue his work. To name but three –
Nijinsky, Ravel, Stravinsky. Nijinsky had had no predominant role in any
of the 1909 ballets – even in *Les Sylphides* he was only one of four principals,
and his striking appearances in *Le Pavillon* and *Cléopâtre* had been subsidiary. Diaghilev longed to create great opportunities for him. He also longed
to initiate new works of art, to draw miraculous new scores out of Ravel,
Stravinsky and, if possible, Debussy. It is probable, besides, that Diaghilev
was eager to put on Rimsky's *Coq d'or* in Paris, not to mention his *The City
of Kitej* and *Sadko* and Mussorgsky's *Khovanshchina*. So long as the Russian
Establishment, Duma or no Duma, remained rigid as a gilded iconostasis,
his stage was bound to be Paris.

Benois, Diaghilev's first mentor in the ballet field – and who thought that
his *Armide* had been the chief reason for showing Russian ballet to Paris
– was now great friends with Fokine and insisted that 'there could be no
talk of opera'.[1] Nuvel, obviously, would take the opposite point of view.
Diaghilev was determined to present both opera and ballet. In his Black
Notebook we have his list of projects and dancers, his accounts, his estimates
and his ideas for programmes.[2] The operas *Khovanshchina* and *Sadko*, as
well as *Boris* and *The Maid of Pskov*, occur along with names of ballets under

consideration. *The Firebird* and a *divertissement* called *Etudes*, which later became *Les Orientales*, were among the first ballets mentioned.[3]

From the time of their first talks in Zamiatin Pereulok a year before, Benois had considered it desirable to show Paris a Russian folk ballet, a fairy story more magical and less childish than the Mariinsky's *Little Humpbacked Horse*.[4] Many people had a hand in what eventually became *The Firebird*.[5] Fokine read through Afanasiev's collection of folk tales and began to combine elements of several.[6] Benois thought the basis of the story was provided by the young poet Potemkin[7] – with whom Nuvel was hopelessly in love:[8] 'The working out of these elements was undertaken by a sort of conference in which Tcherepnine (who was supposed to be writing the music), Fokine, the painters Steletzky, Golovine and I took part. Our excellent writer Remisov, who was not only a great crank but a great lover of all things Russian, was carried away by our idea.'[9] Remisov at least contributed to the court of the evil magician the Bellyboshkies – 'evil sort of creatures, some with tails and some without'.[10] Fokine, who was eventually credited with the scenario, as usual thought he had written it single-handed: 'We met very often, during the evening hours, at the home of Alexandre Benois for tea. During some of these tea-drinking sessions, I narrated the story of the Firebird. Every time some artist visitor appeared who was not familiar with the new ballet, I had to repeat the libretto ... and I would describe the ballet and be carried away by my own fantasy. With each description I added new details. ...'[11] Grigoriev too may have a claim to co-authorship, even if he only borrowed the books of Afanasiev for Fokine, for he wrote many years later, 'I obtained several collections of Russian fairy tales; and between us we evolved a story by piecing together the more interesting parts of several versions. This took us about a fortnight.'[12] Eventually, Benois describes, Tcherepnine, 'who was prone to inexplicable changes of mood, and whose attitude was in those days cooling towards ballet in general', lost interest.[13]

Impervious to these tea-parties, Diaghilev had already written from Venice to his old professor of harmony, the composer Liadov: 'I want a ballet and a *Russian* one; there has never been such a ballet before. It is imperative that I present one in May 1910 in the Paris Opéra and at Drury Lane in London. We all consider you now as our leading composer with the freshest and most interesting talent.'[14] When Diaghilev accepted Fokine's scenario in the autumn of 1909, it was agreed that Liadov should be invited to compose the score. But Liadov was a slow worker, and after a few weeks had done little but buy the music paper.[15] Diaghilev must have anticipated this, for he had meanwhile discussed the new fairy-tale ballet with young Stravinsky. Liadov was persuaded to relinquish the commission; and when, in December, Diaghilev rang up Stravinsky to tell him he was to compose *The Firebird*, Stravinsky admitted that he had already begun it.[16] He would finish the composition in March, and the orchestration a month later: the complete work (apart from a few retouchings) would be posted to Paris in mid-April.[17] Stravinsky wrote, 'Fokine is usually credited as the librettist of *The Firebird*, but I remember that all of us, and especially Bakst, who was Diaghilev's principal adviser, contributed ideas to the plan of the scenario.'[18] He was not attracted by the subject of the ballet, and disliked the idea of producing 'imitation Rimsky-Korsakov' music,[19] though, of course, glad to have his first big commission. It was taken for granted by all the collaborators that Pavlova the birdlike would dance the Firebird.[20]

Fokine had intended that Prince Ivan, the hero of *The Firebird*, should bewitch the magician and his retainers, with a magic *guzli* (a kind of zither or psaltery), and make them dance till they fell exhausted, but because Diaghilev was hoping to take *Sadko* to Paris, and it was with a *guzli* that Sadko charmed the inhabitants of the Kingdom of the Sea, Fokine was persuaded to substitute a feather from the Firebird's breast as the instrument to subdue Kastchei's court of evil spirits.[21] Stravinsky urged a more fundamental change in the libretto. Fokine wrote, 'Yielding to the wish of Igor Stravinsky, I agreed to substitute a coronation for the gay processional dances with which I had wanted to end the ballet.'[22]

In the old days, music for ballet had been ordered by the choreographer from the composer bar by bar. For instance, when Petipa worked with Tchaikovsky on *The Sleeping Beauty*, he had given him specifications such as the following:

No. 14. Suddenly Aurora notices the old woman who beats on her knitting needles a $\frac{2}{4}$ measure. Gradually she changes to a very melodious waltz in $\frac{3}{4}$, but then suddenly a rest. Aurora pricks her finger. Screams, pain. Blood streams, give 8 measures in $\frac{4}{4}$, wide. She begins her dance, – dizziness. ... Complete horror – this is not a dance any longer. It is frenzy. As if bitten by a tarantula she keeps turning and then falls unexpectedly, out of breath. This must last from 24 to 32 measures.[23]

Fokine's pioneering notions did not prevent him from trying to work in a similar dictatorial way; and *The Firebird* has been quoted as an example of close collaboration between composer and choreographer.

Stravinsky played, and I interpreted the role of the Tsarevitch, the piano substituting for the wall. ... Stravinsky, watching, accompanied me with patches of the Tsarevitch melodies, playing mysterious tremolos as background to depict the garden of the sinister immortal Kastchei. Later on I played the role of the Tsarevna and hesitantly took the golden apple.... Then I became Kastchei, his evil entourage – and so on. All this found most colourful interpretation in the sounds that came from the piano, flowing freely from the fingers of Stravinsky. ...[24]

It seems hardly probable that Stravinsky improvised an accompaniment to Fokine's miming, then went and wrote it down. Nevertheless, Stravinsky recorded, 'I like exact requirements. ... In spite of his wearying homiletics, repeated at each meeting ... Fokine taught me much, and I have worked with choreographers in the same way ever since.'[25]

Tamara Karsavina had returned from London with a new contract for appearances at the Coliseum in her pocket. She had been a great success and Oswald Stoll wanted her back. Diaghilev had not warned her that he was planning another Paris season in 1910. 'Great was the annoyance of Diaghilev when he heard this,' wrote Karsavina.

Mutual recriminations began; he reproached me with not having kept myself free for him; I retorted that he should have warned me of his plans. The anguish was great on both sides. I would have willingly given up the material benefits of the London engagement not to miss anything of the Paris season; but I was bound by my signature. In Diaghilev's agreement with the Opéra my name had been stipulated. ... In pursuance of the common cause we left off reproaches and started devising means how to get out of the difficulty. Frantic telegrams, many of them, I sent to Marinelli. The same answer came – there can be no question of shifting the Coliseum dates. ... I bore a very considerable part of the Mariinsky repertoire, rehearsed new parts for the spring, and was being literally tormented by Diaghilev. I dreaded the telephone, as it was not easy to resist Diaghilev's pressure. He would wear out his opponent, not by the logic of his arguments, but by sheer stress of his own will. ...[26]

Giselle had been one of the first ballets Diaghilev had thought of bringing to Paris.[27] He must have been in some doubts whether this old ballet, with a score by Adolphe Adam, first given in Paris in 1841, had a place in his modern repertory. *And yet*, it was Pavlova's greatest role and brought out *all* her extraordinary qualities. With Diaghilev, a real man of the theatre, this was a deciding factor. He would probably have revived Adam's opera *Le Postillon de Longjumeau* if he thought it had a perfect part for the tenor Smirnov. So he allowed Benois to persuade him, and was half-prepared to be persuaded, that *Giselle* must be shown in Paris. Benois pointed out that in taking *Giselle* to Paris they would be paying a compliment to France. (He was certainly earning his *Légion d'honneur* in retrospect. Who cared about compliments to France?) Bezobrazov and Svetlov were all in favour. 'Diaghilev made a face and said "Shura is quite right, of course. But *Giselle* is too well known in Paris. ...' (This was untrue. It had not been given since 1868.) He thought it would not be likely to interest the public. (Here he proved quite correct.)[28]

It must have been late in January or at the beginning of February 1910 that Pavlova told Diaghilev she could not take part in the Paris season as she had signed a contract with Alfred Butt to appear at the Palace Theatre, London, in April.[29] (In any case, she disliked what she heard of Stravinsky's music.) To lose your star in this way is a knock-out blow. I suggest this approximate date because it was on 10 February that Diaghilev cabled

Astruc, 'All well here. Giselle replaced by short version La Belle au bois dormant with Kchessinskaya.' *The Sleeping Beauty* had the best score of any of the old ballets, and Aurora was one of Kchessinskaya's roles. But this plan fell through. On a page of the Black Notebook, evidently about this time, he crossed out 'Pavlova' and wrote the name of the Moscow ballerina Gelzer in its place.[30] If Diaghilev could not count on Pavlova, Karsavina or Kchessinskaya, how could he fulfil his contract with the Opéra? Nijinsky begged to be allowed to dance the Firebird. When Diaghilev protested that it was for a dancer on points, he argued that he could dance very well on his toes.[31] (He did, in fact, perform exercises *sur les pointes*.) But Diaghilev knew where to draw the line. Despairingly, he pinned his hopes on the most malleable of the three ballerinas, who also happened to be the most intelligent and to have the nicest character. Karsavina *must* be released by the London music-hall (where he had seen performing dogs and a fat lady playing a silver-plated trombone), so that she could dance the Firebird and possibly Giselle in Paris.

Sadko was not the only work of Rimsky's that Diaghilev had in mind: there was also the symphonic poem *Schéhérazade*. Benois had loved this composition for many years, though he was ignorant of the very sketchy programme on which the composer had based it. He always associated the turbulent fourth movement, which Rimsky called 'Festival at Baghdad: the Sea', with 'the voluptuaries of the harem and their cruel punishment'.[32] (His mind rather ran on harems, as drawings in *The World of Art* bore witness.) From the beginning, it was agreed that Bakst should design the scenery and costumes.[33]

The authorship of *Schéhérazade* was as disputed in later years as that of *The Firebird*. Benois had been hurt during the first Paris season at being given no credit as part-author of *Cléopâtre*. Now, as the scenario of *Schéhérazade* came to him, he wrote down his ideas on the score itself. 'I did this solely to help my memory. One evening, however, as Argutinsky and I were returning home from one of these creative evenings I said to him half-jokingly: "This time my notes are in black and white, which will guarantee that this work will be considered *mine*."'[34]

Schéhérazade had become the subject of general discussion among the friends by the time Fokine was told about it, and the choreographer thought it had been conceived by Bakst.[35] Some astonishment was caused when Diaghilev announced that the third movement must be cut: but when he and Nuvel had played it over on the piano it was agreed that its long, meditative passages would hold up the action.[36] The first movement was to be played twice: initially as an overture, then as the first part of the ballet. Bakst wanted the unfaithful wives to be sewn in sacks and thrown into the sea, but Fokine was not alone in thinking sacks a restriction to choreography. 'A mass slaughter of lovers and faithless wives in front of the spectators presented a much more enthralling problem for me.' This was agreed on.[37] Ida Rubinstein would be the Sultana Zobeïda; Bulgakov, who had been an impressive Marquis in *Le Pavillon*, would mime the Shah; and Nijinsky would be the Negro slave who was the Sultana's lover. Nuvel said to Diaghilev, 'How odd it is that Nijinsky should always be the *slave* in your ballets – in *Le Pavillon d'Armide*, in *Cléopâtre* and now again in *Schéhérazade*! I hope one day you'll emancipate him.'[38]

Six months before his death in 1908, Rimsky-Korsakov had written of Isadora Duncan, 'What I dislike about her is that she connects her art with musical compositions dear to me. ... How vexed I should be if I learned that Miss Duncan danced and mimed to my *Schéhérazade*. ...[39] When we consider, looking ahead, what shocks Debussy and Stravinsky would sustain when they saw dancing to the accompaniment of scores actually commissioned for ballet, it seems inconceivable that Rimsky could have been pleased with what happened to his *Schéhérazade*. When Fokine, taking his cue from Isadora, had arranged dances to Chopin, he was breaking fresh ground. But *Les Sylphides* had no story. By imposing a passionate drama on an elaborate symphonic composition complete in itself, Fokine and his collaborators were going much further – committing a different kind of outrage. This bending of music to serve an action for which it was not intended would become a common practice in the next half century.

In Rimsky's autobiography we read,

The programme I had been guided by in composing *Schéhérazade* consisted of separate, unconnected episodes and pictures from *The Arabian Nights*, scattered through all four movements of my suite: the sea and Sinbad's ship, the fantastic narrative of Prince Kalender, the Prince and the Princess, the Baghdad festival and the ship dashing against the rock with the bronze rider on it. ... The final conclusion of Movement IV serves the same artistic purpose. In vain do people seek in my suite leading motives linked consistently with ever the same poetic ideas and conceptions. ...[40]

Leaving, for a moment, the creation of a new repertoire, let us follow, in Diaghilev's correspondence with Astruc, a chart of his hopes and fears. After (as I believe) Pavlova had announced her London engagement on, or just before, 1 February, Diaghilev, reluctant to break the news to Astruc, had sought to please him by cabling the offer of three performances of the popular *Cléopâtre* at the Châtelet during the Metropolitan Opera season, for 50,000 francs.[41] On 8 February Astruc replied implacably – perhaps he smelt a rat – that he would pay 45,000 francs for three performances, comprising *Les Sylphides*, *Cléopâtre* and *Le Festin*, provided that Kchessinskaya, Pavlova, Karsavina, Rubinstein, Nijinsky and Fokine all appeared, and provided that these three works were exclusive to him and not performed at the Opéra.[42] Impossible conditions: for Diaghilev could not relinquish half his repertoire for the Opéra season, he could not produce Pavlova, he had come to no arrangement with Kchessinskaya, and he might not be able to induce Karsavina to break her London contract. On 10 February, as we have seen, Diaghilev, hopeful of Kchessinskaya's collaboration, had cabled that he was substituting *The Sleeping Beauty* for *Giselle*.[43] On 11 February he cabled bravely, 'Everything else is going all right.'[44] This was an exaggeration. On that same day, one of Astruc's contacts in St Petersburg wrote to Astruc about the possibility of getting him a Russian decoration (Brussel had just received one), and mentioned that Diaghilev was totally failing to raise money in St Petersburg, that Kchessinskaya had refused to appear, that the Grand Duchess Marie Pavlovna (Vladimir) had withdrawn her patronage because of all the scandals surrounding Diaghilev's name, and that the Paris season could not possibly take place.[45] In what sceptical spirit must Astruc, after reading this letter, have asked Diaghilev to name the dates of his *générale* and *première* at the Opéra?[46] On 16 February the desperate Diaghilev gave him two dates, without an inkling of what dancers or ballets he was going to be able to present. The dates, chosen perhaps almost at random, were not adhered to.[47]

During his visit to St Petersburg Robert Brussel had reason to believe that Baron Dmitri de Gunsburg, Diaghilev's new business associate, who clearly helped him to pay some of his 1909 debts, was trying to prevent a *rapprochement* between Diaghilev and Astruc, for on ·12 January 1910 he had telegraphed to Astruc, 'Tapir [Gunsburg] is getting Valet [Calvocoressi] to write to Chemineau [Diaghilev] to prevent agreement insisting that you are trying to take over Russian season in order to make it fail. I have parried the blow'; and Astruc had replied 'Tapir's behaviour in keeping with his past record. Reassure Chemineau who will be certain to understand it is in my interest to make both affairs succeed.'[48] Gunsburg (who would later be suspected of trying to separate Diaghilev and Nijinsky at the time of the latter's marriage), was a dilettante, balletomane and amateur painter, and he may well have seen himself at the head of a ballet company (a solvent one, which Diaghilev's could never be); but Diaghilev, who may not have trusted him further than he could see and did not care whether he was a rogue or not, was well able to charm him into believing himself an essential partner in the enterprise. It was probably Gunsburg who enabled Diaghilev on 14 February to pay Astruc 5,000 francs, and on 10 March to honour a bill for 17,432 francs.[49] A month later, Diaghilev, who had continually been postponing a visit to Paris, cabled to Astruc that Nuvel and Gunsburg, his powers-of-attorney, would be leaving on the morrow.[50] Nuvel went to Paris, but Gunsburg did not follow till the last week in April.[51] They had instructions to persuade the directors of the Opéra that it would be an advantage to confine the season to ballet; they were also to make Diaghilev's peace with Calvocoressi, for he was needed. Nuvel and Calvocoressi heard Ravel play some of *Daphnis et Chloë* in a house near Fontainebleau.[52]

Possibly the sums of money advanced by Gunsburg were only borrowed by Diaghilev: at any rate, there was a limit to what the Baron was prepared to fork out, for Diaghilev, having failed to finance the future season at the Russian end, left for Paris just before Easter. There, at first, he met with such setbacks and disappointments and sent such unhappy cables to Benois, that, when these ceased and there was a lull, the friends feared he might commit suicide.[53] But Astruc somehow contrived to make the Paris season possible. As before, Diaghilev accepted all financial responsibility, simply hiring the Opéra for so many days, and hoping the box-office takings would cover his expenses. Astruc would have his percentage, but he also helped to raise money as a guarantee.[54] We can imagine that in these negotiations Misia, Mme Greffuhle, Mme de Chevigné, Mme de Béarn, Mme Ephrussi and others played their parts.

On 5 March the magazine *Satyricon* had held in the Pavlov Hall a ball for which Fokine had been asked to stage a ballet. Fokine suggested that Schumann's *Carnaval* would be an appropriate score for the eve of Lent.[55]

Apart from the actor Meyerhold, all those who took part in *Carnaval* were members of the Imperial Ballet: but they wore masks to preserve a fiction of anonymity, for they were not allowed to appear in private engagements during the theatre season. Leontiev was Harlequin, Karsavina was Columbine, Nijinsky was Florestan, Schollar was Estrella, Alexander Shiriaiev was Eusebius, Vera Fokina was Chiarina, Bronislava Nijinska was Papillon, Alfred Bekefi was Pantalon and Meyerhold was Pierrot. The ballet was accompanied by the piano score, as Schumann wrote it.[56]

It was this work that Grigoriev proposed to Diaghilev, when he got back from Paris, as an addition to the repertoire.

I found him drinking coffee in his dressing-gown, busy writing in his black exercise book. I sat down and waited, till after about five minutes, realizing that he was not likely to speak himself, I broke the silence by saying that I had had an idea for the ballet that was still wanted. This was ... *Le Carnaval.* Diaghilev looked up from his exercise book and said that he did not particularly care for Schumann, and that though he had not seen Fokine's ballet, he had heard that it was arranged for only a small number of dancers and would therefore be unsuitable for a large stage. However, Benois arrived at this point, and, on hearing of my suggestion, supported me. ... Diaghilev did not argue with us. He merely went on thinking. I could not tell whether we had succeeded in persuading him or whether he was just tired of the subject – when he suddenly made up his mind and wrote down *Carnaval* in the black book. Then, looking much happier, he turned to Benois and asked: 'What about *Giselle,* Shura?'[57]

It seems to me likely that Astruc had said something in Paris to restore Diaghilev's confidence in the power of the old Romantic ballet to please, even though they both knew that Pavlova would not be dancing it.

'Do you still insist on *Giselle*?' 'I do indeed,' said Benois. 'I feel sure it would give our repertoire variety and show our dancers at their most brilliant. Besides, I should like to paint you a *décor* for it!' Diaghilev gave a sly smile and wrote *Giselle* in large ornate characters in his exercise book. I must have guessed aright: that the question of *Giselle* had already been decided in his mind.[58]

It turned out that Schumann's *Carnaval* had already been orchestrated by Rimsky-Korsakov, Liadov, Glazunov and Tcherepnine: this had been done as far back as 1902 for a concert in memory of Anton Rubinstein.

For the *divertissement*, which was now called *Les Orientales*, Diaghilev had himself chosen music by Glazunov, Sinding and Arensky,[59] and had commissioned for seventy-five roubles[60] an orchestration of Grieg by Stravinsky. The repertoire for 1910 – which included the ballet items of 1909, minus the singers in *Prince Igor* – was now complete. The company were to have a short season in Berlin on the way to Paris, and *Carnaval*, which the Germans ought to like and by which Diaghilev did not set much store, would have its *première* there. Columbine was to be danced by the young Lydia Lopukhova, just out of the ballet school; *Schéhérazade* was for Rubinstein and Nijinsky; and *The Firebird* and *Giselle* must wait till Karsavina was granted leave by Oswald Stoll.

If she was granted leave – for everything depended on a personal plea and her beautiful big dark eyes! Karsavina had begun to be admitted to sessions of the committee. Benois was mad about her. 'Tatochka now really became one of us; she was the most reliable of our chief artists and one whose entire being was suited to our work. ... Tamara Platonovna was not only a beautiful woman and a first-class, highly individual artist, but had as well a most attractive personality, was open to varied interests and infinitely more cultured than most of her comrades. ... Unlike Pavlova, with whom one could not talk except in a half-coquettish ballet fashion, Karsavina was capable of sustaining a serious conversation.'[61] The admired ballerina had always longed to be 'behind the scenes' at Zamiatin Pereulok, the sorcerer's kitchen where so many spells were brewed, and suddenly there she was.

In Diaghilev's small flat beat the pulse of his formidable enterprise [wrote Karsavina]. ... Around the table sat wise men; the Artistic Committee drinking weak tea and hatching daring ideas ... he [Diaghilev] kept a vigilant eye on his collaborators. 'Gentlemen, you are wandering off your point,' came now and then from his corner. Diversions constantly occurred. Tradesmen burst in; alarming news arrived: unless Anisfeld has more canvas at once, he won't be able to finish painting the scenery.[62]

Diaghilev told Karsavina how once, when things looked black owing to the defection or scheming of some lady (Kchessinskaya or Pavlova?), Vassili, who 'would come unbidden constantly in and out of the rooms', had 'suggested direct action'. ' "Barin [Master], shall we do away with the villainess?" "What do you mean?" The hand moved in dumb show, brushing something aside, "What can one do, Vassili?" "Shall I, Barin ... ?" Another dumb show demonstrated the action. "Just a little powder." '63

When in May, Karsavina was about to leave for London – her agent Marinelli having vainly appealed several times to Stoll to release her – 'a more than usually pressing "come to talk things over" brought me again to Diaghilev's flat.'

I think he wanted to re-exercise the almost hypnotic power he had over me before I could escape from his influence. There the air was tense, all nerves worn down, as usual nothing ready and time short. He took me to his room, the only uninvaded spot. ... Diaghilev reminded me of my promise. We had both outlived the strife, if there was one; mutual anxiety had brought us closer. Diaghilev spoke affectionately; we cried a little. I looked round. The image lamp [before the ikon] was lit; Diaghilev looked weary, a mere human. The room was bare of adornment, I had expected it to be fastidious. I could not realize then that the glamour of his personality spent itself in creations of fancy. His gentle words had a touch of resignation. He knew that on his way one obstacle hardly removed another will arise.64

King Edward VII had died on 6 May, thus blighting all Diaghilev's hopes for a London season in 1910. Karsavina saw the funeral procession65 on 20 May, the day after her appearance at the Coliseum. Preobrajenska was at the Hippodrome and Pavlova was at the Palace.

The twentieth was also the day when Diaghilev's company opened with *Carnaval* in Berlin. Before they left St Petersburg, there had been one or two dramas. Diaghilev could not find the money for their fares. In desperation he went to see the Finance Minister, Count Kokovtsov (who became President of the Council on the assassination of Stolypin in the following year), who advised the Tsar to grant Diaghilev ten thousand roubles, and the Tsar signed the paper. The friends heard of this about three in the afternoon, a day or two before the company was due to depart. 'Diaghilev went hurriedly to a banker of his acquaintance, and on this surety borrowed £1,000 for a few days. The tickets were bought.' But the Tsar withdrew the small subsidy. The banker had to be repaid. Prince Argutinsky and another loyal friend, Ratkov-Rognev, signed a bill for the sum needed in order to repay the banker.66

Then Benois made one of his scenes. He was not really as grateful as he should have been that, by assuming command, Diaghilev, his former 'pupil', had spared him and his colleagues all the work of administration, to allow them to get on serenely with their jobs. Diaghilev, who had so much on his mind, sometimes assumed, out of impatience, a high-handed manner. When, on the day before the company's departure, Benois called at the passport office to collect his passport for Germany and France and found

Diaghilev had not made arrangements for him, he went home, and, losing his temper, broke a window-pane with his fist and severed an artery. He was lucky not to lose the use of his hand. He missed the Berlin visit and the Paris opening and, after an operation, went to convalesce with his family in Lugano.[67]

The Russians' Berlin theatre was the Theater des Westens in the quiet suburb of Charlottenburg, near the palace and gardens of the Prussian kings. The contingent from Moscow did not include Karalli this year: another prima ballerina, Ekaterina Gelzer, a pretty, plump and excitable lady,[68] who had a strong classical technique but little else, was there instead, with her partner, Alexander Volinine. Sophie Feodorova was again with the company. Bolm was not.

Fokine's Commedia dell'Arte characters in *Carnaval* gambolled and flirted before the simplest of backgrounds – a deep-blue curtain adorned at the top with a black, red and gold frieze of huge stylized poppies. Just as it was left to the audience to decide whether the dancers were representing Harlequin, Columbine, Pierrot and Pantalon, or were impersonating characters at a ball impersonating them, so there was room for doubt (and poetic ambiguity) as to whether the curtains were those of a fairground booth, a tent erected for a ball, or a mysterious passage linking a ballroom and a garden where the real action was taking place unseen. We know that Schumann represented two sides of his character in the impetuous Florestan, who pursues capricious Estrella (himself and Ernestine von Fricken), and in the solitary dreamer Eusebius, with his shy, reverent love for Chiarina (himself and the fifteen-year-old Clara Wieck, whom he later married).

The girls all wore flounced crinolines, with poke bonnets or lace-trimmed caps. Papillon being younger than the others, her flimsy skirt was shorter and she had wings. Columbine's big, swaying white silk skirt had cherries painted on one of its innumerable scalloped flounces. These matched the apple-green, vermilion and white lozenge pattern on Harlequin's tights. The men, mostly top-hatted, wore frock coats with high collars, nipped-in waists and full skirts in the d'Orsay style, with peg-top trousers. But long-haired Eusebius the poet was hatless in his short salmon-pink velvet jacket; and Pierrot, with his shapeless, floppy white pyjamas and limp black ruff, had a black skull-cap, like Harlequin.

Carnaval had only just enough story to give an extra point to the dancing: an ideal balance was kept. (Diaghilev felt obliged to cut only the short number 'Réplique'.) There were hints of satire, sadness and even cruelty to add spice to the pretty comedy. Harlequin took nothing seriously, even love; and the moon-struck yearning of Eusebius, the despair of Pierrot and Pantalon's elderly flirtation were to be seen from his point of view.

The German audience were delighted with the Frenchified version of the Italian comedy which the Russians had brought them.[69] There were at least two magical inventions. One was the tip-toe *pas de trois* of Estrella and two friends, who, in a group like the Three Graces, with arms raised and gloved hands touching, to the nocturnal tune called 'Chopin', celebrated the mysteries of their virginity, soon to be lost for ever. The other was the entry of Columbine and Harlequin linked together, to the tune 'Reconnaissance', with his high-hopping, knees-up steps, which followed the *animato* melody on flute and clarinet, in counterpoint to her rapid *pas de bourrée* to the string accompaniment. These had the simplicity of genius.

Fokine had been clever in spotting Lopukhova's special quality: she was not so much pretty as effervescent, and Jean-Louis Vaudoyer would write that her ingenuous virtuosity was 'tempered by the imperceptible awkwardness of youth'.[70] Vera Fokina, with her rather affected romantic sweetness, and Bronislava Nijinska, with her speed and strength, were well suited to the roles of Chiarina and Papillon.

The German Emperor, who fancied himself as an Egyptologist, was so struck by the beauties of *Cléopâtre* that he ordered a congress of archaeologists to attend a performance.[71]

The company arrived in Paris at the beginning of June. Lopukhova was one who had never been there – or anywhere outside Russia – before. 'As she was stepping out of the railway carriage, emotion overcame her. She fainted right away on the piles of luggage. It had been her dream to be in Paris, she told the alarmed Bakst, who had rendered her first aid; the lovely sight (of the Gare du Nord) was too much for her.'[72]

For those who had not taken part in the gala at the end of the previous season, the gorgeous Opéra, with its luxurious dressing-rooms, was a new experience. Once again Diaghilev and Astruc had to rally the press and society to their support. This season they had no Chaliapine and no opera. They were dancing three nights a week, alternating with the French opera company. They had the Metropolitan Opera and Caruso at the Châtelet in rivalry with them. They had no Pavlova, and for the beginning of the season at least, no Karsavina. If the French proved fickle, this would probably be Diaghilev's last season.

There was to have been a *répétition générale* in aid of charity to launch the Paris season on Thursday 2 June, but some scenery had not arrived, either that of *Schéhérazade* from Russia or that of *Carnaval* from Berlin, and the charity had to wait for the dress rehearsal of *Giselle* (matinée of Friday 17 June), while the press were convoked for a 'working rehearsal' at 9 pm that Thursday instead.[73]

The first-night programme on 4 June 1910 began with a *divertissement* which was a mixture of *Le Festin* and the Polovtsian Dances from *Prince Igor*. *Carnaval* followed, with Fokine as Harlequin, Lopukhova as Columbine, Fokina as Chiarina, Pilz as Estrella, Nijinska as Papillon, Bulgakov as Pierrot, Orlov as Pantalon, Scherer as Eusebius and Vassiliev as Florestan.

(The orchestration of Schumann's piano composition did not escape adverse comment.)[74] The evening ended with *Schéhérazade*.

What was the most potent element in *Schéhérazade*, to conquer a public already rendered susceptible to Oriental excesses by *Cléopâtre* the year before? Was it the theme of the Shah's vengeance on his faithless harem, the mass slaughter, on his unexpected return from hunting, of women surprised *in flagrante delicto* with their Negro lovers? Was it Fokine's choreography and his new kind of vivid mime, bereft of the old sign language? Was it the performances of Bulgakov as the Shah, of Rubinstein as Zobeïda and of Nijinsky as the Golden Slave? Was it the surging crescendo of Rimsky's music, in which the movement called 'Festival at Baghdad: the Sea' became a bacchanalian orgy followed by mass execution? Was it the setting and dresses of Bakst, with juxtapositions of colour hardly guessed at before in the West? It is safe to say that it was the combination of all these elements by Diaghilev, his inspired decisions, his care for detail, his desire to realize some ideal he had seen in his mind's eye, that did the trick.

Grigoriev wrote of the ensemble dances in the orgy, 'By means of intricate evolutions for the various groups of dancers woven in with a number of individual moves, Fokine contrived to endow this dance with such rich variety that its climax was tremendous.'[75] Benois thought that the tall, ivory-pale, black-bearded Bulgakov, whose heart broke when Zobeïda killed herself with a dagger, was 'a king from head to foot'.[76] Of Rubinstein's Zobeïda Fokine wrote,

Everything was expressed with one single pose, with one movement, one turn of the head. Nevertheless, everything was outlined and drawn clearly.... She is displeased by the departure of her husband, and expresses her displeasure with a single movement, turning away her head when he comes to kiss her farewell. She stands in front of a door through which her lover is momentarily due to emerge. She waits for him with her entire body. Then (and to me the most dramatic scene) she sits utterly still while slaughter takes place around her. Death approaches her, but not the horror nor the fear of it. She majestically awaits her fate in a pose without motion. ...[77]

Fokine thought that 'the lack of masculinity which was peculiar to [Nijinsky] and which made him unfit for certain roles ... suited very well the role of the Negro Slave. ... Now he was a half-human, half-feline animal, softly leaping great distances, now a stallion, with distended nostrils, full of energy, overflowing with an abundance of power, his feet impatiently pawing the ground.'[78] Pages could be filled with the tributes of other writers to Nijinsky's extraordinary interpretation.[79]

I have written above that, studying Vrubel's watercolour *An Oriental Tale*, which shows a seated Shah in his harem, with a new slave girl standing bashfully before him on a rich carpet, I thought it might have inspired the designs of Bakst for *Schéhérazade*.[80] The subject is similar, and the range of colour is as wide, but, whereas Vrubel applied his paint in jewelled drops, Bakst, in the setting, swept his paint on with a fat, full brush. His architecture was nebulous, and it would be hard to produce a plan of such a room. What suggestions of solidity there were – related to the tiled mosques and the pavilions of Shah Abbas at Isfahan, with their slender columns and coffered ceilings – was screened by the immense swags of curtains, muffled by piles of cushions on the carpeted floor and dominated by huge pendant lamps.

Sert, Cocteau, Misia and Diaghilev in a box at the Opéra. Drawing by Jean Cocteau.

Not form, but colour reigned, and its reign was as debauched as that of Heliogabalus. An unheard-of violence of peacock-green and blue was the main theme (which gave the jeweller Cartier the idea of setting sapphires and emeralds together for the first time since the Moghul Emperors), but this was defied by the subsidiary theme of coral-red and rose-pink. Against this chromatic jungle, with its patches of light and shadowy depths, stood out the royal blues and crimsons of the turbaned brother kings, the green and pink Odalisques who began the drama (to the surprise of their interpreters)[81] with a dance seated on the floor, the diaphanously clad, patterned and bejewelled ladies of the harem, the scarlet Chief Eunuch, who was bribed by pearls to open the doors of the slaves' quarters, the braceleted Negroes, with their strange encrusted brassières linked to metallic lamé trousers by ropes of beads, and the orange-vermilion and chrome-yellow high-capped janissaries who sliced their way into a snake-pit of writhing flesh to effect the final slaughter.

Marcel Proust was present with Jean-Louis Vaudoyer and Reynaldo Hahn, and a few days later he wrote to Reynaldo, 'I never saw anything so beautiful.'[82]

Calvocoressi, as a musician, should have been shocked by Diaghilev's use of Rimsky's composition, but he wrote:

In principle, I know, my critical sense ought to have made me feel that it was absolutely wrong to use a symphonic work, intended for the concert platform only, for the purposes of a ballet – and especially a ballet whose subject had nothing to do with the composer's avowed poetic and descriptive intentions.... I could see that Rimsky-Korsakov's widow and eldest son had very good reasons for angrily protesting against the travesty in both the French and the Russian Press. And I, myself, deeply loving the music of *Schéhérazade*, ought to have felt that there must be something wrong somewhere. But what I actually did feel was that stage atmosphere, stage action, and music were never at cross purposes.... Like everybody who saw it, I considered it purely and simply amazing. ... Nijinsky showed for the first time ... at least in France – that he was as superb a mime as he was a dancer.[83]

Now, in response to 'insistent letters' from Diaghilev, Benois left his family in Lugano and travelled to Paris to see his sets for *Giselle* and the rest of the repertoire on stage. Of course, he was impatient to see the fruits of all the winter's work and to enjoy the acclaim.

How great was my amazement when, having taken my seat in the stalls of the Paris Opéra, I unfolded my programme and read under the title *Schéhérazade* the words 'Ballet de L. Bakst'. I was so amazed I could hardly believe my eyes, but at the first sounds from the orchestra and the raising of the curtain I forgot everything and gave myself up entirely to intense enjoyment of the performance. My enthusiasm was so great that when I went on the stage to embrace Bakst and Diaghilev after the performance I was quite unconscious of having been hurt by them. It was only after I had reread the programme in my hotel that ... my heart was filled with bitterness and indignation. This disappointment of mine had nothing to do with practical considerations. ... In spite of my age – forty – I had only a vague idea of the existence of 'royalties'.... Next day I was finally flabbergasted by Serioja's answer to my question as to how this could have happened: 'Que veux-tu? Bakst had to be given something. You have *Le Pavillon d'Armide* and he will have *Schéhérazade*.'[84]

Diaghilev never claimed credit for himself: his satisfaction came in seeing a ballet come to life, as he had planned it, on the stage. He had made the mistake of riding roughshod over the feelings of his old friend, who was getting touchy about being elbowed out of the Russian Ballet, which he had helped to inaugurate. Diaghilev probably thought that, as his friends pooled their ideas, they might as well divide the credit and the payments between them. On his return to Lugano, Benois wrote to Diaghilev, telling him that he was 'breaking with him for good'.[85] Diaghilev had too much on his mind to spare time for quarrels, but he was indignant about Benois' temperamental behaviour, and ruled him out of his life for the time being.[86] Benois wrote a generous article about the ballet and about Bakst's décor in the Russian magazine *Rech*.[87]

Karsavina's despairing eyes, backed by the kind prompting of her agent Marinelli, convinced Stoll that he must let her go for a month – she admired his fairness of mind – on condition that she returned in July.[88] She probably travelled to Paris on Sunday, 5 June 1910. That gave her a fortnight to rehearse *Giselle*. (*The Firebird* would follow after another week.) Oddly enough, it was a short version of *Giselle* which she had been dancing at the London Coliseum with Koslov and Baldina. Now she had to rehearse the whole two acts of the old ballet with Nijinsky. Their parts were of equal importance and difficulty.

Karsavina had learnt the role of Giselle from her old teacher Sokolova. Pavlova, who had almost a monopoly of the role in St Petersburg, could have helped her, but did not.[89] Nijinsky was less at home in the straightforward role of prince and lover – such as was common to most of the nineteenth century ballets – than in the quaint, original conceptions of Fokine.

Giselle on our stage was a holy ballet [wrote Karsavina], not a step to be altered. ... I loved every bit of it. I was sadly taken aback when I found that I danced, mimed, went off my head and died of a broken heart without any response from Nijinsky. He stood pensive and bit his nails. 'Now you have to come across towards me,' I suggested. 'I know myself what to do,' he said moodily. After ineffectual efforts to go through the dialogue by myself, I wept. Nijinsky looked sheepish and unmoved. Diaghilev led me off to the wings, proffered a handkerchief and told me to be indulgent: 'You don't know what volumes he has written on that part, what treatises on its interpretation.'[90]

Diaghilev was probably exaggerating: Nijinsky may just have kept a notebook. But he was not good at thinking out a role: he had to *feel* it, and this 'feeling' could not be rushed. Sometimes it only happened at the last moment.[91] His imperfect adjustment to normal life (which would later break out in schizophrenia) made it difficult for him to portray a straightforward man–woman relationship; and we can imagine that his second act, when Giselle was a ghost, came easier to him that his first, when she was a pretty girl to be flirted with. In the second act the heroine was unattainable, like the diaphanous woman in *Les Sylphides*, which made possible an atmosphere of strangeness, in which he flourished. In *Schéhérazade*, though his Negro was a symbol of desire, he had expressed a hyper-aesthetic refinement of lust,[92] and had been in a way more feminine than the rigid Rubinstein. In *Cléopâtre* he had been the Queen's devoted but cringing slave, snarling at strangers, but permitted outbursts of gaiety. In *Le Pavillon d'Armide* he had been a glittering plaything, the *bombe surprise* at Armida's banquet of dance, living only for three intense minutes a day, when wound up like a mechanical nightingale.

Svetlov, who had seen many Giselles, compared Karsavina's to that of the dramatic Pavlova, and observed that she 'took the part in another key. In her interpretation there enters no deep tragedy. On the contrary, it is the lyrical song of a woman's grief, sad and poetic. The pathos is tender, restrained. In the mad scene it is an almost timid complaint. In the Act of the Wilis, in all her dances there is something soothing, almost a quiet satisfaction, a submission to fate and a hope for a happier future.'[93]

When, at length, Benois, who had designed two perfect, nostalgic décors, the first an autumn landscape with a distant castle on a crag, the second a deep-blue moonlit forest with tangled trees, came to see the old ballet whose revival he had urged, he thought Karsavina 'almost outshone Pavlova'.[94] The critic of *Le Gaulois* recorded 'ovation after ovation' for Karsavina, for Lopukhova, who danced the flute solo in Act I, and for Poliakova, the Queen of the Wilis, and commended Nijinsky not only for the strength of his dancing but also for his expressive mime. He felt obliged, however, to state that he preferred the Russians in their national works.[95] (Was *Schéhérazade* a national work?) Diaghilev was right in doubting whether the French would be bowled over by *Giselle*: they were not. Karsavina summed up: it was 'a great personal success for the chief interpreters – nothing more'.[96] Yet Proust liked it: and he wrote from Cabourg in July to reproach Reynaldo Hahn for calling it insipid.[97] When, that summer, he began *A l'Ombre des jeunes filles en fleur* with descriptions of Balbec's (Cabourg's) hotel, casino and *plage*, he gave the name Gisèle to one of the girls in Albertine's 'little band'.

If Diaghilev had known Pavlova was not to dance in *The Firebird*, he would certainly have made a ballet with a dominant role for Nijinsky instead. When it became evident during rehearsals that *The Firebird* was going to be a success, he was more than ever determined to give Nijinsky an outstanding role in the following year. He pinned his hopes on *Le Dieu bleu*, which Cocteau and Hahn were planning together. The new work must have an oriental theme, since he had brought the East into fashion; it must have a décor by Bakst even more fantastic than that of *Schéhérazade*; and Nijinsky must have a role, like that of Karsavina in *The Firebird*, which isolated him from the other characters, a supernatural being subsidiary to no ballerina. Eager for any clues he could pick up, the ambitious Cocteau asked Karsavina to tell him the story of *The Firebird*, and borrowed several of its elements for his libretto.[98]

Benois thought *The Firebird* too short; Stravinsky thought it too long. Benois considered that Diaghilev's stipulation that the ballet should last no more than an hour restricted Fokine, made the action too precipitate and prevented the development of the principal characters.[99] Stravinsky disliked the padding and atmospheric linking passages that a story ballet necessitated;[100] and as soon as he was able (in 1911) carved out a concert suite, scrapping what he considered inessential. (He made a second concert suite for smaller orchestra in 1919; and a third 'ballet suite', also for small orchestra, in 1945.) Diaghilev too disliked story ballets, and either his conscious preference or an unconscious instinct was leading him towards a more compressed art form than the old three- or five-act ballet lasting all evening, something more in step with this revolutionary time. *The Firebird* was a transitional work, as would be Ravel's *Daphnis* (which never satisfied him). Diaghilev's ballets were to get much shorter.

Stravinsky remembered that Diaghilev would have liked Vrubel to design the ballet, but Vrubel had died nearly three months before the opening night.[101] Golovine's décor had something of him in it: in reproduction, it strikes one as a tapestry woven of green, gold, russet and silver thread. The anti-Moscow Benois did not like that either. 'No one could *penetrate* into such a forest – indeed, it seemed scarcely a forest at all.'[102] He had rather a literal mind. The costumes were as rich as the set: 'Everything was submerged in uniform, sumptuous luxury,' complained Benois.[103] Diaghilev was dissatisfied with Golovine's costumes for the Firebird, the Prince and the Beautiful Tsarevna, and Bakst made new designs for them.

During the final week Stravinsky had been present at eight orchestral rehearsals under Gabriel Pierné's baton. The great day, Saturday 25 June, came at last when his first ballet would be performed, and when his music would be heard in Western Europe for the first time. He was even more struck by the perfume than by the glitter of the audience.[104]

This audience heard the mysterious introduction, with its hint of night terrors; they saw the Firebird flash across the dark clearing in the orchard to her incandescent music, watched her struggle in the arms of Prince Ivan. Then, by moonlight, stole on the captive Princesses to play catch with golden apples, and Ivan joined them in a stately round dance. Dawn drove the girls back into the Magician's castle, and Ivan battered at the gate, thus bringing on the Court of Kastchei for their Infernal Dance. Before Kastchei could turn him to stone, Ivan summoned the Firebird, and her Lullaby put the crowd of demons to sleep. It only remained for Ivan to smash the egg containing Kastchei's soul; then he and his Tsarevna could celebrate their wedding and coronation to the sound of a folk song which became a hymn of thanksgiving, with crowds of boyars and soldiers coming and going.

Fokine, dancer and choreographer, acknowledged the acclamations of Paris, with Karsavina on one side of him and Vera Fokina on the other, the old love and the new. Stravinsky was called on stage to bow several times. He was twenty-eight. 'I was still on stage when the final curtain had come down, and I saw coming towards me Diaghilev and a dark man with a double forehead whom he introduced as Claude Debussy. The great composer spoke kindly about the music, ending his words with an invitation to dine with him.'[105]

As we have remarked, the East was in fashion – if it had ever been out of fashion since the youth of Hugo and Delacroix. In fact, the *divertissement* which followed *The Firebird* on 25 June bore the same name as Hugo's second book of poems, *Les Orientales*. Gelzer and Volinine appeared in this, and Nijinsky was given two numbers. In one, 'Kobold', danced to the piano piece of Grieg, which Stravinsky had orchestrated, he was a capering goblin clad in all-over tights of green-blue *paillettes*. The other was a series of poses based on Fokine's memories of the visit of the King of Siam's dancers to St Petersburg in 1901. In his costume for this, which Bakst had designed, Nijinsky was much photographed and painted.[106]

Diaghilev had paid Stravinsky fifteen hundred roubles for *The Firebird*, and, although Igor could ill afford it, when two extra performances were announced at the Opéra after Diaghilev's two-day Brussels engagement, he sped home to Russia to fetch his wife and children. He obviously foresaw further collaborations with Diaghilev and felt a golden age was dawning. Already, when he had been finishing the orchestration of *The Firebird* two months before, he had had the idea of a new ballet. 'I had dreamed a scene of pagan ritual in which a chosen sacrificial virgin danced herself to death. The vision was not accompanied by concrete musical ideas, however. ...'[107] Before leaving St Petersburg for Paris, he had talked to Roerich, the dreamer of ancient Russian mysteries, about the scenario. A letter to the painter, begun at Ustilug, Igor's family home near the Polish border, and finished at La Baule, on the west coast of France, after the final performance of the extended Paris season, gives us a glimpse of the hatching of *The Rite of Spring*.

Naturally, the success of *The Firebird* has encouraged Diaghilev for future projects, and sooner or later we will have to tell him about the 'Great Sacrifice'. In fact, he has already asked me to compose a new ballet. I said I was writing one which, for the moment, I did not wish to talk about, and this touched off an explosion, as I might have guessed. 'What? You keep secrets from me, I who do my utmost for you all? Fokine, you, everyone has secrets from me.' Etc., etc. I had to tell him, of course, but I begged him not to repeat it. As soon as I said that I was working with you, both Diaghilev and Bakst were delighted, Bakst saying he thought our idea was a noble one. They were greatly relieved, obviously, to hear that my secret did not concern Benois: Diaghilev would have been greatly offended if Benois had been involved.

Later. I have had to complete this letter in La Baule, having found no time in Paris, where we spent only three days. Again *The Firebird* had an immense success, and I was greatly pleased, but I must say that some of Golovine's work, and some of the lighting, was not very fortunate. I had thought, from the very first, when I saw Golovine's costumes and his beautiful sets, that he had failed to create anything satisfactory for the spooky Kastchei dance, and this opinion was also shared by Andrei Rimsky-Korsakov and Kolya Richter, who came for the final performance. Music and costumes are at odds in this scene, and the dancers look like dressed-up actors. Diaghilev took charge of the lighting himself, but with imperfect results. ... I do not know the exact reasons for it, but the quarrel between Diaghilev and Fokine began because of difficulties in producing *The Firebird*. ... If the Fokine feud is not settled soon Diaghilev thinks we should work with a certain Gorsky, of whom I know nothing. ... I cannot find the paper on which I wrote the libretto of the 'Great Sacrifice'. For God's sake send it to me, registered. ...[108]

After just over a fortnight back at the Coliseum, Karsavina, bombarded by telegrams from Diaghilev, managed to beg more time off from Stoll, so that she could dance at one of the two performances in Brussels. During her absence from Paris Gelzer had been given the valse in *Les Sylphides* and Fokine had persuaded Diaghilev to allow Lopukhova to dance *The Firebird*. Her big jump suited her for the role, but her interpretation was quite different from Karsavina's, 'a delicate humming-bird rather than a flaming phoenix'.[109]

In Brussels Diaghilev welcomed Karsavina 'like a fond father' and 'his joy was touching'. At luncheon with her and Nijinsky on the day of her performance, Diaghilev asked her not to be cross that Gelzer, who had helped him out while she was in London, danced her valse that night in *Les Sylphides*: he felt he could not take the part away from her this season. Karsavina, who, a year and a half before, had been so shy of Diaghilev that she hardly dared open her mouth for fear of saying something stupid, 'raged and stormed for form's sake, meaning all the while to meet his wishes'.[110] That evening, while she was making up, she saw him in her looking-glass. He never knocked on doors. She was no longer angry but thought her dignity required her to look daggers. He said, 'You have slapped one cheek. Here is the other.' Then he added sadly, 'Tata, I am desperately in love.' 'Who with?' 'She doesn't care for me any more than for the Emperor of China.'[111] A loaded silence would be for both the safest way to follow up this semideclaration.

To protect himself from the threat of London music-halls, Diaghilev offered Karsavina a contract to dance for him from 1 May to the end of August, during the summer recess of the Mariinsky, in 1911 and 1912.[112] She hesitated to tie herself down. He raged at her for 'prostituting her art' by appearing in a music-hall. He was possessively jealous, saying, 'I hate your family. It takes you away from me. Why could you not have married Fokine? You would both have belonged to me.' He resented the fact of my still clinging to the Mariinsky. 'I can't see what is the lure of St Petersburg to you. Is it Teliakovsky's waxed moustache or the hysterical ovations of the greenhorns in the gallery? Or maybe you just like to show yourself off in your new carriage and pair.'[113] Then he complained that Fokine's work was out of date. He did not like Fokine, resenting his self-sufficiency, as well as the fact that he had begun his 'revolution' independently. With his longing for new experiments, Diaghilev had already begun to see the limitations of Fokine's devotion to local colour, and he was wondering whether he could not replace him by someone more malleable – either Gorsky or Nijinsky. Karsavina could not believe her ears. So soon after Paris had been overwhelmed by the novelty of the *Polovtsian Dances* and *Cléopâtre*, Diaghilev was calling Fokine old-fashioned. ' "What are you going to do with Fokine's ballets, Sergei Pavlovitch?" "Oh, I don't know. I may sell it all, lock, stock and barrel." ' She felt Diaghilev was trying her out, and she assured him of her fidelity.[114]

Diaghilev could no longer count on Calvocoressi's fidelity, however. Calvocoressi wrote:

At the end of the season I discovered Diaghilev had decided not to adhere, in the future, to the terms made with me on his behalf by Gunsburg and Nuvel. Then I made up my mind for good and all; and on the very day when my work was finished, I resigned, treating him to a grand scene *à la Diaghilev*. I must have imitated his own way of expressing fury quite well: for he never retorted a word except: 'And I who was going to ask you to take charge of my London season!'[115]

The 1910 season had not been a financial disaster like the previous one. Astruc, once bitten twice shy, had exercised effective control: but it is obvious that the chief reasons for Diaghilev's new experience of solvency were that he had dispensed with an opera company, and with Chaliapine – who cost the earth – and that he had not had to transport and lodge a Russian orchestra. He had had nearly two hundred fewer souls to cope with, less scenery and fewer costumes. What is more, he had proved that he could fill the house without opera: the ballet on its own was acceptable. However, for the rest of his life he would seek subsidies to enable him to present opera as well as ballet, or to mix singing and dancing.

At the end of July 1910 the 'Diaghilev Ballet' once more dispersed, but its creator was negotiating for another season in Paris, as well as seasons in London and New York; and he told Grigoriev that in the following year they would work longer together. As Grigoriev and the other members of the Mariinsky and Bolshoi Ballets had devoted three of their four months' leave to working for Diaghilev, the *régisseur* could not imagine what he meant.[116] In fact, Diaghilev was hoping to form his own company, independent of the Tsar. The chief difficulty about this was that, in return for their eight-year training and their board, lodging and clothes, members of the Imperial Ballet were expected to dance for a minimum of five years after they left school. After that they were free to leave, and give up their pensions. But Nijinsky and other dancers had to do a year or two more of work to fulfil their obligations.

Lydia Lopukhova was the first Russian dancer to break her agreement with the Mariinsky, and cut herself off from Russia. She had signed a contract to dance in the United States, and, although she was to rejoin Diaghilev during the war, she would never return home. Ida Rubinstein had developed grandiose ambitions; tired of miming, she wanted to dance and speak. So she parted company with Diaghilev, in order to finance with her own money, and later that of her lover, Walter Guinness, immense spectacles of her own. Diaghilev feared this rivalry, especially as she lured Bakst to work for her (and paid him better); but he soon realized she had made a fool of herself.

During the summer of 1910 the friends were scattered for work or pleasure. Diaghilev and Nijinsky visited Benois at Montagnola near Lugano to make up the quarrel,[117] then went on to Venice. Encouraged by Diaghilev, Vaslav was trying to work out a new kind of choreography. Stravinsky stayed with his family at La Baule in Brittany, then moved to Switzerland.[118] In September the Stravinskys moved from Vevey to a clinic at Lausanne, where their second son was born. Igor had interrupted work on his first sketches for *The Rite of Spring* to compose a *Konzertstück* for piano and orchestra. He worked on this intended piano concerto in an attic studio opposite the clinic, and when Diaghilev and Nijinsky arrived towards the end of September, hoping to hear how the music of *The Rite* was getting on, Stravinsky played them the new composition, which he proposed to call *Petrushka's Cry*.[119]

Petrushka was the Russian Punch, who beat his wife, killed people and was finally hauled off to Hell by the Devil. While one man, hidden, worked the puppets, the organ-grinder provided music and dialogue. He would continually warn Petrushka, 'Look out! You'll get into hot water,' and Petrushka would merely give a shrieking laugh, 'He, he, he!' When speaking Petrushka's lines, the organ-grinder put into his mouth 'a little contrivance which gave a nasal tone to his voice', and it was the strange sounds thus produced that Diaghilev heard in the new composition. The puppet-shows were a feature of the Butter Week fairs in St Petersburg (which preceded Lent), when temporary wooden theatres, *montagnes russes* (switchbacks) and roundabouts appeared in the Square of the Winter Palace.[120]

Stravinsky had up his sleeve the beginnings of another piece – a Russian Dance – for piano and orchestra, which he intended as a companion to the first,[121] and, when Diaghilev heard this fragment, he at once had the idea of using the two compositions as the basis for a ballet about the Russian carnival. All agreed – oddly, in view of Diaghilev's recent aversion to his old friend and Stravinsky's remarks in his letter to Roerich – that Benois, with his nostalgia for the old architecture and traditions of St Petersburg, would be the only man to plan the story and make the designs. Diaghilev wrote to Shura, who was by then back in St Petersburg, a day or two later. Although Benois had been reconciled with Diaghilev at Montagnola, he had still insisted (like Calvocoressi) that he would work no more for him, little suspecting that his most famous ballet was about to be born. He had to be coaxed, but Diaghilev knew very well that the idea of Petrushka would prove irresistible.

Benois wrote,

Petrushka, the Russian Guignol or Punch, no less than Harlequin, had been my friend since my earliest childhood. Whenever I heard the loud, nasal cries of the travelling showman: 'Here's Petrushka! Come, good people and see the show!' I would get into a kind of frenzy to see the enchanting performance.... As to Petrushka in person, I immediately had the feeling that it was a duty I owed to my old friend to immortalize him on the real stage. I was still more tempted by the idea of depicting the Butter Week Fair ... the dear *balagani* [fairground booths] which were the delight of my childhood, and had been the delight of my father before me. The fact that the *balagani* had for some ten years ceased to exist made the idea of building a kind of memorial to them still more tempting....[122]

Stravinsky moved along the Lake of Geneva to Clarens, where, in another attic, he completed the Russian Dance. Diaghilev went to Paris for discussions with Astruc[123] and to London to make a plan for the following year with Joseph Beecham, the pill-maker, whose son Thomas was an aspiring conductor.[124] Diaghilev was in London on 10 October, but back with Nijinsky in Paris on 27 October, as is proved by the postmark on the following letter-card. After a lunch spent plotting *Le Dieu bleu*, the collaborators were suddenly seized with a superstitious fear that, if the secret of their new work leaked out, something might happen to prevent its realization; so they wrote to Astruc from the Restaurant Le Grand Vatel, 275 rue St-Honoré, 'In the name of all you hold dear, not a word to *anyone* about the ballet we are planning, and especially about the possibility of including it in the Coronation celebrations, Yours ever, Reynaldo Hahn, Serge Diaghilev, Leon Bakst, Jean Cocteau, Nijinsky.'[125]

Fokine had presented Stravinsky with a complete libretto of *The Firebird* (only slightly modified later), and the music had been composed to fit it, but Benois wrote his libretto for *Petrushka* around the two pieces which had already been composed. Before Stravinsky and Benois met again several months later, more music was composed and more story worked out, and they were in continual correspondence. Diaghilev was back in St Petersburg in November, and discussions began in the absence of the composer. Other friends took part, but Bakst was in Paris being 'unfaithful', planning *Le Martyre de St Sebastien* with Ida Rubinstein, D'Annunzio and Debussy. Fokine was not called in till a later stage, but Nijinsky was now a silent member of the committee. Benois wrote:

We met daily in Diaghilev's flat in Zamiatin Lane, where at the traditional evening tea with *boubliki* ... *Petrushka* took shape and fitted ultimately into four fairly short acts without any intervals. The first and last acts were to take place at the Carnival Fair; the two middle ones were to show the interior of the Conjuror's theatre. The puppets that had come to life in the first act under the magic spell of the Conjuror, were to continue living a real life in their own quarters, where a romance was to begin between them....[126]

Benois had already invented the pretty, empty-headed Ballerina, with whom poor, uncouth Petrushka would be in love, and his rival, the flamboyant Blackamoor, whom the Ballerina would prefer. The last was inspired by the traditional interlude in Petrushka performances, when 'two Blackamoors, dressed in velvet and gold, would appear and would start unmercifully hitting each other's wooden heads with sticks'. Petrushka was to lose his character of a knockabout bully like Punch, and acquire a soul. 'If Petrushka were to be taken as the personification of the spiritual and suffering side of humanity – or shall we call it the poetical principle? – his lady Columbine would be the incarnation of the eternal feminine; then the gorgeous Blackamoor would serve as the embodiment of everything senselessly attractive, powerfully masculine and undeservedly triumphant.'[127]

The Stravinskys had moved in October to Beaulieu, between Nice and Monte Carlo, where more music was written. When in December Stravinsky visited his mother in St Petersburg, Benois heard the new parts of the score. 'Igor played them to me in my little dark blue drawing-room; the piano was my old, fearfully hard Gentsch.... What I now heard surpassed my expectations....'[128]

After Stravinsky's return to France (where, by March, he had written three-quarters of the score)[129] Benois set about designing his sets and costumes for the new ballet, the period of which was not to be that of his own childhood in the 1870s, when he had first seen the travelling puppet-shows and the pre-Lent fairs, but a period forty years earlier, in the days of the Emperor Nicolas I, his father's patron. He was living near to the palace of Count Bobrinsky and the room he had taken to work in was directly over the lodgings used by the Count's coachmen. 'Unceasing revels and dancing went on there all day long to the sounds of the balalaika and the laughter of gay ladies. At any other time this would have greatly disturbed me, but in the present case all the noise, shouts and stamping only helped to inspire me. It was almost a gift of providence.'[130]

CHAPTER 10

1911–12

Diaghilev forms his own Company – Nijinsky leaves the
Mariinsky – The Coronation Season, London –
Nijinsky's First Ballet – Departure of Fokine

DIAGHILEV HAD INVENTED a new art form, the ballets as *Gesamt-kunstwerk*: an entertainment, not more than an hour long, in which all the elements, story (if any), music, décor and choreography, were commissioned by himself to form a complete whole. Adam, Delibes and Tchaikovsky had composed longer ballets which were works of theatrical art; but who, except a few ballet historians, remembers their designers? Isadora had danced to the music of Gluck, Beethoven and Schubert, but she had commissioned no living composer. In *Schéhérazade* Diaghilev had perverted an existing score of Rimsky's to make a powerful musical drama. But in *The Firebird* everything had been started from scratch. *Petrushka* would carry the new art-form one step further towards perfection.

Yet Diaghilev had already sensed in Fokine the beginnings of decay; and he wanted to get rid of him. It was surely less the fact that Fokine had evolved choreographic theories of his own before he met Diaghilev, than his pigheadedness, conceit and limited vision, that made Diaghilev despair of finding in him the collaborator of whom he dreamed. Perhaps, though, there was a touch of pride in Diaghilev's desire to create a choreographer all of his own. Naturally, it was to Nijinsky that he first looked.

From his experiences of the past season and from discussions with Astruc, Diaghilev had decided what might be possible in the future. Not all his wishes were to be immediately fulfilled, but from his Black Notebook – as well as from talks with Karsavina and Grigoriev quoted above – we can see what he had in his mind. Four wishes.

1. He wanted his own ballet company, for which he would accept financial responsibility, for which he would create a new repertory, and which would function all the year round, apart from holidays.

2. He wanted to continue to present Russian opera in the West (and no doubt to commission and present new operas). But he could not possibly

afford to keep going his own opera company, so opera would only be performed in the summer with borrowed artists.

3. He wanted his company, sometimes giving opera and ballet, sometimes ballet alone, to perform in Paris, Monte Carlo, Rome, London and New York. He was already in touch with managements in these cities. He also planned symphony concerts.

4. He wanted Nijinsky to invent choreography. But until Nijinsky was ready, Fokine must continue to work on the new ballets.

No. 1 came true in 1911. No. 2 had to wait two years. No. 3 was fulfilled as regards the European capitals. Diaghilev's ballet company danced in South America in 1913. They would not visit the United States until 1915. No. 4 came true, but the public did not see Nijinsky's first ballet until 1912. Fokine left on cue, immediately after it.

Which dancers were prepared to leave the Imperial Theatres, renouncing the pensions they would have earned by the age of thirty-five, in order to join Diaghilev? Karsavina had in 1910 been promoted to prima ballerina at the Mariinsky. Apart from an increased salary, this meant that her appearances would be less frequent (and more carefully prepared); and she would have the right to dance as guest artist abroad. She could plan her appearances with Diaghilev to suit their mutual convenience; and she was sufficiently loyal to him to give up her music-hall career in London, highly profitable as it was, and to resign herself to frequent journeys backwards and forwards. Adolf Bolm, having graduated in 1904, had served well over the necessary five years and was at liberty to hand in his notice. He was intelligent enough to realize that the new Fokine repertoire offered him greater opportunities than that of the Mariinsky; and he renounced security for a chance to see the world and score new triumphs such as he had earned in *Prince Igor*. Naturally, Diaghilev had to offer more money than the Imperial Theatres. Sophie Feodorova from Moscow was one who decided to throw in her lot with Diaghilev. Grigoriev considered that to enlist a corps de ballet was harder than to secure the services of a few principal dancers.[1] He might have added that to train them and make them work together was harder still. There would be Fokine and Cecchetti to lick them into shape; and to Grigoriev himself would fall the task, on top of his other work – signing contracts, transporting dancers and scenery, supervising the stage staff – of remembering and rehearsing the repertory of previous years. 'General' Bezobrazov was despatched to Warsaw on a recruiting campaign.[2] Diaghilev cabled Astruc about a touring troupe, led by one Molodsov, believed to be in Paris, about whom Fokine expressed doubts.[3]

It was inconceivable that Nijinsky should not be the star of the new company, but he could only be available all the year round if he broke his agreement with the Imperial Theatres, as Lopukhova had done. This probably meant exile. But it will be seen that things turned out luckily for Diaghilev.

A corollary to the craving for rapid change, which marks our accelerating century, is the desire of young artists in every medium to be original. To question, rather than to learn from, their professors is the tendency of young writers, just as the budding painter, instead of serving an apprenticeship in the studio of his master, longs to strike out a line of his own. Fokine had rebelled against the academy: in 1910 Nijinsky, abetted by Diaghilev, began to doubt the doctrines of Fokine, of whom he had become so remarkable an interpreter. Diaghilev's and Nijinsky's dissatisfaction probably expressed itself in different ways, if, indeed, it found a precise definition.[4] Diaghilev foresaw a dead-end to the ballet of local colour, the evocation of past periods and distant lands. Fokine, happily yoked with Benois and Bakst, had conjured up both the eighteenth century and the 1830s. He had made a 'Polovtsian', an Egyptian, a Persian and a Russian ballet. When Ravel's *Daphnis* was ready, he would no doubt make a Greek ballet, and with Reynaldo Hahn's *Le Dieu bleu* he would make an Indian ballet. These fairy-tales, however appealing to a public greedy for varied flavourings, had little to do with the new world which was being born. The words 'modern' and 'contemporary' were acquiring a new prestige in the currency. Better, thought Diaghilev, to reinterpret past eras, rather than merely to evoke them: better still to speak for your own. Must ballet forever be a matter of fairy-tales? He felt the breeze of a new spirit which was ruffling the hair of artists throughout Europe, giving them the impulse to look at the changing world in a new way.

In a dancer's mind, in Nijinsky's, the rebellion was differently fomented. Although Fokine had given him something to interpret in such roles as the Golden Slave in *Schéhérazade*, he disapproved of the disordered sprawl of the orgy and slaughter.[5] There was no pattern of his movements that could be put on paper, no defined form in his attitudes or gestures. The ballets of Petipa at least had their architecture, if they had nothing else. Fokine had sacrificed much to achieve his 'realism'.

How was he to devise this both classic and expressive new form of movement, Nijinsky must have asked himself, this *durable* choreography? How do you invent a new language? Where is the starting-point? The young creative artist in the twentieth century is so afraid of doing something that has been done before that he is inhibited from starting at all. Then what, at twenty-three, had Nijinsky to 'say'? Diaghilev could hardly help him with a new grammar of movement. He had never learnt the secrets of the body, which only a dancer knows.

Every dancer (I think) must envy the perfect poses he sees in the painting and sculpture of the great masters, must despair while adoring, say, Botticelli's Venus or Michelangelo's Adam, Bernini's Apollo and Daphne, the Parthenon frieze. When he comes to consider being a choreographer, the dancer must often (I think) have the idea of stealing certain poses or groups from the old masters and devising graceful movements to link one pose, one group, with another. Fokine certainly looked for inspiration in museums; Massine's starting-point, a few years later, would be the memory of ikons and the sight of Italian *duecento* painting; in summer 1910 Nijinsky had been to the Louvre.

To explain why Nijinsky, when he set out to make a ballet on a Greek subject, used the attitudes of Egyptian paintings and reliefs, in which the head, arms and legs are shown in profile, the torso full on, Diaghilev told a story, perhaps partly true, about Nijinsky going to the wrong section of the Louvre, and becoming lost in admiration for the Egyptian sculptures, while Bakst waited for him in vain on the floor above. This was repeated by Larionov in later years.[6]

Which came first, Nijinsky's wish to invent movements in this two-dimensional style, or the decision to make a ballet to the existing music of Debussy's *L'Après-midi d'un faune*? The two ideas had been bracketed together by September 1910. We know that until Diaghilev and Nijinsky visited Stravinsky in Lausanne at the end of September, they were expecting *The Sacrifice*, which was the early name for *The Rite of Spring*, to be Stravinsky's new ballet for 1911; then, when they heard his two pieces for piano and orchestra, *Petrushka* was substituted and *The Sacrifice* postponed. On page 123 of Diaghilev's Notebook, *Faune* and *Sacrifice* are included in plans for 1911.[7] I therefore guess that Diaghilev had his notebook with him in the West, and that this entry was made in Venice in August or September, before he heard the beginnings of *Petrushka* at Lausanne a few weeks later.

During the last two months of 1910 Nijinsky worked with his sister on what became *L'Après-midi d'un faune*. They were both pleased with the result. At the end of December Bakst returned to St Petersburg; and a few days later, probably at the beginning of 1911, Vaslav and Bronislava, at their flat, showed Diaghilev and Bakst what had been evolved in the way of a moving Greek frieze.[8] There was only one jump in this *bas relief* of a ballet, made up of walks and runs and stiff-armed poses in profile. The human figure was dehumanized, and the dancers – there were to be several nymphs and one faun – were elements in a two-dimensional composition. Nijinsky's angular comings and goings cut across the fluid music, although the drama of the Faun's passion built up parallel with the music's rise to a climax, and diminished with its ebbing. Instead of the law-ordained married bondage between music and dance, the possibility of a freer union, a more felicitous concubinage, could now be perceived. In retrospect, we can say that a step had been taken which might lead to dancing without any musical accompaniment at all.

Was Diaghilev already so practised an augur that he could see what Nijinsky had done was good? Did the remote relationship of music and dance give him a shock? After all, it was he who had suggested the use of

Debussy's music. He said he was delighted. Bronislava had a foreboding that the right wing of Diaghilev's Committee, the balletomanes Svetlov and Bezobrazov, might persuade him to modify Nijinsky's stark movements, lacking in conventional 'grace', and she urged him not to allow any changes.[9]

Partly because Tcherepnine was working on a Greek ballet, *Narcisse*, which Fokine would arrange (since Ravel had not finished *Daphnis et Chloë*) and which would provide a star role for Nijinsky, and partly because Diaghilev was afraid Fokine would walk out if Nijinsky was brought forward as a choreographer even more radical than himself, *Faune* was postponed until 1912.[10]

On 10 February 1911 Diaghilev telegraphed Astruc. 'Debussy replaced by Spectre de la Rose. Théophile Gautier music Weber Nijinsky Karsavina only. Gautier's anniversary.'[11] The French poet Jean-Louis Vaudoyer had written an article on the Ballets Russes in *La Revue de Paris*, which appeared on 15 July 1910, just before the end of the Paris season.[12] Because of the rose Chiarina threw to Eusebius in *Carnaval*, which he referred to, he had, on an impulse, placed at the head of his text two lines from Gautier's poem 'Le Spectre de la Rose'.

> Je suis le spectre d'une rose
> Que tu portais hier au bal.

The 'ball' then made Vaudoyer think of Weber's piano piece *L'Invitation à la Valse*, for Weber was a composer Gautier had admired. This piece had been orchestrated by Berlioz; and Vaudoyer wrote to Bakst suggesting that a ballet might be made out of it.[13] Bakst then told Diaghilev, who liked the idea; and Fokine invented the *pas de deux* very quickly at the Catherine Hall.[14] Bakst watched the rehearsals and began to plan his setting,[15] which was a girl's bedroom of the Charles x or Biedermeier period.

Nijinsky, who had never danced the principal male role in *Giselle* in St Petersburg, was to do so on Sunday, 5 February. He decided to wear the costume Benois had designed for his appearance in Paris. In the first act, when Count Albrecht was disguised as a peasant, he wore a green and red tunic ending in a skirt over the thighs,[16] which Diaghilev had ordered to be shortened by two inches.[17] It was not unlike the costume that Perrot had worn in the original production, but ballet fashions had changed in Russia since the Romantic period, and it had become customary to wear trunks over the tights in medieval and Renaissance-style ballets. However, Benois had not included these in his sketch, so Nijinsky had worn none in Paris: but in St Petersburg the omission, plus the shortened tunic, made the dancer appear unexpectedly nude. When he appeared on stage before the performance, Krupensky protested at the revealing costume, but Nijinsky refused to make any addition or deviate from Benois' design, and danced the first act wearing it.[18]

During the interval Karsavina was summoned by the Dowager Empress, and congratulated on her success in music-hall in London.[19] Either Teliakovsky was away, or he took no direct part in the argument with Nijinsky, but two friends of Kchessinskaya's probably telephoned to her, hoping to make trouble.[20] Either Kchessinskaya took steps to have a rival for popularity removed, or Krupensky availed himself of the chance to humiliate Diaghilev through Nijinsky, or a Grand Duke gave orders, hoping to discredit Diaghilev's boy-friend. Next morning, Nijinsky was told to apologize or resign. He refused to apologize and was dismissed. It looks as if the management realized almost immediately what a loss they were sustaining, and gave Nijinsky a chance to rejoin the company. Possibly Teliakovsky, if he had not been initially involved, was angry at his subordinates' drastic action. But Nijinsky, prompted by Diaghilev, was adamant.[21]

It is almost impossible to believe that Diaghilev had not engineered this dismissal, which released Nijinsky to be the star of his new company. Perhaps by making Nijinsky late for the opening of the season, and by urging him to wear the shocking costume, he had been provoking the authorities to quarrel with his friend. Anyway, he had got his heart's desire. One might think that he would have put off forming a company until he knew Nijinsky was free, but this was not the case. He had begun to sign contracts as early as 1 December 1910.[22]

Diaghilev, in a high state of exaltation, set about making what use he could of the incident; by arousing resentment and sympathy abroad, he could gain publicity for his own enterprise. On 10 February 1911, when it is beyond doubt that Nijinsky was well and truly dismissed, he telegraphed to Astruc, 'After triumphant début presence all Petersburg Vestris was dismissed within twenty-four hours. Reason costume Carpaccio designed Bakst. Monstrous intrigue. Press indignant this morning. Interview director announcing willing take back Vestris who refused. Appalling scandal. Use publicity. Acknowledge receipt. Serge.'[23]

Knowing how Diaghilev was apt to exaggerate, Astruc naturally wondered whether he was telling the exact truth, particularly as he had attributed Nijinsky's costume to Bakst, when it was by Benois. Since *Schéhérazade*, which he had also 'given' to Bakst, Diaghilev knew what publicity value the name of Bakst had in Paris. Astruc cabled Gunsburg for confirmation. The same evening Gunsburg replied, 'Costume revealing ['Costume décolleté'] but responsibility of direction. No difficulty bookings abroad nevertheless foresee possible trouble London Gala.'[24]

Gunsburg was referring to the relationship between the Empress Marie Feodorovna and Queen Alexandra. The direction of the Imperial Theatres had spread the rumour that the Dowager Empress had been shocked by Nijinsky's appearance, and it is said she later denied this.[25] On Friday 13 February Diaghilev telegraphed again, 'Try to obtain and send me at once letters or interviews with Duncan and Zambelli about Nijinsky and his grotesque dismissal. Reply.'[26] Then, the next day, 'Incriminating costume same as Paris Giselle style Carpaccio. Worried Direction invent Dowager demanded dismissal. Let's stir something up ['Moussons'].'[27] An hour later: 'Whole family present applauded. Mother seeing for first time declared she had never seen anything like it. Next day direction gave out Mother shocked insisted dismissal. Acknowledge receipt. Send me press interviews.'[28] Before leaving his office that Saturday, Astruc wrote back:

> I enclose all the articles that appeared this morning about the Nijinsky affair.
> I must admit that your telegram worried me quite a lot. I cannot see why you want us to take this Carpaccio-Bakst line when the real reason is Giselle-Benois? You must have your reasons, but I can't give the French press information which differs from what Nijinsky and Benois told the Russian press in great detail in the columns of *Novoe Vremya* and the *St Petersburg Journal*.
> Anyway, you will see that I got going in a big way within half an hour of receiving your telegram. Paris seethed. Every columnist and balletomane in Paris arrived at the Pavillon de Hanovre. So we have [a list of articles follows] ...
> I am very anxious for detailed information about your programmes.... Let me know also how you stand over your tours and whether you reckon to be in a position to keep all your promises.[29]

All that now remained of Diaghilev's opera plans for 1911 was the ballet of sea monsters in the submarine act of *Sadko*. Fokine had prepared the choreography for this, and Boris Anisfeld, who had hitherto only painted and interpreted the décors of other artists, was given the undersea kingdom to design.

Tcherepnine was finishing *Narcisse*, for which Bakst had designed a landscape setting and some bold-patterned Greek peasant costumes. Benois was completing his designs for *Petrushka*, while in Beaulieu Stravinsky worked on with the score. In Paris Ravel was far from having finished the score of *Daphnis*, although he played extracts from it to the English writer Arnold Bennett, then living in the Forest of Fontainebleau, on 27 February.[30] Reynaldo Hahn, however, had written most of *Le Dieu bleu*, and by way of reward Diaghilev invited him to St Petersburg and made a fuss of him. On 28 February Diaghilev gave a big dinner for Hahn chez Cubat, after which the composer and Baron Medem of the Conservatoire played *Le Dieu bleu* as a piano duet.[31] This was the nearest Diaghilev ever got to presenting any of his new repertoire in St Petersburg. He who had so successfully taken the music of Russia to the West could now be seen in his own capital, which had snubbed him, as a patron of French composers. Three weeks after Nijinsky's dismissal the 'decadents' were keeping their end up!

Diaghilev had signed contracts to present his Ballet at Monte Carlo before the end of its annual winter season, and in Rome during the World Exhibition of Art. The Paris season would follow in June; and he was negotiating for a Coronation season in London in the summer, and a visit to America. Five weeks before his Monte Carlo season opened and eleven weeks before his Paris season (which was to be at the Châtelet, as in 1909), Diaghilev's proposed repertoire for Paris was: *Schéhérazade*, *The Firebird*, *Narcisse*, *Petrushka*, *Sadko*, *Le Dieu bleu*, *Le Spectre de la rose* and a ballet to Liszt's Fourteenth Hungarian Rhapsody.[32] There would be additions, subtractions and indecisions. It was also planned to show *Le Pavillon d'Armide*, *Les Sylphides* and *Giselle* in Monte Carlo, Rome and London. Diaghilev had had a lavish new idea: symphonic *entr'actes* – with illustrations. That is to say that a painted curtain would be lowered to keep the audience quiet while the music was played. One was to be Liszt's *Orpheus*, with a decorative panel by Bakst – for it was Liszt's centenary as well as Gautier's;[33] another *The Battle of Kerjenetz*, an interlude in Rimsky's *The City of Kitej*, with a painting by Roerich.[34] Only the second of these was realized, but Serov painted a big curtain, in the style of Persian miniaturists, to hold the attention during the overture (that is, the first playing of the first movement) of *Schéhérazade*.[35]

Tcherepnine would conduct in Monte Carlo and Rome, but Diaghilev had to find two other conductors for Paris. He negotiated with Cooper in Moscow, and, through Astruc, with Pierné in Paris.[36] As things turned out, neither of these conducted *Petrushka*, but a newcomer to the Ballet, Pierre Monteux.

On 13 March Bakst arrived in Paris to paint the décors of *Le Dieu bleu* and *Le Spectre de la rose*[37] and to start his enormous job (five scenes) for Rubinstein's *St Sébastien*. On the fifteenth Diaghilev telegraphed to Astruc that he would be in Paris on Sunday.[38] Could they lunch together and would Astruc book two stalls for the Colonne concert that afternoon? When he and Nijinsky set off together on the night train, Vaslav was leaving Russia for good.

They stayed a week in Paris. Probably because he was jealous that Rubinstein should successfully have commissioned Debussy before he had managed to do so, and out of frustration at the slowness of Ravel, Diaghilev lamented to Astruc (as I think) that *Le Dieu bleu* would be his only French ballet to be presented during the first season of his very own company. Astruc had a pianist play over to Diaghilev and Nijinsky the score of *La Péri* by Paul Dukas.[39] Diaghilev liked the composition and at once decided to give it as a ballet during his Paris season. This decision was the beginning of a long and futile saga.

Diaghilev and Nijinsky broke their journey to Monte Carlo at Beaulieu and spent three nights there at the Hôtel Bristol, having discussions with Stravinsky.[40] The Riviera (eastwards from Nice, only a French possession since 1860) was only visited in winter and spring, and the coastline, which Nijinsky was seeing for the first time, was one of isolated villages and scattered villas. Travelling backwards and forwards between Beaulieu and Monte Carlo, Diaghilev had talks with Raoul de Guinsbourg, the Director of the Monte Carlo Theatre, rented a disused theatre, Le Palais du Soleil, for classes and rehearsals, and booked rooms for Vaslav and himself – not at the smart Hôtel de Paris, near the Casino, where he was always to stay in post-war years, but at the Riviera Palace at Beausoleil, high on the steep mountain slope above the town.[41]

The St Petersburg dancers in the charge of Svetlov, the Moscow dancers, the Polish contingent under Bezobrazov, and the Molodsov troupe from Paris converged on Monte Carlo, with barely a fortnight in which to rehearse before their opening on 9 April 1911.[42] They constituted a smaller and weaker group than Diaghilev had presented in the two previous years. Ten of them had been at the Châtelet in 1909: Nijinsky, Karsavina, Bolm, Schollar, Rosaï, Vassilieva, Nijinska, Grigoriev, Alexandrov and Semenov. (Vassilieva and Alexandrov had been in *Boris* in 1908.) A few old hands, such as Kremnev and Orlov, would be joining later. Bolm had been with Diaghilev in 1909, but not in 1910. It was the scratched-together corps which might prove weak. Cecchetti's lessons helped to strengthen them.[43]

Diaghilev had stipulated that Fokine should confine himself to choreography.[44] Did he fear Fokine as a rival to Nijinsky or dislike him as an interpreter? (Karsavina always praised Fokine's dancing highly, but Bronislava Nijinska told me he was 'terrible in everything'.)[45] Fokine fought hard for his right to dance, but in vain. He was given the title of Choreographic Director and a large salary to compensate him for leaving the Mariinsky.[46] Besides this, he was to be allowed to devise a dance in *St Sébastien* for Rubinstein. He was annoyed at having to arrange *Narcisse* in place of his long-planned *Daphnis*; and he knew how little time he had for everything.

About the size of his repertoire Diaghilev had been optimistic rather than realistic. Fokine had arranged certain ballets so quickly in the past – *Prince Igor* for one, and a few groups in the St Petersburg production of *Les Sylphides* had been shown to the dancers just before the curtain rose – that Diaghilev thought, or hoped, that he might yet break his speed record.[47] But preparing new ballets in the peace of the Catherine Hall on the Ekaterinsky Canal was one thing: preparing them on tour, while performing, was another. The bigger Diaghilev's repertoire grew, the more ballets had to be constantly rehearsed. Fokine could but plunge in and hope for the best.

There was a long telegraphic correspondence between Diaghilev and Astruc over the next two months about *La Péri*, which Paul Dukas had insisted should be danced by his mistress, Trouhanova. Diaghilev would agree to this on certain conditions. But there were endless stipulations and counter-proposals. Diaghilev demanded the right to give the ballet, after his Paris season, in every country throughout the world. He claimed that

Nijinsky would only dance if Dukas conducted. Otherwise *La Péri* must be replaced by the Fourteenth Hungarian Rhapsody of Liszt.[48]

The friends were gathering at Monte Carlo. Besides Svetlov and Bezobrazov, there was Diaghilev's cousin, Pavka Koribut-Kubitovitch, with the perfect manners, who ran errands and was nice to anyone who was difficult.[49] Benois was present in his capacity as Artistic Director to supervise productions. Stravinsky came over from Beaulieu.[50] Gunsburg was supposed to keep an eye on finances. Bakst was absent in Paris with Ida Rubinstein, but his two nieces, the daughters of Dr Botkine, were there to enjoy themselves.[51] Then, the Aga Khan, who sighed in vain for Karsavina, had a villa at Monte Carlo and was sometimes drawn into conferences by Diaghilev, who hoped for his support.[52] From their palace on its rock, the Grimaldis, the princely rulers of Monaco, kept an eye on their Russian guests.

The Théâtre de Monte Carlo, where the Ballet were to perform, was built in the pastry-cook style of the 1870s, with tiled and pinnacled domes, and stood on a terrace overlooking the sea. Its main entrance on the landward side, which it shared with the Casino, faced a garden with palms and giant magnolias, flanked on the west by the Hôtel de Paris, on the east by the Café de Paris, with its terrace of tables and awnings. The interior of the theatre, though small, was rectangular, ornate and golden, with big mirrors down each side and with carved chairs upholstered in red plush.

Diaghilev spent the day of 5 April in Paris with Astruc, travelling there and back on the night train.[53] Among other problems to deal with, he had to persuade Ida Rubinstein to come to Monte Carlo to appear in *Schéhérazade*: this was necessary for Diaghilev to fulfil his contract. As she had probably never been paid for previous performances, she felt no strong obligation.[54] He also had to persuade Bakst to take two days off from his work for Rubinstein in order to set up *Le Spectre de la rose* at Monte Carlo. Next day, 6 April, was the dress rehearsal.

Anticipating the non-appearance of Rubinstein, Diaghilev had made Karsavina study the role of Zobeïda in *Schéhérazade*, so at the dress rehearsal and – as Rubinstein did not appear till 23 April – at the *première* on 9 April 1911, she and Nijinsky danced the principal roles in both *Giselle* and *Schéhérazade*. What very different roles they were, too!

It was a happy, constructive spring season, and the company, delighted with Monte Carlo and their comfortable dressing-rooms, looked forward to many more seasons in later years. Although Diaghilev was anxious about *La Péri* and *Le Dieu bleu* and about Fokine's rehearsal time, and although he was also resentful about the defection of Bakst, he could see that a good beginning had been made by his company, and he only occasionally vented outbursts of temper by telegram on Astruc. After the day's work he, Nijinsky, and Karsavina often had supper with Chaliapine at the Café de Paris, where there seemed to be a friend at every table.[55] Kchessinskaya was in Monte Carlo,[56] and one night four Grand Dukes, George and Sergei Mikhailovitch, Boris and Andrei Vladimirovitch, were seen dining together at the Hôtel de Paris.[57] It may have been the Grand Ducal menace that had made Diaghilev settle further up the hill. An English visitor who was to become a dear friend, and who arrived with her husband in time for the first night of *Le Spectre de la rose*, was Lady Ripon's daughter, Lady Juliet Duff.[58]

Le Spectre de la rose, which had its first performance on 19 April, was a freak ballet in that it only had two characters, one of whom – the Girl back from her first ball – was asleep throughout most of the action, while the other – the Ghost of the Rose her partner had given her – was a sexless spirit, neither male nor female. Then, the setting of the Girl's bedroom, with its blue and white flowered wallpaper, its curtained bed, and open, muslin-hung French windows, was more like the décor of a play than that of a Russian ballet. Nijinsky's non-stop dance to a series of waltz tunes was perhaps the longest ever invented. From the moment he bounded in at the right-hand window – to leap and twist round the room, to lead the sleeping girl through a hypnotic duet, and then to soar through the left-hand window out into the night – he hardly came to rest.

In St Petersburg, when Bronislava Nijinska had watched Fokine arranging *Le Spectre*, she had been disappointed by the banality of the movements.[59] Indeed, we can well see how a man capering alone in waltz time to Weber's 'tum-ti-ti, tum-ti-ti' could have looked silly. In the course of rehearsals Nijinsky transformed his role.[60] (Even Diaghilev can hardly have foreseen what he would do with it – and yet perhaps he gave the necessary hint.) Nijinsky instinctively realized that he must de-sex himself, soften every line, keep continually swinging, curving and circling like a leaf caught in a whirl of wind. He distorted the correct classical *port de bras* to wrap his arms and hands round his head and face, and when he extended an arm upwards or sideways, he sagged at the elbows, let his wrists loll and his fingers curl like petals.[61] Bakst had had dyed and sewn to the pinkish-purple leotard the limp silk petals of various pinks, reds and purples, which merged into each other like the colours of Gallé or Tiffany glass, abolishing contours and camouflaging sex. Nijinsky devised his own make-up. 'His face was like that of a celestial insect, his eyebrows suggesting some beautiful beetle which one might expect to find closest to the heart of a rose, and his mouth was like rose petals.'[62] When costumed and made up, as ever, he became possessed. The photographs of Bert and Baron de Meyer have perpetuated the magic of his interpretation. Nobody who saw Nijinsky as the Rose ever got over it.

When Fokine danced the Rose later on, he must have looked like a handsome man acting effeminately; and we have Mme Bronislava Nijinska's word that he was 'terrible'.[63] When Idzikovsky did it, his tiny stature and his dazzling technique made him acceptable. We have seen some embarrassing performances in our own day. Perhaps the most thrilling attribute of Nijinsky's performance was its strangeness – a quality of movement like the soaring song of the great *castrati*, whose voices have long ceased to sound upon the earth.

There had been more than one panic at the dress rehearsal. When Nijinsky's costume arrived at the eleventh hour from Paris, it was found to have been badly interpreted by the dressmaker. (Bakst had a tendency to create difficulties by thinking more of how his design would look on paper than of how it could be adapted to a human body.) Benois recalled that

important corrections had to be made there and then. There was no other course but to pin the silk rose petals direct to the flesh-coloured *tricot*. Naturally this could not be done without pin-pricks and scratches, which caused poor Vaslav to squirm and cry out in pain. Diaghilev, in evening dress and top hat, looking very pompous and solemn as he always looked on first nights, stood by, giving directions with growing anxiety, while the role of costumier was being improvised by our stage-manager [the scene-painter] O. P. Allegri, as the professional costumier seemed no good at all. Kneeling on the floor with his mouth full of pins, Allegri cleverly performed the complicated and responsible operation of correcting the costume on a living body....[64]

When Bakst arrived, he found that his bird cage, which was to hang in one of the open windows, had been removed because Nijinsky said it would impede his jump, but he was determined to place it somewhere. Diaghilev exclaimed, 'Levushka, for God's sake, chuck the canary, the public is growing impatient. Oh, don't be ridiculous; canaries don't stand on the chest-of-drawers.' 'You don't understand, Serioja: we must give the atmosphere.' The interval was prolonged while the cage was hoisted up to cornice height.[65]

The exceptional success of *Le Spectre de la rose* took Diaghilev and his friends by surprise. It would become the most popular work in the repertoire, and within a year Nijinsky was fed up with it.

Rubinstein arrived from Paris on 23 April to give two performances of *Schéhérazade* and two of *Cléopâtre*. In the latter, Preobrajenska, who had come from Russia earlier in the season to make what turned out to be her only appearances with Diaghilev's company, took Pavlova's role of Ta-Hor, the temple attendant.[66] Rubinstein never worked for Diaghilev again: her rival spectacles, richly subsidized, which followed year after year, aroused his jealousy, but this in time gave way to contempt. Nijinsky had intended that she should be the first Nymph in his *Faune*,[67] because he wanted someone taller than Bronislava; it soon became clear that this was not possible. Although Rubinstein's performances in Monte Carlo coincided with the *première* of *Narcisse*, Fokine invented the dance she would perform as St Sebastian before she returned to Paris.[68]

Fokine had been reluctant to undertake *Narcisse* because he was holding all his Greek ideas in reserve for *Daphnis et Chloë*, whose scenario he had written over two years before. It was Bakst, who had never got over a trip to Greece with Serov in 1903,[69] who was importunate for a Greek ballet in 1911; and Tcherepnine had been inspired to write what Benois considered his finest score.[70] Then, Diaghilev naturally liked the legend of the beautiful youth in love with his own image (as the homosexual Caravaggio, almost alone among Renaissance painters, had done three centuries before), and saw its possibilities for Nijinsky. Yet Benois wrote,

The performance of *Narcisse* proved to be a beautiful and noble spectacle, but it was not a great success. The reason, I think, was that the subject is entirely unsuitable for ballet. The two characters are the most static in Greek mythology – Echo is imprisoned in her cave and Narcissus is immobilized in the contemplation of his own beauty. I remember how difficult it was for Fokine to get some variety in Narcissus's interminable 'choreographic soliloquy' in front of his own reflection; even Karsavina's beauty and her genuinely classical poses did not prevent the melancholy mood demanded by Echo from becoming tedious. Both dancers seemed to be the victims of a strange fancy and one felt sorry for them. . . . The most successful part of *Narcisse* is the music. . . . The images which flitted in the composer's imagination are evoked far more convincingly than when one actually *sees* them on the stage.[71]

Karsavina as Echo was not, in fact, 'imprisoned in her cave', but posed and repeated the movements of Nijinsky's Narcissus on the stage level. Diaghilev had given her a hint which evoked the image of Echo for her. ' "Don't trip lightly as a graceful nymph; I see rather a monumental figure, a tragic mask, Niobe." "In my vision," she wrote, "the heavy metric structure of the tragic name became the mournful tread of sleepless Echo." '[72]

Nijinsky, in a white *chlamys* and a wig of long blond ringlets, gave a fine impression of Greek youth and beauty, but the large artificial flower which rose from the pool into which, in love with his own reflection, he sank at the end, had a ridiculous effect.[73] The woodland monsters, too, were rather funny.[74]

Diaghilev was in Rome ahead of the company,[75] and Fokine followed him.[76] The talks they had about the ballets still to be invented brought matters to a head. The company arrived at the end of the first week in May, with a week to rehearse before their opening. At the station Grigoriev was handed a note from Diaghilev, summoning him to the Excelsior for a talk.

I found him in a very bad mood [wrote Grigoriev] and much preoccupied. He said that very little time remained before our opening in Paris, and that Fokine must be made to finish the remaining ballets at once. I replied that this was not feasible. He could not devote himself entirely to the new ballets, because of having to rehearse our recruits in the old ones. 'That's nothing to do with *me*!' Diaghilev interrupted angrily. 'Fokine shouldn't have wasted his time rehearsing the old stuff. He should have worked at Monte Carlo on *Petrushka*; and he must find time now, even if he has to keep at it morning, noon and night!' Having learnt by experience that when Diaghilev was in one of his black moods it was useless to argue, I refrained from doing so. But I could not help wondering what had upset him; and I discovered later that Fokine ... had told him that he could not possibly manage all his work in time for the opening in Paris [that is, *Sadko*, *Petrushka*, *Le Dieu bleu* and *La Péri*]. Later the same day Benois, Stravinsky, Tcherepnine, Fokine and I met in order to work out a programme for our perform-ances in Rome such that it might lighten Fokine's task. He sulked and refused to speak, however.... Yet when he began composing [*Petrushka*], as he shortly did, he turned out to be full of ideas; and the rehearsals went quickly ahead. Only when he reached the third scene, where the Moor is left by himself for a time, did his invention fail him. He could not think what to make him do, and lost his temper, throwing the music on the floor and leaving the rehearsal. Next day, however, he appeared looking happier, and said he had thought of some 'business' for the accursed Moor: he would give him a coconut to play with – which would carry him at least through the first part of the scene.[77]

Petrushka was rehearsed in a shabby buffet in the basement of the theatre. The heat was intolerable,[78] and Benois sketched Stravinsky seated without his coat at the piano. He did another drawing of Diaghilev, fully dressed, leaning back in his chair with an expression of patient weariness. In the margin of his drawing of the composer, Benois wrote, 'Fokine can make *nothing* of the rhythms of the Coachmen's dance!'[79]

The happy summer days live for us in the reminiscences of Benois and Karsavina. Benois and Stravinsky were staying at the Albergo Italia, near the Quattro Fontane, and their rooms overlooked the Barberini Gardens. 'Every morning,' wrote Benois, 'I used to hear ... a confused tangle of sounds, interrupted from time to time by long pauses. This was the maturing of the last bars of the fourth act.'[80] *Petrushka*, which we can see as the epitome of the *World of Art* movement, a glimpse of old Russia through modern spectacles, had been designed in St Petersburg; it had been composed mostly by the Lake of Geneva and on the Côte d'Azur; and it was finished and choreographed in Rome, before being staged in Paris.

Karsavina was staying at an hotel opposite the Queen Mother's palace, near the Borghese Gardens.[81] She wrote,

Diaghilev often came round in the morning to fetch me on his way to the Teatro Costanzi. 'Maestro [Cecchetti], you say? The old man will wait; it is a sin to be indoors on such a morning,' and he would take Nijinsky and myself for some enchanting drive, point out here and there an arch, a view, a monument. He would hand us over to the Maestro with a request not to scold his children for being a bit late. Maestro, with unusual blandness, would excuse his unpunctual pupils; he knew he could make up for time lost.... For the sake of discipline, though, Maestro would go through a show of disapproval; twirling his cane, thus giving time for escape, he would sling it at my feet; a well-timed skip cleared the missile.... He was in a frenzy of teaching, and an equal frenzy of learning possessed both Nijinsky and myself.[82]

The Russian Ballet opened at the Teatro Costanzi on Monday 14 May, with *Le Pavillon d'Armide*, *Les Sylphides* and *Prince Igor*, and was well received. Diaghilev cabled to Astruc next day about the smart audience and the sixteen curtain calls. The King of Italy, the Queen and the Queen Mother attended the second performance, which was greeted with 'infinite ovations'.[83] It had been difficult, however, owing to the hostility of the theatre managers and the absence of nearly all the technical staff – not only difficult, in fact, but dangerous. During *Le Pavillon* Benois had to stand by the switchboard himself to signal the different changes and press buttons. Diaghilev, *under* the stage, was controlling the lighting.[84]

Once the opening was over Diaghilev turned his mind to Paris. It is probable that, when on 22 May he wrote the following (typed) letter (sending a copy to Bakst), he had already realized that Fokine could not arrange *La Péri* and *Le Dieu bleu* in time for Paris, and was initiating a lightning campaign with the intention of putting the blame for a change of programme on Astruc and Bakst. It may have dawned on him that to present both ballets in addition to *Schéhérazade* would be an excess of Orientalism; but he may still have been clinging to the hope that Fokine might manage to complete one or the other. If *La Péri* and *Le Dieu bleu* could not be staged, he did not want to have to pay Bakst for his designs.

This is the situation: we have a fortnight till the Paris opening, and there are still two ballets we have not even touched for reasons which have nothing to do with me or my company.

First Péri. I have still not received Trouhanova's contract signed.... Mlle Trouhanova, having given her word to come to Monte Carlo, never managed to do so during the entire two months [that is, just under six weeks] we were there.... Obviously we can't plan a work without the co-operation of its chief interpreter.

I have certainly received the piano score (in which there are some obvious mistakes), but it is of no use to me for the reasons given above and above all for the following reason, which I must now put to you most seriously.

You have followed my work for five years and you know the principles on which it is based. I am not a professional impresario, and my speciality is to make painters, musicians, poets and dancers work together.

Of all my collaborators the most indispensable has always been Leon Bakst, my childhood friend, who has taken part in all my enterprises. [When they first met in 1890, Diaghilev and Bakst were eighteen and twenty-four respectively.] He owes his Paris reputation entirely to the Russian seasons which, as you well know, have cost me such superhuman efforts.

This year I gave him four productions to do. One, Narcisse, we all worked out together. As for the second, le Spectre de la Rose, Bakst watched the rehearsals in Petersburg and saw it arranged choreographically. So he had only to adapt his décor to a ready-made work.

As for 'Dieu bleu' and above all 'Péri' we have had nothing but vague suggestions, possible treatments – nothing more, not even a pencil sketch.... In short I know nothing about the construction or the very idea of the décor. And it is under these conditions that Fokine, Benois and myself are supposed to devise a production?

As far as Péri is concerned the situation has become absolutely ridiculous, for we are in total ignorance of whether the action takes place in a palace, on a mountain-top or in the clouds – and this is two weeks before the first night. Bakst claims that we lack confidence in his work, but I must say that I have never seen so astounding a betrayal of every artistic and aesthetic principle as he has shown in his dealings with us. When Bakst took on the production of S. Sébastien he swore to me that it would in no way interfere with our work, which he held much dearer. Now I declare that we have been completely sacrificed to the work of Rubinstein and d'Annunzio. We are paying for having trusted him so completely. Certainly Kchessinska never played us such a dirty trick as you have done over this negotiation, which, as you will remember, I was so helpful about. Kchessinska never obliged us to abandon anything we had undertaken. Now, thanks to you and Bakst, at the last moment we are forced to give up the production of two ballets planned for a season beginning in a fortnight's time, and I warn you that you must take the consequences.

I need not remind you that by giving up the *répétition générale* of Dieu bleu we lose almost a hundred thousand francs. But what hurts me most is not to be able to give Paris the whole splendid repertory we planned – and you know that that is the one thing I really care about.... Now I am in the most embarrassing position with regard to Dukas and above all Reynaldo Hahn, who took the trouble to come to Petersburg; and I must ask you to make your excuses for what has happened and to explain to them the reason for this delay. I have suffered too much from the financial and moral worries that you and Bakst have brought upon me.

PS. [in manuscript] Copies of this letter have been sent to Bakst and Reynaldo Hahn.[85]

Diaghilev may have timed this letter to arrive on the breakfast tables of Astruc and Bakst with the press notices of Rubinstein in *Le Martyre de St Sébastien*. Posts were quicker in those days.

Bakst protested vehemently.[86] Astruc's reply does not survive, but he appears to have strongly resented any change in the announced programme. On the night of Friday 25 May, Diaghilev, Benois, Fokine and Grigoriev sat up till the early hours, discussing possibilities; and next day Diaghilev telegraphed to Astruc, 'After discussion entire night decided definitely renounce revival Firebird in favour following programmes. First Carnaval with Nijinsky Harlequin Narcisse Rose Sadko. Second Schéhérazade Péri Kerjenetz Rose Petrushka. Stage director Allegri arriving Paris Sunday with music.... Begin rehearsals Monday.'[87]

Having officially abandoned the idea of putting on the complicated *Dieu bleu*, Diaghilev, in the letter Allegri took to Astruc that Sunday 27 May, renounced *The Firebird* and, knowing how easily he could manage *not* to come to terms with Dukas and Trouhanova, prepared the way for giving up *La Péri* by blaming Bakst and Trouhanova for the state of affairs. As a sop, Nijinsky was to dance for the first time in *Carnaval*. Diaghilev did not mention that Karsavina would be dancing Columbine in the place of Lopukhova, and Bolm Pierrot (a role he made great) in the place of Bulgakov.

Your telegrams full of words like disastrous, immoral and deplorable are getting on my nerves. You seem to be willing disaster on our season.... It is obvious that if Bakst and Trouhanova had come to Monte Carlo for a few days Péri would have been arranged already.

Now the unanimous revolt against this intruding ballet has reached its climax. Karsavina refuses to come to Paris to dance alongside Trouhanova. Fokine declared yesterday that to put on Péri with Trouhanova would be the most idiotic thing he had ever let himself in for and something he could never forgive himself.... Yesterday, after hearing the music Fokine declared that he would need at least twelve rehearsals to arrange it, not counting orchestral ones!! He doesn't feel ready to start work on it because the libretto is quite inadequate and he has no idea how to produce it.

Under the circumstances I realize that the revival of Firebird, our most complicated ballet and one we have not danced for a year, is a physical impossibility if we do Péri. I had to decide between the two and to give up the work put in on the revival of Firebird.

I made that decision against the wishes of all my colleagues as a result of all the abusive words in your interminable telegrams.

And now I hear from you that the cancelling of Firebird is deplorable too. ...

There is one thing I must ask you to do. See your friend Bakst and let me know by telegram which scheme you decide together is likely to be less damaging to my reputation and financial prospects. ...

I must know by Monday at the latest. ...[88]

It was awkward that Trouhanova had already been photographed for the programme, wearing her Bakst costume for *La Péri*, and that the designs for this and for Nijinsky's costume had been reproduced in colour – and the scenery had been painted; but there was really no need to give *The Firebird*, and the second of the two programmes telegraphed by Diaghilev on 26 May was quite long enough without *La Péri*. Besides their favourite *Schéhérazade* – with Karsavina instead of Rubinstein – and *Carnaval* with (for the first time) Nijinsky, Parisians would have three new works in two programmes, plus *The Battle of Kerjenetz* as a musical interlude with Roerich's curtain. On 31 May Diaghilev cabled to Astruc that Tcherepnine would conduct the first and Monteux the second programme; that he needed twenty men, twenty women and eight children as walkers-on for *Petrushka*; that an extra rehearsal room would be necessary besides the stage, as there would often be three rehearsals a day; that the company would arrive in Paris on Friday morning [the following day] and begin rehearsals at the Châtelet at once.[89]

'At once' was none too soon. The *première* was on Tuesday. The dancers got off the night train from Rome to face a weekend of hard work. At frantic times like this so much depended on co-ordination by the methodical and imperturbable Grigoriev; yet it was always he who had to bear the brunt of Diaghilev's rages when anything went wrong.[90]

There was an incomplete rehearsal on the Monday, at which *Carnaval* was not given.[91] On 6 June Nijinsky danced Harlequin in *Carnaval* at the Châtelet Theatre, and although Leontiev took over at least in the second of the four performances of the first programme,[92] it was to become one of Nijinsky's most famous roles.

Not only was Karsavina dancing Columbine, a more mature and romantic coquette than that created by the impetuous Lopukhova, but Bolm, as Pierrot, created such a tragic figure within the scope of the comedy that he almost stole the show, and Cecchetti made a living portrait of the dapper, fussy, self-satisfied Pantalon, with his well-brushed moustache and green gloves.

That night, after dancing in *Carnaval*, Nijinsky went on to dance, for the first time in Paris, *Narcisse* and *Le Spectre de la rose*. Of the last, Cocteau wrote,

In his costume of curling petals, behind which perhaps the Girl perceives the image of her recent dancing-partner, he comes through the blue cretonne curtains out of the warm June night. He conveys – which one would have thought impossible – the impression of some melancholy, imperious scent. Exulting in his rosy ecstasy he seems to impregnate the muslin curtains and take possession of the dreaming Girl. It is the most extraordinary achievement. By magic he makes the Girl dream she is dancing and conjures up all the delights of the ball.[93]

In the submarine act of *Sadko* the hero, who descended into the Kingdom of the Sea to seek the hand of the Sea King's daughter, was sung by Issachenko, the King by the familiar bass of the last two seasons, Zaporojetz, and Kupava by Sapanova-Shevtchenko. The undulations of the sea monsters, some with faces covered and with trailing finny sleeves, in marvellous tones of green, red and mother-of-pearl, and the subsequent storm, comprising some of Rimsky's most pungent passages, made a strong impression.

It is odd that, after this evening of remarkable dancing, the critic of *Le Gaulois* should have chosen to emphasize the role of the painter. 'He devises the décor, costumes and lighting effects and he is the real magician behind these animated visions.' The critic described 'the enchanted clearing and beautifully shaped white clouds' of Bakst in *Narcisse*, Anisfeld's 'green rocks and tumbling tresses of aquatic vegetation, his horizons of blue, luminous and fairy-like waves' in *Sadko*, the 'blue and white room, in perfect taste' of *Le Spectre de la rose*. In the latter Karsavina was allowed 'charming subtlety' and Nijinsky 'surprising virtuosity'. But in *Narcisse* 'the handsome young man in a white tunic' was 'a little too reminiscent of Diana the Huntress'. Of *Carnaval* he would not write, firstly because it had not been given at the dress rehearsal, which he attended, secondly because he could not approve the transfer of Schumann's intimate little piano pieces to the stage.[94] The critic of *Commedia* repeated last year's complaints about orchestrating Schumann, and thought it was lazy of Diaghilev to have used the Weber–Berlioz music, instead of commissioning a new score for *Le Spectre de la rose*.[95]

Fokine had had trouble making out Stravinsky's score for *Petrushka*, and never really liked it.[96] His admiration for the composer, like that of so many other people, stopped short with *The Firebird*. (For that matter, Stravinsky never thought that Fokine's loose handling of the crowd scenes was a correct interpretation, or that Benois' costumes were what they should be. Benois, on the other hand, thought everything perfect.) When the musicians began to rehearse the music, they burst out laughing. Monteux had trouble convincing them that it was not a joke.[97] Benois' scenery had arrived from Russia, but the black set of Petrushka's cell was damaged in transit. Fokine had only one two-hour rehearsal with the crowd, including the French walkers-on, who, when photographs were taken, tended to stare at the camera – particularly the children.[98] When Cecchetti mimed the Magician playing his flute solo before bringing the puppets to life, a girl in the crowd, as if hypnotized by the music, was drawn forwards into the open centre of the stage. Fokine liked this and 'wrote in' the episode.[99]

Benois had an abscess on his arm and was in pain. Because of this it was Bakst who retouched the décor of Petrushka's cell. In doing so, he repainted the portrait of the old Magician; and he painted him in profile, instead of full-on with staring, hypnotic eyes. When Benois came to the theatre for the dress rehearsal he made another of his scenes.

Petrushka opened the wound that had hardly healed after *Schéhérazade*.... According to my plan, this portrait was to play an important part in the drama: the Conjuror had hung it there so that it should constantly remind Petrushka that he was in his master's power, and must therefore be humble and submissive. But it is just this portrait of his master that arouses Petrushka's indignation when he finds himself in solitary confinement: he shakes his fists at him and pours on him maledictions and curses.... I saw instead of 'my' portrait of the Conjuror a totally different one, showing him in profile.... My fury expressed itself in a loud shout across the theatre, filled with a highly select audience: 'I shall not allow it! Take it down immediately! I can't bear it!' After which I flung my portfolio full of drawings on the floor and rushed out into the street and home....

My state of fury continued for two whole days. It was in vain that Serov immediately offered to give the portrait its original form and executed it with touching diligence; it was in vain that Nuvel kept coming to explain that it had been a misunderstanding and that both Serioja and Bakst were very sorry about what had occurred. I would not listen, nor give in. . . . I sent in my resignation to Serioja, giving up my post of Artistic Director, and announced my refusal to go to London. . . .[100]

Like *Schéhérazade*, *Petrushka* should have been pickled for posterity in its splendid music, but has failed to retain its vitality on stage. The Oriental work looks ridiculous today, and the Russian work has only an historical interest. This is sad, but the passing of famous works of theatrical art leaves the stage empty for us to replace them. No doubt but that *Petrushka* was wonderfully novel and thrilling in 1911. Then we have Fokine's word for it that in his lifetime no one came near to equalling the interpretations of Nijinsky, as the tormented puppet, dehumanized as he was by grotesque make-up, mittened hands and stilted movements, or of Karsavina as the doll-ballerina, although she had so little and such commonplace dancing to perform.[101] Their performances – together with Orlov's as the stupid swaggering Moor and Cecchetti's as the equivocal Magician – the ballet's Hoffmannesque theme, the picture it gave of St Petersburg in the 1830s, the colour and life of the crowd, the strident bustle of the music, were together overwhelming.

First there was the crowd circulating among the booths of the pre-Lenten fair, with tippling grooms and coachmen, aristocratic couples, cadets saluting their officers, pedlars selling tea or pretzels, boys playing the harmonica or teasing an old man, girls cracking sunflower seeds with their teeth and the rival street-dancers performing to their commonplace tunes on barrel-organ or cornet. Then followed the revealing of the three puppets by the Magician and their pantomime of love and jealousy. In his cell Petrushka's convulsions were a soliloquy of loneliness and despair. Into the gorgeous tropical apartment of the Moor, scarlet with green palm-trees, Petrushka burst to interrupt his rival's flirtation with the Ballerina, only to be ignominiously expelled. The final scene in the fairground took place in growing dusk: the dance of Nursemaids in their traditional finery and the entries of a bear with his keeper and a drunken merchant with two gypsies were followed by the squatting, kicking dance of the two booted coachmen. After the procession of carnival revellers, snow began to fall, and at last the puppets ran out of their booth, circling the stage, and the Moor struck Petrushka dead, while the Ballerina held her hands to her ears. The crowd which surrounded the body enabled a dummy to be substituted for Nijinsky, so that, when at last the cloaked Magician dragged the sagging sawdust puppet away and the stage was empty of satisfied customers, Nijinsky, as the soul or ghost of Petrushka, could appear in a green light on top of the booth in which he learned to suffer, threatening to live for ever – before he fell forward to hang with swinging arms.

In spite of rows and resignations, Benois saw two performances of *Petrushka* before leaving Paris and 'derived considerable pleasure from them'. He wrote,

I was particularly enchanted with Nijinsky at the first performance of *Petrushka*. He had not been successful in the part during rehearsals and it seemed as if he did not completely understand what was needed. He even asked me to explain his role to him, which was very unusual for Nijinsky. But in the end he amazed us as he had in *Pavillon*, *Sylphides*, *Schéhérazade* and *Giselle*. This time also the metamorphosis took place when he put on his costume and covered his face with make-up – and it was even more amazing. I was surprised at the courage Vaslav showed, after all his *jeune premier* successes, in appearing as a horrible half-doll, half-human grotesque. The great difficulty of Petrushka's part is to express his pitiful oppression and his hopeless efforts to achieve personal dignity *without ceasing to be a puppet*....[102]

Diaghilev's third season of ballet was almost more successful than the preceding two.

The Russians were beginning to realize what the life of a touring company would be like. They had arrived in Paris from Rome with a weekend in which to rehearse before their opening. After a fortnight in Paris, when they had given their eighth performance – the fourth of the second programme – on Saturday 17 June, they were off across the Channel the very next day. They were to open at Covent Garden on the Wednesday and perform at the Coronation Gala on Monday 26 June.

To have arranged a season at Covent Garden to be shared with the summer opera company was one feather in Diaghilev's cap. To have the ballet included in the Coronation Gala programme, which would otherwise have been devoted to opera, was another. This unheard-of event was largely due to Lady Ripon, who had seen what Russian ballet could be like on a visit to the Dowager Empress in St Petersburg, and who had witnessed the success of Diaghilev's company in Paris.[103] (Her daughter, Juliet Duff, as we have seen, had been in Monte Carlo for the *première* of *Le Spectre*.)

Lady Ripon was a daughter of Sidney Herbert, Secretary for War and sponsor of Florence Nightingale in the Crimea, son of Catherine Vorontzov, daughter of the Russian Ambassador at St James's. Her first husband was the Earl of Lonsdale, who died in 1882, leaving only a daughter, Juliet; she then married Lord de Grey. It was as Lady de Grey, in the nineties, that she had established the London opera seasons for the de Reszkes and received the dedication of Oscar Wilde's *A Woman of No Importance*. On the death of her father-in-law in 1909, she had become Marchioness of Ripon. E. F. Benson thought she knew nothing about music. Yet, describing an informal supper in the nineties at which Réjane recited and both de Reszkes sang, at which the old Duke of Cambridge dozed imperturbably, and at which Wilde said to a new arrival, 'Oh, I'm so glad you've come. There are a hundred things I want not to say to you,' he wrote that the actress and the singers might possibly have sung at the Duchess of Devonshire's or at Lady Londonderry's for a colossal fee, 'but there was no one but Lady de Grey for whom they would have rollicked like this, just for the fun of it.' He added, 'At heart she was a Bohemian, while socially a great lady on a pinnacle ... higher than any other.... She wanted a definite "stunt" to occupy her.... When the Russian ballet appeared in England her interest in the affairs of Covent Garden swiftly revived.'[104]

Of course, Diaghilev realized that Lady Ripon was not typical of the London audience he was setting out to captivate. He probably thought the country of Gainsborough, Turner, Burne-Jones, Beardsley and William Nicholson, where the American Sargent's portraits had been almost all he found to admire at the Academy of 1901, had sunk to the condition of a cultural desert. Diaghilev was aware that Kyasht (now a *protégée* of Lady Ripon's brother-in-law, the sporting Lord Lonsdale), Karsavina, Pavlova and other Russian dancers had been successful in London music-halls, but, knowing the kind of truncated ballets and showy numbers they presented,

Nijinsky and Astruc. Drawing by Sem, from *Le Figaro*, 1911.

he had reason to fear that they might have given Londoners the wrong impression. In fact, in June 1911 there was a Russian ballerina at every one of the big music-halls near Leicester Square,[105] except at the Coliseum, where the Danish Adeline Genée – for years the terpsichorean queen of the music-hall stage – held the fort.

The boats and trains were full of foreign dignitaries converging on London for the Coronation festivities. Diaghilev and Nijinsky could not get in at the Savoy, so spent the first week or so at the nearby Waldorf. Most of the Russians were accommodated in small hotels in Bloomsbury, where, according to Grigoriev, they were amazed by the plainness of the brick and stone squares and terraces, with their locked gardens. Equally surprising were the 'curious two-wheeled vehicles, with the driver seated behind the passengers, called hansom cabs' and the situation of the Opera House (with its unraked stage), 'hemmed in by greengrocers' warehouses and vast mountains of cabbages, potatoes, carrots'.[106]

A small audience, invited to witness a dress rehearsal on the afternoon of Tuesday 20 June, were told that the wardrobe staff had been detained at Folkestone by the Immigration Officer, which made it impossible for the costumes, wigs and properties to be correctly issued. It was decided that the company could not dance in plain clothes, even in front of Diaghilev's friends, so 'the little group of people in the stalls filed reluctantly out of the theatre as the orchestra started to play.'[107]

The next day, Wednesday, 21 June 1911, the Diaghilev Ballet gave its first performance at Covent Garden. In *Le Pavillon d'Armide* Karsavina was partnered by Bolm, Nijinsky had his usual role and Maestro Cecchetti was the Marquis-magician. In *Carnaval* Elsa Will was the first Columbine to be seen in England, dancing with Nijinsky and the Paris cast. *Prince Igor* was given with only three singers, Petrenko and Zaporojetz, who had sung Khontchakovna and the Khan in 1909, and Issatchenko, who replaced Smirnov as Vladimir. Bolm, Sophie Feodorova and Rosaï led respectively the Warriors, the Girls and the Boys; Gatchevska was the leading Persian Slave. Diaghilev wrote in later years, exaggerating for his own purposes (to show how he had brought about successive revolutions in taste), that during *Prince Igor* 'at least a hundred old ladies, covered in diamonds like ikons, went out past me with a look of disgust on their faces', and that the business manager complained that he had spoilt everything with the 'barbarian horror' of 'savages prancing about':[108] but there can be no doubt that the English public reacted as whole-heartedly to the marvellous Russians as had the Parisians.

The Coronation took place next day, but this did not prevent the Russian Ballet from receiving its first notice in *The Times*. The English critics were music critics, like their French colleagues; they were just as appreciative, but wrote more intelligently. George Calderon, the anonymous critic of *The*

Times, and Richard Capell of the *Daily Mail*, in particular showed remarkable foresight, as well as giving proof of acute observation, their detailed comments proving a marked contrast to the rhetoric and hot air of the French.

The critic of *The Times* wrote,

It has been obvious for some years that Russians are the ideal dancers of the world....

The Schumann *Carnaval* was an unqualified joy from the beginning to end, with never a moment when one felt that the music had been treated with anything but complete sympathy.... M. Nijinsky dances with incredible virtuosity during the number called 'Paganini', and at the wonderful point where the dominant seventh on E Flat emerges by the deft use of the pedal, the dancer represents the effect to absolute perfection by suddenly sitting down.... The stage-management of the whole was among the most purely artistic things the stage has ever seen.[109]

So Nijinsky's (*ritardando*) *pirouette*, which ended with him seated cross-legged on the floor, can lay claim to being the first actual movement of the Russian Ballet to be singled out for praise in England. By 'stage-management' the critic meant what we now call 'choreography', a term not yet in common use. The programme announced merely, 'Scenes and Dances by M. Michel Fokine'.

In the *Daily Mail* Richard Capell judged the spectacle 'Little less than a revelation'.[110]

The *Daily News* made more than one good point:

The first ballet presented was *Le Pavillon d'Armide*. When the orchestra began the prelude, under the direction of the composer, people looked at one another in surprise. They had evidently come expecting the jingling tunes associated with the ballet in this country, and found they were listening to a wonderful piece of orchestration, restless, passionate, at times almost poignant, which might have been the prelude to a serious opera. It was the first indication that the ballet, as developed in Russia, is a serious form of art, and not merely a frivolous excuse for showing pretty girls and dresses behind the footlights.

The scene is entrancing. The glitter of spangles and glare of colour which offend the eyes in most ballets in London were absent, and the combination of exquisite colouring, graceful movement, sprightly, but never banal, music, made a spectacle surpassing in artistic feeling and charm anything yet seen in this country.[111]

The *Morning Post* even approved the orchestration of *Carnaval*: 'The music has been admirably scored for orchestra by MM. Rimsky-Korsakov, Liadov, Glazunov and Tcherepnine, who have but accentuated its salient features for the purposes of the dancer.'[112]

There were no performances on Coronation Day or on the 'Procession Day' which followed. On that Friday Diaghilev cabled Astruc, 'Announce unparalleled triumph ... audience indescribably smart. London has discovered Nijinsky and given warm welcome Karsavina, Will, Fokine, Tcherepnine.'[113]

On certain nights during this season the opera company gave short operas, such as *I Pagliacci* or *Il Segreto di Susanna*, on the same bill as Russian ballets. At the second performance of Diaghilev's company on Saturday 24 June, Leoncavallo's opera preceded *Le Spectre de la rose*, *Carnaval* and *Prince Igor* (without the singers). Of *Le Spectre* Richard Capell wrote of 'the exquisite Mme Karsavina' and of Nijinsky's 'leaps of elfin grace which suggest the whole of youth's untrammelled joy'.[114] The *Observer* (on Sunday) described the work as 'a dream of perfect beauty and all too quickly over'.[115]

On 24 June there appeared a long and thoughtful article by George Calderon (who had still seen only three of Diaghilev's ballets) on the 'new and enchanting pleasure' provided by the novel art form. (How rare in any age are 'new' pleasures!) As early as his first paragraph the writer even envisaged a time when British artists might 'arrive at some imitation of it on our own stage'. The critic went on:

What then are the essential characters which differentiate the art of the Russian Ballet from that which we have hitherto known in England? That they dance better – the simplest explanation – is one of the most misleading, for the elusive differentia does not lie in technique. Certainly their technique is exquisite; all of them can do the most wonderful things with no appearance of effort, and they can do many sorts of wonderful things. But technique is no more the source of the highest pleasure in dancing than it is in painting, in music, or any other of the arts. It is a channel of communication [for] the conveyance of choreographic ideas. Russian ballet-dancing never for one moment escapes from its subjection to ideas – and, moreover, to artistic ideas, ideas, that is, conceived at a high pitch of emotional intelligence....

For all his admiration of Pavlova, the intelligent critic was aware of the shortcomings of her programme.

How much of the work of a ballet-master suffers from being given piece-meal may be seen by comparing the effect of the detached 'turns' of Pavlova and her company at the Palace Theatre before an irrelevant purely 'decorative' back-cloth, with the effect of *Carnaval* in its entirety at Covent Garden. *Carnaval* is an exquisitely delicate artistic whole, from the first coy scamperings and hidings of Chiarina and Estrella to the good-natured *grand rond* in chase of the Philistines; and not a detail of it could be spared; least of all the black dado with the giant golden tulips and the two little roguish Pierrots of sofas, crouching against the wainscot, which make one alert from the beginning for the airy mockery of the whole intention. It is the sum of all these details which leaves us in the end with a quite new and brilliant vision of Schumann's work, purged of all possible suspicion of any Germanic seriousness of purpose.... This is an aristocratic tradition, with something of Boucher and Beaumarchais clinging to it, arch, mischievous, *gouailleur*. It is immensely serious as Art, but never for a moment serious as Life.[116]

206

The only English *dancer* – as opposed to critic – whose opinion of the Russians can be quoted is Phyllis Bedells, who was appearing in *Sylvia* at the Empire, with Kyasht, and who wrote her memoirs years later. She had seen Karsavina at the Coliseum, but her sight of the whole ballet at Covent Garden was an overwhelming experience.

When the Diaghilev Ballet made its first appearance at Covent Garden with the full company it was maddening not to be able to see them as there were no matinée performances. [But because of the Ballet's success matinées were introduced quite soon after the beginning of the season.] All London was raving about their success, and eventually I had to go to the Empire directors and say that as part of my education I must be given the opportunity to see them. Very reluctantly it was agreed that I take one night off which, unless one was ill, was an almost unheard-of thing. I booked a seat in the circle – just one. I could not afford to pay for another seat on my small salary. My father took me to the theatre and collected me when the performance ended.... As long as I live I shall not forget that night. I could hardly keep still in my seat. Because people who were sitting in neighbouring seats would keep chatting away in a blasé manner I worked myself into a state of fury. It seemed impossible to believe that anyone could behave like that while the magic of those artists filled me with such delight. Several times, young as I was, I asked them to be quiet.... I cannot write about Nijinsky. It is useless. Then he was at the very height of his powers. I was breathless as I sat there in my seat and watched him dancing.[117]

An intelligent, artistic member of the audience was the Duchess of Rutland, whose youngest daughter, Diana Manners, was coming out that season. She had always despised ballet, which she had thought of as a silly after-dinner entertainment for vulgar men. Her first sight of Karsavina had been a revelation, and the Diaghilev Ballet turned her into a passionate devotee.[118]

A more obscure enthusiast was Florence Henderson, the daughter of a wealthy Scottish businessman, who went to the opera, to plays or to concerts nearly every night of her life, and had been to Paris and twice to Bayreuth. Florence kept an album into which she stuck the press announcements or fragments of the programmes of every entertainment she attended, writing her own brief but perspicacious comments underneath. She went to see Pavlova (without Mordkine) at the Palace on the afternoon of 21 June. The same evening she saw the first English performance of the Diaghilev Ballet, and wrote, 'Father and I went to the Russian Ballet, which was undoubtedly the most beautiful, at the same time the most amazing performance I have ever seen....'[119]

It was announced that a third of the seats for the Coronation Gala on Monday 26 June had been taken for the King's guests and their suites: for the remaining tickets there had been an unprecedented demand, and Americans had offered in vain £1,000 and £500 for boxes.[120] The house was to be decorated with 100,000 roses, but most of these were to be artificial, for fear of overpowering the audience with their scent.[121] According to Diaghilev, there were almost as many maharajahs as roses.[122] 'The audience began to assemble at seven o'clock, Lady Ripon and her daughter, Lady Juliet Duff, being very early on the scene.' Upstairs 'the gallery slips were much sought after for their view of the audience'. Queen Mary wore rose-pink embroidered with jewels, with the huge Cullinan diamond and the Star of Africa on her bodice.[123]

Destinn and Kirkby Lunn sang the duet from *Aïda*, Melba the second-act aria from *Roméo et Juliette*, Tetrazzini and McCormack the music lesson from *Il Barbiere*. Then came the ballet. *Le Pavillon d'Armide* was given without the third scene, and ended 'happily' with René and Armida united.

Richard Capell wrote in the *Daily Mail*,

> The regal spectacle ended with one of the most enchanting creations ever seen on any stage. ... Both the King and Queen freely used opera glasses and the interest of the whole assembly was excited. The pauses after the various dances, meant for applause, were at first silent. As the marvellous ballet progressed there was more and more admiration for the delicious Mme Karsavina, M. Nijinsky, who seems the incarnation of youthful joy, the astonishing company of buffoons and the others.[124]

Queen Mary wrote in her diary, 'The music and ballet were both extremely good.' 'The performance excellent,' commented King George.[125]

Diaghilev's later recollections of the audience's reactions, although perhaps exaggerated, may be given. 'Our reception was icy, and neither Karsavina's variations, nor even those of Nijinsky ... received the slightest applause. It was only after the dance of the buffoons that the strangest of sounds came to us: the public was gently clapping its kid-gloved hands.'[126] Of course, applause was restricted in those days when Royalty was present, and kid gloves were the general rule in the lower parts of the house.

On the following night, Tuesday, *Les Sylphides* was given for the first time in England. 'How gloriously the familiar music gains when offered in the guise of the charming ballet!' wrote the *Daily Telegraph*.[127] Richard Capell thought that although a music-lover naturally looked askance at this 'free-handling of the masterpieces of the immortal dead ... the imponderable Karsavina floats once more across the stage and he is conquered utterly.'[128] It is curious that throughout the season Karsavina yielded her role of Columbine in *Carnaval* to Elsa Will: there can have been no question of rivalry, for the two ladies were sharing a flat near Baker Street.[129]

On 30 June *Les Sylphides* was 'a good recompense' in the eyes of Florence Henderson for a 'disgracefully given' *I Pagliacci*. She went to Covent Garden with her father and Mr Grenfell, a banker twenty years older than herself, whom she was to marry in 1913.[130] It was as Mrs Edward Grenfell that she became after the war a friend and loyal supporter of Diaghilev's.

Cléopâtre, with Serafina Astafieva (who was not very good) in the principal role, and *Schéhérazade* (which Florence Henderson 'simply hated')[131] with Karsavina, were introduced into the repertoire on 7 and 19 July. Both were given on the last night, the thirty-first. Tcherepnine conducted every performance during the season.

Diaghilev had captivated the rich but dowdy English by the imagination of his ballets and the fire and style of his artists. He may already have guessed that he could venture longer and more frequent seasons in London than in pampered, impatient Paris – indeed, he was bringing his company back to Covent Garden after their summer holiday; and he hoped that the London public would take to the old-fashioned classical ballets as readily as they had to the modern ones. He had a production of *Giselle* which he did not want to waste (and which he would not risk boring Paris with again); he had also arranged to show London Kchessinskaya (who had not yet chalked up that capital on her score-board) in *Le Lac des Cygnes*, thus including an important work by Russia's greatest composer, his 'Uncle Petia', in the repertoire. Musical friends in England would have told him that the orchestral suite of *Casse-Noisette* had long been popular there. There was another reason for including classical as well as modern ballets in his autumn programmes. Karsavina would have to return in mid-season to fulfil her obligations in St Petersburg, and it was a golden opportunity to persuade Pavlova to dance her special role in *Giselle* in the West. Her guest appearances would be followed by those of Kchessinskaya in *Le Lac des Cygnes*; and Karsavina would return to finish the season. Diaghilev would thus have shown London three outstanding ballerinas, all partnered by Nijinsky, within two months. He was successful in bringing off all these plans. In only one matter had he miscalculated: the English would find *Giselle* just as insipid as had the French, and they would be bored by *Le Lac des Cygnes* too.

When Grigoriev asked how Diaghilev could afford the scenery and dresses for so big a ballet as *Le Lac des Cygnes*, the latter told him that he had arranged to buy the entire Moscow production, which had been designed by Korovine and Golovine as early as 1901.[132] Kchessinskaya may have helped to make this transaction possible.

Diaghilev also had the ambition of showing his new repertoire in Russia. This would not only be one in the eye for the Mariinsky; it might also be a step towards his taking it over. There was no question, of course, of his company performing at the Mariinsky during the winter season. The only other theatre large enough to house a ballet company was the People's Palace, Narodny Dom, a big modern building neither attractive nor fashionable, but which Diaghilev might have contrived to make smarter, just as he had refurbished the Châtelet. After his summer holiday with Nijinsky in Venice, he travelled to St Petersburg and had completed negotiations by 29 September, when he telegraphed to Astruc, asking if he would undertake to organize the St Petersburg season of twelve or fifteen performances between 29 December and 1 February.[133] This Astruc refused.

Leaving St Petersburg on 7 October, Diaghilev was in London by the tenth.[134] He had been unable to persuade Tcherepnine to conduct another London season, and he had some trouble over engaging Monteux. He negotiated with Carlotta Zambelli, of the Paris Opéra, whom he hoped to secure as a replacement for Pavlova if she let him down.[135] He was in Paris a few days later, but back with Nijinsky at the Savoy Hotel in time for the opening of his second London season at Covent Garden on 16 October 1911.[136] There were a few changes in the company. Elsa Will was gone, but Maria Pilz, who was tall and handsome, had been engaged; Max Frohman, whose sister had been with the company in Paris since the spring, had come from Moscow; and Grigoriev had brought some Poles from Warsaw[137] to replace the inadequate Molodsov dancers. Frohman was extremely good-looking in a classical way and it was not long before Diaghilev 'had his eye on him'.[138] Covent Garden had taken the trouble to improve the lighting,[139] to install a hydraulic curtain and to lay a new oak stage for the ballet.[140]

On the first night Karsavina and Nijinsky danced *Giselle* and *Schéhérazade*, as they had on the opening night at Monte Carlo in April: but in the early part of *Giselle* Calderon of *The Times* thought 'the audience hardly seemed to know what to look for.'[141] Capell of the *Daily Mail* tried to be nice: 'Were the dancing anything less than perfect "Giselle" would, truth to tell, be a thought tedious. ... Even this wonderful troupe of dancers cannot always steer clear of that incongruity which rightly rendered the old ballet a laughing-stock.' He thought Karsavina 'truly pathetic', admiring not only Nijinsky's flying leaps and *entrechats*, but also the 'deep-dyed villain' of Bolm's rejected lover, and saw in Cecchetti, who played Giselle's mother, 'an actor of singular and sinister power'.[142] The *Observer* could not think how 'these fine dancers were attracted by their parts'.[143] The familiar *Schéhérazade* was a different matter, although Capell complained of people talking during the 'overture'. 'The splendid and cruel spectacle made an overwhelming effect.'[144] 'In its wonderful expression of pent-up passion let loose in flood,' wrote the music critic of the *Sunday Times*, 'and in the unity of all its constituents ... "Schéhérazade" is *sui generis*; its impression bites deeper into you every time you see it.'[145]

On the season's second night Karsavina danced Columbine in *Carnaval* for the first time in London. Indeed, in the seven performances before her return to Russia on 27 October, she danced in every ballet, following those mentioned above with *Le Pavillon d'Armide*, *Les Sylphides* and *Le Spectre de la rose*. *Prince Igor* was the only ballet in the regular repertoire in which neither she nor Nijinsky appeared, but that was not given until after she was gone. The Russians performed two, three or four times a week, alternating with Wagner operas.

On Saturday 28 October Pavlova appeared once more with the Diaghilev Ballet. She danced Giselle; and, in *Cléopâtre*, oddly enough, took not her old role of the tragic, forsaken Ta-Hor, which perhaps Feodorova did not wish to give up, but Karsavina's role of Nijinsky's fellow-slave, the dancer with the scarf. Cleopatra was mimed by Serafina Astafieva, as in the summer. The critic of *The Times* thought Pavlova's two roles gave her 'no proper scope'.[146] Her Giselle was much praised, however, in spite of the 'weakness' of the old ballet, and the *Daily News* recorded that 'The extraordinary intensity of Mme Pavlova's acting in the mad scene lifted the performance to a dramatic significance that seemed almost an intrusion amid the polite conventions of the remainder.'[147] Capell gives us an idea of how Nijinsky appeared as Loys-Albrecht. 'A young faun from some Slav Arcadia, straying here among mortals, was her fantastic cavalier.'[148] During her seven performances Pavlova danced also *Le Pavillon d'Armide*, *Les Sylphides* (both of which she knew from 1909), the Blue Bird *pas de deux* (now called *L'Oiseau d'or*), and, twice, Columbine in *Carnaval*. Florence Henderson, who saw her in the first three of these on 3 November, noted that 'it was immensely interesting to see Pavlova in all Karsavina's roles & was *v. much* to the former's advantage. She dances with so much more emotion & has such far greater personal charm.'[149] On Saturday 11 November, in Tchaikovsky's and Petipa's famous *pas de deux*, Pavlova danced with Nijinsky and for Diaghilev for the last time.

Kchessinskaya had by then arrived at the Savoy Hotel, attended by her lover the Grand Duke Andrei, her son Vova, her faithful jester Baron Gotch (who did female impersonations), a doctor, a dresser and a maid. Her jewels had travelled separately,[150] but the ballerina was childishly pleased to show them to a reporter of the *Daily Telegraph*. ' "A million roubles, my jewels?" Yes, I suppose so. I have two sapphires on a chain that alone are worth 45,000 roubles. This is the bandeau I mean to wear on Tuesday night. See how big the sapphires are!'[151]

Kchessinskaya made her London début on 14 November in the *grand pas de deux* from the last act of *The Sleeping Beauty*, which Diaghilev called *Aurore et le Prince*. Eager to oblige in every way, he had helped her choose a blue costume to go with the sapphires. Her 'undeniable success' was not as great as she hoped.[152] 'What would the public say ... if it knew nothing of the sapphires of fabulous size ... and if it had not been told that she is the wealthiest woman on the stage? Probably that she is a competent dancer of the stereotyped kind.' 'She does not display that added touch of exquisite inspiration shown by Mme Pavlova.' 'Extraordinarily skilful, but often quite unlovely gymnastics.'[153] The same evening she danced Columbine in *Carnaval*, which was surely one of the few roles in Fokine ballets to suit her very well. However much Diaghilev sought to please and to make use of Kchessinskaya, he and his friends tended to regard her as the relic of a past age of ballet and to make fun of her. When she danced Columbine, Bakst was in Lady Juliet Duff's box and so was the Grand Duke Andrei. Sensing a lack of enthusiasm in the designer of the ballet, Lady Juliet urged him to say something civil to the Grand Duke about his mistress. He managed to lisp a remark about her costume: 'Montheigneur, tha robe a l'air bien fraîche.' ('Her dreth lookth very new, Thir.')[154] Nor was Florence Henderson enthusiastic. 'The new woman Kchessinska was a great disappointment, she was fat & passée, not on the same plain with either Kasavina or Pavlova.'[155]

There was a gap to fill between the end ot the London season on 7 December and the January season at Narodny Dom. On 17 November Diaghilev was in Paris, arranging with Astruc for three special performances at the Opéra around Christmas.[156] He was also negotiating for visits to Amsterdam, Vienna and Budapest, and for a German tour.

Diaghilev had compressed the four-act ballet of *Le Lac des Cygnes* into two acts, substituting a Fiancée for the Prince's Prospective Bride and having Fokine arrange for Nijinsky a solo to the Sugar Plum Fairy's dance from *Casse-Noisette*. How a man could dance effectively to that tinkling tune on the celesta is a puzzle, but the *Lady* thought his performance 'exquisite' and 'his appearance in a 15th century Italian dress a vision of fairyland'.[157] Another anomaly was the insertion by Kchessinskaya into the ballroom scene of one of her favourite flashy numbers, to a violin solo of Kadletz. 'Diaghilev agreed with me,' she wrote.[158] The poor man well knew that she was the one dancer he could not argue with. To play this solo and Tchaikovsky's own, which accompanies the Petipa *pas de deux* in the lake scene, Kchessinskaya engaged Mischa Elman, a pupil of Leopold Auer, the first violin at the Mariinsky, who was in London for some concerts.[159] Because more rehearsals were needed, the *première* of *Le Lac* was postponed from 28 November to the thirtieth.

The first English reaction to this ballet, which Ninette de Valois was going to force the English to like a quarter of a century later, was boredom. 'Some of the early dances are exceedingly dull and ... full of padding,' wrote the critic of *The Times*.[160] 'The music is of little account,' wrote the critic of the *Daily Mail*. But the national dances were 'fascinating',[161] and the *Morning Post* praised the Spanish Dance of Feodorova and Bolm.[162] Kchessinskaya 'did some extraordinary feats of precisely calculated design with *finesse* and a mathematical exactness which suggested a pair of magic compasses controlled by a fantastic philosopher with a taste for humour as well as a sense of beauty.' Was this George Calderon's way of describing the thirty-two *fouettés*?[163] Kchessinskaya, at any rate, was satisfied. 'It was a real feast,' she commented.[164]

On the day of Kchessinskaya's final appearance Diaghilev had lunch, along with Karsavina and Nijinsky, with Lady Juliet Duff in Upper Brook

Street. All three signed her birthday book. Diaghilev wrote after his name, 'L'ami des dieux' – 'The friend of the gods.' Nijinsky wrote, '*Le Spectre à la rose*,' which was very polite, though the idea of the tall, angular, aquiline Lady Juliet as a rose is rather far-fetched.[165]

Her mother, Lady Ripon, had taken Nijinsky and Karsavina down to Sargent's studio in Tite Street, Chelsea, to be drawn. The artist made a charcoal head of Nijinsky in the turban and jewelled choker of *Le Pavillon d'Armide*. The exaggerated length of the neck, the arrogant backward tilt of the head, the mocking eyes and the parted, provocative lips convey vividly the impression he gave in this ballet of being a visitor from Olympus.

Charles Ricketts, the distinguished painter, stage designer, printer, connoisseur and collector, left us a description of the Russian Ballet's last night on Saturday 9 December, when Karsavina and Nijinsky danced *Carnaval*, *Les Sylphides*, *Le Spectre de la rose* and *Schéhérazade*. He wrote to a friend, a few days later, 'I am bitter and melancholy ... the Russians have left us! ... On that last night they danced as they dance only in Paradise – Karsavina destroyed utterly all the diamonds which the Tsar had given to the rival lady! (I forget her name), and Nijinsky never once touched the ground, but laughed at our sorrows and passions in mid-air. It was I who got the encore for Chopin's ironical and immortal valse.' After *Carnaval*, *Les Sylphides* and *Le Spectre* there was 'thunderous applause', but the drama of *Schéhérazade* almost overwhelmed the spectators. Of the final slaughter Ricketts wrote, 'They put such beauty into their deaths that we became amorous of death. ... The audience was cowed and applauded silently, one faded round of sound, whereupon that pimple of a French conductor struck up "God save the King", which of course suggests to the Britisher coats, hats and trains to the suburbs.' Poor Monteux doubtless knew that after an evening prolonged by an encore and applause, the orchestra were impatient to get away. Ricketts was not to be foiled. 'I was white with rage and, the moment he ceased, I yelled "Karsavina" twice at the top of my voice; there was a pause, then came the roar from the gallery, like the boom of a distant gun, and the house applauded for twenty minutes.'[166] Richard Capell confirmed this in the *Daily Mail*, for he himself stayed to join in and time the applause.[167]

Next day Diaghilev was off across the hated Channel to sign his contract for the company's Paris appearances, which he did at the Crillon Hotel.[168] While in Paris, he cabled to London to discover Pavlova's whereabouts.[169] The season in St Petersburg had been deferred till February: so the company would spend January in Berlin. Diaghilev was there to clinch the deal on Monday 11 December.[170] He was in St Petersburg on the fifteenth[171] and back in Paris for the first performance at the Opéra on 24 December.

Nothing new was given at the three Opéra performances or at a charity gala which followed, but the last was notable for an encore of the entire twelve minutes of *Le Spectre de la rose*. 'Diaghilev sent me before the curtain,' wrote Karsavina, 'and I delivered my maiden speech to the effect that we would like to please our public by encoring, and that we entertained a hope that a charity collection about to begin would be generously supported.'[172] This may have been the occasion which inspired Cocteau to make his caricature of Nijinsky being fanned by Vassili's towel, like a boxer in the corner of a ring, watched by Bakst, Misia, José-Maria Sert and an anxious but benign Diaghilev.

By 4 January 1912 Diaghilev and his company were in Berlin.[173] He had signed with a German impresario to give fifty-three performances in Berlin during the year: these would be divided between two seasons, one at the beginning and one at the end of 1912.[174] Pierre Monteux had come from Paris to conduct. Diaghilev was busy preparing his Russian season, which was to begin on 24 February and continue into March. Through Astruc he opened negotiations with two exotic dance recitalists, whom he wished to fill Ida Rubinstein's roles in St Petersburg and to take part in *Le Dieu bleu* when it was given in Paris. He settled with Mata Hari – who was later shot as a spy – for three thousand francs plus her fare, but failed to secure the services of the other lady, Napierkovska.[175] To replace Karsavina when she was appearing at the Mariinsky, he engaged the star of the Paris Opéra, Zambelli, who had been a guest artist in Russia in 1901, to dance seven performances for twenty thousand francs.[176]

Stravinsky had spent part of the previous summer with Roerich, staying at Talashkino, Princess Tenishev's property near Smolensk; and Roerich had copied some of his costumes for *The Rite of Spring* from old originals in her collection. Then, in Russia and at Clarens by the Lake of Geneva, Stravinsky had completed, apart from the orchestration, the score of his great primitive ballet. Arriving in Berlin at the end of January 1912, he found that Diaghilev could not mount it, as he had hoped, that spring. It was to be postponed for a year, but Diaghilev urged him to score it for a huge orchestra. Stravinsky was reconciled to this postponement because he had already begun thinking about another work on a Russian peasant theme which became *Les Noces*.[177]

Fokine at last began rehearsing *Le Dieu bleu* in Berlin; and it was during the company's stay there that Nijinsky and his sister heard of their father's death in the Ukraine. A Mass was sung, for which Diaghilev ordered music by Bach.[178]

On 20 January Diaghilev heard that Narodny Dom in St Petersburg had been burnt to the ground.[179] This was not only a financial blow, but a blow to his ambitions. Although he knew well that there was no other non-subsidized theatre with a large enough stage for his ballet, it seems that he racked his brains and made desperate efforts to devise some scheme, for it was not until 9 February that he cabled the news to Astruc, saying that he had 'done the impossible to find a replacement without success', and asking him to break the news to Zambelli and Mata Hari that he could not fulfil his contracts with them.[180] The company now had no engagements until they went to Monte Carlo in April.

Diaghilev did not waste time: he had to pay his dancers. The Berlin season was nearing its end. At the shortest of notice, the German impresario managed to book three days at Dresden in mid-February, eight performances in Vienna and a week in Budapest. But Karsavina had to be at the Mariinsky by mid-February and Diaghilev needed a ballerina for the Austrian and Hungarian capitals. There was no one to fall back on except Kchessinskaya. She consented to dance *Le Lac des Cygnes* and *Carnaval* and perhaps stipulated that she should also be allowed to appear with Nijinsky in *Le Spectre de la rose*, for in Budapest this was added to her repertoire. (Pilz danced Karsavina's role in Vienna.) As a reinforcement, Diaghilev summoned Kyasht from London.[181]

But who was to be the company's ballerina in Dresden? If Karsavina did not appear at least once, Diaghilev might be considered not to have fulfilled his obligations. Just before the end of the Berlin season Diaghilev remarked to her 'quite casually', ' "You are not of course going to leave us, Tata; they have made stipulations for your appearance." "My leave will be over, Sergei Pavlovitch." "Nonsense, it is carnival now, nobody in the Mariinsky but moustacheless youth, send a telegram asking for prolongation of leave." Though it was only a matter of matinée performances for schools, my reiterated demands were refused. Through side channels Diaghilev addressed high circles in Petersburg. It was of no avail; Teliakovsky was adamant. There was nothing for me but to go.'

Svetlov was travelling with the company and he comforted Karsavina by taking her side against Diaghilev; she felt that she would have been powerless to resist the iron will of her implacable master without his help. She spent ten days, it seemed, in tears in a telephone kiosk; and every evening Diaghilev 'got hold' of her 'to talk things over'. She wrote:

His arguments exhausted, he bowed to the inevitable, and it was heart-breaking to see his dejected face. On the last night [in Berlin] he sat in my dressing-room. My eyelids were swollen with continuous crying, and looked like little red sausages. Diaghilev sucked the knob of his stick, a sign of depression, and then very wearily, on the off-chance, he said 'Let us look up the A B C.' He then calculated that starting on the night after the [first] Dresden performance and travelling by the North Express I could arrive at Petersburg early in the morning on the day of my matinée. It seemed a Heaven-sent solution.

The last ballet on the programme on 12 February, the opening night in Dresden, was *Cléopâtre*. Karsavina wrote,

I rushed off the stage immediately after the performance, threw a shawl over my ringlet wig, a coat over my Egyptian dress, and arrived at the station just in time to catch the last train.... The express sped on till, on the second day, when a snowdrift caused a delay, the train was six hours late. From the station, I hurried to the theatre. My understudy had been got ready, but there still remained ten minutes of interval. When, in the costume of Sugar Plum Fairy, I came on the stage, the overture had finished and the curtain was going up. Teliakovsky thought it sporting of me.[182]

Although the Ballet appeared in the pretty baroque Royal Theatre in Dresden, they were not greatly appreciated by the provincial public. While members of the company visited the picture gallery to see Raphael's Sistine Madonna, Diaghilev and Nijinsky drove to the suburb of Hellerau to investigate Dalcroze's School of Eurhythmics. They were always eager to explore any possibility of enlarging the language of the dance and seeking new relationships between dance and music. It was in Dresden that Grigoriev heard that Nijinsky had been secretly working with Bronislava and Vassilievska on his ballet to Debussy's *L'Après-midi d'un faune*: he connected this quite wrongly with Dalcroze.

The reason [he wrote] for the secrecy in which this activity had been shrouded was that, owing to Diaghilev's exclusive interest in Nijinsky, he and Fokine had been getting on less and less well, and that before allowing anyone to know about it, Diaghilev wished to make sure that the experiment would succeed. I must confess that I was somewhat disquieted by this discovery, foreseeing what might happen when Fokine learnt of it. But I did not let this perturb me for long, since my leave from the Mariinsky would in any case expire in the autumn, when my service with Diaghilev's company would come to an end.[183]

After the successful opening night at the Hofoper, Vienna, on Monday 19 February, Diaghilev could sit back and relax. With him, relaxation took two forms: sightseeing and the planning of new works. Sometimes one would lead to the other, for pictures or architecture could inspire ballets, and the contemplation of old masterpieces always spurred Diaghilev to initiate new ones. Stravinsky had never been in Vienna before, and Diaghilev must have enjoyed showing him and Nijinsky the Hapsburg Titians, the Infantas of Velazquez, the flower of Breughel's work and the giant-guarded palaces of Fischer von Erlach. He had conceived the idea of doing a ballet to Debussy's 'Fêtes' – at least, that is how Benois put it in his *Reminiscences*; but we can safely assume that, of the three pieces in Debussy's orchestral suite *Nocturnes*, Diaghilev would have used at least the first two, 'Nuages' and 'Fêtes', to make a twenty-minute ballet, possibly omitting the third, 'Sirènes', which might be difficult to arrange for fin-less dancers. Although the sound of the procession which is heard passing in 'Fêtes' has no period flavour, Diaghilev's mind must have been running on French eighteenth-century festivals, for otherwise there would have been no particular reason to summon Benois, the acknowledged expert on the period of Boucher,

Fragonard and Hubert Robert. Strange that Diaghilev could not yet quite see his way to juxtaposing a French painter (even one without previous experience of the stage – say, Monet, Renoir or Bonnard) with his French composer.

Benois came from St Petersburg, obedient to the call. The music was played over to him several times on the piano, but did not suggest any definite story. 'Its vivid colours only evoked visions of a fête in general.'

Very soon [wrote Benois] – perhaps because of my daily visits to the Kunsthistorische Museum, where there is a wonderful collection of Venetian art, 'this general fête' began to take a definitely Venetian aspect. Speaking of Venice and its pageantry – what can be more festive and inspiring than the art of Paolo Caliari? That is why I suddenly conceived the definite desire to create a ballet *à la Veronese*. The décor seemed to come of itself; it was to represent a Palladian villa somewhere on the Brenta. A sumptuous banquet was to be in progress; the Doge himself was to arrive and be received with unheard-of splendour.

Unfortunately the music was too short to produce the final effect. Diaghilev did not doubt that he would be able, without trouble, to get the twenty or thirty bars that were needed from Debussy, but he was mistaken. The composer stubbornly refused to add anything to his music. In consequence Diaghilev suddenly cooled off towards the whole idea although he was delighted with my designs for the costumes and décor.[184]

One does not know whether to be more astonished that the sensitive Benois should have thought of imposing ponderous Renaissance ceremonial on Debussy's iridescent cobweb of a score, or that Diaghilev, with his fine ear, should dare to ask the composer to add a conventional climax. But I dare to read between Benois' lines. I think Diaghilev soon realized, as sheaf after sheaf of Venetian designs appeared on the table in his hotel bedroom after Benois' morning visits to the art gallery, that his old friend had got completely out of hand, that Debussy was being submerged. I believe that he never really asked the composer to lengthen his score, but only invented a correspondence with him to appease the designer, who had made the trip to Vienna (highly enjoyable, no doubt, and all expenses paid) to no avail. Debussy's music was much too short for a *ballet d'action* and there was absolutely nothing Venetian or Renaissance about it.

The idea of a 'Veronese' ballet was realized, however, though in an unexpected way. While in Vienna, Diaghilev talked to Hugo von Hofmannsthal, Richard Strauss's librettist, about the possibility of Strauss writing a ballet for Nijinsky.

During the two weeks I spent in Vienna [wrote Benois] I used every day to meet Hugo von Hofmannsthal, who was a great admirer of our ballets.... In conversation with him I developed my Veronese ideas and he greatly encouraged them.... Hofmannsthal *did* see their fulfilment, but in his own ballet *La Légende de Joseph*, with music by Richard Strauss, for which he demanded a Veronese setting. Serioja did not think of entrusting me with the production and so deprived me of the joy of rendering public homage to one of my favourite artists of the past.[185]

Joseph would not see the light of day till 1914. The first subject Hofmannsthal proposed to Strauss on 8 March 1912 was very different.

Will you, my dear Dr Strauss, allow yourself to be inspired by the vision of this central event in ancient tragedy and write a tragic symphony, a symphony of thirty to thirty-five, at the most forty minutes duration, *Orestes and the Furies?*

Please read the enclosed sketch and tell me whether this is not an occasion for wonderful, sombre, grandiose music – a synthesis of your symphonies and your two tragic operas. And now imagine Orestes created by Nijinsky, the greatest miming genius on the modern stage (next to Duse, and as a mime above Duse) – the whole thing, as a pantomime, as a scene, as a tableau based on your music – just as a symphony of yours would be based on a vision, and growing out of it – think it over and please don't refuse me this....

... A note is enclosed which contains an outline of the terms which Diaghilev, the artistic director of the Russian Ballet, takes the liberty of submitting to you for the composition of these Furies.[186]

But Strauss, who had dealt with Elektra, the sister of Orestes, only a year or two before, did not like this idea. This was a misfortune. If Nijinsky had made a tragic ballet to the music of Strauss, it might have been a masterpiece, and it might with luck still be with us today. In the one tragic ballet he did bring off (to Stravinsky's *Rite*) there was no part for himself, and because of his marriage and parting from Diaghilev it has not survived.

Nijinsky had been unwell in Berlin – he was prone to influenza – and at the end of the Vienna season he was again feverish.[187] He travelled on with the company to Budapest, nevertheless. Talks with the agent for a proposed South American tour kept Diaghilev an extra night or two in Vienna.[188]

It was during this first short visit of the Ballet to Budapest that a Hungarian girl, Romola de Pulszky, saw them and Nijinsky for the first time. She is our evidence for the fact that Nijinsky did not dance on the first night. When she went to the theatre on the second, eager to see this fabulous star, she thought the name 'Nijinsky' was that of a woman.[189] Then she saw him in *Carnaval*. She described her sensations later: 'Suddenly a slim, lithe, cat-like Harlequin took the stage. Although his face was hidden by a painted mask, the expression and beauty of his body made us all realize that we were in the presence of genius. An electric shock passed through the entire audience.'[190]

Romola was an intelligent girl, although spoilt and used to having her own way. Her mother, Emilia Markus, was Hungary's most famous actress; her father, long since dead in exile, had been Director of Hungary's National

Gallery, and had brought her up not on fairy-tales, but on Vasari's *Lives* of the Renaissance painters.[191] She had had acting lessons – her sister had married a celebrated Danish tenor – and she was perhaps in search of some artistic movement to attach herself to. She fell in love with the Russian Ballet and sought introductions to its members. Bolm became a friend and brought other dancers to her mother's house. Nijinsky, however, remained unattainable, hedged round by Diaghilev in sacrosanct privacy at the Hungaria Hotel.[192]

From Budapest the Russians travelled to Monte Carlo. Diaghilev was in Paris on Friday 15 March and back at the Riviera Palace Hotel, Beausoleil, on the day following.[193] There were three new ballets to rehearse in the three weeks before the spring season opened: Fokine's *Thamar*, to the symphonic poem of Balakirev, his *Daphnis et Chloë*, of which Ravel had at last completed the score, and Nijinsky's *L'Après-midi d'un faune*. Now that everyone knew Nijinsky was making his choreographic début, Fokine was in a bad mood. Although Karsavina, who was to dance the role of Thamar, the cruel and amorous Georgian Queen of Lermontov's poem, was still in Russia, Fokine was obliged to start rehearsing the Caucasian dances, which her attendants performed while she made love, without her, and these took up most of the company. When Nijinsky wanted his chosen nymphs for *L'Après-midi*, there was a tug-of-war.[194] The six girls were Bronislava Nijinska, Tcherepanova, Khokhlova, Maikherska, Klementovicz and Kopyshinska. Bronislava's short stature and snub nose lost her the role of principal Nymph: a stranger, Lydia Nelidova, was engaged at her mother's private dancing school in Moscow. She was also to be the Goddess in *Le Dieu bleu*. *L'Après-midi* needed many rehearsals, but this was not because of Nijinsky's slowness in working out the movements, as some writers have alleged: as we have seen (and it was Mme Bronislava Nijinska who told me), the ballet had been completely worked out a year before. The dancers found it extremely hard to adapt their ballet-trained bodies to Vaslav's new way of moving. Also, being used to dancing on the beat of the music, they got lost when obliged to move through and across Debussy's eddies of sound. Nijinsky was better at demonstrating than at explaining what he wanted.[195]

Yet, even at the beginning of April 1912, it was still taken for granted that it would be Fokine who would arrange the dances for *The Rite of Spring*. Stravinsky wrote to his mother in Russia,

Diaghilev and Nijinsky are mad about my new child, *Le Sacre du printemps*. The unpleasant part is that it will have to be done by Fokine whom I consider an exhausted artist, one who has travelled his road quickly and who writes himself out with each new work. *Schéhérazade* was the high point of his achievement and, consequently, the beginning of his decline. I have seen all of his ballets since *Schéhérazade* [that is, *Narcisse*, *Sadko*, *Le Spectre de la rose*, *Petrushka*], and all of them are immeasurably inferior and weaker. *Schéhérazade* was an inspired spectacle....

New forms must be created, and the evil, the gifted, the greedy Fokine has not even dreamed of them. At the beginning of his career he appeared to be extraordinarily progressive. But the more I knew of his work, the more I saw that in essence he was not new at all. There is no salvation in *habileté* [mere cleverness]. Genius is needed, not *habileté*....[196]

Unfair to Fokine? After 1912 the unloved – at least, by Diaghilev and Stravinsky – choreographer would make only one more highly successful work for the company he had put on its feet. Yet, of the many ballets he created after his connection with Diaghilev was severed, none has survived or been thought worthy of revival in recent years, and all are consequently lost and forgotten. Fokine never afterwards commissioned a score from a living composer.

Ravel's First Suite from *Daphnis et Chloë* was played at the Colonne Concert in Paris on 2 April. It may have been another cause of exasperation for Fokine that the cream of Ravel's music for *his*, Fokine's, Greek ballet, a score which had taken so long to write, should be enjoyed by the musical public of Paris before his ballet could be mounted. Diaghilev had failed to prevent this. Fokine had already been obliged ·to stage one Greek ballet, *Narcisse*, in 1911, which was to be included in the Paris repertoire for 1912, and, now that he was able to work on *Daphnis* at last, Nijinsky's Greek ballet was going to divert attention from it. That would make three Greek ballets in all in the repertoire.

Diaghilev and Fokine had a long talk, and Fokine decided to leave the company after the Paris season. In allowing this, Diaghilev was taking an enormous risk: Nijinsky's first short ballet had not yet been shown to the public; yet Diaghilev was gambling on his being capable of creating at least two new works for the season of 1913, of which one would be the difficult *Rite of Spring*.

Grigoriev wrote:

Now that Fokine had decided to leave the company in June, he grew more and more restless and nervy, till it became almost impossible to work with him. He suspected everyone who stood close to Diaghilev of being his enemy, including myself. I was obliged by my work to be constantly referring matters to Diaghilev; and my doing so never failed to arouse Fokine's wrath. He even began accusing me of treachery; and a particularly painful incident led to a final quarrel between us. Diaghilev insisted on Nijinsky having a great many rehearsals for *L'Après-midi*; and however hard I tried to do so, it proved impossible to avoid refusing Fokine the services of the same dancers at the same time. He flew into a rage with me; and the quarrel that ensued was the end of our friendship, a close friendship of many years. I was so much upset that I asked Diaghilev to relieve me of my duties; and though he, of course, refused, he agreed to provide me with an assistant, in the person of N. Semenov, the *régisseur* from Moscow; and this relieved me of some of my responsibilities.[197]

Kchessinskaya arrived from Russia in time for the first night of the Monte Carlo season on 8 April, at which she danced *Carnaval* and *Le Spectre*, but, as her son was ill, she was obliged to travel backwards and forwards between Monte Carlo and the Grand Duke Andrei's villa at Cannes.[198] Lady Ripon and Lady Juliet Duff had joined Diaghilev and Nijinsky at Beausoleil.[199] Karsavina danced three performances of *The Firebird* on the last three nights of the Monte Carlo season. Bronislava had been dancing the Doll in *Petrushka* in her absence.[200] The company left for Paris on 6 May,[201] and Bezobrazov waved them off. They were never to see him again, for he died of diabetes in Monte Carlo shortly afterwards.[202] Serov had died during the autumn. Diaghilev wept for days on hearing the news.[203] Valerien Svetlov still survived from the 1908 Committee, and during 1912 he looked after the Ballet's accounts.[204] He also produced in Russia and France a handsome book, *Le Ballet contemporain*, whose fine illustrations are precious documents for the study of Diaghilev's early seasons.[205]

The Russians opened for the third time at the Châtelet. If you count the few performances at the Opéra at the turn of the year, it was Diaghilev's fifth season of ballet in Paris, but he was including *Boris* and the concerts when he announced it as his 'septième saison russe'.

There were to be four programmes, each given four times. In each there would be a new ballet. Diaghilev set more store by impressing Paris than any other city and one can see how his mind worked by studying the souvenir programme, published, as all his illustrated programmes had been since 1910, by Brunoff's *Comoedia Illustré*. First, omissions. *Le Pavillon d'Armide*, *Les Sylphides*, *Carnaval*, *Giselle* and *Le Lac des Cygnes*, good enough for England or Central Europe, were not to be allowed to run the risk of boring Paris. Everything had to be either exotic – that is to say, Russian, Greek or Oriental – or sensational in another way, like *Le Spectre de la rose*, with Nijinsky's virtuoso marathon of waltzing. The exotic ballets were almost devoid of the classical dancing which was the general rule in Russia before Fokine's revolution. Greek ballets were performed in sandals or barefoot, Russian or Oriental ballets in various kinds of boots and shoes. Here we may assess the extent of Isadora's influence. The only female dancer – with two minor exceptions – who would be called on to dance *sur les pointes* during this Paris season was Karsavina: in *Le Spectre*, as the inhuman, drifting Firebird; and as the brainless Doll – whose role was a kind of parody of the old conventional ballet – in *Petrushka*. The two other exceptions were Nijinska and Schollar as the two Street Dancers in *Petrushka*, whose numbers were also parodies. And yet – how perverse, when you consider it – Nijinsky, both as Petrushka and as the Golden Slave, had padded tips to his slippers and rose occasionally on point in order to convey the wooden structure of the Puppet or the animal ecstasy of the Negro paramour.[206]

Three of the four new works had music by French composers, and two of these scores had been commissioned by Diaghilev. This was a cause for self-congratulation. Yet Reynaldo Hahn's score did not, in fact, amount to much; and, curiously enough, Diaghilev was never completely satisfied with Ravel's, although it came to be acknowledged as one of the masterpieces of modern French music.

Diaghilev set great store by *Le Dieu bleu*, not only because of its music, but because it was to glorify Nijinsky as a godlike being – which he could hardly be said to have appeared in *Petrushka*. Bakst had been urged to excel himself, to produce his most fantastic, his most Oriental, his most sadistic designs: in this he was successful. Reynaldo Hahn could only try his hardest in a genre which was outside his scope, and although Brussel found no fault with the result in his *Figaro* article, writing that the composer, a lover of Mozart, 'tended to write with increasing simplicity',[207] what could be further from Diaghilev's requirements than Mozart or simplicity? Today the score sounds more reminiscent of Delibes and Massenet. In Cocteau's story, borrowed partly from *The Firebird*, he brought off none of the miracles – such as the resurrection of an ancient myth in the idiom of 'today' – for which he would later become famous.

Bakst unleashed his most savage colours upon the setting. He designed an open place with a pool, overhung by hot orange crags, carved into the heads of Hindu gods, beneath a boiling sky of ultramarine. Instead of the looped curtains and lamps of *Schéhérazade*, he hung aloft an immense swag of sacred snakes. The basic colour of most costumes was white. To many of these were applied patterns in slate-blue, purple, magenta, yellow and green; and never had there been devised such towering, wired turbans and head-dresses, such yards of pleated gauze or such endless festoons of pearls.[208]

The story concerned a young man, the handsome Max Frohman, about to be initiated to the priesthood. For trying to dissuade him, his abandoned girl-friend, Karsavina, was condemned by the Priests to death. The monsters who emerged at night to torment her (a reminiscence of *The Firebird*) were quelled by the apparition first of the Goddess, Nelidova, then of Krishna, the Blue God himself, Nijinsky, who, after he had reunited the lovers and been adored by the priests, ascended to heaven.

Fokine invented a good dance for three Bayadères with peacocks perched on their shoulders, and a spinning number for Dervishes, who had white ropes attached to their hats and shoulders which appeared to form discs in the air as they rotated:[209] but the chief beauty of the ballet, apart from the spectacle, was Nijinsky's pseudo-Indian 'dance of divine enchantment' to a flute solo. This was mainly posturing, but with his blue flesh, skirted yellow costume and tall gold head-dress, he indeed seemed like a being from another world. The monsters who tormented Karsavina were inevitably absurd.[210]

Thamar, presented on 20 May, was the second novelty of the season. Calvocoressi, who had not been too much of a musical purist to condemn the use of Rimsky's *Schéhérazade*, was shocked at the abuse of Balakirev's masterpiece, a symphonic poem, which, after Glinka – in fact, it was first performed twenty-five years after Glinka's death – was a milestone in the development of Russian national music.[211] To Calvocoressi, the music historian, *Thamar* appeared sacrosanct, although to Diaghilev, the propagandist of Russian music, it evidently did not. Though the mysterious languours of the score might match the brooding of the lustful queen with an insatiable appetite for passing travellers, and the louder rhythmical passages certainly provided occasion for outbursts of Caucasian dancing, *Thamar* had a bloom which could be rubbed off by choreographic manhandling. Bakst seized his opportunity to design another extraordinary set: he succeeded, by ignoring perspective, in giving spectators the impression that they were gazing up the inside of a high, reddish-purple sandstone tower, at the bottom of which, amid piles of cushions, the action took place. Against this lurid interior, the dark-blues and purples of the costumes, the tall, conical black felt hats of the men and the Parma-violet silk of Karsavina's costume stood out. The warriors rose on the toes of their soft boots and flung their daggers into the floor; the women glided in veils; and the noble, passionate Bolm was loved and stabbed by Tamara – Tamara, to whom Diaghilev had recommended a 'livid face – eyebrows in a single line . . .'. He told her: 'Omission is the essence of art.' It had been enough to 'touch the spring' and make her 'see all Thamar in a flash.'[212]

Until he had seen it dressed, lit and correctly performed on stage, Diaghilev could not be sure whether Nijinsky's peculiar experiment, *L'Après-midi d'un faune*, due to be revealed to the public on 29 May, was indeed a perfect work of art; and perhaps even then the reaction of the public – or rather, of the chosen few – might influence his judgement one way or the other. But who were the chosen few, whose approval he sought to gain? Bakst, who had made the designs, was presumably in favour of the experiment: Benois, who left only vague expressions of doubt about Nijinsky's invention, less so.[213] The balletomane Svetlov may well have been totally opposed to the new work. Fokine was naturally antagonistic. Stravinsky thought it beautiful.[214]

All Diaghilev could do was to *will* the public to like Nijinsky's ballet. He invited the press and all his friends to a midday rehearsal on 28 May. Debussy's score (first performed in 1894) was a familiar and accepted masterpiece of French music. If we are to believe Fokine, who had been shocked at one of the final rehearsals by Nijinsky's last erotic movement, the audience received the ballet in silence: this may have been because they were awed by its beauty or shocked by its ending. 'After a few strained minutes, during which a hurried backstage conference was held in whispers

... Gabriel Astruc appeared in front of the curtain. He explained to the audience that such a new exhibition could not be understood in a single viewing, and therefore the administration had suggested that the ballet be repeated. This was done, and there was some scattered applause.' Such was Fokine's account. For the first time at a dress rehearsal, champagne and caviare were served in the foyer.[215]

The landscape Bakst designed was less realistic than his sylvan sets for *Narcisse* or for *Daphnis*. It was as if he had tried to match Debussy's 'Impressionism' with a dappled 'Nabi' counterpane of russet, grey and green, in which rocks, trees and a waterfall all merged without shadow or contour. This painted backcloth was hung far forward 'on the line of the second wings', but the wings were black, as was the floorcloth in the front part of the stage as far back as the Faun's rostrum, which stood to the left of the stage and was camouflaged to look like a grassy bank fading into the background: beyond this the floor was green. To someone seated on the level of the lower boxes, or above, the stage picture would be framed in black. The dancers were lit so as to appear flat.[216] Their costumes, however, were *not* intended to fade into the background: the Nymphs' pleated tunics of white muslin, variously stencilled in blue or rust-red with stripes, spots, waves, leaves or checkers, hung in straight lines which matched the angular movements Nijinsky had devised, and the frieze of figures was as clearly defined as one on a Greek vase, although its background was far from plain. Nijinsky's Faun, it is true, was piebald, like the mottled landscape, with dark-brown patches on his white and flesh-coloured tights, but his wig, which incorporated horns lying flat against his head, was metallic gold, and he wore golden sandals.

Nijinsky extended his ears upwards with flesh-coloured wax, and made them pointed like a horse's; he exaggerated his naturally faunlike bone-structure with make-up, underlining the slant of his eyes, emphasizing his chiselled mouth, and growing into the mask of an indolent, sensual creature, half-animal, half-human.[217]

The action of *L'Après-midi d'un faune* can be summarized in a sentence. The idle Faun observes seven Nymphs, and his desire is aroused by one who undresses to bathe in the stream; but when he confronts her, she flees, and he has to console himself with the scarf she has left behind. The Seventh Nymph's nudity was represented by a brief, sleeveless undergarment of gold material. The Faun's token love-making with the scarf, which he carried back to his rock, culminated in a stylized jerk of the pelvis, which suggested orgasm. The whole episode was supposed to represent his first sexual experience.[218]

From a moment after the curtain went up and the Faun raised a pipe to his lips to parallel Debussy's initial warble on the flute, action and music parted company, only to unite at a *fortissimo* when the Nymph (Nelidova) ran away and the Faun became conscious (at the moment of losing her) of his passion: here the climax of music and action coincided. It is worth noting that the 'falling in love' constituted the climax, and that the orgasm on the scarf *faute de mieux* took place to a 'dying fall'. Yet, although the movement for the most part ignores the music, they go marvellously together – as even Fokine conceded – and certain 'surges of sound convey the pulse of desire and summer joy in the breast of this pagan creature, just as certain musical scurries suggest little encounters and disappearances among the trees.'[219]

The sophisticated first-night public were completely taken by surprise. There was no 'dancing'! Nijinsky had only one little jump – which was intended to denote his crossing the (imaginary) stream in which the Nymph bathed. (The waterfall which formed it was painted on the backcloth.) What had this coming and going of distorted bodies to do with the dreamlike music of Debussy? Anyone who was in two minds as to what he thought of the short new ballet, and was inclined to reject the choreographic innovations or disapprove of the abuse of the score, could well be swayed to total rejection of Nijinsky's work by the too explicitly sexual ending. The ballet was performed in silence, but, when the curtain fell, applause was mixed with sounds of disapprobation. No Diaghilev ballet had ever been booed before. Diaghilev was 'visibly put out' and went on stage.[220] Nijinsky thought his first work must be a failure. Then they heard through the curtain a group of supporters who had got together to shout 'Bis!' (I cannot help thinking that this may have been Valentine Gross and her friends.) Diaghilev gave orders for the work to be repeated, as it had been at the rehearsal.[221] Now that he had seen the work performed – and it was exactly as Nijinsky had planned it – he knew it was beautiful, and was confident that everyone must sooner or later come round to his opinion.[222] So the 'encore' was a way both of 'persuading' the public and of encouraging Nijinsky.

The editor of *Commedia*, the daily paper which covered all theatrical events in detail, was persuaded. Pawlowski himself wrote the three-column article which appeared on the front page on 30 May; he also printed two more articles, several photographs and three of Manet's line illustrations to the poem of Mallarmé which had inspired Debussy's *Prélude*.[223] Other papers were warm in praise. Not so Gaston Calmette, editor of *Le Figaro*.

Calmette probably had reasons for attacking *L'Après-midi d'un faune* which had nothing to do with art. The desire to cause a scandal may have been one: an indirect attack on the Franco-Russian alliance another. Brushing Robert Brussel aside, he himself wrote the front-page denunciation.

UN FAUX PAS [literally, 'a wrong step']

Our readers will not find in its usual place on the theatre page an account by my esteemed colleague Robert Brussel of the first performance of *L'Après-midi d'un faune*, a choreographic scene by Nijinsky, arranged and danced by that amazing artist.

I am not printing that account. This is not the place to assess the value of Debussy's music. ... [etc., etc.]

I am, however, certain that any of our readers who were present yesterday at the Châtelet will join with me in protesting against the extraordinary exhibition which they had the audacity to serve up to us in the guise of a serious work, decked out with all the refinements of art and imagination.

Anyone who mentions the words 'art' and 'imagination' in the same breath as this production must be laughing at us. This is neither a pretty pastoral nor a work of profound meaning. We are shown a lecherous faun, whose movements are filthy and bestial in their eroticism, and whose gestures are as crude as they are indecent. That is all. And the over-explicit miming of this misshapen beast, loathsome when seen full on, but even more loathsome in profile, was greeted with the booing it deserved.

The true public ['Le vrai public'] will never accept such animal realism.

M. Nijinsky, ill-suited to such a role, and little accustomed to such a reception, took his revenge a quarter of an hour later with an exquisite rendering of *Le Spectre de la rose*, so delightfully conceived by M. J.-L. Vaudoyer.

This is the sort of show to give the public, with its charm, good taste, *esprit français*. ...[224]

There was a side of Diaghilev to which the scandal was welcome. He snorted and prepared to do battle. He went straight to Rodin and to Odilon Redon, who had been a friend of Mallarmé, and it is easy to imagine that he had a hand in the letters they were persuaded to write in defence of Nijinsky's ballet, incorporated in his own letter of protest, which he took round at once to the offices of *Le Figaro*, to be published without delay on the thirty-first. Rodin's piece was ostensibly written for *Le Matin*, which printed it in full, and only part of it was quoted in *Le Figaro*.

Next morning Calmette wrote

I had not expected to return to the subject of the Châtelet affair, but among the hundreds of letters which my readers have been so flattering as to write to me, and which have given me so much pleasure, there has come one from M. de Diaghilew, the director of the Russian Ballet Season, which I print in the interest of impartiality.

Paris, 30 May 1912

Sir,

I cannot in a few lines defend a ballet which is the fruit of several years' work and of much serious research.

It seems simple in view of the article by M. J.-E. Blanche published by you on Tuesday to submit to the public the opinion of the greatest artist of our day, M. Auguste Rodin, together with that of another master, M. Odilon Redon, who was so close a friend of Stéphane Mallarmé.

First of all, here is the letter I have received from M. Odilon Redon:

Sir,

Joy is often coupled with sorrow. I could not help regretting, amid the delights of this evening's performance by your company, that my illustrious friend Stéphane Mallarmé was not with us. More than anyone, he would have appreciated this wonderful evocation of his thought. ... I recall how Mallarmé was always bringing dance and music into his conversations. How happy he would have been to recognize, in that living frieze we have just been watching, his faun's very dream, and to see creatures of his imagination wafted by Debussy's music and brought to life by Nijinsky's choreography and the passionate colour of Bakst. ...

ODILON REDON

Here now is an important passage from the article published by M. Auguste Rodin [in *Le Matin*]:

Nijinsky has never been so remarkable as in his latest role. No more jumps – nothing but half-conscious animal gestures and poses. He lies down, leans on his elbow, walks with bent knees, draws himself up, advancing and retreating, sometimes slowly, sometimes with jerky angular movements. His eyes flicker, he stretches his arms, he opens his hands out flat, the fingers together, and as he turns away his head he continues to express his desire with a deliberate awkwardness that seems natural. Form and meaning are indissolubly wedded in his body, which is totally expressive of the mind within. ... His beauty is that of antique frescoes and sculpture: he is the ideal model, whom one longs to draw and sculpt. When the curtain rises to reveal him reclining on the ground, one knee raised, the pipe at his lips, you would think him a statue; and nothing could be more striking than the impulse with which, at the climax, he lies face down on the secreted veil, kissing it and hugging it to him with passionate abandon. ...

I wish that such a noble endeavour should be understood as a whole; and that, apart from its gala performance, the Théâtre du Châtelet would arrange others to which all our artists might come for inspiration and to communicate in beauty.

AUGUSTE RODIN

I call attention [Diaghilev continued] to these authoritative opinions and to our obstinate experiments, of which *L'Après-midi d'un faune* is the culmination, in the belief that our works are worthy even of the respect of our enemies.

I have the honour to be, Sir, etc.,

SERGE DE DIAGHILEW

I do not want to argue with M. Serge de Diaghilew [Calmette went on]: he is the impresario of the business and is bound to find the programme chosen by himself very good. This programme contains beautiful works, I admit, and we have only instanced one 'faux pas'. About this 'faux pas' there can be no argument. ...

Calmette next turned the attack on Rodin, whom he accused of living at the tax-payers' expense in the old Hôtel Biron (now the Rodin Museum) and exhibiting indecent drawings in the former chapel of the Sacred Heart which adjoined it, surrounded by a court of swooning lady admirers and self-satisfied snobs. 'There is the real scandal,' he concluded, 'and it is for the government to put a stop to it.'[225] Calmette had lost the battle and was trying to change the subject. The police attended the second performance of *L'Après-midi* on 31 May. Nijinsky modified his final movement. Instead of sliding his hands under his body, he allowed them to remain along his sides, and, when he lowered himself on to the scarf, it was with a less perceptible jerk. The police approved the ballet, which had its third and fourth performances on 1 and 2 June.

The controversy was diverted to Rodin, to whose defence sprang Pierre Mortier of *Gil Blas*, who declared that the Faun was the leading motif of all his art, and suggested that instead of expelling him from the Hôtel Biron, as Calmette suggested, the State should give him the house as a studio for life and convert it into a Rodin Museum, on condition that he left his work to France. This indeed, happened later. Forain published a caricature in *Le Figaro*, showing the sculptor confronted by a nude model, holding her dress over her arm and asking, 'Oh, Master, where can I put my clothes?' Rodin was made to reply, 'Over there in the Chapel.'[226] This provoked more indignation and protests. Calmette was murdered by a jealous mistress two years later.

Meanwhile, everyone in Paris wanted to see the scandalous ballet, and the Châtelet was sold out.

Fokine was very angry. Who would be interested in his long-planned *Daphnis et Chloë* now? Its first night was announced as part of the fourth programme on 5 June, a week after that of *L'Après-midi*, and there should be four performances, as there had been of the other three programmes, the season finishing on 10 June.[227] Although – apart from the last dance of general rejoicing – Fokine had finished the choreography of *Daphnis* before the *première* of *L'Après-midi*, Diaghilev sought reasons for postponing Fokine's ballet. He had once been so thrilled at the prospect of having a score from Ravel: but Ravel was obstinate and refused to allow Diaghilev his favourite game of cutting. (One obvious small cut that was needed was the repeat in Dorkon's bucolic solo.) Then, for a three-scene ballet with a story, there was a surprising lack of dramatic conflict. (Not Daphnis but Pan rescued Chloë from the pirates.) *Daphnis* was the first new ballet Diaghilev had given which did not preserve the Unities of Time and Place. The story, with its rival lovers, dance competition and raid of pirates, with the captivity of Chloë, her near-rape and her restoration to Daphnis by the god Pan, must have seemed to Diaghilev, in comparison with Nijinsky's 'choreographic reverie', too reminiscent of the old Mariinsky ballets. Perhaps Diaghilev realized late in the day that another Greek ballet would be one too many. Perhaps, if he could 'postpone' the production, it would be possible, when Fokine left the company, for Nijinsky to work on the Ravel score. Diaghilev, of course, wanted to give more performances of *L'Après-midi d'un faune*. For one or many reasons *Daphnis* was put off till 8 June. This meant that, as there was a performance on the seventh (including an extra *L'Après-*

midi), there could be no *générale* of *Daphnis*; and as 9 June was a *relâche* (that is, the theatre was closed) and the season ended on the tenth, *Daphnis* could only be given twice. Ravel was annoyed. It is remarkable that the first performance of one of the most famous scores Diaghilev commissioned, now an acknowledged masterpiece, should have been attended with such delays, dissatisfaction and doubt.

If Wagner is the most Dionysian of composers, the one whose music – in the Love-Death of *Tristan*, for example – most nearly offers a musical parallel to sexual ecstasy, Ravel in his *Daphnis* took up the challenge on behalf of France.

Fokine's talent was equal to the occasion, and Nijinsky rehearsed his role of Daphnis in his usual submissive, devoted way: but off-stage there was an atmosphere of animosity between the two men, which Diaghilev had been at no pains to dispel. The company took sides and were divided into two camps. Fokine abused Diaghilev at the last rehearsal and (so he himself reported) called him a bugger.[228]

Fokine averred that, when 8 June arrived, he had to make a scene to prevent Diaghilev from placing *Daphnis* first on the programme,[229] but I cannot believe that this was ever intended. New ballets were always given in the middle. There were murmurs and an 'altercation' in the wings after the first ballet, *Schéhérazade*, because, according to Fokine, part of the company were protesting against a presentation which was to be made to him, but 'The ballet [*Daphnis*] was performed perfectly, by the dancers loyal to me and by my enemies, alike. A whole herd of sheep walked across the stage. They were tended by shepherds and shepherdesses. The prayers, the offerings of flowers and wreaths as gifts to the nymphs, apotheotic dances, pastoral peace, harmony – how far off this was from the belligerent atmosphere and the narrowly averted riot just a few seconds before!'[230]

Nijinsky's solo was performed with his arms twined round a crook which rested on his shoulders. This we know from surviving sketches by Valentine Gross; and other drawings suggest that Karsavina, in the mournful dance of supplication to her captors, adopted poses similar to those of Isadora, whom she despised. Compared with Nijinsky's *L'Après-midi*, we must remember, *Daphnis* was a huge production, with an orchestra of eighty, and with a chorus whose wordless who-hoo-ing contributed immeasurably to the subtle musical texture.

Brussel was allowed his say in *Le Figaro*, and he saluted Ravel's masterpiece. 'The work was received with acclamation. M. Fokine and his interpreters were recalled several times: but M. Maurice Ravel modestly avoided the ovations.'[231] 'And so I left Diaghilev,' wrote Fokine.[232]

The Russians crossed the Channel on Tuesday, 11 June 1912 and opened at Covent Garden on the following day. Their third London season was awaited with rapturous expectation by their devotees. Charles Ricketts described in a letter to the poet Gordon Bottomley how he and Charles Shannon looked forward to the Russian dancers.

They have been something like a passion during the past [two] seasons. ... All that the antique world thought and said about the famous male dancers who were seduced by Empresses, etc., is quite true. Nijinsky outclasses in passion, beauty, and magnetism all that Karsavina can do, and she is a Muse, or several Muses in one, the Muse of Melancholy and of Caprice, capable of expressing tragedy and even voluptuous innocence; the wildness of chastity and the sting of desire; she is the perfect instrument upon which all emotion can be rendered. Nijinsky is a living flame, the son of Hermes, or Loge perhaps. One cannot imagine his mother – probably some ancient ballerina was answerable; but I prefer to believe in some sort of spontaneous nativity, at the most a passing cloud may have attracted some fantastic and capricious god.[233]

Richard Capell of the *Daily Mail* admitted to having seen *Carnaval* in London and Paris about thirty times, and was as fascinated this June as ever. 'The Russians are back at Covent Garden. This means that the Londoner of 1912 is offered a series of pantomimic and choreographic spectacles of a complete and luxurious beauty such as was beyond the command of Nero and Sardanapalus. These three great arts of music, of painting and of dance contribute to these incomparable shows – all three in their most daring and sumptuous expressions.' On the first night *Il Segreto di Susanna* preceded *Carnaval*, which was followed by *Thamar*. Capell wrote of Karsavina, 'lithe in miraculous lilac clothes and of a dreadful pallor – the victim of her own cruel voluptuousness.'[234] Thomas Beecham, son of Joseph, was 'warmly received', wrote the *Daily News*, 'on his first appearance (as conductor) at Covent Garden in any other season than his own'.[235] When the curtain rose on *Carnaval*, wrote *The Times*, 'a thrill of joy went through the house'.[236] The critic of the *Pall Mall Gazette* disliked *Thamar*. 'One is oppressed by the endlessness of this orgy of perverted desire. Somewhere, one feels ... this horrible woman is waving and waving her scarf for evermore. ... Why are all the dramas of Bakst pitched on the same note? Why is there always this inhuman delight in kisses with a taste of blood?' But 'the music of Balakirev ... was rich in barbarous colour, it had a throbbing undercurrent, and it rose to passionate heights.'[237]

When *Thamar* was repeated on 18 July, there was a new recruit to the battalion of balletomanes in the house. The twenty-one-year-old Cyril Beaumont had been trained as a research chemist, but his obsession with the theatre, then the apparitions of Karsavina, Pavlova and Mordkine in musichall, had made him throw caution to the winds and open a small bookshop in theatre-land, the Charing Cross Road. His first sight of the Diaghilev Ballet changed his life. *Thamar* was his first experience of Diaghilev's new art-form.

The opening notes of Balakirev's score set the mood. . . . The air seemed suddenly heavy and the darkened theatre charged with foreboding. . . . The lighting was subdued, save for the dull glow of a dying fire. . . . [On] a huge divan . . . reposed Karsavina. . . . Stretched at full length, she occasionally stirred uneasily in her sleep. A waiting-woman sat near her couch, other retainers stood in the shadows, their attitudes strained and watchful. . . . It was as though a terrible menace had been halted, leaving behind a perceptible tenseness which suggested that the threat was about to be renewed. . . . The curiosity aroused was intense. . . .[238]

By Nijinsky in *Les Sylphides* Beaumont was overwhelmed.

He danced not with his limbs, but with his whole body, and the sequence of his movements composing the dance flowed one into the other, now swift, now slow, now retarded, now increasing in speed, with a suggestion of spontaneity that had all the quality of melody. . . . These were not mortals. It was the poet's shade visiting, in company with the spirit of his dead mistress, the moonlit grove which had once inspired his imperishable odes.[239]

This was the night when, with the first English performance of *The Firebird*, the music of Stravinsky was first heard in these islands. Florence Henderson was present, and thought it 'the most beautiful large ballet' she had seen.[240]

Beaumont, who was the same age as Miss Henderson, though he loved *The Firebird*, retained his critical sense. He admired the music, the atmosphere, the encounters of Prince Ivan with the Bird and with the Tsarevna, but he thought that 'from the moment the gates closed upon the princesses, the ballet became stagy. The demons and Kastchei (even though played by Cecchetti), the dance with which the Bird of Fire forced the demons and their leader to dance until they fell exhausted, were all too obvious . . . the ballet was no longer a choreographic poem.'[241]

Hugo von Hofmannsthal had not ceased to correspond with Richard Strauss about the possibility of a ballet for Nijinsky; and Diaghilev had not ceased to hope that his love for Nijinsky might be 'crowned', as it were, with a glorious score by the most celebrated living composer. On 23 June we find Hofmannsthal writing to Strauss:

At the time of my *Orestes* suggestion, which I sacrificed quickly and readily enough to your objections, I said all that is necessary to broach the ballet question. You were by no means altogether disinclined. . . . Together with Kessler, who possesses a most fertile, and quite specifically a designer's imagination, I have produced a short ballet for the Russians, *Joseph in Egypt*, the episode with Potiphar's wife; the boyish part of Joseph of course for Nijinsky, the most extraordinary personality on the stage today.

Tomorrow or the next day I shall send you the sketch in typescript. . . . Even if you are not willing to set it to music, I cannot withdraw yet another piece from the Russians (Diaghilev and Nijinsky know the sketch!). But I would endeavour

231

to modify, as far as possible, my collaboration with the Russian or French musician of Diaghilev's choice, so as to make it quite clear that I was concerned to be of assistance only to the dancer, and not to the musician concerned.[242]

The blackmail, if such it was, appeared to work. Strauss accepted the idea of *Joseph in Egypt*; and on 28 June Hofmannsthal wrote again: '... I am very glad that you take to the idea of *Joseph* as an interim work. ... Diaghilev will come to see you in Garmisch from London to settle the business side, but will inquire beforehand when this discussion would suit you best. He is a Russian of the most attractive kind, much more like a country gentleman than a manager. ...'[243] It was arranged that Count Harry Kessler should take Diaghilev to see Strauss at Garmisch on 3 August.[244]

Narcisse appeared in the repertoire in London on 9 July. Although it had both good and bad reviews, it was more favourably received in London than in Paris. *The Times* thought there was 'something irritating in the insensibility of Narcissus to the charms of the Nymphs who wreathe themselves around him and literally lay themselves at his feet' and judged the latter part little more than 'a prolonged tableau', but praised the groups, the Bacchantes and 'the unsullied joy of the first dances of Narcissus', which were 'as captivating as anything which the Russians have given us'.[245] Praise came from the *Morning Post*[246] and *Daily Express*,[247] while in the *Daily Mail* Richard Capell considered Nijinsky's role 'the most elaborate' in which he had yet been seen, 'curious and wonderful', and the whole ballet 'a glimpse of the antique world, a Theocritan idyll'.[248] The *Sunday Times*, however, found Nijinsky's 'every pose, every movement, every gesture ... instinct with sexless insensibility and vacuous complacency. ... You feel the punishment fits the crime.'[249]

As usual, Charles Ricketts wrote most vividly about the ballet. To a friend he reported, 'Karsavina surpassed herself as Echo in *Narcisse*. She creeps on to the stage, enamoured of Narcisse, and approaches silently, hiding behind trees; she dances in a trance and sinks at Nijinsky's feet at the end of each musical phrase. He leaps like a faun, with such rare clothing on that Duchesses had to be led out of the audience, blinded with emotion, and with their diamond tiaras all awry. ...'[250]

In the excitement of such aesthetes as Ricketts may be measured the degree of Diaghilev's achievement.

Diaghilev, Nijinsky and Bakst made a new friend in Lady Ottoline Morrell, whom they had met briefly in Paris. Her timorous, loving heart, and longing to do good, were concealed beneath a fantastic exterior. She was tall and wore unfashionable clothes, brilliant coloured shawls and trailing brocades, in which she was often drawn and painted by Augustus John and Henry Lamb. The writers and painters of 'Bloomsbury', for entertaining whom she was to become famous, and who had an unattractive custom of mocking her behind her back, were still almost unknown. 'Lytton [Strachey] and most of my friends,' she wrote, 'were such enthusiastic admirers of [Nijinsky] that I . . . rather pooh-poohed him, but when I saw him dance I was completely converted, for I saw that anyone who so completely lost himself was not just a good ballet dancer . . . but became the idea he was representing.'[251]

The difference between Lady Ottoline and Lady Ripon was extreme – in fact, all one can find that they had in common was high birth, height, a tendency to have unconventional love affairs and a passion for the Diaghilev Ballet. Glwadys Herbert had never cut herself off from the world of palatial country houses, sport and splendour, and had made two conventional, loveless marriages to rich men, while Ottoline Cavendish-Bentinck, brought up in a similar society, where a girl invited comment by reading a book, had fled from it into the arms of a middle-class Liberal MP. When Lady Ottoline, who could face D. H. Lawrence without a tremor, drove down in the car of the amusing *littérateur* Maurice Baring to meet Diaghilev and Nijinsky at lunch with Lady Ripon at Coombe, she felt rather shy. But when she was placed next to Vaslav at luncheon they got on like a house on fire. Friendship ripened.

Lady Ottoline wrote,

He was very nervous and highly-strung, and his guardian and jailer, Diaghilev, did not allow him to go out into society as it tired and upset him, and I was one of the few people that he was allowed to come and see, as at my house he could be quiet and only meet other artists. 'He is like a jockey,' I laughingly told Lytton, but really I grew very fond of the little figure with long, muscular neck and pale Kalmuk face, and the hands so expressive and nervous. He always seemed lost in the world outside, as if he looked on as a visitor from another world, although his powers of observation were intensely rapid. For on entering a room he would see all the pictures hanging in it before he had been there but a few minutes. It was not easy to talk to him as he didn't speak English and his French was very vague, but we managed to understand each other, and he was glad, I think, of real understanding and appreciation of his serious work. I was lamenting one day that I was not able to create anything myself and he quickly answered, 'Oh, but you do create, Madame, for you help us young artists to create.'

There were at this time fantastic fables about him: that he was very debauched, that he had girdles of emeralds and diamonds given him by an Indian prince; but on the contrary, I found that he disliked any possessions or anything that hampered him or diverted him from his art. He was incessantly thinking out new ballets, new steps; also he was absorbed by the ideas of the old Russian myths and religions which he wanted to express in his ballets as he did in *The Rite of Spring*. Such ballets as *Le Spectre de la rose* did not interest him; he said it was *trop joli* and was rather annoyed when people admired it.[252]

Lady Ottoline invited Nijinsky to tea in Bedford Square, and Duncan Grant came to play tennis in the square the same afternoon, half hoping to see Nijinsky leap over the net.[253] This may have been on 12 July, when Vaslav and Bakst signed the Visitors' Book.[254] Though Nijinsky and Bakst did not play tennis, they sat in the square's gardens and watched others playing it. I am sure that the Georgian terrace architecture of Bedford Square, seen over the 'dreaming garden trees', was transmuted in Bakst's design for Nijinsky's next ballet, *Jeux*, and the tennis party may have suggested the ballet itself. Lady Ottoline wrote that, as Bakst and Nijinsky watched Duncan Grant and some others playing tennis, they were 'so entranced by the tall trees against the houses and the figures flitting about playing tennis that they exclaimed with delight "Quel décor!"'[255]

Three days later, on 15 July, Bronislava Nijinska was married to the dancer Alexander Kotchetovsky at the Russian Orthodox Church in Buckingham Palace Road. Diaghilev, *in loco parentis*, gave her away, and he bought her a ring set with sapphires and brilliants, which he stated firmly was to 'wed her to her art'. (She had to sell it during the Revolution.) Sapphires were Diaghilev's favourite stone – or so it would appear from the rings he bought not only for Bronislava but Vaslav, and later Massine.[256]

On 17 July, Diaghilev was at Lady Ottoline's, presumably with Nijinsky (who did not sign her book again).[257] From Jacques-Emile Blanche, who was in London for the season, we have a description of Nijinsky hatching the egg which became *Jeux*. The worldly Blanche ridiculed Nijinsky's novel ideas, and gave the impression in his reminiscence, perhaps misleadingly, that Diaghilev was not too happy about them either.

Chaliapine [wrote Blanche] was one day entertaining Lady Ripon to lunch in the large hall of the Savoy, and I was among the guests. A waiter brought me a note from Diaghilev; I opened it and read, 'Dear friend, we are in the grill-room with Bakst. Vaslav would like to see you; he wants to talk to you about a mad scheme, but you know his fancies – he wants us to collaborate in a "games" libretto and Debussy is to do the score. Come as soon as you leave the table. We have a rehearsal at the theatre at four o'clock.' Vaslav was drawing on the tablecloth when I reached the grill-room. Diaghilev looked as if he were in one of his cross moods (he was biting his fingers); Bakst looked at the drawings on the cloth aghast – but Nijinsky understood only Russian, and it took me some time to find out what was in the wind. The 'cubist' ballet – which became *Jeux* – was a game of tennis in a garden; but in no circumstances was it to have a romantic décor in the Bakst manner! There should be no corps de ballet, no ensembles, no variations, no *pas de deux*, only girls and boys in flannels, and rhythmic movements. A group at a certain stage was to depict a fountain, and the game of tennis (with licentious *motifs*) was to be interrupted by the crashing of an aeroplane. What a childish idea![258]

The idea of three dancers representing a fountain is so enchanting an idea that it is hard to read the painter's words without irritation. He did consent, however, to act as intermediary with the composer. 'I sent the scheme to

Debussy,' he wrote, 'who replied: "No, it's idiotic and unmusical; I should not dream of writing a score." Diaghilev pleaded Debussy's cause; Nijinsky was obstinate, and threatened to dance no more in London. Debussy was again wired to; his fee was to be doubled.' When Blanche saw and heard *Jeux* in the following year he thought it 'a bad score'![259]

The account of this scene at the Savoy makes clear more than just the origin of a lost ballet, whose music is now famous. Diaghilev was obviously still devoted to Nijinsky; he listened to his projects and, even if they alarmed him, helped them to come true. It is at the same time evident that Nijinsky was developing a mind and will of his own. This summer perhaps saw the dawning of a need to be independent of Diaghilev.

Vaslav sometimes snubbed Diaghilev. 'One day at luncheon at the Savoy,' Juliet Duff recalled, 'Diaghilev embarked on a somewhat lengthy anecdote. Nijinsky bore it with ill-concealed impatience and at the end of it looked up and said with firmness and finality, "Histoire longue mais pauvre".'[260]

That Diaghilev was capable of being made unhappy by Nijinsky, whether they still went to bed together or not (which is not really very important), we know from another reminiscence of Lady Juliet. Diaghilev, she observed, 'was an odd mixture of ruthlessness and vulnerability. He could make others cry, but he could cry himself, and I remember a day at my mother's house [Coombe] on Kingston Hill when he had had a disagreement with Nijinsky, who had refused to come, and he sat in the garden with tears dripping down his face and would not be comforted.'[261]

The Russian Ballet had so captured the imagination of the British that even a matinée performance on Gold Cup Day at Ascot, Thursday 20 June, was sold out.[262] When a short version of *Le Pavillon d'Armide* was given on 2 July, it was noticed that Paderewski was in Lady Ripon's party, and that 'Master Anthony Asquith', the ten-year-old son of the Prime Minister and the irrepressible Margot Tennant, were in the audience.[263] Russian dancers were in demand to perform at parties. Kyasht and Volinine had danced at Lord Londesborough's, at St Dunstan's, Regent's Park, two nights before the Diaghilev Ballet opened.[264] Lady Ripon had a dinner for fifty people at Coombe, after which Karsavina and Nijinsky danced.[265] Admiral and Mrs Beatty staged a short play by Rostand at Hanover Lodge, Regent's Park, after which Karsavina's valse in *Les Sylphides* was interrupted by rain.[266] Early in July Karsavina, Zambelli and Nijinsky danced for the Aga Khan at the Ritz.[267] On 17 July Pavlova and Novikov appeared for Lady Michelham at Strawberry Hill.[268] Dmitri de Gunsburg had Pavlova as well as Karsavina and Kyasht to dance at a party he gave at the Carlton Hotel.[269] Then, the Fine Art Society held the first English exhibition of the stage designs of Bakst at their handsome Bond Street Galleries, and published the English version of the massive French folio on his work which had just appeared. The photographer Hoppé, who had first known Diaghilev in Munich years before, exhibited his photographs of the Russian dancers in Baker Street, besides releasing an album of his studies, published by the Fine Art Society. These included Karsavina, Feodorova and Bolm: but as Nijinsky was the only dancer who could not be lured to his studio, Hoppé was obliged to include one photograph of Vaslav in *Le Spectre de la rose* by Bert.[270]

That summer the young poet Rupert Brooke fell in love with the Russian Ballet. Both Geoffrey Keynes[271] and Cathleen Nesbitt, whom Brooke adored, remember going to Covent Garden with him. One night, as he left the theatre with the beautiful actress, he exclaimed, 'Do you realize you have seen a miracle? Nijinsky actually stopped still in the air.'[272] Shortly afterwards he wrote to Eddie Marsh, Winston Churchill's Private Secretary, about the Russians, 'They, if anything can, redeem our civilization. I'd give everything to be a ballet-designer.'[273] He meant he would like to be Diaghilev.

When the London season ended on 1 August 1912, there were five performances to give between 6 and 22 August at Deauville, the new seaside resort on the Normandy coast; then a peaceful stretch of holiday lay ahead, for the autumn—winter tour was not to open at Cologne until 30 October. Yet Diaghilev was kept busy planning and darting about Europe, and Nijinsky was working out a new language of the dance. No fairy with her three wishes, not Hadrian for Antinous, had ever had such rare gifts in store as Diaghilev had for Nijinsky that summer. It was three years since they had decided to live together, and ballet scores by Strauss, Debussy and Stravinsky, commissioned for Vaslav by Diaghilev, were being planned or composed during August, September and October.

Diaghilev had arranged to see Strauss at Garmisch on 3 August, but he postponed his visit.[274] On the fifteenth Astruc's office, who reported daily to him during his holiday in south-west France, believed Diaghilev still to be at Deauville.[275] He did not wait for the last Deauville performances, but joined Stravinsky at Bayreuth, where they heard *Parsifal* together on 20 August.[276] With Nijinsky, who may also have missed the last performance at Deauville on the twenty-second, they spent a few days at the Park Hotel, Lugano, visiting Benois and his family, and Igor played *The Rite* on the piano. Shura, who took no part in the Russian Ballet's activities during 1912 and 1913, was thrilled by the new music.[277] On 25 August Diaghilev, Stravinsky and Nijinsky were at Stresa on Lago Maggiore, took the steamer to Isola Bella and photographed each other on its terraces. They must have been on their way to Milan, where they briefly parted company, for by the twenty-seventh Diaghilev was at the Hôtel Crillon, Paris, telegraphing Bessel, the St Petersburg music publisher, about the rights of Mussorgsky's operas.[278] By 30 August Diaghilev was in London[279] for talks with the Beechams about the two 1913 seasons, the second of which would consist of both opera and ballet. Within a day or two Sergei Pavlovitch had joined his friends in Venice. On 2 September (probably) Stravinsky played him the 'Danse des Adolescents', the first number of *The Rite*, in the ballroom of the Grand Hôtel des Bains on the Lido.[280] Stravinsky left almost immediately for Russia,[281] while Sergei and Vaslav spent the first three weeks of September in Venice.

On 25 September Diaghilev was in Paris at the Elysée Palace Hotel, writing to Durand to reserve his rights in Ravel's *Daphnis* for the following year. On 4 October he took the train to Rouen and drove out in a hired car to visit Maeterlinck at the Abbaye de Saint Wandrille. The project he wished to discuss with the Belgian poet, whose Symbolist play *Pelléas et Mélisande* had been metamorphosed into Debussy's opera, remains a mystery. It may have been related to *Jeux*, but the telegrams Stravinsky was receiving from Diaghilev at this time were urging him to return from Russia for discussions with Maeterlinck, so the best guess I can offer is that a ballet version of the play *L'Oiseau bleu*, first performed in 1909, was envisaged – birds being in the air, so to speak, at that time. In mid-October Diaghilev was in St Petersburg, and on the twenty-fourth he cabled anxiously to Astruc about the necessity of Monteux starting rehearsals at Cologne on Sunday the twenty-seventh.[282] He missed the opening at Cologne on the thirtieth and in Paris on the thirty-first he called on Debussy at four o'clock to ask him to prolong the ending of *Jeux*. Nijinsky had decided he wanted the ballet to close as it had begun, with a ball bouncing on the stage. Diaghilev begged the composer to reintroduce at the end the chords of the opening Prelude. This Debussy did with a subtle variation.[283]

Diaghilev and Nijinsky were concerned with the problem of establishing a new relationship between music and dance. The choreography of *L'Après-midi* had gone against the music. This was clearly viable, but a way should be found of following the sense or phrasing of symphonic music without being enslaved by the metric beat. Of one thing the two men were convinced: 'dance music', as it had been known to the nineteenth-century ballet-masters, was dead.

The Russian Ballet opened at the new Kroll Opera House, Berlin, on 21 November (after their visits to Cologne, Frankfurt and Munich), and Stravinsky came from Switzerland to join Diaghilev and Nijinsky at the Adlon Hotel. He had just finished the piano score, though not the orchestration, of *The Rite of Spring*.[284] On Sunday 8 December, the friends heard Arnold Schönberg's *Pierrot Lunaire* at the Choralionsaal[285] – and a few days later Stravinsky, dining with Schönberg, met Alban Berg and Anton Webern.[286]

L'Après-midi d'un faune was so well received on 11 December that it was repeated, and Diaghilev cabled boastfully to Astruc that all Berlin had been present – Strauss, Hofmannsthal, Reinhardt, Nikisch, the whole Secession group, the King of Portugal, ambassadors and the Court. He had had a long talk with the Kaiser, who had congratulated the company and was coming again with the Empress and the Princes on Sunday.[287] But the most important talk that took place, from the point of view of new developments in ballet, was one between Hugo von Hofmannsthal, Diaghilev and Nijinsky about Strauss's worries over the traditional demands of dance music, for Hofmannsthal was able to write to the composer on 13 December:

> I fear it is the idea of ballet, of the need for accentuated rhythms which has misled and confused you. Therefore I must make myself the spokesman of Nijinsky, who implores you to write the most unrestrained, the least dance-like music in the world, to put down pure Strauss for this leaping towards God which is a struggle for God. To be taken by you beyond all bounds of convention is exactly what he longs for; he is, after all, a true genius and just where the track is uncharted, there he desires to show what he can do, in a region like the one you opened in *Elektra*.[288]

Hot in pursuit of new clues to the interpretation of music by dance, Diaghilev and Nijinsky paid their second visit to Hellerau. The headquarters of Dalcroze, which they had first visited when passing through Dresden, was a two-hour journey from Berlin, and it is a measure of the extent to which Diaghilev was anxious about finding an equivalent in dance for the incredibly difficult score of *The Rite of Spring* that he thought the exertion worth while. Dalcroze's system, which was not really to do with the art of dancing, but was a highly organized method of analysing music by bodily movement, might hold the key Diaghilev and Nijinsky were looking for. Dalcroze always insisted, according to his pupil Beryl de Zoete (who later wrote with insight about Oriental dancing), that 'his *méthode rhythmique*' was devised for the unrhythmical bodies of Europeans and was entirely superfluous for peoples who had not lost their sense of rhythm. He had listened to Arab drummers in North Africa, and would perhaps not have included Russians in his category of 'Europeans'.[289] The school at Hellerau, to which Dalcroze had moved from Geneva in 1911, had been built for him by German admirers, and the great hall in which Diaghilev watched a demonstration of rhythmical exercises had been designed by Adolf Appia, whose new simplicities in stage design had influenced Gordon Craig, the lover of Isadora. That summer Dalcroze had staged the Inferno scene of Gluck's *Orfeo*. (In the following year he would produce the whole opera.) Among the pupils who had taken part in this was a Polish–Russian Jewish girl, Miriam Ramberg,[290] who was intelligent and well-read, who had studied ballet in Warsaw, danced barefoot in Paris, and even travelled in January 1911 with Dalcroze and a group of his pupils, at the invitation of Prince Sergei Volkonsky, to give demonstrations in St Petersburg and Moscow.[291] Dalcroze was an enemy of ballet, few of his pupils had any connection with the dance, and he used to tell Ramberg, 'Tu es trop extérieure.'[292] It was perhaps her tendency to give a performance when doing her exercises that attracted the attention of Diaghilev and Nijinsky. They spoke to Dalcroze about her (and Diaghilev probably asked about her character, anxious to make sure that she was 'serious' and not prone to frivolity and flirtation). Ramberg was amazed to hear that Diaghilev considered engaging her 'for special work'. She was given a ticket to Berlin, and on Thursday 19 December 1912 saw the Russian Ballet for the first time on the last night of the Berlin season.[293]

Ramberg's reactions to the programme were mixed, and being (in her own phrase) 'badly brought up', she did not hesitate to express her views to Diaghilev over supper.

He listened politely, even sympathetically, to my stupid prejudiced criticism. I said I thought that the procession in *Cléopâtre* should have corresponded more exactly to the rhythm of the music, which was how Dalcroze would have done it. I know now that the great Fokine was absolutely right in his looser treatment of the passage. Diaghilev, however, did not defend him – they had fallen out at that time – and said: 'Yes, they walk like cooks – we must improve that.' (As though I was ever capable of improving on Fokine!) *L'Après-midi d'un faune* was also in the programme. Here the discrepancy between the impressionistic music of Debussy and Nijinsky's absolute austerity of style quite shocked me. ... *Carnaval* ... enchanted me. ...[294]

Ramberg was also moved by the Polovtsian Dances from *Prince Igor*. She 'readily accepted Diaghilev's invitation to join the company to acquaint them with Dalcroze's method, to help Nijinsky in applying it in the production of Stravinsky's *Sacre du Printemps*' and to dance in ballets for which she was 'suitable'. She signed on a few days later at Budapest, where the Ballet performed over Christmas.[295]

And at Budapest Romola de Pulszky saw again the Ballet which had so thrilled her a year before that she had followed them to Paris, given up her acting lessons with Réjane, and taken dancing lessons instead.[296] The word 'fan' (short for 'fanatic', and first applied to the supporters of baseball teams in the United States in 1889) was not yet in common use for followers of theatrical stars. Yet Misia Edwards had been a 'fan' of Diaghilev since 1908, Robert Brussel of Karsavina since 1909, Lady Ripon and her daughter Juliet of Diaghilev, Karsavina and Nijinsky since 1911, and Romola of the Russian Ballet in general and Nijinsky in particular since March 1912. The difference between Romola and the others, apart from her youth, was that she wanted to associate herself *actively* with the new artistic movement, which she saw as comparable to the Italian Renaissance in painting and sculpture. Thirty or forty years later she might have aspired to be their Press Representative, for her genuine talent, as time would show, was for publicity.

CHAPTER 11

1913–14

The Rite of Spring – South America: Nijinsky's
Marriage and Dismissal – Re-engagement of Fokine –
Massine's Début – The Beechams' Great Season –
Diaspora

ON 2 JANUARY 1913 Diaghilev telegraphed automatically to Astruc
from the Hungaria Hotel to let him know – and, through him,
Paris – that *L'Après-midi d'un faune* had been repeated after its first
performance in Budapest.[1] On 4 January Stravinsky arrived in Budapest
and made a scene with Monteux after a performance of *Petrushka*. Monteux
went straight to Diaghilev and resigned. Next morning everything was
patched up.[2]

At the beginning of this crucial year, 1913, Diaghilev had reason for self-
congratulation – his company had conquered all the major European capitals
except Madrid, Athens and Amsterdam, glorious new works were in the
offing, and his favourite, Nijinsky, the greatest dancer in the world, was
turning into a choreographer: but do artists, do creative geniuses (and Diaghilev *was* a creative genius, although he neither composed nor painted, nor
made choreography) ever congratulate themselves? Not very often and not
for long at a time. Bitter experience had cured Diaghilev of the temptation
of complacency. There would always be work; there would always be
worries. His bookings were good right up to the holidays, but an anxious
time lay ahead: to put on Rimsky's *Ivan the Terrible* and Mussorgsky's *Khovanshchina* – parts of which Ravel and Stravinsky were going to re-orchestrate
– as well as *Boris* was a huge undertaking; and there were the heavy problems
of interpreting Debussy's and, particularly, Stravinsky's ballet scores. It was
to be hoped that Ramberg, who was to work so closely with Nijinsky, would
not complicate matters by falling in love. Diaghilev well knew that in private
life the quality of his ordinary-looking friend became manifest in a guileless
simplicity which was irresistible. Since the beginnings of the new Russian
Ballet nobody had enjoyed the privilege of intimacy with Vaslav except his
mother, his sister (now married), Diaghilev, Nuvel, Benois, Bakst and Karsavina. Karsavina's beauty and intelligence made Vaslav rather shy. 'Mimi'

Ramberg was no beauty, but she *did*, in fact, fall under Nijinsky's spell. Yet the danger, the influence that was within the year to disrupt the lives of Diaghilev and Nijinsky and threaten the existence of the Russian Ballet, would come from another direction; and of Romola de Pulszky's underground operations Diaghilev had no more suspicion than the Tsar had of Lenin's.

When, in the first week of 1913, Stravinsky and the Diaghilev Ballet moved to Vienna, Romola followed them.³ Karsavina had rejoined the company in the Hungarian capital, and in Vienna she danced not only *Thamar*, which was well received, but, with Nijinsky, the Bluebird *pas de deux*, now renamed *La Princesse enchantée*, and *Petrushka*.⁴ Stravinsky's score for the last named was pronounced *Schweinerei* (filth) by the Opera orchestra, who at first refused to play it. When, at a rehearsal, the violinists threw down their bows, Diaghilev advanced on the orchestra pit and said, 'Gentlemen, in ten years you will be proud to have been the first Austrians to play Stravinsky's music.'⁵ At the first performance of *Petrushka*, the musicians tried to sabotage the score.⁶ Stravinsky fled Vienna next morning for Switzerland.⁷

Romola was already friends with Bolm and Maestro Cecchetti. At a rehearsal in the Opera House she persuaded a lady journalist to introduce her to Nijinsky.

In the ensuing conversation there was a bit of confusion, which was greatly aided by the diversity of languages spoken. Nijinsky misunderstood my identity, and thought I was the prima ballerina of the Hungarian Opera, whose name had been brought into conversation at that moment. ... It was probably due to that error on his part that he greeted me with so charming and respectful a bow. For many, many times after that first introduction I was introduced to him, and never was there more than a polite, fleeting acknowledgement. ...⁸

In order to get closer to Nijinsky, Romola de Pulszky decided to approach Diaghilev. She wanted him to allow her to travel with the company, take lessons with Cecchetti and perhaps walk on in small roles or in the crowd; but she was subtle enough to hope the suggestion would come from him. (This was Diaghilev's own technique.) Romola's strength was her social position, dependent partly on the eminence of her father's family, partly on her mother's fame. Diaghilev's weakness was snobbery. So battle was engaged. Romola had done a service to a kind, fat, old music critic, Ludwig Karpath – he was afraid of the dark and she had seen him home one night after dinner.⁹ It was he whom she persuaded to introduce her to Diaghilev at the Hotel Bristol. They were received in an empty drawing-room in the depressing middle of the afternoon. Romola wrote,

Diaghilev ... made us feel absolutely that nothing interested him more than my intention to be a dancer. ... Apparently a young society girl had come to the great artistic organizer with a request. In reality, two powerful enemies had crossed swords for the first time. Diaghilev held the thing I most wanted – Nijinsky. ...

'I think Bolm is wrong in advising you to go to the Wiesenthals' [Diaghilev told her]. 'The ideal thing for you would be to become a pupil of the Imperial Dancing School in St Petersburg. But of course it is not feasible, even with the greatest possible pull, for you are not a Russian, and you are long past the required age. ... I think the best thing for you to do would be to take private lessons from Fokine in St Petersburg.'

With apparent joy I jumped at the idea. ...

He then asked my impression of the different ballets and the artists of his company. My answers must have been correct. He smiled approvingly. During all this time I felt gradually that I was falling under his spell. ... With a desperate effort I began to rave about Bolm as a man, not as an artist, like any little 'flapper' would. And then Diaghilev, with unexpected strategy, turned and asked, 'What about Nijinsky?'

Without hesitation I answered, 'Oh, Nijinsky is a genius. As an artist he is incomparable. But somehow Bolm is more human to me' – and I continued my extravagances about Bolm. By this time he was convinced of my good faith, and then said the fatal words:

'I will speak to Maestro Cecchetti. ... I am sure he will take you as a special private pupil. This way you will have not only a marvellous teacher, but also the possibility of travelling with us and closely studying our work.'[10]

Romola had won 'her first battle'. When, in 1932 and 1933, she wrote the life of Nijinsky from which these lines are quoted, she was hoping it would be made into a film.[11] (She needed money to care for her sick husband.) 'Diaghilev held the thing I most wanted – Nijinsky' was a romantic exaggeration (just as were statements in Nijinsky's *Diary*, on which we have commented above, which she published two years after her biography). But when I asked her whether she was in love with Nijinsky in 1913, she quickly answered 'No', adding that because of his goodness she came to love him later, after their marriage.[12] She was a fan – and who can blame her for that?

After the last night in Vienna, when *Petrushka* was given a second performance, Diaghilev took the trouble to telegraph to Stravinsky that it had gone much better and that there had been four curtain calls.[13] He then set off at once for St Petersburg,[14] where he had to see Sanine (who was to stage the operas), the designers, Chaliapine and other singers. The company went on to perform twice in Prague, twice in Leipzig and once in Dresden on the way to London. From Dresden on 27 January Nijinsky telegraphed to Astruc, asking for the dimensions of the stage of the new Théâtre des Champs-Elysées,[15] at which the Ballet's Paris season was to take place (and which was to open with a production of the *Benvenuto Cellini* of Berlioz on 31 March). Although the February–March London season was once more at Covent Garden, the first rehearsals of *The Rite of Spring* were held, during the few free days the company had in England before the opening night, on the stage of the Aldwych Theatre.[16]

When Stravinsky first came to one of our rehearsals [wrote Rambert, as she later called herself] and heard the way his music was being played, he blazed up, pushed aside the fat German pianist, nicknamed 'Kolossal' by Diaghilev, and proceeded to play twice as fast as we had been doing it, and twice as fast as we could possibly dance. He stamped his feet on the floor and banged his fist on the piano and sang and shouted, all to give us an impression of the rhythms of the music and the colour of the orchestra.[17]

To dancers, who, before the invention of recording music on tape, were obliged to rehearse to piano scores, the orchestrated music of a ballet, which they seldom heard until a day or two before the first public performance, often came as a nasty shock. The devoted artist, Valentine Gross, thought that some of the incongruity of Nijinsky's *Jeux*, as finally presented on the stage, was due to its having been rehearsed to a piano score which gave little idea of Debussy's instrumentation.[18]

Diaghilev only arrived in London at the last minute. On 2 February he had telegraphed to Stravinsky from St Petersburg, not knowing he was already in London, asking him to come for the first English performance of *Petrushka* on the fourth.[19] For he had decided that the English were ready for *Petrushka*, which had already been seen in Paris, Berlin and Vienna. On 4 February there were 'startled expressions on the faces of the audience', as Cyril Beaumont noticed; and even he thought at first that Stravinsky's music sounded 'incredibly daring and uncouth', though he soon fell under its spell.[20] *The Times* found the ballet 'refreshingly new and refreshingly Russian';[21] Stravinsky told the *Daily Mail* that his score had never been better played than by Thomas Beecham's orchestra;[22] and Beecham's doting supporter, Lady Cunard, wore a 'Russian diadem' with her blue and gold brocade dress on the first night.[23] Beaumont was as fascinated by the way in which Nijinsky, when supported under the arms by the iron stand inside the Magician's booth, gave his legs 'a looseness suggesting that foot, leg and thigh were threaded on a string attached to the hip', as by his putty-coloured make-up, with a thickened nose, wavy eyebrows, and lidless, boot-button eyes, which composed 'a sad and unhappy mask, an expression which remained constant throughout the ballet'.[24] The young Osbert Sitwell applied the epithet 'genius' to all the creators and interpreters of *Petrushka*, and came later to think that the fable was prophetic of the fate of European man.[25]

Diaghilev, in his infinite fecundity – or was it duplicity? – had invented yet another name for the Bluebird *pas de deux*, and on 11 February, the day that the death of Captain Scott in the Antarctic was announced, it was danced by Karsavina and Nijinsky under the name of *L'Oiseau et le prince*.

L'Après-midi d'un faune was given its first English performance in the same programme. There were a few hisses, but there was also much applause, and the short ballet was repeated, as it had been in Paris, Berlin and Budapest. The critics were not shocked; and the *Daily Mirror* suggested that 'the fuss made over this ballet in Paris was largely a "put up" business'.[26] Capell guessed that the inspiration of the 'miracle' performed by 'the fabulous Nijinsky, the peerless dancer, who as the faun does no dancing', came from Greek pottery in the British Museum and a study of 'the gambols of chamois or goat'.[27] *The Times* judged Nijinsky's 'stiff poses, and particularly his last action when he lies down to dream beside the scarf ... extraordinarily expressive' and acclaimed 'a new phase' in the art of ballet.[28] When Queen Alexandra was brought by Lady Ripon, on 19 February, to see the controversial work, it was again repeated.[29] On the twenty-first the *Daily Mail* reported an exchange of telegrams, which was undoubtedly initiated by Diaghilev.

M. Nijinsky, having telegraphed to M. Debussy, the composer, news of the success at Covent Garden of the new ballet 'The Afternoon of a Faun' – which is now being regularly encored – has had the following telegraphed reply: 'Thanks, my dear Nijinsky, for having sent me that telegram, whose words flame like the gold of victorious trumpets! Thanks to your peculiar genius for gesture and rhythm the arabesques of my "Prélude a l'Après-midi d'un faune" have been endowed with a new charm. Congratulate the English on having understood it.' [30]

Hilda Bewicke, an exceptionally intelligent girl with a gift for languages, had been the first English dancer in Diaghilev's troupe.[31] Now he engaged three more, along with two Russian men who also formed part of Koslov's ballet at the Coliseum. Hilda Munnings, who was to become celebrated under another name, described the occasion.

It was arranged that four of us girls, with Zverev and Tarasov, should be given an audition to show our ability, if any, at the awful hour of ten o'clock on a Monday morning. ... We had to face a committee more terrifying than any first-night audience: they sat with their backs to the towering safety curtain on the stage of the Royal Opera House, Covent Garden. Diaghilev, of course, was there, and Nijinsky, Maestro and Madame Cecchetti and Grigoriev. We had no music, and nothing arranged. We girls lined ourselves up to do some of our dances from *Schéhérazade*. Just as we started I caught my uncomfortable shoe in something, and down I went with a crash. ... At last Diaghilev suggested that Cecchetti should give us some classroom steps to do, and with these I got on better. ... That same evening during our performance we got the news that five of us had been accepted: Anna Broomhead (later Bromova), Doris Faithful, Zverev, Tarasov and myself.[32]

Before leaving London on 9 March Diaghilev gave an interview to the *Daily Mail* in which he announced his future plans. In the summer London was to hear Chaliapine in *Boris* and *Khovanshchina*, as well as seeing the new Nijinsky ballets. He hoped 'on a future visit to produce an English ballet for which Dr Vaughan Williams is writing music; Mr Gordon Craig will be responsible for the scenery and staging.'[33]

There had been a luncheon at the Savoy to discuss this collaboration, which proved abortive.

Nijinsky proposed that he should dance both Cupid and Psyche, which was the story Gordon Craig wanted to use. Ralph [Vaughan Williams] objected very strongly to this idea. When the party broke up he and Craig walked home [to Chelsea] together. 'Let me have the music,' said Craig, 'and I'll fit the story.' 'Impossible,' said Ralph, 'you must let me have the scenario and I will write music for it.' 'Impossible,' said Craig, 'just send me the music' – and so they parted. Neither sent anything to the other. ...[34]

On the last night of the season, 7 March, the persistent audience succeeded in having the final ballet, which was *Le Spectre de la rose*, repeated.[35]

The Diaghilev Ballet gave one performance in Lyon on their way to Monte Carlo, where they arrived without Diaghilev, who had business in Russia.[36] Not only were there details to be settled about the operas, but since Nijinsky was a slow worker, he had decided not to depend on him alone, and he wanted to discuss the possibility of Boris Romanov and Alexander Gorsky arranging new ballets for him. He engaged Romanov as a dancer and as choreographer of *La Tragédie de Salomé* to the existing score of Florent Schmitt: this was to be for Karsavina and to console her for Nijinsky's predominance. For in Munich in November Diaghilev had received a letter from Lady Ripon which aroused his indignation.

Diaghilev swept into my room [wrote Karsavina], a letter in his hand. He threw the letter on the table with an imperious 'Read!' and started pacing up and down the room. Now and then he hurled at me bitter accusations. I was a 'snake in the grass'. I was 'an ungrateful child'. I was 'trying to cause trouble between him and his friends'. The letter was from Lady Ripon. I could hardly read it through my tears, but the gist of it was this: she had espoused my cause in asking Diaghilev to retract his policy and give me my proper place in his productions. 'N'exaspérez pas Karsavina,' she wrote. I freely admitted that I had confided in Lady Ripon, but ... only after having pleaded with Diaghilev himself. He was too angry to listen to my arguments, and left unreconciled. Luckily there was no performance that evening; a look in the mirror told me I was not fit to be seen in public.... We made it up over supper....[37]

In Diaghilev's absence Nijinsky was left to work alone with his sister or with Mimi Rambert. Not that he was ever alone for long with the latter, for there was the German pianist, and Vassili Zuikov, under instructions from Diaghilev, came and went to supervise 'the temperature' in the studio at the Casino where they worked.

We couldn't rehearse for twenty minutes [wrote Rambert] without Vassili coming in and saying, 'Vaslav Fomich, we'd better open the window. It's very stuffy in here, it's not good for you.'... But half an hour later he would come in again and say, 'Vaslav Fomich, you know, I think it's rather draughty now, we'd better shut the window.' He was really spying on us, though there was nothing to spy on, because Nijinsky didn't take the slightest notice of me as a woman....[38]

Nijinsky stayed at Beausoleil, and Ramberg at the Hôtel Ravel, along with a number of other dancers, lower down the hill; and although they parted company when their work was done, they sometimes met for chocolate and cakes chez Pasquier. It had been understood that Bronislava Nijinska would dance with Karsavina and her brother in *Jeux* and would be the chosen Virgin in *The Rite of Spring*. Her great strength and her powerful jump suited her for this taxing role, in which beauty of face was not important. One day Rambert saw Nijinsky arrive chez Pasquier, 'looking as pale as a ghost'.

'What on earth is the matter?' I asked.
'I very nearly killed a man.'
'How can you say such a thing? Anyhow, who was it?'
'A blackguard, a brigand, who has prevented Bronia from dancing *Jeux* and *Sacre*.'
'But who is he?'
'Kotchetovsky.'[39]

Bronislava's husband had taken the awful responsibility of making her pregnant. Her roles in *Jeux* and in *The Rite* would have to be danced by pretty little Schollar and by Maria Piltz, a tall, good-looking girl with Slav features. One afternoon Ramberg watched Nijinsky teaching Piltz the Sacrificial Dance, and was dismayed to see how little she understood of his intentions. When Vaslav demonstrated the dance, Mimi thought how wonderful it would have been if only *he* could play the Chosen One instead of a girl. With clenched hand across his forehead, he threw himself into the air in a paroxysm of fear and grief. Although his movements were stylized and controlled, he exuded tragic power. (When Piltz danced the role in public, she 'kept the bones' of Nijinsky's demonstration and made a profound impression, but Ramberg thought her merely 'a poor copy, a postcard reproduction' of what she had seen that afternoon.)[40]

Neither Piltz nor any other of the dancers appreciated what Nijinsky was trying to do. He was as bad as ever at explaining to the company what he wanted, and they were as slow as ever at adapting their classically trained bodies to his novel distortions. Yet he needed them, for only dancers with the strength and skills learnt from the academic class could perform the feats he demanded. How difficult, how paradoxical it was! His ideas were so much more revolutionary than Fokine's. When Fokine devised a series of steps, there was always a logical flow. Nijinsky invented contrary movements for the head, torso, arms and legs, which sometimes seemed to be working independently of each other: he had the pig-headedness and perhaps the insecurity of youth – there had never in history been a twenty-four-year-old ballet-master before – and, if questioned, he tended to go off the deep end.[41] Because he was firstly very young, secondly very famous (a big star, like Chaliapine), thirdly in a special position in relation to Diaghilev, fourthly both sure that what he was doing was important and unsure if he was doing it right, and fifthly bad at making clear the why and the wherefore of his new movements, arranged to new and mystifying music, he tended to treat his interpreters as puppets – and they resented this.

When Nijinsky was composing his ballets, the idea of virtuosity, of showing off brilliant steps, never entered his head – not even when he was arranging a dance for himself. He first looked for a basic position, then kept to it right through the work. In *L'Après-midi* it had been that Egyptian combination of a full-on torso with heads, hands and legs in profile. In *Jeux*, the ballet about flirting tennis-players which he was planning, it was the sideways and upwards swing of two arms across the body – a sort of composite sport movement. (In fact, since tennis-players use one hand and not two, this movement was more like golf – but Nijinsky hardly knew the difference between the two games.) In *The Rite* the awkward closed fists half supporting a lolling head, the turned-in bent knees and turned-in feet (reminiscent of Petrushka's) gave the idea of a prehistoric species at the mercy of the weather, the harvest and their own fearful superstitions.[42]

Mimi Ramberg was supposed to give rhythmical lessons, but few of the overworked dancers turned up for these, and Grigoriev abolished them. She was rather laughed at by the company in general, who gave her the nickname 'Rithmitchka'; and everyone took for granted that she was flinging herself at Nijinsky's head.[43] Vaslav's mother noticed the growing intimacy between Mimi and her son, and warned him that she thought Mimi was attracted by him: but Vaslav told her there was 'no danger'.[44] Yet although Ramberg adored Nijinsky's genius, their relations were so impersonal that it had never occurred to her to be in love with him.[45] She knew all about his alliance with Diaghilev and respected it; but she was too naive to realize that the other newcomer, Romola de Pulszky, was making friends with her in order to learn more about Nijinsky's character and habits. Romola had her private lesson with Cecchetti after the company's class. Karsavina's and Nijinsky's private lesson followed at noon.[46]

Tamara Karsavina travelled back from Russia with Diaghilev, leaving on the night train of 4 April, and arriving in time to rehearse for the first night at Monte Carlo on the ninth. 'I had a powerful attraction in my compartment,' she wrote, 'an ornamental bucket of caviare, brought, together with chocolates, flowers and a small ikon, as a farewell gift.' She decided that for once the greedy Sergei Pavlovitch was in her power and set about 'reforming' him.

As the express, without undue hurry, progressed from Petersburg to Monte Carlo, we ate caviare and talked. 'Do you say your morning prayers, Sergei Pavlovitch?' I asked rather timidly. 'Yes ... I do,' he said after a slight hesitation. 'I do kneel down and think of all I love and all who love me.' Some silence and some more caviare, and then again, with a somewhat bolder show of proselytism, 'Do you ever search your conscience, Sergei Pavlovitch, for hurts you may have inflicted?' 'I do' – emphatically and warmly. 'So often I reproach myself for lack of consideration. I think of how many times I went out in a hurry without saying good-night to Nanny, forgetting to kiss her hand.'[47]

During the Ballet's Monte Carlo season there took place the accidental drowning in the Seine, through the failure of a car's brakes, of Isadora's two children: her daughter by Gordon Craig and her son by Paris Singer. This awful event, which happened on 19 April, like some god-inflicted punishment in Greek tragedy, aroused the pity and horror of every artist in the civilized world. Ravel wrote to Stravinsky, whom he had just left in Switzerland, 'I'm going to see poor Isadora tomorrow. I dread this visit. It's really too appalling – too unjust.'[48]

Bronislava Nijinska said that Nijinsky invented *Jeux* with a volume of Gauguin reproductions open before him.[49] At first he intended, perhaps with the idea of abolishing sexual differentiation in this strange work, to dance in point shoes, like the women: but he soon decided this was wrong. During one of the rehearsals Karsavina asked him a question, and he lost his temper. Tamara walked out of the room without a word. Vaslav complained to Diaghilev that she had the mentality of a prima ballerina. Then it was Diaghilev's turn to lose his temper. 'How dare you insult that great artist? You are nothing but a guttersnipe to her. Go at once and beg her to forgive you.'[50]

The creation of Diaghilev's epic season at the Champs-Elysées, the creation of Nijinsky's new choreography, even the creation of Karsavina's role in *Jeux*, put a strain on the equanimity of all three: it was a testing time for will-power, artistry, friendship and love.

Diaghilev was in Paris on 30 April, ahead of the company. He and Nijinsky were to stay at the Elysée Palace Hotel, which was convenient for the theatre.

The Théâtre des Champs-Elysées was Astruc's greatest endeavour. Built in a modern style which presaged the ornamental cubism of Metro-Goldwyn (now called 'Art-Deco'), it was decorated without by carved reliefs of Bourdelle inspired by the Dionysian Isadora, and within by frescoes of Maurice Denis depicting the insipid festivals of a bourgeois Parnassus. It stood in the Avenue Montaigne near the Pont de l'Alma, miles west of any other Paris theatre. This fact, and its economic impracticality, which soon dawned on its optimistic sponsors, spelt its doom. Astruc had lavished his most grandiose ideas and the millions of his well-wishers on making the opening season a feast not only of French but also of German, Italian and Russian music.

The Russian season was to open with two performances of ballet on the fifteenth and nineteenth. On Sunday 4 May Diaghilev had a row with Gabriel Astruc, which was reported by Ravel in a letter to Stravinsky in Switzerland: 'Don't worry: the acoustics of the Théâtre des Champs-Elysées are perfect – one can hear all the subtlety of Berlioz's harmony. The really frightful things are the show, the sets, the audience, Van Dyck [producer of *Benvenuto Cellini* and *Der Freischütz*] and Gabriel himself. Serge and he had a deadly quarrel yesterday and parted company for good. It was all patched up in five minutes.'[51]

Astruc had absolutely needed the Russian Ballet for his opening season at the new theatre, and, according to him (telling the story years later), Diaghilev took advantage of this to make him pay through the nose. How much were the Opéra offering, he had asked Diaghilev: was it 12,000 francs a performance, his usual price? 'Yes,' Diaghilev had replied, 'but you must understand that people are saying that Astruc invented the Russian Ballet. That, my dear friend, must be paid for.' Astruc claimed that he was obliged to settle for 25,000 francs a performance. 'This folly,' he wrote, 'which I had not the right *not* to commit, made possible the creation of *Le Sacre*, but cost me the life of my management.'[52] He was over-simplifying, of course: but the fact remains that he went bankrupt in August 1913.

Jeux was not finished, and on Diaghilev's orders a rehearsal was called as soon as the company arrived. But, according to Grigoriev, it was one of Nijinsky's bad days. 'He stood in the middle of the practice-room, his mind an obvious blank. I felt that the situation was desperate and suggested a run-through of what had been composed, in the hope of stimulating his invention. This luckily produced the desired effect.'[53]

At the first dress rehearsal of *Jeux* the set and costumes of Bakst were seen on the big stage. Diaghilev was sitting in the middle of the *corbeille*, and on the appearance of Nijinsky in the red wig, rolled-up shirt-sleeves, red tie and long, knee-length, red-bordered shorts held up by red braces, and with the red-topped white stockings which Bakst had designed, Diaghilev blew up. 'No, no, it's quite impossible!' Bakst was seated further to the left, and Rambert heard the two men abusing each other in an affectionate way. 'He can't go on like that!' 'How dare you say he can't go on, Serioja? It's designed, and it's made, and it's going to go on. . . . I won't alter a stitch.' 'All right, Levushka, but they are not going to appear in these costumes.'[54]

In fact, the two women did dance in Bakst's plain white dresses with short sleeves and skirts ending at the knee – a prophecy of post-war fashions, for even in 1913 women wore longer dresses for tennis – and these were made by Paquin. Diaghilev redesigned Nijinsky's costume himself, retaining the white shirt and red tie, but abolishing the braces and giving the dancer white trousers cut like the black ones worn for class, which ended just about the ankle and were buttoned tight round the calf.[55]

249

Behind the heavy summer trees seen at dusk rose the long building with its many windows, into which Bakst put something (as I believe) of his memory of Bedford Square. Bronislava Nijinska told me that she thought the setting had too much sense of space and that the choreography demanded something more confined.[56] This was a way of saying that Nijinsky's intentions would have become clearer on a smaller stage. Diaghilev knew the originality of Nijinsky's mind (which Ansermet, who was an advanced thinker in higher mathematics, as well as a musical philosopher, would later describe as being 'always several jumps ahead of the mind of ordinary people'[57] – that is, elliptical, and missing out transitional stages) and in putting over Nijinsky's ideas to Debussy and Bakst to the best of his ability Diaghilev had perhaps gone astray. To Bakst he may have said, 'The characters of this ballet are like moths in the night, like children who do not know the rules of the game they are playing': and Bakst had created a space filled by huge trees and a towering building to make the dancers smaller. Debussy had complained in the previous September that his score had to make acceptable a rather improper situation (such as Noël Coward, speaking of his *Design for Living*, called 'a triangular carnal frolic'); but added that 'in ballet, immorality escapes through the dancer's legs and ends in a *pirouette*'. When he saw *Jeux* on stage, he grumbled, 'Before I composed a ballet I didn't know what a choreographer was. Now I know – he is a very strong and mathematical gentleman.'[58] Debussy was perhaps slightly ashamed to find himself composing a ballet, and made jokes about what Diaghilev and Nijinsky expected of him. Neither he nor Stravinsky understood that dancers have a way of counting which has nothing to do with musical counting, and which is necessary when the choreography goes against the music.

It was disastrous that Nijinsky should have had to work on *Jeux* and *The Rite* in the same year. It was the fault of Diaghilev, with his megalomania. *Jeux*, I feel, was sacrificed to the vast Stravinsky ballet, which was more thoroughly worked out. As it is, neither has survived in Nijinsky's choreography.

On the opening night, 15 May, *Jeux* merely puzzled the public. The subject, the strange poses, the music so loosely tied to the dance, the lack of virtuoso steps, the inconclusive brevity of the work, left them with an unfamiliar sensation, as if they had just tasted Japanese food for the first time. Was it meant to be funny?

The fact that the reluctant composer, conjuring up – with his dance numbers and their wisps of melody 'developed against an infinitely flexible background of sudden glissandos, trills, tremolandos, all the subtle stock-in-trade of Debussy's orchestra'[59] – equivocal games of tennis and love, had written a masterpiece, occurred to no one, possibly not even to himself. But Diaghilev had commissioned and paid for that masterpiece.

Even with such a childish libretto [wrote Henri Quittard in *Le Figaro*, hoping perhaps to please his proprietor, Calmette, or under orders] one would think this haphazard essay in affectation might provide something graceful or pretty to look at. But the new art, of which M. Nijinsky is the prophet, manages to turn even the insignificant to absurdity.... It goes without saying that modern dress does not enhance these poses inspired by Greek vase paintings [*sic*]. ... The public, apart from a few quite lively interruptions, submitted good-humouredly to these mystifications.... Composer and choreographer take absolutely no notice of each other in this ballet....[60]

Immediately after dancing *Jeux* Nijinsky, seated on a divan with broken springs in his dressing-room, which smelled faintly of scent and was decorated 'only' by 'a few designs of Bakst and some sketches of Rodin', gave an interview to *Gil Blas*. He was 'rather surprised and sad' at the public's reaction to *Jeux*, as he had not expected them to laugh at his 'experiments in stylized gesture'. 'The rather unkind reception of the ballet has not discouraged me, because ... there have been one or two whose judgement I value who have liked what I did.... I shall just keep trying....'[61]

A fortnight later Debussy wrote to a friend,

Among recent pointless goings-on I must include the staging of *Jeux*, which gave Nijinsky's perverse genius a chance of indulging in a peculiar kind of mathematics. This fellow adds up triple crotchets with his feet, checks them on his arms, then suddenly, half-paralysed, he stands crossly watching the music slip by. It's awful. It's even Dalcrozian – for I consider Monsieur Dalcroze as one of the greatest enemies of music and you can imagine what havoc his method can create in the mind of a young savage like Nijinsky![62]

The ballet may have been as unsuccessful as Debussy thought it, but nothing could have been less Dalcrozian than to 'watch the music slip by'. Fokine, Nijinsky's harshest critic, had been able, a year before, to admire the way in which, during *L'Après-midi d'un faune*, Nijinsky had the courage to stand still when the music seemed to demand agitated movement.[63]

The *première* of *The Rite of Spring* was to be two Thursdays later, on the anniversary of *L'Après-midi*, a date chosen by the superstitious Diaghilev. In the meantime, *Boris Godunov* had to be got on. Stravinsky had arrived with his wife and a child, and Ravel had taken two rooms for them at the Splendid Hotel, just below his flat in the Avenue Carnot.[64] Ravel was the first and warmest French admirer of *The Rite of Spring*. One afternoon in the last week of May Diaghilev, Vaslav and the pregnant Bronia went to see him, and Stravinsky, that keen photographer, posed Ravel and Nijinsky playing the piano *à quatre mains*.[65]

The revival of *Boris Godunov* took place on 22 May 1913, the hundredth anniversary of Wagner's birth (celebrated at the Opéra by a performance of *Tristan* which Messager conducted). Quittard in *Le Figaro* thought Chaliapine as complete an artist as ever, and the chorus incomparable, but had reservations about other singers, whom he obviously considered inferior to those of 1908.[66] He did not mention Konstantin Yuon's décors, which, from the reproductions in the programme, look more picturesque than tragic – though the Forest of Kromy is a fine landscape. Diaghilev had seen to it that Repine's living likeness of Mussorgsky on his death-bed should be included among the many illustrations of the programme.

The best analysis of Nijinsky's choreography for *The Rite of Spring* was that of Jacques Rivière, editor of *La Nouvelle Revue Française*. As this was only published in November 1913, it did little to help the public understand the ballet, but it helps us.

This is a biological ballet. It is not only the dance of the most primitive men, it is the dance before man.... Stravinsky tells us that he wanted to portray the surge of spring. But this is not the usual spring sung by poets, with its breezes, its bird-song, its pale skies and tender greens. Here is nothing but the harsh struggle of growth, the panic terror from the rising of the sap, the fearful regrouping of the cells. Spring seen from inside, with its violence, its spasms and its fissions. We seem to be watching a drama through a microscope....[67]

The bejewelled Parisian public of the stalls and boxes did not go to the Russian Ballet to watch the regrouping of cells as seen through a microscope. They went to admire the artistry of Nijinsky, the grace of Karsavina and the colour of Bakst. This thirty-four minute work, in which neither Nijinsky nor Karsavina appeared and which took place against a bleak northern landscape, would be accompanied by a score such as no one had heard before. It is possible that Nijinsky's awkward peasants, with their bunched garments and strapped leggings, who formed circles to learn spells, competed in war-like games, trembled with awe before their Elders, leaped and stamped to make the earth fertile, chose a virgin to be sacrificed to the Sun God, and, after evoking the spirits of their ancestors, watched her dance herself to death, might have been accepted as merely quaint, like painted Russian toys, if they had cavorted to a sweet, coloured rhapsody on a series of folk-tunes by Rimsky-Korsakov. But they were in bondage to a score in which the whole traditional rhythmic system was overthrown, in which from bar to bar the time signature changed unaccountably, in which the vast orchestra specially demanded by Diaghilev[68] (determined to impress by scale) indulged in a variety of special effects – the use of both strings and woodwind in their highest registers, harmonics, *col legno*, flutter-tongue on the flute and *campanella in aria* on the French horn. (There were eight horns.) At the very beginning of the introduction there was a woodwind solo so weird that even the music critics could not agree between them what instrument was playing.[69] (It was a bassoon in its highest register, something seldom heard.) The snatches of melody, Russian, Oriental or chorale-like, and the steady rhythmic passages, for which it was easiest for Nijinsky to arrange dances, were interrupted by terrifying arpeggios, squawks, shrieks and glissandos, intended to represent spurts of growth, vegetable birth-pangs, convulsions of nature or the explosion of sap, and I doubt whether Nijinsky tried to find a parallel for these in human movement.

Of course, there were young people – artists, students and 'fans' – who were prepared to align themselves with Diaghilev on his boldest charges into battle against the old guard. Counting on their support, he had given them free tickets – standing passes. It was the presence of these bloodthirsty enthusiasts *in the middle of* the elegant occupants of the boxes which was partly responsible for the *battle* which took place in the theatre on 29 May. On the first night of Victor Hugo's *Hernani* at the Comédie Française in 1830, of which we have his own description, and at the first performance of Wagner's *Tannhäuser* at the old Opéra in the rue Le Peletier in 1861, the young aesthetes who supported their rising heroes against the academic reactionaries had been isolated in the upper section of the house. The Théâtre des Champs-Elysées was constructed in a novel way. Between the *loges avec salon* and the *fauteuils* and *loges de corbeille*[70] there was an ambulatory, and it was here that Diaghilev's favoured young friends of the *avant-garde* were standing to applaud and defend Stravinsky and Nijinsky. Cocteau thought the reaction of two sections of the public to the ballet and to each other was inevitable, almost as if Diaghilev had planned the juxtaposition of diverse groups. 'All the elements of a scandal were present. The smart audience in tails and tulle, diamonds and ospreys, was interspersed with the suits and *bandeaux* of the aesthetic crowd. The latter would applaud novelty simply to show their contempt for the people in the boxes.... Innumerable shades of snobbery, super-snobbery and inverted snobbery were represented.... The audience played the role that was written for it....'[71]

Nothing that has ever been written about the battle of *Le Sacre de printemps* [Valentine Gross later recalled] has given a faint idea of what actually took place. The theatre seemed to be shaken by an earthquake. It seemed to shudder. People shouted insults, howled and whistled, drowning the music. There was slapping and even punching. Words are inadequate to describe such a scene. Calm was briefly restored when the order was suddenly given to put up the house lights. It amused me to see how certain boxes whose occupants had been so noisy and vindictive in the dark quietened down when the lights went on.... I saw Maurice Delage [the composer], beetroot-red with indignation, little Maurice Ravel truculent as a fighting-cock and Léon-Paul Fargue [the poet] spitting out crushing remarks at the hissing boxes. I cannot think how it was possible for this ballet ... to be danced through to the end in such an uproar. Standing between the two middle boxes, I felt quite at ease at the heart of the maelstrom, applauding with my friends. I thought there was something wonderful about the titanic struggle which must have been going on in order to keep these inaudible musicians and these deafened dancers together, in obedience to the laws of their invisible choreographer. The ballet was astoundingly beautiful.[72]

Stravinsky was sitting in the fourth or fifth row, on the right of the stalls.

The image of Monteux's back is more vivid in my mind today than the picture of the stage. He stood there apparently impervious and as nerveless as a crocodile. It is still almost incredible to me that he actually brought the orchestra through to the end. I left my seat when the heavy noises began – light noise had started from the very beginning – and went backstage behind Nijinsky in the right wing. Nijinsky stood on a chair, just out of view of the audience, shouting numbers to the dancers. I wondered what on earth these numbers had to do with the music for there are no 'thirteens' and 'seventeens' in the metrical scheme of the score.[73]

Diaghilev had ordained a pause between the two scenes; during this the lights were turned up and police were called in to eject the most violent demonstrators; but no sooner had the curtain risen on the trembling group of girls in Part II, with their in-pointed toes, their bent knees and their right fists supporting their sideways-bent heads, than a voice called out, 'Un docteur!', then another, 'Un dentiste!', followed by a third with 'Deux dentistes!'[74] A lady slapped the face of a man in a neighbouring box, gentlemen challenged each other to duels, Comtesse René de Pourtalès declared that she was sixty years old and that nobody had dared to try to make a fool of her before,[75] Florent Schmitt shouted at the boxes, 'Taisez-vous, les garces du seizième!' (the *seizième arrondissement* being associated, like Kensington, with the upper middle class), someone called Ravel 'a dirty Jew',[76] and Carl van Vechten, the Paris music critic of the *New York Times*, became conscious that a young man standing behind him was, out of excitement, drumming with his fists on top of his head.[77] Astruc leaned from his box and implored, 'Ecoutez d'abord. Vous sifflerez après.'[78] Rambert, dancing in a group of girls, heard Diaghilev's voice, coming from very far away, calling, 'Je vous prie. Laissez finir le spectacle!'[79]
Nijinsky had to get dressed for *Le Spectre de la rose*, which followed, and the evening ended with *Prince Igor*.

After the performance [Stravinsky remembered] we were excited, angry, disgusted, and ... happy. I went with Diaghilev and Nijinsky to a restaurant. So far from weeping and reciting Pushkin in the Bois de Boulogne as the legend is [spread by Cocteau], Diaghilev's only comment was: 'Exactly what I wanted.' He certainly looked contented. No one could have been quicker to understand the publicity value and he immediately understood the good thing that had happened in that respect. Quite probably he had already thought about the possibility of such a scandal when I first played him the score, months before, in the east ground [floor] room of the Grand Hotel in Venice [on the Lido].[80]

Except for the perceptive Gaston de Pawlowski, editor of *Commedia*, who saw in the galvanized movements of Nijinsky's dancers a kind of reflex action,[81] for Louis Schneider in *Le Gaulois*, who reserved judgement on the audacities of Stravinsky, wonderfully embodied by Diaghilev's astounding dancers,[82] and for Auguste Mangeot in *Le Monde Musical*, who found the choreography 'grotesque and absurd' but 'oddly impressive',[83] the critics dismissed *The Rite* and ridiculed Nijinsky. The stock joke was to call it 'le massacre du printemps'.[84] The horrible Quittard in *Le Figaro* resented the fact that 'this frantic beginner', Nijinsky, had supporters who dared to express their adherence. 'This new art form, such as it is, already has its admirers. If only their enthusiasm were less noisy! *Le Sacre du printemps* was rather badly received yesterday and the public was hard put to restrain its mirth. It would therefore have been in better taste if those who thought differently – and there were not many of them – had refrained from applauding the authors on stage in a way everybody found not only impertinent but absurd.'[85]

Diaghilev had found that he could not put on *Khovanshchina* on 30 May as announced. It was postponed till 5 June and an extra performance of Fauré's *Pénélope* substituted. To atone for this, as it were, the Inn scene in *Boris*, omitted by Diaghilev in 1908, was given for the first time in Paris on the thirty-first. In subsequent performances, it was announced, this scene and the Polish Fountain scene would be sung at alternate performances.[86] (In London, in June and July, the Inn scene would always be given, and both Polish scenes omitted.)

We have seen how Ravel was attacked for his partisanship of Stravinsky at the first night of *The Rite*. Frederick Delius had also been present. He had been unable to attend the rehearsal, and wrote to Stravinsky, saying that as he had no ticket for the *première* he would pick him up on the way to the theatre, 'so as to get in with you, as I did last time'.[87] Debussy and his wife wrote vainly (on 31 May and 4 June) to press Stravinsky to come to dinner, but received no reply, as Igor had developed typhoid fever.[88] Ravel wrote (on 5 June), reporting that the third performance of *The Rite* had passed without interruption, and that it had been possible to hear the whole work.[89] But Stravinsky missed the first performance of *Khovanshchina* on the fifth, through illness. Diaghilev went to visit the invalid every day, but would not go into the room, through fear of infection.[90]

The sets of Feodor Fedorovsky for *Khovanshchina* – the exterior of the Church of St Basil the Blessed, whose turbaned towers loom theateningly, the street hillside of the Streltzy quarter, the interior of Prince Khovansky's palace and the wooden monastery of the Old Believers – were far more dramatic than Yuon's for *Boris*, and they were called 'magnificent' by Schneider.[91] 'Superb spectacle ... powerful work ... considerable success ... a page of history ... music based on popular songs which breathes the soul of a country.' The score was 'less idiosyncratic' than that of *Boris*, but contained 'superb pages'. The critic named the sunrise, the soldiers' songs, the *Lied* of Marfa (Petrenko), the chorus of pleading (which was acclaimed and repeated), the dance of Persian slave girls (arranged by Bolm), the scene of assassination (of Prince Khovansky) and the liturgical chants of the Old Believers as they burned to death. Diaghilev had once more been successful in his tribute to the genius of poor Mussorgsky.

Karsavina's special ballet, *La Tragédie de Salomé*, to Schmitt's music, which Trouhanova had danced in 1911, was not a success, although Sudeikine had made striking designs in purple, black and silver, very much influenced by Aubrey Beardsley. It was a tentative work with choreography by a young character dancer from Moscow, Boris Romanov, and we may guess Diaghilev had been too preoccupied to give much of his attention to it. There were no Herod, no Herodias and no John the Baptist – although the prophet's severed head was represented on a pedestal: apart from a few Negroes and Executioners, it was a long solo for Karsavina as Salome, who made an impressive entrance down a staircase, with a glittering train unfolding behind her, then moved in a trance-like way as if, according to Svetlov, she were not so much dancing as reliving in Hell her dance before Herod as an expiation of her crime.[92] Tamara wore long, false eyelashes (an adornment she claimed to have invented); her breasts, covered by the filmiest gauze, appeared almost bare; and a rose on her bare knee was painted afresh at every performance either by the designer or by Baron Dmitri de Gunsburg.[93]

'None of the three ballets of our fifth season in Paris,' wrote Grigoriev, 'was approved of either by the public or by the press.' This, in the eyes of the *régisseur*, constituted failure, and he thought it was the reason that Diaghilev, when preparing the year's second London season, which Sir Joseph Beecham was presenting at the Theatre Royal, Drury Lane, 'laid greater emphasis on the operas'.[94]

Shortly before the end of the Paris season, the last in which Nijinsky would appear in Paris with the Diaghilev Ballet, Valentine Gross went backstage after *Le Spectre de la rose*. It was perhaps the night of Saturday, 21 June, when the programme consisted of *Salomé*, *L'Après-midi*, *The Rite*, *Le Spectre* and *Prince Igor* – the final ballet night of the Russian season. If so, she must have been carrying one of the sketch-books in which she jotted down innumerable impressions of Nijinsky's ballet, which give us a faint idea of this forgotten work, and which are now in the Theatre Museum, London. The house was still applauding, and she found Nijinsky curled up on the floor, alone, in the wings, like a bird fallen from its nest.

He was like a crumpled rose in pain, and there was no one near him. I was so touched that I left him alone and said nothing. Then he saw me and sprang up like a child taken by surprise and came smiling towards me. As he stood beside me in his leotard sewn with damp purplish petals, he seemed a kind of St Sebastian, flayed alive and bleeding from innumerable wounds. In a halting but quite accurate French he began to tell me how pleased he was with some pastels I had made of *Jeux* and to thank me for the article I had written to go with them in *Comoedia*

Illustré. I was almost the only person to appreciate his choreography. When I said good-bye he took my hand in both of his in such a charming way that for the rest of the evening I kept glancing down at it in wonder – this hand which had been covered in dew on contact with the miraculous dancer.[95]

She would never see him dance again.

Diaghilev was already in London, for the Drury Lane season opened with *Boris Godunov* on Monday, 24 June, and frantic preparations, rehearsals of orchestra, chorus and lighting were necessary before Chaliapine could work his magic and London could hear Russian opera for the first time.

Although Romola de Pulszky had continued her classes with Cecchetti in Paris, and continued to cultivate the friendship of Mimi Rambert, hoping to learn more about Nijinsky's habits, she had not been told that Diaghilev had left Paris, and when she boarded the midday boat-train at the Gare du Nord, and managed to get seats for herself and her maid Anna in the carriage next to Nijinsky and Nuvel, she hid behind her newspaper, expecting to be spotted by Diaghilev.

Cautiously smoking a cigarette in the corridor, I passed the window of Nijinsky's compartment. He was with Nuvel, reading and talking. I wondered where Diaghilev was, but, throwing all caution aside, I remained. Nijinsky looked exceedingly smart in a greyish-green travelling-suit, with light grey cap, suede gloves, unbottoned ... he did not notice me; at least I think he did not. After a while he stood up, came out, bowed, and passed before me.... I sat on a *strapontin* and gazed out.... Suddenly I felt the same painful electric shock as when I saw him entering the stage, and turned slowly round and looked into Nijinsky's fascinating oriental face. He smiled ... he stood near me, overpowering me as I sat there. In his broken French he said, 'Mademoiselle, vous connaissez Londres? Content voyager?' I answered with a torrent of French all about London – my school years there, England, its charm. He did not understand a word, but listened indulgently ... then suddenly Nuvel called him in – and I became frightened, but Nijinsky not in the least; softly, naturally, he opened the door ... and went in.[96]

Romola braved the wind and her fear of sea-sickness to continue her 'conversation' with Vaslav on the Channel steamer. Then, as the train drew in to Victoria Station, she saw Diaghilev, 'smartly dressed as always, standing there with a group of distinguished looking men'. As she passed Nijinsky on the platform, he took off his hat and waved goodbye. 'Diaghilev turned round and looked at me. I was surprised at Nijinsky's courage.'[97] Romola stayed at the Stafford Hotel, St James's,[98] and made a point of getting her friends to take her to supper in the evenings to the Savoy Grill, where she watched Diaghilev hold court, with Lady Ripon and his other friends, at a large table by the fireplace.[99]

London was given two performances of *Boris*, two of *Khovanshchina* and two of *Ivan the Terrible*; *Jeux* was performed five times, *La Tragédie de Salomé* four times, and *The Rite* four times.[100] Bakst wrote to Astruc that the opera was as popular as the ballet:[101] Chaliapine was acclaimed; *Jeux* was thought funny;[102] and *The Rite* had a mixed reception.[103]

Misia was in London. Diaghilev apparently considered cutting *Le Sacre*, which the English orchestra anyway did not like playing, and he had trouble at a rehearsal with Monteux, whom the composer had appointed as his champion. Misia blamed Stravinsky for this. On the eve of the first performance she wrote to Igor, 'The orchestra made a big scandal ... and Monteux lost his temper ... Serge always has your best interest at heart, and, in keeping such things from you, simply does not want to worry you ... *Le Sacre* is the justification of his life. ....' After the performance she cabled Igor, who was in Berlin on his way back to Russia: 'Complete success *Sacre* spoilt by your letter Monteux unjustly wounding Serge'. Back in Paris on 15 July, Misia wrote: 'I left Serge overwhelmed with troubles, defeated, exhausted ... Nijinsky is intolerable and *mal élevé*, and Bakst no longer speaks to Serge ... Monteux ... said publicly ... in front of Nijinsky and the whole ballet, on the day of the first performance, "I am Stravinsky's representative ..." The incident deprived Serge of all authority. The dancers did not want to continue rehearsing, and Nijinsky spoke to Serge as if he were a dog. The unhappy man left the theatre alone, and spent the day in a park. . . .'[104] Misia's devotion to Diaghilev was greater than her regard for the strict truth: but in spite of her exaggerations we can at least divine that Diaghilev and Nijinsky were no longer always seeing eye to eye.

The company were on the whole distressed to learn that, after a fortnight's holiday following the close of the London season, they were to dance in South America. Karsavina was one who dreaded the long sea voyage; others probably wondered what was the point of dancing for a crowd of savages. It was because several dancers begged off the tour that Romola de Pulszky, recommended by Cecchetti, got her chance to join the company, on trial as a member of the corps de ballet.[105]

Diaghilev, Nijinsky and Nuvel, however, went to Baden-Baden and stayed at the Hotel Stéphanie, where Diaghilev summoned Benois from Lugano to join them. The latter had taken no part in the ballet seasons of 1912, and although, as we have seen, Igor had played him *Sacre* at Lugano in the previous August, he had never seen it on stage. He had been busy working for the Moscow Arts Theatre, and had himself produced Molière's *Malade Imaginaire* and *Le Mariage forcé*. A new project was to be hatched for 1914 in complete contrast to Strauss's *Joseph*, which was obviously going to have a highly coloured score. Diaghilev wanted to make a ballet to baroque music, which would enable Nijinsky to show that he could work in the formal academic technique and in the grand manner. This would provide a spectacle in contrast to the Russian, Oriental and Greek ballets. Since the visit of the brothers Casadesus and their ensemble to St Petersburg in 1909 Diaghilev and Benois had been attracted by the music of a forgotten early eighteenth-century composer, called Montéclair, found in the library at Versailles. The Casadesus had, however, only given permission for its use as a ballet if it was played by their own group on ancient instruments, and although Benois welcomed the idea, Diaghilev was afraid the sound would be too thin to accompany a modern dance company in a big theatre.[106] Diaghilev's next notion was to have Ravel orchestrate some of Domenico Scarlatti's sonatas for harpsichord.[107] But Ravel did not answer Diaghilev's letter about this till September, and at Baden-Baden – where perhaps the works of Scarlatti were not easily available – Diaghilev switched his attention to Bach.[108] A German pianist was engaged; he and Nuvel took turns to play through most of Johann Sebastian's keyboard compositions. Within a week a choice of pieces to form a ballet had been made:[109] a Sarabande, a Gavotte and Musette, a Gavotte en rondeau, a Bourrée, Prelude 1 from the First Book of the Forty-eight Preludes and Fugues, Prelude 21 and Prelude 2 and Fugue 2.[110] The work made up of these short pieces was, according to Benois, to have 'all the elaborate splendour of Court festivals of the rococo period – the splendour of pageants and fireworks and illuminations'. The friends made expeditions to see Vierzehnheiligen, Bruchsal and the Archbishop's palace at Würzburg, with its superb Tiepolo frescoes. The ceiling of the Kaisersaal, perhaps the masterpiece of the Venetian painter, depicted the Triumph of Apollo, and the scenario Benois proposed for the new ballet was 'an echo of Bach's comic opera *Phoebus* [Apollo] *and Pan*'.[111]

Diaghilev, who had not yet received the letter in which Ravel refused to orchestrate Scarlatti, was now counting on him to direct his attention and skill to Bach.[112] This was one reason why he decided not to go with the Ballet to South America. He also had to keep Strauss up to the mark, and, as Stravinsky was busy finishing his opera, *Le Rossignol*, resumed after a gap of three years, for production at the Free Theatre, Moscow, and had no new ballet ready, Diaghilev had to hatch more eggs of novelty for the 1914 season. Sergei's fear of the sea, though great, was therefore a secondary reason for his remaining in Europe. It goes without saying that if his feelings for Vaslav had not outgrown the stage of obsessive infatuation, he would have risked the ocean wave and even the defection of Strauss in order to accompany him: but, as Benois observed, 'their romance was coming to an end'.[113] There was no reason to suppose, however, that their friendship and artistic collaboration would not continue for years to come.

Diaghilev, Nuvel and Nijinsky went to Paris, and Vaslav joined the *SS Avon*, on which the Russian Ballet had embarked at Southampton the day before, at Cherbourg on 16 August.[114] Benois went back to his family at Lugano, where he expected Diaghilev to join him, with Ravel, in a few weeks' time.[115] He had to produce Goldoni's *La Locandiera* for the Moscow Arts Theatre that winter.[116]

Diaghilev had made a profitable deal with the South American management, and could afford to relax for a few weeks. From Paris he made for Venice, possibly stopping at Bayreuth and Salzburg on the way, and he may have motored with Misia (still Mme Edwards, though her ex-husband was married to the actress Lanthelme) and Sert. What a price he had to pay for that period of peace! Within a fortnight of his parting from Nijinsky Vaslav would be engaged to Romola de Pulszky, and in less than another fortnight the two would be married.

What happened on board the *Avon* has been told in detail elsewhere. As the ship crossed the Atlantic in calm summer weather, Nijinsky, with the conductor Rhené-Baton at the piano, worked on the Bach ballet. Romola, who had procured for herself a first-class cabin on the same deck (while her maid Anna occupied the second-class one which the Ballet provided), continued to stalk her prey. She did not really believe (and, indeed, hardly wished) that her pursuit would end in marriage, but there was a group of ready matchmakers on board: these were Dmitri de Gunsburg, who was in charge of the company, his middle-aged mistress, the *divorcée* Ekaterina Oblokova, and their foolish, pretty friend the dancer Josefina Kovalevska, who had been a mistress of the Aga Khan. As Vaslav became increasingly conscious of the attractive Romola's presence, and his desire for a woman's caresses and companionship – never completely suppressed – was revived by his unaccustomed sense of independence and by the equatorial sun, so the conspirators amused themselves by bringing him and the Hungarian girl together. Nijinsky was easily led in worldly matters – as opposed to questions of art – and in some respects could be said not yet to have emerged from the nursery. The engagement could never have happened if Diaghilev or Eleonora Nijinskaya or Bronislava or even Karsavina had been on board. But Bronia was in St Petersburg, expecting her baby in October, and her mother was with her. Karsavina had decided to travel separately on a faster boat. (The *Avon* put in at Vigo, Lisbon, Madeira and Rio de Janeiro – where Nijinsky bought the rings.) Vassili Zuikov, the perpetual nurse and bodyguard, must have been taken by surprise by the suddenness of the engagement on Saturday, 30 August, on the eve of landfall at Rio.[117] Who would not have been surprised, for the young couple could hardly converse? Vaslav knew very little French, Romola no Russian or Polish. 'How can you talk to her?' asked Rambert. 'Oh well——she understands,' was Vaslav's vague reply.[118] Bolm, as a friend of Romola's family, felt it was his duty to warn her of the nature of Nijinsky's relationship with Diaghilev. She knew all about that, and, having succeeded beyond her wildest dreams in attaching herself to the artist she so admired, she did not intend to relinquish her hold.[119] Also she foresaw for herself – loving, as she did, not only dresses, jewels and furs, but admiration and power – a pre-eminent place in European society. Beside this, the fate of the Russian Ballet was of small account. When she thought about Diaghilev's reaction, she must have told herself that he could not dispense with Vaslav's services in the company.

When the Russian Ballet disembarked at Buenos Aires on 6 September and set about preparing for the opening performance of their tour on the eleventh, Zuikov (and probably Grigoriev) telegraphed the news to Diaghilev.[120] Nijinsky had already dispatched a cable by radio to Emilia Markus, asking for Romola's hand.[121] Gunsburg sent out printed invitations to a wedding breakfast at the Majestic Hotel on 19 September.[122] Then somebody had second thoughts. Was it Gunsburg or Romola de Pulszky who suddenly realized that, if the wedding did not take place for twelve days, Diaghilev might find some way to prevent it? The date was put forward to the tenth, and presumably a notice was pinned on the call-board of the theatre to announce the party's changed date.[123]

It had been thought for several years by Astruc and by certain members of the company that Dmitri de Gunsburg wanted to detach Nijinsky from Diaghilev in order to form around him a new troupe; and Diaghilev himself told Benois later in the year that Gunsburg had engineered Vaslav's marriage with this intention.[124] Yet Gunsburg never did have a company of his own – too sensible, perhaps, to think that he could hope to rival the inventions of Diaghilev – and when Nijinsky got together a small troupe in 1914, Gunsburg had nothing to do with it.

Diaghilev was in Venice when he heard the news. Misia described how he asked her to come to his room one sunny morning to play over a score which had just arrived.

I can see myself entering his room, dangling a parasol, in a dress of white muslin. He was still in his nightshirt, with slippers on his feet.... Performing elephantine capers across the room, in his enthusiasm he seized my parasol and opened it. I stopped playing with a start, and told him to shut it, as it brought bad luck to open it indoors and he was madly superstitious. Barely had I time to utter my warning when somebody knocked at the door. A telegram....

Diaghilev turned livid: the wire announced that Nijinsky was marrying Romola Markus [*sic*], a Hungarian, who had sailed on the same boat. . . . Serge, overcome with a sort of hysteria, ready to go to any extreme, sobbing and shouting, gathered everybody around – Sert, Bakst etc. When the council of war was complete, the terrible event was discussed with greater calm. What had been Nijinsky's state of mind when he left? Did he seem preoccupied? Not at all. Sad? Certainly not.

'This is all very silly,' interrupted Bakst, 'the important thing is to discover if he bought any underpants.'

But if he had, did that prove anything? Yes, something serious and premeditated.... A deadly silence ensued – somebody vaguely remembered hearing him order shirts. But as to underpants ...

Diaghilev burst into a fit of rage: he told them to go to hell.... Could they not do something useful, instead of coming out with such insane ideas. They must telegraph at once! Find out! Act! Forbid the banns!

Alas! numerous confirmations continued to arrive: the marriage had taken place.... We immediately took Diaghilev, drunk with grief and rage, to Naples, where he launched himself on a frantic bacchanalia....[125]

What were Diaghilev's thoughts when he heard the news? Even if Benois was right that his 'romance' with Nijinsky was on the wane, we know that the threat of loss revives desire. Vaslav had been stolen from him by a twenty-year-old girl, whose intentions he had not even suspected. He, the great Diaghilev – for he must have seen himself as great – had been outwitted. His company had lost its chief ornament. The experiments that he and Vaslav had embarked on together were at an end. A young married man could hardly be separated from his wife, and there could be no question of including Romola de Pulszky in the Ballet's secret councils. Was there any reason to carry on the company?

Well, he had commissioned a ballet from Richard Strauss.

If Diaghilev's first impulse was to vent his rage by dismissing Vaslav by telegram, he overcame it. If Nijinsky did not fulfil the South American engagement, Diaghilev's contract would be broken and a large sum of money would be lost. Diaghilev took no action. We have proof of his attention to business in Venice in the second week of September. Hugo von Hofmannsthal, the chief librettist and promoter of *Joseph*, was in Venice, and one of Diaghilev's problems was to persuade him that Fokine would be as desirable a choreographer for Strauss's ballet as Nijinsky. The question of who should now dance the title role was presumably left in abeyance, but it was important that Hofmannsthal should keep Strauss interested. On 30 September – that is, three weeks after Nijinsky's wedding – Hofmannsthal wrote from Munich to the composer, 'In Venice I saw a lot of Diaghilev, Bakst and the very charming Lady Ripon, and the conversation came round to *Joseph* over and over again.... I entirely approve of Diaghilev's intention to employ Fokine and not Nijinsky as *metteur-en-scène* of this ballet.'[126]

Fokine, who was at daggers drawn with Diaghilev, had not yet heard the good news.

Jacques de Brunoff, the editor of *Comoedia Illustré*, whose father Maurice published the Russian Ballet's programmes, was in Venice, and he had all the gossip from the sociable Bakst. On the evening of Sunday, 14 September – Nijinsky had been married on the Wednesday – he wrote to Valentine Gross.

Bakst is on the Lido and I went to see him today. He had some strange stories to tell. Diaghilev has got a divorce. The ballet, with Nijinsky and Gunsburg, is in South America. Our poor faun is reduced to *premier danseur*. Diaghilev is going to engage Pavlova and Fokine for the three big new ballets, the first of which, Putiphar, will be designed by Bakst and given at the Munich Festival, then in London and finally in Paris. This year they begin in London – I bet you will want to be there!! Diaghilev can get backing in London which he can't get in France. Apparently the great new star is the dancer Simonov from St Petersburg. Bakst was at Baden Baden with Pavlova and is mad about her. He says she is far more *poetic* (?) than Karsavina.

Dear Stravinsky is producing a little *Chinese*!! opera this year!

Diaghilev is at Florence (I don't know with whom), where I shall doubtless have it out with him this week. Naturally he is still the head of the Nijinsky–Karsavina ballet.

Apart from that Bakst has been designing Venetian parties with the Marchesa Casati's crowd....[127]

An account of Diaghilev's first reactions to Nijinsky's marriage thus comes to us – at second hand, but perhaps accurately – via Bakst. Nijinsky was still to be allowed to dance but not to be a choreographer. In this supreme post he must be replaced by the hated Fokine; and his starry eminence was to be shared with Pavlova. (Pavlova, however, was not engaged; nor did the Strauss ballet open in Munich; nor did the company dance in London before Paris. There was, indeed, a Semenov in the Russian Ballet during the 1913–14 season, but he was given no leading roles.) Diaghilev had evidently set off with Misia and Sert – who liked to motor round Italy every summer, looking at works of art – in a southerly direction, taking in Florence and perhaps Rome on the way to Naples. Misia's lurid style of writing makes us often doubt her veracity. By 'Bacchanalian orgies' she may have implied drink, drugs or boys, but it was against Diaghilev's nature to drink to excess and he was not promiscuous.

On this journey south Diaghilev engaged a young Italian servant, Beppe Potetti, who had been a Florentine baker. Whether their first encounter was connected with the 'orgies' is not clear.[128] Vassili Zuikov was with Nijinsky, and Diaghilev had no one to look after him or run errands. Beppe gradually became part of his life, and he stayed on even after Vassili had returned to Europe; he also brought his wife Margherita to work in the Ballet's wardrobe, of which she eventually assumed command.

Nijinsky's marriage had, of course, been widely reported in the newspapers. It was generally assumed that Romola was a rich heiress who had been his pupil and now wanted to be his partner and a star. The headline 'Un mariage bien ... parisien' seemed to imply that any reason other than love must account for an alliance between Diaghilev's favourite and a girl of whom no one had heard.

Within a day or two of his reading the first rumours in the Press, Benois wrote from St Petersburg to Stravinsky in Switzerland, hardly taking the marriage seriously. Igor had been commissioned for a large sum to complete his *Le Rossignol* for the Free Theatre, Moscow, and hoped Benois might design it, but the Free Theatre was the rival of the Arts Theatre, for which Benois was working, and which was keeping him busy. At that time the question of Diaghilev staging Stravinsky's opera had not arisen.

Serge is the Devil knows where. After discussing the Bach ballet with me in Baden, he was to have come to see me in Lugano and to have brought Ravel with him. But I have heard nothing from him, and since he has disappeared without a note, I am inclined to believe those charming gossipers (their news has probably reached you too) who say that Vaslav married a Hungarian millionairess and Serge, in his grief, has sold the company to an impresario. Have you any news of our dissolute genius Serge? Valetchka, who went to Paris (cursing his fate, poor fellow), also does not know anything.[129]

Stravinsky had the news of Nijinsky's marriage from Diaghilev, who spent two days with him at Clarens on 1 and 2 October, and he wrote confirming that it had taken place. Benois replied:

I was in Moscow and found your letter only on my return. The news about Nijinsky's marriage struck me like a thunderbolt. When did it happen? None of our friends is here in town at the moment, and I know of no one who can give me any information about it, since I do not want to talk to a stranger like Svetlov. I saw Serge and Vaslav almost on the eve of Vaslav's departure for Argentina, and there was no hint then about the coming event. Nijinsky was very attentively studying Bach with us, preparing the Bach ballet. Is it possible that he had no idea of it then? Be kind and tell me one thing: was it a complete surprise for Serge, or was he prepared for it? How deep was his shock? Their romance was coming to an end, and I doubt that he was really heartbroken, but if he did suffer I hope it was not too terrible for him. However, I imagine he must be completely bewildered in his position as head of the company. But why can't Nijinsky be both a ballet master and a Hungarian millionaire? The whole story is such a phantasmagoria I sometimes think I have read it in a dream and am an idiot to believe it.[130]

The Ballet appeared for a month in Buenos Aires, gave two performances in Montevideo, then went by sea to Rio de Janeiro, where they spent the second half of October, and where Romola became pregnant. They sailed for Europe early in November. While the company travelled on to Cherbourg, the Nijinskys left the ship at Cadiz and made for Paris, where Vaslav hoped to meet Diaghilev. But Diaghilev was by then in St Petersburg. Vaslav and Romola went on, via Vienna, to Budapest. After meeting his mother-in-law and her family, Vaslav intended to take his bride to spend Christmas in Russia with Eleonora Nijinskaya and Bronia, who had had a baby girl in October.[131] He was still unconscious of Diaghilev's feelings, and, being anxious about the staging of *Joseph* and the Bach ballet, he telegraphed to Diaghilev.

Only part of Grigoriev's account of the sequel is likely to be true.

When we arrived in Petersburg, deep in winter snow, we were so sunburnt ... that people in the streets turned to look at us. Hardly had I unpacked when

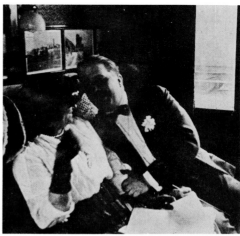

13 (*above*) Diaghilev and Nijinsky in Venice, 1911.

14 (*top right*) Misia Edwards and Diaghilev in a train, probably from Dover to London, 1914.

15 (*middle*) Diaghilev returning from America on the *Dante Alighieri*, 1916.

16 (*bottom*) Khokhlova, Larionov, Diaghilev, Kremnev, Shabelska and Kashuba at San Sebastian, 1916.

17 (*opposite*) Massine in *La Légende de Joseph*, 1914.

18 (*above*) Leonide Massine as the Chinese Conjuror in *Parade*, 1917.

19 Igor Stravinsky, Rome, 1917. Drawing by Picasso.

20 (*opposite above*) Massine and Lopukhova in *La Boutique fantasque*, London, 1919. Drawing by Picasso.

21 (*opposite left*) Picasso and Massine at Pompeii, 1917. Photograph by Jean Cocteau.

22 (*opposite right*) Lydia Lopukhova in *La Boutique fantasque*, 1919. Photograph by Hoppé.

23 Stanislas Idzikovsky and Lubov Tchernicheva in *Les Femmes de bonne humeur*.

24 (*opposite*) Lydia Sokolova and Leon Woizikovsky in *Le Tricorne*.

25 Olga Spessivtseva in *The Sleeping Princess*, London, 1921. Photograph by Stage Photo Company.

I received a note from Diaghilev asking me to call on him the following day. I had imagined Diaghilev to be in Moscow, where I had expected him to remain for a time. However, I called at the flat as instructed; and the door was opened by Zuikov, who asked me to wait. Diaghilev, he said, now lived at the Hôtel de l'Europe, where he had an Italian valet looking after him. I inquired how he was. But all Zuikov would say was, 'You'll see for yourself.' I did not have long to wait; and when Diaghilev came in he seemed pleased to see me. Then, after a few inquiries about the tour, he handed me a telegram, saying, 'Look at what came yesterday.' The telegram was from Nijinsky. It asked when rehearsals were to start and when he was to begin work on a new ballet, and requested Diaghilev to see that during rehearsals the company should not be employed on anything else. When I had read the telegram Diaghilev put it on the table and covered it with the palm of his hand. This was what he always did with any communication that annoyed him. Then, looking at me sideways with his ironical smile, he said, 'I should like you, as my *régisseur*, to sign the telegram I propose sending in reply to this.' He then took up a telegraph form from the table, and screwing his monocle into his eye and biting his tongue (as he would when worked up), he wrote his answer. It read: 'In reply to your telegram to Monsieur Diaghilev I wish to inform you of the following. Monsieur Diaghilev considers that by missing a performance at Rio and refusing to dance in the ballet *Carnaval* you broke your contract. He will not therefore require your further services. Serge Grigoriev, *Régisseur* of the Diaghilev Company.'

I now understood why Diaghilev had summoned me so urgently. By causing the answer to Nijinsky's telegram to go from me, he wished to show that their former friendship now counted for nothing and that their relationship had become purely formal. When I had read it he took the telegram from me again, and turning to Zuikov, who was in the room, said to him 'This is what it means in Russian' (for the telegram was in French), and translated it for his benefit. After a short pause he then handed it back to me and said it must go off at once. When showing me out and helping me on with my overcoat, Zuikov remarked, 'Your telegram won't improve Madame Nijinsky's sleep I dare say!' I turned and saw he was silently laughing.[132]

Although Grigoriev's chronicle of the Diaghilev Ballet was published twenty years after Romola Nijinsky's sensational life of her husband, I think that Grigoriev, a loyal servant but a sometimes unreliable chronicler, was still anxious to gloss over Diaghilev's homosexuality; and I believe that he invented the missed performance of *Carnaval* in order to play down Diaghilev's jealousy. As he was responsible for paying the company he must have known better than anyone that since 1909 Nijinsky had never had a contract to break.

A communication from St Petersburg to Budapest was certainly sent and received. (Romola Nijinsky maintained that the missed performance was an invention,[133] but she also wrote that the telegram was signed by Diaghilev.)[134] Perhaps to tell the world that he was open to other offers – and possibly on the suggestion of his wife, who never believed in waiting for things to happen – Vaslav telegraphed to Astruc, 'Please inform the news-papers that I shall not be working any longer with Diaghilev.'[135] Of the text of this message, received in Paris on 5 December 1913, there can be no doubt, as Astruc kept it. Yet Nijinsky in his naïveté was still puzzled by Diaghilev's reaction, and on 9 December he wrote to Stravinsky, whom he believed to be in St Petersburg, but who was working on *Le Rossignol* in Switzerland.

I went with my wife to her parents' home in Budapest and there I immediately sent a telegram to Serge asking him when we could see each other. The answer to my telegram was a letter from Grigoriev informing me that I shall not be asked to stage any ballets this season, and that I am not needed as an artist.

Please write to me whether this is true. I do not believe that Serge can act so meanly to me. Serge owes me a lot of money. I have received nothing for two years, neither for my dancing nor for my staging *Faune*, *Jeux*, and *Sacre du Printemps*. I worked for the Ballet without a contract. If it is true that Serge does not want to work with me – then I have lost everything. You understand the situation I am in. I cannot imagine what has happened, what is the reason for his behaviour. Please ask Serge what is the matter, and write to me about it. In all the newspapers of Germany, Paris, and London, etc., it is reported that I am not working any more with Diaghilev. But the whole press is against him (including the *feuilletons*). They also say that I am gathering a company of my own. In truth, I am receiving propositions from every side, and the biggest of these comes from a very rich businessman, who offers one million francs to organize a new Diaghilev Russian Ballet – they wish me to have sole artistic direction and large sums of money to commission décors, music, etc. But I won't give them a definite answer before I have news from you.

My numerous friends send me letters of revolt and rage against Diaghilev – and propositions to help me and join me in my new enterprise. I hope you will not forget me and will answer my letter immediately.[136]

This letter, as veering in its attitude towards Diaghilev as certain pages of Nijinsky's *Diary* written in 1919 on the brink of breakdown, may have been sent without Romola's knowledge, though the tempting reference to large sums of money, calculated to arouse the cupidity of Igor, who was reputed to think of nothing else, could well have been suggested by her. Equally, the telegram to Astruc might have been sent by Romola without reference to Vaslav.

It was a season of unparalleled gaiety in St Petersburg. 'One entertain-ment succeeded another. Fancy-dress balls, balls where coloured wigs were worn, parties at the Embassies, and in the Grand Dukes' palaces.'[137] There was a ball given by Countess Betsy Shuvalov[138] at the palace on the Fontanka which had once belonged to Marie Narishkin, mistress of the Emperor Alexander I. There was the fancy-dress ball given by Countess Kleinmichel, at which the Persian Quadrille of sixteen beautiful young women with their partners was led by Grand Duchess Cyril and Grand Duke Boris.[139]

Anatoli Nekludov, who had been Russian envoy in Bulgaria throughout the last difficult years, and was on his way to represent his country in Sweden, found himself standing next to the former Minister, Count Witte. They commented on the lovely sight, then Nekludov remarked, referring to a dramatic poem of Pushkin's, 'But tell me, my dear Count, do you not feel as if you were assisting at the "Festivity during the Plague", or rather "before the Plague"?'

I had hardly spoken these words [wrote Nekludov] when Witte's face assumed a terribly serious expression. He seized me by the arm, exclaiming: 'Then you also have that impression?'
'Most certainly. Ever since I have been in St Petersburg, I cannot get rid of the feeling.'
'I know! I know!' returned the Count excitedly. 'We are going God knows where; God alone knows to what abyss! It is impossible to go on like this.'[140]

To Diaghilev, at the Europa Hotel, looking down on the Nevsky Prospekt, there seemed to be no alternative to the unpleasant step of persuading Fokine to return to the Ballet. There are two versions of the way in which he set about this. Grigoriev wrote that when Diaghilev told him of his intention he protested:

'But you're on the worst possible terms with him.' 'What does that matter?' said Diaghilev. 'Fokine's an excellent dancer and a no less excellent choreographer. . . . Let's ring him up and see what he says' – on which he went to the telephone and, wiping the receiver with his handkerchief as was his habit, obtained the number. . . . There was a to me ominous pause before a conversation started. It lasted no less than five hours. . . . Fokine was venting his wrath and bitterness. . . . The result was that . . . Diaghilev wore him down and obtained his promise to call the next day. As he replaced the receiver Diaghilev heaved a sigh of relief. 'Well, that's settled, I think. He was a tough nut to crack, though, all the same.'[141]

Fokine wrote,

At first I did not want even to meet Diaghilev. But one day Valerian Svetlov, who lived in the same apartment house as I, telephoned me to say that Diaghilev was at his flat and would like to come down and see me. . . . A few minutes later, Diaghilev rang the bell. It was a very embarrassing moment. He made a most eloquent speech, trying to convince me that he was now wholeheartedly on my side, that his infatuation with his favourite was now long forgotten, and that it was only I who could now save the art of the Russian ballet which I myself had created. . . . After a few meetings we signed an agreement to restudy the old repertoire with the company and to stage seven new ballets.[142]

There was some hard bargaining. Fokine demanded the dismissal of four or five members of the company, including Grigoriev, his wife Tchernicheva and Bronislava Nijinska. 'That's quite absurd, of course,' Diaghilev told Grigoriev. 'On the other hand, you two must make peace.' The reconciliation of choreographer and *régisseur* took place at Diaghilev's flat: they shook hands 'without a word'. Diaghilev consented to exclude Nijinsky's ballets from his repertoire. (The simple Grigoriev thought he did not like them anyway.) Fokine agreed that Diaghilev should be allowed to employ other choreographers, such as Romanov, after consultation with himself. He was to be called 'choreographic director' and to dance the leading roles, which he had not been allowed to do in 1912.[143] His wife Vera was to alternate with Karsavina in certain ballets. The third movement of Rimsky-Korsakov's *Schéhérazade*, cut by Diaghilev, must be restored, and new choreography – a long *pas de deux* for Zobeïda and the Negro Slave – invented for it.[144]

One rich bribe which Diaghilev had to offer, apart from the refurbishing of the repertoire, was the new score by Richard Strauss. Such princely opportunities did not come the way of *maîtres de ballets* at the Mariinsky. On the other hand, the mature Fokine could not himself play the youthful Joseph, the simple shepherd boy who was to be seduced at the Egyptian court by Potiphar's lustful wife, so there was a casting problem. And what were the other six ballets to be? If the Bach ballet was discussed, nothing came of the project.

Fokine had staged a ballet to Schumann's *Papillons*, which was a kind of sequel to *Carnaval*, for a special occasion at the Mariinsky in March 1912. This Diaghilev agreed to take over.

Sir Joseph Beecham had demanded a second season of mixed opera and ballet at Drury Lane, and, in addition to Mussorgsky's two great operas and Rimsky's *Ivan the Terrible*, Diaghilev intended to give, for the first time in the West, Mussorgsky's *May Night* (finished by Rimsky after his death), in which there were dances, and Borodin's *Prince Igor*, whose Polovtsian Dances were already familiar. In all of these except *May Night* Chaliapine would sing. In the Paris Opéra season, which preceded that of London, only ballet would be performed.

Benois was travelling backwards and forwards between Moscow, where he was exhaustively rehearsing his Goldoni play, and St Petersburg, where, apart from seeing his family, he was making sketches for Stravinsky's *Le Rossignol*, which he had not been able to resist taking on.[145] Then, suddenly, at the end of the year, the Moscow Free Theatre, who had commissioned Stravinsky to finish his opera, collapsed. When Benois brought the news to Diaghilev, the latter jumped at the possibility of including *Le Rossignol* in his 1914 repertoire.[146] Then he and Benois began to plan something else. Both were enthusiastic admirers of *Coq d'or*, Rimsky's last opera and probably his masterpiece, which, because of its satire on royalty, had never been publicly performed in Russia. (The march from the last scene had provided the opening number of *Le Festin* in 1909.) Benois suggested staging it in a novel manner: the action should be mimed by dancers, while the singers sang off-stage.

The question at once arose as to whether the singers would agree to limit themselves to the part of 'orchestral instruments', for their only function would be to 'accompany' with their voices the real performance on the stage. But I knew that our 'Peter the Great' would overcome greater difficulties than these, if he wanted to. One had only to egg him on by pointing out what the difficulties were.... Sergei set to work with enthusiasm.

Eventually, it was decided that the singers should be placed neither in the wings, where they would be imperfectly audible, nor in the orchestra pit, where there was no room for them, but on benches raised on steep ramps to either side of the stage. 'It was necessary,' wrote Benois, 'to dress them all in the same costumes.... Diaghilev succeeded in persuading the opera artists to accept the sacrifice demanded of them. The production was completely organized in Moscow and St Petersburg.'[147] Whether, as Benois claimed, it was he who suggested Natalia Gontcharova – since he himself had so much on his plate at the time – as designer for *Coq d'or*, seems more questionable. Diaghilev had exhibited her work, along with that of her friend Larionov, in Paris in 1906. Benois was usually averse to the excesses of Moscow artists, and, as he pointed out, she had been going through 'a period of rather absurd experiments of a modernist kind': but she had recently 'turned with enthusiasm to popular imagery and ancient ikon painting' and he claimed that he 'nominated her' as his 'successor'.[148]

Impetuously, Diaghilev accompanied Benois back to Moscow, taking Fokine and Vera Fokina with him. The choreographer (who claimed that it was himself who had suggested to Diaghilev putting on *Coq d'or*, as well as the method of staging it),[149] was apprehensive of what Gontcharova might do to the opera.

I had heard that she and Larionov, who worked with her, belonged to a set of 'Moscow Futurists' who painted their faces, organized violent lectures on 'new art' and 'the art of the future', and that at these lectures, as the strongest argument, pitchers full of water were tossed into the audience....

After all the horrors I had heard ... I found myself in the company of the most charming people, modest and serious. I recall the degree of admiration with which Larionov described the beauty of Japanese art.... And the thoroughness with which Gontcharova discussed each detail of the forthcoming production.... Her paintings at first shocked me. In a large dark studio of a gloomy suburban house, we ... were introduced to her work by candlelight.[150]

Gontcharova, the daughter of an architect, came of an old noble family, and she was the grand-niece of Pushkin's wife, who bore the same name as herself. She and Larionov, the son of a chemist, were both born in 1881 (the same year as Picasso) and both came to Moscow in 1891. They studied together at the Academy of Painting, rebelled together, went through successive stages of experiment together and apart, and exhibited continually. That summer of 1913 Gontcharova had held a 'retrospective' show of eight hundred pictures in Moscow.

Once the production of *Coq d'or* had been set in motion, Diaghilev left hot-foot for Paris, and summoned Stravinsky from Switzerland to talk about *Le Rossignol*.[151] The composer had been paid ten thousand francs for his score, and Diaghilev could have it for nothing. Most of Benois' designs had already been made. On the night of 20 January Stravinsky played the first two acts of his opera to Diaghilev and Misia. Diaghilev sat talking to him till 3 a.m., then left the same morning for Moscow.[152]

In Paris Diaghilev had signed his contract with Strauss's agent and asked Ida Rubinstein to interpret the part of Potiphar's wife. He thought she had agreed – though, in fact, she never took the part – for he telegraphed the news to Hofmannsthal. The latter wrote to Strauss at Garmisch on 31 January, congratulating him.[153]

The role of Joseph had still to be filled. While he was in Moscow talking to Gontcharova and Benois about *Coq d'or*, Diaghilev went to several performances at the Bolshoi Theatre. Both in Gorsky's *Don Quixote* and in *Le Lac des Cygnes* he noticed the face of a handsome young man, who played the Knight of the White Moon in the former and danced the tarantella in the last scene of the latter.[154] This young man showed no outstanding skill as a dancer and his legs were imperfect in shape, but he had a presence, and his big dark eyes gave him the look of St George in an ikon.

Whether Diaghilev merely fell under the spell of Leonide Miassin's Byzantine eyes or whether his divining rod signalled some latent power of interpretation or invention in the young man, it was one of the most sensational feats of 'talent-spotting' in history. Diaghilev, however, was not the first to sense a special quality in Miassin, for the old actor Sadovsky had said of him, 'There is a boy who has God's spark.'[155] Miassin was thinking of giving up dancing to become an actor, and was even being considered for the role of Romeo in Shakespeare's play at the Maly Theatre.[156]

Once Diaghilev had made up his mind that he could 'do something with that face',[157] that he had found the young shepherd whom Potiphar's wife must seduce, events moved with incredible speed. Diaghilev told Mikhail Savitsky, a dancer in the Bolshoi company whom he had engaged for the coming season, to send Miassin to him on the following day at the Metropole Hotel, which was on the same square as the theatre.

When I walked into the ornate, gilded lobby [wrote Miassin] I felt as though I were entering a larger-than-life world of fantasy. Timidly I made my way through rows of potted palms and porters in gold braid.... [Diaghilev's door] was opened by a young Italian with curly black hair and beady eyes. He smiled when I gave him my name, and showed me into a formal little sitting-room.... I sat down stiffly on a plush sofa. The Italian disappeared into another room, and I heard him say 'Signore Barone, Signor Miassin is here to see you.' A moment later Diaghilev appeared in a dressing-gown. At first glance he appeared tall and imposing, but when I stood up I realized that he was only of medium height, but that he had an unusually large head and broad shoulders. The next thing I noticed was the streak of silver-white hair, like a feather, over his fore-head. Peering at me through his monocle, he looked to me like a creature from another world.

He told me that he had enjoyed my performances in *Don Quixote* and *Swan Lake*. He was looking for someone to dance the title-role in his new production, *La Légende de Joseph*, and he thought I might be suitable. If his choreographer, Michel Fokine, approved of his choice he would want me to join the company immediately. Before I had a chance to reply, Diaghilev explained that he was leaving Moscow in two days' time, and that he had to have a quick decision. He told me to go away and think it over, and to come back and see him again the following day.[158]

Miassin talked the offer over with his friends, who, no doubt, explained Diaghilev's morals to him, and although he assumed that his engagement with Diaghilev would only be for a few months, he was afraid of ruining his career in Moscow. When he returned to the Metropole he had 'definitely decided to refuse Diaghilev's offer'.

I walked in, he peered at me through his monocle, smiled and waited for me to speak. I was just about to tell him that I could not accept his offer, when, almost without realizing it, I heard myself say, 'Yes, I shall be delighted to join your company.'...

I still cannot comprehend why, almost involuntarily, I changed my decision at the crucial moment.... I was eighteen at the time.[159]

Diaghilev, Miassin and the valet Beppe left Moscow on the following evening by night train for St Petersburg. In his 'quiet persuasive voice', but with 'conviction and self-confidence', Diaghilev described Fokine's choreography and explained the new art-form which had emerged from the academic style. Miassin wondered what he would be able to contribute to these ballets he had never seen.[160]

Two days were spent in St Petersburg. On the first, Miassin had his audition with Fokine, which took the most curious form. 'I felt very nervous as I entered his room, where the only splash of colour among the carefully arranged white furniture was a mural of the Nine Muses by Giulio Romano.' The 'immaculately dressed' Fokine in his 'well-tailored English suit' received the young aspirant 'with measured politeness'. He asked Miassin to repro-duce the positions of the Muses in the mural. Miassin did his best. Then Fokine asked him to demonstrate his *élévation*. Miassin jumped over a chair. That was all. Next day Diaghilev told Miassin he had passed the test and took him to a photographer's studio, where he was dressed in a simple white tunic, and Fokine gave him some poses appropriate to Joseph's role.[161]

While these events were taking place, the Diaghilev Ballet had already begun their second German tour at Prague. They went from there to Stuttgart, and Diaghilev intended to catch them up in Cologne. In the train to Cologne Diaghilev explained to Miassin his intentions for *Joseph* and the way in which it was to be produced, with a sumptuous setting by José-Maria Sert and costumes of unparalleled richness in the style of Veronese by Bakst. Miassin was not quite sure what the word 'Renaissance' meant. By the end of their journey he had begun to feel more at ease with Diaghilev, whose well-cut English suit he noticed was rather shabby, and who had holes in the soles of his shoes. But at the Domhof Hotel, Cologne, the young dancer was overpowered by the size and luxury of his bedroom, and embarrassed to be served by waiters of his own age. There were, however, some dancers he knew from Moscow in the company: Savitsky, Fedorov, Zverev, and Max Frohman, who used to play New Orleans jazz between rehearsals at the Bolshoi.[162]

Fokine had been detained by his duties at the Mariinsky, and he too joined the company in mid-tour. Watching the Russian Ballet rehearse the Fokine repertoire, Leonide Miassin felt very conscious of his limitations. The flowing movement of Fokine, which Diaghilev told him derived from Isadora Duncan,[163] was so at variance with the familiar stiff academic style, which he now studied under Cecchetti.[164] He was given the small part of the Night-Watchman in *Petrushka*, a ballet which impressed him more than any other. Fokine danced Petrushka, and, Miassin wrote, 'Although I heard glowing descriptions of Nijinsky's performance, I did not see how Fokine's interpretation could have been improved upon.'[165] Miassin had a very reserved character. From the first, the other dancers, particularly the women, found him fascinating.[166] If, in full-face, Miassin was like an ikon, in profile he resembled one of the ripening boys whom Baron von Gloeden photographed at Taormina. Diaghilev's interest soon turned to love. He had found the son he could educate, the pupil he could mould: and to nurture talent – just as much as to devise and present ballets – was his vocation. So he was happy.

The Ballet visited Hamburg, Leipzig, Hanover and Breslau before performing in Berlin, after which they were to make a stop in Zürich on the way to Monte Carlo; but Diaghilev returned once more to St Petersburg, leaving Miassin in the care of Kremnev and Hilda Munnings.[167] Diaghilev engaged Pierre Vladimirov, a leading classical dancer of the Mariinsky, as a reinforcement, and Bulgakov, the mime, who had excelled in *Armide* and *Schéhérazade*, to play Potiphar in *Joseph* and King Dodon in *Coq d'or*. It was Diaghilev's last visit to Russia.[168]

Nijinsky, meanwhile, had accepted an invitation from Alfred Butt, of the

Palace Theatre, London; he had formed a company of twelve, with his sister as ballerina, and with her husband Alexander Kotchetovsky as the only other male dancer. They rehearsed in Paris a small repertoire to which they were hardly entitled, as it included works created for Diaghilev, or variations on them. Bakst had been forbidden to collaborate, but Ravel orchestrated some Chopin pieces to make up a new *Les Sylphides*, for which Boris Anisfeld designed a silvery birch forest. This, followed by Vaslav's old Oriental solo to music of Sinding, danced by Kotchetovsky, and *Le Spectre de la rose* made up the first three-quarter-of-an-hour music-hall 'number', which started at 10.5 and was followed by the Bioscope at 10.50. It is absurd to suggest, as Romola Nijinsky did, that Nijinsky had signed his contract without realizing that the Palace Theatre was a music-hall,[169] for he had seen Pavlova dance and had applauded the clown Little Tich there, and the theatre's official writing-paper announced it as 'London's Leading Music Hall': but the organization of this season proved a taxing task for Nijinsky, who had never borne the cares of management before. There were temperamental scenes, both with Bronislava and her husband and with Alfred Butt.[170] Although some newspapers greeted Nijinsky with rapture, Cyril Beaumont felt that 'something of the old magic had departed'.[171] The Fine Art Society held an exhibition of pictures of Nijinsky, which included Sargent's drawing, a big painting in the costume for *Les Orientales* by Blanche, studies by Glyn Philpot and a number of pastels by Valentine Gross.

A new programme, including *Carnaval* and *L'Oiseau et le prince*, was published for the second fortnight, beginning on 16 March, but in the middle of that evening's performance Alfred Butt was obliged to come on stage and announce that he had just heard Nijinsky had a temperature of 103 degrees and could not appear. The rest of the troupe filled in as best they could, but two nights later their contract was considered broken.[172] Nijinsky paid all his dancers for a full year's work,[173] and this must considerably have reduced his savings. (Although in the Russian Ballet he had not been given a proper salary, he had earned large sums for dancing at private parties.)[174] Diaghilev had tried unsuccessfully to prevent Bronislava from appearing at the Palace;[175] further action he intended to take to prevent Vaslav presenting Fokine's ballets was rendered superfluous by the abrupt ending of the season. On the other hand, Nijinsky's losses may have prompted him or his wife to claim arrears of salary from Diaghilev, and Sir George Lewis, the solicitor, was instructed to institute proceedings.[176]

By the time the Russian Ballet arrived in Monte Carlo, to give intermittent performances between 16 April and 6 May, Fokine had decided that he had too much work on hand, and Boris Romanov was named as the choreographer and producer of *Le Rossignol*. Diaghilev allowed Monte Carlo the privilege of seeing the first performance of *Les Papillons*, for which Dobujinsky had designed a formal garden with a circular temple, and

Bakst some pretty Victorian costumes. In this slight work Fokine had the only male role, that of a Pierrot who mistook some dancing girls for butterflies and was stricken with grief when his favourite – Karsavina – returned with a male escort and raised her mask to smile at him.

Although hindsight makes it almost too easy to read the signs, the 1914 season was indeed the end of a period; and the *ne plus ultra* of the Ballet's first phase coincided with the end of *la belle époque*, the end of *art nouveau*, the end of the *World of Art* movement, the end of empires. *Les Papillons*, with its Schumann music and Bakst dresses, which opened the Monte Carlo season, was a mere pendant to *Carnaval*. *La Légende de Joseph*, for which two German intellectuals had provided the libretto (for Count Harry Kessler had joined forces with Hugo von Hofmannsthal), and whose expensive score by the composer of *Salomé*, *Elektra* and *Der Rosenkavalier* was such a feather in Diaghilev's cap, was planned to be more stupendous a spectacle even than *Schéhérazade* or *Le Dieu bleu*; and Diaghilev, piling Pelion on Ossa, had found it necessary to employ two designers. The idea of evoking a banquet in the style of Veronese, which, as we have seen, had been conceived by Benois in another context, was interpreted by the Catalan Sert with his typical Baroque excess, and the columns of his palace were twisted like those of Bernini's *baldacchino* in St Peter's; while Bakst, in his Renaissance costumes, combined with his own incomparable audacity of colour the perversity of Beardsley and the incrustation of Gustave Moreau. Benois, who arrived on the stage of the Opéra 'straight from the train' and saw 'the fully illuminated face of Richard Strauss at the conductor's desk, standing out against the dark background of the empty theatre', thought the composer 'failed to conceal his inner emptiness beneath the flash and thunder of the orchestration'.[177] Not Ida Rubinstein, but the opera singer Maria Kusnetzova, who was the mistress of Bakst,[178] mimed Potiphar's wife, but she had little success, and Karsavina took over in London. Miassin, whose role Fokine had simplified almost to nothing, was inevitably a disappointment as a substitute for Nijinsky, and the brevity of his white sheepskin garment, suggested by Benois because Diaghilev had not liked the design of Bakst, prompted the Paris wits to dub the new ballet 'Les jambes de Joseph'.[179] The fact that both Rimsky's last opera, *Coq d'or*, and Stravinsky's first opera, *Le Rossignol*, were most acclaimed for their spectacular beauty as stage pictures could be brought forward as evidence that Diaghilev was relying too much on show. Although Misia 'actually wept with delight' at the scene when the court worshipped the Emperor in a ring of lanterns,[180] the opera-ballet 'failed to make any great impression'.[181] *Midas*, with music by Rimsky's son-in-law, Maximilian Steinberg, and a scene by Dobujinsky representing Parnassus, veered between the serious and the comic, and a ballet whose climax is reached by its hero growing ass's ears must be handicapped from the start.

Yet even amid the egregious profusion of the Paris season, during which *Cléopâtre*, *Petrushka* and the new extended version of *Schéhérazade* were danced, along with the new works, there was one shining landmark in the history of Diaghilev's company. In *Coq d'or* another marvel from Russia was given to the world. It was Fokine's last contribution to the Diaghilev repertoire. Not only were his ordering of Dodon's grotesque court, of the languorous enticements of the Queen of Shemakhan, which became Karsavina's favourite role,[182] and of the final processions, wonderfully effective, but the use of static singers as a frame for the dance proved a happy solution, and Gontcharova's scenes and costumes, overlaid with big childish flower patterns in yellow, orange and red, revealed a new aspect of Russianness and brought a new artist of genius into the theatre. Benois had reservations about Gontcharova's use of 'motley Asiatic colours', but he observed, as he sat in Misia's box at the *première*, among all the principal 'amis des russes', how 'every new effect evoked from them a chorus of exclamations. The greatest sensation of all was the appearance of King Dodon's silver steed on wheels. That supreme *arbiter elegantiarum*, Boni de Castellane, fell into a sort of ecstasy, and his fluted 'Versailles' voice could be heard throughout the theatre ejaculating 'C'est trop joli!'[183]

Nijinsky, returning from dancing at a party for Kermit Roosevelt's wedding at the American Embassy in Madrid, had been at the *générale* of *Joseph* on 14 May. His presence in the stalls was noted by the Press.[184] He visited Misia in her box, and, according to Romola, who was in Vienna expecting her baby, had a cool reception from some of his old friends, including Cocteau.[185] While in Paris, he took a class at the Opéra with Cecchetti. Diaghilev sent Miassin to join in the class and watch him work. Leonide noticed how meekly Vaslav accepted correction.[186]

Lady Ripon wrote from London to Misia that Nijinsky's marriage had 'prediposed everyone here in his favour'; she was sure that if Diaghilev would only re-engage him, Nijinsky would be quite content to dance alternately with Fokine and not insist on making ballets; she wondered if it were not Diaghilev who had made Fokine insist on Nijinsky's exclusion, and asked to what extent he was committed to Vladimirov. Misia admired Lady Ripon enormously, but she was loyal to Diaghilev as to no one else, and she thought the uncalled-for marriage had produced in London 'a wave of fine Puritan approval'.[187]

Through Jacques de Brunoff Valentine Gross asked Diaghilev if she could meet and draw Miassin, but received a curt refusal.[188]

The singers who took part in *Coq d'or* at the Opéra on 28 May had to scuttle off to be in time for *Boris Godunov* in London on the thirtieth. The dancers had two more performances in Paris, on 2 and 4 June, while, on the third, *Ivan the Terrible* (*The Maid of Pskov*) had its first English performance, with Chaliapine.

While the reader should be warned of the inaccuracy of Thomas Beecham's memoirs – for he included *The Rite of Spring* in the 1914 season, attributed the décor of *Le Rossignol* to Bakst, and stated that he and Diaghilev had decided that *Prince Igor*, with its mixed cast of singers and dancers, should be the first Russian opera given, when it was the third – we can take his word for the chaos which preceded the *première* of Borodin's work on Monday, 8 June.

It still remains a mystery to me not only how we ever reached that first night, but how everything during it went with such accuracy and swing. The few final days beforehand Drury Lane was more like a railway station than a theatre, with scenery arriving from three or four different quarters, and, when unpacked, disclosing frequently the awful fact that the artist had gone no further than indicate the design on some cloth sixty feet long without adding a stroke of paint. As Russians work on a flat floor instead of a vertical frame ... this meant finding ... some horizontal space large enough to accommodate such huge areas of canvas.... The orchestral parts were full of blunders with most of the cuts marked wrongly.... The proceedings were interrupted every five minutes by the agitated appearance of a small legion of dressmakers, wigmakers and bootmakers.... The leading singers quarrelled, the temperamental Chaliapine had a fisticuff encounter with the baritone who sang the title role [Andreyev], and the chorus took sides.... The actual day before the production the final rehearsal began in the early afternoon, went on throughout the evening well into the morning hours [it was indeed a Sunday], and came to an end only because the conductor [Emile Cooper] had an attack of hysteria.... It now seemed humanly impossible that the work could be ready in time; and yet such is the calibre of this remarkable people that fifteen hours later everything fell into place ... and yielded a performance as flawless as exhilarating. It is true that while the first act was being played some of the scenery for the last was still in the hands of painters, but it was all finished with a good half-hour to spare.... I have figured both as actor and spectator in a goodly number of stirring episodes in the theatre, but can recall none to match the tumult among the audience that followed ... the great scene in the Tatar Camp at the close of the third act....[189]

Beecham himself conducted the ballet.

The first all-ballet night was on 9 June, with *Thamar*, *Daphnis et Chloë* (given for the first time in London) and the expanded *Schéhérazade*. That morning a letter from Ravel was printed in *The Times*, complaining that Diaghilev was presenting in London 'a makeshift arrangement [of *Daphnis*] which I had agreed to write at M. Diaghilev's special request in order to facilitate production in certain minor centres'.[190] He meant that the *bouche fermée* singing of the invisible chorus was being omitted. Diaghilev replied the next day that in the original Paris production of 1912 the singing had been 'an experiment' which in his view had proved 'not only useless but actually detrimental'.[191] Detrimental to his budget, certainly.

Late at night, after seeing the first performance of *Coq d'or* in England on 15 June, Charles Ricketts wrote in his diary,

Delighted beyond all reason ... the music is exquisite, enchanting and original, the idea of the singers ranged on either side of the stage in oratorio fashion while the action is mimed and danced in the centre is admirable.... Karsavina looked like a bewitching Hindu idol, her dancing and miming were incomparable. The intelligence of the management and the choreographic invention is also incomparable – at times, ever so slightly, on the side of too much movement....[192]

On 18 June *Le Rossignol* and *Midas* were given. Neither made a sensation, and Osbert Sitwell observed Stravinsky, 'with an air both worldly and abstracted, and a little angry', bowing to the audience of 'clustered, nodding tiaras and the white kid gloves, that applauded him sufficiently to be polite'.[193]

The composer then returned to Clarens in Switzerland. Even when he was working on *The Rite* in 1912, Igor had had the idea for a cantata about a peasant wedding. That June he left his family in Switzerland and returned to Russia to pick up a book of popular poems and a dictionary of Russian phrases which he needed for his text.[194] This was his last visit to Russia until his old age.

In London there was a Strauss concert conducted by Nikisch on 21 June; and, after a dress rehearsal at which 'all little London was present and ... Lady Diana Manners clambered over the balcony from one box to another before an enraptured house',[195] the great man conducted *La Légende de Joseph* at Drury Lane on the twenty-third.

Karsavina had taken over the role of Potiphar's wife without any of her 'usual doubts' of her fitness; and she thought Miassin 'quite remarkable. His very lack of virtuosity in those days lent pathos to the image he created....'[196] Miassin himself was 'now feeling much happier in Joseph'; Diaghilev had built up his self-confidence; and the English gave him a 'warm reception'.[197]

As usual, Charles Ricketts left a more vivid impression of the ballet's good and bad points than any newspaper critic. He described the excess of gold on columns, table-cloths and apples. First the 'Oriental slave dealer', who acted as *compère* for the cabaret staged at the banquet, introduced a dance of odalisques, then wrestling gladiators, over whom the guests 'gloated' but who were driven off by whips. Joseph, who was carried on asleep in a hammock on poles, aroused the attention of Potiphar's bored wife. She followed him with her eyes 'like a cat watching a mouse', and bought him for a string of pearls. In the second scene Joseph was revealed asleep on a couch by moonlight.

The music then shudders like wind in a prison corridor, and Potiphar's wife in her shift, with streaming strands of hair ... passes through the columns against the sky.... She leans over Joseph.... He awakes ... she unties her hair in count-

277

less monstrous strands or ropes of living gold, and with this she starts smothering him, stinging him and half wrapping him, until he darts from his couch and covers his head and body with his black cloak. She ... writhes about his body ... till he leaves the cloak in her hands, escaping dressed in skin tights only, with a black band across his chest, giving thereby a more startling impression of starkness than sheer nakedness itself. She then dashes at him with a dagger but cannot strike him.... Her attendants rush in.... Slaves with torches appear, attending Potiphar ... the dagger is shown to him, and to wind-like sounds – wind through a key-hole – Potiphar's wife lies to Potiphar with her smiles and her fingers, whilst her rigid body and revulsed head is twisted into an incredible half-snake, half-Lot's wife pose which would have fascinated Burne-Jones.... At a gesture from Potiphar a burning cauldron is brought on to the stage, Joseph wrapped in chains, and irons heated.

Then the music becomes vulgar beyond belief, a light breaks upon Joseph, the chains fall off, and a golden archangel passes across the upper stage, descends, and leads Joseph off to the Savoy Hotel – I believe – to a sort of parody of Wagnerian apotheosis music of the worst type.

If the Russians had not been the inspired interpreters of the thing, it would have been intolerable and fatuous. Karsavina as Potiphar's wife was superb. A creature of gold and marble at the start, her sinister repelling of the begging dancer was evil but passionless; it suggested the avoidance of something unclean. When she strangled herself with her pearl necklace, the act was spontaneous and spasmodic like a moth meeting a flame.[198]

If *Joseph* looked back to Beardsley, its equivalent half a century later would be Fellini's film *Satyricon*. The Russian Ballet's first phase, the Fokine period, with its emphasis on local colour, was over: but the seeds of the new period were already planted. Moreover, Russian opera had taken root in England, and the 1914 season went down to history for the great interpretations of Chaliapine – five roles in four operas. Of him Ricketts wrote that he was 'the finest dramatic actor of my lifetime, and I saw Salvini when I was a boy!'

In *Boris* he is the ideal Macbeth. . . . As Ivan he has Lear-like moments and touches of grandeur in admonition, introspection, and disdain; but the character ... is outwardly sinister and melancholy. His part in *Khovanshchina* [Dosifey] expresses the most stately and simple sense of piety with almost humorous touches here and there. In *Prince Igor* he impersonates two different persons: [Galitsky] a burly blackguard, every inch a prince – a very bad one.... He transforms himself [as the Khan] into a small wiry and wily, yet genial, Tartar ... at once polite, cordial and strange, with something feline hidden....[199]

That season was the apotheosis of the basso to whom Mamontov had given his first chance, and whom Diaghilev had first brought to Paris in Russian opera in 1908.

The twenty-three-year-old Sergei Prokofiev was in London to witness Diaghilev's stupendous season. It was his second trip abroad. He had heard

Stravinsky play a piano arrangement of *The Firebird* in Moscow two years before, and had been bold enough to criticize it as pastiche Rimsky-Korsakov to the composer's face. Nevertheless, he was fascinated by the effectiveness of the new ballets on stage. Nuvel took him to play his Second Piano Concerto to Diaghilev. Sert thought the music 'fauve', but Diaghilev was stimulated to consider it as a ballet. Prokofiev wanted to write an opera on a Dostoievsky subject – *The Gambler*: but Diaghilev said 'Opera is *passé*. Contemporary taste demands ballet and pantomime.' He asked the young man to write him a ballet 'on a Russian fairy-tale or prehistoric subject'; and told Nuvel to put him in touch with the St Petersburg poet Sergei Gorodetsky immediately. Prokofiev watched with a critical eye as many performances as possible of *The Firebird*, *Petrushka* and *Daphnis et Chloë*, hoping to learn the secret of writing ballet music. He lingered in London until well into July.[200]

The murder of the Arch-Duke Franz Ferdinand at Sarajevo on 28 June preceded by three days the first *Khovanshchina* (whose spelling, like that of all difficult Russian names, Diaghilev simplified in the West).[201] Nijinsky, whose daughter Kyra had been born on 19 June, was on his way to England at Lady Ripon's request. She was certain she could make Diaghilev re-engage him. Romola reported that Vaslav was cold-shouldered by most of the company and returned to Vienna,[202] but it seems sure that Fokine, not Diaghilev, was the stumbling-block.[203] Within a few months Diaghilev would be moving heaven and earth to arrange Nijinsky's return to the company. In July 1914, with the most complicated season of opera and ballet on his hands, he could not risk disarranging the programmes by antagonizing Fokine.

On 7 July Sir Joseph Beecham bought 'the heart of London', as a newspaper called it[204] – that is, Covent Garden, including the Royal Opera House. Diaghilev had arranged that the Tsar should award him the Order of St Stanislas, but he could not receive this unless he belonged to the hereditary nobility, and he was only a knight.[205] (His son Thomas had also been knighted in the previous year.) King George compliantly made Sir Joseph a baronet on 17 July. On the twenty-fifth, the last all-ballet evening, Diaghilev arranged for the dancers to drag Sir Joseph before the curtain and give him a huge gilt laurel wreath. The pill-maker had spent a fortune – to further not only his son's career, but the cause of Russian opera and ballet. After the safety curtain had been lowered, Diaghilev lured Karsavina from her dressing-room, where she had begun to change, to take more calls in the auditorium. 'I stood for a brief moment, oddly confused; feeling as if I had violated the ethics of the theatre. The excited audience rushed forward: I turned and fled.'[206]

Diaghilev had not paid Karsavina a penny for two years. He carefully mentioned this fact to Sir Joseph Beecham, who visited the ballerina one evening in her dressing-room and gave her £2,000 in notes. Diaghilev then asked Tamara to lend him £400. With an apprehension of the possibility of war, she was longing to get back to Russia, but she put off her departure from London until after the weekend, so as to go to the bank and draw out some money for him.[207] This delay was to be the cause of considerable hardship for her. Diaghilev had ignored the hints of Count Harry Kessler that the projected autumn tour in Germany might not take place,[208] just as Nijinsky misunderstood Lady Ripon's telegrams, begging him to move his family to London.[209]

On Friday, 24 July, the last night of *Boris Godunov* and of the season, Lady Cunard took Paul Cambon, the French Ambassador, to Chaliapine's dressing-room. The young *attaché*, Paul Morand, who was with his chief, described the scene.

The huge Chaliapine, bigger than any of us, is covered in vaseline, removing his make-up. He announces that he is off to the war. The Duchess of Rutland cries. Nancy Cunard and Diana Manners wail as if they were losing a father. Maud Cunard exclaims 'The French have the best army in the world. They'll beat the Germans!' Edward Horner says he's going to join the Navy, and Thomas Beecham, humming Mozart ['*Non più andrai*'?], whispers 'Hold on tight! We'll be with you soon.'[210]

Karsavina, because of the extra day spent in London, was turned back at the German–Russian frontier.[211] She and her fellow travellers had a hard time, transported by goods train to Holland, and shipped thence back to England. She eventually reached Russia through Scandinavia. This Diaghilev never heard till years later.

PART V

The Massine Period

CHAPTER 12

1914–August 1918

Massine becomes a Choreographer – Wartime Tours and Tribulations – The United States and Spain – Picasso – South America: the Last Nijinsky Tour – Down and Out – Rescue by King Alfonso and Oswald Stoll

ANY THOUGHTS Leonide Miassin may have had of returning to Moscow to join up were soon dispelled by Diaghilev, who, like most people, did not think the situation was very serious, or that Germany and Austria, trapped between France and Russia, could hold out for long.[1]

Diaghilev's war work would be to turn Miassin into Massine – the new name he gave Leonide to mark his birth as a choreographer; Stravinsky's would be to write *Les Noces*, *L'Histoire du Soldat* (which did not concern Diaghilev) and *Renard*. The war years would bring Picasso, through Cocteau, into the orbit of Diaghilev, and lead to further involvements of the Russian Ballet with the School of Paris. Diaghilev would be cut off from Russia, first by war, then by revolution and the Peace of Brest-Litovsk. The supply of dancers would almost dry up: and yet he would contrive to keep his 'Russian Ballet' alive.

Massine and Stravinsky – and, later, Picasso – provided the incentives for Diaghilev to carry on. But in August 1914 Diaghilev had no company. Perhaps he thought he had – the Russian Ballet were due to assemble on 1 October in Berlin after their holidays – but he had not. For the time being he would show Massine the treasures of Italy. Their long holiday together began, incongruously, at the seaside resort of Viareggio on the Gulf of Genoa. The Cecchettis came with them, so that Leonide could have daily classes. Such *spiaggie* as Viareggio were not popular 'holiday camps' as they are today: they had a more select character, for the lower classes did not go on holiday. 'When I was not practising with Cecchetti,' wrote Massine, 'I often used to go to the Viareggio open-air marionette theatre, a favourite spot with the summer visitors and their children. Sometimes I would stand there for hours, totally absorbed in the antics of Pulcinella,

Diaghilev and Massine. Drawing by Mikhail Larionov.

Pimpinella or Il Capitano. I was intrigued by their grotesque masks and their jerky, loose-limbed movements. . . .'[2]

The friends' next destination was Florence; but, driving in a hired motor, they made a leisurely tour, stopping on the way at Pisa to see the Campo Santo, at San Gimignano, with its hilltop towers and frescoes by Benozzo Gozzoli, and at Monte Oliveto to see the frescoes of Signorelli and Sodoma.[3] Massine wrote to his old art teacher Bolshakov, who had first aroused his interest in painting, to describe the journey: 'Travelling by car is much more exciting than going by train, for you can see the landscape unfolding around you as you speed along the winding roads. There is a certain moment, just before twilight, when the countryside takes on its purest colouring and everything becomes more intense and more clearly defined. . . . Truly this country is, as Dostoievsky described it, a "cemetery of miracles". . . .'[4]

Diaghilev took a flat in Florence, 4 Viale Torricelli, and began to show Massine the pictures and sculpture he himself knew so well. 'In spite of his erudition, Diaghilev always carried his faithful Baedeker with him, and as soon as we entered a room in the Uffizi he would open the guide-book and say, "Let us see what Mr Baedeker has to say about these pictures."'[5] At the age of eight Leonide had received a profound impression from the Byzantine frescoes in the monastery of St Saavo near Moscow,[6] and in Florence it was the 'primitive' painters, whether Florentine or Sienese, who stirred him most – Cimabue, Duccio and Pietro Lorenzetti.[7] From a trip to

Pescia and Lucca he brought back an admiration for the Berlinghieri family, and in Ravenna, to which he and Diaghilev made an expedition that summer, he saw, in the mosaics of Sant' Apollinare in Classe, a Byzantine art older than that of Russia. He was particularly stirred by the Miracle of the Loaves and Fishes, 'with its gleaming golden background and the stylized grouping of Christ and the four disciples, tightly placed together, with stylized arm and torso movements'.[8] Diaghilev encouraged Massine to reproduce the poses and movements of figures in the paintings they most admired. Leonide's response to works of art was ready and serious. He was quick to grasp the styles of different periods and the way an artist revealed his character and beliefs in his work. Perhaps Diaghilev hesitated for a while to broach the subject of Massine attempting choreography. The day came when he could wait no longer, or when he judged the time was ripe.

One afternoon in the Uffizi [wrote Massine], while I was looking up at Fra Filippo Lippi's Madonna and Child, Diaghilev said to me 'Do you think you could compose a ballet?' 'No,' I answered, without thinking, 'I'm sure I never could.' Then, as we passed into another room, I was suddenly aware of the luminous colours of Simone Martini's Annunciation. As I looked at the delicate postures of Gabriel and the Virgin Mary, I felt as if everything I had seen in Florence had finally culminated in this painting. It seemed to be offering me the key to an unknown world, beckoning me along a path which I knew I must follow to the end. 'Yes,' I said to Diaghilev, 'I think I can create a ballet. Not only one, but a hundred, I promise you.'[9]

It follows that in this Renaissance atmosphere Diaghilev and Massine should begin to plan a religious ballet. They discussed whether to create a Life of Jesus or a danced version of the Mass. Perhaps it could be performed in silence. Work on this ritual ballet proceeded for six months in Italy, and continued after Diaghilev had assembled a company. The Serbian sculptor Mestrovic had a studio in Rome and Diaghilev conceived the idea that he should design the ballet, which they began to refer to as *Liturgie*. He wrote to Mestrovic about it.[10]

Throughout August, September and October Diaghilev was constantly telegraphing to Stravinsky in Switzerland, begging him to come to Florence and enquiring after *Les Noces*, none of which he had yet heard.[11] On 1 November he wrote,

You awful pig.
I wired you that I have signed the American contract, and that Mestrovic answered that he expected me in Rome in November. And you, not a word. You force me, an old man, to take up my pen. We stay here until 10th November, then go to Rome. We were in Ravenna and were overwhelmed by this magnificent cemetery. I have received a mad telegram from Misia saying she will not leave Paris because it is now the most beautiful city in the world. I have received a telegram from Nijinsky too. He has no right to leave Budapest

for the moment because of the war. Prokofiev is working with Gorodetsky and it seems he will finish his piano concerto. Kussevitsky is going to conduct in Rome and I shall see him. I received from your Mr Fokine an amiable enquiry about my affairs. The Fokines are at Biarritz. Well, and you? Which scene of *Noces* have you reached? Write, dog.[12]

This letter makes necessary several comments. If Diaghilev had signed an American contract (about which he may have been exaggerating, or even lying), he had done so without having a company to present. Then, Misia had been 'in action' in the Battle of the Marne.[13] Diaghilev seems slow to realize that Nijinsky, whom he was now prepared to forgive, particularly as the Americans would demand to see him, was an enemy alien in Austro-Hungary and that his movements were restricted. Prokofiev would shortly be coming to Rome from Russia. Fokine was about to return with Vera to St Petersburg, where he would be Ballet Master throughout the war. He played no further part in the Diaghilev company, though his works continued to be given until it came to an end.

In Rome Diaghilev and Massine stayed at the Grand Hotel, near the Museo delle Terme. Leonide was carried away by the Holy City and felt 'the spirit of God' everywhere.[14] Diaghilev at once went to see Conte di San Martino, who had organized the International Exhibition in 1912, when the Ballet were rehearsing *Petrushka*. He was President of the Accademia di Sta Cecilia, the Roman conservatoire, which presented Sunday concerts between September and May. Diaghilev planned to have Stravinsky and Prokofiev invited to take part in these. He needed to see them both and it would be a help if San Martino could pay some of their expenses. His first project for a concert on 3 January fell through for financial reasons. Diaghilev tried to make the best bargain he could for Stravinsky, whom he knew to be hard up. At first San Martino jumped at the idea. He offered between six and seven hundred francs. Diaghilev pointed out to him, as he wrote to Igor on 25 November,

that the train ticket costs 240 francs and your sojourn in Rome seven days at 50 francs a day, 350, i.e. 600 francs, the sum he proposed. All I can do is to invite you to stay with me so you will have no expenses in Rome, and argue you into accepting 1,200 francs. He agreed with me and said that to get the money he would shrink his budget (!!) (he has also invited Strauss, Debussy, and Kussevitsky from Moscow and others) so that the concert could take place. I even spoke with him about the order of the programme and I insisted that they give you twelve rehearsals.[15]

San Martino again said he could not afford this and Diaghilev intended offering to pay Stravinsky's travelling expenses himself if San Martino would give a fee of a thousand francs. 'If this also fails to work out, then to hell with him.'

We absolutely must see each other [wrote Diaghilev].... If you pass the [Christmas] holidays here, you can have a little, quiet room in our apartment, and one eats not badly here.... Our plan with Mestrovic is progressing. Mestrovic is a timid man with an exaggerated *amour propre* and a distrust of everything one does. He has a genius for fulfilling his work, but his advice is mediocre.... We must take care of everything ourselves. Your being at such a distance makes this all impossibly difficult. I work together with him and Massine. Bless us, I want Massine to stage this ballet!

Nijinsky behaves so stupidly. He didn't even answer my detailed and, in my opinion, fair letter, and to my modest telegram requesting, reply paid, whether he had received it, he answered only: 'Letter received: cannot come.' I am sure his wife is busy making him into the first ballet master of the Budapest Opera. As for *Noces*, do not worry. I will write him a second, less modest and less reasonable letter and this miserable person will understand that now is not the moment for joking. The invention of movement for *Noces* is definitely for Nijinsky, but I will not discuss the thing with him for several months yet. As for Massine, he is still too young, but each day he becomes more and more ours, and this is important. I am not going into any details now, but let me tell you that what I have in mind is a performance of the MASS in six or seven short tableaux. The period will be Byzantine, which Mestrovic will arrange in his own way. The music should be a series of *a cappella* sacred choruses, inspired, perhaps, by Gregorian chant, but more of that later....

The frescoes in the Roman underground churches of the first century are really astounding....

The main thing is that you come. Please reply immediately to the Grand Hotel. I embrace you.[16]

'As for *Noces*, don't worry!' How typical of Diaghilev! He had no company, no money. Europe was at war. Nijinsky, the potential choreographer, was interned. Mountains would be moved, the world would be traversed, thrones would topple and empires decline and fall, bankruptcy would more than once be faced before he produced the new ballet. All Stravinsky needed to do was to finish *Les Noces*, and not worry. The 'finishing' of the great choral ballet, its scoring, rescoring and re-rescoring, its designing, redesigning and re-redesigning would take eight years. By the time Diaghilev presented it on a stage Nijinsky would be mad, Massine dismissed and married, and its eventual choreographer would have passed the war years in Russia, endured the Revolution and escaped. Of course, Diaghilev could not foresee the long purgatory of this ballet's gestation: but, for the time being, all Stravinsky had to do was to get on with the composition, and not worry. He also had to feed his wife and family, but Diaghilev never considered that such mundane distractions presented much of a problem.

Two concert performances of *Petrushka* were being given in Geneva under the baton of a new friend of Stravinsky's, Ernest Ansermet; and after the second of these on 4 February Stravinsky left for Rome. Diaghilev invited a distinguished audience, including Rodin, who was in Rome to sculpt the Pope, to the Grand Hotel, where Stravinsky and Casella played a four-handed version of *The Rite*. Igor also played part of *The Firebird* and accompanied Marya Freund in some of his songs.[17] The next day Casella conducted *Petrushka* at the Augusteo Theatre, and at the end Marinetti, the leading Futurist, whose famous manifesto had been printed on the front page of *Le Figaro* on 20 February 1909, shouted from a box, 'Abasso Wagner! Viva Stravinsky!'[18] Igor then returned to Switzerland. Massine remembers his meeting with Rodin at the flat of Khvotchinsky, of the Russian Embassy. Mme Khvotchinsky was a good-looking woman and the first to arouse Diaghilev's jealousy with regard to Massine.[19]

As the only son of a widow, Prokofiev had not been called up: on the other hand, his friend Miaskovsky, with whom he had been working on his opera *The Gambler*, was at the front. Prokofiev and the poet Gorodetsky, with whom Diaghilev had asked him to work, persevered with the ballet on a 'prehistoric' subject, *Ala and Lolli*. The composer played part of it to Nuvel and Alfred Nurok in Petrograd early in 1915 and Nuvel wrote to Diaghilev, 'Prokofiev is writing muddled music on a muddled subject.'[20] But Diaghilev wanted to judge for himself and he wrote to Prokofiev, asking him to come to Rome, promising to pay his fare and arrange a concert. The composer travelled through Roumania, Bulgaria and Greece – all still neutral – arriving in Rome in March 1915.[21]

Diaghilev wrote to Stravinsky on 3 March, replying to a suggestion that San Martino should 'buy' some of his music. This Diaghilev thought highly unlikely. He held out some hopes of Henry Russell, founder of the then closed Boston Opera House, who in 1915 acted as an agent for the Metropolitan, and had been in Rome; but he counselled against sending the score of *Le Rossignol* back to Russia with Prokofiev. 'You are not so much mad as ridiculous. If Teliatina ['veal' – that is, Teliakovsky] stages it at all he will not do so earlier than 1917, when everybody will have forgotten about the war. Why in hell should Prokofiev (who is coming today) drag the material with him so that it can stay two years in Petrogrrrrad [joke about the new patriotic Slav name of St Petersburg]?'[22]

Diaghilev did not like *Ala and Lolli*: perhaps he thought its 'primitive' story and some of the scoring too like Stravinsky's *The Rite*. On Sunday, 7 March, at a Sta Cecilia concert, Prokofiev played his Second Piano Concerto under Bernardino Molinari. The work had a mixed reception,[23] but there were no demonstrations, as there had been at its first performance in St Petersburg.[24] Massine found Prokofiev's 'unique blend of boyish high spirits and Russian intensity very appealing'.[25]

In his letter of 3 March Diaghilev had told Stravinsky that he and Massine planned to go to Naples and Palermo on 8 March for ten days or so, then visit him in Switzerland to 'take' *Les Noces*, which 'must be finished by that time'. 'Have a big ballet ready,' he commanded, adding, 'You left "an indelible mark", as they say, here.'[26] He wrote again on the eighth, telling him about Marinetti's experiments which anticipated *musique concrète*.[27] But the trip to Naples did not take place. What happened instead was that Stravinsky returned to Rome. Prokofiev remembered that Diaghilev and he were somewhat apprehensive of Stravinsky's attitude to his new music, but the elder composer was 'well-disposed'.[28] Stravinsky backed out of helping with *Liturgie*, partly because he disapproved of presenting the Mass on the stage, partly because Diaghilev wanted him to compose its music and *Les Noces* for the same price.[29]

Diaghilev asked Prokofiev to write him a ballet of Russian folk-lore. They studied the tales of Afanasiev together, and picked out one called 'Chout' – 'The Buffoon'. Diaghilev, who was not interested in anti-clerical satire, deleted the characters of the priest and his wife from the story. A contract for a ballet on this subject was drawn up and signed by Prokofiev, who was to receive three thousand roubles. 'Please write me Russian music,' Diaghilev demanded. 'In your rotten Petrograd they have completely forgotten how to write Russian music.' Diaghilev scoffed at Prokofiev's wide range of musical appreciation. 'In art you must learn to hate. If you don't your own music will lose its character.' 'But', argued Prokofiev, 'this will inevitably lead to limitations.' Diaghilev replied, 'A gun fires far because its aim is narrow.'[30] Prokofiev returned to Russia to work on *Chout*. From the rejected *Ala and Lolli* he carved out a selection of music, which became the *Scythian Suite*, and Ziloti undertook to play this in spring 1917.[31]

Naturally it was from Russia and Poland that Diaghilev set about recruiting his company. His two recruiting officers were Grigoriev and Trubecki. But Grigoriev heard nothing from Diaghilev until early in 1915, when he wrote himself to enquire his intentions.[32] Trubecki must have been busy in the meanwhile. He had both Polish and German passports, which, in some way which is incomprehensible, facilitated his coming and going.[33] Grigoriev began to receive frequent telegrams from Diaghilev, asking him 'to see to certain matters'.[34] Diaghilev must have got some money from Russia to live on. 'The affairs of the Ballet seemed to be shaping well,' wrote Grigoriev – a phrase which appears meaningless when we read on to learn that it was only at the beginning of May (the *Lusitania* was sunk on the seventh) that he received a telegram summoning him to Switzerland 'for an important discussion'. He travelled via Finland, Sweden, Norway, England and France; it took him a fortnight.[35]

Diaghilev had rented a house in Switzerland from some old English ladies.[36] This was the Villa Bellerive at Ouchy, the lake-side village which was the 'port' of Lausanne on the north of Lake Geneva. At the centre of Ouchy rose the huge bulk of the Hôtel Beaurivage. To the west of this was a suburb of villas and gardens, where Diaghilev's new home stood in a small park off a lane leading from the water-front. The Swiss lakes had been a favourite holiday resort for well-to-do Russians since early in the nineteenth century. Dostoievsky, fleeing from his creditors, had written part of *Crime and Punishment* at Vevey, and a Count Shuvalov had built a Russian church in memory of a daughter who had died there. Stravinsky, who had more than once visited Switzerland as a child, found several temporary homes on the lake. He had written *The Rite of Spring* at Clarens, outside Montreux, and the last scenes of *Le Rossignol* higher in the mountains at Leysin. In the late summer of 1914 he had begun *Les Noces* at a cottage in Clarens; and in spring 1915 he was living at the Château d'Oex, east of Montreux. This was what he called 'the bicycle stage' of his life.[37] It would have taken him over two hours to reach Diaghilev at Ouchy, but he enjoyed the exercise.

Now at last Diaghilev heard the beginnings of *Les Noces*, which Stravinsky played to him at the Villa Bellerive. He burst into tears and exclaimed that this cantata would turn out to be 'the most beautiful and the most purely Russian creation' of his company. He was right. Igor was so happy that his strange work was so spontaneously appreciated that he resolved to dedicate it to Diaghilev.[38]

Stravinsky had made friends before the war with a Swiss neighbour at Clarens, Ernest Ansermet, a teacher of mathematics who, since his childhood, had lived entirely for music, and with his friend, the writer C. J. Ramuz, had founded an intellectual periodical, *Les Cahiers vaudois*, in 1914. It would not be till 'after the vintage' of 1915 that Ansermet introduced Stravinsky to Ramuz,[39] who would write the French texts of his *L'Histoire du soldat* and *Renard*. Meanwhile, since Pierre Monteux had enlisted in the French army, Stravinsky brought Ansermet to Diaghilev as a potential conductor; and Diaghilev thus acquired a great musician as *chef d'orchestre*.

It was on the Villa Bellerive at Ouchy that dancers from Moscow, Petrograd, Warsaw and London converged to form Diaghilev's new company. Grigoriev spent only a week there before returning to Russia. In Petrograd his first visit was to Karsavina, but she had found love at last with H. J. Bruce, a tall, handsome *attaché* at the British Embassy, and was having a baby.[40] He next approached the up-and-coming star of the Mariinsky, Olga Spessivtseva, who was 'somewhat reminiscent of Pavlova', and she was on the point of agreeing to join Diaghilev when the critic Volinsky, who influenced all her decisions, persuaded her that Diaghilev's modern repertoire was unsuitable for a purely classical dancer like herself. Grigoriev tried Moscow. The leading ballerina of the Bolshoi, though far from ideal, was willing. Diaghilev cabled, 'Continue looking for someone better, but failing that engage Makletsova.' Grigoriev did.[41] The Polish contingent arrived in Lausanne first.[42] From Petrograd came the old hands, Tchernicheva (Grigoriev's wife), Bolm, Burman and Gavrilov, with several new faces;[43]

and from Moscow the familiar Zverev, with eight unknowns.[44] The new star from Moscow, Xenia Makletsova, travelled separately. Passing through London, Grigoriev picked up Bewicke, Faithfull, Muningsova, her lover Kremnev, who had remained with her on the outbreak of war, and a brilliant little Pole whom they had met in class and recommended, Stanislas Idzikovsky, with his English girlfriend, Wanda Evina.[45]

All the dancers were paid the same, four hundred Swiss francs a week each. This was enough to feed them and to pay for simple lodgings in *pensions* or private houses.[46] Classes under Cecchetti were begun; Grigoriev and Bolm began to revive the old repertoire. The company had to climb the hill to their afternoon rehearsals, which took place in a hall which had been used as a market in the morning.[47]

The English girl, Hilda Munnings, who had suffered under the mongrel name of Muningsova, wrote,

During the past nine months in London, Kola [Kremnev] had taught me to speak Russian quite fluently, and in Lausanne, where the company was so much smaller than before and we all lived on rather more intimate terms, Diaghilev was much surprised to discover this. . . . He decided to give me solo roles to learn. The first was Papillon in *Carnaval*: it was not easy for me to follow Nijinska in this. One day Diaghilev told me he had included my pictures with those of other principals and soloists sent to the States for the advance publicity of our tour. He said 'I have signed your photographs myself with the name of Lydia Sokolova, and I hope you will live up to the name of Sokolova as it is that of a great dancer in Russia. Please forget from now on that you have ever been anything but Russian.'[48]

The newly named Sokolova later considered that of all her years with Diaghilev 'those six months in Switzerland were the happiest', and she thought 'the Old Man', as she called him, would have said the same.[49] Yet it is a curious thing for a ballet company to pass six months without giving a performance.

A young neighbour, Maurice Sandoz, who had studied under Ansermet, telephoned Diaghilev with an introduction from the pianist Vladimir Tchernikov, who had warned him, 'Beware of the snake concealed beneath the roses.' He was invited to call.

The big Louis XVI house, spread out on its terraces, dominated the grassy slopes. Huge clumps of trees, judiciously planted by English gardeners a hundred years or so ago, did not hide the house or deprive it of its famous view. . . . I caught a glimpse of three people strolling up and down the lawn in front of the wide-open windows. . . . Happily for me I suddenly recognized the silhouette of my former teacher of arithmetic at college. . . . It was indeed Ernest Ansermet who came to meet me and was kind enough to introduce me. . . 'An old pupil of mine. His music is better than his algebra.'. . . 'Are you sure he might not say the same of you?' replied Diaghilev, looking me straight in the eyes and taking hold of me rather roughly by the arm, not out of friendship but because he limped and leant on anything that was in reach. Suddenly, he added: 'Are you thirsty?' I was thirsty and said so. I saw at once that my affirmative had gained me a good mark.

'Léonide,' called out the big man who was weighing on me more and more ... 'Be kind and ... tell somebody to go and find some burgundy and some crystallized cherries....' This little speech was addressed to a thin young man with hair shaved short like a convict's, looking like a youthful St Francis....

Léonide Massine, for it was he, went off in a casual way ... and did not condescend to reappear. None the less a servant brought in a jug of burgundy, miraculously warmed to the right temperature, and in a glass salad bowl a pyramid of crystallized cherries looking like huge Burmese rubies.

Sandoz thought it odd to be drinking burgundy on such a warm evening, and when the conversation turned to ballet, he could not understand Diaghilev's 'affectation of belittling the productions which had won the greatest success a few years previously'. When Sandoz tried to defend *Schéhérazade*, Diaghilev said,

'Would you care in these days to furnish a room in pure Regency [*Régence?*] style or in that of the *Directoire*? I should find the idea intolerable.... What is true of a room is true of a ballet. Fokine's choreography is undoubtedly perfect of its sort but it has now got to make way for something else. One will come back to it later on, in fifty years, when, like everything else that has been lost and found again, it will seem amusing and then become a classic.

'What we need now is "emancipated" dancers, that is dancers who know all the technique of the school but have freed themselves from it. They will have to evolve new gestures to the sound of such music as has never before been heard.'

'*Le Sacre du printemps?*' I asked.

'It was a step in the right direction,' replied my host, 'but too daring perhaps for our public. But what can you expect? Nijinsky was first and foremost the God of Dancing. What I am looking for now is the God of Dancers: a choreographer. And Massine, who understands everything (even French) if he is given half a hint, fills me with the highest hopes.'

Diaghilev propelled the young Maurice into a dark room where there was a grand piano, and commanded him to play his Suite. The question of light did not arise. Twenty minutes later Diaghilev said, 'If you were Borodin's son, and your music reminds me very much of his, do you know what he would have said to you? He would have said: "My son, you have lots of talent; nevertheless you have not as much as your father." '[50]

The question of Nijinsky's release was all-important, for he was the star Americans would expect to see when the Ballet went to the States. Mme Greffulhe, Lady Ripon, Queen Alexandra, the Dowager Empress of Russia, the King of Spain, the Austrian Emperor, even the Pope were expected to play a part.[51] Surviving telegrams to or from the Russian Legation in Berne, the Hungarian Consuls in Berlin and Karlsruhe and the American Consulate in Budapest are slight indications of the efforts involved.[52]

Diaghilev had a new associate and backer, Randolfo Barocchi, the owner of a marble statuary business, an amateur of music and the theatre, who had already been secretary to Henry Russell, when he took his so-called San Carlo Opera Company on a tour of North America. Doubtless he advanced money to Diaghilev on the understanding that it would be repaid out of the takings of the projected tour.[53] Nevertheless, Diaghilev found it necessary to make occasional trips to Paris. As Sokolova pointed out,

Everything was short in those days, and we had difficulty in getting the make-up and shoes we needed. Before the war we had always been given a very generous allowance of shoes – a new pair every four days, with pink satin ribbons to sew on to them: those lavish times were never to return. We always knew when Diaghilev had been successful after one of his Paris trips, because Massine would be wearing another sapphire ring on his little finger. Massine, like Nijinsky, collected several of these, but whereas Nijinsky's had been set in gold, Massine's were set in platinum.[54]

Bakst came from Paris on a visit; but Gontcharova and Larionov came to stay, and were given a studio in the garden of Villa Bellerive.[55] Mikhail Larionov had novel theories on every branch of art and on every branch of the theatre, and he worked with Massine on the movement of *Liturgie*. Massine wrote:

The first scene ... was the Annunciation, danced by Lydia Sokolova and myself. For this I devised a succession of angular gestures and stiff open-hand movements inspired by Cimabue's Virgin. For the Ascension I arranged two groups of angels with their hands crossed to create the illusion of wings ascending to heaven.... Diaghilev arranged for Larionov to supervise my work, and we began work in the little rehearsal hall in Ouchy, going through the steps together and paring them down drastically to achieve an organic simplicity.[56]

Many of Gontcharova's handsome designs survive, angels with vermilion wings, and three-eyed seraphim plated with gold and silver, but it is hard to imagine how the sharp Byzantine-Cubist shapes of their draperies, unless cast in plaster, could have been realized on the stage. After Stravinsky had refused to co-operate, Diaghilev and Massine decided that the several episodes of the ritual should be performed in silence, with Russian church music played in the intervals. '[Diaghilev] even had some specific music in mind – some ancient chants which he had heard in Kiev. He wrote for copies of them, but because of the upheavals of war was unable to obtain them. As he decided the music was essential for the success of the ballet he decided to abandon it.'[57]

Massine was 'bitterly disappointed' that his religious ballet came to nothing. 'For me *Liturgie* had been not only a technical challenge, but even more the first artistic realization of a theme which had taken root deep in my subconscious when I was a child.'[58] He was to make more than one ballet along similar lines to *Liturgie* after the death of Diaghilev.[59]

Racking his brains for another ballet on which Massine could try his hand, Diaghilev thought of the dances from Rimsky's *The Snow Maiden*. Massine did not know the opera, so Diaghilev played it through for him, and he liked it. 'It conjured up for me the singing games of my childhood.'

Larionov was again asked to supervise my choreography and to design the sets and costumes. He ... suggested that it should revolve round the person of the sun-god, Yarila, to whom the peasants pay tribute in ritual ceremonies and dances, fusing with it [as Rimsky did in the opera] the legend of the Snow Maiden, the daughter of King Frost, who is destined to melt in the heat of the sun when she falls in love with a mortal. I also decided to incorporate into the action the character of Bobyl, the 'Innocent' or village half-wit, and to end the ballet with the traditional dance of the Buffoons. . . . Working on *Soleil de Nuit*, Larionov and I seemed to inspire each other.... For the dances I drew on my childhood memories of the *khorovod* and of 'Gori, gori jasno' ['Burn, burn, brightly'], which he helped me to embellish with suitably primitive, earthy gestures. I think it was through Larionov that I first came to understand the true nature of these old ritual peasant dances.[60]

The Chairman of the Metropolitan Opera House, New York, was Otto Kahn, a financial genius who happened to love the arts and was extremely generous to the Metropolitan. He was also a Jew, and, as such, not received in the most exclusive American society. He may have wanted the Russian Ballet not only for its own sake and for the sake of dazzling America with a new art form, but as a stepping-stone towards social acclaim. His Managing Director, Giulio Gatti-Casazza, was an Italian who had brought Toscanini with him from La Scala, and who had made the Metropolitan pre-eminent in the opera world. He had, however, an old mistrust of Diaghilev, as a telegram of 14 December 1910 bears witness – 'Diaghilev said earlier he could do without Fokine. Now says exactly opposite. Not my way handle business matters such frivolous and incoherent manner';[61] and as his mistress, Rosita Galli, the chief dancer of the Metropolitan, had good reason to fear competition, he was in opposition to the Russian Ballet, in spite of his friendship for, and dependence on, Otto Kahn.

Gatti-Casazza, his Press representative William J. Guard and Henry Russell were in Milan in August 1915, when Toscanini arranged a big charity concert at La Scala. It was then that Diaghilev came to an agreement to present his company, headed by Nijinsky, in America in the following year. In an article (written later to publicize the Russians in the *New York Times*) Guard, who was of Irish descent, gave a highly-coloured version of the discussions with Diaghilev, which took 'seven hours – including an hour and a half for *déjeuner*....'

When he was told in the plain language of American 'business' that he must
... have his troupe on hand at such an hour on such a date, and see that his
scenery is at the theatre ... on such a morning, he almost turned pale with amazement.... 'Why, if I have to be bothered with these details imposed on me in a
country I never saw and of which I know nothing, I'll tear up the contract!...
This is not a "show" ... it is an art exposition.... If you are going to hamper me
in this absurd way, then in Europe I stay and America will have to get along
without my Ballet Russe.' [62]

Although extravagant with other people's money, Diaghilev was as
practical and businesslike as the toughest American, and we may guess from
Guard's portrayal of a stock Russian 'type' that Diaghilev, who depended
absolutely on an American contract, staged some kind of scene and played
hard to get.

William Guard also described a visit he paid to Villa Bellerive two weeks
later. He had merely stopped at Lausanne to 'pass an hour between trains
with Mr Diaghilev', but when he found the latter in 'a charming but simple
dwelling house, hidden away in what seemed a little park', his 'cordial
Russian host' would not hear of him leaving before the next day.

Others ... have said he is irresistible. I found him so, and speedily changed my
plans. So first of all he showed me all over his temporary house and the grounds
around it – an ideal spot of several acres, abounding in dates and oleanders,
pines and maples, lilacs and roses. Following a little path through the miniature
woodland, we emerged on a little garden surrounding the smaller villa. 'Here,'
he said, 'is where most members of my colony live,' and then, leading me within,
we visited half a dozen rooms, in each of which I found a young woman or man
busy with pen, pencil or brush. All were Russians. One of the women – a striking
Slav type – I learned was the grand-daughter of the Russian novelist Pushkin,
Natalie Gontcharova [She was in fact the great-grand-niece of Pushkin's wife.] ...
while a tall young painter I found to be another of Diaghilev's 'discoveries', Michel
Larionov....

Guard was shown a class and Massine having a private lesson with
Cecchetti. Then, to complete the picture, there appeared in time for tea, on
a bicycle, 'a young man about 30 years of age, keen of eye, prominent of
feature, nervous in movement, quick in observation, rapid in speech'. This
was Stravinsky. Ernest Ansermet, who was to go with the Ballet to America,
soon followed.

Stravinsky ... did most of the talking ... but everyone else had his share, while
the 'Maître', as they all called M. Diaghilev, with his timely question or objection
or counter-argument, played with the mentalities of his friends ... as an organist
with the stops of his instrument. The discussion was resumed at the dinner table,
and was only terminated when Mr Diaghilev insisted upon taking the party a
thirty-mile motor-ride to the interior of the country. There we found a lonely
lake surrounded by hills. We sat on a big log watching the dark water below for

nearly half an hour, during which my host hardly opened his mouth. 'Time to return,' he said at last, as the full August moon peeped from behind a cloud. It was midnight when we parted at my hotel and I wished him 'au revoir' in New York.[63]

Towards the end of their happy stay at Ouchy Gontcharova gave Massine two ikon-like watercolours of *The Flight into Egypt* and *Christ in the House of Mary and Martha*, which were added to some Futurist pictures, acquired in Rome, to form the nucleus of what became a considerable collection. These were clearly related to her work for the unrealized *Liturgie*. On the back of the first she wrote, 'To dear Leonid Fedorovich Miassin in memory of our life and work at Bellerive, December 1, 1915.... This is quite a springlike day.'[64]

It still remained for Diaghilev to find a beautiful woman who could mime the old Ida Rubinstein roles of Cléopâtre and Zobeïda. Bakst went to hear *Tosca* in Geneva, and was struck by the appearance of the soprano Flora Revalles, a handsome friend of Ansermet's.[65] Diaghilev engaged her.

Diaghilev arranged for the Ballet to give two performances before they left for America. The first was a matinée at the handsome old Grand Théâtre in Geneva on 20 December. Stravinsky, coached by Ansermet, had conducted in public for the first time at a subscription concert on Sunday, 3 December, the piece being a selection from *The Firebird*. At the Ballet's performance he conducted it for the second time, but as an *entr'acte*, for he was not yet trusted to conduct for dancers.[66] Ansermet himself made his début as conductor for the Russian Ballet. In *Carnaval* Makletsova and Idzikovsky danced their first Columbine and Harlequin, and Sokolova her first Papillon, with the old-stagers Bolm and Cecchetti, and Makletsova danced *L'Oiseau bleu* with Bolm, who must have felt very miscast. Sokolova thought it was fun to dance in the first performance of Massine's first ballet, *Soleil de Nuit*, but

Although the costumes were vivid in colour and wonderful to look at, they were appallingly uncomfortable. All our abandon and zest for dancing was nipped in the bud. We had horrible thick pads tied round our waists, then there were tight heavy costumes on top of them. The tall, mitre-shaped Russian head-dresses, once they had slipped slightly to one side, just refused to stand up straight again.... The boys had a delightful number led by Kremnev [as Bobyl, the 'innocent']. They carried pigs' bladders on the end of sticks, which they banged on the ground.... Massine [as the Midnight Sun], wearing clappers on his hands painted with great sun symbols, performed all those eccentric jumps he liked so much....[67]

Massine thought the *khorovod* was vigorously danced and that Zoïa Rosovska, the contralto who sang the 'Song of Lel', had a 'child-like buoyancy'. 'Before my entry . . . I was in a state of extreme tension, but as soon as I stepped on to the stage my nervousness vanished and I felt that

I had made instant contact with my audience.... In order to sustain the illusion of a revolving sun I was forced to keep every muscle in my body in constant motion until the end.... But I could feel power pulsating within me, and by the end I had reached a fever pitch of excitement.'[68]

The last ballet was *Prince Igor*, in which Bolm could show his true quality. Felia Litvinne had come from Paris to sing Franck's 'Procession' as an *entr'acte* – a lavish, if incongruous, supplement to the programme.

Massine was pleased with the public's response to his ballet and said something to that effect to Diaghilev. Even in those he loved Diaghilev could not tolerate a momentary glow of self-satisfaction. 'I didn't hear them cheering,' he remarked coldly.[69]

The first notice of Massine's first ballet appeared in the *Journal de Genève* on 22 December 1915: '*Le Soleil de Nuit* ... was a delight. It was like a box of Russian toys brought to life and laughter, shining with gold paper and splashed with colour. Comic costumes for peasants and clowns, with, among them, Bobyl, a simpleton in a white blouse, and Massine, the much applauded choreographer, as a puppet with cymbals and a vermilion face.'[70]

While the British prepared to evacuate Gallipoli; while the Germans, Austrians and Bulgarians swept the defeated Serbians into the Albanian mountains; while the Russian army, driven out of Poland, came under the command of the Tsar himself; while the Germans prepared their spring offensive towards Verdun; and while Christmas was celebrated along the line of trenches on the Germans' 'Western Front' by fraternization and football matches, Diaghilev's dancers packed their bags and prepared to leave their lake-side asylum for North America.

The second performance Diaghilev had arranged for his Ballet to give before they left for the United States – which would also be their second and last in 1915 – was to be in Paris. Queen Alexandra was behind this, for the gala would be in aid of the British Red Cross, of which she was President, and of the united Red Cross of France and Belgium. The Opéra was lent for the occasion. An evening performance – which might encourage certain ladies to indulge in an unseemly display of magnificence in time of war – was considered out of the question.[71]

On Christmas Day Stravinsky played the first scene of *Les Noces* at Misia's flat to Diaghilev, a few Russian friends and Jacques-Emile Blanche. Tea was served in the rococo décor. Outside, in a violet dusk, the setting sun lit up the roof of the Pavillon de Flore across the river. Massine turned the pages of the music, and the composer attempted to sing as he played. Massine could hardly keep pace. Soon Stravinsky and his audience were equally breathless. Stravinsky drank tea with lemon and strode up and down the room. The second scene was attempted, but Massine lost the place – sheets of music were falling about the floor and the lamp was rocking. Stravinsky collapsed on a sofa, mopping his brow.[72]

The gala matinée of ballet on 29 December was supposed to start at half-past three but began at four. The crowds outside the Opéra were slightly surprised to see programme-sellers in costume and make-up who ventured as far as the entrances of the Métro to hawk their wares, calling out, 'Five francs! A work of art for five francs! Don't forget the war-victims!' The programme was *Schéhérazade*, *The Firebird* conducted by Stravinsky, *Soleil de Nuit*, the Blue Bird *pas de deux* and *Prince Igor*. Blanche thought the audience 'drab, modern and colourless', but in the interval he saw a few old friends and overheard conversations which were typical of the time.

Astruc threw himself upon me, exclaiming 'How right we were! Isn't it beautiful? What money I should have taken at my theatre [the Champs-Elysées] if only it hadn't had that *boche* façade. It's all very well Maurice Denis saying its style was Greek – people will always say I had a *boche* theatre and played *boche* music....

Misia, the Muse of the Russian Ballet, consoled Astruc, who is now director of the Radio–Guerre agency.

Everyone was running down pre-war *boche* taste. 'The only mistake Diaghilev made was to commission *Joseph* from Strauss.'

The young editor of *L'Envol*, a magazine which goes in for symbolic-cubist art, took Astruc aside, saying '*Cher maître*, you got out just in time! This kind of art is finished – *Schéhérazade* is dead as mutton. Give us cubism in the theatre. My colleagues and I will have some ideas for you when the war is over....'

The name of Nijinsky was much spoken in the corridors. 'Without Nijinsky this company has lost its soul.' 'Massine does not make up for the loss of Nijinsky.' 'But don't you know Vaslav is a prisoner in Hungary?' 'I was expecting to see him. The King of Spain has persuaded the Kaiser to restore him to the dance. The Duke of Alba acted as intermediary. Nijinsky is leaving with the Ballet for America.... He must be in the audience, dressed as a woman....'

Passing a group of aesthetes, I heard one say 'They haven't the nerve to take a chance with *L'Après-midi d'un faune* or *Le Sacre*.' Another said 'One can see the results of the income-tax going up this morning. If this is a sample of tomorrow's fashions – what a crowd!'

People left the Opéra as if they had just heard Bach's Passion on Good Friday.[73]

During *Soleil de Nuit* Grigoriev had overheard Diaghilev say to Svetlov, as they stood near him in the prompt corner, 'You see? Given the talent, one can make a choreographer in no time.' If correctly reported, this was a flippant remark which hardly expressed Diaghilev's immense satisfaction at having found so receptive a pupil as Massine.[74]

The Ballet set sail from Bordeaux on 1 January 1916. It was to be an eleven-day voyage, most of which Diaghilev spent shut up in his cabin, holding long discussions with Barocchi and Trubecki. When he ventured forth, he wore his life-belt. To be so long at sea was a nightmare to him. But Massine felt there was a 'pervading sense of expectancy and optimism in the company'. He himself paced the deck, 'gazing at the wintry seascape on which the rolling Atlantic breakers formed vast hillocks of foam'.[75]

As the ship approached New York on 11 January the weather grew foggy. Suddenly there was a sound of sirens and foghorns. Diaghilev thought the end had come. He ran with Massine to his allotted lifeboat – only to learn the ship was passing the Statue of Liberty.[76]

Lydia Lopukhova, who had danced Columbine and the Firebird for Diaghilev in 1910, had been in the United States, dancing and acting, ever since. She was to join the company in New York. Only a few old-stagers, Grigoriev, Tchernicheva and Kremnev, had known her, but Hilda Munnings, now called Lydia Sokolova, had toured with her under Mordkine in 1910 and 1911. (The English Lydia was the only member of the present company, except Barocchi, who had been in the States before.) Lopukhova had had many admirers in the United States, and she accepted a proposal from Heywood Broun, the popular baseball and drama critic of the *New York Tribune*, beside the reservoir in Central Park, a few days before the Ballet landed.[77]

In all the years of my friendship with Lydia Lopukhova [wrote Sokolova], I have never known her say or do an unkind thing either in the theatre or out of it. She was sweet to everybody, never jealous and never coveting another dancer's roles; but she always seemed to be hopping off somewhere, and obviously valued her private life as much as her life in ballet. She had a quick brain and was very witty, and her best friends were often intellectuals.... She never sold her soul to Diaghilev, fond of him as she was.[78]

The Century Theatre, where the Russian Ballet were to appear – for the Opera season was in progress at the Metropolitan – stood on Central Park West at 63rd Street, near Columbus Circle. It was several blocks further north than any other 'Broadway' theatre. The dancers had five days to rehearse before they opened, and Massine arranged a special extra solo dance for Lopukhova in *Soleil de Nuit*.

The Metropolitan were giving *Il Trovatore*, *The Magic Flute*, *Prince Igor* and *Manon Lescaut* – Caruso, Destinn and Hempel were singing. Sousa was conducting for an Ice Ballet at the Hippodrome, in a show which included Irene and Vernon Castle. Ethel Barrymore was at the Lyceum and Gaby Deslys in *Stop! Look! Listen!* at the Globe.[79]

There was a dress rehearsal on Saturday, 15 January, and on the Sunday Diaghilev spoke to a few journalists from the more serious papers about the *World of Art* movement; he also gave his views on America.

'We were all revolutionists ... when we were fighting for the cause of Russian art, and ... it was only by a small chance that I escaped becoming a revolutionist with other things than colour or music.'

The heavy features of the speaker, features curiously suggestive, like the immense frame, of unlimited animalism and latent energy, lit up, or rather smouldered, with a smile.... The neck and lips are thick, the eyes are those of a dreamer and artist.

'We began ... by questioning and overthrowing every precedent.... And we were right.... All the traditions of educated Russia were against us.... Where did we go for inspiration? We went where you in America will have to go – to the people. You have asked me about the future of American art. Dear Sir, there is plenty of American art, virile, characteristic art. The only difficulty is that America doesn't know it. In America' – Mr Diaghileff paused reflectively – 'In America it seems to me that what is vulgar, parvenu, affected and insincere is considered beautiful, and what is beautiful – vulgar!'

'For instance?'

'For instance when I am shown an immense mansion which is an ugly imitation of Gothic architecture, and am asked to admire its beauties. For instance, when I marvel at Broadway at night time, the life, the power, the endless variety of beauty to be found there, and I am laughed at! They think I am joking. Well, I am not joking. It is time that the American people realized themselves. Broadway is genuine. It is certainly a powerful influence for an American art. But in the drawing rooms they think it well to deprecate all this. They want to copy Europe, just as we in Russia insisted for so many years on copying Europe....

'I have made extensive researches, at first hand, in the development of Russian art of the 16th, 17th and 18th centuries. During that time every manifestation of culture not Russian was encouraged and fostered in the courts. (French culture dazzled us. Italian music was our passion. Later on, German literature found ... an influential following.) ... Even then, the people were becoming articulate....

'I found the most naïve indications of the real art – sometimes grotesque, sometimes very beautiful.... In objects of utility (domestic implements in the country districts), in the painting on sleds, in the designs and the colours of peasant dresses, or the carving around a window frame, we found our motives, and on this foundation we built.

'And this self-realization in Russia, consequent on a movement which had its inception some years previous in the creations of Russian authors and musicians, has borne considerable fruit. I remember that in the year 1905, the year of our revolution, I had collected 2,800 portraits of Russian nobility, most of them painted by foreign artists or in imitation of foreign art, and these portraits we displayed in the Palais de la Tauride, built by Catherine II. It has always seemed wonderful to me that in the same year the portraits of the nobility went out of the Palais, and the Duma, representative of the people, came in.'[80]

Diaghilev had been in America only four days when he gave this interview, and his knowledge of New York may have been limited to the sight of a few mansions on Fifth Avenue and of Broadway by night. Yet in what he said about the folk art beginnings of the artistic revival in Russia he seemed to be preaching the same gospel of craft-before-art that Oscar Wilde had delivered in his American lectures thirty-three years before, with the difference that Wilde was speaking for William Morris and Ruskin, and

Diaghilev for Mamontov's Abramtsevo. When Wilde turned to praise the water-works of Chicago – 'The rise and fall of the steel rods, the symmetrical motion of the great wheels'[81] – he foreshadowed Soviet Constructivism and even a late ballet produced by Diaghilev. Diaghilev's acclaim of other modern manifestations, the steel-framed skyscrapers, brash posters and coloured lights of Broadway, heralded the Pop Artists of the 1960s.

The first-night programme on 17 January consisted of *The Firebird*, danced by Makletsova (who was quite unsuitable), Bolm and Tchernicheva; *La Princesse enchantée*, with Makletsova and Bolm (who was quite unsuitable); *The Midnight Sun* and *Schéhérazade*, with Revalles, Bolm and Cecchetti. A few old friends were present: Prince Paul Trubetskoy, the sculptor, Adolf de Meyer (who had taken a series of photographs of Nijinsky in *L'Après-midi* in 1913) and his wife Olga, and Carl van Vechten, who had sent back reports of the pre-war Russian Ballet to the *New York Times* from Paris. The long list of the socially eminent who filled the boxes and stalls included the well-known names of Mrs John Astor, Mr and Mrs Theodore Roosevelt, Mr and Mrs Julius Bache; of Drexels, Tafts, Winthrops and Havemeyers, besides, of course, the Otto Kahns. Miss Elsie de Wolfe (later Lady Mendl), who had designed the interior of Henry Frick's mansion, which housed his growing collection of European works of art, was there too.[82]

Although the public seemed slightly puzzled by the new art form – so different from Pavlova's ballets, recently seen at the Hippodrome – the notices were laudatory and generous. But Diaghilev knew something was missing – and if, talking to Massine, he blamed the audience, saying that 'Americans still seemed to think of ballet as light entertainment to be enjoyed after a hard day at the office'[83] – he knew that it was Karsavina and Nijinsky. The *New York American* found Makletsova lacking in 'the airy grace of Karsavina'.[84] The *Globe* thought that, if the classical *pas de deux* (*La Princesse enchantée*) had been included as a kind of sop to New Yorkers, it was 'a mistake, perhaps, for here we have seen Anna Pavlova in that sort of thing and in that sort of thing Anna Pavlova is incomparable.'[85] The *Tribune* wrote that 'Makletsova is an accomplished technician, but she displayed little fancy or poetry.... M. Bolm was no Mordkine, and certainly no Nijinsky.' The *Tribune* also praised the settings of Golovine and Bakst.[86] The *Sun* thought Larionov's décor for *Soleil de Nuit* a 'tour-de-force',[87] but the *Journal of Commerce* thought it childish.[88] Grenville Vernon of the *Tribune* stated frankly that 'the remarkable impersonation of the Negro favourite of Zobeïde ... by M. Bolm will render the ballet impossible of production south of Mason and Dixon's line. Even to Northern minds it was repulsive. Yet it is a scene whose Oriental splendor, color, animality and lust will long remain with all who saw it....'[89] This was the sort of notice to fill the house, and the house was filled, even though the Metropolitan's season was in progress, and 'at almost opera rates'.[90]

The novelties on the second night were *L'Après-midi d'un Faune* and *Prince Igor*. If the critic of the *Tribune* had anticipated the impossibility of presenting Fokine's *Schéhérazade* in the South, it was in Puritanical Boston that he feared Nijinsky's *Faune* would give offence.[91] The Metropolitan had mounted Borodin's opera *Prince Igor* for the first time a few weeks before, which took the edge off the Borodin-Fokine Polovtsian Dances, and a critic thought the Ballet contained 'no woman dancer of the skill and agility' of Gatti-Casazza's favourite, Rosina Galli.[92]

On Monday, 24 January, another interview with Diaghilev appeared, this time in the *New York Post*. In Diaghilev's words we recognize his usual paradoxical style: 'In Russia we have schools of dancing and traditions, but they are Italian traditions ... the present Ballet Russe is not Russian at all. The company is assembled from everywhere. The ballets we are giving here have, many of them, never been seen in Russia. Russians have never seen *Daphnis and Chloë* [not given in America], nor the ballets for which Stravinsky has written music. . . .' He spoke of the growing importance of ballet and the difficulties of presenting opera as an acceptable music drama.

'Talent collects round ballet, not opera. Stravinsky has two new scores. One of them, which is already finished [untrue], is entitled *Les Noces Villageoises*. The other, which is unfinished, is to be mystical.' This, since it was said to be the combined work of Stravinsky, Massine and Gontcharova – wrongly described again as the granddaughter of Pushkin – must have been the abandoned *Liturgie*.

The twenty-year-old Prokofiev, 'our future', was writing for the ballet – not to mention Debussy, Ravel, [the late] Rimsky, Tcherepnine, Dukas, Roussel, even Strauss. 'Whom have you writing for opera now? Puccini, who hardly merits consideration, musically, and Richard Strauss.'

At the betrayal of Diaghilev's old hero, Puccini, the cock must have crowed thrice, as it would have reason to do regularly throughout the years to come. 'The problem before us,' he concluded, 'is to engage every organ of the body sensible to art, every sense. . . . Our material difficulties are great. . . . The human body is beautiful only in youth ... spoiled by life at thirty. A singer only begins in his thirtieth year ... there must be a revolution in opera.' Asked if he had ever had aspirations to be a painter, Diaghilev admitted, 'I never even drew a cat or a house and a chimney!'[93]

At 11 a.m. on 25 January Diaghilev was summoned to answer a complaint about 'alleged objectionable features' of his ballets before Judge McAdoo at 300 Mulberry Street.

M. Serge de Diaghilev and the Russians listened with the grave patience and the puzzled amusement with which intelligent folk from Continental Europe have often watched the workings of the censorship of municipal authorities over the American theatre. . . . 'I believe,' said M. de Diaghilev, half-amused and half-perturbed, 'that my mind and the minds of those who planned and executed the ballets are less vicious than the minds of those that made the protest.'[94]

He had to say something, but whether or not Fokine's *Schéhérazade* and Nijinsky's *Faune* were successful works of art, no one could deny they were about a sexual orgy and masturbation. 'A moral *Schéhérazade* is about as possible of realization as a continent Don Juan,' the *Tribune* aptly pointed out.[95] That night, instead of lying down on the Nymph's scarf, Massine 'placed the drapery gently on the rocks and sat gazing at its silken folds'.[96] 'When the audience had ceased applauding,' wrote the critic of the *Times*, 'after the ushers had carried out huge armfuls of flowers sent to Leonide Massine, M. de Diaghilev came smiling from his seat in the orchestra circle, down the aisle to where Mr Gatti-Casazza, John Brown [Business Manager] and other heads of the Metropolitan were standing, and said in French "America is saved." '[97] The miming of the Negro Slaves in *Schéhérazade* was toned down, and the *Tribune* thought it had become dull in consequence.[98]

The tour began at Boston, which, with its neighbouring university of Harvard, was the intellectual capital of the United States. It had an opera house, which Henry Russell had been instrumental in building, and it had one of the ablest music critics, H. T. Parker, to write about the Ballet. Diaghilev took special trouble over the lighting. Mayor Curley gave instructions to Chief of Police Casey that the Russians were to show no bare flesh except their toes,[99] a ban which presumably did not extend to the arms of Columbine and Papillon in *Carnaval*. In Boston, jealous of Lopukhova's success with the public, Makletsova walked out. Nobody was sorry – except the Bostonian critics, who complained of the last-minute programme changes which were necessitated, and of the cancellation of *Le Pavillon d'Armide*, which had aroused little enthusiasm in New York and was given no more.[100] Lopukhova had deputized for Karsavina in *The Firebird* in 1910 and she took over Makletsova's roles in this and in *La Princesse enchantée*, for which Bakst had designed a special setting of scarlet trees against a purple sky.

The repertoire for the tour was not large; without *Le Pavillon*, there remained eight ballets and the *pas de deux*. It looks as if Diaghilev had decided not to present *Le Spectre de la rose* until Nijinsky arrived. Then, during rehearsals on tour, it perhaps became clear to him that Gavrilov could dance it adequately and that Lopukhova could easily replace Karsavina.

Plotted on the map, the tour looks well planned. In two months the Ballet covered most of the principal northern cities, going no further west than Minneapolis and Kansas City, and no further south than St Louis. Nowhere did the company have to retrace their steps or cross their own tracks. In Boston they played ten days, in Chicago a fortnight, in St Louis, Cincinnati, Cleveland, Pittsburgh, Washington and Philadelphia several days each. They can only have spent about twelve nights out of sixty on the train; and the only big cities on their route for which they were not booked were Buffalo, Baltimore and Newark. The company, the orchestra and certain key technicians travelled in state, with their scenery and wardrobe, on three special trains. Otto Kahn spared no expense. It was, nevertheless, the most arduous tour Diaghilev ever had to experience.

After Albany and Detroit the Ballet arrived in Chicago, where they stayed longest, dancing at the Auditorium of the University, and had least success. Before the opening Diaghilev was warned, à propos of Schéhérazade, that miscegenation was 'not a misdemeanour appropriate to the Eli Bates Settlement', a charity which was to benefit from the first night's takings, so 'his continental cunning asserted itself' and he 'bleached Le Nègre a trifle'.[101] The smart first-night audience were talkative. 'The music ... proved a most wonderful accompaniment for conversation.... Lots of people were talking at the top of their voices during the overture to the Firebird, and some of the box-holders, too, were in great form all evening.'[102] After the first week, although the Chicago Sunday Tribune printed a photograph of Revalles and Bolm which reached from the top to the bottom of the page, its critic reported that 'numbers were small'.[103] Not even Lopukhova's appearance on 23 February with Gavrilov in Le Spectre – which may have been a desperate expedient on Diaghilev's part, and which 'did, in fact, really draw applause' – made any difference.[104]

In Milwaukee we get a glimpse of Diaghilev snatching a combined breakfast and lunch in the café of the Hotel Pfister, delighted to find that the reporter of the Milwaukee News could speak French. (He couldn't write it.) ' "Ah, vous parle Française!" – and the dapper Russian's brown eyes were aglow with joy and friendliness. "Si vous ne parle pas trop vite," pleaded the interviewer.... Anyone who thinks this aristocratic Russian might be nursing a grouch because his spectacular ballet is a losing venture financially ought to see the man. He couldn't be cornered into saying anything uncomplimentary about America or American audiences....'[105]

The Russian Ballet travelled north-west to St Paul and Minneapolis. Arriving at St Paul from Milwaukee,[106] where he had conducted in a vast icy hall, Ansermet felt so ill – with influenza, no doubt – that he could hardly climb out of the train. At his hotel he fainted and was put to bed. The doctor told him that there was no question of his getting up for at least a week. Then outside his door he heard the voice of Diaghilev, who was too afraid of infection to come in, but who asked, 'Ansermet, you're not going to let me down tonight, are you?' The courageous musician replied,

'No, you can rely on me. But have an armchair put behind my desk.' When Ansermet took his place that evening, he felt the hand of his doctor on his shoulder, and heard the kind words, 'Don't worry. I'm here. I'll keep an eye on you.'[107]

From Minneapolis the Ballet plunged south for four hundred miles to Kansas City. As this was the furthest west that Diaghilev, the son of Perm, was ever to travel, it is of interest how he spent his day at the confluence of the Missouri and Kansas rivers, where the first log cabin had only been built seventy years before.

Diaghilev and his company had passed the night of 3/4 March in their special train. This was divided into three sections, with nine Pullman coaches for dancers and orchestra and fourteen baggage cars. The first section, due to arrive at 7 a.m., came in as late as 11.30. The *Kansas City Star* described the scene.

A door opened and emitted a large managerial person, who enquired abruptly about the advance sale. The managerial one took four steps, spotted a railroad official and gave decisive directions that the next train should be rushed to the unloading track, despite the fact that two Pullman coaches were with the long line of baggage cars. It was suggested that the occupants of the coaches would have to walk a few blocks. 'I don't care if they walk a mile,' snapped the manager. 'Shoot the whole train and be lively with the baggage – that's what we're after.' The Union Station 'red caps' [porters] trusted to their intuition to spot the aristocrats of the party.... As the Ballet Russe in street clothes swarmed through the station, pattering along in rubber-encased shoes, the principals began coming through the swinging doors. These were the great names of the posters. Ahead of each man or woman possessed of a name walked ushers buried deep under luggage. ... At the Hotel Muehlebach, where the principals, about a score in number, immediately registered, hotel attendants had never seen such luggage, queer handbags and portmanteaux.... The hotel had reserved its best and most expensive rooms for the ballet principals. But the artists demanded cheaper rooms in a confused chorus. A spokesman [probably Kremnev] thrust himself to the front. He knew this much English: 'Two, two-fifty.' This he repeated with great vigour. A hotel clerk who knew a little French explained that every room ... except the expensive rooms reserved, had been taken by persons from Kansas and Missouri, who had come to see the ballets. The artists had to take the reserved rooms at prices akin to the prices prevailing for their own ballet [$5 top].[108]

Merle Armitage, a young enthusiast for Stravinsky's music, who had persuaded Otto Kahn to engage him to help with the tour, described the problems of performing in a theatre which was not a theatre.

We were booked to play the vast Convention Hall, an oval building without a permanent stage. Therefore, after our late arrival it was necessary to curtain off one end of the great auditorium, install a gridiron on which to hang the scenery, erect a proscenium arch, and hang all the complicated décor and connect our own portable switchboards.... Diaghilev insisted that the audience [were] not to be admitted until he had completed checking scenery and lights. And it was a rainy day!

Four thousand people had booked seats for the matinée, which was due to begin at 2.30 and started at 4.15. Armitage was sent out four times to assure the wet crowds that the doors would soon be open.[109] Mr Fritschy, the manager, begged Diaghilev to let the performance start, but in vain. Diaghilev kept his head and he kept the crowds waiting. This needed courage. The potential audience went off to drink in bars and hotels, and even passed the time in picture-houses and theatres. Meanwhile Diaghilev had to pacify Captain Ennis of the police department, who told the *Kansas City Star*, 'I dropped in to see Dogleaf before the curtain went up. Dogleaf, or whatever his name is, couldn't understand plain English.... I told a fellow [interpreter] "This is a strictly moral town and we won't stand for any of that highbrow immorality. Put on your show, but keep it toned down...." What's more, I told him we didn't want to make trouble, but if the show was too rank I'd come right up on the stage and call down the curtain. ...'[110] The audience bore no grudge, though the curtain did not fall on *Schéhérazade* till 6.50. 'Spontaneous applause' followed every ballet. 'After dinner another rehearsal of scenic and lighting effects for the night's performance kept the audience waiting out in Thirteenth and Central Streets until 9.15 o'clock, and it was 9.35 when the curtain rose on *Carnaval*.' But the Convention Hall was filled to its capacity – 4,300. 'Colour that dreams, that is virginal or abandoned, that murders or restores, that weeps or laughs, that sings or is silent – that is what Leon Bakst brought to our astonished eyes,' raved the *Times*.[111] As the dancers journeyed on, next day, south-east to St Louis, they could read in their Sunday *Star*, 'BALLET WON KANSAS CITY.'[112] Diaghilev's perseverance had not been wasted.

St Louis was pleased;[113] Indianapolis was happy.[114] In Cincinnati the Ballet had a free Sunday, and the reporter of the *Times-Star* was astounded to find the dancers at class with Cecchetti at nine on the Monday morning.[115] In Cleveland the company enjoyed the luxury of a big stage on which to spread themselves.[116] Arriving at the William Penn Hotel, Pittsburgh, Diaghilev, 'said to be of royal birth', was too 'shy' to give an interview; but Pittsburgh's 'fashionable set' had returned from wintering in Florida specially for the two performances, and the ladies' dresses were described at length in the *Gazette*.[117] In the *Pittsburgh Post*, though, *Petrushka* received the worst notice it had ever earned. 'Of all drivelling European crudity submitted to American view the *Petrushka* pantomime of yesterday afternoon ranks with the worst. The scenic nightmare showed a Benois attempt at Bakst delirium by enveloping the stage in wash-day blueing.'[118]

Most of the women in the company thought Massine attractive, but he showed little response. One lady, however, proved irresistible. Grigoriev's wife, Lubov Tchernicheva, had 'the most wonderful, quivering brown velvet eyes with yellow flecks in them', and Massine was attracted. 'The silent but ardent flirtation was obvious to the whole company.' Things came to a head in Washington, DC.[119]

In the capital Diaghilev stayed with Bakhmetev, the Russian ambassador,[120] and he must have thought himself in touch with civilization once more. The President and Mrs Wilson attended the ballet on 23 March, saw *Cléopâtre*, *Le Spectre*, *Carnaval* and *Soleil de Nuit*, and met the artists on the stage. There was a Russian Ball afterwards at Rauscher's Hotel in aid of sick and wounded Russian soldiers.[121] Several numbers, including the dance of nursemaids from *Petrushka*, were given in the middle of the ballroom before the dancing became general. Sokolova's partner led her out of the crush into a little room empty of people.

Almost immediately we were followed by Massine and [Tchernicheva]. We were all laughing and flirting and having a wonderful time, when to our horror we saw Diaghilev standing in the doorway, a champagne bottle under his arm and glasses in his hand. We froze. He had seen enough; he turned and walked away. The following morning a message came round via the bush telegraph – that is, by Vassili, Diaghilev's servant and spy – that anybody who interfered with the peace of the company by disturbing Massine in his work would be expelled immediately. Leonide and [Luba] did not speak to each other for many a day after that. As for the rest of us, any girl who valued her position in the company was careful to steer clear of Massine.[122]

After a few days at Philadelphia and a performance at Atlantic City, the Russian Ballet were back in New York.

Nijinsky had been released – the Metropolitan Opera House had announced this on 2 March – but he would still arrive late for the opening of Diaghilev's season at the Metropolitan, which began on Monday, 3 April, the day after the company's return. On that night *Le Spectre de la Rose*, the only novelty to New York, was danced by Lopukhova and Gavrilov.[123] But all the interest of the public and the Press was focussed on the overdue Nijinsky, whose name meant more than the rest of the Ballet put together.

Vaslav and Romola Nijinsky, with their little daughter, had spent a year in 'open arrest' in Budapest. In January 1916, while the Ballet were sailing to America, they were sent to Vienna in preparation for their release. In February the Nijinskys were summoned to the American Embassy in Vienna and told that they might travel 'on parole' to the United States to join Diaghilev, provided Nijinsky did not return to Russia. He and his wife and daughter passed the frontier into neutral Switzerland, to stay first at Berne, then at Lausanne, where they were met by Henry Russell, who was to conduct them to New York. In Lausanne two things happened. Vaslav heard from Sir George Lewis, his London lawyer, that the action he had brought against Diaghilev in 1914 for arrears of salary had been won. The sum specified was (according to Romola) 'half a million gold francs: but as Diaghilev was not a resident in any country, there would probably be great difficulty in collecting it.'[124] Sir George under-estimated Romola, who knew how necessary her husband was to the Diaghilev Ballet at this time. Gratitude to Diaghilev for engineering her husband's release never entered into her calculations. Then, at Lausanne, Vaslav and Romola saw Stravinsky, who also had a grievance against Diaghilev. Needing money as he did, Igor was waiting for Diaghilev to invite him to conduct his ballets at the Metropolitan Opera House, but he had received no sign. He tried to persuade Vaslav to make his own appearance in New York conditional on Stravinsky's. On his side, Vaslav asked Igor and Catherine to take little Kyra into their home while he and Romola were in America. Each friend refused the other's request.[125] On 24 March the Nijinskys spent a day in Paris and Romola had a shopping spree.[126] They sailed from Bordeaux on the French ship *Espagne*[127] at the end of March.

Diaghilev was at the quay-side to greet Nijinsky and his family on Tuesday, 4 April 1916. Officials of the Metropolitan were present, and so, in force, were the Press. On the surface everything was amicable. Diaghilev presented flowers; Nijinsky handed him his child.[128] Diaghilev had moved heaven and earth to bring Vaslav to New York. He did not know what he was in for.

Apart from European heads of Church and State, the three most important factors in the release of Nijinsky had been the Austrians who had let him go, the Americans who through their ambassadors and consuls had given him a visa to their neutral country, and Diaghilev, who had planned the whole operation. On Wednesday, 5 April, Romola embarked on a tirade against the Austro-Hungarian authorities, whom she accused of half-starving her family and depriving her child of milk.[129] By Friday Nijinsky was expressing surprise that he was advertised to dance in America with the Diaghilev Ballet, with whom he had no contract. Otto Kahn had referred him to Diaghilev and Diaghilev referred him to the Metropolitan's John Brown. Nijinsky refused to allow *L'Après-midi d'un faune* to be performed in the way it was being given in New York; and he wanted to rehearse the company in certain Fokine ballets.[130] He demanded 'a salary several times as large as Diaghilev's representative mentioned to him yesterday afternoon'.[131] On that Saturday, the *Globe* reported, 'lawyers and reporters swarmed at the hotel headquarters of Nijinsky.... Dancers and mere opera directors stood aghast around Diaghilev five blocks below.'[132]

Diaghilev had contracted to produce Karsavina and Nijinsky. Karsavina had not come, and Diaghilev had been excused. Nijinsky had missed the fortnight at the Century and the first tour, and still no penalty had been exacted. After all this, Nijinsky had arrived, only to make these impossible demands. Diaghilev could neither pay him eighty thousand dollars down, the alleged debt, nor a salary like Caruso's. It did no good to his company to have headlines like 'NIJINSKY AT ODDS WITH BALLET RUSSE – FAMOUS DANCER SAYS THAT HIS FINANCIAL AND ARTISTIC TERMS HAVE NOT BEEN MET' in the *New York Times*,[133] or 'NIJINSKY'S DEBUT IN STRIKER'S ROLE – NOT A TOE WILL EX-WAR PRISONER TWINKLE TILL ANTE IS RAISED' in the *New York Tribune*.[134] Diaghilev could not explain to the Press or public that, because of his special relationship with Nijinsky, he had, in lieu of salary, fed, lodged and clothed him, and paid all his and his mother's expenses for four years; and he did not explain.

Somehow, on Saturday 8 April and on Sunday 9 April (when Mahler's Eighth Symphony was performed under Stokowski at the Metropolitan), the affair was settled between Laurence Steinhardt, a lawyer employed by Nijinsky, and Alfred Seligsberg, representing the Metropolitan Opera Company.[135] Details were not announced, but the *Telegraph* reported Diaghilev as saying that '\$3,000 a week was enough even for a Nijinsky',[136] and Romola recorded that, in addition to his salary, Vaslav was to receive a proportion of the company's weekly receipts from the Metropolitan in repayment of the debt owing to him.[137] It is likely that Otto Kahn himself put up a considerable initial payment – this would have been in character.

At the matinée on Wednesday, 12 April, Nijinsky made his American début, dancing *Le Spectre* and *Petrushka*. He received an ovation and his Petrushka was especially praised. It is curious that although nearly all the critics acclaimed him, they did so in spite of what they considered his effeminacy in *Le Spectre de la rose*. 'That Mr Nijinsky is effeminate at times is obvious,' wrote the *Herald*. 'But . . . he is a great artist, probably the greatest that the present generation has seen here.'[138] The *Times* considered that 'a super-refinement of gesture and posture amounted to effeminacy. The costume of the dancer, fashioned about the shoulders exactly like a woman's *décolleté*, with shoulder-and-arm straps, even helped to emphasize this, as did certain technical details . . . such as dancing on the toes, which is not ordinarily indulged in by male dancers.'[139] 'While the effeminate quality, almost inseparable from the male ballet dancer, is quite visible . . ., he has at the same time a certain masculinity of strength and rhythm which counteracts the other impression,' wrote the *Evening Post*.[140] The critic of the *Tribune* summed up very neatly Nijinsky's special qualities:

His movements flow one from another without effort and without break in a sort of muscular legato. His lightness of limb is controlled by a tremendous muscular power, so that when he leaps into the air he appears to float, and when he touches the ground it is but to bound upward again. . . . In his mastery of detail, his insistence that each step, each movement shall be given, not for its own sake, but for the total effect, Mr Nijinsky shows himself the consummate artist.... The Russians have now secured a great dancer ... a force which appears able to galvanize the proceedings into a life which they have not hitherto possessed.[141]

Carl van Vechten, who had been disappointed by the Russian Ballet's performances at the Century, thought Vaslav had 'surpassed himself' and that 'from the day of Nijinsky's arrival the ensemble of the Ballet improved.'[142]

That Wednesday evening *Thamar* was given for the first time in New York, and was judged Bakst's most gorgeous spectacle.[143] On Friday, 14 April, Nijinsky danced *Les Sylphides* and *Carnaval*; on the fifteenth, *Schéhérazade* and *La Princesse enchantée*, in which 'he seemed not to touch the stage more than ten times during the whole ballet.'[144]

The opinion of Massine, who had been dancing some of Nijinsky's roles without ever having seen him in the flesh, is worth quoting.

I was astounded by the way his whole personality became transformed on the stage. He had an instinctive effortless control of his body; every gesture expressed the most tender and complex emotions.... Although I had identified myself with Petrushka, I soon realized that the role came more naturally to Nijinsky.... In the Blue Bird *pas de deux* ... to convey the quivering motion of the bird's wings he fluttered his hands at such a dazzling speed that they seemed to have exactly the pulsating action of humming-birds....[145]

When Nijinsky appeared in *Narcisse*, however, on 22 April, people giggled. 'Mr Nijinsky', wrote the *Tribune*, 'succeeded in being offensively effeminate, but at most he succeeded in being nothing else.'[146] (Benois' original objection to the subject of the ballet comes to mind.) After two more performances[147] *Narcisse* was given no more in America.

L'Après-midi d'un faune had to be cancelled because Diaghilev would not agree to Nijinsky's request to substitute Flora Revalles for Tchernicheva as the Chief Nymph.[148] Although *L'Après-midi* looked simple, it was hard to dance, and as Revalles was not trained as a dancer, however effective as a mime, it is surprising that Nijinsky should have thought her preferable. Perhaps he was trying to take a line against Grigoriev, whom he rightly felt was antagonistic towards him, through his wife, and perhaps Diaghilev was trying to defend Grigoriev.

After the tour and the trouble with Nijinsky, Diaghilev was 'so tired that small things quickly irritated him, even the fact that as soon as he sat down in a restaurant a glass of ice-cold water would be put on the table without his having asked for it.'[149] Otto Kahn, too, had been through much during the stay of the Russian Ballet in America: the initial absence of the stars, the exigencies of Diaghilev, the difficulty of organizing the tour and its cost, the temperament and demands of Nijinsky, the complaints of the Metropolitan's subscribers at the substitution of ballet for opera, and the constant changes of programme. Yet Kahn was determined to persist in his philanthropy, if that is the right word – it was Romola Nijinsky who maintained that he was merely trying to get into society[150] – and show the Ballet to an even wider audience in the autumn. He may have been right in assuming that, as the Nijinskys and Diaghilev were at loggerheads, it would be better for business if they were kept apart. There was no question but that Nijinsky was the big attraction for the public, so, if Kahn had to choose between him and Diaghilev, it would be Diaghilev who must be left out. An arrangement was come to by which Nijinsky should have complete control of Diaghilev's company during the next engagement.[151]

Diaghilev had two motives for agreeing to this: the dread of another even longer tour and the need for money. If Nijinsky was to rent Diaghilev's company, it would probably be Kahn who paid the rent. While the Ballet were in America, his money would keep Diaghilev and Massine alive in Europe – and not them only, for Diaghilev insisted on retaining a small group with him, so that Massine could evolve new works. Massine, Grigoriev, Tchernicheva, Woizikovsky and his girlfriend Antonova, Idzikovsky and his English girlfriend Evina, Maria Shabelska, Khokhlova and Novak were eventually chosen.[152] This was the happiest part of the scheme. Nijinsky, on his side, stipulated that Grigoriev should not accompany the Ballet.[153] This was the most unfortunate part of the scheme. Three men together – Barocchi, Trubecki and Kremnev were selected – were inadequate to take his place.

Meanwhile, Diaghilev had received an invitation from King Alfonso to present his Ballet in Madrid:[154] this was welcome as it provided work for the company in Europe and the prospect of a summer holiday there before they returned to the United States. Before the Ballet sailed on 6 May on an Italian ship, the *Dante Alighieri*, which was going to put in at Cadiz especially for them,[155] they heard that Lopukhova, having rejected Heywood Broun, was married to Barocchi. Besides the Nijinsky family, Flora Revalles, whom Otto Kahn admired, remained in New York, hoping to further her singing career.[156] Tchernicheva took on for Spain her roles in *Cléopâtre* and *Schéhérazade*. Even Diaghilev found the weather warm during the crossing, and slept on the bridge between Massine and Ansermet, who had constantly to reassure him that there was no danger. When he went ashore at last, he knelt down and kissed the earth of Spain.[157]

The Ballet had suffered no attack from submarines, but, after their safe arrival, the Spanish dock hands let fall the crate containing the scenery for *Thamar* into the sea, and the original décor of Bakst was ruined beyond repair.[158] The company travelled to Madrid, which they found surprisingly small,[159] and prepared to give their first performance at the Teatro Real ten days later.

Diaghilev made a quick dash for Paris.[160] This was a momentous visit.

Ever since his invention of the short-lived *Le Dieu bleu*, Cocteau had been longing to work on another ballet for Diaghilev. A project for a circus ballet called *David* had been turned down both by Diaghilev and by Stravinsky, whom Cocteau had visited at Leysin in January 1914 to talk about it. In late autumn 1915 Cocteau had been introduced by Edgar Varèse to Picasso,[161] who from then onwards he rightly classed with Stravinsky as one of the giants of the age. Picasso's Cubism, an entirely new way of rendering the visible world in paint (or collage or sculpture), invented in 1908, had been evolving and developing greater complexity ever since. Into the Cubist milieu Cocteau plunged whole-heartedly: it was a society on its own, concentrated in Montparnasse, where the artists met at the Dôme or the Rotonde, and on the Butte Montmartre, where Picasso lived from 1904 till 1909 in one of the studios of a ramshackle building known as the Bateau Lavoir. (Juan Gris still lived there in 1916.) The Cubists were a world apart from the Russian Ballet and its admirers; and Cocteau was to be the link between them. Moreover, on 18 October 1915 Valentine Gross had introduced Cocteau to Erik Satie,[162] whom Diaghilev had heard play at Misia's flat in summer 1914,[163] and Cocteau had pressed Satie into collaborating on a ballet which he hoped Diaghilev would stage.[164] Now, Picasso had never seen a Russian ballet: but in the third week of May 1916 the Chilean, Mme Errazuriz, patron of the Cubists, took Diaghilev to Picasso's studio (soon abandoned for another in Montrouge) in rue Schoelcher, overlooking the cemetery of Montparnasse,[165] and the two men met – the two worlds came together. Diaghilev never forgot the impression made by this encounter in the sinister milieu,[166] when he first beheld the thick-set little Spaniard with twinkling eyes among stacks of Cubist canvases. It would be three months before Picasso committed himself to joining Cocteau and Satie in the creation of what became *Parade*, but Diaghilev's meeting with the painter brought that project a step nearer to realization.

On 26 May (five days before the Battle of Jutland) the Russian Ballet opened in Madrid in the presence of King Alfonso, Queen Victoria Eugenia, their children and the Queen Mother, giving *Schéhérazade*, *Les Sylphides*, *Soleil de nuit* and *Carnaval*.[167] From that day onwards the King became their most faithful patron. He would refer to himself as 'Godfather to the Ballet'. 'Queen Ena was so lovely,' wrote Sokolova, 'that we used to take it in turns to peep at her round the drop curtain.'[168] Performances in Madrid began at ten in the evening,[169] but the Ballet did not dance every night, only eight times in a fortnight. The King and Queen were present at every performance, usually with the Queen Mother and other members of the Royal family. *La Epoca* devoted as much space to 'Los Bailes rusos' as to 'La Guerra', and regularly recorded the names of noble box-holders.[170] On the first night, besides the Prime Minister, Conde de Romanones, the American Ambassador and Mrs Willard, the British Ambassador and Lady

Hardinge and the Argentine Minister, several 'refugees' from belligerent countries were in the boxes – including Diaghilev's old acquaintance, the Marquise de Ganay. The presence of the last Russian Imperial Ambassador, Prince Alexander Kudashev, was not recorded, but Baroness Konrad Meyendorff, whose husband had been Second Secretary in Madrid since 1914, represented Russia.[171]

From the accounts of smart audiences at the Teatro Real, as well as from newspaper descriptions of the King attending a bullfight (with Belmonte) at Aranjuez on 29 May, when there was no ballet, of the Royal celebration of Ascension Day on 31 May, and of the two Queens' attendance at a party given by the Duquesa di Montellanos that afternoon, at which Artur Rubinstein played *Carnaval* and Stravinsky's *The Firebird* – after which the Royal guests, their hostess and the pianist went, as well as the King, to see the second performance in Madrid of *The Firebird* on stage[172] – one gets a picture of Spain as a serene paradise garden undisturbed by the baying of the dogs of war.

On the first occasion that Diaghilev, with his principal colleagues and dancers, were received at Court, King Alfonso asked him, 'Now, what do you do in the company? You don't conduct. You don't dance. You don't play the piano. What *do* you do?' Diaghilev replied, 'Your Majesty, I'm like you. I don't work, I do nothing, but I am indispensable.' When the King offered him a cigarette, Diaghilev, who had never smoked one in his life, puffed instead of inhaling, and blew out the King's match.[173] King Alfonso fell in love with Tchernicheva.[174]

Stravinsky had been summoned, and arrived in Madrid in time for the first performance of *Petrushka* on 6 June, which he did not conduct.[175] He was received at Court, and the Infanta Isabella, aunt of the King, said to him, 'I'm deaf. Come close, sit right up against me.... I love your *Petrushka*.' She then began to hum a tune like nothing Stravinsky had ever composed, but which Diaghilev thought he recognized as Gounod.[176] Mme Errazuriz was in Madrid,[177] and she made friends with Stravinsky, to whom she later gave an allowance.[178] Igor had a flirtation with Lydia Lopukhova.[179]

Diaghilev had never seen the Prado before, with all its treasury of Velazquez and Titian, or the Goya tapestries in the Royal Palace. Who could set eyes on the vast canvas of Velazquez, *Las Meninas*, without it being a landmark in his life? The immediate result of the impact of Spanish painting was an urge to produce a Spanish ballet. This would also be a gesture of gratitude for the patronage of King Alfonso.

On the day after the last night of the Madrid season on Friday, 9 June, at which *Petrushka* was given a second performance, Diaghilev telegraphed to Otto Kahn, hoping to impress him, 'Season ended yesterday admirably. Their Majesties attended every performance. Lopokova, Tchernicheva,

Bolm and Massine were introduced by me to the King, who spoke enthusiastically to them. He wants us to return next spring. Has twice received Stravinsky, asked him to compose Spanish ballet. His Majesty wants us to give a few gala performances at San Sebastian in August.'[180]

The company went on holiday. Diaghilev and Massine went to Sitges,[181] a fishing village near Barcelona, where Sert was planning decorations for a medieval hospital converted into a villa by Charles Deering, a Chicago millionaire. Diaghilev therefore had the pleasure of Misia's company that summer.[182] He also lost no time in sending for Gontcharova and Larionov from Paris.[183]

To what music should the new Spanish ballet be arranged? Should it be by Albéniz or Granados? A number of designs by Gontcharova labelled *Triana*, which implies Albéniz, and *Rapsodie Espagnole*, which implies Ravel, as well as many paintings of Spanish dancers, survive. There was the 'Spanish' music of Glinka (who had travelled to Spain in 1845) and of Rimsky-Korsakov. Perhaps Diaghilev thought that all the best Spanish music was written by French composers.[184] There were Lalo's *Symphonie espagnole*, Chabrier's *España*, Fauré's *Pavane*, Debussy's *Iberia* and Ravel's *Pavane pour une Infante défunte*. Diaghilev was 'stimulated', as Massine put it, 'by his first visit to Spain'. 'When he suggested that we should use Fauré's *Pavane*, with its haunting echoes of Spain's golden age, I immediately thought of the Velazquez paintings which I so much admired. Diaghilev approved . . . and commissioned Sert, himself the epitome of a Spanish grandee, to design the costumes.'[185]

Others might question Sert's right to this flattering description: apart from his bald head, his whole body was covered in black hair. (As Cocteau said, Misia had a taste for monsters—and he named her previous husband, the gross half-Turkish millionaire Edwards, and Diaghilev as two other examples.)[186] Nor would one think it was Sert's painting, a vulgarization of Goya and the Baroque, that appealed to Diaghilev so much as his being Misia's husband. However, he was Spanish (Catalonian) and, being rich, would presumably design five costumes, which were needed for the Spanish ballet, for nothing.

Something Spanish having been agreed on, it was natural that something Russian should be concocted. Diaghilev suggested that one of the *Fairy Tales* by his old teacher Liadov should be put to use.[187] 'Kikimora', whose score today sounds like a precursor of *The Firebird*, was chosen. This was about a hideous young witch who made her cat rock her cradle, then, in an outburst of rage, chopped off its head. Larionov was ordered to design a scene for this, which turned out to be a kind of Abramtsevo peasant interior in Cubist terms, with primitive costumes for the two dancers. Diaghilev also wanted to revive *Sadko*, but no one could remember Fokine's choreography, so Bolm was invited to work out a new version,[188] for which Gontcharova designed new costumes.

During the holiday, Grigoriev returned to Russia to fetch his young son. After a month's stay he found that, although he was exempted from military service, the authorities were unwilling to allow him to leave. Diaghilev had to intervene through the Minister of War.[189] It is surprising that his influence, at this stage of hostilities, should still have been effective.

The company reassembled at San Sebastian on the Basque coast in August, and the final touches were put to the Fauré ballet, which was named *Las Meninas* after the paintings of Velazquez. It was really only a court dance for two couples, but, to make it more interesting, a sinister spying dwarf was to be introduced – to a pizzicato cello which threads its way through the music.[190]

In a simple setting by the scene-painter Socrate, the little ballet had its first performance at the Teatro Eugenia-Victoria, San Sebastian, on 21 August. The two pairs of courtiers who performed the *pavane* were Sokolova and Massine, Khokhlova and Woizikovsky. The women wore immensely wide hoops which could not be got into the dressing-rooms and had to be put on in the wings; their wigs were twice the width of their shoulders. Sokolova wore purple and gold, Khokhlova salmon pink and silver. Sokolova loved dancing *Las Meninas*, although the costumes were 'so heavy that when you turned round you had to do it very carefully all in one piece'.[191] *Kikimora*, with Maria Shabelska as the witch and Idzikovsky as her cat, was given on the twenty-fifth, two days before Roumania declared war on Austria and Germany.

From San Sebastian the Russian Ballet moved to Bilbao, to give a gala performance when the King came to review the Spanish fleet. The principal dancers were taken to the Royal withdrawing-room in the interval, to be presented. King Alfonso, to make conversation, used to ask people where they came from – in Madrid he had said to Ansermet, 'It's easy to see by your beard that you are from Moscow!', only to receive the reply, 'Non, Majesté, je suis Suisse.'[192] In Bilbao Diaghilev warned Sokolova, 'Hilda, don't mention your nationality. I have just told the King all my artists are Russian.'

We went through several small rooms into a bigger reception room with a parquet floor. Tchernicheva ... went up first to be presented to the Queen; she was followed by Lopokova and her partner Idzikovsky. The rest of us were taken to the King. Everyone conversed with the Royal couple in French, but Diaghilev, no doubt thinking my French would give me away as being English, said to King Alfonso, 'You can speak to her in English,' which he did.... The King remarked 'But surely you are English?' ... I replied 'No, Your Majesty, I was brought from Russia at an early age and educated in England.' I knew he did not believe me.... I went on to be presented to the Queen, and while I was making my curtsey,

I saw to my horror the impression of Idzikovsky's red lips on her beautiful, long, white gloves. At the same moment I heard Lopokova saying to the King in a clear voice full of affection and enthusiasm, 'Yes, isn't she wonderful? She's the only English artist we have in the company.'...[193]

Stravinsky had again joined Diaghilev, and they saw together a Charlie Chaplin film. 'Chaplin was an event in my life,' wrote Igor, 'as he was in Diaghilev's.' In Massine's, too, he might have added.[194]

While the Ballet were in Spain, William Guard, the Press Officer of the Metropolitan, who had visited Diaghilev at Ouchy a year before, made the difficult journey to Russia and succeeded in persuading Olga Spessivtseva, the Mariinsky ballerina, and Margarita Frohman, who had been with Diaghilev before the war, to join the Ballet in America.[195]

On 8 September the Russian Ballet sailed on the *Lafayette* from Bordeaux for New York;[196] Diaghilev and Stravinsky saw them off. It was a stormy night,[197] and the dancers were less optimistic than on their last voyage out. They had a longer tour ahead to face, and neither Diaghilev nor Grigoriev would be with them. To be under the orders of Nijinsky was a new experience. Monteux, who had six months' leave from the French army in order to conduct for the Ballet, was to follow them a few days later.

During his summer holiday at Bar Harbour in Maine, Nijinsky had been working on two ballets, conceived when he was still in semi-captivity, to the scores of Strauss's *Till Eulenspiegel* and Liszt's *Mephisto Valse*.[198] These he intended to rehearse with the company and present in New York. In fact, only the former would see the light of Broadway, the sole work presented by his Russian Ballet that Diaghilev never set eyes on. It had a difficult delivery. In the absence of Diaghilev and Grigoriev everything seemed to go wrong.

The season was due to open, with *Till* on the programme, on 9 October, at Oscar Hammerstein's Manhattan Opera House (formerly called the Lexington Theatre) on 6th Avenue at 35th Street. When Monteux arrived on 26 September, he refused to conduct the Boche music of Strauss. An extra conductor, Anselm Goetzl, had therefore to be engaged.[199] The scenery designed by Robert Edmond Jones, a talented American painter whom Nijinsky had commissioned, did not fit the stage and had to be adapted.[200] On 3 October Nijinsky sprained his foot, and it was thought he would not be able to dance for 'some weeks'. The opening was postponed from the ninth to the sixteenth.[201] This dire step was bound to put the box-office in a turmoil. The Ballet's first night took place without Nijinsky: *Les Sylphides*, *Le Spectre*, *Schéhérazade* and the new *Sadko* were given.[202] There was a warm welcome for the company, and both Rimsky's music and Gontcharova's gold-encrusted, fishy costumes for *Sadko* were praised.

Following the scenario of Strauss, Nijinsky had taken the little phrase on the clarinet, which is like a mocking question-mark, as the *leitmotiv* of

Till, the medieval German Puck, and had involved his hero in a series of skirmishes with noble ladies, learned doctors and the law. He diverged from the composer's programme in treating the epilogue not as the people's recollection of the dead mischief-maker, but as a hint at his immunity from hanging, like the apparition of the dead Petrushka. Sokolova wrote that during the rehearsal period Nijinsky used to vanish unaccountably, to the despair of her friend Kremnev, the acting *régisseur*, and that the company had to work out the final section (the brief epilogue?) of the ballet without Nijinsky's detailed instructions.[203] She may have been right about this, but she failed to state that *Till Eulenspiegel* was a marked success with public and critics, and she was wrong in writing that it was rapidly dropped from the repertoire. After its first performance on 23 October, at which there were fifteen curtain calls,[204] it was repeated once more in New York and twenty times on tour.[205] H. T. Parker of Boston later wrote, 'It is the handiwork of an intellect, invention, and emotion that make Mr Nijinsky more than the master dancer of our time....'[206] Romola Nijinsky thought *Till* was her husband's best ballet.[207] On the twenty-fourth Nijinsky danced *L'Après-midi d'un faune* for the first time in America, with Flora Revalles as his chief Nymph, and Olga Spessivtseva made her American début in *Les Sylphides*.[208] On the twenty-eighth the New York season ended. On Monday, 30 October, the four months' tour began at Providence, Rhode Island. Barocchi, Trubecki or Kremnev telegraphed to Diaghilev or Grigoriev nearly every day.[209]

Much has been written about the disasters of the tour under Nijinsky, but, to judge from the Press, it was more successful than the previous shorter tour. Nijinsky's name was a big draw, of course, but his presence and his care as a producer must have had a beneficial effect on the company. In cities they had visited before, such as Boston, Minneapolis and Chicago (where they appeared briefly twice, on 28 January 1917 between visits to Milwaukee and Indianapolis, and on 15 February between Grand Rapids and Cleveland), they were thought greatly improved.[210] In cities they visited for the first time, such as Fort Worth, Texas,[211] and Denver, Colorado,[212] and on the West Coast, they were greeted with rapture. The orchestra was continually praised; and San Francisco was bowled over by the lighting.[213] Barocchi (whose beard was shaved off by mistake in Denver, while he slept),[214] Trubecki (who fell sick in Minneapolis on the return journey and went to New York)[215] and Kremnev, whom even Sokolova thought unfit for a position of authority, may have had their troubles with Nijinsky behind the scenes, but the only evidence the public had of these anxieties were some late starts and occasional changes in the order of programmes. Otto Kahn's bold venture brought the relevation of a new art-form to hundreds of thousands of Americans.

In September Diaghilev and Massine had motored with Sert and Misia, visiting Verona, Bologna, Padua and Venice, before establishing himself, with his group of dancers, in Rome.[216] He was always happiest in Italy. Massine, too, came to love everything Italian. After his daily class with Cecchetti in the little old Teatro Metastasio, he used to watch the craftsmen in the Via Margutta 'hammering and polishing as they laughed and shouted to each other'. He was fascinated by the traditional skill with which the wood-carvers reproduced baroque furniture, and he delighted in 'their gaiety, in their natural sense of style, and the expressiveness of their gestures, their wit and buffoonery'.[217] The walks of this observant young man would not be wasted. Diaghilev's headquarters were the Grand Hotel, and it was here, mostly, that he entertained: but he found it more economical to rent a furnished apartment on the Corso Umberto, and this was his home for the winter. At the Caffè Ariana, across the way, Diaghilev and Massine sat for hours with Mikhail Semenov, a former music critic in St Petersburg, 'reminiscing about Russia and discussing plans for new ballets'.[218]

Some rare old books on choreography came up for sale at an auction in Paris, and Diaghilev bought them for Massine. They included first editions of Carlo Blasis, Raoul Feuillet, Louis Pécour, Malpied and Jean-Philippe Rameau. 'At first,' wrote Massine, 'I found it almost impossible to decipher the intricate seventeenth- and eighteenth-century notations invented by these authors, but after some concentrated study I began to discover certain choreographic patterns which they had set down. . . . My introduction to those early authors came at a most opportune moment in my career. . . . I was anxious to forge ahead. . . .'[219]

On 25 August, in Paris, Picasso had agreed to join Cocteau and Satie in the creation of *Parade* for Diaghilev.[220] By 15 September the composer observed that the painter had begun to have ideas of his own which were at variance with those of the author.[221] On 7 October Paul Morand, the young diplomat, friend of Misia and Proust, who dined out in all the most interesting houses and was always the first to hear the latest news, recorded in his diary, which is so precious a record of Paris in 1916 and 1917, that Cocteau was working on a ballet with Satie and Picasso, 'which Diaghilev will give in Rome'.[222]

In November 1916, while his Ballet danced in New England,[223] then headed south,[224] Diaghilev burrowed in Roman libraries for old music. He suggested to Massine that he should make a ballet out of Goldoni's comedy *Le Donne di buon'umore*, and Massine decided to put into practice the dance techniques he had studied in his old choreographic manuals.[225] Diaghilev could have adapted music from the operas of Paisiello, Pergolesi or Cimarosa, but he was understandably drawn to the younger Scarlatti. Undeterred by the fact that Domenico Scarlatti wrote almost exclusively for the harpsichord, he hired a pianist to play through the approximately five hundred sonatas. Massine and he took their time and made their choice;

and the young Roman composer, Vincenzo Tommasini, was asked to orchestrate the twenty which were chosen. With Massine, the working out of this ballet was a laborious intellectual process. He decided to give his characters 'broken, angular movements for the upper part of the body while the lower limbs continued to move in the usual academic style'. Because of the difficulty of containing the typical complicated plot, with its 'use of masks, flirtations, deceptions and disguises', in one act, Massine attempted 'to balance the action simultaneously on both sides of the stage'. Although this 'worked well in the supper-party scene', there was obviously a difficulty in having two different actions going on to the same music. Diaghilev made Massine study Guardi, Longhi and other Venetian painters, to get the feel of eighteenth-century behaviour, but it was to Watteau's 'Fêtes galantes' that the choreographer looked for the 'languorous gestures of the women, their delicate hand movements, and the ineffable sadness of their backward glances'. The languor and sadness were most in evidence in Costanza's solo (which would be for Tchernicheva) to the only slow sonata used (Longo, Vol. I, No. 33) to make a contrast. Massine gave the waiter (Woizikovsky) the 'floppy loose-jointed movements' of the puppets he had seen at Viareggio in 1914.[226]

In December[227] Bakst, who had been invited to design the Italian ballet, left a Paris which was becoming increasingly conscious of Cubism to arrive in a Rome where Futurism, in the person of Giacomo Balla, was still alive. The Milanese Marinetti, the chief propagandist of the movement, which attacked society, tradition and academies, and sought inspiration in contemporary life, machines and speed, had welcomed the war and was serving in the army. He would be seriously wounded in 1917. The most vigorous Futurist painter and sculptor, Umberto Boccioni, had died from a fall during military manoeuvres in summer 1916. Both Carrà and Severini (who lived in Paris and was married to the daughter of the poet Paul Fort) made war paintings. Balla had painted his flamboyant *Flag on the altar of the fatherland* in 1915 and was the mentor of a new generation of Futurists and a friend of Diaghilev's.

Bakst was anxious not to be left out of these new movements, whose principles he hardly grasped and whose methods of painting it was hopeless for him to imitate. His designs for the Italian ballet's rich eighteenth-century costumes, sharp yellow or glowing crimson, covered in ruched ribbon or gold embroidery, were drawn in an exaggerated, angular and grotesque manner, which Massine's talk of puppets must have suggested. (This did not, however, affect the way in which they were made up.) When it came to designing the setting Diaghilev had asked for – a small Venetian *piazza*, or *campo*, with a bell-tower – Bakst had the idea of painting it as if reflected in a concave mirror, so that all the buildings curved inward. The consequent distortion and blurring seem to have been an attempt to emulate the dynamism of the Futurists – a mistaken attempt, as Diaghilev soon decided, for what has architecture to do with speed?[228]

In December 1916 Lloyd George became Prime Minister of Great Britain in succession to Asquith and a small War Cabinet was formed which led to a more effective prosecution of the war. Briand remained in power in France, but Joffre was retired, Lyautey made War Minister and Nivelle given command of the armies on French soil. The aged Austrian Emperor Franz Josef had died in November, and his young successor Karl was anxious for peace. Food was beginning to get short in Germany. A million Russian soldiers were absent without leave, living unmolested in their homes. On 4 December in Paris a Borodin quartet was played at Princesse Edmond de Polignac's.[229] On the twenty-seventh, in Paris, Misia, Cocteau and Paul Morand looked in at a music-hall performance at the Alhambra, at which a fight between the champion of the Californian orange-packers and the champion of the crate-makers was announced by a manager with a megaphone. Misia commented, 'The invasion of American style has begun.'[230] On 30 December Rasputin was assassinated by the Tsar's nephew, Grand Duke Dmitri, and Prince Yusupov.

Having danced their way from Texas, through Oklahoma, Missouri, Iowa, Nebraska, Colorado and Utah, the Russian Ballet arrived from the cold of the Rocky Mountains in the sunshine of California.[231] They performed on Christmas Day in Los Angeles, and remained there until New Year's Eve, when they moved to San Francisco. Charlie Chaplin came to see the ballet, and some of the dancers visited him on the set in Hollywood.[232] In California Nijinsky had his first flight in an aeroplane,[233] and Sokolova found she was pregnant.[234]

Massine had been able to work out his entire ballet *Le Donne di buon'umore* with the dancers who were in Rome, most of whom would play the principal parts in it: only Lopukhova, destined for the *soubrette* role of Mariuccia, was missing. Diaghilev next proposed that Massine should use more of Liadov's music to add further episodes to the short ballet (*Kikimora*) he had arranged in Spain.[235]

The resulting work, *Contes russes*, was arranged as follows. There was a short prologue in which a Street Vendor hawked his puppets – the characters who would be seen enlarged in the ballet. Next came the scene of Kikimora killing her cat. In the central episode the Swan Princess was rescued from the three-headed dragon by the knight Bova Korolevitch. An interlude was filled by the dragon's funeral, at the end of which a couple performed a number called 'I danced with a mosquito.' The final story was of a little girl lost in a forest and attacked by the witch Baba Yaga, with her three attendant demons, whom the girl vanquished by making the sign of the cross. All the characters danced a *khorovod* in the busy finale.[236]

There was trouble about the knight's steed. Although Larionov had designed vivid sets and amazing make-ups for the ballet, it was to young Fortunato Depero, a follower of Balla, that Diaghilev turned for a non-realistic but workable sculpted horse. Massine wrote, 'Eventually we were summoned to his studio on the outskirts of Rome. As we walked into the room the artist pointed proudly at his construction – a bulbous outsized elephant! We stood staring at it silently for a few moments until Diaghilev, in a sudden outburst of rage, smashed the papier-maché animal with his walking-stick.'[237]

In January 1917 Diaghilev went to Paris. He arranged a three weeks' season to take place in May, and he came to terms with Picasso, Cocteau and Satie, thus making sure that he would be able to give *Parade* in Paris, as well as his new Italian ballet and *Contes russes*. On 11 January Picasso wrote him a letter to serve as contract:

Confirming our verbal agreement, I accept to undertake the production (sets, curtains, costumes and properties) of the ballet 'PARADE' by Jean Cocteau and Erik Satie.

I will make all the necessary designs and models and I will personally supervise all the work of carrying them out.

All the designs will be ready by 15 March, 1917.

For this work you are to pay me the sum of five thousand francs, and if I have to go to Rome, a thousand francs extra. The drawings and models remain my property.

Half the sum named must be paid me on delivery of the designs and models, and the other half on the day of the first performance.[238]

The terms agreed in the letter written by Cocteau for himself and Satie on the following day were more complicated. The piano score was to be delivered on 1 February, the orchestral score on 1 April 1917.[239]

On the way back to Italy Diaghilev visited Stravinsky at Morges.[240] In January 1916, a few days after Diaghilev and the Ballet had sailed from New York, Stravinsky had solicited or been given a commission by Princesse Edmond de Polignac. The Princess had the idea that 'after Richard Wagner and Richard Strauss the days of big orchestras were over', and she planned to commission from different composers works for a small orchestra[241] – which could be performed in the music-room of her house at the corner of the Avenue Henri Martin and the rue Cortambert. The work Stravinsky undertook to write for her became *Renard*.[242] Diaghilev was very jealous of this, and, during the summer of 1916, Ansermet's letters from Spain to Stravinsky had reported Diaghilev's recriminations.[243] Now Diaghilev asked Stravinsky to make a version of his opera *Le Rossignol*, without singing, which could be used as a ballet. Stravinsky had long been unhappy about the difference in idiom between the music of the first act and that of the second and third, written years later, and he admitted that he had been thinking of 'making a symphonic poem for orchestra by combining the music of Acts II and III'. Diaghilev 'warmly welcomed the suggestion'.[244] *Les Noces* was still not finished, but the 'short score' would be completed at Morges in April.[245]

In Milan Diaghilev signed a contract for the Russian Ballet to appear, with Nijinsky, in South America in the late summer. He then returned to Rome, where he commissioned Depero to design a set for the ballet which was to be called *Le Chant du rossignol*. The model for this 'fantastic garden scene' was later destroyed by an unpaid landlady.[246]

During January the Russian Ballet crossed the Canadian border to dance in Vancouver, British Columbia, before appearing in Seattle, Tacoma and Spokane, Washington (where Bing Crosby was growing up), and heading east (via Buffalo, Montana) for Minneapolis.[247] During the tour Romola Nijinsky had noticed increasingly that her husband was under the influence of two male dancers, Kostrovsky and Zverev, who were disciples of Tolstoy.[248] Vaslav became a vegetarian and took to wearing a Russian peasant shirt. He also began to distribute the principal roles among the corps de ballet in a democratic manner. Thus the Russian Revolution was foreshadowed in the microcosm of the Russian Ballet. Gavrilov had for long alternated with Nijinsky in *Le Spectre*. Now Zverev danced it – sometimes, he claimed, under Nijinsky's name,[249] but in Pittsburgh, at least, under his own.[250] Both Sokolova and Vera Nemtchinova were given their chance as Nijinsky's partner.[251] Vera Nemtchinova was the girlfriend of Zverev, but Romola thought that both she and Kostrovsky's quiet little wife were neglected by their menfolk for Vaslav, while she, Vaslav's wife, had to sit silent, listening to hour-long Tolstoyan sermons in Russian.[252] When the Ballet reached Chicago on 28 January, she rebelled and went back to New York, where she had left her daughter in the care of friends.[253] The company swooped south through Indiana, Missouri, Tennessee and Kentucky, back to the great cities of Cincinnati, Detroit, Toledo, Cleveland and Pittsburgh – having a free Sunday to visit Niagara Falls on the eighteenth – and so, via Syracuse and Albany, to New York.[254] At the Diaghilev Ballet's last performance in the United States, in the Harmanus Bleecker Hall, Albany, on Saturday, 24 February 1917, Flore Revalles danced Cleopatra, with Gavrilov as Amoun, Sokolova as Ta-Hor and Zverev in Nijinsky's old part of the queen's Favourite Slave; Nijinsky and Lopukhova performed *La Princesse enchantée*; and, in *Schéhérazade*, Revalles had Zverev as her Negro, while Nijinsky played the Chief Eunuch.[255]

Picasso and Cocteau had left Paris to join Diaghilev in Rome on 17 February.[256] It was to be a historic excursion. Bakst was already there and both Stravinsky and Ansermet would soon join the little circle centred round Diaghilev and Massine in the Corso Umberto. Picasso stayed at the Hôtel de Russie in the Via Babuino,[257] and rented a studio in the Via Margutta, the old artists' quarter, with a window looking towards the Villa Medici,[258] where Ingres had presided over the French Institute. Massine gave Cocteau a vellum-bound notebook in which the author of *Parade* jotted down his thoughts for the ballet.[259]

A *parade* was the sample given outside a fairground booth of the entertainment to be seen within. The scene was a suburban street in Paris. A Chinese conjuror, a precocious little American Girl and an Acrobat would perform extracts from their turns, to lure the public inside. Satie's music was what Ansermet called 'learned popular music'.[260] There were satire and a hint of mystery behind its easy tunes. Cocteau's intention of implying hidden depths to his popular entertainers, so that the spectator might feel 'the Chinaman was capable of torturing missionaries, the little girl of being drowned on the *Titanic*, and the acrobat of communing with the stars',[261] was thwarted by Picasso's insistence on a more superficial *divertissement*. Cocteau had asked Satie to introduce real noises from everyday life – typewriters, pistol shots and ships' sirens – in his score; and these became an integral part of it. Between the three numbers Cocteau wanted an amplifier – the modern equivalent of a classical tragic mask – to spout publicity in the form of gibberish: 'Come up and see the truth about America, the earthquakes, the short-circuits, the Hudson detectives, Ragtime, factories, derailed trains and sinking steamers! A moment's hesitation and you're lost!'[262] This was replaced at Picasso's suggestion by three stamping Managers who would announce the acts in dumb-show.[263]

In later years Ansermet recalled the 'dazzling lunch-parties' when Stravinsky, Cocteau, Bakst and Picasso sat round Diaghilev's table, and 'Cocteau's wit bubbled over for hours on end.'[264] One afternoon Diaghilev noticed Picasso studying a conventional eighteenth-century court painting which hung over the sofa in his flat, and asked, 'Why are you so fascinated by that picture, Pablo?' 'I am studying it carefully,' replied Picasso, 'in order to learn how not to paint.'[265] Then there were the rehearsals in a studio in the Piazza Venezia, where Picasso drew groups of dancers, the walks and the explorations of Rome. Picasso drew Diaghilev, Bakst and Massine seated on chairs in a park (perhaps the Borghese Gardens), and on Easter Sunday he drew Cocteau, seated, in a dressing-gown, holding a book.[266] And Cocteau never forgot Picasso's studio, where 'the model of the set for *Parade*, with its buildings, trees and booth, was in a small box, while Picasso painted the Chinaman, the Managers, the American Girl and the horse on a table facing the Villa Medici'.[267]

About the end of the first week in March Diaghilev dispatched Grigoriev to Spain to meet the Ballet.[268] Meanwhile he took Stravinsky, Picasso, Cocteau and Massine to Naples for a few days' sight-seeing. Picasso drew Massine in the train.[269]

The friends explored Herculaneum and Pompeii.

Picasso was thrilled by the majestic ruins [wrote Massine], and climbed endlessly over broken columns to stand staring at fragments of Roman statuary. Diaghilev was somewhat less enthusiastic. He had seen it all before, and the long afternoons in the hot sun exhausted him. But Cocteau thoroughly enjoyed it all. He brought a camera and took a number of photographs of us all leaning against statues and broken blocks of marble.

On 8 March, in Petrograd, the bakers' shops had been broken into by hungry crowds. Three days later, when the huge city garrison were ordered to clear the streets, soldiers of the Guards' Regiments abandoned their officers to join the people. On 12 March the Winter Palace was invaded and the Fortress of St Peter and St Paul, the Russian Bastille, where so many political prisoners had languished and died, fell to the rebellious crowd. The Duma refused to be prorogued. On 15 March the Tsar abdicated.

A few days later, in Paris, Mme de Chevigné, the close friend of Grand Duchess Vladimir, had a dinner-party, at which her son-in-law, the Belgian Jew Franz Wiener, who had adopted the name of Francis de Croisset, teased her, saying that the Grand Duchess would be sure to arrive penniless in Paris and would have to be put up, waited on and provided for for the rest of her life. A few moments after Croisset had said goodnight, pretending to be leaving, the butler entered to announce, 'Her Imperial Highness, the Grand Duchess Vladimir!'[270]

Back in Rome in mid-March, Diaghilev was cabling Grigoriev in Madrid, trying to arrange a Spanish season. With the increasing menace of German U-boats, shipping was naturally a danger as well as a difficulty, and Trubecki had warned him that the scenery could only arrive at the end of March.[271] Diaghilev left for Monte Carlo in search of bookings, and was in Paris at the Hôtel Edouard VII at least from 20 to 24 March.[272] He turned down the offer of a Spanish manager[273] and was back in Rome when the company arrived about the last week in March.[274] They had travelled nearly half-way round the world since Christmas. America was to declare war on Germany on 6 April.

Roman sculpture, the frescoes of Pompeii, Michelangelo and the neo-classical Ingres fused in Picasso's mind to produce, a few years later, a new 'period' in his development. There was another influence. Although he wrote to Gertrude Stein at the beginning of April, 'I go to bed very late. I know all the ladies of Rome. I have done many rather naughty and fantastic things in a Pompeiian manner, as well as caricatures of Diaghilev, Bakst, Massine and some of the dancers',[275] there was one lady in particular with whom he had fallen in love. The oval-faced, auburn-haired Olga Khokhlova, one of the group who had been working under Massine, was a colonel's daughter, better born and educated than most of her colleagues. She was also virtuous. Ansermet and the dancers were staying at the Hotel Minerva, looking out on Bernini's obelisk-bearing elephant, and the church containing

Michelangelo's *Christ the Redeemer*. 'Picasso took the opportunity,' wrote Ansermet, 'of seeing me back to my hotel, then, after a few moments, went out, saying "I'm going to see Olga." I heard Picasso in the passage knocking at her door, and Olga on the other side of it saying, "No, no, Monsieur Picasso, I'm not going to let you in." '[276]

It was even more surprising that Cocteau should step out of character to have a flirtation with Maria Shabelska, the lively, intelligent dancer who was to embody his Little American Girl in *Parade*. They went for walks together in Rome and he made drawings of her in the notebook Massine had given him.[277] Maria was one of the only three women he loved a little. Madeleine Carlier (the heroine of his book *Le Grand Ecart*), who had been at the first night of the Russian season in 1909, and Natalie Paley were the others.[278]

Nijinsky and Romola had remained in Spain. This was presumably because one of the conditions of Nijinsky's parole was that he should not dance in any of the Allied countries. Although Diaghilev must have known this, it appears that he still hoped Nijinsky might have been persuaded to come with the company to Italy, for in one of his telegrams to Grigoriev in Madrid he wrote, 'Participation Nijinsky Italy and Paris desirable.'[279]

One of Diaghilev's first problems after greeting his troupe was to cope with Sokolova's pregnancy. He advised her to have an abortion. She had been knitting baby clothes all the way back on the boat, and she refused. 'He gave in gracefully and said, "Very well, we must get you married as soon as possible. Your parents will be horrified." ' She then had to break the news that Kremnev was married already to a gypsy. In Russia, however, the law allowed divorce if a husband and wife had not seen each other for three years, which was the case with the Kremnevs. The Russian Ambassador, M. de Giers, was helpful and drew up a contract.[280]

Diaghilev arranged a few performances at the Teatro Costanzi of which the first was to be on 9 April. Lopukhova learned her role of Mariuccia in *Le Donne di buon 'umore*, and the two groups worked again together under Cecchetti.

While the Russians in Rome were in doubt about their position with regard to their country's new régime, the world at large was wondering whether Russia would continue to prosecute the war. Diaghilev had always been a liberal, and he had suffered under the autocracy. Was a new golden age, such as the Decembrists had died for and so many writers from Pushkin to Tchekhov had dreamed of, about to dawn? Rodzianko, President of the last Duma, headed a list of signatories, which included Benois, Bilibine, Steletsky and Gorky, to a telegram asking Diaghilev to return to Russia as Minister of the Fine Arts.[281] He hesitated. The lawyer Kerensky, who had become head of the Russian state, held the Tsar and his family in custody at Tsarskoe Selo. It was expected that they would seek refuge in England.

In the meantime, it was clear to Diaghilev that the old Tsarist hymn could not be played, along with the Italian National Anthem, at the opening night in Rome. What should take its place? Out of a thousand Russian songs that Diaghilev and Stravinsky could think of, which was most representative of the toiling masses and deserved to become Russia's *Marseillaise*? They picked on one which was not yet famous – though familiar in Italy, as Giordano had introduced it into the second act of his opera *Siberia* – the melancholy dirge of the Volga Boatmen. Stravinsky sat up all night to orchestrate it.[282] On 10 April, the day after the Roman opening, Misia, in Paris, who had seen Diaghilev two or three weeks before and had perhaps heard from him since, reported news that filled her with hope – though she got muddled over the details. Morand described her excitement as she sat in bed (she had a cold) amid lace and pink cushions.

Misia speaks with enthusiasm of the Russian revolution, which she sees as a vast ballet. She says that Bakst finds his brother-in-law is Minister of War. Diaghilev is related to Rodzianko, who has telegraphed to him in Rome, offering him the Fine Arts. All the group headed by Gorky, Argutinsky, Benois, Bakst, are coming into power. In Rome Stravinsky has been commissioned to write the National Anthem on the theme of the 'Song of the Volga Boatmen'.[283]

The remote connections of Bakst and Diaghilev with members of the new government were not to prove of much use to them. Alexander Gutchkov, formerly President of the Third Duma and for the first two months of Kerensky's government Minister of War, had married a sister of Alexander Ziloti, whose wife, like Bakst's ex-wife, was a daughter of P.M.Tretiakov, founder of the Museum: but he was forced out of office at the end of April. The wife of Rodzianko's elder brother Paul was a Princess Galitzin, who had been divorced by a Khitrovo, related to Diaghilev on his mother's side. Kerensky, despite his talent for oratory, only held on to power by making concessions to the Soviet party extremists, and in November he would be swept away.

The first charity gala at the Costanzi was attended by the cream of Roman society – also by the spectacular Marchesa Casati and by Colette.[284] On Wednesday the eleventh Stravinsky conducted an afternoon concert of his work, during which pictures from Massine's collection, by Picasso, Braque, Balla, Carrà, Depero and Gontcharova, were exhibited in the foyer.[285] The second gala took place on the following day.[286] So great was the Ballet's success that an additional performance at popular prices was given on the Sunday afternoon.[287] While Stravinsky's new hymn was being played that Sunday, 15 April, Lenin, after ten years' exile in Switzerland, was travelling in a sealed train through Germany. The Germans were sending him home to further a more extreme form of revolution, which they rightly reckoned would remove Russia from the war. He arrived in Petrograd – soon to bear his name – on Monday, 16 April.

We have seen how Diaghilev, before the war, had commissioned paintings to 'accompany' musical scores. Benois' front-curtain for *Petrushka* also served as an act-drop. In 1911 (not in 1910) the audience were given Serov's 'Persian miniature' curtain to look at during the long 'overture' of *Schéhérazade*. But the *Battle of Kerjenetz* of Rimsky, played as a symphonic interlude, had had a painted curtain by Roerich all to itself. In 1917, for his Roman performances, Diaghilev went further and staged with Giacomo Balla the first 'happening', to accompany Stravinsky's short early composition, *Feu d'artifice*. In March 1915 Balla had issued with the twenty-three-year-old Depero a manifesto entitled *The Futuristic Reconstruction of the Universe*. After painting a number of pictures suggesting 'the speed of automobiles' and the 'essential laws and lines of their force', he had found the painted canvas inadequate, and created abstract 'reconstructions' in various materials, which even made noises. For *Feu d'artifice*, Balla built a composition of jagged and curved shapes, surmounted by a stylized flower or Catherine-wheel, and lit both from without and within. There were fifty lighting cues, worked out by Balla and Diaghilev. The colouring was as violent as that of Pop Art in the 1960s, mainly scarlet and emerald green. Whether this glowing, flashing object was a help or a hindrance to the appreciation of Stravinsky's vertiginous little piece, it was the sort of adventure that made Diaghilev feel the opposite of stagnant.[288]

The Scarlatti ballet, first called by the Italian name of Goldoni's play, but better known later as *Les Femmes de bonne humeur* and *The Good-humoured Ladies*, was a hit with the Romans, as it would be in France and England. Prepared at leisure, it was the most meticulously thought-out of ballets. Apart from *Carnaval*, Fokine had never made a comedy of manners, and Nijinsky's *Jeux* could only just squeeze into that genre. Massine's comedy was something new for the Russian Ballet; new, too, in being neither Russian nor Oriental. It was as perfectly cast as any Fokine ballet had ever been. By some fortunate alchemy, Diaghilev had made Miassin into Massine, transformed a scratched-up company into a team of ideal interpreters, chosen the right subject for the right moment – why a Goldoni comedy with music by Scarlatti should have been just right in spring 1917 we cannot guess, but it was – and even presented it in the right country. It is hard to say whether the flickering movement of Massine's carefree, superficial characters was a conscious reflection of the early cinema. Today Scarlatti is sacred, and the cult of ancient instruments has been much evolved since 1917. To clog and retard the master's sonatas by orchestration seems as irreverent to us as Diaghilev's former manipulation of Chopin to make *Les Sylphides*: for what dancer could keep time to the original sparkling tempo of the harpsichord? Nobody worried about this, however, at the time. Diaghilev felt that Bakst's distorted décor was the only unsatisfactory element.

After the performances in Rome five more were planned for Naples. Bakst and Cocteau returned to Paris after the Roman season, but Picasso remained behind.[289] The Russians and Poles saw for the first time the blue bay, Vesuvius and the islands; as did the pregnant English Sokolova, who thought Naples stank of 'garlic, Macedonia cigarettes, olive oil which had been cooked in several times over, and inadequate sanitation'.[290]

The Teatro di San Carlo was 'opened up' for the first time in years to receive the Russians, but the Neapolitan aristocracy and the critics (perhaps wishing to know better than Rome, as Chicago had at first reversed the verdict of New York) could find nothing to admire in the Ballet. *Il Giorno* judged Stravinsky's 'hymn' funereal, *Las Meninas* a bad joke, *Soleil de nuit* a piece of madness, and thought *The Good-humoured Ladies* must have resulted in some 'ill-humoured gentlemen', one at least being the man who initiated the work, and who probably wished he had had second thoughts.[291] The last three performances were cancelled.

Massine went on alone to stay with Mikhail Semenov and his wife at Positano in its sheltered cove to the south of the Sorrento peninsula. Diaghilev called Positano 'the only vertical village he had ever seen'. Out at sea Massine saw the jagged rocks, I Galli, reputed to be the Siren Islands of Ulysses. He was rowed out to visit them, and at once coveted them as a romantic home.[292] He later bought them, and the passion to cultivate and build on their reluctant soil became a driving force in his life, the spur to herculean labours for over half a century to come.

On Friday, 11 May, the Russian Ballet began its only wartime season in Paris (apart from the one gala in December 1915) with a *répétition générale* at four in the afternoon. Once more they were at the Châtelet. Morand described the scene.

What a step back into the past! A crowd in the square [Place du Châtelet] – cars, bustle, excitement. Sert, of course, at the door ... Misia, dressed to kill, in a silver tiara, chatting with Mme de Chabrillan [Vice-president of the French Red Cross]. Emotional atmosphere. This very morning a little blackmailing newspaper launched an attack on the performance.... A packed house.... At 4 the Marseillaise, followed by a sad song which nobody knows, and which turns out to be the Song of the Volga Boatmen, the new Russian National Anthem recently composed by Stravinsky in Rome. Protests from [Etienne de] Beaumont [just back from Russia], who says it is a fake which no one in Petrograd has ever thought of using....

L'Oiseau de feu begins.... Alas, from the moment he jumps over the wall Massine's performance makes one regret Nijinsky. At the end, when he smashes the egg, symbol of the old grey and gold sorcerer's evil power, someone says 'It's the break-up of the old régime.' For the first time in France we see a vast red flag borne by a moujik in red. The audience mutters. Little applause, but no booing.

The lights go up. Marigny, annoyed, grumbles 'they dance, but they don't march.'... [A reference to the new Russia's separate peace.] Mme de Chabrillan very nervous, looking to right and left.

Uproar in the corridors. The whole of Montparnasse in flannel, with shorn heads, and blue and black nails. Mme Errazuriz dressed as a Spanish nun, Maurice Rostand, Princess de Polignac, Valentine Gross, ... Drian, ... Bakst, etc. ... Then *Les Femmes de bonne humeur* of Goldoni. Delightful Scarlatti music. Décor by Bakst – a Venice seen as if distorted in a glass paper-weight. Violent colour-scheme – plaster and zinc – dazzling white lighting from the side at floor level, bulging houses, a stormy sky. Within this frame the maddest comic ballet, in costumes sparkling with gold and silver, absurd colours, orange velvet, chalk-white stockings, pink feathers. At the Opéra they perform Italian slapstick so wretchedly that the jerkiness of these puppets is a joy....

Its oddity makes the ballet a great success. A Mme Bauvillat is dressed as an Inca priestess with slicked-down black hair, outlined eyes and a dress of coarse material cut all in one piece. Poiret's sister, Mme Groult [wife of the great collector], looking like the Vatican Heliogabalus.

The third ballet was four Russian fairy-tales in a cubist décor; rather overdone. Finally the Polovtsian Dances from *Igor*. We come out at 8.[293]

Léon Bailby voiced conservative opinion in a letter of protest to Diaghilev about the red flag.

A considerable portion of French society, in the person of the upper classes, were disagreeably impressed at yesterday's matinée by an exhibition which at best they deemed pointless.... The people who yesterday scrupulously refrained from protesting, in order to avoid any disturbance which might have involved those respected figures [Mme de Chabrillan] under whose patronage the performance was given, are of a mind, when the production is public and commercial, to express their feelings with the utmost clarity, should the red flag again appear on the stage....[294]

Diaghilev's reply, in a letter to *Le Figaro*, was specious and fantastic.

Some people have written to me after the première of the Ballets Russes, asking what was meant by the red flag at the end of *L'Oiseau de feu*.

In Russia today the red flag is the emblem of those who recognize that the well-being of the world depends on the freedom of its people, which can only be ensured by a fight to the finish.

Pacifist revolutionaries sport the black flag....[295]

Diaghilev knew that what the French dreaded more than a Communist Russia was that its rulers would make a separate peace. The black flag was a pure invention.

On the afternoon of Friday, 18 May, *Parade* was shown to Paris at last. Cocteau had wanted something mysterious and eternal to shine through an episode of everyday life. Picasso had been willing to settle for an amusing but commonplace entertainment, transmuted, as might be a guitar or a coffee-pot standing on a newspaper, by the Cubist eye. Satie had written tunes of 'today', with hints of ragtime and satire, which could only be French, but which owed nothing to Debussy. Diaghilev had wanted to show that the Russian Ballet was capable of taking new turnings. All were to some degree successful. Even if the resulting ballet was rather light-weight after all the *Sturm und Drang* attendant upon its birth – and the big front curtain of Picasso would have been appropriate for something more portentous – it opened the gates of the twenties, during which Diaghilev's company would be identified not only with the painters of the School of Paris, but with a group of young composers who revered Satie and were to be known as 'Les Six'.

Picasso's curtain, in a naïve but old-fashioned style, like the decoration of a nineteenth-century fairground, gave no hint of the Cubist novelties its rising would reveal. Framed in crimson draperies, with foliage, ruined architecture and a distant view of Vesuvius – all of which might be intended as stage scenery – seven fantastic figures were grouped round a table on the right: a torero, a harlequin, a priest, a turbaned Negro, a sailor and two girls. To the left, a Sylphide-equestrienne, poised on the back of a winged white Pegasus with feeding foal, reclaimed a monkey from a ladder striped like a barber's pole in red, white and blue. Curtains painted on a curtain, a scene depicting stacked scenery, was the same kind of poetic joke as Benois' stage-within-a-stage-within-a-stage in *Petrushka*, of which Picasso knew nothing. The *forains* were clearly picnicking on stage, for Picasso had painted its boards, on which there lay a big blue ball adorned with white stars – foretelling the costumes of the Acrobats – and a dog curled in sleep beside a silent drum. But the meadow beyond, which gave to this picture, already comparable, because of the loving girls, to Renoir's *Déjeuner des canotiers*, an outdoor atmosphere like that of Manet's *Déjeuner sur l'herbe* – was it composed of real grass or of the artificial grass mats used in the theatre? Either way, it was on this pasture that Pegasus, symbol of the divine heights attainable by even the humblest entertainers, must graze.

The setting for the action was a Cubist streetscape. The elements – characterless *immeubles* typical of the outer *arrondissements* of Paris, trees, an improvised booth conventionally painted with a lyre and barley-sugar columns, and its flanking balustrades – were all shuffled together in such wise as to make hay with perspective. Some were even reversed, seen, as it were, from the back or in negative, so that the windows of the building at the top centre appeared lit up as if by night, while those on either side were black rectangles in a sunlit wall. The colours were traditional Cubist ochres and greys, with some dull green in the trees.

Massine's scarlet, yellow and black Chinese Conjuror's costume (later used as a device on posters of the Ballet), the blazer, pleated skirt and bow of Shabelska's Little American Girl (bought the day before at Williams, the fashionable sports shop) and the sky-blue and white leotards of Lopukhova and Zverev as the Acrobats – all caused astonishment, but none more than the towering Cubist structures worn by the stamping managers, which were three-dimensional sculptures incorporating portraits of two men, two cities – almost two civilizations. The French Manager, with his top-hat, starched shirt-front, pipe and stick, carried a background of Paris chestnut-trees around with him. The American Manager, a robot crowned with a stove-pipe hat like a ship's funnel and with flags, had the skyscrapers of Manhattan on his shoulders, wore a red-pleated shirt-front and the cowboy chaps of Buffalo Bill, and he carried the megaphone Cocteau had seen at the music-hall in December.[296] The third Manager had been intended to be a Negro on horseback, the horse being two men in a canvas skin. At the final rehearsal the dummy Negro kept falling off the 'horse' and was abolished.[297] Chance – even mishaps – played a part in the evolution of this ballet.

Massine's act consisted in swallowing an egg, retrieving it from his foot, breathing fire, and walking in a jerky manner round the stage. Shabelska imitated Charlie Chaplin, had adventures typical of early films like *The Perils of Pauline* – jumped on a moving train, swam a river, had a pistol fight, was drowned at sea – and ended up playing in the sand at the seaside.[298] Zverev and Lopukhova executed *pirouettes* and *arabesques* and pretended to be walking the tightrope. The finale was 'a rapid, ragtime dance in which the whole cast made a last desperate attempt to lure the audience in to see their show....'[299]

The uproar that greeted *Parade* has been greatly exaggerated. Cocteau heard a lady saying, 'If I had known it would be like this I should have brought the children;'[300] and he told me that the noise was so great that 'Diaghilev, who was behind the scenes, thought the chandelier had fallen.'[301] Certain adverse critics equated 'Cubism' with the atrocities of the 'sales Boches', which made Cocteau overreach himself by proclaiming his ballet as 'the greatest battle of the war'.[302] We have Paul Morand's account of the *première*, ignored by art historians:

A full house yesterday at the Châtelet for *Parade*. Canvas scenery [that is, not constructed] in circus style by Picasso; pretty music by Satie, partly Rimsky, partly *bal musette*. The Managers, cubist constructions, were surprising. The Little American Girl and the acrobatic dancers had charming costumes. Massine too, as the Chinese juggler. But Cocteau's idea of replacing the stereotyped movements of ballet with fragments of everyday behaviour, and his stylized modern actions – starting up a motor-car, taking a photograph, etc – did not seem quite worked out. Much applause and a few whistles.[303]

Guillaume Apollinaire had written the programme note, prophesying that '*Parade* will upset the ideas of many people.... They are sure to be surprised, but in the most agreeable way, and, being charmed, they will come to know all the grace of modern movement, of which they have never dreamed.'[304] But the press was antagonistic; *Le Figaro* was condescending.[305]

Henri Bidou, in the *Journal des Débats*, thought *Parade* was a failure, but not without interest.

It was during this Paris season that Cocteau remarked how Misia, on ballet nights, looked as if she were marrying off her daughter.[306] On 30 May Paul Morand noted that the young dressmaker Coco Chanel, mistress of the popular Englishman, Boy Capell, was 'definitely becoming a personality'.[307]

Awaiting the Ballet in Madrid, the Nijinskys had had a peaceful holiday, reading the poems of Oscar Wilde and Rabindranath Tagore, wondering about the future of Russia – 'Of course they must ask Sergei Pavlovitch to be Director of the Mariinsky now,' said Vaslav – playing with their child and watching the spring come in the gardens of the Prado.[308] When Diaghilev arrived and 'burst into the lobby of the Ritz', he showed nothing but friendship towards Nijinsky, and embraced him affectionately. Vaslav was delighted, thinking a new period of creative collaboration was about to begin. Picasso, too, was there, and Romola observed that, when he wanted to explain anything, 'he became full of excitement, and used to draw on the table-cloth, the menu card and on top of Sergei Pavlovitch's ivory walking-stick'. To her Diaghilev behaved like a 'fatherly friend, protective and kind'.[309] Indeed, she was just the sort of woman with whom Diaghilev got on – intelligent, artistic, well-dressed and amusing. Although Diaghilev did not see eye to eye with Nijinsky about opening a school and a dance laboratory, or holding an annual festival at which many of the seats would be free – which were his latest ideas – the two men were so at ease together on their sight-seeing excursions and were so united – with Stravinsky – in irrepressible admiration for the art of fat, middle-aged Pastora Imperio, who, when she began to sing and move and play the castanets, 'offered the history and soul of Spain', that all seemed blissful as Paradise.[310] But Romola had one less attractive quality – suspicion: and this, heightened no doubt by jealousy, was the serpent in the garden.

When the Madrid season began on Sunday, 2 June, Nijinsky made his début in that city, dancing *Le Spectre de la rose* with Lopukhova; and the critic of *La Epoca* wrote next day that 'although our public on the whole does not admire male dancers, when they dance as Nijinsky did last night they are acclaimed'.[311] *Prince Igor* was followed by *Carnaval*, and no doubt few of the Madrid public realized how lucky they were to see Nijinsky (as Harlequin) and Massine (as Eusebius) in the same ballet. One of the numerous duchesses present, however, the red-headed Duquesa de Durcal, whose husband was a cousin of the King, fell in love with Nijinsky.[312] On the following night *Sadko* aroused interest, but Nijinsky's dancing in *La Princesse enchantée* brought no comment from the critic.[313] *The Good-humoured Ladies*, given both on the Tuesday and Wednesday nights, was said to be much better appreciated on its second showing, especially by writers and painters.[314] *Schéhérazade* remained the prime favourite of Spanish audiences,[315] and the critic, seeing Nijinsky in it for the first time, found him 'worthy of his reputation – an extraordinary artist'.[316]

Nijinsky put himself out to coach Idzikovsky in *Le Spectre de la rose*.[317] He also greatly admired Massine's Italian ballet, and told him so. He went round to his dressing-room one night, embraced him, and offered to dance Battista, Idzikovsky's role. Massine was taken by surprise, and greatly honoured.[318] The two men, living and working at closer quarters than in New York in 1916, had a chance to appreciate each other's qualities. Leonide had watched Vaslav rehearsing *L'Après-midi d'un faune*. 'I was thrilled by the way he demonstrated the most minute details of gesture and movement, correcting each dancer with calm assurance and complete understanding. He was an extraordinarily gifted choreographer.'[319]

Diaghilev, Massine, Stravinsky, Picasso and the Nijinskys went together to bullfights, met the heroic Belmonte, watched the gypsies dance in cabarets till the early hours of the morning. The King and Queen came regularly to the ballet; and sometimes there were small-scale performances in a little private theatre at the top of the Teatro Real, at which the Court sat round informally.[320] Romola did not at all resent the Duquesa de Durcal's infatuation with Nijinsky: she welcomed any sign of 'worldliness' in her husband as a counterbalance to Tolstoyan asceticism.[321]

For the Tolstoyans, Kostrovsky and Zverev, were at work on Nijinsky again. Romola not only resented their long visits and sermons in Russian, during which she was compelled to keep silent; she was also jealous of them, as she could not help being of Diaghilev. She told her husband that he must choose between them and herself and went out into the night. At the theatre one evening, 'in a dark corner near the stage', she saw Diaghilev talking in what she considered a conspiratorial manner with Zverev.[322] This (to my mind) was the second turning-point in the story of Diaghilev and Nijinsky. Brooding over what she had seen, Romola came to the conclusion that Diaghilev was trying to destroy her husband. As Sokolova wrote, 'This absurd idea could only have occurred to a woman who was herself undergoing severe mental stress.'[323] Why, it may well be asked, should Diaghilev try to destroy his chief breadwinner, the glory of the Russian Ballet? Because he wanted the decks cleared for Massine, Romola might have answered. How was Nijinsky to be destroyed? By Tolstoyan vegetarianism which would make him too weak to dance – so she wrote – or by a Tolstoyan 'return to the soil', which would remove him from the Ballet.[324] Romola decided to persuade her husband not to go on the South American tour.

On Sunday, 10 June, King Alfonso was obliged to form a new government. The Marques de Alhucemas having refused the premiership, Eduardo Dato accepted.[325] As the King wanted to go to the races in the afternoon, he was late for the ballet – and subsequently apologized to Nijinsky, who was dancing in *L'Après-midi d'un faune* that night, while Massine played in *Petrushka*, with the words, 'Je viens d'accoucher d'un nouveau gouvernement.'[326] The latest developments had not yet been made public when he arrived at the Teatro Real, and, when Ansermet struck up the National Anthem, the King was booed.[327]

That Sunday night's performance should have been the last in Madrid, but, at the request of the King, extra ones were given, the first on Wednesday, 13 June. The critic of *La Epoca* thought *Cléopâtre* the most beautiful of all Diaghilev's spectacles; and it is curious to note that, while Tchernicheva played the cruel queen as usual, Lopukhova was Ta-Hor and Nijinsky danced Amoun for the first time.[328] The impresario Serran, who had arranged all the performances in Spain up till then, had reason to be pleased with his enterprise.

During the last fortnight in June the Russian Ballet performed for the first time in Barcelona before sailing for South America on 4 July. Vaslav and Romola Nijinsky had left it rather late to announce that they did not wish to go on the tour. If Romola's account, which follows, is true, the contract signed in New York can only have applied to North America. They were lunching one day with Diaghilev, Romola wrote, when the latter began to talk about the trip to South America. But, according to Romola, Vaslav declined, as follows:

'I am not sure I will go, Sergei Pavlovitch, I need a rest, and do not like the idea of being separated from my child in war-time. South America will not be a creative trip artistically.'

Diaghilev, with a freezing smile, returned, 'But you have to go, you are under contract.' 'Have to?' said Vaslav. 'I have no contract.' 'You cabled me from America agreeing in principle. That is a contract.' 'But I also cabled that we would discuss the matter in Spain.' 'That is beside the point. In this country a cable is a binding contract.... I will force you to go.'[329]

Nijinsky may not have wanted to be separated from his daughter, but the idea of his needing a rest was ludicrous. After the sea voyage back from New York, he had spent three months in Madrid doing nothing. There had then been a few performances (by no means nightly) in Madrid and Barcelona. Whatever excuses he may have had for letting down the company and not going to South America, overwork was the most futile.

That afternoon Romola and Vaslav packed their bags and booked seats on the Madrid express. But there was another Spanish law of which they were ignorant. An artist billed to appear in a theatre must do so, unless incapacitated by illness. Diaghilev had taken steps. Nijinsky was arrested. He danced that night and finished the Barcelona season.[330]

Grigoriev's story is different. 'In Diaghilev's publicity he laid more stress on the artistic merits of the company as a whole than on any individual performer; and this deeply displeased the Nijinskys, who at once concluded that it was Diaghilev's intention to minimize Nijinsky's importance. They

334

grew more and more hostile until one morning ... as Diaghilev was crossing the entrance hall of the hotel, he noticed their luggage piled up near the door. He therefore telephoned to his local lawyer.... They called on the governor of the city....'[331]

Diaghilev telegraphed to the South American impresarios that Nijinsky's arrival in the Argentine was improbable, that everyone else had got visas except Massine, and that he himself was prevented from coming by the Russian 'governmental committee'. He offered to take 45 per cent. instead of 50, the 300,000-franc guarantee remaining as before.[332]

Nijinsky, however, signed a contract for South America, agreeing to the same salary as in the United States, with the proviso, insisted on by Romola, that he be paid in gold before every performance. (She had taken this tip from Fanny Elssler.)[333] On 30 June, at the Teatro Liceo, Barcelona, Diaghilev saw Nijinsky dance for the last time.[334] Olga Khokhlova remained in Europe, for she was engaged to Picasso. When the Ballet left Barcelona for Cadiz, the lovers were on the station platform to wave them goodbye. The Nijinskys sailed with the company from Cadiz on 4 July. This time Grigoriev was in charge, and Ansermet was conducting. The company had been supposed to travel to Rio de Janeiro on a British ship, but Diaghilev had insisted that they should sail on the neutral Spanish *Reina Victoria-Eugenia*. Unfortunately this landed them at Montevideo in Uruguay. The impresario Mocchi told Grigoriev and Barocchi that he considered this a breach of contract. To pacify him, they agreed to give three extra performances in Montevideo without payment, before sailing a thousand miles north to Rio to begin their tour proper.[335]

Diaghilev and Massine had become friends with the Spanish composer Manuel de Falla, whom Stravinsky had met in Paris in 1910 and described as 'even smaller than myself, and as modest and withdrawn as an oyster ... unpityingly religious' and the shyest man he had ever met.[336] Massine thought he 'might easily have passed for a university professor', but found him 'extraordinarily inspiring'.[337] In Barcelona, Falla had taken Diaghilev and Massine to see a one-act farce by Gregorio Martinez Sierra, *El Corregidor y la Molinera*, for which he had written the incidental music. This was based on a nineteenth-century novel, *El Sombrero de tres picos* (*The Three-cornered Hat*) by Alarcon, and was about the attempted seduction (in the eighteenth century) of a miller's wife by the local governor.

Falla's score [wrote Massine], with its pulsating rhythms, played by eleven brass instruments, seemed to us very exciting, and in its blend of violence and passion was similar to much of the music of the local folk-dances. Both Diaghilev and I felt that the story and the music offered us the potentials of a full-length Spanish ballet. When we talked to Falla about it, he seemed ... ready to collaborate with us, to the extent of omitting some of the pastiche writing in the music for the Corregidor's dance, and expanding the ending into a fuller, more powerful finale in accordance with Diaghilev's suggestions. He said, however, that he would have to spend some time studying native dances and music before he could successfully translate the *jota* or the *farucca* into a modern idiom.[338]

Massine had another new friend, a young Spanish dancer, Felix Fernandez Garcia, met on an expedition from Madrid to Granada. 'One evening, at our favourite café, the Novedades, we noticed a small, dark young dancer whose elegant movements and compelling intensity singled him out from the rest of the group.... Diaghilev invited him to join us.... He was a nervous and highly strung creature with a very original talent.' Felix was a printer by trade. Diaghilev took him to Madrid, where the Ballet was a revelation to him. He joined it, and in Barcelona had begun to give Massine lessons in Flamenco dancing. He also introduced Massine to his old teacher, Molina, who instructed the insatiable Russian in the secrets of *zapateado*, the rhythmical heel-tapping which is an essential part of the male gypsy's art.[339]

While Diaghilev paid a rapid visit to Paris and to Stravinsky in Switzerland – where, in a railway carriage between Leysin and Aigle, on 25 July, Igor compelled him at last to sign a provisional contract for *Les Noces*[340] – Massine continued to work with Felix in Barcelona.

Felix was not only an excellent teacher but a delightful and intelligent companion. It was really through him that I first learned to speak Spanish fluently, and began to achieve a basic understanding of the manners and customs of the country.... He had perfected his mastery of Spanish dancing to the point where it had become a highly refined art. Not only had he devised a written system of notation for the *zapateado* ... but he had taught himself to sing the difficult *seguidilla* and *alegria* songs while dancing. This was a most remarkable feat, but I often felt that it must have imposed a terrific strain on his nervous system.... To help me in my work Diaghilev arranged for us to take a trip through Spain to study the infinite variety of native peasant dances. With Falla and Felix as our tutors, Diaghilev and I were eager and receptive students. During the whole of that hot, dry, Spanish summer we travelled at a leisurely pace....[341]

So the four oddly assorted pilgrims set off, Diaghilev eager for Massine to create a masterpiece, Falla eager to collect material, Massine eager to learn, Felix eager to teach – but also dreaming of glory and acclaim for himself in far lands. The price of the masterpiece would be the eventual sacrifice of Felix.

They visited Saragossa, Burgos, Salamanca, Toledo, Seville, Cordova and Granada, 'sight-seeing in monasteries, museums and cathedrals ... watching the local dancers' and planning the ballet which became *Le Tricorne*. Wherever Felix went he was accepted as a friend by local dancers, and he opened doors for his companions. Falla was fascinated by what he saw and heard. In Seville the four watched the famous Ramirez and Macarona, and saw a *sevillana* performed by two couples on a roof by moonlight. In Cordova Felix organized a show in a cave, at which 'a group of cobblers, barbers and pastrycooks' demonstrated their skill. 'After a meal of raw ham and Jerez they danced with such pleasure, spontaneity and native fire that the performance went on until the early hours of the morning.' That morning the friends moved on to Granada. 'We decided to hire donkeys and tour the Alhambra Palace and the Gardens of the Generalife … with Felix and Falla leading the way we climbed the first slopes; then Falla and I noticed that Diaghilev was no longer with us. We turned round and saw him at the bottom of the hill, prodding his donkey which had collapsed under his weight.'

Returning from the Moorish courtyards and fountains of the Alhambra, one afternoon, on their way back to the hotel, Falla and Massine stopped to listen to a blind man playing a guitar. Falla asked him to repeat 'the mournful little tune', and he did so several times. Falla stood with his eyes closed, humming the tune, then wrote it down in his notebook. He used it for the *sevillana* in *Le Tricorne*.[342]

Back in Madrid, Diaghilev, instead of allowing Massine to get on with the creation of his Spanish ballet, began to talk about a very different work. Perhaps he thought Massine's hoard of new knowledge needed to be stored away for a few months before being put to use. During the previous winter in Rome the composer Ottorino Respighi had shown Diaghilev a series of unpublished short compositions by Rossini, written in his retirement in Paris to entertain the guests at his succulent Sunday dinner-parties. These he called 'Les Riens', or 'Péchés de vieillesse'. There were about 180 of them, and when Diaghilev began to play them, Leonide at once saw their possibilities. Remembering *Coppelia* and the old ballet *Die Puppenfee*, they conceived a toyshop 'which offered its customers a wide range of dancing dolls'. Diaghilev urged Massine to adopt as simple a libretto as possible. There was a tarantella for two Neapolitan dolls – and Massine, with his new love for the carefree city on its blessed bay, wanted the toyshop to be situated in Naples in the nineteenth century. There was a mazurka, for which Massine imagined two Kings and two Queens from a pack of cards. There was a can-can, a parody of Offenbach, which prompted a dance in the style of Toulouse-Lautrec's paintings. 'We all agreed that the ballet should be taken at top speed, the dances following each other without a break.'[343]

In Rio, where the Ballet gave twelve performances, the Nijinskys met the new French Minister, the poet Paul Claudel, who had been present when his *Partage de midi* had been performed in Paris only nine months before. He had brought as one of his secretaries the young composer Darius Milhaud, and together Claudel and Milhaud had devised a ballet, *L'Homme et son désir*. Claudel took Nijinsky into the Brazilian jungle to explain the work to him, hoping he would produce it.[344] Milhaud noticed how beautiful

Nijinsky was 'when he turned to speak to someone behind his chair. He turned his head, but his head alone, so precisely and rapidly that he seemed not to have moved a muscle.'[345] But there was increasing friction between Romola Nijinsky, who liked power and thought her birth and her position as Nijinsky's wife entitled her to make decisions, and Grigoriev, who regarded both her and her husband as obstacles to the smooth running of the company. Romola developed persecution mania, interpreting every accident – a rusty nail on the stage, a falling piece of scenery – as an attack on Nijinsky; and she hired a private detective to guard him.[346] Grigoriev and others thought Nijinsky was already showing signs of mental disorder.[347] This Mme Romola Nijinsky always hotly denied;[348] and certainly the friends Nijinsky made outside the ballet – Claudel, Milhaud, the composer Estrade Guerra and his wife – saw nothing odd in Nijinsky's behaviour. Grigoriev, and the usually accurate Sokolova, may have been wise in the light of later events.

In a railway tunnel between Rio and São Paulo a spark set fire to the scenery in an open wagon, and the sets of Le Spectre and Cléopâtre were completely destroyed.[349] In São Paulo Sokolova had her baby, a daughter, under difficult circumstances.[350] In Buenos Aires the company found Pavlova; and on 10 September the Nijinskys celebrated their fourth anniversary at a dinner given by the priest who had married them.[351] On the twenty-sixth the Diaghilev Ballet gave the last of twenty-three performances at Buenos Aires, and Nijinsky, dancing Le Spectre and Petrushka, appeared with them for the last time.[352] When the company sailed for Spain a few days later, Nijinsky saw them off, but he stayed behind to give a performance for the Red Cross, in which Artur Rubinstein participated.[353] This was the last time he danced in public. On their return to Europe the Nijinskys took a villa in Switzerland, and Vaslav played no more part in the history of the Russian Ballet.

Diaghilev felt that he had almost squeezed Spain dry. He decided in October to try his luck in England, and travelled there with Sert, who was decorating a room (with allegories of Allied victory) for Lady Ripon. It cannot have been easy to negotiate a passage on a troop-ship across the Channel; and we only know of their excursion through the diary and a letter of Charles Ricketts. Diaghilev must have played the scores of The Good-humoured Ladies, Parade and perhaps Contes russes to Thomas Beecham and other friends.

In his diary Ricketts described Diaghilev's visit with 'the Spanish Decorator'.

He has been delving in Italian libraries for the scores of 18 century Italians now forgotten, save Scarlatti. He has also hunted down Rossini. . . . He has joined the anti-German propaganda . . . and wants an Italian revival & a Russian propaganda.... I ... could not deny the great Germans, who, even during this war, had been my great consolation. That I would none of the Saint-Sæns point of view, that I admired the element of ridicule and comedy in being bombed while listening to Tristan.... We talked in a circle with Sert sympathizing on both sides.[354]

To a friend, Ricketts wrote,

Diaghilev ... came here to try and plant his recent productions on Beecham; one of them to music of Scarlatti is excellent, but none of the stars are there and one of the ballets is staged by Picasso. We quarrelled over German music, which he wants to persecute and suppress; he means to scrap *Carnaval, Papillons* and the *Spectre of the Rose*. I would hear nothing of the kind, said that Schumann and Wagner had been the friends of all my life ... that Art had no frontiers (this is not true), that I hated nationalism in Art, and that the tables might be turned against Russia. This actually happened. Beecham's excuse not to have a Russian season was that he wished to encourage national British art, so the boomerang returned to roost within a few hours of my lecture.[355]

Reading this, we cannot feel much sympathy with Diaghilev's anti-German attitude, with Beecham's determination exclusively to push British music – mostly Delius, of course – or with Ricketts' 'but' preceding the information that Picasso was working for the Ballet. The perceptive Ricketts had his limitations: for instance, he placed Degas (who had just died) below Rossetti.

On 11 October 1917 at Morges Stravinsky finished an orchestral version of *Les Noces*. This was later discarded, as were several others.[356] He had been corresponding for some months with André Gide about music for a new *Antony and Cleopatra*, which came to nothing, and he soon began work with Ramuz on *L'Histoire du soldat*.[357] Diaghilev, when he heard of the latter (first performed in Lausanne on 28 September 1918), was jealous beyond all reason. It was a tragic flaw in his character that the uncontrollable possessiveness he showed in his personal relationships should be extended to matters of art. Far more than with Bakst or Benois, he resented that Stravinsky – a greater genius and his own 'discovery', his 'first son' in music – should be unfaithful. When he heard *L'Histoire du soldat* played by Igor in 1919 he professed to dislike it. He might have contrived a striking production of the work (as he did with *Renard* when he was allowed to take it over from Princesse Edmond de Polignac). The first Paris production of *L'Histoire*, put on, without his aid, at the Théâtre des Champs-Elysées in 1924, was a near disaster.

Picasso had spent the last four months since the Ballet departed visiting his family and old friends in the neighbourhood of Barcelona, and introducing Olga to them. He and Olga were there to welcome the company back. Under Olga's influence he had become temporarily less bohemian, and Ansermet watched him gazing in an amused way at his appearance in a mirror – he was wearing a dinner-jacket and a bowler hat – and heard him murmur, 'Monsieur Ingres!'[358]

Diaghilev assembled his troupe and told them that, beyond a few performances in Barcelona, Madrid and then Lisbon, he had no engagements to look forward to.[359] Italy was in no state to receive them. Up to that summer the Italians had battered ineffectively against the Austrians in their Alpine fortresses from the Trentino in the west to the Isonzo in the east. On 24 October the Austrians, augmented by seven German divisions, broke through the Italian lines at Caporetto and General Cadorna's army retreated behind the Piave, whose mouth was twenty miles east of Venice. In France the Third Battle of Ypres was raging. The Russian war effort would soon peter out, and the Russian dancers would cease to be citizens of an Allied country. In Spain the epidemic which was to sweep Europe and to cause more deaths than the war itself, 'Spanish 'flu', had begun to rage; and some of the dancers went down with it.[360]

In November, when the Bolsheviks staged their revolution and Lenin became Premier, the Ballet were dancing in Madrid;[361] and in December they travelled for the first time to Portugal. They were to perform in a vast arena called Coliseu dos Recreios.[362] Almost immediately after their arrival revolution broke out. Diaghilev, Massine, Grigoriev and a Portuguese balletomane were walking back one night to their hotel on the main square when they heard shouting and rifle fire, and shells began to explode in the street. The manager of their hotel asked them to take shelter under the main staircase, as their front rooms were exposed to fire, and they remained there throughout the three days and nights of the revolution. 'Diaghilev was more irritated than frightened, and complained bitterly that we were wasting valuable rehearsal time.'[363]

Sokolova had succumbed to Spanish 'flu in Madrid. She, Kremnev, her baby, the Catalonian wet-nurse and Felix, whose passport had been delayed, arrived by train in Lisbon a few days after the company, to be greeted by firing. Because of the Portuguese revolution or because Felix now knew that he was not to be the star dancer of the company he had joined, he began to show signs of instability. When there was a further outburst of revolution in the square, he barricaded himself inside a back room with furniture against the door, and was eventually only persuaded by hunger to come out.[364]

The Ballet's season began a fortnight late, and the unheated Coliseu was never full. Diaghilev contrived to have the Royal Theatre specially opened for two performances of the ballet. This, too, was icy cold and so dirty that the dancers' shoes, tights and costumes were 'almost ruined'. The shows they gave in Lisbon were the worst the Ballet put on in a capital city,[365] though even shabbier performances would take place later on tour in Spain.

Massine had found himself stimulated by the Portuguese revolution. He had begun rehearsing his Rossini ballet. A Venetian waltz, learned by Soko-lova and Gavrilov, was thought too mild and was discarded, but Leonide's imagination was busy at work. He remembered two fox-terriers he had watched 'coquettishly chasing and teasing each other' on the beach at Viareggio on his first visit to Italy in 1914, and he transformed them into Poodles for another number in the dolls' *divertissement* of his Rossini ballet. He had soon worked out most of *La Boutique fantasque*.[366]

But Diaghilev had to find bookings for his troupe and he set off with Massine and Barocchi for Madrid.[367]

When 1918 dawned, the company was without prospects. Diaghilev's con-tracts with his dancers stipulated that they were obliged to spend one month of the year rehearsing on half-pay. This clause he enforced during January. At his wit's end, Grigoriev began rehearsals of *Daphnis et Chloë*, which had not been given for years, and which nobody took seriously.[368]

The rehearsals were rather a farce [wrote Sokolova]. . . . However, our time was not wasted, as it gave some of us a good opportunity to study Spanish dancing under Felix. Woizikovsky, Slavinsky and myself worked particularly hard . . . what money there was in the company circulated, but in the end we were all living on credit. . . . Most of us were determined to be faithful to Diaghilev. . . . One small group of dancers, however, were lured into signing a contract with a theatrical agent and . . . went to Spain. . . . They only danced a few performances and had little success. They were soon glad to come back to us. . . . Diaghilev was very angry about this desertion because it made it much more difficult for him to negoti-ate the new tour; in fact he was only able to conclude a new contract for the com-pany when the renegades had agreed to return.[369]

Weary winter days. The company were cold, hungry, bored and hopeless for the first time since the war began. Never had Diaghilev's responsibility weighed so heavily upon him. But the dancers and staff helped each other along. Vassili Zuikov, Diaghilev's servant, who looked after the wardrobe, noticed that Sokolova's shoes were shabby, and gave her the high-heeled purple shoes she had worn in *Las Meninas*.[370]

On 3 March the Peace of Brest-Litovsk was signed between Lenin and the Central Powers. Russia, which had already lost Poland, gave up Finland, Esthonia, Livonia, Lithuania and the Ukraine. Diaghilev, like most of his dancers, became a stateless exile. He had probably long ago reconciled him-self to losing his pictures and papers, including letters from so many eminent men, living and dead.

At last Diaghilev arrived in Lisbon to announce that he had arranged a tour of Spain. The company were not only to visit large cities, but smaller towns where theatrical performances of any kind were scarce, and where little money was to be made: but it was a relief for all to be going on the road and working again. The Russian Ballet had spent three unprofitable months in Lisbon. The tour began at Valladolid on 31 March.[371]

The Ballet travelled clockwise round Spain, visiting Salamanca, San Sebastian, Bilbao, Logroño, Saragossa, then, as the spring came on, travelling south through Valencia, Alcoy, Alicante, Cartagena, Murcia, Cordova, Seville, Malaga, Granada, and back, via Madrid, to Barcelona. In whatever sense dancers, who live between train, hotel and theatre, can ever be said to 'see' a town or a country, the Russian Ballet saw Spain. Everywhere they went Massine was watching and studying; and Diaghilev encouraged the whole company to observe and learn from regional dances. In Bilbao they saw steps and miming inspired by bullfighting,[372] which Massine incorporated in the crowd scene of *Le Tricorne*. In Saragossa they watched the leaping, cabrioling *jota* performed in soft slippers:[373] this became Massine's finale. In Seville they drove in carriages to a café situated amid orange groves, with pavilions built in tree-tops. In the light of the setting sun gypsies vied with each other, and 'each dancer seemed to be better than the last'. One young man particularly aroused the interest of Diaghilev. Felix grew jealous and 'began to dance as we had never seen him dance before. He tapped his heels faster and faster in an amazing variety of rhythms, and cracked his fingers as though they were castanets. He danced on his knees, leapt in the air, fell crashing on the side of his thigh, turned over and jumped up with such speed that it was incredible that the human body could stand the strain without injury.... It was not until the gypsies closed in and surrounded him that he would give up.'[374] Massine took 'one step towards the end of his *farucca*' from Ramirez, the king of Sevillian dancers. But the *farucca* he regarded as a dance 'about life and death', and he put into it much of the drama of the bullfight.[375]

The company continued to work under Felix, who screamed at them when they failed to execute a step; but no one could master the art of playing castanets correctly. 'Massine wrote down in a book every step, movement and footbeat he learned from Felix.'[376]

The tour ended in Barcelona. Nobody had any money. Diaghilev realized that he had exhausted the possibilities of Spain for the time being. He released the dancers from their obligations. He telegraphed to Paris to Misia, his dearest friend, asking if she thought he should continue the struggle of keeping the Ballet going. 'Give it up, Serge,' she replied. Massine noticed that her discouraging answer seemed to make Diaghilev keener than ever to weather the storm. 'But then, Picasso was there and that always gave Diaghilev hope,' Massine told me.[377] It is not certain that Picasso *was* in Barcelona in May 1918 (at the time of the last big German attack), though he had been there before the Ballet went to Madrid and Lisbon; but *Le Tricorne* was coming to life with Picasso's aid, and that was almost the same thing; and Falla had arrived with the completed score. Massine himself was there.[378] And Stravinsky was in Switzerland, with *Les Noces* still unperformed.

It was doubtful, even, how much the Russian Embassy in Madrid could help their compatriots, for their own position was in the balance. Anatoli Nekludov, who had succeeded the last Imperial Ambassador in summer 1917, resigned in a telegram to Kerensky on 12 September, and when his successor, Stakhovitch, arrived after Lenin's coup d'état, his situation was highly ambiguous.[379] Soloviev, the Councillor, was pro-German.[380] It seems to have been Baron Konrad Meyendorff who did what he could to help.

Diaghilev had already been in touch with Oswald Stoll, of the London Coliseum, when he was received by King Alfonso on his way north at the beginning of June. The question was how to transport – and how to get permission to transport – the Russian Ballet through France to England in time of war. The King of Spain exercised himself on their behalf. The British Ambassador in Madrid and the Spanish Ambassador in London obtained permission for the company to enter England.[381] On 30 June Meyendorff telegraphed to Diaghilev at the Hôtel d'Angleterre, Barcelona, 'Entry troupe authorized for England. At present seeking authorization passage through France.'[382] Diaghilev rushed to Madrid, where he stayed at the Palace Hotel. On 4 July the King's secretary, Torres, wrote to him 'By order of His Majesty the King, my august Sovereign...' that the French Ambassador had telephoned permission for the company to pass through France.[383] Next day Diaghilev cabled the news to Stoll and asked for an advance. Stoll sent a thousand pounds.[384] Thomas Cook in Barcelona informed their London headquarters that the Ballet's baggage was in cases weighing approximately fifteen thousand kilos,[385] but on 17 July the French Consul in Barcelona still had no order concerning transport.[386]

We have only Sokolova as witness of how Diaghilev behaved during those anxious days in Madrid, when the survival of his company was at stake. She had travelled from Barcelona to Portugal to fetch her baby, left with a peasant woman near Lisbon during the long tour, and on her return journey she was met by Kremnev at the frontier. They had just enough money to get them to Madrid, where they took a room in a *pension*. It was with joy that they discovered Diaghilev was in the capital.

> We used to meet him at ten o'clock at night in the park where the cafés were [wrote Sokolova], and I came to love him dearly as a person during that anxious time. He often used to carry the baby himself and let her play with his monocle. One day Natasha was so ill I thought her last hour had come. Diaghilev took me to his bedroom, opened a wardrobe trunk and brought out a little bag. He undid the string and emptied on the bed a heap of copper and silver coins from various countries. This, I suppose, was all the money he had left. He picked out all the silver coins and gave them to me, telling me to get a doctor.[387]

In Barcelona a few of the dancers had been tempted away by theatrical agents. Grigoriev, with no money to give them, was powerless to keep them with the company, but he succeeded in persuading Woizikovsky to stay, for which the Pole was subsequently glad, as he soon danced leading roles.[388] Nearly twenty dancers left, including Vera Nemtchinova and Nicolas Zverev, who returned later, and Maria Shabelska, who remained in America for good. At last everything was arranged.

Diaghilev and Massine travelled ahead of the Ballet. Arriving in Paris off the night train from Barcelona, they lunched at the Meurice with the Serts, and told them all their past tribulations and future plans. Massine wrote:

Misia, who had for a long time been urging Diaghilev to give up the unequal struggle and disband the company ... was delighted to hear that I was planning a ballet on Rossini's music.... José was more interested in Diaghilev's idea for a new production of Cimarosa's opera *Le Astuzie Femminili*, and was obviously eager to do the décor for it.... We could have talked for hours, but had to rush away to catch our train.... Just as we turned into the rue des Capucines we saw a house receive a direct hit. Its walls and windows burst and splintered in the air, and fragments of glass and stone pattered on the roof of our taxi.... Victoria Station, when we arrived there, was a scene of perpetual motion ... rather like one of my early finales with too much movement....[389]

What remained of the Ballet left Barcelona for Paris on 4 August. 'For the last time during those years of war,' wrote Sokolova, 'we lined up at a frontier while Grigoriev produced his album – known as the "Rogues' Gallery" – containing all our photographs and particulars, calling out our names in turn to summon us before the officers....' They arrived in Paris in the early morning and found lodgings near the Opéra. That night they had their first experience of black-out.[390] Within a few days they had passed through the mine-sown waters of the Channel and docked at Southampton.

CHAPTER 13

August 1918–January 1921

Post-war Triumphs in London and Paris – *Le Tricorne* – Break with Massine

LADY RIPON, Diaghilev's closest English friend, was dead; and so, of course, were many of the young men who had admired the Russian Ballet before the war, including Rupert Brooke. A few friends, mostly middle-aged ladies, were glad to welcome Diaghilev back: to name a few – Juliet Duff, who had lost her husband in the war, and had been working in a soldiers' canteen; Ottoline Morrell, who had employed intellectual pacifists on her farm at Garsington near Oxford; Thomas Beecham's passionate adherent, Lady Cunard, the sparkling tamer of the most splendid lions; the Duchess of Rutland, whose daughter Diana was shortly to marry Duff Cooper; Cathérine d'Erlanger, in her big Piccadilly house near Hyde Park Corner; Hazel Lavery, the painter's wife, as spectacularly beautiful as ever; and Margot Asquith (not yet Countess of Oxford), whose husband had ceased in 1916 to be Prime Minister, but who, with her intelligence, chic and unbridled tongue, could claim to rule a large section of London society.

The Savoy Hotel still stood; and here Diaghilev, Massine and Beppe, the Italian valet, took up their residence.

It was arranged, with the concurrence of Eric Wollheim, whose theatrical agent's office was in St Martin's Lane, opposite the Coliseum, that the Russian Ballet should give one work, afternoon and evening, in each of the two daily performances of mixed music-hall acts at the Coliseum. If Diaghilev felt humiliated at such an arrangement, Oswald Stoll would soon be astonished at the new public his theatre attracted.

Auditions were held, for, after the Barcelona desertions, Diaghilev was short of dancers. Among the English girls engaged, Miller became Pavlovska, Murray Muravieva, Grant Grantseva, Thomas Istomina, Pettit Petipa and Wilson Olkina.[1] Vera Clark, who, as Savina, was to outstrip them all, kept her own name for the time being. Among the men, little Leighton

345

Lucas, who would be better known as a musician than as a dancer, concealed his identity beneath the mask of Lukin. The old drill hall in Chenies Street was in use for its military purpose, so, for classes and rehearsals, a club-room on the first floor of a house in Shaftesbury Avenue was hired. (This was just opposite where the ABC Cinema – formerly the Saville Theatre – stands today, 1978.)[2]

Stoll had saved the Russian Ballet's existence, but this did not induce Diaghilev to behave in other than a lordly way. He told the Managing Director that his gaudy Coliseum drop-curtain, sewn with a blaze of sequins, would kill the romantic picture of *Les Sylphides*. 'As it rose you would see the two effects at the same time, and this was an impossible beginning.' Stoll was reluctant to mutilate his precious curtain; but Diaghilev insisted. The curtain was lowered, and throughout an August Sunday a crowd of women cut off most of the sequins.[3]

The Russian scene-painter Vladimir Polunin, who had worked for Beecham before, but never for Diaghilev, was summoned by telegram, on about 22 August, to the Savoy Hotel. He remembered the *World of Art* exhibitions and the Historical Portraits at the Tavrichevsky Palace in St Petersburg and was proud to collaborate.[4] Diaghilev had decided to revise the décor of *The Good-humoured Ladies* and Bakst had produced a design without distortion.

This had to be executed quickly [wrote Polunin]. Without concealing the difficulties of working in wartime, financial troubles, and so on, Diaghilev clearly showed that the success of this ballet would enable his company to rise in every respect to its former eminence. There remained a fortnight.... All the difficulties of finding a studio, procuring canvas and other materials (by no means easy at this period) were quickly surmounted, thanks to Diaghilev's untiring energy and his gift of inspiring all those with whom he came in contact. The studio, at the top of the fruit baskets store at Covent Garden market [opposite the stage-door of the Opera House], at first hired for ten days only, became the repository of Diaghilev's scenery, and there my wife and I worked uninterruptedly for over two years.[5]

When the dancers arrived from Paris, they settled into lodgings or board-ing-houses in Soho and Bloomsbury. Sokolova felt so linked to Diaghilev in friendship after the privations they had shared in Madrid that she looked forward fondly to their reunion.

My heart thumped when I saw him standing on the stage of the Coliseum. But when I went up to him, he said, quite casually, 'Glad to see you. You've arrived safely?...' Then, as he moved away, he asked as an afterthought 'How is Natasha?' I realized that the episode of our closeness in Spain was to make no difference to our relationship in the future – in fact, it was never to be mentioned again.... No one was ever to know that the great Diaghilev had lived through those anxious weeks in Madrid, or sat on a park bench holding a sick baby. I told no one until after he died.[6]

London was hungry for the Diaghilev Ballet, but its old favourites, Karsavina and Nijinsky, were no longer to be seen. Much depended, as Diaghilev had explained to Polunin, on how Massine's new type of ballet and the new dancers he had trained were received. Massine was known to London only as the shy youth of *La Légende de Joseph*: as a choreographer, he had yet to make his name. Not only Lopukhova (always written 'Lopokova' in England), but Woizikovsky and Idzikovsky were new names to the ballet public. Tchernicheva was not associated with such important roles as Cleopatra and Zobeïda.[7] Who could be expected to identify, in her new metamorphosis, the Cockney-born Sokolova?

To transfer a design by Bakst into suitable proportions for the stage [wrote Polunin] proved to be a difficult task, for he often painted his effective designs with more regard for their pictorial effect than for the use of the scene painter. . . . The nearest houses of the backcloth [for *The Good-humoured Ladies*] would have appeared so small that the heads of the dancers would have been on a level with the roofs. . . . On the other hand, if the buildings were to be of normal size, the top of the tower would have been then cut off by a sky-border. Diaghilev, who came several times a day to the studio, . . . immediately decided that the tower should be 27 feet high, and he was right. . . . He looked over the details of the drawings, criticized the height of the buildings on both sides of the backcloth (which were not in the design), chose another type of fountain. . . . Bakst's 'inky tone' [of sky], as Diaghilev termed it, was to be changed to a pure Italian blue. . . .[8]

When the décor was finished, Diaghilev examined it carefully and remarked that 'the water-colour blotches' in Bakst's design had not been reproduced. The effect was achieved by wiping parts of the canvas with a damp sponge. This delighted Diaghilev. Polunin received a telegram of congratulations from Bakst in Paris: he assumed that Diaghilev had instigated this.[9]

On the afternoon of 5 September 1918 *Cléopâtre* was given in a new setting by Robert Delaunay, with two new costumes by his wife, Sonia, and many old ones by Bakst. In the evening London saw its first Massine ballet, *The Good-humoured Ladies*.

The *Times* had wondered how a music-hall audience (normally rowdy and boozy) would respond to the art of ballet – not that ballet was a novelty in music-halls; but there was a difference between ballet *à la Diaghilev* and the Genée or Pavlova kind. 'There was not a sound as the action unfolded itself. Drury Lane or Covent Garden could not have behaved better.'[10] Tchernicheva's Cleopatra, thought Cyril Beaumont, 'was a cold, enigmatic, sadistic being, quite different from the voluptuous woman presented by Astafieva. . . . Massine was at his best in the death scene.'[11] Sokolova wrote, 'Luba's costume had a round mirror in the middle of her stomach, and as Massine, dying from the poisoned cup, struggled up clutching at her body all he saw was his own face in the glass before falling dead at her feet.'[12]

Massine, who took good care of himself, was worried about the Spanish 'flu. 'I was naked except for a loin-cloth. After my death scene I had to lie on the ice-cold stage for several minutes, and I could feel the chilliness penetrating my bones. ... As it turned out I stayed perfectly well, but next day I was told that the great sturdy six-foot-high policeman who had been on duty at the front of the theatre had died at the first onslaught of 'flu.'[13] Sokolova played Ta-Hor, Pavlova's old role, and the *Dancing Times* commented that 'her anguish over the dead body of her fickle lover held the huge Coliseum audience spellbound'. In the Bacchanale Lopukhova had 'danced like a Maenad and electrified the audience with the sheer joy and seemingly boundless vitality of her movements'.[14]

Massine loved the violent colours of the new Delaunay setting.[15] Charles Ricketts, one of the old faithfuls who hastened to the Coliseum, did not.

Cleopatra was a tragic medley [he wrote to Shannon]. The hideous setting was by the post-Impressionist round the corner, pink and purple columns, a pea-green Hathor cow, and yellow Pyramids with a green shadow with a red spot; curiously enough, like many efforts at intensive colour, the effect is not coloured. A few of the old dresses, grown grey and tired, stood out amongst the new ones. ... These were eked out with dresses from *Le Dieu bleu*, *Thamar*, even *Joseph*, worn by very British supers with expressions on their faces signifying 'If you think I like these clothes you are blooming well mistaken.' Massine dances well, but he is uninspired; he has huge square legs. . . . He is stark naked except for rather nice bathing drawers, with a huge black spot on his belly. Two or three idiot girls in the gallery shrieked with laughter when he came on. . . . Will the masses turn Bolshevist or suffer in silence this intrusion of art in their National Shrine?[16]

Of the success of *The Good-humoured Ladies* there could be no doubt. The cast was the same as in Rome and Paris, except for Olga Khokhlova, who had been married to Picasso in Paris on 12 August, and whose role of Felicita was taken by Sokolova. 'Not only a very brilliant work of art,' wrote the *Observer*, 'but a most exhilarating entertainment.'[17] Grigoriev thought the maid Mariuccia was Lopukhova's finest part.[18] She immediately captured the heart of London, and remained its favourite dancer for five years. Cyril Beaumont was at first taken aback by the speed and jerky movements of Massine's ballet, but he came to love it. 'Accustomed to the sweet sadness of Karsavina ...' he found Lopukhova 'a complete surprise'. But she was 'a born comedienne'. 'Yet her soubrette had a mellow quality, the glaze of a past epoch....'[19]

Nearly all the Ballet's scenery had to be repainted or renewed, and Diaghilev signed a year's contract with Polunin. Every set presented a different problem (but the scene-painter's detailed notes are too long to be repeated here). 'Each time that a scene had to be renovated, Diaghilev gave his instructions regarding the repainting and the former aspect of it. He had not retained the original designs . . . so that all his instructions were most important.' As *Carnaval* (9 September), *Prince Igor*, *La Princesse enchantée* (16 September), *Papillons* (19 September), *Schéhérazade* (10 October) and *Sadko* (31 October) took their places in the repertoire, so each was smartened up. *Schéhérazade* was extremely complicated, and Diaghilev 'entered wholeheartedly into the smallest details', besides visiting the British Museum to check up on Persian architecture and design. Not much work was done on *Papillons*, 'because Diaghilev did not attach any importance to this ballet'. The set for *Las Meninas* had to be converted into one for *Les Sylphides*. When it was finished and Diaghilev set about lighting it, he exclaimed, laughing, 'Why, that is not Socrate, it is Polunin.'[20] Beaumont missed 'the lovely Benois setting' and thought the 'avenue of green trees relieved by a stone fountain set in the central pathway' inappropriate.[21]

At the *première* of *Sadko* – 'Fishiness, scaliness, greenness, wetness, underwaterness,' wrote *The Times*[22] – it was reported by the *Lady* that 'Baroness d'Erlanger had a Byzantine headdress of metallic tissue and upstanding leaves. . . . Lady Juliet Duff was wearing a black velvet picture gown, and Lady (Arthur) Paget had a black tuft in her hair, and a long black velvet wrap, with a deep ermine collar, over a black dress.'[23]

In spite of the French, British and American advances between July and September, and the collapse of Bulgaria, no one outside Germany and Austria guessed how close the end of the war had come. On 3 October the new German government asked the President of the United States to negotiate peace terms. On 27 October the Emperor Karl wrote to the Emperor Wilhelm that he was determined to make a separate peace. There was revolution in Germany, and on 9 November the Kaiser abdicated.

On 11 November, when the Armistice was announced, Diaghilev and Massine were dining with Osbert Sitwell, a Captain in the Grenadier Guards, in Swan Walk, Chelsea. Miss Ethel Sands, a well-to-do American amateur painter, and Mme Vandervelde, the art-loving wife of a Belgian politician, were among the guests. Mme Vandervelde foresaw the whole of Europe becoming Bolshevik – for the Germans, who had returned Lenin to Russia, had been themselves infected and weakened by his doctrines. Osbert Sitwell thought at the time how clever the Russians had been to make a separate peace, then to provoke revolution in Germany. 'But I said little, for Diaghilev and Massine were Russians. . . . And Diaghilev, indeed, dwelt on the low cunning of the Bolshevik leaders, and remarked how strange it was to have been born and to have lived in a great country, to think that you knew by sight, or at least by name, every prominent leader of opinion, and then to wake up suddenly one day and find your country ruled by men of whose names, both real and assumed, you and the large majority of your fellow-countrymen were totally ignorant.'[24]

After dinner, Sitwell, Diaghilev and Massine were lucky enough to find a taxi. They had been invited to a party by Montague Shearman, who lived between the Strand and the river. It was not till they emerged through Admiralty Arch into Trafalgar Square that they realized how whole-heartedly the people of London and the servicemen on leave were celebrating the occasion. 'The crowd, sometimes joining up, linking hands, dashed like the waves of the sea against the sides of the Square, against the railings of the National Gallery, sweeping up so far even as beyond the shallow stone steps of St Martin-in-the-Fields.... The northern character of the revellers ... was plain in the way they moved, the manner, for example, in which the knees were lifted, as in a *kermesse* painted by Breughel the Elder, as well as in the flushed and intent faces. ...' Diaghilev, 'with something of the importance of a public monument attaching to his scale and build ... bear-like in his fur-coat, gazed with an air of melancholy exhaustion at the crowds. ...' Massine, 'so practical an artist, and ... so vital in the manner in which he seizes his material from the life around him, was watching intently the steps and gestures of the couples. ...'[25]

Eventually we reached the Adelphi. The spacious Adam room, covered with decoration as fine as a cobweb, was hung inappropriately with a few large pictures of the Paris school – by Matisse, for example – and by several of the Bloomsbury Group.... Tonight, the Bloomsbury Junta was in full session.... Lytton Strachey, Clive Bell, Roger Fry, Mark Gertler, Lady Ottoline, D. H. Lawrence and his wife, Maynard Keynes, Duncan Grant, Lydia Lopokova and David Garnett.... All equally, soldiers, Bloomsbury beauties and conscientious objectors – all except Diaghilev – danced. I remember the tall, flagging figure of my friend Lytton Strachey, with his rather narrow, angular beard, long inquisitive nose ... jigging about with an amiable debility. He was, I think, unused to dancing....'[26]

Osbert Sitwell's younger brother, Sacheverell, also serving in the Grenadier Guards, came into Diaghilev's life at this time and fell in love with the Ballet. He suffered from always having to catch the last train back to Aldershot, and Diaghilev became exasperated and asked, 'Qui est cette Aldershot?', thinking it was a mistress.[27]

The Ethel Sands who was at Sitwell's dinner on Armistice night was already a friend of Diaghilev's. In several letters to her great friend Nan Hudson she mentions lunches or dinners that he was coming to, with or without Massine, and her anxiety because of his 'discriminating greed'. In December Diaghilev was to meet Logan Pearsall Smith, among others, at her house in Chelsea.[28]

Much of Diaghilev's life at this time was lived in the neighbourhood of Trafalgar Square, which the Coliseum overlooked. The Savoy lay just to the east, and Lady Ottoline Morrell, who was temporarily without a London house, stayed at Garland's Hotel at the dead-end of Suffolk Street, off Pall Mall East. Here 'in her old-fashioned sitting-room, furnished with plush, and a marble clock on the chimney-piece, the ballerinas would be found after the first house, eating strawberry or raspberry jam in silver spoons, dipped previously, after the Russian mode, in tea without milk.'[29]

Massine entirely changed the last scene of *Contes russes*,[30] which, following the première of *The Midnight Sun* (*Soleil de Nuit*) on 21 November, was to be shown to London as *Children's Tales* on the day before Christmas Eve. Much of the scenery had been burnt in a railway tunnel in South America, and had to be replaced.[31] A new act-drop was planned for the episode of Bova Koralevitch and the Swan Princess; and Larionov's design for this arrived from Paris at the last moment. Diaghilev decided to have the set for the third act, 'Baba Yaga', repainted in green instead of yellow. 'I want it to be spring-like instead of looking like a banana forest,' he told Polunin, who gave it the required colouring, 'much to the displeasure of the designer', as Polunin heard later. Diaghilev pacified Larionov by telling him that it was impossible to procure ochre in London because of the war.

The back-cloth of the second act ['The Swan Princess'], which consisted of an enormous red sky, required to be carefully repainted ... and the following dialogue ensued:

POLUNIN: It is impossible to find any vermilion, and the other red tones available are all very bad.
DIAGHILEV: There is no interest in achieving the possible, but it is exceedingly interesting to perform the impossible.
POLUNIN: How can that be?
DIAGHILEV: Did you think it was possible for me to come to London with my company and remain here for six months instead of a few weeks? The impossible becomes possible. I am not interested in what is available or what is not, all I know is that the work must be done.
The impossible was performed – but at what cost.[32]

Children's Tales became a favourite ballet in England, and remained in the repertoire on and off for ten years.

The most unusual number [wrote Beaumont] was the Kikimora scene, an extraordinary presentation of venomous hate, most forcibly rendered by Sokolova, whose striped make-up gave her a fiendish appearance. Idzikovsky's remarkable *élévation* was admirably suited to the cat.... The whimsical manner in which he despondently shook his head [at the Dragon's funeral], and dabbed his eyes with an orange handkerchief dangling from a trembling hand, used to make Diaghilev shake with laughter.[33]

The year 1919 was to be calm and happy for Diaghilev, and during its course he would produce two of his greatest and most popular ballets.

On 6 January Diaghilev left the Coliseum at five o'clock, meaning to visit Ricketts and Shannon in Holland Park, but by 6.15 he had still not found a taxi. Anxious to apologize, he wrote to Ricketts inviting him to lunch or dinner at the Savoy, so that they could go on to the ballet together.[34] In his letter of refusal Ricketts admitted that he liked *The Good-humoured Ladies* so much that he had been to see it four times.[35]

Beaumont had made friends with the polyglot Barocchi, whom he found 'a whole theatrical entertainment in himself' and who gave a good imitation of Diaghilev, compressing his mouth into a certain shape and placing an imaginary eye-glass in his eye. It is also clear that Beaumont was a little in love with Lopukhova. She 'had no exalted ideas as to her importance. As soon as she had taken leave of those who came to pay homage, she would wipe off her make-up – she never put very much on – and change into a simple short skirt, woolly jumper and tam-o-shanter, skipping home like a schoolgirl let out of school.'[36]

In contrast to Lopukhova, Massine had developed a definite consciousness of his position. Beaumont was standing by the stage-doorkeeper's office one evening when he observed the poster announcing a charity performance, on which Lopukhova's name was printed in much larger type than Massine's. Massine arrived, noticed this too, 'visibly snorted with indignation', unlocked his dressing-room and shut the door. When Diaghilev arrived, he found Massine's door locked, imagined that he was late in arriving and went in search of Grigoriev.

Together they crossed to Massine's room and tried the door once more. They called to him, but all was silence. They banged on the door with their fists, but there was no reply. ... Tall, slight Grigoriev and massive Diaghilev, as though actuated by a mutual impulse, sank on their haunches and tried to peer through the keyhole, bumping their heads in the process. ... Massine finally consented to open the door and go on stage.[37]

Bakst had designed the Russian version of *Die Puppenfee*, which the Legat brothers had staged at the Hermitage Theatre in 1903. Naturally he wanted to design the Rossini ballet on a similar subject which Diaghilev had told him about in Rome in spring 1917. The setting of the former had been a toyshop in the St Petersburg arcade off the Nevsky Prospekt, and that of the second was to be a shop set in an improbable arcade overlooking the Bay of Naples. It is not clear whether Diaghilev disliked the first sketches sent him by Bakst, and deliberately asked for the remaining designs 'immediately', knowing that Bakst would demand more time, or whether Bakst had still shown Diaghilev nothing and was serious when he wrote to him on 24 March 1919, accusing him of a long silence and refusing to execute the designs in a hurry. He ended with the words: 'Since you are in such a rush, order the *mise-en-scène* from another painter. Perhaps he will throw it together for you in double-quick time. As for me, I shall have the consolation of having done something important, which in due course I shall have published under the title *La Boutique fantasque*, or perhaps *Naples Reverie*,

1832.'[38] Although the tone of this letter was playful, Diaghilev was perhaps glad to take it seriously. He sent Massine to Paris to talk to André Derain.

Massine found Derain to be 'a tall man with the robust good looks of a French peasant, who spoke in a soft, gentle voice, and waved his hands about like an excited child'. Derain was proud of a marionette theatre, bought at a country fair, and he gave a demonstration for Massine in his flat in the rue Bonaparte, manipulating the strings of the puppets. Massine hummed Rossini's tunes, and the painter made rapid sketches of the court cards, the tarantella and can-can dancers.[39] The date of the action was moved forward from 1832 to the 1860s, the crinoline period.[40]

Bakst was 'hurt and indignant'[41] when he was told that the job had been given to Derain. He and Diaghilev were estranged for two years. Massine had often heard Diaghilev say that 'in the theatre there are no friends', and he was not surprised by Diaghilev's ruthlessness, realizing that, if the Ballet was to keep up with the times, it meant 'a change from lavish splendour to simplicity and rigid artistic control'.[42]

Les Sylphides and *Thamar* were staged before the long Coliseum season closed on Saturday, 29 March. There were seventeen curtain calls on the last night; and Diaghilev was able to publish the news that he was beginning another season, but this time a proper one, with three ballets a night, at the Alhambra in Leicester Square – also run by Oswald Stoll – on 30 April. But before that the Ballet was booked to appear at the Manchester Hippo-drome, another music-hall, at which they would dance one ballet at each of the three daily performances.

When Diaghilev received from Switzerland the news that Nijinsky had become insane, he told Massine that Botkine had long ago predicted this: he was not surprised that it had happened, only that it had happened so soon.[43] Marie Rambert was shocked, when he told her at tea at the Ritz that Nijinsky 'was walking on all fours', and thought him callous: but, of course, he would not wish to join the emotional lady in her demonstrations of dismay.[44]

Ansermet arrived to conduct the Alhambra season. Throughout May and June Stravinsky, in Switzerland, used him as an intermediary in his attempts to extract from Diaghilev money which was due for performances of *The Firebird* and *Petrushka* during the war. In August Ansermet was able to take him ten thousand francs.[45]

The company was now rejoined by some of the deserters to South America – Vera Nemtchinova and her boy-friend, Nicolas Zverev, Anatol Burman and Leokadia Klementovicz. What is more, Karsavina's return was announced, as well as guest appearances by Lydia Kyasht, who had spent the war in England. The Moorish decorations of the Alhambra, which stood on the east side of Leicester Square (where the Odeon Cinema stands today), amazed the Russians. At the *première, Petrushka* was given for the first time in England since the war.

La Boutique fantasque was taking shape. It was finely wrought. Not only was each musical number, from the 'Marche slave' of the overture to the galloping finale, perfect of its kind; the variety of the tunes and of the dances arranged to them was infinite. Not only were the Shopkeeper (Cecchetti) and his loose-limbed, light-fingered, nose-picking Assistant (Gavrilov) characters of Dickensian eccentricity; each of their customers, English, American or Russian, had a life of his or her own. The tarantella of Soko-lova and Woizikovsky, the mazurka of the four Court Cards, Idzikovsky's Snob (a caricature of an English dandy), who is run over by the Melon-vendor's cart, the Cossacks led by Zverev, the two Poodles of Clark and Kremnev, and the can-can of Lopukhova and Massine – who was made up chalk-white and imitated the inhuman contortions of Lautrec's *Valentin le désossé* – were all vivid interpretations. 'Most of the doll characters,' wrote Massine, 'were the direct results of conversations between Diaghilev and myself.'[46]

The fact that the male and female Can-can Dancers were bought by the two different families, Russian and American, to be parted for ever on the morrow, made possible the contrasting sweet sorrow of the middle scene, when the shop was closed for the night. Massine could not think how to end the ballet, and it was Derain, walking with him beneath the trees of Leicester Square, who suggested that the dolls should rebel and attack the shopkeeper and his customers.[47]

Felix Fernandez had been getting more and more peculiar. It was hard on him to be far from Spain, isolated in a crowd of foreigners, and he obviously found it difficult, as a highly personal artist whose potency depended much on improvisation, to fit into the schedules of company life: on top of this he must have suffered a mortal blow when he discovered that it was Massine, not himself, who was to be the Miller and dance the *farucca* in Falla's ballet. He had wanted to dance the tarantella in the Rossini, but he could not be trusted to stick to the script and do the same thing two days running. He enjoyed fooling around as the Pedlar in *Petrushka*; and this was almost his only 'role'. Massine gave him a metronome and he could be seen walking down Shaftesbury Avenue, 'keeping time, time, time'.[48]

Much had happened to Karsavina since Diaghilev had caused her such tribulations by delaying her return journey to Russia by one day, in order to borrow money, in 1914. She had left her first husband, Mukhin, for Henry Bruce, of the British Embassy in Petrograd; she had married him and had a son; she had danced at the Mariinsky throughout the Revolution; she had escaped with husband and child via Murmansk in the extreme north; she had spent time in Tangier, where Bruce was *en poste*. Tamara was naturally out of practice, but Diaghilev wanted her to dance the Miller's Wife in the

Spanish ballet; and, to interest her, he arranged a demonstration by Felix at the Savoy Hotel.

It was fairly late when, after supper, we went down to the ballroom, and Felix began. ... He needed no begging, and gave us dance after dance. In between, he sang the guttural songs of his country, accompanying himself on the guitar. I was completely carried away, forgetful that I was sitting in an ornate hotel ballroom till I noticed a whispering group of waiters. It was late, very late. ... They went over to Felix too, but he took not the slightest notice. He was far away. ... A warning flicker and the lights went out. Felix continued like one possessed. The rhythm of his steps – now staccato, now languorous, now almost a whisper, and then again seeming to fill the large room with thunder – made this unseen performance all the more dramatic. We listened to the dancing enthralled.[49]

Poor Felix! It was his last performance.

Sokolova had been trained for the part of the Miller's Wife. She was now ordered to teach it to Karsavina. Tamara also found Massine, whose Joseph she remembered as 'an image of youth and innocence', 'a very exacting master'.[50] Leonide was twenty-four.

Karsavina made her return to the London public on 4 June in *Carnaval* and *Schéhérazade*. On the next evening, Thursday the fifth, took place the first performance of *La Boutique fantasque*.

A full house was to be expected, but Beaumont was not prepared for what he saw. 'The promenade at the back of the stalls was so packed that you could hardly cross from one side to the other.' It was the same on the upper tiers.

Everywhere you looked, you could see nothing but rows of white faces blurred by the haze of cigarette smoke. It was a critical audience too, for I recognized many faithful ballet-goers and many well-known critics, painters, sculptors and composers. There was an air of jollity and buoyancy which seemed to promise success. ... The first ballet [*The Firebird*] was well received, but it was obvious that everyone was impatiently awaiting the *Boutique*. I crept through the pass-door. ... The large table in the greenroom had been covered with papers, on which the evening's bouquets were set out in order. In a corner there was a silent sewing-machine. ... As the dancers emerged from their dressing-rooms and came on to the stage, Derain passed them in review. He was very particular on the subject of make-up and each artiste had placed on his or her dressing-table a tiny sketch of what was required. There was a shout of *orchestre!* ... I went back to the auditorium where the buzz of conversation was almost deafening. ... Suddenly the house-lights began to dim.[51]

Even the sketchy drop-curtain of Derain, with its draperies, potted palms and double-bass, its guitar-player and mid-nineteenth-century girl with long pantaloons under her skirt, flanking, like heraldic supporters, a charming still-life, was a signal to Bloomsbury and to young painters that the Russian Ballet was now in alliance with the *avant-garde*. Beaumont thought 'the naïve

355

treatment of the two figures poised against the broad masses of harmonious earth reds and browns resembled the decoration of an early Victorian pencil-box.'[52] That this banner of Post-Impressionism waved in the face of the British public should have a nineteenth-century subject was perhaps no more paradoxical than that the most startling success of the new school of English writers, published in 1918, should be Lytton Strachey's irreverent bio-graphies of four *Eminent Victorians*. So *La Boutique fantasque* was to London what *Parade* had been to Paris two years before.

For once Grigoriev, who had little taste, had been right in foreseeing the drawbacks of Derain's much praised toyshop décor, though his objections were practical, while mine are artistic.[53] The main point and beauty of the set lay in its backcloth, with a paddle-steamer in a hill-girt bay very unlike the Bay of Naples – Diaghilev said the toyshop was more like a restaurant overlooking the Lake of Geneva.[54] (Admittedly, the wings, painted with towering flower arrangements, were also delightful.) But this landscape was cut up by the architecture of the shop-front through which it had to be seen. Grigoriev, who could not imagine how this shop could be shut up for the night, waited – not in vain – for the expression on Diaghilev's face when the problem presented by 'two vast windows and a doorless doorway' had to be faced. The unsatisfactory solution was to draw tall blue-grey curtains across the gaping apertures.[55] The landscape, which in the first and third tableaux was obstructed, in the second was totally concealed. If Diaghilev had crossed the Channel to talk to Derain, instead of merely sending Massine, these problems might have been obviated.

Under Olga's influence, Picasso had undergone a worldly transformation. He wore expensive suits and went to parties. On his first visit to London he discovered the tailors of Savile Row and the shirt-makers of Jermyn Street. He also made, as usual, a number of portrait drawings, sketched the dancers in rehearsal and drew several dazzling impressions of Lopukhova and Massine in the final pose of their *pas de deux* in *La Boutique fantasque*.[56] Polunin was astonished at Picasso's elementary set for *Le Tricorne*, but appreciated its merit. 'Having dealt so long with Bakst's complicated and ostentatious scenery, the austere simplicity of Picasso's drawing ... was astounding. ... Diaghilev and Picasso approved my model without any alteration, and the work proceeded in a spirit of exultation. Picasso came to the studio daily. ...'[57]

Picasso painted much of the drop-curtain himself. After working on this picture – it was the group of a man, four women and a boy fruit-seller, in a box overlooking a bull-ring – for more than a fortnight, he asked Polunin to stop him when he thought he had gone far enough. This Polunin did. 'Diaghilev expressed his admiration to Picasso, embracing him, and thanked us for the execution of the scene.'[58]

Elizabeth Polunin, known as 'Violet', made many portrait sketches of the dancers and was responsible for the only decent oil portrait (done from photographs) of Diaghilev to survive outside Russia.[59] The Polunins gave a party for the principal dancers, to meet some of their friends from beyond the footlights. This was held in a rope-maker's loft off Monmouth Street, and it was here that Sokolova remembered meeting for the first time the tall Mrs Edward Grenfell, wife of the banker[60] (later Lady St Just), who became a close friend to Diaghilev and to several of his dancers in later years. Juliet Duff used to say, 'We never quite knew who she was,'[61] implying that she was not 'in society', and I sensed in this a certain rivalry over friendship with Diaghilev. She 'was', in fact, the Florence Henderson who, as a girl of twenty-one, had made notes in her album about the early performances of the Russian Ballet in London in 1911. Other new friends met through the Grenfells were the portrait-painter Oswald Birley and his handsome wife Rhoda.[62]

A few days later, on 10 July, Lydia Lopukhova, who was bored with Barocchi, eloped (to St John's Wood) with a Russian officer.[63] Diaghilev was in Paris.[64] The newsvendors' hoarding announced, 'FAMOUS BALLERINA VANISHES.'[65] Massine and Grigoriev gave Vera Nemtchinova Lydia's role in *La Boutique fantasque*.[66] It was her big chance.

Every century, or every half-century, or, as time grows short, every few years, northern countries are obsessed by the thought of Spain. *Le Tricorne* (called in England *The Three-cornered Hat*), the work of Falla, Diaghilev, Felix, Massine and Picasso, was to open the gates to a new epidemic of Hispanomania. London would soon be full of Spanish dancing schools, and Ernest Hemingway would be at the *corrida*. Massine described his ballet, first given on 22 July, praising Karsavina:

The languorous, seductive movements of her first entry quickly established the character of the miller's bored dissatisfied wife, and her tentative flirtation with the young nobleman [Idzikovsky] prepared the way for her later adventures with the lascivious old Corregidor, superbly danced by Woizikovsky, who made him a wonderfully grotesque character, all trembling lust and licentious leers. In my *pas de deux* with Karsavina after we have driven off the flirtatious Corregidor, I tried to achieve that quality of pursuit, of tension, teasing, advancing and retreating, which is a salient feature of so many Spanish dances. As we whirled and leapt round each other Karsavina flashed a provocative smile at me and I responded by leaping higher and higher. Although the dance was mainly inspired by the *fandango* with some *flamenco* passages, I added to it a variety of classical movements. Then, at the first lyrical strains of de Falla's *sevillana*, I brought a number of dancers on stage. . . . At the end [of their dance] they disposed themselves gracefully about the stage and I was left alone for my Miller's dance [*farucca*]. I began by stamping my feet repeatedly and twirling my hands over my head. As the music quickened I did a series of high jumps, ending with a turn in mid-air and a savage stamp of the foot as I landed. Throughout the dance my movements were slow and contorted, and to the style and rhythm which I learned

357

from Felix I added many twisted and broken gestures of my own. I felt instinctively that something more than perfect technique was needed here, but it was not until I had worked myself up into a frenzy that I was able to transcend my usual limitations. The mental image of an enraged bull going into the attack unleashed some inner force which generated power within me. I felt an almost electrical interaction between myself and the spectators. Their mounting excitement had the effect of heightening my physical strength until I was dancing with a sustained force that seemed far beyond my reach at other times. For one moment it seemed as if some other person within me was performing the dance.[67]

Perhaps the 'other person' possessing Massine was Felix Fernandez, who had been found by the police three months before, dancing furiously on the altar steps of St Martin's-in-the-Field. He was certified as insane, then taken on 13 May to the Long Grove Hospital at Epsom in Surrey, where he remained until his death in 1941.[68]

Le Tricorne was an enormous success. Massine created over a hundred ballets in his long life, but it remained the work of which he was proudest.[69] So much of his experience of Spanish life and art had been filtered through his subconscious to produce this ballet, 'plus vrai que le vrai' – to use a favourite phrase of Cocteau's. *Le Tricorne* was also the culmination of Diaghilev's five years of tuition: now Leonide had gone beyond the point where Diaghilev could help him.

Margot Asquith had a habit of waking up early and writing letters in bed. The following note, written on the morning after the first night of *Le Tricorne*, must have been delivered by hand by a footman at the Savoy Hotel; and it may well have been the first 'notice' of the new ballet, arriving with his morning coffee, that Diaghilev ever read. (It was written in pencil and is copied without corrections.)

20 Cavendish Square, W.1.

Mercredi 23rd
Dear Mr Diaghileff

A great succès last night. Just *one* word of criticism. When they all kneel down – Carsarvena & Massine move down the centre – *all sh be down* — last night one or two stood up which looked ragged – also when the men cry out it is very nice and enthusiastic but the cries were *feeble* and not at all *spontaneous* they s^d be *sharp* & *all together*. The castagnettes were not quite *in time*: & I think the finale when the curtain falls finds the hero too *far back* – not quite *near* all of us – when Carsarvina came in with her *tiny* little head all close close – & no tail to her hair, it was *more* chic – but why not have her hair nice all *close*, & in the next dance (if you prefer it) have the little tail? – *It was all quite beautiful*.

The Massine dance the *most wonderful* I ever saw=Dont let him go too far away from the front: – Can you Déjeuner to-day 1.30? or tomorrow jeudi 24th & bring *Mme Bruce* Please do

Yrs
Margot Asquith[70]

There were laudatory notices in most newspapers.[71] The provincial-minded Ernest Newman, however, who knew a lot about Wagner, but little about anything else, and who was to prove an irritating critic of Diaghilev until the latter ceased to send him tickets, wrote in the *Observer*, 'I am not sure that it is quite de Falla at his best. ... The drop scene and the background of M. Picasso I frankly did not like. ...'[72]

Diaghilev telegraphed to Torres, King Alfonso's secretary, asking him to bring to the attention of 'our august protector' the fact that the Ballet had just given a new Spanish work, with the collaboration of two great Andalusian artists, Falla and Picasso, which was a triumph with the London public and press.[73] He would be grateful to the King to the end of his days.

On the Monday following the first night of the new ballet, Diaghilev, the Picassos and Massine had lunch with Lady Ottoline at Garsington Manor, near Oxford. Aldous and Maria Huxley were there, having spent the weekend.[74] On Wednesday, 30 July, the successful Alhambra season came to an end. Another London season had been arranged with Sir Alfred Butt at the Empire Theatre (on the north side of Leicester Square), to start on 29 September. The Ballet had two months' holiday. Diaghilev and Massine made straight for Italy, spending a week or two in Naples before going to Venice.

Massine's determination to possess I Galli, the islands off Positano which Diaghilev called 'Les Sirenouzi'[75] – a transaction which was delayed because they belonged to several members of the same family[76] – was the first sign of his need to make a life apart from Diaghilev. Other signs would appear during the next year and a half. In the meantime, there was more work for them to do together. Massine was fascinated by the old Italian comedy, the *Commedia dell' arte*, which still survived in Neapolitan puppet theatres, and he did some research in the library of the Royal Palace, adjoining the San Carlo, where he found many eighteenth-century scenarios for the improvised plays. He realized that because the players in the old comedy wore masks their movements and gestures had to be exceptionally expressive.

I decided that the character of Pulcinella would best lend itself to balletic treatment. ... During that summer in Naples I went often to watch the puppet-plays in which Pulcinella played the chief part. I delighted in his ever-changing gestures, his dangling legs, and his hook-nosed mask, with one side of the face laughing and the other crying. From an old Italian actor I bought an authentic Pulcinella mask which had originally belonged to Antonio Petito, the eighteenth-century *commedia dell' arte* actor and producer. I put it on and began trying to reproduce Pulcinella's gestures and movements.[77]

Diaghilev thought this comic ballet should have music by Pergolesi. He and Massine studied printed scores and manuscripts by that composer in the library of the Conservatorio of S. Pietro a Maiella, and chose eighteen pieces which were suited to their purpose.[78]

359

The evolution of *Pulcinella* may have begun earlier than this summer of 1919, for Ansermet had referred to a 'Pergolesi-Picasso ballet' in a letter to Stravinsky in May:[79] but Stravinsky was not asked to orchestrate the Pergolesi until the autumn.

Before returning to London, Diaghilev and Massine visited Henri Matisse at Nice, to ask him to design *Le Chant du rossignol*. 'One of the best rooms', wrote Massine, 'was occupied by a giant birdcage. He had hundreds of exotic birds ... and was so proud of them that he even carried about an official document testifying to the vocal range of his favourite nightingale. He was naturally delighted at the idea of doing the décor. ...'[80]

During the season at the Empire, London, which lasted from 29 September till 2 December, King Alfonso came to see *Le Tricorne*,[81] there was a gala to which King George brought the Shah of Persia, and *Parade* was given for the first time in England. During the gala for the Shah Diaghilev talked to Kathleen Scott (widow of Scott of the Antarctic, and a cousin of Karsavina's husband) about the play J. M. Barrie had written for Karsavina, *The Truth about the Russian Dancers*, which was to be staged in 1920.[82] On 18 October Margot Asquith had wanted to ask Diaghilev to change the programme of the matinée, so that her son Anthony and his friends could see the Spanish ballet during his half-term holiday from Winchester College; and she invited Diaghilev and Massine to hear some Spanish music at Cavendish Square and have tea on the afternoon of the twenty-second.[83]

Matisse came to London in October to supervise Polunin's painting of the Chinese décor for *Le Chant du rossignol*. He arrived 'without any sketches or any definite plans', wrote the patient scene-painter. 'After having visited with me different museums, he set to work in the studio, scissors in hand, cutting out and piecing together a model. This work took a fortnight. His complete ignorance of the stage was surprising. ... He left me to paint the scene and departed for Paris, saying I should do it much better in his absence.'[84] The stage picture turned out simple and original.

Against a background mainly white, outlined in black, with touches of sky-blue, the Chinese costumes stood out in the clear colours of Ming porcelain, green with pink as on a *famille verte* vase, saffron yellow or white barred with orange and black. The grotesque soldiers, whose armour Matisse sketched from originals in the Musée Guimet,[85] were sky-blue and white. Karsavina's costume as the real Nightingale was not that of a bird (Diaghilev disliked realistic animal costumes), but that of a white rose; Idzikovsky, as the Mechanical Nightingale, was encased in a globular carcase and had a long beak; as Death, Sokolova wore scarlet tights, with a necklace of skulls and another on top of her head. There was a fine moment when the supposedly dead Emperor, mimed by Grigoriev, was restored to life by the Nightingale's song. He rose to his full height on his up-tilted bed, and from his black-and-gold figure an immense vermilion cloak unrolled, covering half the stage. He then slowly stepped into the wings on the bowed backs of his white-and-black-clad mourning courtiers.[86]

When Diaghilev decided *Le Chant* must have a drop-curtain, as *La Boutique* and *Le Tricorne* had done – it was his way of commissioning the best painters to produce their biggest pictures – Matisse had to come back to London. He brought only a pencil sketch, representing two kylins flanking a panel with three masks against a flowered background. 'Having begun the lion on the left,' wrote Polunin, 'he presently gave it up as he thought that the one on the right, painted by me, was more successful.'[87]

Diaghilev had arranged that his company should give forty performances at the Paris Opéra, divided into two seasons, in the first half of 1920, with visits to Rome, Milan and Monte Carlo in between.[88] The Ballet had performed only three times at the Opéra, on Christmas Eve, the twenty-seventh and the thirtieth, when an orchestra strike interrupted their season for three weeks. At these performances the French saw *La Boutique fantasque* for the first time, with Karsavina in Lopukhova's role; and Vera Karalli, whom Diaghilev had hardly set eyes on since she eloped with Sobinov in 1909, danced the Polovtsian Girl in *Prince Igor*.[89]

Every kind of difficulty attended the evolution of *Pulcinella*. Diaghilev had given Massine to understand that Stravinsky was scoring the Pergolesi numbers for a large orchestra 'with harps', whereas the composer had settled for a small string orchestra and a wind quartet, with songs for soprano, tenor and bass. There were no harps, no clarinets and no percussion instruments. The 'volume' of Massine's choreography had to be reduced in consequence. Stravinsky made several trips from Switzerland to adjust matters.[90] Diaghilev himself was astonished by the transmutation of Pergolesi into Stravinsky. This was no straightforward orchestration, such as Ottorino Respighi had made of Rossini: it was a new composition. Even the composer did not realize at the time that it was the gateway to his new classical period, 'my discovery of the past, the epiphany through which the whole of my late work became possible'. He wrote, 'That the result was to some extent a satire was probably inevitable ... but ... I did not set out to compose a satire. ... Diaghilev ... went about for a long time with a look that suggested The Offended Eighteenth Century. ... People who had never heard of, or cared about, the originals cried "sacrilege". ... To them all my answer was ... You "respect", but I love.'[91]

Picasso's first idea of designing a contemporary setting for the Italian comedy was rejected by Diaghilev. He next thought of creating a theatre within a theatre. When he had been in Naples in March 1917, he and Stravinsky had gone to puppet shows, music-halls and probably the San Carlo Opera House together; and he may have returned for the Ballet's curtailed visit in April. Designs executed between 22 January and 1 February 1920 represented a Neapolitan street scene, framed by a classical theatre with boxes. These sketches were followed by another for a white and gold (more Parisian) theatre, enclosing a similar scene, with people in the evening dress of 1860 in the boxes.[92] Costumes for the *Commedia dell' arte* characters were of the same period. 'Picasso's first designs were for Offenbach-period costumes with side-whiskered faces instead of masks. When he showed them, Diaghilev was very brusque: "Oh, this isn't it at all," and proceeded to tell Picasso how to do it.' The evening concluded with Diaghilev actually throwing the drawings on the floor, stamping on them, and slamming the door as he left. The next day all of Diaghilev's charm was needed to reconcile the deeply insulted Picasso, but Diaghilev did succeed in getting him to do a *Commedia dell' arte Pulcinella*.[93] Luckily, the painter came to see eye to eye with Diaghilev, for the finished result, a Neapolitan street scene conceived in Cubist terms and painted blue, grey, dark-brown and white, the houses framing a view of the bay, with a boat, Vesuvius and the full moon, is one of the most beautiful stage settings ever made. But *Pulcinella* would not be shown before the spring.

Reviewing the first performance of *Le Chant du rossignol* on 2 February, *La Vie Parisienne* thought the designs of Matisse too sketchy.[94] Diaghilev himself considered that Massine had tried to be too clever in 'imposing a rhythm on the dance steps that was independent of the musical rhythm, having the dancers move against the music'. The consequence was that the company, who had been worked very hard, 'gave the impression of having been poorly rehearsed and led people to say that the dancers "had no ear"'.[95] Massine's ballet did not long survive.

The company's subsequent visit to Rome was rendered sad by the death, after an operation, of Margherita, wife of Diaghilev's valet, Beppe Potetti. She had for several years run the wardrobe, and Diaghilev was very fond of her. The whole company attended her funeral and Diaghilev wept without restraint.[96] The Roman season was followed by the company's first visit to Milan, where they were received without enthusiasm.[97]

Rehearsals of the Cimarosa opera, with its awkward name *Le Astuzzie Femminili*, 'Feminine Wiles', caused trouble between Diaghilev and Massine. Cimarosa had worked for the Empress Catherine in Russia – which must have been one reason why Diaghilev was interested in him – but Massine's idea of arranging the 'Ballo russo' in the last act as a danced *divertissement*, which was quite in keeping with eighteenth-century tradition, for some reason displeased Diaghilev. 'This led to a heated argument,' wrote Massine, 'but I finally persuaded Diaghilev to let me have my way and the dances remained in. That was our first real disagreement, and the beginning of a gradual decline in our relationship and in our artistic collaboration.'[98] Every relationship, every collaboration has to come to an end, and the reason given to the world may be the whole story or merely an incident which was the symptom of some hidden unrest.

Barrie's play, which had necessitated Karsavina's return to London, only ran for a month, so Tamara was free again to appear with the Russian Ballet during its first post-war season in Monte Carlo, when the plums from Massine's repertoire were shown in the Principality.

There was a railway strike in France, and the train in which Diaghilev, Karsavina, Matisse and Massine were returning to Paris, by an unusual route, on 1 May, was derailed because a striker had cut the line. The carriages were thrown on their sides, and Massine was woken by an ashtray hitting his nose, but no one was hurt. As they stood by the wreckage in the light of early morning at Bar-le-duc, they were photographed.[99] The rest of the company just managed to squeeze on to the only available train, already crowded,[100] and arrived to perform *Schéhérazade* (with Ida Rubinstein) at a gala on 4 May, four days before the opening of the Opéra season on the eighth. At this performance Massine danced in *Les Sylphides* for the first time – with Karsavina.[101]

In Paris Jean Cocteau, now known as the author of *Le Cap de bonne espérance*, held court. His circle of young friends included the musicians who would be called 'Les Six'; Valentine Gross, recently married to the painter Jean Victor-Hugo, great-grandson of the poet; Paul Morand; Lucien Daudet; and the youngest among them, who soon took first place and was the disciple whom Cocteau loved, Raymond Radiguet. The friends went to the cinema, to see the Fratellini clowns at the Cirque Medrano, and to the fair at the Barrière du Trône. Every Saturday they dined together.[102]

For *Pulcinella*, first performed on 15 May at the Opéra, Picasso had ordained a white floor-cloth, to give the effect of moonlight.[103] This was repainted for each performance[104] and no footlights were used. The dancers enjoyed dancing their strenuous steps to the breezy music of Stravinsky. Paris was enraptured. Nobody seemed to mind the absurd *imbroglio*, with its disguises and feigned deaths, which would seem tedious a few years later.

Young Sacheverell Sitwell was just back from studying baroque architecture in southern Italy. On the first night he told Picasso that all the *graffiti* on the walls of Lecce in Puglia were of Pulcinella.[105] Another occupant of Misia's box was the dandy Boni de Castellane, who lived in reduced circumstances since his rich American wife, Anna Gould, had left him (to become Duchesse de Talleyrand), but who had plotted with Misia's cousin Retinger, during the war, when he lived in two rooms at the Hôtel Meurice, to have himself made King of Poland.[106] Sitwell was amused to overhear Boni remark to Picasso, '*I'm* not an anarchist.'[107]

The party after the first night of *Pulcinella* was given by a sociable young Persian, Prince Firouz, who was attached to the Embassy and had become the pet of Paris society. It was held at Robinson, an extraordinary bogus castle south of Paris, rented by a crook called René de Amouretti, who ran illicit night-clubs, and whom the surveillance of the police obliged to keep continually on the move. A visit to Robinson was described, though without mentioning *Pulcinella* or its creators, in Radiguet's masterpiece *Le Bal du comte d'Orgel*, published after his death. Jean Hugo told the true story over half a century later.

We went to Robinson in a string of cars, as in the novel, directed at cross-roads by men with electric torches. René greeted us on the steps. Besides Stravinsky, Picasso and his wife, Diaghilev and Massine, there were Misia and Sert, Princess Eugène Murat – called 'Princesse d'Austerlitz' in *Le Bal* – Lucien Daudet, Jean Cocteau, Auric, Poulenc, others whom I have forgotten, and Radiguet, who immortalized the party. Prince Firouz – Mirza in the novel – was a marvellous host. A lot of champagne was drunk. Stravinsky got tight, went up to the bedrooms and, collecting all the pillows, counterpanes and mattresses, flung them over the banisters into the hall. There was a pillow-fight and the evening ended at three in the morning.[108]

Prokofiev had arrived in Paris from America, where he had been giving piano recitals. He was touched to find that Diaghilev had had his first version of the score of *Chout* handsomely bound. Both Diaghilev and Stravinsky were helpful with their comments; and Diaghilev said he was prepared to produce the ballet if Prokofiev would make some changes. The composer recognized the weaknesses Diaghilev pointed out in his score, and was impressed by his exceptional knowledge and understanding. He agreed to

Picasso and Stravinsky.
Drawing by Jean Cocteau.

rewrite the unsatisfactory parts, to compose five symphonic *entr'actes*, so that the six scenes could be given without interruption, to revise completely the finale and to rescore the whole. 'The very beginning of the ballet, with all its whistling and rattling sounds, as if someone were "dusting the orchestra" before the beginning of the spectacle' was to be left intact.[109]

Meanwhile six Italian singers were rehearsing the Cimarosa opera, and the principal Russian dancers were working on the final *divertissement*. *L'Astuce feminine* was first given (with *Prince Igor*) on 27 May. Diaghilev's own description, though not published till a month later in an English newspaper, may be inserted here.

The first scene is an eighteenth-century interior, influenced by the Chinese importations which one met with in palaces such as Aranjuez. The second is a colonnade in a garden. A tree in the centre looks like a tree of coral. ... The third scene, in which the ballet takes place, is a broad terrace with a panoramic view of Rome. The costumes are ... of the opening year of the nineteenth century. ... I am of the opinion that the principles of choreography are equally applicable to the action in opera, and I wanted to put this theory to the test and show how it could be done. So the action in this opera has been invented and directed by M. Massine.

In 1789 Cimarosa went to St Petersburg and took the place of his fellow countryman Paisiello as director of the Italian theatre. He conducted there for three years, composing much music ... and seeing many things, amongst which may be included the Russian peasant dances. [The work, produced in 1794] is a typical comic opera of the eighteenth century. ... There is the usual kind of intrigue, and the vocal numbers include a love duet and a laughing trio. The story winds up with a wedding, and when it is a question of celebrating the wedding the last line of the libretto is 'And now let us have a Russian ballet.' ... Cimarosa ... makes use of a tune called 'Kamarinskaya', a dance which no doubt he saw the peasants dance at weddings in Russia. Forty years later, Glinka, the father of modern Russian music, used the same tune for an orchestral fantasy which is looked upon as the starting-point of the modern Russian school.[110]

And which – one might add – had been included by Diaghilev in the programme of his first concert of Russian music in Paris in 1907 (though it was not played until the second).

At the beginning of June Darius Milhaud, who had talked to Nijinsky in Brazil about *L'Homme et son désir*, the ballet which he had composed to Claudel's libretto, played it to Diaghilev and Massine at Misia's; but they did not like it.[111]

The Russian Ballet returned to Covent Garden for the first time in seven years on 10 June, and opened triumphantly with *Pulcinella*. They played alternately with the opera; and at another gala for King Alfonso on 7 July danced *Le Tricorne* after a performance of Ravel's *L'Heure espagnole*. Prokofiev had travelled to London with Diaghilev, and when Walter Nuvel, whom

Diaghilev had not seen since 1914, escaped out of Russia via Finland, the young composer went with Diaghilev to meet him at the station.[112] Valetchka was immediately absorbed into the Ballet's organization. He made his headquarters in Paris in the small Hôtel Pasquier, behind the Madeleine,[113] and, since he spoke not only French but German, he became indispensable in dealing with agents and railway companies. The Cimarosa opera (out of which the ballet *Cimarosiana* was later carved) was very well received in London; *Le Chant du rossignol* less so.[114]

Diaghilev pretended to be quite aloof from the private lives of his dancers, but he longed to know who loved whom and to hear all the latest gossip. Sokolova had been having a difficult time for several years with Nicolas Kremnev, who drank and was obsessively jealous; she and Woizikovsky were secretly in love. Woizikovsky's girlfriend Antonova had found some letters, Woizikovsky had denied the whole affair, Sokolova was miserable and began taking overdoses of laudanum. Diaghilev knew all about this and, besides, he could not help noticing that Lydia looked ill and was always crying. He sent for her to the Savoy Hotel and received her in the lobby between the entrance hall and the restaurant. 'He was very kind. He made me tell him what I could through my tears, and then he said, "I want you to think of me as a father, and remember I will come to you at any time of the day or night if you should need me." ... I went back to work feeling braver.'[115]

Stravinsky had still not found what he considered to be the right orchestration for *Les Noces*, so Diaghilev decided to revive *The Rite of Spring*. Nobody could remember Nijinsky's choreography, so Massine was to make a new version.

The London season ended on an unpleasant note. The Covent Garden management were not fulfilling their financial undertaking in the exact manner laid down. Diaghilev's lawyer advised him that if a certain sum of money was not forthcoming, the final performance on Saturday, 31 July, should be cancelled. The house was fully booked, but Diaghilev took his lawyer's advice, and the show was cancelled on the day itself. Diaghilev at once realized that he had made a mistake, but it was too late to reverse his decision. Masses of bouquets had arrived for the dancers from their devoted London public; money was refunded; disappointment was caused; and the episode made a bad impression. To take a lawyer's advice on such a matter in South America (as had actually happened) was one thing: in London, with its possessively affectionate public, it was fatal.[116]

On 2 August, rather tardily – for they had lived together for several years even before the death of Edwards in 1914 – Sert and Misia were married. Their honeymoon was another of many habitual summer tours in Spain and Italy, for Sert loved looking at works of art. This time they took with them, to cheer her up, Coco Chanel, who had not easily survived the death of her dashing English boyfriend, Boy Capell, on 22 December. Paul Morand had noted the steps of Chanel's conquest of society: she had cut her hair short; she had 'definitely become a personality.'[117] Then, the simple, comfortable clothes she made for the rich were in keeping with the spirit of the age. Cocteau had been quick to realize that she was to *couture* what Picasso was to painting.[118] She was vastly successful. But this child of peasants in the Auvergne gave not a damn for the millionairesses who made her fortune. Her description of Misia is the best that exists, so, although it may seem late in the day to provide a portrait of Diaghilev's sphinx-like best friend and staunchest supporter, 1920 is the year when Chanel became a figure of importance in both their lives, and it must be given here. The new Mme Sert was as easily bored as the former Mme Edwards – with Italian sightseeing as with other occupations.

'To hell with these damned Botticellis and Leonardos,' said Misia. 'Let's go and buy some coral and make Chinese trees.' [Sert's coral tree in the Cimarosa opera had echoed a fashionable mania. People were also beginning to make flowers out of shells.]
She was my one real friend, but my feeling for her was more than friendship. . . . She came into my life at the moment of my greatest sorrow. Other people's suffering attracted her as certain smells attract bees. We like people for their defects of character, and Misia gave me good cause to be fond of her. Misia was only fascinated by what she could not understand – and she understood most things; but she always found me mysterious, so she clung to me desperately, and if we had a row she was soon back, close as ever. . . . Misia never opened a book. 'I wonder how you find time for reading,' she said. She didn't even read her own letters. Misia had a sickness of the soul. . . .
'She likes you, Madmachelle,' said Sert, 'because she has never been able to understand you.' She never found the chink in my armour – which was there nevertheless. The resulting frenzy of exasperation brought excitement into her life. . . .[119]

When the three tourists arrived on the Lido at Venice, they found Diaghilev lunching alone with the young Grand Duchess Maria Pavlovna.[120]

Massine went to Switzerland to discuss the new production of *The Rite of Spring*. Stravinsky told Leonide that he thought 'Nijinsky had made a mistake in following too closely the rhythms of the score.' This, of course, had been due to the influence of Dalcroze.

After studying the music for several weeks I came to the conclusion that I could perhaps avoid Nijinsky's error by attempting a counterpoint in emphasis between it and the choreography, and while Stravinsky played selected passages from the score on the piano I demonstrated my idea. Stravinsky approved. . . . I returned to Paris and discussed the project at length with Diaghilev, who thought that Nijinsky had failed because he had attempted to do too much at once. As Diaghilev said, he had not realized that the eye and ear cannot absorb simultaneously as much as the ear alone.

367

Massine could find no justification for Nijinsky's bent wrist and ankle movements in old ikons or wood-carvings, so he decided to base his production on simple peasant round dances, with some angular Byzantine poses; and he thought his choreography might also have been influenced by 'the captivating spirit of cubism'.[121]

Diaghilev still had Roerich's sets and costumes for *The Rite of Spring* – which was one reason for reviving the ballet – and the latter were in good condition, having been danced in only eight times in 1913. This made it unnecessary to pay for a new production. Yet the enormous orchestra demanded by Stravinsky's score would cost more than any décor or set of fifty costumes. Misia, who had introduced Diaghilev to Coco Chanel in Venice, may have spoken a word. One day at the Hôtel Continental Diaghilev was told that Mlle Chanel was asking for him. He could not remember at first who she was. She gave him 300,000 francs to stage *The Rite*, on condition that Diaghilev never mentioned it to herself or to anyone else again.[122]

There was a problem how to keep the Ballet busy in the autumn. London had had a spate, and Germany was too poor in 1920 to afford a visit from the Russians. An English provincial tour was all that could be arranged. This was dismal: three nights at Bournemouth, three at Leicester, one night each at Nottingham, Sheffield and Leeds. In Liverpool, where the Ballet performed for two weeks at the Olympia, things improved.[123]

It was in Liverpool that matters came to a head between Woizikovsky and Sokolova. She was one of the captive women in *Prince Igor* and as he lifted her he stroked her bare waist. After the ballet she slapped his face in front of the whole company, and Grigoriev fined Sokolova '£5 for assault'. Diaghilev told Woizikovsky and Sokolova that, since they had to work together in the company, if they could not get along without causing disturbances they must not speak to each other any more. Sokolova thought he was secretly amused.[124]

Massine cast Sokolova as the Chosen Virgin in his new *Rite of Spring*, and Diaghilev gave them permission to return to London to rehearse, so that they missed the last few days in Liverpool and three days (29 November till 1 December) in Birmingham. Vera Clark, now renamed Savina, went with them, to study the mazurka of *Les Sylphides* under Massine. Whereas Sokolova was essentially a character dancer (though she could pass muster as Columbine in *Carnaval*, which she had been dancing on tour), Savina had a lovely classical style and 'a wonderful quality of lightness', and Diaghilev looked upon her as his future prima ballerina. The three dancers worked daily in a basement room in Maiden Lane: but Sokolova was too busy learning her Sacrificial Dance to notice that Massine had fallen in love with Savina. The unsophisticated English Vera was probably the only person in the company who had no idea of Massine's special position.[125]

From the last performance in Birmingham on 1 December 1920 till the opening performance of Diaghilev's Paris winter season at the Champs-Elysées, when *The Rite* was to be given, the company had a fortnight to put the finishing touches to Massine's difficult work, which Ansermet came to conduct. Stravinsky, too, attended the orchestral rehearsal, and pranced up and down the central aisle of the theatre in a terrifying manner.[126]

After this rehearsal Sokolova witnessed an encounter on the stage between Vera Savina and Misia Sert. Savina told Misia that she was to meet Massine at the Arc de Triomphe, but that it was such a big place she did not know exactly where she should go. Misia advised her to stand right in the middle under the arch; and presumably went straight off to tell Diaghilev.[127]

The dress-rehearsal passed off successfully [wrote Sokolova].... At the end of it I was going back to my dressing-room when I heard Massine calling to me. His room was next to mine, and the door was open. As I walked in Leonide Feodorovitch congratulated me for the first time in my life. He said 'We could not have achieved this work without each other.' I was surprised and touched. I told him I was grateful for all he had done for me. He put his hands on my shoulders and kissed me quite naturally on each cheek. This was done with such sincerity, and I was so overwhelmed to hear these words from the handsome Massine, who never praised anybody, that I returned his embrace with emotion. As he moved away he suddenly froze. Looking round, I saw Diaghilev standing in the doorway. Without a word, he walked past me. I mumbled something and slipped out, leaving an icy atmosphere behind.[128]

On Wednesday, 15 December, the Ballet opened with *Pulcinella*, *The Rite of Spring* and *Le Tricorne*. Sokolova had to dance Karsavina's role, Pimpinella, in the first ballet before undergoing her ordeal in the second. Before she began to dance in the scene of the sacrifice she had to stand still with her left hand across her body, clenched fist in the air, and with her feet turned in, for twelve minutes, staring across the heads of the audience. The only way she could stop herself blinking was to keep her eyes fixed on a red exit light at the back of the auditorium. When she began to dance her exhausting solo, the forty other dancers remained motionless in a semicircle behind her, with hands arched over their brows, as if shading their eyes to watch her. Not only had she to execute her strenuous movements: she had to think, act and keep counting.

At last I came to my final spinning jumps round the stage. These consisted of *grands jetés en tournant*, in themselves difficult steps to do, but between each, on landing, I had to bend sideways and place one hand on the stage while I raised the other in the air and beat my breast twice. Coming to a sudden halt in the middle, I pulled myself up on my toes, waiting for the curtain to begin to fall. I dropped to the ground and lay backwards, raising my body in a taut arch, like a victim meeting the knife, resting on my shoulders, elbows and toes. Just before the curtain touched the stage the last moment of music sounded, and I collapsed.[129]

Stravinsky kissed the twenty-four-year-old Sokolova's hand before the applauding audience. When she got back to her dressing-room, she found that Diaghilev and Massine had given her their little *griffon* dog Micky, which they may have been glad to be rid of, as it suffered from eczema.[130]

There was a supper party at the Hôtel Continental, where Diaghilev and Massine were staying. In the big private dining-room a long table had been laid. Diaghilev sat at one end and Stravinsky at the other. Misia, Coco Chanel and the company's staff and principal dancers were all present. Vera Savina looked very English in a short pink dress, and Diaghilev began to rag her, urging, 'Have a little more champagne, Verotchka.'[131] Massine, for once, must have been drunk, for all he could remember afterwards was burning Picasso's hand with a cigarette. ('Picasso never moved.')[132] Leonide suddenly leapt on the piano to make a speech. 'Quiet, everybody! I have an announcement to make. The time has come. I have made up my mind that I am going to run away.' There were cheers and people shouted, 'Come on! Tell us who with!' 'There's no secret about it,' cried Massine. 'I'm going to run away with Sokolova.' There were embarrassed cheers and laughter, while Massine ran round the table to kiss Lydia's hand.[133] Massine may have been saying thank-you to Sokolova in a light-hearted way for all her good work, but he was not going the right way about giving her, or the jealous Kremnev, or Diaghilev – or possibly Savina – a good night's rest.

Grigoriev had noticed that Diaghilev had recently been irritable and lost his temper easily, and he asked Vassili Zuikov what was the matter. 'Quarrelling with Massine,' was the laconic reply.[134] Over Christmas in Paris Diaghilev must have been in some doubt whether Massine was carrying on a flirtation with Savina or Sokolova.

From the time the Ballet arrived in Rome on New Year's Eve, to begin an intermittent series of performances at the Costanzi on 1 January 1921, Sokolova found herself followed by a pair of detectives.[135] Massine was at the Grand Hotel as usual with Diaghilev (rooms 325 and 327),[136] and the other dancers were at the Minerva. It was here that Sokolova first noticed the two men who took their meals at the next table to hers and Kremnev's, and whose motor-bicycles, parked outside, appeared again outside the rehearsal room. One afternoon Massine told Diaghilev he was going to look at some monuments down the Appian Way, hired a *carrozza*, and drove Savina to a café where rooms could be hired. The detectives were apparently switched, but the only report they were able to bring back to Diaghilev was one of Savina's implacable virtue.

In a way, history was repeating itself. Nijinsky, in pursuit of a woman's love, had to settle for one who was an outsider to the company, a Hungarian camp-follower. Vera Savina was a very pretty girl, and a fine dancer, but she was English, spoke no Russian and hardly knew the facts of life. It is difficult to believe that one of the Russian or Polish girls, particularly if she were in training to become the company's ballerina, would have given up her prospects or risked Diaghilev's wrath by having an affair with Massine. Savina did not understand the situation: she was bewildered, flattered, and no doubt attracted by Massine. She confided in Sokolova, and could not see why the latter thought the romance was a calamity.[137] Diaghilev apparently tried to come to terms with Savina, offering her a special contract and leading roles if she gave up Massine, which she refused to do.[138] Another story is that Diaghilev invited her to his room, made her drunk, stripped off her clothes and threw her, naked, into Massine's room next door.[139] On the day after this crisis, when Massine arrived for rehearsal, 'Grigoriev took him aside and quietly said something to him. Leonide Feodorovitch went deathly pale, turned and walked out of the room.... The rehearsal was cancelled.' Massine had been dismissed. Savina was told she must dress upstairs with the corps de ballet.[140] She left the company, to be followed shortly by several other dancers, who, under Massine, formed a group to visit South America. Massine and Savina were married in London on 26 April.

After the banishment of Massine Diaghilev did not appear in public for several days.[141] He had lost not only his friend but his principal dancer and choreographer – to some extent, the breadwinner of the company. He had again been defeated by youth. Apart from the servants, Vassili and Beppe, only Nuvel was a witness of Diaghilev's breakdown. Whatever excesses there may have been of drinking, tears and despair, all Nuvel ever reported was that he feared not only for his friend's health, but also for his reason.[142] But the Roman season had to be carried through: Massine and Savina had to be replaced in their roles. Diaghilev had to make an effort. When he emerged, he had such black rings under his eyes that he was barely recognizable.[143]

On 4 February the Ballet gave a gala in aid of Russian refugees, of whom Rome was full. On the sixth they danced *Schéhérazade* after a performance of Strauss's *Salomé*. They left Rome on Sunday, 13 February, for Lyon, where they were to give ten performances. Here Idzikovsky danced for the first time in *Les Sylphides*, and for the first time Woizikovsky danced Amoun in *Cléopâtre*. Woizikovsky had to learn all Massine's roles in the Massine ballets: the Miller, the Can-can Dancer and Pulcinella.[144] The company were booked for a season in Madrid following Lyon, but Diaghilev went to Paris on business with Nuvel on 18 February, leaving the dancers to finish their performances in Lyon and travel to Spain without him. It was a day or two before he left the Grand Hôtel, Lyon, where the bedrooms opened on to a balcony which looked down on to the central hall, that Sokolova overheard Diaghilev telling the contralto, Zoia Rozovska, the story of his estrangement from Massine, and was relieved to hear that no blame attached to her 'for having flirted with Massine or betrayed Diaghilev's trust'. Diaghilev ended by saying, 'There is nobody indispensable in this world. I shall find someone else.'[145]

PART VI

The Kochno Period

CHAPTER 14

February 1921–February 1922

Kochno appears – Temporary Measures – *The Sleeping Princess* – Disaster

MIRACLES MAY HAPPEN by chance or from necessity. We have seen how, in the winter of 1913–14, Diaghilev enlisted a young dancer, Miassin, who became first his friend and later his choreographer. Just as his Ballet needed a choreographer to keep it going, so did Diaghilev in private life need the companionship of a young man – a son, as it were – whom he could instruct and guide. Was it by chance or from necessity that Miassin turned out so well? With his departure in January 1921, there was again a gap to fill. It is extraordinary that within one month it was filled, not by a choreographer, certainly, but by another young man chosen at first as an intelligent companion, appointed secretary (which might mean anything – and there were already Nuvel and Barocchi), but who became so close an artistic collaborator that he soon shared all the secret processes of Diaghilev's mind.

Boris Kochno came of the same class as Diaghilev; but his family were ennobled in the course of Catherine's journey through the Ukraine. His father was a Colonel of Hussars, and, as the result of some act of distinction performed at the time of the Tsarevitch's birth during the Russo-Japanese War, was awarded the Oriental-sounding title of 'Godfather to the New-born'. Born in 1904, Boris was educated at the Imperial Lycée of Moscow (closed in 1917). He saw and was thrilled by the modern French paintings in the Shchukin and Morozov collections. After the Revolution he and his mother wandered in a south-easterly direction in search of food. In the small town of Elizabetgrad he met the pianist Szymanovsky, later famous as a composer. Szymanovsky and another friend played *à quatre mains* to the young poet – for such he aspired to be – early compositions of Stravinsky: *Petrushka* and *The Rite of Spring*.[1]

Boris left Russia with nothing but a few volumes of modern poetry wrapped in his clothes. In Constantinople he met the painter Tchelitchev, and the young composer Dukelsky, who was impressed by his elegance and sophistication.[2]

Boris and his mother reached Paris on 9 October 1920. Among his friends in exile were the painter Sudeikine and his wife Vera. Sudeikine, of course, was an old acquaintance of Diaghilev, who had brought him to Paris for the Russian Exhibition of 1906, and commissioned him to design *La Tragédie de Salomé* in 1914. Vera, on the other hand, although she had met Diaghilev once in Moscow in 1914, had only recently made friends with him. What is more, Diaghilev had, during the previous autumn, introduced her to Stravinsky. Taking her to dinner one night with Bakst and Nuvel, he had said, 'Stravinsky will be there. Do you know him?' She said, 'No.' 'Then be kind to him, because he is very moody.' Vera and Stravinsky had got on so well that a month or two later Diaghilev had occasion to ask her, 'You are married. Stravinsky is married. What is going on?' To which she had replied, 'Love.' It remains to be said that the Sudeikines had lived in extreme poverty in Paris until the arrival of their fellow expatriate, the producer, Nikita Baliev, who signed a contract with Sudeikine to design for his *Chauve-Souris*.[3] Such was the situation when Kochno entered their lives.

To Sudeikine and Vera Boris spoke continually about Diaghilev, whose picture he had frequently cut out of newspapers in Russia, and whom it was his ambition to meet.

While the handsome Kochno sat for his portrait, Sudeikine devised a little plot to satisfy his young friend. Kochno should go to Diaghilev's hotel with a message from Sudeikine, asking some question about the performing rights of *La Tragédie de Salomé*. Boris had already seen the Russian Ballet twice at the Théâtre des Champs-Elysées. He had even caught sight of Diaghilev as the lights were dimmed at the end of an interval. Sudeikine spent half a night teaching Boris what he should say when he called on Diaghilev, making him repeat, like a catechism, question and answer. Sudeikine stuffed a cushion into his coat to suggest Diaghilev's girth, walked in a pompous way and adjusted an imaginary monocle. This imitation, as Kochno soon found out, bore no resemblance to the reality.

On 27 February 1921, a Sunday, Boris called at ten in the morning at the Hôtel Scribe. The porter told him that Diaghilev had not stayed there for some years, but that he was probably at the Continental. Kochno walked to the Hôtel Continental at 3 rue Castiglione, between the Place Vendôme and the rue du Rivoli. He asked for Diaghilev. The clerk raised his eyes from the ledger he was studying, looked at the clock, and told him to go straight up. Diaghilev was expecting someone who never came. Boris Kochno arrived instead.

The door of Diaghilev's room was opened by the valet Beppe, who had opened the door to Massine at the Metropole in Moscow seven years before. Beppe's face expressed astonishment: Kochno was told to wait outside.

Whatever account of the unexpected stranger's appearance the valet gave Diaghilev, it must have been favourable. In a few minutes Diaghilev emerged, fresh from his *toilette*. He showed no surprise that an unknown young man had called upon him, and it was he, not Kochno, who spoke first and made excuses. 'I'm so sorry to keep you waiting.' He led Kochno to a sitting-room, *le salon turc*, downstairs, and it was here that Kochno began his act: 'I have come on behalf of Sergei Yurevitch Sudeikine. . . .' But Diaghilev asked none of the questions to which Kochno had learnt the answers. Chewing his tongue, he gazed into the air above the young man's head, as if the voice of this new arrival from Russia, the first he had met for years, prompted thoughts of home. Kochno told his story. He described the new poets and the Constructivist painters and sculptors. He had known on the one hand the Acmeists Mandelstam and Akhmatova, on the other hand Mayakovsky and Essenin. The two greatest experiences in his life so far had been seeing Picasso's portrait of Vollard in Moscow and Lydia Sokolova in *The Rite of Spring* in Paris. Boris recited his own poems. When he left at one o'clock, Diaghilev escorted him to the door and said, 'We shall meet again.'

Next morning, when Kochno returned to the Continental, Diaghilev asked him if he would like to be his secretary. The dream began. On the Tuesday he met Stravinsky at lunch. Three mornings running he reported punctually at eight o'clock, and, seated in a Second Empire armchair, watched Diaghilev reading the newspapers, answering the telephone, writing letters. At last he summoned courage to ask what were his duties. He never forgot Diaghilev's reply. 'Il faut qu'un secrétaire sache se rendre indispensable.' From that moment Boris Kochno took the initiative, and tried to forestall Diaghilev's wishes. In the course of time he succeeded in making himself indispensable. Diaghilev, who disliked smoking, gave him a small tortoise-shell cigarette-case, which held only six cigarettes, saying, 'This will hold your ration for the day.'

On 11 March Boris tried on new suits. On the sixteenth he left with Diaghilev, Stravinsky and Beppe for Madrid, where the Ballet were to have a fortnight's season. At a rehearsal in Madrid Kochno called Diaghilev 'tu' for the first time. Since the departure of Massine, there was no one else in the company who did that. The opening night in Madrid was only the third time he had seen a performance by the Diaghilev Ballet. One night *Carnaval* was the first work on the programme, and he longed to see it (the word 'carnaval' held every kind of enchantment for him): but Diaghilev was reluctant to go so early to the theatre and felt no urge to see his old ballet. They arrived after it was over, and Boris suffered a child's disappointment at missing the rise of the curtain. He was seventeen.[4]

Diaghilev had no choreographer and it was necessary to prepare at least two novelties for the next Paris season. One was to be Prokofiev's *Chout*.

He decided that the dancer Taddeus Slavinsky, who had no choreographic experience but made a good impression on the stage, should work on this under the direction of the painter Larionov. The latter was as eager as ever for new experiments. On 15 March Larionov, in Paris, had signed a contract as artistic director of the company.[5] On the twenty-fourth he wrote that he was full of ideas, but held up at Hendaye for lack of a visa.[6]

Meanwhile Diaghilev, Stravinsky and Kochno went to Seville for Holy Week. Luggage being deposited at the Hôtel Alfonso XIII, Diaghilev took Boris straight to the picture gallery. This consisted of one long room in a derelict building, rarely visited. A bell was rung and an urchin was sent for the key. Boris had visited the museums of Moscow and Paris: this neglected conventual barn made a more powerful impression. Diaghilev had his Baedeker and knew all the pictures. The place was full of dirty paintings by Murillo and Zurbarán, 'flapping in their frames'. There were holes in the roof and the windows were broken. Boris watched swallows flying in and out and around Zurbarán's big picture of monks at dinner.[7]

They had come in search of *flamenco* music and dancers. During the Féria, in the week after Easter, night after night and in many cabarets they watched wonderful performances. Stravinsky wanted to write a modern *Barbiere di Siviglia*: it was referred to as *Sevilsky Bradobreï*. This opera would be scored mainly for guitar and castanets; and there was to be a bullfight. In the end both Stravinsky and Diaghilev thought the *flamenco* music so perfect in itself that the idea was abandoned. Diaghilev decided to engage a small troupe of dancers and singers to present, in Paris and London, a *cuadro flamenco*. There were difficulties not only in the choice of artists – for many were superb – but in coming to arrangements with them. Night after night the gypsies poured in to dance for Diaghilev in a private room at a cabaret.[8] According to Kochno, 'Diaghilev's task was complicated by the fact that most of these artists had not the slightest intention of signing a contract or of leaving Spain; they came for the pleasure of being applauded.'[9] No sooner was one dancer engaged than he demanded double and would not come without his friend or mistress. The illiterate gypsies had no idea of time or money. One day several of them marched in a body to Diaghilev to present a protest: he had concealed from them the fact that to reach Paris they would have to cross the ocean. Who had told them this? 'The barber in the corner shop.' One evening Diaghilev, Barocchi and Kochno were driving down the avenue when they saw coming towards them, in another carriage, a Russian Diaghilev knew, a small-scale impresario. He had with him a Spanish girl of extraordinary beauty. Diaghilev asked to be introduced. She was a dancer, Pepita Ramojé. Diaghilev engaged her and renamed her Maria Dalbaicin. The English showman, Charles Cochran, was in Seville and this gave Diaghilev the idea of 'seducing' him. 'Daily we had wonderful lunch-parties in the brilliant sunshine at the Venta Antequera,' wrote

Cochran of Diaghilev's favourite restaurant, where there were fifty kinds of *hors d'oeuvre*. After giving a typical menu, he concluded: 'It was not surprising, after a luncheon such as the one described above, preceded by a bottle of Manzanilla as an *apéritif* and with the best coffee I ever tasted, and a cigar to follow, that Serge Diaghilev should persuade me I needed a season of Russian Ballet at the Prince's Theatre. . . . He could charm a dead man to life.'[10]

The other enthusiasm of the moment was Tchaikovsky. Stravinsky and Diaghilev played over and over, on the upright piano in the hall of the Alfonso XIII, the score of *The Sleeping Beauty*. Because Diaghilev was afraid to give this old work, or part of it, without something modern also in the programme, it was planned that there would be a short curtain-raiser in the form of an opera by Stravinsky to a libretto by Kochno. The subject chosen was Pushkin's story in verse, 'The Little House at Kolumna', about the daughter of a middle-class family, living in the outskirts of St Petersburg, who persuades her mother to engage her lover, a hussar dressed as a woman, as cook. The dénouement is brought about by the cook being found shaving. This work was first referred to by the title of the story; it was next called *La Cuisinière*, and finally *Mavra*.[11]

Diaghilev's original intention was that, if he could stage a production of *The Sleeping Beauty*, Benois, the expert on the Louis XIV style, should design it, but Benois was at that time Director of the Hermitage and would have to be lured out of Russia.[12]

Larionov had arrived in Madrid, Falla was there, and so were Robert and Sonia Delaunay. Rehearsals for *Chout* were begun.[13]

The weeks between the end in mid-April of the Madrid season (the Russian Ballet's last in that city) and the opening in Paris were spent by Diaghilev between Paris and Monte Carlo.[14]

Boris Kochno returned from Spain sadder than he went; from a physical point of view, he was not Diaghilev's type, though he had other qualities to hold the interest of his hero. Vera Sudeikina understood the situation.[15] That Boris was a gentleman may have been a little off-putting to Diaghilev; and the very intelligence which made him so precious a friend diminished his desirability as a lover. But there were ways in which he could make himself indispensable to Diaghilev without wearing the official badge of favourite. Boris Kochno resigned himself to a different vocation, and his work behind the scenes was destined often to steal the show, to the greater glory of the Russian Ballet, from star performers who basked briefly in the twin spotlights of Diaghilev's infatuation and popular acclaim.

Diaghilev never paid Kochno a salary, but he lodged, fed and clothed him well;[16] and, as people noticed, Boris did not mind asking Sergei Pavlovitch for a few francs to buy cigarettes.[17] It was not such a bad life; it was the one for which he was predestined; and he would not have exchanged it for all the Easter eggs Fabergé ever made – although he had a greed for rare and precious objects.

Prokofiev had at last made arrangements with Mary Garden (the first Mélisande), the new Director of the Chicago Opera, for the production of his *Love for Three Oranges* in the autumn of 1921. Now, in the spring, he returned to Paris.[18] Diaghilev sent him to Monte Carlo, where rehearsals for *Chout* were in progress.[19]

Diaghilev had decided to invite Juan Gris – like Picasso, both Spanish and a Cubist – to design the décor for his *Cuadro Flamenco*, and Picasso approved his decision.[20] Diaghilev telegraphed to Gris on 14 April.[21] But a day or two later, when Diaghilev visited Picasso in the rue la Boétie, he found that Picasso had made all the designs himself.[22] It was as if the painter could not bear to be left out of so Spanish a manifestation as gypsy dancers. The décor was adapted from one of the rejected projects for *Pulcinella*. The curtains of a nineteenth-century theatre were parted to reveal a still-life of flowers in a vase. In three of the four surrounding stage boxes were groups of spectators in evening dress, that on the lower left being a variation on the theme of Renoir's *La Loge*. On the ceiling of the theatre (painted in false perspective) was the figure of Fame, blowing her trumpet.

Barocchi had been left in Seville to come to terms with the gypsies, and from 27 April till 10 May Diaghilev received a series of comical, despairing telegrams.

Seville, 27 April. 'Attitude Ramirez and Macarona unbelievable. Will not discuss money.... Madness to count on them because at last moment will not come. Malena asking hundred pesetas a day. Vez with performing husband two hundred. Estampillo forty. All discussion of fees useless.'

27 April. 'Have spent entire evening with Macarona and Ramirez. They decided finally to tell me their fee tomorrow, therefore am slightly hopeful. Do nothing but embrace them entire time.'

28 April. 'Macarona asking minimum one month contract three thousand pesetas.... Ramirez thousand five hundred ... essential they leave with me.... If you approve wire travel advances also money for trousers shoes for Ramirez.'

28 April. 'Ramirez now insisting on identical terms Macarona.'

5 May. 'Trying one solid week engage Manolo called Huelvano who declines even thousand five hundred pesetas a month. Husband Minarita magnificent performer great friend Manolo but also unable persuade him sign.'

7 May. 'Minarita and Vez do not dance. Prefer Vez because prettier better voice but insists singing songs with orchestra plus six thousand pesetas a month.... Ramirez has lost wits. Refuses sign unless we engage Rosario who will not come without aunt or Macarona or Malena who now asking six thousand with husband performer.'

Madrid, 8 May. '[La Rubia] refused flatly before police and Tovar [Governor of Madrid] to leave before Tuesday night. Nasty disposition therefore unwise insist.'

Madrid, 10 May. 'Absolutely indispensable you meet me station Thursday with address cheap pension and bus transportation for entire flock for they are all repeat all dotty.'[23]

The Paris season was to be at the Gaieté Lyrique, and would last only one week. Diaghilev was fearful that, without Massine and with only one new ballet apart from the Spaniards, he might not be able to fill the house even for that short time. 'Maria Dalbaicin' had travelled separately from the other Spaniards, and was with the company at Monte Carlo. Diaghilev hoped that because of her beauty he might be able to build her up into a star of sorts; and Sokolova was told to teach her the role of the Miller's Wife in *Tricorne*.

When Juan Gris arrived at Monte Carlo from Bandol, Diaghilev had to break the news that he had come to other arrangements for *Cuadro Flamenco*. He made the excuse that Gris had answered his telegram too late, and did not mention Picasso. As a consolation prize, Gris was asked to draw portraits of Larionov and Slavinsky. He also made drawings of Dalbaicin and Kochno.[24] These were executed in pencil and in a mannered classical style which had nothing to do with Cubism. Prokofiev went to Nice on 25 April to be drawn by Matisse.[25]

Gris wrote to his friend and dealer, Daniel Kahnweiler, 'I can't stand this sort of Universal Exhibition landscape where one sees nothing but bad architecture, people with idiotic expressions or intriguers. True, I spend a great deal of time with Diaghilev, Larionov or the dancers, but they are all Russians, that is to say eccentrics of one sort or another. . . . I go to bed almost as bad-tempered as I get up.'[26]

There was a competition between Diaghilev and the celebrated *chef d'orchestre* Sergei Kussevitzky as to who should first present the music of Prokofiev in Paris. Kussevitzky won by just over a fortnight, playing the *Scythian Suite* (extracted from the ballet *Ala and Lolli*, which had been first suggested then rejected by Diaghilev) on 29 April.[27]

The Gaieté Lyrique, where the Paris season was to be held, was not the sort of theatre at which Parisians expected to see the Russian Ballet. Situated on the Boulevard de Sebastopol in a working-class district, it was a home of operetta, and catered for a local audience. When *les gens du quartier* saw Diaghilev's regular customers arriving for the first night in top-hats and tails, evening dresses and diamonds, they whistled and booed. Yet, although it was rather a come-down for the Ballet to appear in such a theatre, the result was that a new audience began to appreciate it. One night Misia, in her box, raised a lorgnette to survey the packed house and, recognizing no familiar face, exclaimed, 'There's no one here.'[28]

Diaghilev had arranged that the prodigal Lopukhova should come from London to dance some of her famous roles in Paris, where she had not been seen since 1917; and he made 'big publicity' for her. On the opening night she danced in *The Firebird*; subsequently in *Les Sylphides* and *Petrushka*. The souvenir programme, produced as ever by *Comoedia Illustré*, had a superb pastel of four naked giantesses in Picasso's new classical style on the cover; the illustrations included a new Picasso portrait of Stravinsky drawn on New Year's Eve and those by Matisse and Gris already mentioned.

Among the more expert members of the audience on the first night were Pavlova, Ida Rubinstein, Michel and Vera Fokine, Massine and Savina.[29]

Chout was a farce, whose violence – even cruelty – was echoed in the mocking dissonance of Prokofiev's score. All the characters were male or female buffoons – that is, comic peasants. The chief buffoon of the title sold seven others a supposed magic whip with which, after 'killing' his wife, he pretended to restore her to life. This led to foreseeable complications. The opening phrase of the ballet, a gurgle on the flute, resembled the ultimate 'orgasm' in *The Rite*, but there was a sour taste in Prokofiev's orchestration, coming from the 'wrong notes', which was unlike Stravinsky. There were leading motifs for the various characters, mostly parodies of Russian-style tunes. Linked by the five recently composed *entr'actes*, the action unfolded like some lurid nightmare amid the hurtling rainbows of Larionov. Even with all its crudities, *Chout* could not fail to make a strong impression.

Before leaving for London, Diaghilev and Kochno saw on the afternoon of 24 May the first of three matinées of a *Spectacle Bouffe*, presented by Pierre Bertin and Jean Cocteau at the Théâtre Martin.[30] This show comprised short pieces by Max Jacob, Radiguet and Cocteau, and Satie's *Piège de Méduse*. The jokes were too subtle even for the small, sophisticated public attracted by the names of Satie, Cocteau and Bertin. According to Jean Hugo, when the curtain fell on *Le Gendarme incompris*, a short play about a policeman who mistakes an elderly marquise for a priest, the three actors bowed to an icy public. 'Only Mlle Le Chevrel [a sociable Norman lady who knew everyone], thinking Cocteau was a safe bet, was on the point of clapping. Her hands were already raised when she caught the baleful eye of Misia, whose stony gaze was turned upon her. She was not slow to get the message, and the hands which were about to meet in applause went fluttering to her temples in a gesture of dismay at the fatuity of the piece.'[31] But the twenty-one-year-old Francis Poulenc, one of 'Les Six' (all of whom, under Satie's sponsorship, had contributed to *Les Mariés de la Tour Eiffel*, which the Ballets Suédois would stage less than a month later) was the composer of the slight incidental music for the play by Cocteau and Radiguet. Diaghilev's first hearing of this music by Poulenc led to his commission of a ballet from him shortly afterwards.[32]

Georges Auric, another of the young composers sponsored by Satie, had written some music for Molière's *Les Fâcheux*, which was being hissed at the Odéon that spring; and Diaghilev, after hearing it, had gone backstage to ask him to expand it into a ballet.[33] With these two commissions of Poulenc and Auric, Diaghilev dived into 'les années folles' of the 1920s.

On the first night at the Prince's Theatre, London, on 26 May, Diaghilev gave a popular programme: *Children's Tales, La Boutique Fantasque* and *Les Sylphides*. London was enduring a heat-wave and both Covent Garden and Drury Lane were closed, while the Palace Theatre and the Alhambra were showing moving pictures. Lopukhova danced the Can-can Dancer (and later the Firebird), which was some guarantee of success, in the absence of Massine. The Prince's had been an unlucky theatre until Cochran took it over for this season. It held two thousand, but the stage was too small for the Russian Ballet, and some of the orchestra was accommodated in the stage boxes. Extras had to dress across the road.[34] Ansermet conducted throughout the season.

On 31 May *Cuadro Flamenco* caused a sensation. *The Times* reported:

Before anything has happened at all, you get the novel zest of seeming to peep through a window at an unacted scene of folk-life.

Then (you hardly know how it comes about, so rapid it is) the whole scene changes its spirit. The guitars quicken, the hands begin to clap, and abruptly, without warning or designation, two of the men spring into the middle. The 'Tango Gitano', danced by Rojas and El Tejiro, goes to a sustained tattoo of heels on the hollow flooring that whips the blood like military drums.... Maria Dalbaicin's lovely 'La Farruca' is almost academic in its grace. Of the complex threads that make up the charm of this spectacle her sinuous elegance is, perhaps, the most captivating.[35]

Cyril Beaumont was surprised at the women's unusual method of acknowledging applause by shaking their breasts.[36] The grotesque antics of the dwarf Gabrielita and of Maté 'el sin pies' (the legless), who moved on a trolley with wheels, then performed *Zapateado* on his stumps, provoked indignation in an unexpected quarter. Diaghilev received a letter from the Spanish Ambassador, Marqués Merry del Val, asking him to suppress the whole number, as these two artists brought ridicule upon Spain. This was distressing for Diaghilev, as the *Cuadro* was clearly going to be very popular. (Cochran recorded that the theatre was sold out every time the Spaniards performed.) Diaghilev decided to retain the number in the programme for one more night. Luckily, King Alfonso was in the audience on 1 June, and applauded warmly. The beauty of Dalbaicin found favour in Royal eyes; she was invited to dance at the Spanish Embassy on the following night;[37] and nothing more was heard about the disgrace of Spain, although the footless Maté was left out of subsequent performances. Maria's performance at the embassy followed her first appearance in *Le Tricorne*. She was accustomed, like all the gypsies, to improvising, and found it hard to fit into the formal framework of Massine's ballet; she could not be counted on to execute the same steps two nights running.[38]

As an unintentional introduction to the revival of *The Rite*, the little-known young Eugene Goossens conducted the work at the Queen's Hall on 7 June. This was its first concert performance in England. 'Just as I raised my stick to give the bassoon player his cue,' wrote Goossens, 'a movement in the dress circle caught my eye, and ... Stravinsky, Diaghilev and Massine crept into their seats.'[39] *Le Sacre* was received with 'hysterical enthusiasm', although Bernard Shaw commented to the *Observer* that 'if it had been by Rossini people would have said there was too much rum-tum in it,' and, in the *Sunday Times*, Ernest Newman condescended that it made a great impression, 'especially by the rhythmic energy of the parts of it in which the composer gets away from his tiresome little Russian formulae'.[40]

Massine had been making trouble about money and claiming arrears of pay; and Diaghilev was obliged to telegraph to Rome on 3 June that he had paid into Massine's account at the Comptoir d' Escompte, Paris, which was his own bank, the sums of 35,000 francs, 50,000 francs, 40,000 francs and 19,000 francs between 16 October and 30 December 1920. He also pointed out that the dancers Clark (Savina), Grabovska, Jadinska, Nevitzka, Statkevitch and Kostecki had broken their contracts in leaving him to join Massine, and that he had as yet hardly recovered from this embarrassment.[41]

To introduce Prokofiev and *Chout* to the British public, Diaghilev gave an interview to the *Observer*, which was undoubtedly interpreted either by Edwin Evans or Eric Wollheim, although Diaghilev's typical brash generalizations, verging on aphorism, are easily recognizable:

Mr Serge Prokofiev has started off in a new direction. The only resemblance between Prokofiev and Stravinsky is that both are Russian, and both are living in the same century. Some idea of the story on which this ballet is founded may be gathered from its sub-title, 'How One Young Buffoon Deceived Seven Old Buffoons and a Stupid Merchant'. The scenery and costumes have been designed by M. Larionov, and the choreography is by a young dancer, Slavinsky, after indications by Larionov. In fact, a new principle has here been introduced, that of giving to the decorative artist the direction of the plastic movement, and having a dancer simply to give it choreographic form. Both the setting and the music of this ballet are of the highest modernity and entirely in keeping with Russian characteristic, without the musical themes being derived from folk-lore.

Of the coming revival of Massine's *Rite* he said, 'I have just been giving this ballet in its new form in Paris, and it has established as a classic masterpiece a work which eight years ago was so revolutionary that it almost led to broken heads. After hearing it this time several persons said to me, "Why, it is Beethoven," to which I replied, "No, it is better." '[42]

Two stories are told about the dress rehearsal of *Chout*, which probably took place on 8 June, and to which Diaghilev had invited a select audience. One is that Prokofiev, who was conducting, halted the orchestra to correct a fault, and that Diaghilev, who had different ideas of what a *répétition générale* should be, rushed forward and told him that when the cream of London society was assembled to see his ballet, he must carry on without interruption.[43] Another is that Prokofiev removed his coat because of the heat and that horrified ladies fled in consternation.[44]

The ballet had a mixed reception. Capell, in the *Daily Mail*, reported that 'all "advanced London" was there to cheer';[45] Ernest Newman, of the *Sunday Times*, hated it;[46] the *Pall Mall and Globe* thought the choreography was the weakest of the three elements;[47] and it is easy to believe *The Times* was right in judging that 'in spite of the brilliant Cubist scenery and dresses with which M. Larionov had provided it and the equally brilliant and equally Cubist music of M. Prokofiev, it has the effect of a loosely-improvised charade. . . .'[48] One feels about *Chout*, as about many experimental works being created in Russia at the same time, and of which photographs and designs survive, that the comedy or drama must have been submerged by the new forms, painted or constructed, which were imposed upon them, just as the dancers' movements and interpretations were hampered by their wired, asymmetrical costumes. Yet in one or two carefully taken photographs the dancers' poses, distorted by their costumes, do seem to be an intrinsic part of Larionov's swirling settings, which are what Mamontov's Abramtsevo or Princess Tenishev's Talashkino might have looked like after an earthquake. Cochran treasured the comment of one critic, who thought it might be 'frightfully entertaining to bloodthirsty children and homicidal lunatics'. The generous showman's conclusion about his one Diaghilev venture was that 'to have done the Cuadro Flamenco was worth the £5,007 which I lost on the ten-weeks season'.[49]

It was Diaghilev's devouring passion for artistic activity for its own sake, his drive to make people listen to unfamiliar music which he himself admired, rather than the mere anxiety to give value for money, which caused him to introduce musical interludes into his programmes. Although in 1921 during intervals at the theatre people did not flock to the bar as they do nowadays, most wanted to talk. That Diaghilev should have attempted to silence them – for ten minutes before the curtain rose, at least – in the interests of young or unfamiliar composers, seems remarkably quixotic. Works by Balakirev, Rimsky-Korsakov and Borodin were played; Stravinsky's Symphony for Wind Instruments and Prokofiev's Classical Symphony (the latter conducted by the composer) had their first English performances. Music by Chabrier, Debussy, Ravel, Satie, Poulenc, Auric, Honegger and Milhaud was heard; and British music was represented by Bax, Berners, Bliss, Goossens and Quilter. The pride with which Diaghilev remarked (in the interview quoted above) that fourteen of these twenty-five pieces were being heard for the first time in England was surely justifiable. It was his panache. Moreover, at certain performances in mid-July the tenor Smirnov sang Puccini and Rimsky-Korsakov, while at others the contralto, Zoia

Rozovska, who travelled with the company to sing the songs in *The Midnight Sun*, *Le Tricorne*, *Pulcinella* and occasionally *Prince Igor*, sang Arthur Bliss's *Rout*.

When *The Rite* had been performed by Goossens at the Queen's Hall on 7 June – and he conducted it again on the twenty-third – an attempt had been made to present it as a symphony – that is, as a piece of pure music, independent of choreography. This led to a newspaper controversy. When the Ballet danced *The Rite* on 27 June, the programme note read, '*The Rite of Spring* is a picture of pagan Russia. This work has been divided into two parts and has no definite plot; the choreography has been freely adapted to the music.' Massine's arrangement may have emphasized the story less than Nijinsky's, but he still had a Chosen Virgin who danced herself to death. There was more controversy; and letters from the public applauded Ernest Newman's inanities in the *Sunday Times*. On 3 July Newman had written, 'It was unfortunate for Stravinsky's music that just when it was on trial for its life, as it were, it should have Massine's choreography put in the dock with it as a fellow defendant.' He had admired Massine's 'genius' in the past, but this *Rite* was 'the silliest, dullest stage spectacle I have ever seen'.[50]

An interview with Stravinsky was published in the *Observer* on the same day. He said, 'The choreographic construction of Nijinsky, being of great plastic beauty, was, however, subjected to the tyranny of the bar: that of Massine is based on phrases each composed of several bars. This is the sense in which is conceived the free connection of the choreographic construction with the musical construction.'[51]

Diaghilev and Kochno escaped from stifling London to spend the week-end of 9–10 July at the Branksome Tower Hotel, Bournemouth.[52] By the time they returned there with Barocchi on 16 July, Bakst, too, was with them.[53] For Diaghilev had been having talks with Oswald Stoll, and these had resulted in an agreement to stage *The Sleeping Beauty* – which Diaghilev promptly renamed *The Sleeping Princess*[54] – as a Christmas entertainment in competition with the traditional pantomimes, in London, that winter. It would take place at the Alhambra in Leicester Square, and the board of the Alhambra Company had agreed to put up £10,000 for the scenery and costumes, which, since Benois had refused to leave Russia without a guarantee of 15,000 francs, 'among other guarantees',[55] were to be by Bakst. These would be in the Louis XIV style; but Bakst so longed to be associated with the modern movement in painting and with new works of art, that he only agreed to undertake the vast production on condition that he should design Stravinsky's new opera *Mavra*, too.[56]

One night when Eugene Goossens was dining with Mrs Robert Mathias – the Ena Wertheimer of the Sargent double portrait which Diaghilev had admired at the Royal Academy of 1901 – and her devoted friend Dr Propert, Diaghilev came in after dinner. Goossens had 'stood in' as a deputy violinist in the Covent Garden orchestra when *Petrushka* had been given in 1913, and the enthusiasm for Stravinsky's music which had led him to perform *Le Sacre* at the Queen's Hall was to be rewarded. Diaghilev asked him to conduct *The Sleeping Princess.*[57]

The season ended in a burst of enthusiasm on 30 July, with a kind of apotheosis for the popular Lopukhova, who danced not only the Petipa *pas de deux*, but in *The Good-humoured Ladies* and *La Boutique fantasque*. She had been paid £100 a week throughout the season;[58] and, incidentally, would have a miscarriage before she appeared in *The Sleeping Princess.*[59]

Ernest Newman fired a parting shot after the Russians as they left for their holidays. Reviewing W. A. Propert's handsome book on *The Russian Ballet in Western Europe, 1909–1920* on 31 July, he thought it came at the right time. One does not write a biography of a living person, and 'the Russian Ballet, if not dead, is dying.'[60]

Because of the long rehearsal period needed for *The Sleeping Princess*, the company could be allowed only one month's holiday, and Diaghilev had much work to do in August, before, during and after his short stay in Venice. Indeed, he had a herculean task ahead of him. To stage a new production of an evening-long ballet would have taxed the resources of the Mariinsky, with its vast company, its school and its spacious studios. Diaghilev had an inadequate company and was without a *maître-de-ballet* familiar with the traditional choreography. Luckily Nicolas Sergeyev, a former dancer and ballet-master of the Mariinsky, was living in Paris; and he possessed notes and notations of several Petipa ballets, including *The Sleeping Beauty*. Diaghilev had not even a suitable ballerina, for Lopukhova was not a dancer in the grand manner. His first thought was of Karsavina, who was booked for a Central European tour in the autumn. Even if she consented to cancel this, her husband had just been given a job in Bulgaria, and she decided that he came before the ballet.[61] Diaghilev may also have considered Pavlova, for a telegram from Nuvel to him in Monte Carlo on 20 July was about conversations Bakst had been having with her, though *The Sleeping Princess* was not specifically mentioned.[62] Paris, however, yielded the former Mariinsky dancer, Lubov Egorova, now married to a Prince Trubetskoy. She could be one of Diaghilev's Auroras: he needed several, for no woman could dance so arduous a role nightly for a long season.

The original Aurora was Carlotta Brianza, then teaching in Paris; and Diaghilev, with his passion for historic links, longed to include her in his production. When it was pointed out that she was nearly sixty, he resigned himself to inviting her for the mimed role of the witch Carabosse. He found that Riccardo Drigo, the original conductor of *The Sleeping Beauty*, who had worked on the score with Tchaikovsky, was living at Padua, so, with Kochno, he set off from Venice to visit him. The old man, with his face (and even hair) painted by his family, was brought down into the garden, but proved senile and could remember nothing; so Diaghilev and Kochno returned laughing to Venice.[63]

Bronislava Nijinska had recently left Russia, and Nuvel was despatched to Vienna to discuss the question of her joining the company. He wrote, 'I wonder if she is not the dream choreographer you need'.[64]

Bakst did the research for his baroque and rococo designs in Paris. He could find most of what he wanted in the Bibliothèque Nationale. For instance, his palace setting for the first scene was taken literally from a design by Carlo Antonio Buffagnoti in a volume of engravings of *Varie Opere di Prospettiva*, after Ferdinando Galli, one of the famous Bibiena family. Bakst's great arch in a hall, with marble pilasters and *oeils de boeuf*, are seen at an angle, as in the original, with many details exactly copied, but he added fantastic statues and a distant staircase, flanked by Negro guards, leading to a circular domed hall. The golden barley-sugar columns in his final scene could have been derived from Charles de Wailly's setting for Gluck's *Armide* or from other eighteenth-century décors. Some of the originals of his costumes may be found among designs by Berain, Martin and Boquet. Aurora's wedding-dress, with its pattern of sun-rays, was taken from Martin's costume of Apollo in the *Opéra de Phaëton*. Even the inclination of the head and the extended arm of Bakst's Aurora in his gorgeous gold and silver design are copied from Martin, though in reverse.[65] Bakst had designed an ill-fated *Sleeping Beauty* for Pavlova at the Hippodrome in New York five years before, and some of his old costume designs came in useful.[66] He had so many to do, and time was short.

While Bakst worked on his designs and Grigoriev looked for new dancers, Diaghilev and Stravinsky studied Tchaikovsky's score, and decided on cuts and changes. The Sugar Plum Fairy's dance from *Casse-Noisette* was to be substituted for the Lilac Fairy's variation in the Prelude. New Fairy Tale visitors in the last act were to be devised to the inserted numbers of the Danse Arabe and the Danse Chinoise from *Casse-Noisette*, the former specially for Dalbaicin. The coda of the *Grand pas de deux* would become a character dance for Innocent Ivan and his brothers.

Certain numbers composed by Tchaikovsky had been omitted from the accepted score (not yet engraved), such as the beautiful solo of Aurora in the vision scene and some *entr'acte* music intended by the composer to follow the Panorama music which accompanied the Prince's journey in the Lilac Fairy's magic boat. Of this *entr'acte* Diaghilev remembered hearing a funny story.

Placed as it was between the andantino of the Panorama music and the andante [of Aurora's awakening] it made one long slow number too many. Everyone [in 1890] was aware of this, but no one, not even Vsevolojsky, dared broach the subject with Tchaikovsky. At the dress rehearsal the Emperor Alexander III, seated next to the composer, began yawning during the *entr'acte* and said 'This is getting rather boring, Tchaikovsky.' The result was that this number was immediately suppressed and was not included in the orchestral score.[67]

Diaghilev asked Stravinsky to orchestrate it anew, and eventually placed it between 'The Spell' (when the forest grew) and the Hunting Scene, which was supposed to take place years later. It thus represented the passage of time while Aurora slept. Diaghilev required Stravinsky to write a tribute to Tchaikovsky for the souvenir programme. The conductors would be Goossens and the Polish Fitelberg.

In September Diaghilev heard that Olga Spessivtseva, the young Soviet Russian ballerina whom he had never seen, though she had danced with his company under Nijinsky in America during the war, and of whom he had glowing reports, was in Riga: she had been given a passport to leave Russia and go south, as she had a tendency to tuberculosis. Diaghilev wrote to ask a theatrical agent in Riga to look her up, and the latter found her 'living in a garret with her mother', with no money either for doctors or travel.[68] Negotiations were set afoot, and she arrived in London after rehearsals had begun. Diaghilev made it easier for the English to acclaim her by simplifying her name to Spessiva.

Pierre Vladimirov, who had escaped from Russia with his wife Felia Dubrovska in the previous year, was to be the Prince, alternating with Anatole Vilzak, another new recruit. For the King and Queen it was necessary to find a tall, handsome couple, capable of expressive mime. Diaghilev's flair led him to engage Vera Sudeikina, the painter's wife and Stravinsky's beloved, and an English actor, Leonard Treer: both were to succeed beyond expectation. The Blue Bird *pas de deux*, no longer disguised as *L'Oiseau de feu* or *L'Oiseau et le Prince* or *La Princesse enchantée*, would be danced by its familiar exponents, Lopukhova and Idzikovsky. Some of the Russian names of newly recruited dancers – such as Patrikief (Patrick Kay) and Astafieva 11 (Margot Luck) – concealed the identity of British subjects, but, like the old-stager Bewicke, the newcomers Coxon, Addison and Moreton kept their own names.

Some of the scenes were painted by Allegri in Paris, some by Vladimir and Elizabeth Polunin in London. Polunin had trouble with the fire-proofed canvas with which he had been supplied, and, since Bakst was in Paris, could not easily discuss with him the interpretation of his designs.[69] Most of the costumes were made in Paris by the firm of Muelle, who had worked with Diaghilev for years, those of Aurora by Ludmilla, wife of the actor Georges Pitoëff; others were made in London by Grace Lovat Fraser, whose husband Claud, the illustrator, had just died.

The company needed space to rehearse this spectacular production, so they were back in the drill hall in Chenies Street, off Tottenham Court Road. Here Brianza held her class, Cecchetti gave individual lessons, and Sergeyev rehearsed *The Sleeping Princess*. Dancers who excelled in Massine's ballets proved to be totally without understanding of the style needed for Petipa's choreography. When Diaghilev saw his company at their first rehearsal in September, he nearly gave up the production in despair.[70]

Kochno recorded the first appearance of Olga Spessivtseva in class, after her arrival from Riga:

When I came into the studio with Diaghilev, Spessivtseva was working at the *barre*. Among the other dancers, all of whom were wearing black tunics – the required costume for rehearsals – she appeared quite strange, for she was wearing a full yellow *tutu* and her long unbraided hair fell down her back. She began to rehearse Aurora's variation. The others, who were working all over the room, stopped one by one and stood motionless, watching her dance. Smiling, she moved with an extraordinary serenity and ease, and the virtuoso steps she was executing seemed simple and natural. She never had to reach for balance; she seemed to be sustained by an invisible thread. At the end of the variation there was a long admiring silence, and then the room exploded with applause. Company rules forbade it, but that day it was Diaghilev himself who first gave the signal.[71]

Spessivtseva was followed everywhere by a watchdog from Soviet Russia, who was allowed to walk on in the ballet under the significant name of Kommisarov.[72]

When Nijinska arrived, she was asked to invent new choreography for the dances in the Hunting Scene, a new variation for the Vision of Aurora, which followed, and choreography for the interpolated entries of Bluebeard, Scheherazade and Innocent Ivan.

Later rehearsals took place in the theatre itself. Cyril Beaumont wrote,

The Alhambra had been closed for the rehearsals and there I spent many enjoyable and instructive evenings. The nights were cold and it seemed colder still in the theatre, with the heating cut off and the stalls shrouded in white dust-sheets. There were no lights in the auditorium, which was as dark as the proverbial tomb; only the stage was lit and that by footlights alone.

There were barely a dozen people in the stalls. You could recognize Diaghilev by his broad back, the strangely flat contour of the back of his head, and the astrakhan collar of his overcoat which he had slung round his shoulders. At his side would be Stravinsky, with his slender, stooping shoulders, egg-shaped head, big nose, straggling moustache, and globular eyes peering owlishly through horn-rimmed spectacles: he reminded one of a harassed headmaster.

They would be joined by Bakst, a brisk, blue-eyed dapper little man – what a fine Pantalon he would have made – who walked with that elastic poise which comes from daily fencing exercise. His hair was auburn, his complexion fresh-coloured, and he sported a fine auburn moustache. He wore gold-rimmed spectacles. In the lapel of his coat was the red ribbon of the *Légion d'Honneur*. When Bakst had taken his seat he would rest his head on his chin and gaze at the proceedings with a cold and critical gaze which missed nothing. Sometimes there would be a fourth personage: Sergeyev, short, spare, grizzled, and grim of expression.[73]

Sergeyev was indignant at the insertion of Nijinska's new numbers, and he left Diaghilev shortly before the opening.[74]

Beaumont watched Diaghilev supervising the lighting or examining costumes. At the lighting rehearsal 'Diaghilev would remain hunched in his seat with an electrician to relay his instructions to the stage.' When he had plotted the lighting after hours of work, he would order the grumbling stage staff to lower the curtain, then, after a few minutes, raise it again, so that he could survey the effect with a fresh eye. 'At such times he cared nothing for the mounting cost of overtime, the passing of hours or the fact that he had not eaten for a long period. If the men showed signs of revolt, he would grant a ten or fifteen minutes' rest interval. As soon as the interval was up, he would utter a curt "Continuez, s'il vous plaît". The men would glare and curse under their breath, but they did his bidding.'[75]

At costume rehearsals Diaghilev sat on the stage, with his back to the footlights, while Grigoriev beckoned from the wings dancer after dancer, who advanced, holding the designs for their costumes. They handed these to Diaghilev, who compared them with the finished results and sometimes asked a dancer to execute a few steps. When Vladimirov appeared, gorgeous in his scarlet and gold for the Hunting Scene, it was found that the weight of his costume greatly reduced his *élévation*. Diaghilev shortened the skirts of his coat, altered the sleeves and stripped off gold braid. The tailor wept.[76] Bakst was obliged to submit gracefully. The dancers all adored him, for he was so simple and friendly. He would ask them if they liked their costumes and felt comfortable in them.[77] (The powdered wig he had designed for Spessivtseva was abolished by Diaghilev after the first night.)[78]

Diaghilev had spent all the money advanced by Stoll and the Directors of the Alhambra Company. Twice he had to ask for additional sums of five thousand pounds.[79] Only packed houses for an exceptionally long run could justify such expenditure. The opening, announced for Monday, 31 October, had to be postponed until Wednesday, 3 November: in the theatre this is a desperate action.

So proud was Diaghilev of his magnificent production that he (rashly, as it turned out) invited the principal Paris critics to visit London as witnesses to his certain triumph – one which he counted on repeating in Paris.[80]

It was not the custom in London to have a *répétition générale* with an invited audience – inevitably smarter than the first night – as in Paris: but a large number of those present on 3 November were guests. Sokolova wrote:

On the first night we found that there was so little room backstage ... that the wings could not contain the crowd of dancers to go on in the opening scene, and a number of us overflowed up a dirty, stone staircase. We waited in these drab surroundings as the orchestra struck up the first bars of the majestic score, a shivering procession, but clad in the richest costumes the company had ever worn. Then our cue came, and we suddenly found ourselves on a stage blazing with lights, amid the splendours of the white and gold décor.... One could hear the audience gasp.[81]

Beaumont had gone back-stage to visit the Green Room, and it sounds as if he was somewhat in the way. 'As the bewigged figures strutted to and fro you were reminded of a page of Dumas awakened to life, a picture by Vanloo or Charles Le Brun.'[82] But two disasters happened to spoil all Diaghilev's pleasure after his long battle for perfection.

At the end of the second act, the climbing tendrils, having raised their heads, remained in a state of suspended animation, and ignored the summons of the Lilac Fairy, who waved her wand in vain. Again, at the end of the third act, when the Prince steps into the Fairy's frail barque to be carried to the mysterious abode of the sleeping Princess (an effect produced by a panoramic background which is eventually blotted out by a deepening mist, simulated by the lowering of a succession of gauze curtains), the machinery failed. Instead of the gauzes descending one behind the other, they piled up on a piece of projecting scenery until they resembled a monster bale of muslin on the shelf of a draper's shop. Diaghilev paled with anger at these blemishes and during the intervals burst upon the stage like a Fury.[83]

It was doubtless Grigoriev who had to bear the first onslaught of his rage.

Few Londoners realized that in *The Sleeping Princess* they were seeing for the first time the greatest of all classical ballets, the flower of the academic dance. Bloomsbury intellectuals disapproved of the old-fashioned spectacle; and Lytton Strachey told Sacheverell Sitwell 'that it made him feel sick. The whole thing was so degraded, especially the music.' Sitwell himself fully appreciated the glory of the production.[84] The critics had more to say about the designs than about the dancing. Richard Capell wrote in the *Daily Mail*, 'The major splendour was Bakst's. All the colours of all jewels, of all sunsets, of all flames, are in these stage pictures.... Only babes in the star Sirius can have christenings like last night's Princess, such orange, saffron and moss-green of the court ladies, such glistening azure and ermine of the royalties' robes.'[85] The *Daily Express* thought

the story itself merely trickles through the maze of scenic splendour, but the appeal to the eye and ear amply atones for the lack of dramatic cohesion. Taglioni might have envied Lopukhova her series of ovations (as the Lilac Fairy). A new *première danseuse*, Olga Spessiva – lissom as a veritable fairy – was hardly less triumphant, while M. Stanislas Idzikovski, as Blue Bird, created quite a furore. The demonstration at the fall of the curtain was quite extraordinary. There seemed to be about fifty calls and re-calls.[86]

The Times noted that the finale of Tchaikovsky's Fifth Symphony was played in the first interval, commented on the failure of the machinery, and thought

26 Bronislava Nijinska, Paris, 1922. Photograph by Man Ray.

27 Boris Kochno, Paris, 1921. Drawing by Picasso.

28 Pavel Koribut-Kubitovitch, Monte Carlo, 1925. Drawing by Picasso.

29 Diaghilev at the Grand Hotel, Paris, 1929. Drawing by Mikhail Larionov.

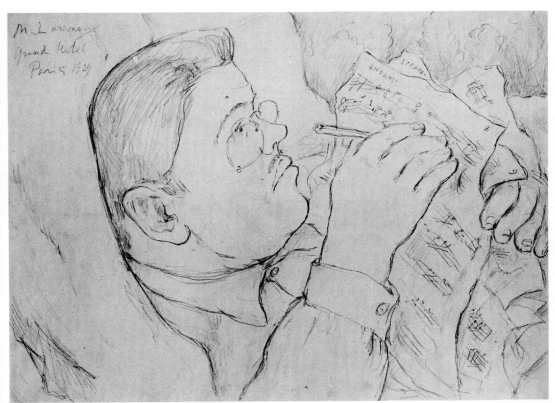

30 (*opposite*) Anton Dolin in *Le Train bleu*, 1924. Photograph by Bassano.

31 (*above*) Serge Lifar and Alexandra Danilova in *Apollon Musagète*, 1928. Photograph by Sasha.

32 (*right*) Vera Nemtchinova in *Les Biches*, 1924.

33 (*opposite*) George Balanchine
in Venice, 1926. Photograph
by Boris Kochno.

34 (*above*) Kochno, Diaghilev,
Lifar, Stravinsky: tea at the
Savoy, 1928. Photograph by
Vera Sudeikina.

35 (*right*) Igor Markevitch,
1929. Cutting from a Dutch
newspaper.

36 Igor Markevitch, 1929.
Drawing by Christian Bérard.

that Spessiva's Aurora 'though danced with perfection, simply did not "come across".' Calderon continued, 'The Prince was meaningless in terms of stage impact. Both these fine dancers were completely outshone by Lopokhova and Idzikovski. . . .'[87] The *Observer* thought 'the spectacle too endlessly and evenly the same to endure four hours' complete attention'.[88] In the *Sunday Times*, Ernest Newman sang 'the suicide of the Russian Ballet'.[89]

Although the masterpieces of Petipa's choreography are contained in the Fairies' solos and the *Grand pas de six* (which Diaghilev made into a *pas de sept*) in the first scene, in Aurora's Rose Adage in the second, and in the Blue Bird *pas de deux* and the *Grand pas de deux classique* in the final scene, Cyril Beaumont used to speak with special tenderness in later years of the autumnal beauty of the Hunting Scene, in which the lovelorn Countess, Tchernicheva, in a yellow velvet riding-habit, tried in vain to distract Vladimirov's melancholy Prince, against a background of courtiers who formed a bluish, greenish, brownish tapestry threaded with gold.[90]

Had the Exhibition of Historical Portraits, had *Boris Godunov*, had the 1909 Russian season of opera and ballet in Paris cost Diaghilev such pains as this attempt to establish Tchaikovsky's genius in the West? Back at the Savoy Hotel, after the first performance, Stravinsky witnessed his friend's despair. 'That night, probably because he had worked so hard and used so much vitality, he had a nervous breakdown. He sobbed like a child, and all around him had difficulty in calming him. With his usual superstition he saw in this incident [of the mechanical failure] a bad omen and seemed to lose confidence in his new creation, to which he had given so much of his soul and energy.'[91]

Diaghilev did, indeed, regard the failure of the 'transformation scenes' as a sign from Heaven condemning his whole enterprise. 'Our opening was ruined,' he wrote seven years later, 'and incalculable sums of money were to be lost. The production of this ballet nearly put an end to my theatrical career in the West. This catastrophe taught me a lesson. I realized that I was receiving an occult warning – indeed our lives are full of such signs – that it was not my business to revive the glories of a bygone age.'[92]

The mechanical shortcomings of the Alhambra stage were rectified. Egorova alternated with Spessiva as Aurora, and Lopukhova danced an occasional performance. Lopukhova and Nijinska alternated as the Lilac Fairy. Matinées were increased from one to two a week. The theatre became a club for the true enthusiasts, who went night after night to compare their favourites, but these devotees mostly occupied the cheaper seats. It was the beginning of Russian 'balletomania' in the West.[93] After the first few weeks business began to deteriorate: but the bills kept coming in. On 3 December Clarkson, the wig-maker, wrote thanking for the promise of a cheque for £167 5s 0d, in settlement of his account, on the following day.[94]

Diaghilev was extremely depressed by the failure of his expensive gamble.

For Bakst it was not so bad: he was working on the 'Sleeping Beauty' murals for the James Rothschilds' dining-room in St James's Place. (These ornate oil paintings, begun some years before, were in no way related to the décors and costumes of the ballet, being Gothic-Renaissance in style.) Bakst arrived every morning in Diaghilev's bedroom with some new idea to make *The Sleeping Princess* more of a draw. One of his projects was tried out. To give the ballet a popular appeal, he suggested introducing real animals (donkeys, sheep and poultry) into the scene of Aurora's Awakening. Because of the noise and the nuisance these creatures made of themselves, and because they failed to adapt themselves to the demands of designer and producer, the experiment lasted only one day. (Years later the son of the English actor, Leonard Treer, who played the King, described to me how he, as a child, had been taken to a matinée of the ballet, to see the stage of the Alhambra crowded with livestock.) Another of Bakst's ideas was to have a comic dialogue written by Bernard Shaw and played in the *entr'acte*. This he suggested should be spoken by the two most popular members of the company, Lopukhova and Idzikovsky, and it was perhaps intended as a sop to the highbrows. A more visually sensational idea, worthy of the Folies Bergère, was to use Maria Dalbaicin, almost naked, as a living figurehead to the ship in which the Lilac Fairy propelled Prince Charming towards the castle of the Sleeping Beauty.[95]

Bakst was mad about Spessivtseva: he particularly approved the way she never smiled on stage.[96] He returned to Paris early in December. Not realizing the full extent of the London fiasco or what would be its consequences, he wrote to Diaghilev that when *The Sleeping Princess* was put on in Paris, it should be advertised frankly as a 'ballet-féerie'.[97]

Stravinsky, too, had reason to be cheerful, for he was with the woman he loved. But Stravinsky did not stay long in London. After he had gone, his love letters were some consolation to Vera for the frantic tirades of Sudeikine, who also bombarded Diaghilev with demands to send him back his wife.[98] ('How ill is she? Is she having every possible care? Should I come?')[99] In mid-January Vera asked Diaghilev to release her[100] and she was replaced by Komarova. Possibly because the latter was taller than Vera Sudeikina and needed an even taller King, Leonard Treer was given notice and Mikhail Fedorov took his place.[101]

Hopes for improved attendances were raised by the announcement of a Royal visit on 12 December. A special programme was printed and the house was packed. The King and Queen brought their newly engaged daughter, Princess Mary, with Lord Lascelles; the Queen of Norway and the Duke of York (later King George VI) were also in the party. Both King George and Queen Mary recorded in their diaries their satisfaction with the spectacle. Spessivtseva recalled: 'During the second interval I had the honour, together with Diaghilev, of being presented to their Majesties. I could not help but notice the strong resemblance of the King to our own Tsar. He said to me, "One should feed you, Madame, you are but a shadow." Perhaps I looked a little pale, for I was still in my Vision Scene costume and had no time to brush the white powder from my face and shoulders before hurrying to the Royal Box.'[102]

Vera Trefilova had arrived in London and was to dance Aurora on the following day. She had retired from the Mariinsky years before, in order to marry a rich businessman. When he died, she began giving lessons. During the war, at night, she used to put on all her woollen clothing and perform her exercises quietly in her room, using the rails of her bed as a *barre*. When she came to join Diaghilev in London, she always 'marked' (that is, walked through) her dances with Vladimirov at rehearsals, then confessed to him that she was afraid to reveal her shortcomings. For a week or two they practised together in private.[103] She was forty-six and had not danced in public for ten years. Kochno recorded:

On the eve of her performance Diaghilev was awakened in the middle of the night by a violent pounding on his door. There stood a Savoy Hotel porter, as pale and stammering as if he had seen a ghost. The man handed Diaghilev a letter from Trefilova. It said 'If you do not release me from my contract, which I signed all unawares and which requires me to appear in *The Sleeping Beauty* at my age, at a time when I have lost all technical skill, this very night I shall kill myself, and you will be responsible for my death. . . .' Diaghilev answered neither Trefilova's letter, nor her incessant telephone calls; and the next evening, looking sixteen, she triumphed in the role of Aurora.[104]

Arnold Haskell thought that Trefilova had the true classical temperament, as well as the training.

It was that very reason that made her performance of *The Sleeping Princess* so full of meaning, and that opened up so many avenues of exploration. It was just because Olga Spessiva, the other great 'discovery' of that season, danced the role with more evident warmth, and so placed something extra between the crystal purity of the role and myself, the something that made her *Giselle* a triumph, that it was Trefilova who moved me, and whom I shall always identify with the role.

Haskell saw *logic* in her performance.[105]

Trefilova and Spessivtseva were partnered by Vladimirov, while Egorova and Lopukhova had Vilzak for their cavalier.[106] A certain rivalry grew up, as was natural, between Spessivtseva and Trefilova, and this was exaggerated by the demonstrations of their respective partisans. One night Trefilova held a balance in the Grand Adage for what seemed like minutes. 'Olga made light of this technical feat. . . ."She just balances against Vladimirov's thigh."' This remark was repeated to Trefilova, who was furious. At her next performance 'when the moment came for the celebrated *arabesque*, Vladimirov, who had been warned beforehand, moved away to the other side of the stage, leaving Trefilova standing perfectly and most wonderfully poised on one point in a supreme *arabesque* position for as long as she wanted, and for that one occasion with a complete disregard for the music. The audience went wild. . . .' This was witnessed by a member of the corps de ballet who later wrote Spessivtseva's life.[107]

The Armenian oil millionaire Calouste Gulbenkian fell in love with Spessivtseva. What would she like as a present? There was a language problem. '*Tutus!*' 'What is *tutus*?' 'Tarlatan.' Yards of tarlatan were despatched. Diaghilev had no objection to his dancers sleeping with millionaires, but Olga proved difficult. Gulbenkian, who might have saved the situation, did not: he only caused trouble.[108]

Vera Nemtchinova, whose usual role was the Carnation Fairy, was tried out as Aurora at a matinée. This was as good as an announcement that she was the prima ballerina-elect. She found that to do her Fairy's role in the evening after dancing Aurora in the afternoon was too exhausting, so Diaghilev allowed her to teach her Fairy variation to Sumorokova and take the latter's part in the corps de ballet on the next occasion. Her 'fans' noticed this and commented anxiously on the demotion. She danced Aurora at three matinées all told.[109] Bronislava Nijinska wanted to dance Aurora and achieved it once. With her high cheek-bones and unusual features, accentuated by an exaggerated make-up, she looked anything but an ideal princess. A voice from the audience was heard to exclaim, 'It's Carabosse', and she never danced it again.[110]

Hopes for fuller houses after the Royal visit were disappointed. On 5 January, however, Cecchetti celebrated the fiftieth anniversary of his first appearance on the stage by playing Carabosse, which he had created thirty-two years earlier, and this was a special night for the balletomanes. Cyril Beaumont prepared a scroll, bound in red and green silk and adorned with miniatures by Randolph Schwabe, of the Maestro in his most famous roles, and this was signed by every member of the company. Silver gifts were presented and speeches made. Of the old man's performance Beaumont wrote, 'This was real miming, with every gesture, every step, timed to perfection.'[111]

Diaghilev was usually kind to Cyril Beaumont, giving him free access to the theatre, descending in a cloud of courtiers on his shop to buy books, or, as happened on one occasion, whisking him off unchanged to watch a ballet with the reassuring comment that 'Dans la nuit tous les chats sont gris.' Yet, so sensitive was he to the failure of *The Sleeping Princess* that he was once moved to insult Beaumont publicly. The latter was lunching with Barocchi at the Isola Bella in Frith Street, Soho, and Barocchi was telling him how Diaghilev had in hand several schemes to make good his losses and fill the Alhambra to capacity, when they were suddenly silenced by the word 'Merde!' 'It was like the vindictive slamming of a door.' Beaumont

Pavlova, Diaghilev, Bakst and Stravinsky. Drawing by Nerman, from the *Tatler*, 1922.

and Barocchi turned, to see Diaghilev, seated a few tables away, glaring at them.[112] 'We became silent,' Beaumont recorded. Barocchi left Diaghilev shortly afterwards, but they kept in touch.[113]

Stoll suggested that Diaghilev should bring over the scenery and costumes of his modern repertoire, so that triple bills could alternate with *The Sleeping Princess*, but Diaghilev, who well knew that Stoll would keep the scenery and costumes of his great production against payment of a debt of £11,000, dared not risk losing the rest of his stock-in-trade.[114] It was decided to close the season on 4 February. Diaghilev placed Nuvel in charge of the company, borrowed three hundred pounds from Hilda Bewicke's mother[115] and left for Paris a week before the end.

Nuvel wrote, 'I shall never forget that dreadful week alone in London. Some of the artists who had not been given their full pay threatened to ruin the last performance by a general strike. Thank goodness, with the help of Grigoriev and the reasonable artists, I was able to ward that off, and the last night, at any rate, was a triumph.'[116] Yet, at that one-hundred-and-fifteenth performance, which Eugene Goossens conducted, one or more of the brass players broke into 'Ach du lieber Augustin' during the final mazurka.[117]

Diaghilev's departure from London a week before the end of his season was a melancholy occasion – a retreat from Moscow. He had sustained the most expensive failure of his career and left behind him a company which might never be reassembled. He had no prospects in view but a season at the Paris Opéra in the spring; and he could not be sure that enough dancers would remain with him to make it possible. He had undertaken to present his Bakst production of *The Sleeping Princess* in Paris, with Spessivtseva: but Stoll held fast to the scenery and dresses and Spessivtseva had announced that, since Diaghilev had not paid her in full, she was going back to Russia.[118] Even Grigoriev was instructed to remain in London and await orders.

The Channel crossing in bitter winter weather was another cause of dread. Even at the best of times Diaghilev prepared to meet death by water three days in advance. Then, he could not be sure that he would escape from the Savoy Hotel without being dunned by his creditors. The final blow was the loss of his valet Beppe.

Although Beppe Potetti had been a Florentine baker, there was a Neopolitan side to him, and his quick wit kept Diaghilev amused. When he called Diaghilev in the morning, his broad jokes would put him in a good mood for the day. The worldly-wise Diaghilev, so shrewd a judge of character, had a childish streak, and Beppe could lead him by the nose. Diaghilev looked upon his valet as someone he had rescued from dire poverty and who would serve him faithfully until death. When he heard in restaurants that Beppe had passed himself off as his son, Diaghilev was merely amused. Beppe, however, lived a double life, and after he had put Diaghilev to bed would make straight for night haunts where he danced, gambled or made love. When he appeared, looking half-dead, in the morning, Diaghilev, suspecting nothing, would rush to the telephone and summon his doctor – Dalimier in Paris, Talariko in London.

On the morning he was to leave London with Kochno, Diaghilev was not called. Beppe, who knew a sinking ship when he saw one, had disappeared. As he had charge of Diaghilev's few poor pieces of jewellery, these had naturally gone too. The servant's room at the Savoy was empty and Diaghilev had to manage his packing and departure with only Kochno's help. Diaghilev could not believe he had been deserted and thought the best way to get in touch with Beppe was through the London police. It took less time to find the missing Italian than might have been expected. Diaghilev soon heard in Paris that Beppe had got a job as a professional dancer in a London night-club. In the course of fulfilling his new duties he stole a woman's necklace, was caught and arrested. The police reported to Diaghilev in Paris that Beppe was in prison.

The Hôtel Continental could only offer Diaghilev a small room, high up, but with a sideways view of the Jardin des Tuileries. As he had no money, he professed to like it better than any room he had ever had before. Boris was given a servant's room. Together they ate at a cab-drivers' restaurant, La Fontaine Gaillon, in the little Place Gaillon. When they considered the *plat du jour*, they used to calculate if they could also afford soup.[119]

CHAPTER 15

February 1922–4

Nijinska as Choreographer – Salvation by Monte Carlo
– *Les Noces* – A French Festival – London after Two
Years – Enter Balanchine, exit Nijinska

IN FEBRUARY 1922 Diaghilev faced another dispersal of his company, such as the war had brought about in 1914. But in 1914 he had the young Massine as an incentive for further productions. In 1922 he had no budding choreographer to help realize his artistic ambitions. On the other hand, Boris, who looked up to him as the embodiment of imagination, ability and courage, was a loyal disciple whom Diaghilev would be reluctant to disappoint. Then there was Stravinsky, whose *Les Noces* had not *yet* been staged, and who was working on Kochno's opera *Mavra*. There was also Prokofiev, who must surely be a fountain of new ballet scores. It was not in Diaghilev's nature to admit defeat for long, and leave the field clear for Rolf de Maré and his Ballets Suédois who had newly aroused interest in Paris;[1] and how, if he allowed his company to disperse, could he ever repay his debt to Stoll?

For the time being, Diaghilev lay very low. He was prey to fears and creditors. For instance, Woizikovsky and Sokolova came over from London to dun him for arrears of salary. The first day, when Woizikovsky rang up, Diaghilev answered the telephone himself – which was unusual – only to say that Diaghilev was not in. On the second day, as the two dancers lay in wait for him in the entrance hall of the Continental, he managed to get from the lift to the swing-doors by passing behind their chairs, and they saw his back view as he vanished into a taxi. At last he gave them a little money: but he made it clear that his plans were uncertain and that he had handed over all business to Nuvel.[2] Back in London, Sokolova and Woizikovsky joined up with Massine and Savina, who had recently returned from a tour of South America, to take part in a musical show.[3]

Diaghilev summoned up courage to give an informal Press conference, and on 18 February *La Vie Parisienne* reported him as saying that he was delighted with the success of *The Sleeping Princess* in London. He hoped to show it 'with new costumes at the Opéra in May, but he was afraid that Perrault's fairy-tale would not please admirers of *Parade* and *Prince Igor*.'⁴ It had occurred to him that he might make a brilliant *divertissement* out of the most striking dances in *The Sleeping Princess*, and that, as few people would remember the garden scene of *Le Pavillon d'Armide*, he might revive Benois' 'Aubusson carpet', with a few additional fairy-tale costumes by Gontcharova.

In March Diaghilev was able to write to Grigoriev in London that he had arranged a short season of twelve performances at Monte Carlo before the Paris season in May.⁵ This would begin on 10 April and continue till 7 May, running concurrently with the opera. Grigoriev's scratched-together company, which nevertheless looks impressive on paper, arrived in Monte Carlo, with ten days to prepare their season. Grigoriev wrote, 'We were overwhelmed with work. I had to rehearse a number of ballets which had not been performed for the best part of a year, and not only had they been to some extent forgotten, but some of the dancers who had before taken part in them had left the company.'⁶

The contract with Jacques Rouché, of the Paris Opéra, signed during the Alhambra season, stipulated that, in addition to *The Sleeping Princess*, two new works by Stravinsky should be staged – namely, *Les Noces Villageoises* (as it was termed) and *Mavra*.

Stravinsky, as we have seen, had begun *Les Noces* as long before as 1913 and had played it to Diaghilev as it progressed during the following years. Originally arranged for a big orchestra, the cantata had been steadily simplified, and only in 1921, when Igor was staying with Chanel at Garches, did he have the idea which led to its definitive scoring for four pianos, percussion and, of course, the human voice.⁷ A similar process of simplification took place with the décor and costumes of Natalie Gontcharova – although people involved in the production told different stories about how their final simplicity was arrived at. What is certain is that the painter had made two complete sets of designs before a third was agreed upon. First, during the war years, she designed the ballet in the raucous reds and yellows she had used for *Coq d'or*; then she made a set of costume designs in pastel blues and pinks, embroidered in gold and silver.⁸

Nijinska came from Vienna to rejoin Diaghilev in Paris early in April;⁹ she found him unexpectedly gay, and they had lunch chez Prunier. Diaghilev told her how, in 1917 in Madrid, Nijinsky and Massine had disputed the right to arrange *Les Noces*. 'To avoid trouble I decided that neither should do it.' (This was probably untrue.) 'Now, I want you to do *Les Noces*, Bronia.' She was thrilled. After lunch Stravinsky played the music to her. But when she saw Gontcharova's gorgeous designs, about eighty of them, laid out on the table of her studio, they struck her as all very well for a Russian opera but the very antithesis of what Stravinsky's music demanded.

'You are very silent,' said Diaghilev, when they left. 'The costumes are magnificent,' she replied, 'but totally unsuited to Stravinsky's music or to the choreography that I envisage.' Diaghilev was very annoyed. 'Then you won't be doing *Les Noces*, either, Bronia,' he said; [10] but this was bluff. If he did mean it for a moment, he did not mean it for long. She must have contemplated starting on the choreography that April, because on the twenty-fourth Stravinsky in Monte Carlo telegraphed to Diaghilev in Paris that he was certain she would never do the work in a month, and urged Diaghilev to deal with Chester, the music publisher, over *Renard*, which only required four dancers and four singers. [11] He was right; and having switched to *Renard*, Nijinska completed it in less than three weeks. Stravinsky anyway did not finish his new orchestration of *Les Noces* till 4 April in the following year. [12]

Renard had been commissioned by Princesse Edmond de Polignac for performance in her music-room, but it had still not been performed. The opera *Mavra* also needed no more than four singers. Diaghilev loved to enrich his ballet repertoire with choral works. His ideal theatrical production, indeed, was one both danced and sung. The jealous Diaghilev had to overcome his repugnance to a work conceived without his collaboration. Not only did Princesse Edmond give him permission to stage *Renard*; she gave or lent him money to tide him over this difficult time. [13]

Perhaps in gratitude for the part he had played in sending him Kochno, or as a recompense for the loss of Vera Sudeikina to Stravinsky, Diaghilev invited Sergei Sudeikine to design *Renard*. Sudeikine, who disapproved of certain recent tendencies in the Russian Ballet, made such stipulations in his reply as would have given him the position of artistic director of the company, with the right to design or supervise every production. This provided Diaghilev, who did not like his sketches, with the pretext for turning him down[14] and handing *Renard* to the ever-eager Larionov, who, indeed, was the obvious choice for this peasant fable.

Bakst had been well paid for his work on *The Sleeping Princess*, but when Diaghilev took *Mavra* away from him and gave it – evidently at Larionov's suggestion – to a young Russian painter, Léopold Survage, he enforced a clause in his contract, which obliged Diaghilev to pay him ten thousand francs for *Mavra*, even though he did not design it. This caused their final quarrel. [15]

Survage was married to the sister of the pianist Marcelle Meyer, later the chief interpreter of the music of 'Les Six'. (It was Marcelle's husband, the actor Pierre Bertin, who had presented the *Spectacle Bouffe* at the Théâtre Michel in May 1921.) Survage had known Larionov at the Academy of Painting in Moscow, and had seen him occasionally in Paris since. One night early in May 1922, as Survage described, Larionov called on him at eleven o'clock.

'Come along,' he said, 'Diaghilev wants to see you.' We set out for the Hôtel Meurice [probably the Continental], and found Diaghilev on the sixth floor in a servant's bedroom furnished only with a bed, a table and a chair. Diaghilev sat on the bed, I on the chair, and Larionov remained standing. Diaghilev explained that he wanted me to make designs for Stravinsky's opera *Mavra*; but he wanted them by the next morning. I thanked Larionov and made two sketches during the night, of which Diaghilev chose one.[16]

Diaghilev made a final effort, through Bakst, to re-engage Spessivtseva, and he drafted an appeal to Poincaré to grant her a work permit.[17] But the difficult lady telegraphed Bakst from Berlin, 'If Diaghilev sends me my London money I go to Paris.'[18]

The rich old people who spent the winter at Monte Carlo – largely English – wanted old favourites rather than disturbing novelties, and that is what Diaghilev, for once marking time and playing for safety, gave them. Every performance was sold out.[19]

Jacques Rouché, of the Paris Opéra, could not quite make out what was going on. Diaghilev had probably concealed from him the extent of his London disaster. On 26 April Rouché wrote to Diaghilev at Monte Carlo:

The information you gave me yesterday about *The Sleeping Beauty* is insufficient, and I should be grateful if you were to give me complete details. . . . You would like to substitute *Renard* for *Les Noces Villageoises*. This is no problem. But in place of *The Sleeping Beauty*, which is a big evening-long ballet, you propose giving me a fragment of the work, *The Marriage of The Sleeping Beauty*. . . . You have neglected to tell me what décor and costumes you will use. . . . Will Bakst be collaborating on them? If, to my great regret, Mlle Spessivtseva cannot come to Paris, her absence would not be sufficient cause for cancelling the ballet altogether. In October you yourself told me that you would have a number of stars performing in the ballet and that in Paris you would perhaps ask me for Mlle Zambelli. The solution you suggest presents nothing but problems: more stars, more sets, more stage designs. Therefore I must ask you for clarification of your new programme. What artist will execute the sets of *The Marriage of The Sleeping Beauty*? Lastly, who will the members of the company be?[20]

Towards the end of the Monte Carlo season Diaghilev went back to Paris, leaving the company to give five performances at the Colonial Exhibition at Marseilles on their way north. Rouché made an attempt to bring him together with Massine, whose musical show in London had been short-lived. When Diaghilev called on Rouché at his office at the Opéra, Massine was 'waiting outside in the passage'. Diaghilev described the encounter in a letter to Grigoriev. 'His object was to ask whether I would take him and all his dancers back into the company. He would not mind what salary he was offered. At the same time he knew that without them my season in Paris would be impossible! I told Rouché that I would give him an answer in a few days' time. It will be in the negative. So that's the position.' Grigoriev thought Diaghilev was taking his revenge for Massine's betrayal.[21] It was not as simple as that, although Diaghilev, so recently in the depths of despair, gave the impression in his letter of crowing over the suppliant Massine. What Grigoriev did not realize, and what Massine did not realize, and what Rouché, who obviously wanted Diaghilev to re-engage the 'star' dancer for the benefit of all concerned, did not realize, was that Nijinska had already given Diaghilev the hope of new developments in choreography. Even though Massine would be a great attraction, Diaghilev's chief interest, as ever, was to create something new. To have two choreographers in his company might cause friction: both Massine and Nijinska were very determined characters. The great prize of *Les Noces* was to be for Bronislava Nijinska, just as, ten years before, it had been so definitely for her brother.

On 14 May 1922, four days before the opening of the Opéra season, there took place an event which was to affect the future of the Russian Ballet: Albert, Prince of Monaco, died. By his first short-lived marriage to Lady Mary Hamilton (great-granddaughter of William Beckford of Fonthill), he had an only son and heir, who succeeded him as Prince Louis II. The only child of this new ruling Prince was a daughter, Charlotte, legitimized in 1919, and in 1920 married to Prince Pierre de Polignac, nephew of the musical Princesse Edmond, *née* Singer. Diaghilev saw no reason why the patronage which the sewing-machine heiress had extended to him should not be exceeded by that of the new Princesse Héritière. Both Princess Charlotte and Prince Pierre, whom he knew, were interested in the arts. Diaghilev had a slightly exaggerated notion of the power of the Grimaldi family within their minute principality,[22] whose revenue derived largely from the Société des Bains de Mer – that is, the Casino: but his idea was a good one and produced results.

On 18 May the Diaghilev Ballet opened their season at the Opéra, and Trefilova made her Paris début. Diaghilev had contrived to put on a show. A company which could present Idzikovsky as Harlequin in *Carnaval*, Trefilova, Nijinska, Egorova, Schollar, Nemtchinova, Dubrovska, Vladimirov and Idzikovsky in *Le Mariage de la Belle au bois dormant*, as well as Stravinsky's new work *Renard* in Larionov's décor, and *Prince Igor* led by Vilzak and Kremnev, could not be said to be without merit.

Fitelberg conducted *Le Mariage*, as he had *The Sleeping Princess* in London; and Ansermet conducted *Renard*. Stravinsky's grotesque music for *Renard*, however, passed the comprehension of most. Tchaikovsky was found, as usual, to be un-Russian, and some critics compared the faded elegance of Benois' costumes unfavourably with the splendours Bakst had created for London.[23]

Renard, although it was by nature a small-scale would-be 'improvisation', unsuited to the gilded opera house, had such thrilling new sounds, and was so aptly staged by Nijinska in Larionov's setting of log hut and snow-laden birch-trees (originally sketched out by Diaghilev), that it pleased the chosen few by its Russian-ness, even if they were slow to realize that it was a masterpiece. The story concerns a Cock who crows on his perch and is twice lured down by the Fox and has to be rescued by the Cat and the Goat: the four characters were played on the stage by dancers and sung in the pit by two tenors and two basses. A feature of the score was the plucked cimbalom, an instrument discovered by Stravinsky in a café band in Geneva. Nijinska herself played the Fox, and Stravinsky was delighted both with her impersonation and her choreography.[24] Idzikovsky was the Cock; Yaz-vinsky and Fedorov were the Cat and the Goat.

Schneider, music critic of *Le Gaulois*, compared Stravinsky's score to a new kind of torture. 'Where are we going to land up, if we follow this talented – and I hope sincere – composer along the perilous paths of unmusical music ["la musique sans musique"]?'[25]

The expatriate Russian critic André Levinson wrote for *Commedia*. He was known as a staunch supporter of the old classical school, and, as such, in the past, had opposed Fokine – though on this occasion he praised *Carnaval* and *Prince Igor*. He was a real expert, and, the limitations of his taste being accepted – he passed over *Renard*, as something outside his range of taste or criticism – his opinions are of particular interest. He considered the 'important fragment' of *The Sleeping Princess* a mere 'succinct *resumé*', with its old beauties interspersed with ingenious new inventions. In the 'rare display' of the 'so-called seven Demoiselles d'honneur' the seven ladies did not execute their *développé à la quatrième ouverte* together. He liked the Fairy Tales of Nijinska – but the 'Princesses de Porcelaine' (Chinese dance) was by [that is, stolen from] Ivanov. He loved Dalbaicin tapping her heels in the Oriental Dance. Then –

Mme Vera Trefilova, whom Paris applauded yesterday for the first time, is a perfect dancer. . . . She had been one of the purest glories of the Imperial Ballet. Her technique is absolute . . . it is the complete expression of a harmonious being. In the Adage the interplay of curves and vertical lines is of incomparable purity: she unfolds her dance like an opening flower. Giddy jumps and outbursts of passion are not for her. If Pavlova is a bird, she is a flower. She is at once the instrument and the musician: a dancing Stradivarius. In the coda of the *pas de deux* she introduced a series of 32 *fouettés* (the hardest and prettiest of *pirouettes*), taken from *Le Lac des Cygnes*. Well, she only did 28 and allowed herself to glide downstage instead of 'biting' the floor, for she was much moved. . . .[26]

Diaghilev hated *fouettés*.[27]

Proust was present at the first night of *Renard*; and after it his friends Sydney and Violet Schiff gave a party at the Ritz for the Ballet and for the four living men of genius they most admired – Proust himself, Stravinsky, Picasso and James Joyce. It was on this occasion that the dying Proust asked

Stravinsky the fatal question, to which he really wanted to know the answer: 'Do you like Beethoven?' 'I detest him!' snapped Stravinsky. 'But surely, the late quartets?' 'The worst things he ever wrote.' Proust got on no better with Joyce – neither had read the other's work – but he sent him home in his private taxi.[28] Sydney Schiff, under the name of Stephen Hudson, translated Proust's last volume, *Le Temps retrouvé*, into English after the death of Charles Scott Moncrieff. His sisters Rose Morley and Edith Gautier-Vignal were friends of Diaghilev and entertained him and his principal dancers in London and the South of France.[29]

There had been a lack of liaison between Diaghilev and Survage, possibly due to Larionov, for, when the latter came to fetch Survage to the scene-painting studio at Belleville towards the end of May, Diaghilev was raging and exclaiming that the first night of *Mavra* would take place at the Opéra in three days' time and a décor had to be painted. 'You shall have it,' said Survage. The painter set to work immediately, and, with the aid of Larionov, began to cover a canvas sixteen by twenty-seven metres. The work took them three days and three nights, and on the third night Survage had a cold sweat and Larionov fed him sugar. The décor, however, was finished in time, rolled up and loaded by the two friends on to a lorry. Survage, on his way home, with his dark-blue suit covered in paint stains, happened to run into Diaghilev near the Magasin du Printemps, in the Boulevard Haussmann behind the Opéra. 'How dare you show yourself in the middle of Paris in such a state?' Diaghilev demanded angrily. 'Go home at once!'[30]

On Friday, 26 May, there appeared in *Le Gaulois* an elegant invitation which might be translated as follows:

M. Serge de Diaghilew

At Home

Monday the 29th at 10 p.m.

Dancing

An editorial explanation was provided. 'In fact the distinguished founder of the Russian Ballet is inviting the Press and the friends of his company to a first hearing of *Mavra*, Stravinsky's latest composition. Music of Glinka, Darghomijsky and Tchaikovsky will also be played.'[31]

In the intimate atmosphere of a party in the ballroom of the Continental, with Stravinsky at the piano, *Mavra* was a great success, but it fell flat five nights later at the Opéra.[32] Diaghilev had the idea that a rousing final quartet, similar to the quintet which brings Ravel's *L'Heure espagnole* to an end, might save the little opera, but he somehow could not bring himself to ask Stravinsky for it.[33]

In spite of the frosty reception of *Mavra*, the Opéra season was so popular that a way was sought to extend it, but no way could be found.[34] Anxious to exploit success, Diaghilev decided to transfer to the Mogador, where he opened on 17 June. The repertoire was the same as that given at the Opéra, with additions, but without *Renard* or *Mavra*. On 27 June Karsavina came from England to dance in a charity gala organized by Comtesse Mathieu (Anna) de Noailles, and remained till the end of the season on 1 July. Grigoriev and his wife resented Karsavina's guest appearances with the company, for, during the war, when Karsavina was in Russia, Tchernicheva had succeeded her in several Fokine roles. They used to stand together, watching her from the wings and making spiteful comments. Dubrovska, who, though she was ten years younger, had known Karsavina well in Russia, noticed this, and Karsavina asked her, 'How can you exist in this snake-pit?'[35]

An experiment made at the Opéra was repeated at the Mogador: Bronislava Nijinska danced her brother's role in *L'Après-midi d'un faune*. She strapped in her breasts and looked remarkably like him, but the result was somehow embarrassing.[36]

Before settling quietly at the Excelsior on the Venice Lido, Diaghilev took Boris on a lightning tour of Italy, waking him daily at dawn so as to show him all the museums and churches. After a stop at Stresa to visit Isola Bella, they spent three days in Florence, three in Rome and three in Naples; they even visited Capri, where Marchesa Casati was in residence.[37] Diaghilev did not accompany the Ballet on its makeshift summer and autumn tour: he was busy negotiating. When Grigoriev, between Ostend and San Sebastian, called on him in Paris, he found him unexpectedly cheerful.

He was drinking his breakfast coffee. . . . Why was I looking so glum, he asked, and without waiting for an answer, said 'Cheer up: I've something to tell you!' He then began by observing that the Ballet simply could not continue as it was, perpetually running into crisis after crisis. Some way out must be found; and he thought he had found one. . . . [He explained about the Grimaldi-Polignac marriage.] 'My idea is to establish ourselves at Monte Carlo, as a base for the winter from November to May. Mme [Edmond] de Polignac has promised to help; and I see no reason why this should not come off.' He went on to explain his scheme in greater detail. This was that we should start every winter with a season of ballet lasting till the Italian opera season opened, when we should dance in such operas as had ballets in them. The advantage of the scheme in general was two-fold: it would give the company employment throughout the winter, and allow Diaghilev ample time to devise new productions. I had begun to congratulate him when he interrupted me. 'Unfortunately there's a slight obstacle in the way of this admirable plan,' he said. 'At the moment the Casino have engaged an Italian ballet company to dance first on their own and then in the operas, so my scheme could not take effect till next year.' 'And in the meantime we should starve!' I put in. 'Yes, if we had to wait, we certainly should,' said Diaghilev. 'That's why I've suggested an interim arrangement. I've suggested that this year we should work *with* the Italians – just *some* of the company, that's to say. And what's more the young Polignacs highly approve, and are going to press the Casino to accept.'[38]

Grigoriev led the company from San Sebastian to Bayonne and Bordeaux, thence to Geneva and Belgium. He was in Brussels when he heard that the Société des Bains de Mer had agreed to all Diaghilev's proposals. The company were very happy: to those weary wanderers the prospect of spending six months of every year by the Mediterranean was like that of the Lotus Island to the companions of Ulysses. 'As two months were always set aside for leave, there would remain only four to fill up with other engagements.' When the Ballet arrived in Paris, before travelling south, Diaghilev eliminated some of the weaker dancers and cut the numbers to thirty. Vladmirov decided to leave.[39] He had been invited to partner Karsavina on her recital tours of Central Europe.

One result of Diaghilev's new official attachment to Monte Carlo was that he began to see himself as a sort of Minister of the Arts to the Principality – if not the whole of France. He planned a Museum of Living Art, for which Braque should design an exhibition hall; and he wanted Picasso to paint portraits of the Princesse Héritière and her husband.[40] The two young French composers, Poulenc and Auric, were already working on ballets for him. Why not plan a whole season of ballet and opera?

One Sunday afternoon he went with Kochno to hear Gounod's little known *opéra comique, Philémon et Baucis,* at the Trianon Lyrique in Montmartre. Although the staging was terrible, Diaghilev fell in love with the music, and decided to plan the choral part of his French season around the compositions of Gounod.[41] Already on 8 August 1922, he was in Lyon in search of singers, and he wrote to Kochno that he had 'heard a work of genius called *Faust*'.[42] The French season was not destined to take place until January 1924, but in the meantime Diaghilev planned productions of two more forgotten Gounod operas, *Le Médecin malgré lui* and *La Colombe.* To these he added Chabrier's *L'Education manquée.* Chabrier was a favourite of his.

The ballets of Poulenc and Auric would represent the twentieth century. The operas of Gounod and Chabrier would stand for the nineteenth century. What could he cull from the seventeenth or the eighteenth – something more recherché than Rameau? He remembered his old enthusiasm for Montéclair, and once more approached Henri Casadesus, the pianist and expert on old music. Together they rifled the extensive archives of the Paris Opéra in search of fragments of this forgotten composer. They put together what they found and adapted this score to the libretto of the danced *divertissement* in Tchaikovsky's *The Queen of Spades,* changing the title from *The Sincerity of a Shepherdess* to *Les Tentations de la Bergère.*[43] Diaghilev asked Juan Gris, who was already commissioned to design *La Colombe* and

L'Education manquée, to provide the décor and costumes for this in his Cubist version of the Louis XIV style. He had written to Russia to ask Benois to design *Le Médecin malgré lui*. (Exit permits were becoming easier to obtain.) He hoped Picasso would design the mythological *Philémon* in his new classic, monumental manner. With Braque decorating the Auric ballet and Marie Laurencin the Poulenc, the list looked impressive. Diaghilev liked to impress people, particularly himself.

He was in the full swing of planning and creation. With Cocteau he was also working on a project which they called 'Plastic Hall' – 'avant-garde music-hall dance performances', a kind of international youth theatre in which dance numbers would alternate with experimental films. This was clearly an extension of Cocteau's *Spectacle bouffe*, and Poulenc's *Gendarme incompris* was included among his notes, along with Satie's *La Belle excentrique* and *Parade*. Naturally, Picasso, Braque, Gris, Derain, Matisse and Delaunay were among the painters he wished to involve, and the Cubist sculptor Laurens occurred in his notes for the first time. The American John Carpenter stands out from a list of otherwise French composers, including Offenbach and Delibes; and among specific compositions named were Ravel's 'Alborada del Grazioso' and Debussy's 'Clair de lune'.[44]

On a cultural expedition to Berlin with Kochno in November, Diaghilev met a number of Russian exiles; there were Russian newspapers, cabarets and concerts in the former German capital. He made friends with the Soviet poet Mayakovsky, and helped him to obtain a visa for France.[45] This came through on 17 November,[46] the day before the death of Proust, and the poet was in Paris to see Proust's funeral procession on the twenty-first. Mayakovsky invoked the Eiffel Tower in a poem, claiming it as a 'Constructivist' object and inviting it to come to the USSR. While Diaghilev had talks with him about possible collaborations, Mayakovsky tried to lure Diaghilev back to Russia.

The year 1923 began with Diaghilev hopeful of security, full of projects – that is to say, with something to live for – and no longer cowering in a servant's room on the sixth floor. Nijinska and the company, at Monte Carlo, sent him New Year's greetings to the Continental in Paris.[47]

On 13 January, after a telegraphic correspondence about visas and money,[48] there arrived from Warsaw five young male dancers who had been Nijinska's pupils in Kiev. Bronislava had spoken so highly of them that Diaghilev had asked her, 'Is there a new Nijinsky among them?' Since it was impossible to reply in the affirmative, she had been embarrassed.[49] At five o'clock they reported at the Hôtel Continental. Serge Lifar, the youngest, who had taken someone else's place at the last moment, described the scene in his colourful prose:

Never before had I seen such regal splendour as that of this hall, crammed with tropical plants. . . . Then suddenly a small group of people began to walk straight over to us, led by a tall bulky man, carrying a walking-stick, who looked a veritable colossus in his fur coat. I saw a large head, a pink, slightly puffy face, big shining eyes full of sadness, yet endlessly mellow and kind, a Peter the Great moustache, a grey lock in the black hair. . . . Then he sat down and began talking, and we were immediately enveloped, subjugated, irresistibly charmed by his luminous soft warmth. . . . In a resounding baritone voice Diaghilev ordered tea. . . .

Diaghilev asked the newcomers about Russia and the privations they had undergone. He was interested in everything they had to say. Could they do double turns in the air? He could not pay them the fifteen hundred francs a month he had promised; things had not been going well lately; he could give them only thirteen hundred francs, but the advance he had sent to Warsaw would be a present. They would sign contracts and leave for Monte Carlo tomorrow.[50]

But when Diaghilev arrived at Monte Carlo and put them through their paces on 6 February, he was bitterly disappointed: their exercises at the *barre* were passable, but their allegro 'centre practice' left much to be desired. The elder four were just corps de ballet material, but young Lifar, though untrained, tried so hard, and was so brimming with vitality, that Diaghilev was appeased.[51] '*Il sera danseur,*' he prophesied.[52]

Serge Lifar was destined to play an important role in the life of Diaghilev and in the final phase of the Ballets Russes: 'destined' by himself, one might say, because from the start he set out to draw Diaghilev's attention. He was vivacious and attractive, crafty but by no means an intellectual. He was (by his own admission) sexless, feeling no physical desire either for men or women, although he aroused the desire and love of both.[53] He craved for admiration, however, and could offer friendship in return. He was devoted to the art of ballet, and it was by his hard work as much as by his dark eyes, high cheek-bones and snub nose that he awoke Diaghilev's interest. Not that he despised other ingenious means of self-dramatization. It was a classic case of the young seducing the old.

So, while rehearsals proceeded, Lifar recorded the stages of his progress, both in the corps de ballet and in class.

Fortunately rhythm was my strong point. . . . Grigoriev approved of my work. . . . But what was most terrifying at rehearsals was Diaghilev's presence. . . . So panicky with fear did I become that I worked alone and at night on the jetty. In that fantastic setting I would practise for hours, while the two coloured harbour-beacons gleamed strangely over the sea, and silhouetted the dark outlines of the rock citadel. . . . Diaghilev soon began to pay attention to my work at rehearsals. Even in February he had praised me and uttered words which filled me with joy and pride: 'That is good, young man, quite good. Go on working hard.' . . . On March 13th I made two *tours* in front of Sergei Pavlovitch, on March 22nd an *entrechat-six* – and noticed in his eyes an expression of gentle approval.

Then, soon after, I almost got a part. At one of the rehearsals of *Schéhérazade* Diaghilev turned to Grigoriev and said 'Put Lifar as the boy dying on the stairs, he seems to suit the part.' . . . But my teacher Bronislava Nijinska intervened: 'No, Sergei Pavlovitch, Lifar is still too inexperienced. . . . Give the part to Slavinsky. . . .' 'Very well,' said Diaghilev, 'let Slavinsky do the part and let Lifar watch: but he'll soon be dancing on his own. . . .' On April 17th our first performance took place, and I made my début in the back ranks of the corps de ballet in *Le Mariage d'Aurore*.[54]

An unusual obsession for watching the sun rise led to a more intimate conversation with Diaghilev.

During that spring at Monte Carlo I went to bed late, rose with the dawn, and, all alone, hurried into the mountains to see the sun rise from La Turbie. . . . I could not tear myself away, could not move. Then, suddenly, I would be seized with terror lest I should be late, and rush panting down, only to arrive long before anyone had reached the theatre. At rehearsal after my lessons, black zig-zag circles would float in front of my eyes, my head reeled. . . . At one such rehearsal, when I could barely stand on my feet, and nothing I did would go right, Diaghilev, in a fury, began shouting: 'What's the matter? Don't you understand what you're expected to do, or can't you dance?' After rehearsal . . . 'What's the matter with you, young man? You look desperately ill. What are you doing about it?' . . . Like a sheep, I began to peer helplessly in all directions, though still unable to utter a word. 'How old are you?' 'Eighteen.' . . . 'The best years! And you probably imagine yourself grown-up, and go whoring after women. Well, in that case, young man, you'll soon philander your talent away and never be a dancer. Shame on you, I had put such hopes on you.' 'Sergei Pavlovitch, I . . . I don't philander.' 'No? What is it then? Why do you look so ill?' 'I'm not ill.' 'But what is it? Tell me a little about yourself, your life. . . . You're not dumb, I hope? When do you get up?' 'At five.' 'Five? What do you do at five when everyone else is asleep?' 'I do nothing. . . . I go for a walk in the hills.' Sergei Pavlovitch burst out laughing, a merry, loud, pleased laugh. 'Why, you must be crazy! Can a dancer lead such a life? A dancer should work and rest. . . . You must promise to obey me, and not do anything so idiotic again.'[55]

Alicia Nikitina, a Russian girl whose real name was Landau, and whom Diaghilev had seen in Berlin, had joined the company on 1 April; and Sokolova and Woizikovsky had returned to the fold on the fourth. The Monte Carlo ballet season began, as Lifar wrote, on 17 April.

In Paris Stravinsky had shown Diaghilev the final wonderful orchestration of *Les Noces*. The great work was at last ready for performance. A year had passed since Nijinska had begun to experiment with *Les Noces*. In April 1923 Diaghilev spoke to her again about this all-important work, which he wished to give in Paris that spring. Nijinska described the conversation.

'Bronia, are you ready to begin rehearsing this ballet? How do you see it? You remember the first scene. We are in the house of the bride. She sits in a big Russian armchair to one side of the stage, while her friends comb and plait her hair.' 'No, Sergei Pavlovitch,' I interrupted, 'There must be no armchair, no comb and no hair!' I took a sheet of paper and sketched the bride with plaits three metres long. Her friends holding her tresses formed a group around her. Diaghilev burst out laughing – which with him was often a sign of pleasure. 'What happens next? How can the girls comb such long plaits of hair?' he asked. 'They won't comb them,' I said. 'Their dance on point and hers will express the rhythm of plaiting.' I went on drawing and explaining my idea of the choreography and staging. Sergei got more and more amused. 'A Russian ballet on point!' he exclaimed, while Kochno listened seriously.[56]

Kochno recalled how all Diaghilev's fears vanished the moment that Nijinska said, '*Les Noces* is a ballet that must be danced on point. That will elongate the dancers' silhouettes and make them resemble the saints in Byzantine mosaics.'[57] Diaghilev saw the advantage at once. Bronislava asked for the simplest possible costumes, 'the same for everyone'.[58] Diaghilev scribbled his ideas, based on the regulation clothes worn in class. 'It was easy to "Russianize" these costumes by lengthening the women's costumes to convert them into sarafans and by changing the neckline of the men's shirts to turn them into villagers.'[59]

Stravinsky wrote, '*Les Noces* is a suite of typical wedding episodes told through quotations of typical talk. The latter, whether the bride's, the groom's, the parents' or the guests', is always realistic ... a collection of clichés and typical wedding sayings . . . in which the reader seems to be overhearing scraps of conversation without the connecting thread of discourse. . . .'[60]

Nijinska found all that she needed in the solemn, even tragic, atmosphere of the score. She well understood that this peasant wedding was no occasion of gaiety, except for a few guests. The bride and bridegroom, who hardly knew each other, were embarking on a perilous journey. The young couple were not so much hero and heroine as victims of a sacrifice, and they were given no solos to perform: the mass groupings were all-important.

The choreography of the earlier episodes had been completed when Stravinsky arrived in Monte Carlo to help analyse the complicated rhythms of the final scene. Gontcharova and Larionov came for three days, and were told what Nijinska and Diaghilev had agreed about the costumes. Diaghilev had said, 'Black and white,' Nijinska thought the plain uniforms should be dark-blue and beige. Gontcharova persuaded her to have them dark-brown and white.[61]

The music of *Les Noces* was given a first hearing, as *Renard* had been, in Princesse Edmond de Polignac's music-room. The whole company were present. Young Lifar sat on the floor 'afire'. 'The powerful sounds enthralled me, swept me on, thrilled me with their mystery, their timelessness. . . . Diaghilev looks at us kindly and smiles the smile of a great, loving, omniscient father. Princess de Polignac embraces Stravinsky and loads him with attentions. . . .'[62] Vera Sudeikina did not like the princess. When she asked her, 'Why don't you invite Chanel?' The Singer heiress, known to her friends as 'Tante Winnie', replied, 'I don't entertain my tradespeople.'[63]

At its first performance at the Gaieté Lyrique on 13 June 1923 *Les Noces* was received by the audience with a rapture which was only equalled by the critics' incomprehension of Stravinsky's music. In the *social* column of *Le Gaulois* on the fourteenth we read of 'a great and deserved success', 'a triumphant evening', 'a genuine ovation for Stravinsky' and 'unhoped for profits' for the Russian charity presided over by the Grand Duchess Marie; and the list of customers includes the Maharajah of Kapurthala and Aga Khan, as well as such familiar names as Polignac, Ganay, Chevigné, Beaumont, Castellane, Sert and Astruc.[64] Three days later the music critic Louis Schneider, after praising the work of Nijinska, wrote 'of new, bizarre effects, whose strident and discordant accents not only fail to charm the ear but by their repetition even provoke it to a state of rebellion. . . . I could hear noise, nothing but noise. Where was the music secreted in all this pandemonium? . . .'[65] No attempt, even, at a comparison with the wedding at the end of *The Firebird*. About the solemn final chime, when four pianos and a bell in unison celebrate the off-stage mating of the married pair – one of the seven wonders of modern music – nothing!

Les Noces was the only new work given that season, Diaghilev's second at the Gaieté Lyrique. But at the end of June Gabriel Astruc organized a fabulous entertainment at the Château de Versailles, to raise funds and draw attention to the need for its restoration. In this 'Fête Merveilleuse' the Diaghilev Ballet inevitably played a part. There were three days of rehearsals, during which the dancers could be seen in costume and full make-up, wandering on the terraces and in the park. It was very hot. The final rehearsal gave Lifar a heaven-sent opportunity to draw attention to himself.

Diaghilev dismissed the company for lunch, and was left alone in the Hall of Mirrors. I crossed the square to a small restaurant, but as I was eating, the thought flashed through my mind that poor Sergei Pavlovitch must be overcome with hunger, thirst and the heat, while completely exhausted with work. So I thought . . . and with my few poor pennies went and got him some sandwiches and a bottle of beer. Then I returned to the Hall of Mirrors, placed the beer and sandwiches in front of him . . . and blushed with confusion. Sergei Pavlovitch looked at me intently, his eyes seemed to jump over his monocle, while I turned pale under his glance. 'How nice of you, young man! I'm very much touched that you should have thought of me,' Diaghilev was saying as a hot maiden flush dyed my cheeks. . . . I turned quickly away. . . .[66]

For the Fête on 30 June, Diaghilev had employed Juan Gris to build a stage in the Salle des Glaces and to design a few costumes. It is extraordinary that Diaghilev's instinct should have prompted him to associate the Cubist painter with the splendours of the *grand siècle*: but his instinct was justified. The vaulted gallery, lined with sober marble, with its seventeen arched mirrors on the courtyard side reflecting as many arched windows giving on the boundless vistas of the garden, was nearly 240 feet long and 35 feet wide. The stage took up a third of the length, leaving two-thirds for the thousand spectators. The performers came down mirror-faced staircases to the dancing area. On either side stood or sat members of the Comédie Française, wearing their own Molière costumes, providing the court of spectators customary in classical ballets. The Diaghilev Ballet danced the first part of *Le Mariage d'Aurore*, and took part in a mixed entertainment of song, recitation and dance that followed. Finally, Anatole Vilzak as Louis XIV, in his blue and gold Roman costume by Gris, topped with feathers, came down the steps to the music of Rameau, while twenty negro pages spread his 35-metre-long blue train, sewn with *fleur de lys*, behind him. He was flanked by two Heralds with trumpets, also wearing Roman costumes by Gris: these were Singaievsky, soon to become the second husband of Nijinska, and Boris Kochno. It was the latter's only appearance on a stage.

Serge Lifar approached Diaghilev at the end of the party and asked if he might have a programme. 'Very well, Lifar, come and see me tomorrow, and I'll give you a programme.' Lifar never knew (or said he did not) what stopped him going for his programme on the next day. In later years Diaghilev would often ask him why he had not come. 'It would all have turned out so differently, and you would never have lost a whole year.'[67] How lucky, though, we can exclaim, with hindsight! If the process of grooming Lifar for stardom had begun a year earlier than it did, Diaghilev might never have engaged Dolin, and the latter might never have attained the experience and the international fame in Diaghilev's Ballet which enabled him (with Markova) to waft the unpromising craft of British ballet off the ground in the 1930s and make it airborne.

As it was, Lifar spent ten weeks' holiday in a village near Chartres, and Diaghilev worked on the plans for his French festival of ballet and opera before going to Venice with Kochno.

When reviving an old work, Diaghilev, as we have seen, could not bear to leave well alone. He felt impelled to cut or add or alter. He could plead the excuse of tradition in having the recitatives in his Gounod operas set to music, for Berlioz had written music for the recitatives in *Der Freischütz* and Guiraud had done the same for *Carmen*: but another reason for abolishing recitative was that Diaghilev thought there had been no singers since Chaliapine who could act.[68] So Diaghilev had commissioned Poulenc to edit *La Colombe*, Auric *Philémon* and Satie *Le Médecin*. The question arose as to who should embellish Chabrier's *L'Education manquée*. Diaghilev and Massine had heard Milhaud play his *L'Homme et son désir* at Misia's house in spring 1920, and they had not liked it. But Satie asked Diaghilev to

employ Milhaud for the Chabrier opera, and he relented. On 21 July Satie
wrote to Milhaud:

Diaghilev charges me to ask your help in completing *L'Education manquée*. I
told my dear employer that you are the only one who can do this work. . . . I
teased him a bit about his neglect of you and he seems to have come round.

What do you think?. . . This small job will earn you 1000 francs. . . . Poulenc
has already done wonders with *La Colombe*. . . .[69]

Milhaud agreed and Diaghilev talked to him before leaving for Venice.
There were three singers in *L'Education*, but the soprano had no aria.
Diaghilev wanted Milhaud to compose one in the style of Chabrier.
The composer's daughter and Enoch's publishing house gave Milhaud
access to Chabrier's unpublished manuscripts, among which he found an
enchanting melody he was able to use, and for which René Chalupt wrote
words. The man's role had originally been sung by a woman *en travesti*,
and Milhaud transposed her part for a tenor. He enjoyed faking the linking
passages, and all went well.[70] The Gounod family, however, rejected Auric's
recitatives for *Philémon*.[71]

Grigoriev spent his summer holiday in London, where he renewed Idzikovsky's contract and signed up an Anglo-Irish girl of good family, recommended by Sokolova, whose professional name was Ninette de Valois.[72]
(Her real name was Edris Stannus.)

Two arrivals from Russia that summer were Diaghilev's cousin Pavel
Koribut-Kubitovitch,[73] who was at once absorbed into the headquarters
staff, and Alexandre Benois. A letter written from Russia a month or two
before makes it clear that Benois was coming expressly to design *Le Médicin
malgré lui*, but he brought his family with him, because he never intended
to return. He was not familiar with the Gounod opera – few people were
– but he looked forward to embracing Diaghilev's 'fresh and voluminous
self' and receiving from him 'a jolt of that superb force of will which always
had so beneficial an effect' on him.[74]

Poulenc was working on his ballet, the ideal name for which came to him
suddenly in a taxi as he sat beside Valentine Gross.[75] In September he wrote
to Diaghilev in Venice, 'How hard it is to get in touch with you! The name
for the ballet has been found – *Les Biches*. So far everyone has been in favour.
I hope you will be. It is *so* Marie Laurencin. . . .'[76]

The company assembled in Paris rather earlier than they might have
wished, on 15 August. For a month, in a large room at the top of the Gaieté
Lyrique, which was in fact the gallery bar, they rehearsed under Nijinska.
The first impressions of Devalois (which was how Diaghilev preferred to
spell her name) included Nemtchinova, now the company's ballerina, in the
mazurka from *Les Sylphides*, and her own difficulty in learning that same
ballet in two rehearsals. She also remembered sitting with Sokolova during
a rehearsal of *Le Tricorne* to watch some boys bent double carrying sacks,

supposedly filled with the Miller's flour. 'Goodness me, look at them,' Sokolova exclaimed. 'Look at those kids from Kiev, they'll never do it, never.' One of those 'worried, perspiring, red-faced small boys' was Lifar.⁷⁷

Astafieva had sent Diaghilev glowing reports of a young dancer called Anton Dolin, who had danced two solos in a display by her pupils in the Albert Hall, London (on 26 June). He was none other than the boy Patrick Healey-Kay, who had appeared under the name of Patrikeef as a page and a village youth in *The Sleeping Princess* a year and a half before. She was invited to bring Dolin over to be inspected in Paris. Early in September Astafieva, Dolin, and a girl pupil were driven by Diaghilev to the rehearsal room at the Gaieté Lyrique. Facing Diaghilev in the car, Dolin was most struck by his eyes and hands. 'They were eyes that looked one through and through, that saw everything, and yet at times gave the impression they were not even looking at you: eyes set wide apart over a full face. His hands, which were small in comparison with the rest of his figure, were white and well kept; and as he spoke they seemed to beat time and express the rhythm of his voice. Fortunately Diaghilev spoke a few words of English.'⁷⁸

Nijinska and Grigoriev joined Diaghilev to watch the two young people dance the *Grand pas de deux* from *The Sleeping Princess*, after which Dolin did a Russian dance and his own arrangement of Rimsky's *Hymn to the Sun*. He heard afterwards that he was accepted and that Diaghilev wanted him to join the company at once. This he could not do as he had an engagement to fulfil at the London Palladium, with Nicolas Legat and his wife Nadejda Nicolaeva.⁷⁹

In mid-September the Ballet gave a few performances in Antwerp, followed by a season in Switzerland, where Ansermet conducted. On the day they returned to Monte Carlo, Diaghilev had the displeasure of seeing two new works given by Les Ballets Suédois at the Théâtre des Champs-Elysées. Jealous of any company which threatened his monopoly, he found it particularly galling that a painter of the calibre of Fernand Léger and a composer who was one of 'Les Six', such as Milhaud, should collaborate, as they did over *La Création du Monde*. *Within the Quota* was a skit on the American way of life, with music by Cole Porter. Diaghilev met Cole Porter in society in Paris, London and Venice, but always pretended to be ignorant of the fact that he wrote music.⁸⁰ Yet, however *avant-garde* the Swedes might try to be – and even temporarily succeed in being in the eyes of *le tout Paris* – it was perfectly obvious that Rolf de Maré's money, which was plentiful, and Jean Borlin's choreographic gifts, which were less so, could avail nothing without Diaghilev's hard-learnt wizardry at making ballets work, eight times out of ten.

During September and October 1923 Diaghilev had discussions with Braque over the Louis XIV designs for *Les Fâcheux*, with Benois over the Louis XIV designs (how different!) for *Le Médecin*, and with Gris over the

Louis XIV designs for *Les Tentations* (a grey-blue and silver stylized Versailles, as against Braque's brown and green village street and Benois' brown and grey, almost monochrome, Paris). The staging of *La Colombe* and *L'Education*, with their small casts of nineteenth-century characters, was less of a problem. The vague, finicky, fussy and affected Marie Laurencin was harder to pin down than the three men, two of whom were great painters and one a theatrical designer of long experience. It was easy enough to use for a front curtain one of her dreamy pastorals of wispy girls caressing a complacent quadruped, and to isolate a slight sketch of a gauze-curtained window in the middle of a plain white backcloth to form a setting. Her suggestions for costumes, on the other hand, were about as helpful to the dressmaker as poems by Verlaine. While Diaghilev lay on his bed at the Hôtel Savoy, certain as usual that he was getting 'flu, Vera Sudeikina and Boris Kochno worked at the writing-table, trying to piece together some practical designs from Laurencin's delicate indications.[81] The firm of Weldy probably had difficulty in reducing Braque's squiggles of colour to patterns of formal appliqué, too.

Diaghilev passionately admired Picasso's paintings of monumental giantesses posed on antique shores, who appeared to 'fleet the time carelessly as they did in the golden world', and he was determined that Gounod's *Philémon et Baucis* should be designed in this style. Picasso never said No to anything, but would sometimes – out of perversity or lack of appropriate inspiration – employ delaying tactics. He did not react (perhaps naturally) to Gounod's music in the way Diaghilev hoped, and when the off-stage bacchanale was played to him, exclaimed, 'Why, it's a can-can!' and began kicking his legs in the air. Reluctantly he agreed to design the opera; he then put it out of his mind.[82]

Juan Gris and his mistress Josette arrived at Monte Carlo and installed themselves at Beausoleil on 11 October; on 5 November the painter wrote to Kahnweiler that his sets for *Les Tentations* were almost ready, but that he had run out of canvas. Diaghilev was expected at any moment and was to bring some more from Paris. Poulenc had arrived two days before and found Monte Carlo delightful. 'He's lucky fellow!' wrote Gris, who hated it.[83]

Diaghilev was full of hopes for Dolin both as an artist and as a friend. He had decided that he should start off as a soloist, without going through the corps de ballet. Dolin arrived back in Paris from London on 3 November. He was bought clothes and taken out to dinner. At a Kussevitzky concert he was introduced to Stravinsky and Vera Sudeikina. That night Nuvel took him to the Gare de Lyon and gave him his ticket for Monte Carlo. Diaghilev was on the train, and after a quarter of an hour came to his compartment. Dolin's luggage, which consisted of one suitcase and an overcoat, was moved to Diaghilev's sleeper, with its twin berths. They had a good dinner together, which included ice cream and sweet biscuits. Patrick, as Diaghilev always called him, understood the ways of the world. He had been seduced by a priest in the confessional when he was a boy.[84]

Boris Kochno had been left behind in Paris, not just because it was convenient that he should be out of the way while Dolin was initiated into the mixed joys of a favourite's life, but to pester Picasso for his *Philémon* designs and for some drawings to adorn the Monte Carlo souvenir programme which he was editing. When at last Picasso showed him a model theatre and raised the curtain, the longed-for décor turned out to be a construction of wood, sacking and string. This was far from Diaghilev's conception and, when he next came to Paris, he turned it down.[85]

Diaghilev gave *Philémon et Baucis* to Benois; but the latter's designs for a peasant's cottage and landscape struck him as suitable for nothing but a provincial production of Wagner. Although Benois' *Médecin* was most satisfactory, the Greek décors were so repulsive to Diaghilev that he never employed Benois again.[86] With Bakst bitterly antagonized, and Benois, as he thought, left far behind the wave of modern experiment in art – for Benois disliked nearly all of Diaghilev's later ballets – Diaghilev had none of his original group to work with except Nuvel. Valetchka had a rich sister living in Paris (married to a Baron van Heekkeren, who was descended from the killer of Pushkin), but she ignored his existence; and he lived alone in the little Hôtel Pasquier in the rue d'Antin, negotiating contracts, facilitating the transport of dancers or scenery, meeting trains, answering telegrams, smoking, breaking in newcomers, and even loving one of the latest, the small, delicate and attractive Konstantin Tcherkass.[87]

Kochno persisted in badgering Picasso for his programme drawings. He had been promised some studies of dancers done during rehearsals in Rome in 1917.

Picasso gave me a date when I could come for the sketches, but when I arrived I found that he had not had time to look for them.... The printer was growing impatient.... I resigned myself to leaving with nothing but the now useless dummy. As I got up to go, Picasso seemed to be struck by an idea. He grew animated, as if he had just realized that since it was a matter of drawings he himself had done, he could remedy the situation with no trouble, without even getting up. He took a stub of pencil from his pocket and, in a few minutes, covered the pages of the dummy with admirable drawings of dancers.[88]

The end of 1923 was a time of furious activity, but also of intense happiness, for Diaghilev. What he hoped would be the first of many seasons of ballet and opera – a perennial festival – was about to flower in Monte Carlo. He was going to see four opera productions he had planned become realities on the stage, and three new ballets. Trefilova was coming to give a few performances of *Le Lac des Cygnes*. And he was in love with Dolin.

Of all his new productions, Diaghilev had the greatest hopes of *Les Biches*;

and that is the work which has survived to the present day (the late 1970s). On 17 November he wrote to Boris in Paris:

> Here everything is going along much better than I expected. Poulenc is enthusiastic about Bronia's choreography, and they get along excellently together. The choreography has delighted and astonished me. But then, this good woman, intemperate and anti-social as she is, does belong to the Nijinsky family. Here and there her choreography is a bit too ordinary, a bit too *feminine*, but *on the whole* it is very good. The dance for the three men has come out extremely well, and they perform it with bravura – weightily, like three cannon. It doesn't at all resemble *Les Noces*, any more than Tchaikovsky's *Eugene Onegin* resembles his *Queen of Spades*.[89]

As soon as he had seen the opening of his winter season at Monte Carlo – not his special French Festival, which would be in January – Diaghilev travelled to Paris, to be in touch with his designers and dressmakers. On 'Friday evening', probably 30 November, Poulenc wrote to him about the progress of rehearsals for *Les Biches*. It should be explained that, apart from a corps de ballet of frivolous ladies in pink and pale blue, with ostrich feathers in their hair, the characters were: three narcissistic Athletes; Nemtchinova, who was perhaps intended to be a page-boy; Nijinska, an older woman, in beige lace and pearls with a long cigarette-holder – perhaps the hostess; and two clinging friends, Tchernicheva and Sokolova, in Sappho grey. One Athlete was attracted to the Page-boy and the other two to the Hostess. The only piece of furniture, a long blue *capitonné* sofa, was used as a vaulting horse and a gazebo, as well as for its usual legitimate and illegitimate purposes.

> Excellency [wrote Poulenc],
> You cannot imagine what you have missed in the last two days. When Nemtchinova's dance is finished – and what a *miracle* – they start the Game. I must say that as *madness* it surpasses anything one could imagine. Nijinska is really a *genius*. Listen to this: having decided that the sofa is a 'star', just as she herself is, she is making it dance throughout the Game!!! Grigoriev asked the Casino for the loan of a magnificent sofa, and they fell to work (in an entirely proper fashion, naturally). . . .
> In a presto movement the women take sitting positions, leap into the air, fall on to the tufted cushions, roll over on their backs (although the two men are straddling the sofa back), and then they drag the poor sofa in all directions. When, in the middle section, the music calms down, the Star [Nijinska] and Vilzak bounce onstage. Thereupon the Girls turn the sofa (its back is now to the audience) into an observatory, their heads popping over the back and then dropping out of sight; when the game resumes – *now listen to this* – the two men quickly turn the sofa around and there are the two women lying in a position that, thinking of Barbette, I can only describe as head to tail. . . .
> At rehearsals I laugh until I cry. . . . Come back soon. A thousand greetings to dear Boris, whom I miss, and to you, Milord.[90]

When a choreographer was to take part in his own ballet, he 'mounted' the role on another dancer. So Nijinska worked out her role of the Hostess (the 'Star', as Poulenc called her) on Ninette Devalois.[91]

Marie Laurencin nearly drove everyone mad. Both Prince Schervashidze, the scene-painter, and Vera Sudeikina, the dressmaker, had to redo their work at her request, then change it back again.[92]

On the opening matinée at Monte Carlo on 25 November, Dolin had danced in the Bacchanale in *Cléopâtre* with Sokolova, Tchernicheva and Woizikovsky, and in *Prince Igor*. At the end of the latter ballet, as he was bowing, he inadvertently stood further downstage than the other dancers in the first line, and the curtain fell behind him, leaving him alone to receive the audience's applause. This Diaghilev took as a good omen.[93]

It was not surprising that senior members of the company, who had worked for years to attain their present positions, should resent the upstart Dolin. He was a cheerful, friendly young man, who doubtless gave the impression of being too pleased with himself. On the day after the Monte Carlo opening Diaghilev announced that Dolin and Sokolova were to study *Daphnis et Chloë* together. 'That was the cleverest thing Diaghilev ever did,' Dolin remarked half a century later[94] – a strange comment, which makes clear how essential it appeared to Diaghilev that Dolin should be accepted by certain key members of the company. If Sokolova became his friend, it followed that Woizikovsky must be also: and the cheerful, irresponsible (in life) but reliable (on stage) Pole got on well with everybody. The revival of *Daphnis* was clearly prompted by Diaghilev's passion for 'comprehensiveness', for completing a series. How could he omit from his French festival a Ravel score he himself had commissioned? Debussy's *L'Après-midi d'un faune*, too, would be included, and *Las Meninas* revived for the sake of Fauré's *Pavane*. Nobody could remember the *pas de deux* of Daphnis and Chloë, so Nijinska invented a new one; and Juan Gris designed a new Greek costume for Dolin. Nijinska tended to judge Dolin redundant. Diaghilev advised Patrick to be very nice to her, and he himself asked Bronislava to coach the young man in private. Dolin turned on the charm, and soon Nijinsky's sister was the best of friends with Nijinsky's successor as *premier danseur classique*.[95]

On 12 December died Raymond Radiguet, the extraordinary boy, Cocteau's friend, pupil and inspiration. Jean had not been able to bring himself to visit Raymond in hospital, nor would he walk in the funeral procession. Boris was in Paris, and, when he made a visit of commiseration, he found Cocteau in bed, surrounded by such a court of mourners that he might have been on his own death-bed.[96] Diaghilev, in Monte Carlo, sent a telegram of commiseration. Jean's reply did not strike quite the right note. 'My condition serious. Think of me. Love. Jean.'[97] Only Radiguet's poems *Devoirs de vacances* and his short novel *Le Diable au corps* had been published. His even shorter novel, one of the most perfect in French literature, would appear posthumously. His death not only affected Cocteau, but also, as will be seen, the Russian Ballet, and Anton Dolin in particular. Diaghilev went to Paris and paid Jean a visit.[98]

It was only in mid-December that Diaghilev asked Juan Gris to do the décor and costumes for Chabrier's *L'Education manquée*. Gris thought – or Diaghilev told him – that Picasso had been supposed to do them, but at the last moment did not. 'They began to rehearse Auric's ballet today,' he wrote to Kahnweiler on 20 November. 'He worries so much about it that he spends all his time at the gambling tables. At any rate I have to some extent saved the situation over *L'Education manquée*, and Diaghilev was very touched, at least for two hours. By now he has forgotten. I *must* soon escape from this centre of incompetence and hysterics. . . .'[99]

The company performed their old repertoire while they prepared the new ballets.

When Vera Sudeikina arrived just before the New Year with the costumes for *Les Biches*, she warned Diaghilev that Marie Laurencin had been visiting her workshop with Misia Sert, that many details had been changed, and that he might get a shock.[100] Much has been written about the perfect collaboration between choreographer, composer and designer under Diaghilev's supervision. The stages by which one of the most famous costumes of any Diaghilev ballet, that for Nemtchinova in the adagietto in *Les Biches*, reached its final form, are therefore of interest. We have seen how Laurencin's nebulous watercolours had been evolved by Sudeikina and Kochno. Laurencin had insisted on further changes. Nemtchinova appeared before Diaghilev's eyes in a long blue velvet frock-coat, like that of a head porter in an hotel. 'Give me the scissors, Grigoriev!' Diaghilev exclaimed. He cut away the collar, to make a wide V-neck. He cut away the velvet, till it barely covered the buttocks. Nemtchinova had never shown so much leg before (what ballerina had?) and she protested. 'I feel naked!' 'Then go and buy yourself some white gloves!' said Diaghilev. The celebrated white gloves became almost a part of the choreography.[101]

The souvenir programme which had given Kochno so much trouble, and for which Picasso had done the drawings, was for the so-called season of 'Ballets Classiques' at the end of 1923, which lasted from 25 November until 31 December. After that, the pencil sketches of dancers making up, having their hair done, pulling on tights and trying out their shoes would be used again in Paris. There was a new programme for the French Festival in January 1924, with a Pierrot by Gris on the cover. Eighteen handsome pages commemorate Diaghilev's final adventure in operatic presentation, which had been inspired by that chance visit to hear *Philémon* at the Trianon-Lyrique a year or more before. The frontispiece, by Gris, a drawing of a fond mother listening to her daughter playing the piano, with the inscription

'Opéra Comique', precedes two drawings by Ingres of Charles Gounod and his wife, made in Rome in 1839. There follow an article by Louis Laloy (now Secretary of the Opéra) on the origins of the operas and ballets being presented, illustrated by ten photographs of singers, Benois' design for the first act of *Philémon et Baucis* (the interior of a peasant cottage), Lamy's pretty poster in colour of the first production of that opera, two pages (in colour) of Benois' third-act décor for *Le Médecin* (with several costume designs), the set for *La Colombe* by Gris and his costume for Horace, and Manet's portrait of Chabrier all in black and white.

Le Médecin, based on Molière's play, contained the minimum of seventeenth-century pastiche and was full of Gounod's charming melody, delicate modulations and vivid orchestration. The roles of Lucinda and Martine were taken by Ines Ferraris and Romanitza, Léandre was Theodore Reich and Sganarelle was Daniel Vigneau, who had sung at the Fête de Versailles. Nothing could be more absurdly artificial than the plot of *La Colombe* (by Jules Barbier and Michel Carré), which concerns the desperate love of Lord Horace for Countess Sylvie. Having ruined himself for her in vain and retired to a humble cottage, he finally wins her love by cooking for her dinner his last possession, the pet dove he had named after her. The two chief characters were sung by Maria Barrientos and the handsome Reich, and it is amusing to compare the Cubist designer's idea of a rustic hovel, its in-sloping walls and window framing the distant view of a cypress and a mountain – which reminded Vladimir Polunin, who painted it, of Picasso's set for *Pulcinella* – with the meticulous design of Benois for *Philémon*, with its view-point so low that the beamed ceiling filled half the décor, its crumbling walls and ladder leading to a loft above, from which tufts of hay hung through the rafters.

The second half of the souvenir programme, devoted to ballet, had its own frontispiece by Juan Gris, an illustration to the ballet he had designed, with a seventeenth-century periwigged nobleman kneeling to a protesting shepherdess. There followed in colour two pages of Braque's designs for *Les Fâcheux*, two of Marie Laurencin's set, curtain and costumes for *Les Biches* and one of designs by Gris for costumes and props for *Les Tentations de la Bergère*. In black and white, models for the set and costumes of the last ballet were reproduced; and there were ten pages of photographs of dancers, of Poulenc and Auric.

Laloy, a precise little man 'like a Chinese',[102] not only wrote the programme note; he wrote a criticism of the season, too. He was therefore bound to be reasonably polite. It is clear, however, that what impressed him most in the first week (*Philémon* and *Les Fâcheux* were given later) was *Les Biches*. The nature of this ballet has already been suggested in the correspondence of Poulenc and Diaghilev. What we have not stated is that the 'Chanson dansée', 'Jeu' and the 'Petite Chanson dansée' were accompanied by nonsensical songs. (These were omitted in Paris.) How would the 'stuffy' public of Monte Carlo receive this work by an unknown composer, which even Paris might have thought controversial?

Here [wrote Laloy], apart from the immediate collaborators of the management and a few friends who had come on a brief visit – about twenty people in all – one looked in vain for a familiar face. As many people were speaking English and Italian as French – if not more – and even those of us who had been most delighted by the ballet during the final rehearsals, could not but feel a certain apprehension as to how this crowd of strangers would take it. However, from the first numbers, applause burst forth from every corner of the theatre. . . .

Nijinska, he thought, had created 'the *Sylphides* of today'; and Poulenc's limpid melodies, so gay but with a hidden melancholy, were the music of youth.[103]

Nemtchinova still felt shy in her abbreviated costume, and in the wings she wrapped herself in a shawl. Once on stage, she forgot everything.[104] Sokolova, who was later to succeed Nijinska as the Hostess, wrote of Vera, '. . . This neat little "Page-boy" entered on tip-toe from the wings, then stood still, with her right hand laid against her right cheek and the other straight down against her leg: her appearance never failed to cause a stir. . . .'[105]

Diaghilev had had the kind thought of inviting Astafieva to come from London to see her pupil, Dolin, as Daphnis.[106] Satie arrived from Paris on Friday, 4 January, to see the results of his own work and that of Poulenc. This excursion was a rare adventure for Satie and Nuvel telegraphed 'Meet him', as if he might get lost.[107] The English music critic Rollo Myers came to hear *La Colombe* and *Les Biches*, and Poulenc talked to him with boyish pleasure about the score of which he was so proud. On an old upright piano behind the scenes the composer played Myers his adagietto, pointing out details of orchestration.[108] Diaghilev had also invited Cocteau,[109] hoping to cheer him up. In this he was at least partly successful, for Jean, who accepted the invitation with the words 'My grief is as violent as ever, but I have decided to come. To me Raymond was the incarnation of poetry. My family of composers is all I have left . . .',[110] later wrote to Poulenc, '*Les Biches* helps me to live;'[111] and again, 'Your compositions are the only things that keep me alive and give me an appetite for life.'[112] It was at Monte Carlo, in the first week of January, that Cocteau learned from Louis Laloy how to smoke opium, which became for him the source of endless *servitudes et grandeurs* in the years to come. Diaghilev asked him to think of a ballet for Anton Dolin, who had not yet had anything specially created for him, and it was while watching Dolin doing acrobatics in the rehearsal room that he had his idea.

Diaghilev's preoccupation with Dolin, whom he took to visit his friends, such as Somerset Maugham,[113] did not entirely put the attractive Lifar out of his mind. Serge had done so well in the czardas in *Le Lac des Cygnes*

that he was given the small role of an Officer in *Les Fâcheux*. Some of Diaghilev's colleagues noticed him and made friends, Cocteau among others, and
when Diaghilev saw Serge in their company at the Café de Paris or in the
stalls of the theatre (the front of house being out of bounds to dancers),
he made angry scenes and threatened to dismiss him.[114]

Of his fellow-collaborators on *Les Fâcheux*, Kochno recalled that, while
Auric used to disappear into the gambling rooms of the Casino during
rehearsals, Georges Braque was seldom out of the scene-painting studio.

He rarely left the workshop where Prince Schervashidze and his assistants were
building the scenery. During the hours when the crew of painters knocked off
work, Braque sometimes joined Diaghilev and me in the Jardin Exotique of the
Casino, but he always seemed worried that he would be late for the resumption
of the work. Seated on a bench in the shade of the palm trees or at a table on
the terrace of the Café de Paris – always wearing a bowler hat – he would tell
stories of his youth and hum 'Je cherche après Titine, Titine, ma Titine', but
his eyes never strayed from the Casino clock....[115]

On 6 January Gris wrote to Kahnweiler:

I have received a number of compliments on *La Colombe*, although the piece
is too long and too tedious. The costumes look well with the scenery, although
they have been badly made.... The Monteclair ballet has been a great success.
The costumes for it are also badly made but they go well with the setting. I had
to take a curtain call, and Nijinska says that she has never seen such a complete
harmony. But oh! how frantic I was during the last days. Except for Nijinska,
who takes her work seriously, and Diaghilev who knows his job, nobody uses his
brains or foresees anything....[116]

Diaghilev's task in co-ordinating the rehearsals, dress rehearsals and
orchestra rehearsals of these operas and ballets was a nightmare of staff-
work. It would have been impossible if there had not been three nights a
week when the theatre offered other attractions, and, even so, there was
rivalry for occupation of the stage. The season did not pass without mishaps.
At a New Year's Eve party at the villa he shared with Sokolova, Woizikovsky
had developed a high fever and a sore throat: he could hardly swallow and
became slightly delirious. On the afternoon of Thursday, 3 January, he was
driven to the theatre, bandaged in Thermogene wool, to play the Shepherd
in *Les Tentations*, and three days later he managed to get through *Les
Biches*.[117] Polunin had trouble with the décor of *La Colombe*. 'Owing to
the peculiarities of construction of the scene and the strong lighting, the
light penetrated the canvas from behind, completely changing the fundamental tones.... The walls, painted with a practically pure white, appeared
to be of a brownish-ochre, the black tones seemed reddish....' The set was
returned to the studio, where, partly by skill, partly by chance, it was possible
to remedy the situation, so that 'Diaghilev was well pleased by the final

result.'[118] Then, Braque had designed for *Les Fâcheux* a front curtain with a hole in the centre, in which a nymph, naked except for some drapery, stood as if in a grotto surrounded by foliage. Dancer after dancer refused to appear in the semi-nude.[119] The part was taken on the first night by Krassovska. After this Braque painted a nymph in the centre of the curtain. Braque had had some of the costumes remade and redyed, then washed several times to achieve the exact tint of his design; when these arrived at the theatre, a few were still damp. Idzikovsky was dissatisfied with his minor role of Lysandre, and, when the dye came off on his body, he made this the pretext for refusing to dance. When he failed to turn up at the dress rehearsal Nijinska put on his costume and played the role herself.[120] Idzikovsky was dismissed.

Princess Charlotte had recently given birth to Prince Rainier and she decided to have some ballet lessons. Diaghilev sent Tchernicheva to teach her. Sokolova also had an amateur pupil, Mrs Reginald Fellowes (daughter of the Duc Decazes and niece of Princesse Edmond de Polignac), famous for her looks, chic, good taste and interest in other women's husbands. Twice a week Sokolova taught her either at the Cinéma des Beaux Arts or at her villa along the coast. One evening Sokolova complained of a headache and Daisy Fellowes, before driving her back to her flat, gave her some powder to sniff.

The headache disappeared and I went to a rehearsal. By the time it came to my turn to dance I was feeling on top of the world: I threw myself into my role ... and enjoyed myself immensely. Diaghilev was watching, and called me over to sit beside him, saying 'You seem very excited. Who gave it to you? ... Weren't you given some powder to smell?' 'Yes ... for my headache....' Diaghilev got up and walked away. From that day onward I never gave that lady another lesson, nor did I ever speak to her again. The 'Old Man' had diagnosed the effects of cocaine: his measures were prompt and drastic.[121]

If Diaghilev was in any doubts as to the public's reaction to the operatic part of his French Festival, the Casino management made the position quite clear to him: the rich visitors wanted 'more ballet'. If they were to have opera, it must be familiar 'grand opera', with famous star singers. Except by the 'vingtaine de personnes en tout', in Laloy's phrase, his efforts had been unappreciated. He had hoped to show the operas along with his ballets in Paris. He decided to give only *L'Education manquée*. 'No more opera!' he decided: it was like the loss of a limb. His great plans for Monte Carlo as a centre of the arts were dashed.

Grigoriev thought that Raoul de Guinsbourg, Director of the permanent Monte Carlo opera season and a clownish character whose pretentions to have shared rooms with Mussorgsky, and so on, no one took seriously,[122] 'had scented in Diaghilev a dangerous rival'. The Casino decided to revert to its former policy of presenting light operas in the autumn, 'grand opera' in the winter and ballet in the spring.[123] But the opera company still needed the co-operation of the ballet; and the delayed opera season of 1924 opened on 31 January with a charity gala in which the ballet took part. After this, while Nijinska and most of the dancers remained in Monte Carlo, Diaghilev, Kochno, Dolin and Nuvel went to Paris.

Dolin travelled by night to London to spend the first weekend of February with his family, and on 4 February telegraphed to Diaghilev at the Hôtel Mirabeau in Paris: 'Arrived safely. Good sleep for my age ten. Patrick.'[124]

Vera Sudeikina, who had been involved in Diaghilev's first encounter with Boris Kochno, was surprised that Diaghilev found it necessary to invite her to tea chez Colombin, at the corner of rue Cambon and rue du Mont Thabor, to tell her that he had a new friend, Dolin.[125] Probably he merely wanted to talk about Patrick to a sympathetic listener. Dolin returned to Paris and studied under Trefilova, while Diaghilev set about preparing the ballet which was to make the young man famous.

Besides the Ballets Suédois, a new rival company was coming into being. Diaghilev's old friend, Etienne de Beaumont, who, although married, was as homosexual as himself, was organizing 'Les Soirées de Paris' with Massine. Diaghilev told Poulenc and Auric that if they worked with Beaumont, he would not present their ballets in Paris.[126] They were young and could be browbeaten: not so Satie, Picasso, Braque and Derain. Diaghilev had reason to be anxious. Stravinsky, however, resisted temptation. When Beaumont asked if he could have the Octet arranged as a ballet, Igor replied that he thought the music self-sufficient.[127]

On about 13 February Cocteau produced the libretto of the new ballet for Dolin, which had the modern subject of sport – tennis, golf and swimming. It was referred to first as 'Le Beau Gosse' ('The Good-looking Fellow'), then as 'Les Poules' ('The Tarts' – literally, 'Hens'), and it finally became *Le Train bleu*.[128] That fast, luxurious train from Paris to Deauville had made its maiden run in the previous summer.

Boris had gone alone to see *Dédé*, the latest musical comedy of Christine and Maurice Yvain, and came away not only enchanted by the songs but raving about the talents of Maurice Chevalier (then thirty-six years old). Diaghilev jumped to the conclusion that Boris was attracted by Chevalier and went secretly to see *Dédé* out of curiosity about the type his friend found irresistible. 'But he's an old man!' he later exclaimed incredulously. Nevertheless, the music fascinated him,[129] and he decided to invite Darius Milhaud, whose adaptability he recognized, to write an *opérette dansée*, whose tunes and sentiment would be as unlike as possible to Milhaud's more solemn music, which he did not care for. Milhaud had begun on 5 February the composition for Etienne de Beaumont of *Salade* (to which Massine was going to arrange another Neapolitan romp, like *Pulcinella*). On 14 February Diaghilev paid him a visit. He enlarged upon the 'immense advantages' which Milhaud would derive from working with him, and urged him to break with Beaumont, whose Soirées de Paris could have no future. Milhaud's was a strict Jewish code of honour. He said that he had a contract with Beaumont which he meant to fulfil, but that, if it contained no clause to prevent him working with Diaghilev, he would do so. 'Diaghilev had no choice, he needed a new work in a hurry to launch Dolin. He knew I worked fast.... Under the circumstances Beaumont behaved perfectly....' Milhaud began *Le Train bleu* on the following day. He finished *Salade* on 20 February and Diaghilev's ballet on 5 March. He thereafter referred to them as his 'twins'.[130] Diaghilev and Dolin returned to Monte Carlo a day or two before they could see Milhaud's finished score.

Braque was to design *Salade* and wrote to assure Diaghilev that he had arranged with Beaumont that it should not be presented before *Les Fâcheux*, which Paris had not yet seen. (This, in fact, did not happen, as the production of *Salade* preceded the first performance of *Les Fâcheux* in Paris by a fortnight.)[131] Cocteau, too, wrote on 29 February to reassure Diaghilev that his work for Beaumont's season at the Théâtre de la Cigale was nothing to do with ballet.

I was so sorry not to have seen you to say goodbye. I wanted to explain to you about a Cigale project which I should think will please you as it changes the aspect of the whole enterprise.

E. de Beaumont wants me to stage *Roméo et Juliette* [of Shakespeare], to alternate with his music-hall programme. I am working with Jean V. Hugo [husband of Valentine Gross], and I am having some Scotch bagpipers sent over from England.

So I am doing nothing that is in any way like your productions, and am confining myself to *theatre* theatre.[132]

There had been clashes between Cocteau and Bronislava Nijinska. On 29 February Jean wrote to Diaghilev: 'Ask Nijinska how she feels about me. I am not going to make a move unless I am sure she will listen to me, for ridiculous diplomatic games are useless. I do not insist that my name appear on the programme as director (although my researches in relation to staging have a logical place in my work), but, in exchange, I do insist on being listened to.'[133]

Meanwhile, Nijinska was busy with opera ballets. On 13 April she staged the dances for Mussorgsky's *La Nuit sur le mont chauve*, which were led by Sokolova and Mikhail Fedorov, and in which Sokolova thought Nijinska 'covered the stage with a writhing whirling mass of bodies and conjured up the most convincing Witches' Sabbath' she had ever seen.[134] Cocteau returned to Monte Carlo for discussions. These were stormy, as Boris Kochno recalled:

Cocteau was used to taking an active part in the staging of his works for the theatre, and he had given Nijinska numerous suggestions for the choreography, which she was to create in his absence. The manuscript of the scenario which he prepared for Nijinska's use was filled with examples she was to follow in developing the ballet. As models, he cited a pair of acrobatic dancers, who that year were appearing at Ciro's late in the evening, snapshots of the Prince of Wales playing golf, slow-motion films of foot-races, and so forth.

But Nijinska was a stranger to the worldly milieu from which Cocteau derived his inspiration, and even disliked it. Her limited French prevented her from putting her own ideas across to Cocteau, and although Diaghilev tried to intervene and translate, their relations were 'tense, even hostile'.[135]

Dolin, as well as Cocteau, had ideas for material that could be incorporated or transmuted in *Le Train bleu*. He had seen Marjorie Moss and George Fontana dancing a number at the Metropole Hotel, and, after failing to interest Diaghilev, enlisted Boris Kochno's help in persuading him to take a look at them. Diaghilev 'eventually agreed, engaged a table for dinner and afterwards with Nijinska stayed to watch them dance'. Nijinska was impressed and Dolin thought the waltz in *Le Train bleu* was largely inspired by these dancers. Diaghilev, however, was reluctant to admit that watching two ballroom dancers had been anything but a waste of time.[136]

When the Ballet went to give a season at Barcelona, Dolin put up, with Diaghilev, at the Ritz. Walking to the theatre, he found everyone stared at him. Diaghilev always insisted on his young friends being dressed in the height of fashion; and Dolin's new plus-fours, a novelty in Spain, were responsible for the sensation.[137] Evening performances in Spain started at 9.45, four ballets instead of three were given, and the dancers left the theatre for supper at two in the morning. The company were kept busy rehearsing *Les Noces* for Paris, and Nijinska made a start on *Le Train bleu*.

About 25 April Diaghilev wrote to Kochno in Paris,

Bronia is staging *Le Train bleu*, and I very much like the first dance, which is quite gymnastic. I made a long speech to the company, explaining just what the word 'operetta' means, what Milhaud's music is about, and what is, in my view, the plastic problem this ballet presents. I was listened to with devout attention. I think everything will be all right, and I hope that, minus Harlequins and Columbines, this ballet will be a true expression of ourselves....

What *really* delights me is Patrick's dancing. He dances in a *really* adorable way. In *Carnaval, Cimarosiana* [the *divertissement* from *L'Astuce féminine*] and *Pulcinella* he is almost better than the other dancers. Perhaps this impression is only due to the novelty of his appearance, but he does possess a true style....[138]

At this time Diaghilev managed to pay back to Oswald Stoll a large part of his *Sleeping Princess* debt: Wollheim cabled Stoll's acceptance of the money on account.[139]

The eleven performances in Spain were followed by eight in Holland. By mid-May the company were back in Paris.

The Russian Ballet was to dance at the Champs-Elysées for the first time since 1920; but rehearsals were held at the Mogador. 'Paris in the heat,' wrote Ninette Devalois, 'working all day and every day on a salary of 1,500 francs per month (the equivalent at that time of £5 to £6 per week) loses its glamour.' She was the only member of the company who had to learn *Les Noces* from scratch, and her 'frantic efforts at memorizing it quickly' were the hardest job she had ever done. All the same, she thought that of all ballets of that period it was the greatest, but so complicated 'that a perfect unity of dancers, orchestra, choir and pianos is out of the question unless [it is] frequently performed'.[140] Nijinska was also rehearsing *Le Train bleu*. Cocteau interrupted continually and kept making changes, so that the dancers did not know whom to obey.[141] A new variation – to a nocturne previously cut by Diaghilev – was inserted into *Les Fâcheux* for Dolin, which, in the part of an affected Dandy, he was to dance *sur les pointes*. He had no physical difficult in doing this, and it was justifiable dramatically, but in the end proved aesthetically displeasing. Sokolova thought that 'the first im-impression one got was the size of his feet. . . . A man has very little flexibility in his ankle and instep and no effortless *relevé* from the flat of the foot to the point, so that one had the feeling that Pat was walking on stilts. . . .'[142]

Diaghilev's publicity campaign for his season of twelve performances,[143] which alternated with those of the Vienna Opera and other companies, was perhaps more extensive than usual, and Laloy boosted him in at least two papers. A visit of Princess Charlotte and Prince Pierre of Monaco to a rehearsal on Saturday, 24 May, was described at length by Joseph Kessel in *Le Gaulois*[144] and by Pierre-Plessis in *Commedia*;[145] both critics were duly impressed. A row of chairs had been placed for their Serene Highnesses, for Princesse Edmond de Polignac, the Duchesse d'Ayen, the Marquise de Ganay, Lord Berners, M. and Mme Picasso with their small son, Auric, Milhaud and Poulenc. When Nijinska jumped and jumped, little Paul Picasso exclaimed, 'Papa, is she going to fly away?' *Les Biches* was followed by *Le Train bleu*. On the entrance of Dolin, 'the rising star', 'the new dis-covery', 'Diaghilev adjusted his monocle, and watched him closely, beating time with his foot;' and 'Nijinska lit another cigarette.'[146]

The first sight to dazzle the eyes of the first-night audience on 26 May was a superb curtain by Picasso.[147] Diaghilev had asked Picasso to let him have copied and enlarged a gouache of two running giantesses on a sea-shore, which he greatly admired. To copy this small work, in which the con-tours of the girls' ruddy flesh were conveyed in hatched strokes of dry paint, was the most demanding task perhaps ever allotted to a scene-painter; but so perfectly did Shervashidze imitate every detail, that Picasso – who could certainly not have enlarged the original so well himself – found not one stroke to alter. Overcome with joy and admiration, he inscribed Shervashidze's work in the bottom left-hand corner, 'Dédié à Diaghilew. Picasso,' thus con-firming the authenticity of the fake. To see one's small sketch enlarged to fill a proscenium arch – even though in this case there was a broad white border – must indeed be intoxicating: and the curtain remains one of the marvels of the twentieth century.[148] Diaghilev ordered from Auric a special fanfare to greet its appearance.

The programme consisted of *Les Tentations de la bergère*, *Les Biches* and *Les Noces*: three ballets in three very different styles. It was the apotheosis of Nijinska. In *Le Figaro* Laloy had quoted Proust's *'jeunes filles en fleur'* (referring to the novel published in 1919) in announcing *Les Biches*. Another critic actually referred to Nemtchinova's role as 'un page'.[149] Paris evidently recognized the ambiguous nature of her *pas de deux* with Vilzak, which would be overlooked in London.

Diaghilev had brought off a coup in persuading the great André Messager to conduct his new French ballets during this season, hoping, no doubt, to create the impression that the old composer and former Director of the Opéra not only paid homage to Montéclair and Chabrier but gave his blessing to the young composers. The Russian works, mostly by Stravinsky, would be conducted by Pierre Monteux.

At a Red Cross fête at the Grands Magasins du Printemps on 28 May members of the Ballet danced in an architectural setting by Juan Gris. This was the painter's last work for Diaghilev.

When *Les Fâcheux* had its Paris *première* on 5 June (sandwiched between *Petrushka* and *Les Noces*), André Levinson gave what was probably the fairest judgement. He could not allow that Nijinska was the Molière of choreography, and thought her imagination was intermittent. The jumping dances of Lysandre (Nijinska) and the Card-Player (Woizikovsky) were witty and attractive. Except for the dance of battledore-and-shuttlecock players, who flapped their crossed rackets behind their backs like wings, and for the original idea of making Tchernicheva, as Orphise, perform her solo walking on the flat of her feet with heelless shoes, the ballet was empty and monotonous. As an intermezzo, Dolin danced a nocturne not without a touch of lyricism. 'This young dancer has a very good *élévation*, performs *entrechats-cinq de volée* with brio, although he sometimes substitutes unbeaten *cabrioles*, and covers the stage easily. A good dancer and a handsome young man. Will he work hard? In *Les Fâcheux* he was foolish enough to dance on point.' The way Prince Shervashidze had enlarged Braque's sketchy design on a huge scale, retaining the painter's personal 'touch', so that the moss greens and grey drawing of the set were as subtle as an enlarged easel painting, was the most successful part of the production.[150]

Other critics wrote of the 'false notes' Auric had introduced into his pastiche of old music, of his accented rhythms and lack of nobility.[151]

On 13 June *L'Education manquée* was booed: not by more than a few people, Robert Brussel recorded in *Le Figaro*, and the singers, who were visibly put out, could console themselves with their six curtain calls; nevertheless, it was clear that a section of the audience wanted 'ballet à tout prix'. Stravinsky heard cries of 'Dance! dance!' The story of sexually inexperienced Gontran and Hélène, thrown into each other's arms by a convenient storm on the eve of their wedding, might not hold much appeal, Brussel thought, but Chabrier's fresh tunes and subtle orchestration justified Diaghilev's including the opera in his season between the *premières* of Poulenc and Auric, to whom its charm must be as irresistible as to André Messager. The wisdom of setting the recitatives to music was arguable: but none could dispute the skill of Milhaud, who had so completely identified himself with the composer.[152]

The booing did not make Diaghilev cancel the second showing of *L'Education* on his next night at the Champs-Elysées a week later, 20 June, when it preceded the *première* of *Le Train bleu*.

Prokofiev was in Paris that summer, but Diaghilev and Stravinsky had not liked what they heard of his *Love for Three Oranges*, so there was a temporary coolness between them.[153] (Prokofiev was not the only person on record as thinking that Diaghilev was influenced in his musical preferences by Stravinsky. Beecham was another.) Other White Russians were drawn to Paris. Naum Gabo, though based on Berlin, exhibited his nonrepresentational sculptures at the Galerie Percier between 19 June and 5 July, and Diaghilev caught his first glimpse of these imaginative constructions. Pavel Tchelitchev, after designing in Berlin décors for Romanov's Russian Romantic Theatre and a production of *Coq d'or* for the Staatsoper, had settled with Alan Tanner, his American boyfriend, at 150 Boulevard Montparnasse. He had already exhibited in Paris and London, and, since seeing *Les Noces* in 1923, he longed, like most painters, to work for Diaghilev, whom he had met in Berlin. A hint had been given to Nuvel, so the message had probably got through,[154] but Tchelitchev's time was not yet come. That spring of 1924 Pavel may have felt a twinge of jealousy at the speedier progress made by the twenty-year-old but fast-working Vladimir Dukelsky, who arrived from the unusual direction – for a White Russian – of America. Dukelsky had already written popular music in the States under the name of Vernon Duke, and his Slav charm and piano concerto had made sufficient impression on Nuvel to inspire an invitation to Diaghilev's box at the ballet on 4 June, the night of *Les Fâcheux*.

The bejewelled Misia, 'with a massive jaw and rather mean mouth', was there, and the benevolent Koribut-Kubitovitch. When Diaghilev appeared, wrote Dukelsky,

I thought instantly of a decadent Roman emperor – possibly Genghiz Khan or even a barbarous Scythian – and lastly, what he really was: a Russian *grand seigneur* of Alexander III vintage. The eyes had a piercing, mocking intensity about them, softened by unusually heavy eyelids, and he was fond of closing them ... but only for a moment; they were soon peering at you again, not missing a thing....

His voice seemed monstrously affected at first – the Imperial Page's voice of aristocratic St Petersburg. . . . He walked straight up to Misia, took her head in his hands and kissed her on both cheeks. 'Mon Serge! Mon ange!' cooed Misia.

Boris, whom Dukelsky had met in Constantinople, came in; then Nuvel, who introduced Dukelsky to Diaghilev.

'Ah, a good-looking boy,' he drawled. 'That in itself is most unusual. Composers are seldom good-looking; neither Stravinsky nor Prokofiev ever won any beauty prizes. How old are you?' I told him I was twenty. 'That's encouraging too, I don't like young men over twenty-five; they lose their adolescent charm and sleep with any woman who gives them the nod. . . . Oh, so you can still blush. . . . Valetchka, I think him a very pleasant young man and I want him to come to supper with us. . . .'

Supper followed at Le Pré Catalan in the Bois, with Daisy Fellowes, Daisy de Segonzac, the Russian Lady (Iya) Abdy (daughter of the actor Gué), Stravinsky, Auric, Poulenc and Cocteau, with his black sleeves turned back to show their scarlet lining. Two days later, in the 'rococo, Marie Laurencin' décor of the Meyers' house, after more than one cocktail, Dukelsky played his concerto.

When I hit the last crashing C-major chord, there was a moment of dreadful, complete silence – I didn't turn round. . . . To my astonishment the great man began clapping his hands thunderously and with such determination that the others soon joined in the applause. 'Bravo, jeune homme. . . . Now, what shall we call your ballet?' . . . '*What* ballet, Sergei Pavlovitch?' 'The one you will write for me, of course. . . .' Kochno . . . declared that he already had an idea for 'my ballet'. . . . A bottle of champagne appeared. . . . I was taken home by Diaghilev himself. . . . He kissed me heartily on both cheeks, and departed.[155]

Kochno's idea, well calculated to appeal to Diaghilev, was that of a mythological ballet performed by serf artists in an eighteenth-century Russian nobleman's private theatre. The subject: Zephyr and Flora, which had already been used for a ballet by Didelot in 1796.

Diaghilev was also talking to Auric about a successor to *Les Fâcheux*, a ballet, for only five dancers, about the loves of sailors. This was to be designed by a young Spaniard, Pedro Pruna, whom Cocteau had met at Picasso's,[156] and whose very slight, school-of-Picasso paintings in pale colours they all admired at the time.

Another twenty-year-old Russian composer – in fact, a connection of Diaghilev's – came into his orbit that summer, though they were not to work together till later. Nicolas Nabokov was dining with his mother at a Russian restaurant, when she spotted Diaghilev at a neighbouring table with a young man. 'Look, look! There he is.' When Diaghilev understood who she was – her second husband's first cousin had married Diaghilev's half-brother

– Diaghilev exclaimed, 'So you are the mother of the second half of Valya's quartet! What are you doing here? Have you any news of Valya and Dasha? I haven't heard anything since 1921. You know, of course, that Pavlik and Alyosha either were killed in the last months of the civil war or have been executed. Valentin, I believe, is still in prison.' When Mme von Peucker explained that her son Nicolas Nabokov wrote music, Diaghilev became bored, gave the young man an icy look and mumbled something about being busy with rehearsals. 'I'd love to listen to your music.... I only regret it can't be now. Au revoir, chère amie, je suis navré. ...'[157]

The décor of *Le Train bleu* was to be by the Cubist sculptor Henri Laurens. He created sloping planes, an irregular frame, lop-sided bathing huts, two dancing dolphins, all in neutral colours. But the costumes, possibly at Cocteau's insistence, had been entrusted to Coco Chanel, who had designed those for his play *Antigone* in 1922.

Fittings for these costumes took place at Chanel's work-room in rue Cambon. Sokolova wrote, 'When I tried on my pink bathing-dress, which we all thought very daring, the question of what I was to wear on my head arose. Three women stood round me, binding my long hair with various pieces of material, until at last they decided on a dark suède. The neat little skull-cap they made for me set a fashion.'[158] Chanel did not like the fawn beach pyjamas Schollar and Devalois were to have worn in their *pas de quatre* with Zverev and Slavinsky, and she took the two ladies to her work-room to try on knitted bathing costumes similar to Sokolova's.

Standing on a chair [wrote Devalois], I was slowly revolved before Diaghilev, Milhaud and Laurens as a means of proving the necessity of introducing another note of colour. ... Diaghilev seemed ill at ease as a connoisseur of bathing costumes, and Schollar, reminiscent in appearance of the pre-war state dancer, added to the tension by complaining that the tight-fitting brown skin bathing-caps were impossible for anyone to wear with long hair. 'Shingle, Madame,' snapped Chanel, 'Everybody else has done it already.'

Devalois thought Schollar won this round, because Diaghilev's horror of shingled Sylphides was well-known.[159]

At the rehearsal on the day before the opening of *Le Train bleu* Cocteau found fault with everything. Nijinska wept. The dress rehearsal took place on the morning of the performance on 20 June.

The weather was colder than it had been a month before, and the theatre heating had not been turned on. The dancers came on-stage in Chanel's bathing costumes, some of which had not been tried on before, and the sight of shivering dancers in their scanty, ill-fitting garments was absurd and tragic. 'When the curtain rose on this dismaying spectacle,' wrote Kochno, 'Diaghilev fled to the last row of the balcony. He felt utterly powerless to remedy the disaster, and asked me which of the other ballets could be substituted for *Le Train bleu*. ...' However, 'after the rehearsal, not one member of the company left the theatre. The few hours that remained enabled Nijinska to revise her choreography, the dancers to learn their new steps, and the wardrobe women to adjust the costumes.'[160] When the stage had to be set for the first ballet of the evening, Nijinska and Dolin retired to a large chorus dressing-room on the top floor, and 'a practically new *pas de deux*' was worked out in place of the old one.[161]

After the dress rehearsal Chanel had told Sokolova she would think up some accessories for her costume. 'I found on my dressing-table the first of the large pearl stud ear-rings which were soon to be seen everywhere. They were very smart but so heavy that they pulled at my ears. . . .'[162]

Nijinska's white tennis dress and eye-shade, in which she imitated the world champion Suzanne Lenglen, and Woizikovsky's Fairisle pullover and plus-fours, which were meant to resemble the Prince of Wales's golfing get-up, had caused less trouble than the bathing dresses.

It is clear from his libretto that Cocteau was trying, typically, to convey in *Le Train bleu* something classic and eternal, as if caught in a snapshot, among the commonplaces of everyday life. The absurd opening chorus of 'Gigolos', who do exercises, and 'Poules', who adopt sentimental poses, 'as in coloured picture postcards', however silly, must have, he wrote, the quality of 'perfect statues'. When the Tennis Champion (Nijinska) entered to a jaunty tune, she held awkward poses – on one leg or with open mouth – as in magazines, but, when she looked at her wrist-watch, 'this classic gesture should have the gravity of ordinary gestures on Greek reliefs'. When, after a quarrel, Beau Gosse (Dolin) and Perlouse (Sokolova) were reunited and mocked the Tennis-Player and Golfer (Woizikovsky), imprisoned in bathing huts, the chorus returned with Kodaks and movie-cameras to watch the release of the captives; and a fugue accompanied the mimed row which took place between the latter. 'As one gesticulates,' wrote Cocteau, 'the other crosses his or her arms and listens with head in the air.' Traditional *commedia dell'arte*! Blows were exchanged, 'with the recipient ducking, and the aggressor losing his balance – as in the fights of Charlie Chaplin'.[163]

What a curious venture – to animate the Parthenon marbles in modern dress!

Pavlova's Paris season had preceded that of the Russian Ballet, and Serge Lifar had run into Diaghilev during an interval at one of her performances, and expressed his admiration for her. Two days before *Le Train bleu* Beaumont's Soirées de Paris presented *Mercure*, an extraordinary series of 'poses plastiques' devised as much by Picasso as Massine, and at this performance Lifar again met Diaghilev, who was with Kochno. (He was going the best way about proving a serious interest in his art.) Most of Beaumont's spectacles had been so ineffective and amateurish as to reassure Diaghilev: but

Mercure, for which Satie had composed the music, was striking enough to worry him. (Most people thought it ridiculous.) This time Lifar noticed that Diaghilev was 'pale, agitated, nervous'.[164]

A day or two later Diaghilev talked to Lifar at the theatre, praised his work and urged him to persevere, because he wanted to make him his leading dancer. 'Come on Monday to see me at the Hôtel St James, but meanwhile keep our conversation a secret, and don't mention it to anyone in the company.'[165]

Perhaps Diaghilev was already beginning to doubt Dolin's high seriousness in matters of art and to resent his incurable independence. ('Diaghilev never broke Pat's spirit,' wrote Sokolova, 'but he tried.')[166] However, Lifar could not know this. After Dolin's triumph in the acrobatic feats of Le Beau Gosse – for it was nothing less – Lifar clearly felt drastic measures were called for. 'On the 24th I called on Diaghilev as arranged.' (Diaghilev had apparently said 'Monday', and the twenty-fourth was a Tuesday – but never mind.) Diaghilev ordered tea for two, and was very friendly. Lifar told him that he wanted to go away. 'Why, where are you thinking of spending your two months' holiday? You know that the whole company has to be back by September 1st. . . . I have a suggestion to make, too. . . . However, tell me your plans first.'

'Sergei Pavlovitch, it isn't for the summer I'm going away; it's for good. I've decided to leave the company —'

'What are you saying?' Diaghilev cries, turning purple and leaping from his seat. Whereupon an incredible thing happens, for he seizes the small table at which we are sitting, crashes everything on it to the floor, and begins to scream out in a choking voice, while the French, English and Americans in the hall sit transfixed.

'You dare to say this to me, you ungrateful puppy? Do you realize all the ingratitude, the meanness of what you are saying? I brought you from Russia, I supported you for two years, taught you everything. . . . Which of the little sluts you are always running around with is depraving you? . . . You're nothing, you're nobody. . . . Well, if you want to resign, resign and go to the devil. . . . To hell with you!'

Lifar played his trump card: 'No, Sergei Pavlovitch. . . . I came here to thank you for all you have done for me, and to say goodbye, for I am going into a monastery.'[167]

The results were all that could be desired. Diaghilev wept, spoke of Russia, called Serge 'Alyosha Karamazov', embraced him, promised to turn him into one of the world's greatest dancers – a second Nijinsky – arranged for him to go to study under Cecchetti in Turin, told him to bring his passport the next day, took him to a tailor, bought him shoes and a straw boater, entertained him to dinner on the night after the last performance of the season, ordered champagne, heard his life story, gave him a parcel of books and his ticket, had a row with Nijinska – who said Lifar could never make a *premier danseur* – then, on 6 July, arrived at six in the morning to drive him to the station.

Lifar was overwhelmed to see 'the scented, well-cared-for Sergei Pavlovitch' walk into his squalid attic room. They had coffee together and drove to the Gare de Lyon. 'We entered a carriage. "Now concentrate." For a minute we were silent, then Diaghilev got up, made the sign of the cross over me with quick, small gestures, embraced me, and gave me his blessing "for the coming work and all that is good"; and lo, there was his white handkerchief, waving, waving, as the monotonous, huge, grey tedious houses began to glide past.'[168]

Three observations may be made about this lightning courtship – the eagle's rape by Ganymede. First: from the moment Lifar appeared at the theatre in his straw hat, the whole company – including Dolin – must have known what was going on, for straw hats were as sure a sign as plus-fours. Secondly: Diaghilev kept his promise about Lifar's future to the best of his ability. He could not turn him into a second Nijinsky, or even give him Idzikovsky's technique: but he made him in time into the brightest star of his company, whose glamour, in the last years of the Russian Ballet, was to outshine that of all the ballerinas. Thirdly: it is clear that Lifar had set himself the task of replacing both Dolin and Kochno in Diaghilev's affections. As regards Dolin, because Patrick did not give a damn and was already on his way out, he was successful. But, with all his energy and enthusiasm, Lifar proved totally incapable of ousting Kochno. How could the well-read, imaginative Boris, with his passion for all the arts, the wise partner in creation who knew the mind of Diaghilev and worked in harmony with him, be supplanted by a youth without an idea – except that of self-promotion – in his head? Lifar never replaced Kochno, and he had to resign himself to live alongside him. Boris possessed self-control, and he knew how to efface himself: but to suffer in silence the steady – if suppressed – rivalry of the younger man did not make life more pleasant. Lifar's hatred of him could not break out until after Diaghilev's death.

Four days after seeing Lifar off at the station Diaghilev left with Dolin for Venice. His Paris season had been more than dazzling. He could enjoy a holiday well earned. A holiday? Chanel said Diaghilev never rested. Business negotiations for the autumn tour would continue. A close eye would be kept on the progress of *Zéphyr et Flore*, which Kochno and Dukelsky had gone to work on together at a village inn in the Chevreuse valley. Yet, for Diaghilev to be in Venice was in itself a relaxation of the spirit, however many letters or telegrams had to be written. He found a letter from Lifar waiting for him at the Excelsior on the Lido. Lifar complained about the food in Turin and found the work with Cecchetti very hard. Diaghilev wrote back:

You must be well fed: that is a matter of prime importance, and you must not neglect it. Please let me know how you are getting on with your reading. Are you returning the books to Paris in order to get them exchanged, and are you getting the Russian papers? Three-hour lessons are certainly very long, but one must take the bull by the horns, and time is precious. I am hoping that old Cecchetti will be able to come to Monte Carlo this winter, but meanwhile get out of him everything that you can. Have you written to your colleagues, and what are they writing to you? How did they take your flight to Cecchetti? ... Write often.

... My departure from Paris was one headlong rush in which I left numbers of things undone. Had I stayed a moment longer I should never have got away at all. Here in Venice, as ever, everything is divine. There is no place on earth like it for me, both for restfulness and because here I conceive all my ideas, which are afterwards shown to the world.[169]

The young Serge must have thought that the apprenticeship for a favourite's life was an arduous one. The books Diaghilev had selected for him to read were works by Tchekhov, Aksakov, Blok, Kuzmin, Ehrenburg, Remizov, Sologub, Biely, Essenin – and Pushkin.[170] Meanwhile, Patrick enjoyed himself on the beach, and Diaghilev occasionally interrupted his dipping into Proust and Radiguet[171] to watch him through binoculars.[172]

In his next letter to Lifar Diaghilev wrote,

I am so glad you are reading so much. Do go on, and even more actively if possible. ... I also spend all my day reading, but only French fiction. ...

By the end of this month I shall have to visit Milan with my agent, with regard to certain engagements, and then we shall certainly be able to meet. That should be in some 8 or 10 days. ... Meanwhile I shall expect to hear from you *more often*. My blessing. ...[173]

In fact, Diaghilev never really read books. Even when he became a collector a few years later, according to Kochno, he merely 'counted the pages'. He admitted preferring the arts of painting and music, which cost him less effort.[174]

Diaghilev had found the Excelsior full of impresarios: this was exhausting, but some good might come of it. There were Gatti-Casazza and Otto Kahn, co-Directors of the Metropolitan; Bodanzky, Musical Director of the same opera house; Morris Gest; Max Reinhardt and Volmüller (of *The Miracle*), and Scandiani of La Scala. There was also the American composer John Carpenter, who wanted Diaghilev to put on a ballet he had written. He came over from America, bringing his score, for two days only. In a letter to Boris on 19 July, Diaghilev described the 'unbelievable circumstances' in which he found himself. There was also a Soviet art exhibition in Venice.

The whole crowd has assembled here to discuss forthcoming theatrical seasons in America. You can imagine the sensation my appearance created. Photographers sprang up on all sides and made us pose in 'colourful groups' etc. ...

436

Diaghilev drawn by Cecil
Beaton from a photograph
taken by Kochno on Isola
Bella, 1921.

Kahn rushed over to me and said point-blank that he would be glad to 'talk business' with me. . . . Carpenter's presence has been a great help in the present instance, for both Kahn and Gest find him a serious and important person. . . . Happily, his ballet is not as bad as I expected . . . it is American de Falla, with appropriate folk-lore. Also, the famous 'policemen's strike' no longer takes place on the Strand but in an American factory, with alarm whistles and workers and such. Carpenter asks whether the décor couldn't be assigned to a Russian *Bolshevik* painter because, in his ballet, he is 'not far away from Bolshevism'. I find this notion amusing. The Bolsheviks are wooing me, by the way. The catalogue of their exhibition here starts out with my name.[175]

Diaghilev never did put on Carpenter's ballet *The Policeman's Holiday*. Gershwin, too, whom Cole Porter introduced to Diaghilev over lunch in Paris, hoped in vain to have Diaghilev stage his *Rhapsody in Blue*.[176] Meanwhile, Dukelsky, Diaghilev's latest protégé, who had affiliations with the world of jazz, which Diaghilev hated, was claiming to be 'deluged with offers from theatre directors and music publishers'. Diaghilev continued, 'I think with interest about your ballet with Dima [Dukelsky]. However, Dima must not become the darling of the business men for a few months; they would drop him later, as they've done with Prokofiev. You will understand, I am sure, that were he to collaborate with the Swedish Ballet, under no circumstances would I compete with them, and I would not work with Dima, no matter what the project.'[177]

437

About *Zéphyr et Flore*, Diaghilev wrote to Boris almost daily. On Sunday, 20 July (he gave the date as 21), Diaghilev wrote in detail about the scenario:

I've received your scenario. The apple orchard I like, as far as style is concerned. The sarafans too, although in Russia, in the eighteenth century, Olympus was described quite otherwise, in a pompous, boring way. Remember Paisiello or the portrait of N. P. Sheremetev dressed as Cupid, at Ostankino.

But this is obviously not important. What does matter is that it will certainly be most difficult to *explain* choreographically about where Zéphyr flies to and why. Among other things, in my opinion the very first dance of Zéphyr and Flore must be a *pas de trois* with Aeolus [Diaghilev at this time referred to the role of Zéphyr's jealous brother, Borée, which he intended for Lifar, as Aeolus]. That will be more original, and perhaps one will be better able to understand Aeolus's share in Zéphyr's departure. With whom will Flore dance her *adage*? No men? Aeolus's scene must be full of seductiveness. It seems to me that Flore must be overcome not only by fear but also by the charm of Aeolus. The climax is utterly incomprehensible. Zéphyr falls – from where? why? – if the Fates are going to carry him? I don't know what to suggest. Would it not be better if he fell on stage? Then the Fates can run up, thinking he has been killed. The ending is good. The absence of Aeolus is unfortunate; he should be puffing from somewhere! And the finale – is it to be danced?

These are my brief comments. In any event, this is a ballet that must be done. It hits the bull's-eye. But who is to do the *mise-en-scène*? A Russian? Braque?[178]

This letter crossed with a revised version of the scenario from Boris, together with Dukelsky's manuscript of part of the piano score, and Diaghilev wrote, misdating his letter 'Monday, July 22, 1924', when it was the 21st,

As rearranged the ballet remains almost the same. I still do not know where to put the *pas de trois*, whether in the second or the last number, but it is indispensable. The other directives I gave you yesterday remain unchanged.

I've just played the score. I like the music, provided it's as simple as your scenario. Actually this is the most important thing. Pruna is simple, and therein lies his complexity. His painting is sweet but at the same time saltier than salt, yet even so it leaves one with a pleasant aftertaste of sugar.

Aeolus is at his best only when he resembles a drunkard heading for the police station. He is as gentle as a Negro and as ambiguous as the god Pan in that turquoise landscape, the most banal in the Adriatic.

I do not know whether Dima will understand this. But you must certainly understand it, for you understand everything; you are even, perhaps, too wise. With you it's the same as with a wise dog – one never knows whether he is guided by his own intelligence or is obeying orders, whether he is guessing or, better still, acting on intuition. Paraphrase this for Dima, or read it to him.

At the moment the sea before me is like the most banal of picture postcards, and my soul is at peace.

P.S. Not long ago, an apple orchard would have suggested to Rimsky-Korsakov, or even to the young Stravinsky, a secret, mysterious place, an impenetrable jungle, whereas in our day the poet seeks an ordinary apple on Olympus, an apple without artifice or complications, which is the most tasty kind. The simplest and soundest is the best.[179]

We have to remember that the 'wise dog' to whom this rather cryptic letter was written was only twenty years old. So was Lifar, and Dolin's twentieth birthday was on 27 July. Diaghilev and Patrick had lunch with Adolf and Olga de Meyer, whom an astrologer had persuaded to call themselves Gayne and Mahrah. Patrick was disappointed by his first birthday present from Diaghilev, a copy of Thomas Mann's *Death in Venice*. That night at dinner, however, there was a nice box with a gold watch from Cartier. Patrick made friends easily. Alice Delysia was on the Lido being photographed by Baron de Meyer.[180] Grace Moore, the singer, was staying at the Excelsior, and flirting with Princess San Faustino's son. Mrs Reggie Fellowes and Elsa Maxwell were also there.[181]

The day before Dolin's birthday Lifar had received a letter: 'I shall be reaching Milan on *Tuesday 29th*. I leave here by the 9.25 a.m., arriving Milan 3.5 p.m. Get yourself a *second-class* ticket, and leave Turin at 10.50 a.m. You will arrive at Milan at 1.30 p.m. Get your lunch at the station, wait for my train and meet me. I enclose what is necessary for the ticket. Acknowledge immediately receipt of this letter. ...'[182]

Lifar met the 3.5 as arranged, and out of it stepped a 'rejuvenated Diaghilev – for Italy always rejuvenated Sergei Pavlovitch, made him look fresher and somehow lighter'. They set about an intensive two-day sight-seeing tour: La Scala, the Galleria (coffee and questions), the Duomo (eternal longings), various frescoes in churches (exhaustion), the Luinis in San Maurizio (deep emotion) and finally Leonardo's *Last Supper* in Sta Maria delle Grazie (a sit-down, calm and delight). Diaghilev wore white trousers, tight in the leg, and shortened by frequent washings, white shoes and a straw hat, 'which he constantly removed to wipe the perspiration from his brow'. In the button-hole of his usual dark jacket was a tuberose. As he walked, leaning on his stick, he puffed, sniffed and eased his inevitable stiff collar. Lifar found that Diaghilev's presence either galvanized or paralysed him. In front of works of art the long explanations might mean nothing, whereas 'two or three words, a hint only, or silence' would make him joyfully receptive.[183] This was natural.

Lifar went back to Turin on the thirtieth; Diaghilev saw to his business and returned to Venice. He had to pick up Dolin, as they were going to spend a night or two at Florence on the way to Monte Carlo. But a matter of the greatest importance had arisen. Olga Spessivtseva, who had once more obtained an exit permit from Russia, and had spent some time in Italy for her health, was in Paris. Diaghilev, who esteemed her as the greatest living dancer, thought her engagement essential to his company. But Bakst, her old admirer, had been writing to her in Italy, pouring poison into her ears, setting her against Diaghilev; and she was now in Paris with Bakst, who was persuading her, abetted by the critic Levinson, to sign with Rouché of the Opéra.

'Beware of Valetchka [Nuvel],' Bakst had written to Spessivtseva in Rome, and Valetchka was now in touch with her, and had made certain proposals on Diaghilev's behalf. On 2 August, Diaghilev cabled to Nuvel from Venice, '[My] Conditions exclusivity for Paris and London. Only tell Spessiva this after she has agreed other conditions.'[184]

In Florence Diaghilev liked to stay at the Palace, an old-fashioned hotel on the south side of the Arno. He and Dolin were there from the fourth to the seventh.[185] Patrick was bored stiff with the museums, and showed it.[186] To Lifar, from whom he hoped for a better response, Diaghilev sent a parcel of booklets on 'the holy' Raphael, on Botticelli, Mantegna ('You remember his Christ?'), Piero della Francesca, Donatello, Filippo Lippi, Francia, Masaccio, Michelangelo, and 'our Milanese' Luini. 'And I consider it your duty', he wrote, 'to memorize all these reproductions so that you will understand the differences between each of these masters, and learn to know them by heart. ... Please acknowledge their receipt, and also the dancing slippers. I am very pleased that you spend so much time with the Maestro, and help him with his little garden. ...' Lifar was shattered at the thought of analysing the differences between all the monochrome reproductions, with the aid only of an Italian text; and he hardly knew how to reply without making a fool of himself.[187]

On 9 August, with Dolin, Diaghilev arrived in Monte Carlo, and there were telegrams from Nuvel and Kochno, sent from Paris, awaiting him. Nuvel's was about the autumn tour: 'Munich reply 600 dollars an evening impossible. Situation depressing. Telegraph best terms.'[188] Kochno, who was back in Paris from his stay with Dukelsky, had seen Spessivtseva and telegraphed, 'Spessiva refuses dance. Believe possible seduce her with new creations. Telegraph instructions. Expect leave Saturday.'[189] Diaghilev drafted his reply at the foot of this message: 'You can seduce her with new creations. Try to make her come now Monte Carlo. Delightful stay. Make sure she does not sign with Rouché.'[190] On the same day Diaghilev informed Nuvel, 'Find agreement Munich essential. Make certain concessions. ...'[191] and to Boris he telegraphed, care of Nuvel, 'Plan début Spessiva Monte Carlo January, also Paris, London. Can also propose two years. Lord Rothermere offers personally arrange London season.'[192]

Rothermere, proprietor of the *Daily Mail*, which he had inherited from his sinister brother, Lord Northcliffe, had a villa at Roquebrune, and Diaghilev had evidently just made his acquaintance.

On 18 August, after sending several telegrams to Olga,[193] Diaghilev cabled Lifar, 'Have sent you 500. Settle up everything at Turin. Meet me

Wednesday evening Milan Hotel Cavour with all your luggage.' The decision, Lifar realized, must have been sudden, for he later received a note from Diaghilev in Monte Carlo: 'Sending cheque. Shall write today or tomorrow. Received today all your four letters together.'[194]

Before leaving Monte Carlo, Diaghilev sent – or drafted, for it was only received on the twentieth – a telegram to Nuvel, saying, '... Offer Spessiva two years 50 shows in 8 months. Begin with 80,000, go up to 100,000 per year. Try to win. Let us persist. I find this engagement necessary to us.'[195]

Diaghilev and Lifar met in Milan on 20 August and took the evening train to Venice. They arrived late at night and, when Diaghilev asked whether Serge would prefer to go to the centre by taxi or by gondola, and Serge begged to go by gondola, he did not know why Diaghilev laughed.

Everything took on a totally different aspect. And Sergei Pavlovitch changed too. As he now was I had never known him, yet thus he was always to be in Venice, as though a veritable Doge, who proudly, joyfully, parades his native, miraculous city. Five days we spent there, five perfect epoch-making days, with Diaghilev all smiles and in a perpetual good humour as he nodded to right and left, with a *bon giorno* for all, since all seemed to know him.[196]

Next day they walked through the city and explored the Grand Canal, while Diaghilev gave a history lesson. Lifar swam at the Lido, but 'Sergei Pavlovitch never bathed, since for nothing in the world would he have appeared naked.' On account of some superstition, Diaghilev never walked, or allowed Lifar to walk, between the two flagstaffs in front of San Marco. That evening they heard *Il Barbiere* at the Fenice and had supper with Isadora Duncan and her young husband, the poet Essenin. On subsequent days they visited the Doge's Palace, the Accademia, churches and palaces.[197] Diaghilev, always in touch with Nuvel, cabled him on 23 August, 'Beat down Spessiva's price. Don't let her go.'[198] On the twenty-sixth, in Padua, before the Giotto frescoes and at the tomb of St Anthony, Lifar felt that his 'rebirth in beauty and art was finally accomplished', his pact with Diaghilev concluded.[199] Meanwhile, Nuvel had come to terms with Munich, and Diaghilev, snatching a mundane moment, cabled him, 'Telegraph if Munich will pay advance.' (Munich did.)[200]

Lifar parted from Diaghilev in Milan on the twenty-ninth, travelling on to Paris, while Diaghilev joined Dolin and Kochno in Monte Carlo. Patrick, besides working with Nijinska, had made friends and gone swimming with two lesbians, and Diaghilev accused him of having an affair with one of them.[201] On 31 August Diaghilev, Kochno and Dolin arrived in Paris to join the company, who assembled there on 1 September.[202]

Spessivtseva had signed with the Opéra.

Rehearsals in Paris took place either on the stage of the Olympia Music Hall or in the foyer of the Théâtre de Paris. One day at the Olympia, some performing seals joined in a rehearsal of *Le Train bleu*. Dolin found that he was to dance *L'Oiseau bleu*, which pleased him, as he did not want to be 'labelled' as a mere acrobat.[203] Nijinska and others noticed the progress Lifar had made after his classes with Cecchetti.[204] He was told that he was to have the part of Borée in *Zéphyr et Flore*, with Dolin and Nikitina in the title roles.[205]

The company left on 14 September, to begin their tour with a fortnight in Munich. Grigoriev thought the poor, shabby Germans were unfriendly to foreigners, but the houses were good and the critics appreciative.[206] Devalois found interest in everything and loved the 'atmosphere of the People's Theatre everywhere'.[207] Meanwhile, Diaghilev was in London, negotiating with Stoll.[208] The latter's letter, concluding their bargain, followed him to Munich. Diaghilev was to pay the Alhambra Company £30 a week during his coming seven weeks' season at the Coliseum; and the balance of the £1,790 owing must be repaid before any subsequent performance of the Russian Ballet took place in London. No further proceedings would be taken against Diaghilev; the whole production of *The Sleeping Princess* would become his property and the £2,000 would be accepted in full settlement of his debt.[209] Whatever sums Diaghilev had been able – with money from Monte Carlo, Princesse Edmond de Polignac or Chanel – to repay Stoll in April, they can hardly have amounted to a first payment of £11,000 on his original alleged debt of £13,000: so Stoll and his fellow-directors were being generous.

The Russian Ballet appeared in Leipzig and Chemnitz on the way to Berlin, where they arrived on 9 October, to perform for a fortnight at the Theater des Westens. At the Adlon Hotel, where he was staying with Diaghilev, Dolin ran into Isadora Duncan in the lift. She had evidently seen *Le Train bleu* the night before, for she exclaimed, 'You are Dolin! Trop beau pour faire de l'acrobatie.'[210] In Berlin Nijinska was married to Singayevsky, with Kochno and Dolin as best men. Patrick hurt himself during *L'Oiseau bleu* on the last night in Berlin, 26 October, and stayed behind to rest, while the company went on to Breslau, Hamburg, Mainz, Cologne and Hanover. Lifar, too, was 'off', as he had caught a disease in Berlin, but he travelled with the Ballet.[211]

Before the tour ended in Hanover, Diaghilev, Kochno and Lifar went to Paris,[212] while Dolin travelled to London with documents for Wollheim and the score of *Le Train bleu* for Edwin Evans, who was to prepare publicity for the new ballet in England.[213] The company followed. The Coliseum season was to open on 24 November.

Another troupe of Russians, consisting only of four dancers and a manager, had been touring Germany that autumn. Political developments had made it easier for Soviet artists to earn money abroad. These four dancers had left Russia in July, to appear in Berlin, but the city was empty and after their first performance the second was cancelled. Their amateur manager, Dmitriev, was hard pressed to find them any engagements. They travelled up the Rhine, to Wiesbaden, Mosel, Ems, Mainz and other cities, dancing where they could in dance-halls or *Biergärten*, at private parties, in summer theatres and once in a lunatic asylum, until summoned to appear for a month at the Empire music-hall, London, in October. They did not appeal to the London public, so were paid their full month's salary and dismissed after the second week.[214] They achieved, however, a brief notice in the *Dancing Times:*

> The first item was a *pas de deux* from the ballet *Don Quixote*, danced by Alexandra Danilova and Nicolai Efimoff. It was very technical and there was little feeling. ... Far more interesting was the 'Egyptian Dance' to music of Arensky by Tamara Sheversheief [Gevergeva, later Geva], whose straight feet would have gladdened the heart of members of the 'Greek Association'. A 'Jester's Dance' by Efimoff introduced typical Russian steps, and a futuristic Indian dance closed the proceedings.[215]

The unnamed choreographer of the troupe was George Balantchivadze. Their work permit having expired, they had to leave England. In Paris, in a small hotel near the Place de la République, they were down to their last few francs. Balantchivadze tended to take everything calmly, having a child-like faith that God would provide. The others were nearer despair, when a telegram arrived from Diaghilev. He had his spies everywhere and was always eager for recruits from Russia. In mid-November Nuvel fetched the four dancers to an audition in Misia Sert's drawing-room. Diaghilev questioned Balantchivadze about the latest tendencies in Russia, about Goleizovsky's choreography (which was 'modern' in a partly German, partly cabaret way), and he watched him dance a Scriabine piece with Gevergeva. He thought some of the movements new and interesting, and asked, 'Can you arrange dances for operas?' 'Yes.' 'Can you do it quickly?' 'Yes,' replied Balantchivadze, not knowing whether he could or not. Danilova was asked what she could show and replied pertly, 'If I'm good enough for the Mariinsky I'm good enough for you.' However, she had danced *The Firebird* in Russia, and she showed a few steps. Danilova told Misia how dirty she thought Paris was. 'There are cauliflowers and tomatoes lying about everywhere.' 'Where are you living?' 'Near Les Halles.' Diaghilev told the group he would consider what offer he could make them.[216]

Soviet Russia was much in Diaghilev's mind at the time, for Mayakovsky was once more in Paris, being shown the sights by Elsa Triolet, and trying to persuade Diaghilev to return to Russia. The poet wrote for him two letters of introduction. In the first, to People's Commissar of Education Anatoli Lunatcharsky, he wrote:

> You know Sergei Pavlovitch Diaghilev at least as well as I do ... nevertheless

I am writing these lines so that S. P. can more quickly get through the secretariat. ... Of course, former Russians turned Parisian have tried to frighten S.P. with Moscow. But his desire has proved stronger, together with my assurances that in delicacy and grace we surpass the French and that we are more 'businesslike' than the Americans. ... It wouldn't do any harm to speak too about our pavilion in the Paris exhibition. ...

To Osip Brik, brother of his mistress Lili, Mayakovsky wrote, 'Be Sergei Pavlovitch's guiding star. ... If S.P. doesn't like Rodchenko, Lavinsky [artists], Eisenstein and others, soften him with caviar (send for it to the shop across the street before lunch); if he doesn't like that either there's nothing to be done.'[217]

Diaghilev did indeed intend to go to Russia and was granted a two-way visa. It was only when he found that the Soviet authorities would not guarantee to allow Kochno, if he accompanied him, to return to France that he abandoned the idea.[218]

On Thursday, 20 November, Diaghilev was at last back in London, and at the Savoy (room 387). His company were to give one ballet every afternoon and one every evening in the music-hall programme at the Coliseum, for seven weeks. On the first night, however, two ballets would be given. Diaghilev made publicity for Dolin, and Friday's papers were full of 'the dancing Irishman'. Sunday's *Observer* carried Diaghilev's traditional interview. '"You know," he remarked, "when I was last here they said the Russian Ballet was dead, and some of the critics [a dig at Newman] even went so far as to compose a requiem and to claim the honour of having killed me. ... The Russian ballet was not dead, not even for a single hour."' He said that *Cimarosiana* would be played 'exactly as it was for the first time, in 1794, in Naples by an orchestra of about twenty performers'. Its designer, Sert, 'had painted the wonderful music-room of Sir Philip Sassoon in Park Lane'. Last came the carefully prepared paradoxes about *Le Train bleu*, which was to be given a new 'frontispiece' in the form of Picasso's glorious curtain:

Now the first point about *Le Train bleu* is that there is no blue train in it at all. The scene is a beach which does not exist, and it is laid in front of a casino which exists still less. Overhead passes an aeroplane which you do not see. And the plot represents nothing. Yet when it was presented for the first time in Paris, everybody was unaccountably animated with the wish to go to Deauville and bathe and perform refreshing exercises.

The ballet, moreover, is not a ballet; it is an *opérette dansée*. The music is composed by Darius Milhaud, but it has nothing to do with the music of Darius Milhaud; and the ballet is danced by the real Russian ballet, but yet has nothing to do with Russian ballet. *Le Train bleu* was invented by Jean Cocteau for Anton Dolin, a classical dancer who does nothing classical. The scenery was painted by a sculptor, Henri Laurens; and the costumes are by the greatest arbiter of fashion, Chanel, who has never made a costume.

The curtain, one of the finest works of Picasso, which serves as an introduction to the ballet, was never painted for this purpose, and it bears a dedication to me, which I have never seen anywhere else. And yet, in spite of these contrary things, the whole ballet is one of the most simple and the most delightful works imaginable. ...[219]

Diaghilev had offered the troupe of four Russians whom he had seen in Paris an engagement, with salaries of fifteen hundred francs a month. On the same Sunday as his interview appeared in the *Observer* he received their reply: 'Acceptons engagement. Attendez détailles par lettre. Balant-chivadze.'[220] One of the 'détailles', or stipulations, made in the letter was that Dmitriev, the stranded manager, should come too. Each of the four dancers would for the time being pay him a fifth of his or her salary. They joined Diaghilev in London just after the opening of the season; took rooms at a Bloomsbury boarding-house slightly superior to their previous one (three guineas as opposed to two guineas a week),[221] and tried out on taxi-drivers various exotic pronunciations of the name of their theatre: 'Kali*zey*oom! Coliss*ee*um!'[222]

London was delighted to have the Diaghilev Ballet back. 'Wonderful Dancing in Two New Pieces at the Coliseum – A GREAT WELCOME' (*Daily Mirror*),[223] 'Brilliant Performances' (*Morning Post*),[224] 'Old Favourites and a New-comer' (*Daily Herald*),[225] 'BATHING BEACH BALLET' (*Daily Mail*),[226] 'DANCING GOLFER WITH PLUS FOURS AND A PIPE' (*Daily Express*).[227] There could be no doubt of the welcome accorded to the company, even if the orchestra of *Cimarosiana*, under Edouard Flament, 'seemed as though it did not know its notes' (*The Times*),[228] and the music of Milhaud, conducted by himself, gave the *Telegraph* 'doubts as to the rights of the caricaturist'.[229] Dolin's victory on home ground was unquestioned. The 'customary dashing curtain by Picasso' (*Daily Telegraph*) had an overwhelming effect on one young sculptor who was present – Henry Moore: it changed his life.[230]

The Faithful Shepherdess (*Les Tentations*) and *Aurora's Wedding* (as *Le Mariage d'Aurore* was called in England) – for which Stoll released Bakst's first white marble palace scene, but no costumes – were added to the repertoire, as well as several old favourites. Diaghilev abbreviated Balantchivadze's name to Balanchine, to make it easier for the public. This newcomer's opinion of the company was low. He thought the corps were awful; and only admired a few soloists, including Dolin.[231]

Patrick had naturally been to visit Astafieva's school at The Pheasantry, King's Road, Chelsea, and he had seen there the progress made by a student called Alicia Marks, just fourteen, whom only an attack of diphtheria had prevented from being enlisted by Diaghilev as a minute fairy in *The Sleeping*

Princess three years before. Alicia's father had just died, leaving his family very poor, and Dolin was anxious to help: but there had been much publicity about the Russian Ballet's English dancers – that is, Dolin himself, Sokolova and Savina (now parted from Massine), who had petitioned successfully to be taken back – and Diaghilev was determined to engage no more. A ruse was therefore resorted to: Astafieva gave a Christmas party for the Diaghilev Ballet and in a lull Alicia danced to Rubinstein's 'Valse Caprice'. 'Her performance was strangely unreal. ... She turned three, four pirouettes on the toe with an ease that was almost uncanny. She jumped high and effortlessly into the air, and her little feet made no sound as they touched the floor.' Diaghilev was won over and consented to employ the girl – whom he renamed 'Markova' – on condition that her mother or a governess travelled with her.[232] Diaghilev had said to Balanchine, 'I have an old ballet that has been arranged twice. It is by Stravinsky. Could you manage it?' 'Yes,' was the automatic reply. 'You are very sure of yourself.' This was *Le Chant du Rossignol*.[233] Balanchine had, in fact, walked on in a production of Stravinsky's opera in Russia when he was a child. His idea that Markova might dance the Nightingale may have been the reason Diaghilev engaged her at such an early age.

'What a choreographer Bronia would have been if only she were a man!' was a saying of Diaghilev's. He admired her and was fond of her, but she was downright difficult and determined, and he found this unacceptable in one of her sex.[234] Nijinska, on her side, strongly resented the engagement of Balanchine. Who was to arrange the dances for *Zéphyr et Flore*, and the other new ballet, *Les Matelots*, which had been commissioned from Auric? The infatuated Diaghilev decided to give Lifar a chance to try his hand as a choreographer on *Zéphyr*. The experiment took place in Astafieva's studio. The nice ugly girl Trussevitch, who sometimes did secretarial work, and whose discretion could be counted on, was invited, with her girlfriend Rosenstein, to act as guinea-pigs, along with Konstantin Tcherkass. Diaghilev had given Lifar the idea that in the *pas de trois* Flora should remain lifted in the air by the two men, without touching the ground throughout the dance. Lifar managed to get a girl on to his shoulder; he then asked, 'What next?' His invention was exhausted. Diaghilev terminated the rehearsal.[235]

But Nijinska had decided to leave the company. Massine was in London. He met Diaghilev at Cecchetti's studio.[236] Sergei Pavlovitch gave Leonide his views on the latter's work for 'Les Soirées de Paris'. He said, 'Don't let's talk about *Le Beau Danube* – that's pure trash.'[237] But he 'had been intrigued by *Mercure* and thought the choreography and lighting of *Salade* had marked a definite step forward'. Massine was amazed when Diaghilev asked him to do two new ballets. He accepted.[238] The Nijinska period was over, but the Balanchine period had not yet begun.

On the evening of 27 December Dolin, opening his dressing-room door, saw Nuvel coming towards Diaghilev in the passage. 'What's the news?' asked Diaghilev. 'Bakst is dead.' The quarrel over *Mavra* had never been made up. Diaghilev wept.[239]

CHAPTER 16

1925–6

Massine as Guest Choreographer – Lifar replaces Dolin as Favourite – An English Slant

O N SATURDAY, 10 JANUARY 1925, the ballet was *Aurora's Wedding*. 'END OF THE RUSSIAN BALLET SEASON – EXTRAORDINARY SCENES AT THE COLISEUM' (*Observer*),[1] ' "Pat Healey!" shouts the London Coliseum' (*People*).[2] Patrick, who had danced *L'Oiseau bleu* with Nikitina, stuck a strip of ticker-tape into his album: '11.24 ONE OF THE MOST REMARKABLE FAREWELLS EVER GIVEN IN A VARIETY THEATRE ... THE LEADING LADIES AND MEN WERE SNOWED UNDER WITH BOUQUETS FLORAL WREATHS AND OTHER FLORAL TRIBUTES. THE APPLAUSE LASTED FOR A SOLID 20 MINUTES AND CONTINUED LONG AFTER THE FINAL CURTAIN HAD BEEN LOWERED.'[3] In fact, the applause continued through the bioscope (film) which followed the ballet. Dolin noticed that Diaghilev looked 'proud'.[4]

Already when he stopped with Dolin for two nights at the Hôtel Wagram in Paris, Diaghilev's duties as Master of Ceremonies to the Principality of Monte Carlo began to close in upon him. There was to be a gala on 17 January, the Monegasque National Day, at which the Duke of Connaught would be present. What dancers could he lend and what would they dance? He suggested a *pas de trois*, to include Nikitina and Efimov, and Markova with Tcherkass in the Red Riding Hood *pas de deux* from *Aurore*.[5] His new dancers were being tried out without delay. Markova learned Red Riding Hood in one rehearsal.[6] Diaghilev arrived 'home' at the Hôtel de Paris two days after his troupe reached Monte Carlo. Within a few days he was faced with a crisis. The dancers held a meeting: they wanted higher wages. Schollar and Vilzak, although they were principal dancers and paid at a different rate to the corps, presided. Grigoriev warned Diaghilev, but Diaghilev already knew what was going on, and on the afternoon of the gala he came very angrily to confront the company. 'I'm very much astonished at your behaviour. You have already been told that I intend considering my budget and seeing what I can do for you. What more can you expect? Each of you has a separate contract with me. If you refuse to perform this evening I shall regard your non-attendance as a breach of contract and shall sue you for damages.'[7] The dancers came in late for the performance, in twos and threes; the programme had to be changed and the curtain went up half an hour late. Lifar said that it was Kokhanovsky who persuaded the dancers not to wreck the performance and jeopardize the whole enterprise – for which Diaghilev remained ever grateful.[8] Schollar and Vilzak stayed away. After the show Woizikovsky led a deputation to Diaghilev and tried to put the dancers' point of view. Diaghilev listened in silence, then said, 'Leon, where are your friends?' Leon looked round – to find the others had all vanished. 'That will teach you to speak for others,' said Diaghilev. 'If you have a grievance come and see me privately.'[9] Schollar and Vilzak were dismissed.

The long annual stay at Monte Carlo looks a peaceful season on paper, but in 1925, as in other years, it was a period of intensive work for the dancers, crammed with incident. Cecchetti continually found fault with Dolin, who was Astafieva's pupil and, he thought, less worthy of promotion than his own English pupil Errol Addison;[10] Dukelsky fascinated all the girls and played 'Lady be Good' to them on the rehearsal room piano – he also tried to persuade Gevergeva to elope;[11] Danilova, who had put on weight since leaving Russia – when Dolin had to lift her, he exclaimed, 'I'm not a piano-mover' – took too many slimming pills and passed out, whereupon Balanchine threw her pills out of the window.[12] One day Lifar appeared in plus-fours and Sokolova told Dolin, 'Your number's up, chum.'[13]

Many of Diaghilev's preoccupations are recorded in surviving telegrams, as well as in his drafts for answers – some of the latter being in Kochno's hand. Braque must come at once, half-price, to Monte Carlo. Auric must be stopped from coming, as his ballet could not be rehearsed yet, but he must send the score of *Les Matelots*.[14] (But Auric arrived three days later, all the same.)[15] Idzikovsky wanted to return and would be free from the end of April: Diaghilev would take him back on the same terms as before.[16] Who was to conduct at Barcelona at the end of April? The conditions of Defosse were absurd. Nuvel must enquire about Inghelbrecht and Baton. Was Ansermet free? He was supposed to sign for the Argentine, but would wait two weeks. Hearing nothing, Ansermet signed with the Argentine. Baton had left for Scandinavia. Nuvel wanted to know whether to await Monteux or engage Defosse at once. Monteux was unavailable; Barcelona would not accept Defosse.[17] To hire a harpsichord from Pleyel would cost two hundred a month, transport – our expense – would take four days.[18] Shervashidze had received his advance and would leave at once.[19] The harpsichord would leave today.[20] Goossens agreed to go to Barcelona.[21]

Pruna's arrival in Monte Carlo would be premature: they could meet in Paris next week.[22] For Paris, Diaghilev would prefer the Champs-Elysées, if not the Vaudeville or Mogador.[23] Stoll accepted the latest proposition.[24] Comtesse Greffuhle begged help with a charity gala.[25]

Massine arrived before the end of January. Diaghilev, who had perhaps not seen him alone in London, stage-managed their reunion, determined to make it clear that their relationship would be formal. Telling Kochno to wait in the entrance hall, he received Leonide in one of the sitting-rooms opening off it. The former favourite rushed at Diaghilev (the latter told Kochno), exclaiming, 'Comment vas-tu?' Diaghilev rejected the familiar form of address. 'Comment allez-vous?' he responded. He soon called Boris in and explained that it was with him, as author of the two new ballets, *Zéphyr* and *Les Matelots*, that Leonide would mainly have to deal.[26]

Diaghilev maliciously cast Massine to dance *L'Oiseau bleu* with Vera Savina. One day, at a rehearsal, Diaghilev sent Kochno over to tell him that he did not think some step he had just arranged was musical. Massine turned round and called out, 'What did you think was unmusical, Serge?' Diaghilev looked with feigned surprise to right and left, then asked, 'Who is called Serge around here?'[27] But Kochno was the peace-maker and diplomat, who 'calmed everybody down'. Danilova thought he was like 'the friend of the family', Diaghilev's 'Gibraltar'.[28] And Diaghilev's great interest at this time, chiefly because of its new composer, Dukelsky, whom he called his 'third son'[29] (Stravinsky and Prokofiev being the other two), was *Zéphyr et Flore*, so, of course, he wanted the best he could get out of Massine. So pleased was he with a solo Massine had arranged for Nikitina that he included a preview of it – with Dukelsky at the piano – in a performance for a party at the palace on 31 January.[30]

Dukelsky made friends with Massine and they went together to a *boîte*, where Dukelsky picked up a girl to whom he lost both his virginity and his watch.[31]

The Ballet were not due to perform between the end of January and April, and this inactivity upset Diaghilev. He arranged to give two shows a week in the small Nouvelle Salle de Musique (also called Salle Ganne), which was attached to the Casino and held only about a hundred. These had only a black curtain for background and a piano, a harpsichord, two pianos or a string quartet for accompaniment, but were extremely popular, and M. Guinsbourg, of the Opera Company, succeeded in having them banned for the following year.[32] Diaghilev took endless pains with the presentation of these miniature performances. Dolin danced *Le Spectre de la rose* at one; at another, coached by Kchessinskaya, Markova danced the second act and Nemtchinova the third act of *Le Lac des Cygnes*, with Danilova and Devalois in their small corps de ballet. Markova's partner was Efimov, Nemtchinova's Dolin.[33]

Meanwhile, Balanchine was 'turning out' his opera ballets in a light-hearted manner. Before April he had arranged dances for *Carmen*, *Thaïs*, *Manon*, *Le Démon*, *La Damnation de Faust* and other operas.[34] He also staged the first production of Ravel's *L'Enfant et les Sortilèges*. In this Markova was the Smoke from the kettle and, with Savina, one of two Squirrels;[35] Danilova danced the Butterfly and told the 'little pianist' 'Faster' or 'Slower' according to the needs of her dance. It was only fifty years later, in New York, that she learned, after enquiring why Balanchine possessed an inscribed copy of the score, that her accompanist had been Ravel.[36] Massine ignored Balanchine and gave instructions that he should not be allowed to watch his rehearsals.[37]

The daily routine was interrupted by a three-day trip to Marseilles. This was the only occasion Sokolova thought Diaghilev was unkind to her. She was to dance in *Les Sylphides* and in *Prince Igor*. Nijinska had inserted for herself a 'spinning, turning, stamping solo' in Fokine's Polovtsian scene, which Sokolova had inherited. She was feeling very ill, suffering from internal pains, and had fainted before the performance, but it was in vain that she begged Diaghilev to let her simplify the solo. She realized as the ballet began that she could not get through it and returned to the original choreography. Diaghilev was in the wings in a flash and raged at her till she was in floods of tears.[38]

Zéphyr et Flore was to be given its 'try-out' *première* at Monte Carlo at the end of the season, before the company left for Barcelona. The store Diaghilev set by it is proved by the invitations he sent out. Braque, of course, was there, as he had designed the scenery – he had to have 3,500 francs in advance before he would leave Paris on 11 April.[39] Picasso had left Paris, escorted by Kochno, on the ninth.[40] Joseph Kessel had come on behalf of *Le Figaro*;[41] and Edwin Evans travelled from London.[42] On 25 April Diaghilev and Kochno telegraphed to Cocteau, 'Do come this Tuesday *première* *Zéphyr*. You can travel back with Picasso. Fine weather and friends will do you good.'[43] But Cocteau was having a disintoxication cure at the Hôtel des Réservoirs at Versailles.

During this visit of Picasso's to Monte Carlo Diaghilev sent Lifar to be drawn by him: but the young dancer returned crestfallen, for Picasso did not want to draw him. (The unflattering drawing he executed of Lifar in 1960 can hardly be said to have made up for this.) To Kochno, however, who had made the arrangements for his visit, Picasso gave not only a cigarette-lighter, but a very special present. Carefully breaking a matchbox into six pieces, he drew on the plain reverse sides six pictures representative of a typical Salon – a banker's official portrait, a still-life, a seascape, a sunset, and so on. Such were the 'perks' of being Diaghilev's lieutenant.[44]

Massine left before the first performance of *Zéphyr*. At a dress rehearsal, a few days before the *première*, Lifar sprained his ankle. He would not hear of Slavinsky dancing his role, and threatened to jump off the rock of Monaco if he did.[45]

It is clear that various things went wrong with *Zéphyr* and why they went wrong. As in several of Diaghilev's later ballets, there were too many plums in the same pudding. The original notion of a classical masque, performed by serfs in a Russian nobleman's private theatre, got lost. Whatever traces there were of eighteenth-century melodies or pastiche in Dukelsky's score were submerged by his amateurish orchestration. ('Too much Glazunov,' Prokofiev said.)[46] The only vestiges of Russia were the simple modernized *kokoshniki*, which the nine Muses wore instead of classic diadems with the ugly modern evening-dresses of coarse woollen material, in murky purples and browns, which were evolved from the draperies in Braque's designs. His simple flickering landscape had nothing to do with Olympus or the eighteenth century. Nikitina, in her tiny *tutu*, her bodice and tights prettily painted with floral sprigs, and Dolin, handicapped by a jockey-cap and loose-hanging tunic of petals, danced with ease and elegance, while Lifar, naked except for gold *lamé* shorts, was impetuous and attractive in a coltish way. Massine's choreography (to judge from photographs) looked more interesting in black-and-white practice clothes than in costume on stage, but its eccentric modernity was at least in keeping with that of the costumes. In a group photograph the Muses have assumed affected poses appropriate to *Les Biches*.[47] Diaghilev realized the ballet had not come off and began thinking how to put it right for Paris.

He, Dolin and the company set off for Barcelona on the following day. Lifar was ill throughout the fortnight in Spain, and Woizikovsky hurt his foot at the end of the Barcelona season.[48] Diaghilev was badgered as usual – Heugel, the music publisher, would not hand over the English text (of the songs) of *Les Biches* until he had been paid for *Le Train bleu*.[49] Pedro Pruna had finished painting his sets for *Les Matelots* and wanted an extra five hundred francs for his journey.[50] Stoll asked for four different ballets during the second week of the Coliseum season.[51] Diaghilev badgered his lieutenants in return. Wollheim must warn Massine, who was in London, that he was expected to start rehearsing the Auric ballet on 20 May.[52] Nuvel must send 5,650 francs for transport and tickets, and should reserve three rooms at the Hôtel Wagram on Friday (15 May).[53]

Diaghilev had complained to the management of the Savoy, after leaving in January, that on three bills he had signed in the Grill Room (then called Café Parisien), items of fruit or liqueurs had been added and charged for after his signature.[54] The Grill Room Manager wrote to Monte Carlo to apologize, saying that, if Diaghilev thought the fruit and liqueurs had not really been consumed, he would deduct the sum of £1 19s from the waiter's wages.[55] It is hardly surprising that Wollheim was told that 'no accommodation was available to offer you for Mr Serge Diaghilev on May 17th, the house being fully booked for the period you mention.'[56] Diaghilev would not accept defeat and obliged Goossens to communicate with Rupert D'Oyly Carte, Chairman of the Savoy Hotel and Theatre. The reply arrived on 12 May, the day before Diaghilev left Barcelona. Rooms were available for the seventeenth; the manager was writing.[57] Diaghilev was always having trouble with hotels: his bills often languished long unpaid, and he did not suffer from Proust's snobbery of over-tipping.

Dolin, with Goossens, who had to rehearse new musicians, and Woizikovsky, who had to see a specialist, were in London a day ahead of the company. Diaghilev and Dolin were drifting apart: there were continual disagreements.

The Russian Ballet were still only appearing as a number in the Coliseum programme. *Carnaval* was to be given at the opening matinée on Monday, 18 May, and again, with *Aurora's Wedding*, which, because of Woizikovsky's injury, had been substituted for *The House Party* (*Les Biches*), in the evening. On the Sunday night, at supper with Astafieva at the Savoy, Diaghilev told Dolin that Idzikovsky, who had rejoined the company, was to dance Blue Bird at the opening. After a heated discussion, Patrick said he would leave the company if this happened. The Russian Ballet had made him famous and he knew he could make far more money in revue. At the theatre next afternoon Grigoriev told him that he had got his way.[58] Of course, Idzikovsky had his chance to shine as Harlequin in *Carnaval*, in which Dolin played Eusebius.

Diaghilev returned to Paris after the Coliseum opening. He was still in doubt about his Paris season and about the length of his stay at the Coliseum. On 22 May Wollheim telegraphed, 'Coliseum June 15th heavily booked. Fear playing here impossible.'[59] Diaghilev, however, found it feasible to arrange a week's season at the Gaieté Lyrique on 15 June, and the Coliseum were able to take him back in the following week.

The general opinion of the London press was that the Russians were better than ever – the orchestra under Goossens was certainly better.[60] *Les Fâcheux* was liked and *The House Party* was liked. There were a few dark hints about decadence and references to young Noël Coward's play *The Vortex*; Sokolova's role (taken over from Nijinska) was called 'a dope fiend';[61] and it was suggested that 'young men in roll-top jumpers who stroll about at the back of the circle and talk and talk and talk should be thrown out.'[62] The *promenoir* at the back of the circle or gallery in certain London theatres was a traditional picking-up place for homosexuals.

Diaghilev was back in Paris a week ahead of the company, leaving Kochno in command in London. He had crossed the Channel six times in three weeks. He wanted to hear the first performance by Kussevitsky of Prokofiev's Second Symphony on 6 June. He was on the look-out for Lord Rothermere, of whom he began to entertain hopes, for on 11 June, Wollheim, replying to an enquiry, telegraphed to him at the Hôtel Wagram, 'Rother-mere at Cap Martin or Paris Claridges'.[63] When Grigoriev asked if he might announce alterations in his Coliseum programmes by projections on the screen, as was common usage in music-halls at the time, Diaghilev cabled, 'Refuse to allow you to make cinematic announcements. Programmes must be exact.'[64]

Prokofiev was upset by the unfriendly reception of his symphony in Paris, and he had the impression that Diaghilev had turned his back on him. Diag-hilev, however, came to see him and asked for a new ballet. 'But,' said the composer, 'I cannot write in the style you like.' He meant in the manner of Auric and Poulenc. 'You should write in your own style,' said Diaghilev. He asked for a subject reflecting life in Soviet Russia. Prokofiev could not believe his ears. Ilya Ehrenburg, then living in Paris, was considered as a librettist. Then Diaghilev spoke of Yakulov, the Constructivist painter, who also designed stage sets, and who had won a diploma at the International Exhibition of Decorative Arts in Paris.

Prokofiev and Yakulov had talks in a small café on the banks of the Seine. They agreed that the ballet should represent the upsurge of industry taking place in Soviet Russia.

We imagined on the stage men working with hammers and axes, revolving fly-wheels and transmissions and flashing light signals. . . . The first part of the ballet would show the breakdown of the Tsarist regime: meetings of workers, speeches by commissars, trains full of black market goods, a former princess bartering her possessions for food, a revolutionary sailor and homeless waifs. The second part would present a picture of Socialist reconstruction, the building of new plants and factories, yesterday's sailor turned worker, and so on.

Once the subject had been approved in principle by Diaghilev, Prokofiev set to work with enthusiasm. The ballet was scheduled for production in 1927, and Prokofiev left for another concert tour of the United States.[65]

The short Paris season was as condensed in its drama as a French classical play. There was Diaghilev's enduring passion to dazzle the aristocracy, in-tellectuals and artists of Paris, whom he regarded as the core of civilization on this largely barbarous planet. Paris would see *Zéphyr et Flore* and *Les Matelots* for the first time, the former being the joint work of Kochno, Dukelsky, Braque and Massine, the latter of Kochno, Auric, Pruna and Mas-sine. In the revised *Le Chant du rossignol*, Balanchine's choreography would be shown for the first time to Paris, and the fifteen-year-old Markova would make her début. Dolin, the falling favourite, was to repeat his personal victory in *Le Train bleu*; while the rising favourite would appear for the first time in the leading roles of Boreas in *Zéphyr* and the French sailor in *Les Matelots*. Dolin was wondering whether or not to remain in the com-pany.[66] His decision, the climax of the drama, must be made before the curtain fell on Saturday.

Goossens could not come to conduct, so Scotto had to be fetched from Monte Carlo. On the first night at the Gaieté Lyrique the programme was *Pulcinella*, *Zéphyr* and *La Boutique fantasque*. In the Stravinsky-Pergolesi ballet Idzikovsky had resumed his old role of Coviello, which Dolin had taken over from him. Neither Dolin nor Lifar was therefore in the first ballet, and they had spent the afternoon finding a hairdresser who would come to the theatre to wave their hair for the second. Ten minutes before the curtain was due to rise, Slavinsky had not turned up. A message came to say he was ill, but he was so irresponsible that he might have been drunk or in bed with a woman. Grigoriev asked Dolin to substitute for him. Patrick refused. Then came Wollheim. 'Come on, Pat....' 'I don't see why I should. I don't want to make a fool of myself at the first performance in Paris....' 'You must do it.' 'I'm sick of being told what I have got to do.... I'm dancing practically every ballet this season, and I haven't time to dress.' 'Do it for me, for old times' sake....' Dolin danced; then ran back to his room, sweating, to change, to make up again, to have his hair curled – while Lifar, next door, kept calling, 'Have you powder, Anton? Please, some black.' Dolin had accepted defeat by Lifar: the two young men were friends, in spite of Diaghilev. Dolin had no time to lace up his cross-garters properly, and one came undone during the ballet. He tore off both shoes and finished in bare feet. Then Nikitina, who was delicate physically, and whose technical training was not equal to her artistry, sprained her foot. Although she finished the ballet, she could hardly walk on stage to take a call; and she danced no more that season. Next day, Dolin was obliged to start rehearsing with Danilova, so that she should be ready by Thursday to dance Flore in the last three performances.[67]

Alicia Markova had to have a special costume designed for her as the Nightingale in *Le Chant du Rossignol*. Diaghilev, Matisse and Balanchine went with her to Vera Sudeikina's flat, where they found Stravinsky. Matisse decided that she was to wear white all-over tights with no skirt – a startling innovation. She would have diamond bangles and anklets, like a bird with a ringed leg. Her white skull cap was to be trimmed with ospreys framing her face. Diaghilev said ospreys were too expensive; Stravinsky and Matisse between them agreed to pay the extra cost.[68]

On Tuesday Dolin threw himself into his role in *Le Train bleu* and gave everything he had.[69] On Wednesday *Les Matelots* was a hit, and Lifar's charm had full expression. Pruna's sets, for the five scenes, called 'Les Fiançailles et Le Départ', 'La Solitude', 'Retour et Variations des Matelots – L'Epreuve', 'La Tentation – Le Bar', and 'Finale', were simple and pleasing like the music, which had echoes not only of sea-shanties but even of *Die Fledermaus*. Nemtchinova as the Girl, Sokolova as her Friend, Woizikovsky, Slavinsky and Lifar as the Spanish, American and French sailors, were the only dancers. In Scene 3, 'Le Retour', each sailor had a distinctive variation. Slavinsky, in his *allegrissimo*, had some peculiar leaps; Lifar's *Valse*, a kind of *barcarolle*, was the most classical; Woizikovsky's *allegro brillante* had some typically grotesque Massine movements.[70] They danced a *pas de trois* with three chairs, on which they jumped and ended by sitting down. At the first performance Lifar's chair gradually came to pieces and he finished by collapsing on the floor. As this fall coincided with the last bugle call and crashing chords of the music, it was thought intentional and he received an ovation.[71] This was the first of several strokes of good luck which, as we shall see, advanced his career. In February, when Auric had arrived prematurely in Monte Carlo and been sent packing by Diaghilev, he had travelled along the coast to stay with friends near Hyères, to finish his final scene. Nina Hamnett, the English painter, who was also there, had whistled him some English sea-shanties, including 'Nautical William', with its bawdy dialogue between Bollocky Bill and the Fair Young Lady. These he had managed to include in *Les Matelots*; and at the first night Diaghilev came up to Nina to ask, 'And how is the fair young lady?'[72] Kochno politely telegraphed to Massine, who was appearing at the London Pavilion, that his ballet had been a triumph,[73] and Leonide received a wreath on stage inscribed 'For *Les Matelots*'.[74]

On Saturday the programme was *Le Train bleu, Zéphyr et Flore, Les Matelots* and *Les Fâcheux*. Cocteau came early to the theatre, and was indignant that his ballet was being given first. He complained to Diaghilev; then Dolin told Jean that he was parting with the Ballet that night. After *Le Train bleu* Cocteau rose from his seat to leave the theatre, saying, 'As Dolin goes, so does *Le Train bleu*. No one shall dance it after him.'[75] Whether he would have been able to prevent Diaghilev staging his ballet is uncertain: what *is* certain is that, back in London, Diaghilev sent Lifar to a teacher of acrobatics 'somewhere up the Tottenham Court Road' and Lifar could not learn the stunts Dolin had done.[76] *Le Train bleu* was never given again. After its last night Dolin was summoned to supper with Diaghilev chez Viel, and arrived very late. Wollheim was still there to hear Diaghilev offer Patrick every inducement to stay – a choice of roles, twice the salary, a new ballet by Stravinsky: but without result.[77] (Lifar wrote, 'Dolin's contract was due to expire on July 1st, and it was common knowledge that it would not be renewed.'[78] Dolin told me that Diaghilev, at the Grand Hôtel, begged him on his knees to stay on.)[79]

Dukelsky travelled with Diaghilev to London (his first Channel crossing), which, because of his companion, he found 'a trying experience'. 'The weather couldn't have been better or balmier; nevertheless Diaghilev was carefully wrapped in a heavy woollen blanket on top of a beaver-fur coat, a cashmere muffler around his neck ... the too-small Lock hat over his eyes. ... He fingered a small ikon of St Nicholas with his left hand and crossed himself repeatedly with his right, his lips moving noiselessly in prayer.' At

Victoria, according to Dukelsky, the bad-tempered Diaghilev 'interviewed' the reporters, asking, 'Why aren't Englishwomen the prettiest in the world? Why is English food inedible? Why are there no English composers?' Only at the Savoy did he relax,[80] to boast to the *Observer* of the Paris reception of his *Matelots* and to describe his new version of *Zéphyr*, with three sets instead of one (which because of Nikitina's injury, would not be shown in London until after the holidays) and to extol his youthful stars.[81] Diaghilev and Lifar were now living together. Back at the London Coliseum, Diaghilev had the idea of including a one-legged ex-serviceman busker, who entertained the queues by making music on spoons, plates and cigar-boxes, in *Les Matelots*. George Peter Dines and his spoons inspired headlines in every newspaper. English popular art was destined to influence the score of this ballet in more ways than one; but no one knew about Nina Hamnett and Bollocky Bill. Writing in the *Queen*, Raymond Mortimer was struck by the 'ephebe' graces of Lifar.[82] Indeed, who was not?

The Ballet gave a performance at a gala for Russian refugees at the Hotel Cecil. Diaghilev made a speech at the London Music Club,[83] had some new clothes made by Gilbert, Piggott & Holding, of 62 South Molton Street, for Lifar, Kochno and himself,[84] and spent a weekend at the Branksome Tower Hotel, Bournemouth.[85] Dining with Eugène Goossens and his wife, Dukelsky made friends with a young composer, William Walton, who had been helped by – and was staying with – the Sitwell brothers at 2 Carlyle Square, Chelsea.[86]

Diaghilev's frequent changes of Paris hotels will be understood when it is disclosed that on 23 June the Grand Hôtel, Boulevard des Capucines, had complained of an unpaid account of 2,996.45 francs.[87] When Diaghilev left London before the end of his Coliseum season, he put up neither at the Grand, nor the Wagram, but at the small Hôtel Vouillemont in the rue du Mont Thabor, which was probably recommended by Cocteau, as its owners were the originals of *Les Parents terribles*.[88] Here he and Lifar stayed from 24 till 30 July.[89] In Paris Lifar had his nose operated on. This he did with the greatest reluctance,[90] but Diaghilev knew what was needed. The fine curved nose which resulted from the operation completed the beauty of his face, which was so well-shaped, with high cheek-bones, fine eyes and full, curved mouth. Even though at first his nose used to run and his colleagues teased him, saying, 'Don't sit in the sun, the paraffin will melt!',[91] it was a step on the ladder to stardom.

From the Hotel Milano, Verona, where they had gone either in search of Romeo and Juliet, or on business, Diaghilev and Lifar moved to the Villa d'Este on Lake Como. 'Our life,' wrote Lifar, 'on the enchanting lake, under the friendly, calm, pale blue skies, seemed to me a veritable ideal.' But at lunch with friends of Diaghilev at Cernobbio, the hostess, Countess Demidoff, paid particular attention to Lifar and, as he liked rowing and was good at it, took him on the lake in a boat. When Lifar returned to the Villa d'Este, he was told that Diaghilev had departed, leaving the message that Lifar could spend the rest of his holidays by the lake alone. He chased Diaghilev to the Hotel Cavour at Milan, arriving only ten minutes after him. It was a relief for both of them to make up the quarrel.[92]

The elder Sergei's love for the younger was all-consuming: and there were terrible scenes of jealousy for the first year or two. Even so, Lifar, who dreamed of the perfect union of two souls, and longed to pour out all his dreams and aspirations, noticed that Diaghilev was reticent about his own. Worse still, 'Soon I found,' wrote Lifar, 'that Sergei Pavlovitch was less interested in my spiritual development than in my sartorial elegance.'[93] In the end, perhaps, Diaghilev's admiration for physical beauty, of which his passion for fashionable clothes was an extension, proved stronger than obsessive romantic love. The shrewd Danilova thought 'Lifar was a beautiful pet, a parrot to perch on your shoulder, who might possibly peck.'[94] Yet, at the beginning of their day-to-day proximity of relationship, Diaghilev's 'winds and waters' were 'greater storms than almanacks can report'. It was very hard on Kochno, who joined Diaghilev and Lifar in Venice, to have to work and live alongside this *ménage*. Does anyone ever like his best friend's lover? Boris kept his own counsel and remained indispensable. He was not pushed out.

In Venice the three men stayed at the Hotel Europa on the Grand Canal.[95] Milhaud had recommended to Diaghilev a young Italian composer called Vittorio Rieti.[96] The latter arranged to play his compositions to Diaghilev at a musical academy, where, he said, there were fifty-two grand pianos at their disposal. 'Let us take fifty-one and leave the other for them,' said Diaghilev. Rieti had written a ballet called *Noah's Ark*, but Diaghilev disliked the idea of all the animal characters. Still, he 'wanted to hear everything, to know everything and to talk about everything',[97] and, when Rieti played him a short *a capella* cantata called *Barabau*, Diaghilev commissioned him to extend it to form a ballet score for orchestra, retaining the original singing.

One morning, in the Piazza San Marco, Diaghilev and Lifar ran into Sokolova and Woizikovsky. The latter had not wished to trespass on Diaghilev's favourite holiday resort, but thought that if they avoided the Lido they might miss him. To their surprise, he seemed delighted to see them. Sokolova wrote, 'We were bundled straight into a motor-boat and carried off to the Lido. We spent a happy day together; and when Leon and I explained that we were only staying four days because of the expense, Diaghilev said, "Nonsense! Now that you are here we will arrange a party and you two and Lifar shall dance." As we had been dancing nine months without a break it was the last thing we wanted to do. . . .'

The Cole Porters were living at the Palazzo Papadopoli. Diaghilev and Boris arranged a stage in their garden, backing on to the Grand Canal, making, as a background, three arches covered with greenery, which framed statues borrowed from a museum. The programme consisted of two male variations from *Les Matelots*, the tarantella from *Cimarosiana* and Sokolova's solo, the Rag Mazurka, from *Les Biches*.[98] Boris had to hum *Les Matelots* to Cole Porter, so that he should be able to play it on the piano, for there was no score available.[99] The performance, Lifar recorded,

was not to pass off without two thunderstorms, one from the skies, the other from Diaghilev. The first burst with tremendous violence [on the eve of the perform-ance], and sank a number of gondolas; but the second burst when the performance was ended. . . . Our grateful, enthusiastic hosts had added to our usual 'envelopes' a few presents. . . . This produced an incredible outburst of rage from Diaghilev, who cried: 'How dare they give presents to my artists – my artists have no need for such paltry sops!' Then, like a raging lion, Diaghilev rushed off to the Piazza San Marco to storm and rave at our hosts, and as a result, created a first-class scandal which soon spread over the town.[100]

Sokolova merely remembered that 'we were each of us sent £25 by Diaghi-lev the next morning.'[101]

Boris and Cole Porter were close friends, and this rather annoyed Diaghi-lev, who found the American's success and opulence unjustified. Lifar, in turn, was jealous that Diaghilev should mind the friendship of Cole and Boris, and he tried to discredit the Casa Porter–Papadopoli in any way he could. He told Diaghilev that some man had kissed his hands passionately at a party there. Diaghilev was furious and ordered Boris to make enquiries. Cole arrived in state to smooth matters out and to affirm that there was no truth in the story.[102]

The rest of Diaghilev's honeymoon with Lifar was spent in Florence, Rome and Naples. Nicolas and Nadine Legat travelled with them, and Lifar had daily lessons from the teacher who had insisted on Vaslav Nijinsky's admittance to the Imperial Ballet School. Lifar was obliged to spend five consecutive days in the Uffizi. (Dolin would never have submitted to that.) He and Diaghilev had dinner at Fiesole, and watched night fall on the city below.[103] Nuvel cabled two suggested programmes for a four-day visit to Antwerp in October. The three men travelled south. In Rome Rieti played them some additional numbers for *Barabau*.[104] From the Hotel Excelsior at Naples they made excursions to Herculaneum and Pompeii.[105]

The company assembled in Paris on 1 October, and, apart from the visit to Antwerp, remained rehearsing there until the twenty-fourth.[106] Having been unable to find an Italian artist suitable for *Barabau*, Diaghilev decided to try the celebrated painter of Montmartre street scenes. It was a known fact that Utrillo, drunk or sober, was simple-minded; and it was rumoured that his latest pictures were copied from picture postcards. His life was organized by his forceful mother, Suzanne Valadon, and her young husband, André Utter, who acted as dealer. Diaghilev shirked an interview with the odd trio and sent Boris Kochno to visit them at their Château St Bernard, near Paris.

I was allowed to see Utrillo for a few moments only. . . . His gentle, melancholy eyes were often vacant. He listened indifferently when I spoke about the ballet; it was enough for him to know that he was being asked to paint 'a landscape with a church'. . . . Utrillo emerged from his torpor only once, on learning that among the ballet costumes he was to design there should be one for an Italian soldier. He seemed to be at a loss and was becoming agitated, whereupon his mother intervened and advised him to copy the uniform of the village gendarme.

Diaghilev never met Utrillo, and, apart from some correspondence three years later about money owing (three thousand francs), had no dealings with him.[107]

With the season at the Coliseum lasting from 26 October till 19 December, Diaghilev would at last wipe out his debt to Stoll. The Queen of Spain and Augustus John were present (separately) on the opening night,[108] when Markova danced Papillon in *Carnaval*. (Nemtchinova had danced the cancan in *La Boutique fantasque* in the afternoon.) Lopukhova returned to dance *Petrushka* with Woizikovsky and Zverev on the twenty-ninth; and on 12 November the refurbished *Zéphyr* was a success – even Dukelsky's score was praised.[109]

Diaghilev had come to realize that, now he was free to hold proper seasons in London, they would have much greater money-making possibilities than any in Paris. He was therefore anxious to devise a ballet on an English subject, though he had no great hopes of English composers or painters.

William Walton was longing to write a ballet for Diaghilev, and Dukelsky arranged for him to play his overture *Portsmouth Point* at the Savoy Hotel. Walton, out of the kindness of his heart, wanted to bring his friend Constant Lambert, too. But Diaghilev had taken a dislike to this young man who had begun haunting him, who had invited him to hear a performance of a suite from Glinka's *Ruslan* which he had arranged and conducted at the Royal College of Music, and who wore an orange shirt with a black tie. Dukelsky smuggled Lambert into the audition with Walton. The latter was a poor pianist and his rendering of *Portsmouth Point* left Diaghilev cold. Lambert then played a ballet he had just written, called *Adam and Eve*, and, being a better performer, gave a spirited rendering of what Dukelsky thought his 'mild' and 'skimpy' music. Dukelsky was surprised to see 'a beatific smile' on Diaghilev's face. ' "Are you English?" he queried. "Yes, I am. Why?" countered Lambert. "That's most surprising. I don't like English music, yet I like your little ballet. I'm going to produce it, but not with that silly title." He took a big red pencil, crossed out "Adam and Eve" and wrote "Romeo and Juliet" over it. Constant burst into uncontrollable tears.'[110]

Dukelsky was in love with the beautiful Canadian actress, Frances Doble, whose sister Georgia was, in December, to marry Sacheverell Sitwell. Diaghilev lunched with Osbert Sitwell in Carlyle Square that December, accompanied by Boris. Dukelsky wrote, 'He sat at the table wrapped in his beaver-fur coat (fear of catching cold) and refused to sample the excellent oysters (fear of ptomaine poisoning). Following lunch, I played my Bogdanovitch songs, which he praised immoderately; Diaghilev then told several wildly improbable stories and departed majestically. Osbert's own majesty paled somewhat next to that of Czar Sergei's....'[111]

One night, at supper at the Trocadero, a dance tune was played which Dukelsky had composed for Cochran's cabaret, staged by Massine. Dukelsky was keeping quiet about his authorship, when one of Cochran's subordinates came up to congratulate him. 'Diaghilev went blue with rage, said nothing, drummed on the table with his knuckles and demanded the bill.... No sooner were we out in the street than Diaghilev knocked my top hat off my head with my own stick, trampled upon it savagely, reducing it to a messy pulp, and with a one-syllable parting shot, "Whore!", disappeared into the dark.'[112]

Diaghilev was repaying Mrs Bewicke's loan of 1922, and her lawyers let him get away with nothing. Acknowledging a cheque on 21 November, they wrote to Wollheim that it was not true that instalments of £35 were to be paid at the end of every week. They were to be paid every Thursday. 'Since your client began the present season on the 26th of October he is now in his fourth week. After your client's last week at the Coliseum is completed no security is remaining to our client should the instalment for that week not be paid.'[113]

On 11 December *Barabau*, conducted by Roger Desormière, was a hit. Woizikovsky, much padded, waddled through the title role of the vineyard owner who feigns death, and Lifar swaggered in grey tights and Napoleonic cocked hat as the sergeant of a passing troop of soldiers. The clownish peasant woman was at first Tatiana Chamié, but Sokolova, shortly afterwards, much improved the role. The singers were 'a chorus of mournful-looking citizens in black bowler hats and gloves who popped up from behind a fence, and sang a deadpan commentary on the action'[114] to a childish nursery-rhyme tune.

The long Coliseum season ended on 19 December with 'a most touching farewell from the public. Several hundred people signed a petition asking for two ballets instead of one on the last night: but they were disappointed.'[115] By 21 December the Ballet were at the Künstlertheater, Berlin.

Perhaps the greatest courage is needed not to confront sudden unexpected disasters but to endure recurrent blows of the same kind monotonously repeated. Diaghilev had paid his debt to Stoll and was now free to hold his first proper London season since 1922: he had made sure that his company would enjoy the security of spending at least four months of the year in Monte Carlo. But 1926 began with financial disaster in Berlin: houses had been 'empty', the Ballet were stranded, without being able to pay their lodgings, and Grigoriev had no money for tickets to Monte Carlo. Funds had to be raised again, either through an advance from the Casino or through loans from friends or businessmen; and Diaghilev found the money in Paris. 'How Diaghilev could have made the necessary arrangements so quickly, and especially at Christmas, said Nuvel, he could not imagine.'[116]

Diaghilev's year, his annual stock-taking, could be said to begin either in the summer, when the dancers' contracts were renewed and holidays taken, or during the hibernation at Monte Carlo – if not on 1 January, at least on the Monegasque National Day, 17 January, by which time the company were always in residence. Yet Diaghilev's disillusion with Monte Carlo as a possible centre of the arts was complete. His venturesome 1924 season of little-known French opera had been totally rejected. The rich, elderly patrons of the Hôtel de Paris, the Casino and the Tir aux Pigeons wanted only the familiar, and they regarded him solely as a purveyor of ballets – preferably rich, elderly ballets like *Schéhérazade*. His ideas for studio experiments and for an art gallery had aroused no interest. It was a disappointment as great, perhaps, as that caused by London's rejection of *The Sleeping Princess*. Not to be able to produce operas as well as ballets, not to open an international workshop, not to have a beautiful museum, whose permanent collection he could build up and where he could arrange temporary exhibitions (for which, of course, Kochno would edit superb catalogues) – it was like losing a limb. Diaghilev would continue to fulfil his obligations to the Principality – indeed, he must, to keep his dancers alive: but his heart was no longer in it.

A new enthusiasm for books took the place of Diaghilev's plans for Monaco. The foundation stone of his library – or Kochno's, for he made no distinction – was the first edition of an early nineteenth-century Russian Almanac containing Pushkin's story 'The Little House at Kolumna', which he had given to Boris one day at lunch with Misia at the time of *Mavra* in 1922. From then on he encouraged Boris to buy Russian books. These were eagerly sought at the shop of Povolotsky in rue Bonaparte, and in London near the British Museum: but the first precious *old* books had been bought at the shop of Rossika in Berlin. Boris kept the treasures in trunks, or, when settled for a few months at Monte Carlo, arranged them in a bookcase in his bedroom. Just as the collection of stage designs given by Diaghilev to Lifar expanded to include fine modern pictures, so did Kochno's few shelves gradually develop into a comprehensive library of Russian literature, continually growing in scale and importance, and at last including both manuscripts and musical scores.[117]

Bibliomania, however, did not possess Diaghilev utterly until 1927. Meanwhile, new ballets must be planned. If he had been content to give his old favourites year by year, without spending money on new ballets, it would have gone far to balance his budget: but, without the work of creation, he would have nothing to live for. As for a hardened captain in the Thirty Years War, battle had become for him a way of life. He had to make wonderful new ballets. There was no lack of talent around for these, if it could be judiciously combined. He must have stars, which the public demanded most of all. Karsavina was no longer young; Lopukhova had married the economist J. M. Keynes; Spessivtseva was at the Paris Opéra. He must therefore create every opportunity for Nemtchinova, Dubrovska, Danilova and Nikitina to shine. He must build up Lifar.

Diaghilev felt that the future of his company depended to a large extent on England – and perhaps America. But the time had not yet come to bring in the New World to redress the balance of the Old – perhaps he kept shirking the big step. He did *not* want the ballet of John Carpenter (who kept bothering him); he did *not* want Gershwin's *Rhapsody in Blue*, which the composer had played him in Paris; he did *not* like jazz. For the moment he concentrated on England. His close friends, though all comfortably off, were not rich enough to underwrite a season, and most were women – Juliet Duff, Lady Ottoline Morrell, Lady Cunard, Mrs Grenfell, Mrs Mathias, Mrs Morley – which made it difficult to ask them for money. What he needed was a man with millions, and a man who admired female beauty would not be a bad idea, for the ballet was not short of that. Samuel Courtauld, the cotton king, answered the description: but his affections were concentrated on Christabel McLaren, wife of the heir to the shipping magnate, Lord Aberconway. And Courtauld was a shrewd man who did not spend money lavishly. Did Diaghilev try the English Rothschilds, or had Bakst turned them against him? Did he try the aesthetic Sir Philip Sassoon? He made advances to Lord Beaverbrook, of the *Daily Express*, without result.[118] He pinned his hopes on Lord Rothermere, of the *Daily Mail*.

Rothermere was soon attracted by young Alice Nikitina; and Diaghilev would live to regret having thrown them together. Just as Kchessinskaya's intimacy with the Imperial Family had enabled her to put spokes in the wheels of Diaghilev's chariot, so was Nikitina's relationship with Rothermere to influence the fortunes of his ballet company in its last years. Not that Nikitina was the first dancer in the magnate's life: Komarova had preceded her in his affections. Rothermere made advances to Sokolova, too. It was Nikitina, though, who became the wielder of power. Then, in the final year of the Russian Ballet, Vadimova took her place.[119]

Diaghilev's saviours in the past had all been people of breeding, or of talent and charm: the Grand Duke Vladimir, Astruc, Comtesse Greffulhe, Dmitri de Gunsburg, Misia Sert, King Alfonso, Stoll, Rouché, Princesse

Edmond de Polignac, Chanel, Princesse Charlotte and Prince Pierre of Monaco. Rothermere could be charming, too, but his underlings were not. Dealing with Rothermere's secretary, Outhwaite, and the staff of the London and Continental *Daily Mail*, Diaghilev had to learn to crawl.

Not only did he need an English backer: Diaghilev needed a London theatre. Covent Garden was his first choice. On 6 February Nuvel cabled, 'Wollheim says Rothermere will come [to the South of France] soon. Will find out cost London week. Between 1350 and 1500 pounds maximum. Bronia signed America. Free till 1st April. Insists 20,000.'[120] Diaghilev had thought Nijinska would be better than Balanchine for *Romeo and Juliet*.

The year 1925 had begun with a strike and the loss of Schollar and Vilzak. Early in 1926 Diaghilev lost his ballerina, Nemtchinova. On 17 February he cabled Wollheim, 'Nemtchinova, Zverev, suddenly left this morning straight for London spreading rumour with permission. Take swift action.'[121] Wollheim replied, 'Nemtchinova, Zverev, Efimov have signed Cochran new revue beginning 17 March.'[122] The reasons given for the two dancers' departure was that, being followers of Tolstoy, they thought it wrong to be bound by any contract. Massine, who was organizing the Cochran show, had, in fact, seduced them.[123] As Nemtchinova was one of the dancers Diaghilev was obliged by *his* contract to present in Monte Carlo, he had some explaining to do. No wonder that, at this time, according to Lifar, 'Sergei Pavlovitch would lie abed for weeks, busy with "little talks and little thinks".'[124] C. B. Cochran received an imperial reprimand.

I was in London in November, also last June, and you could easily have asked me if I needed the leading dancers with whom you were in touch. You must realize that Mme Nemtchinova is my pupil and has learned everything she knows in my company over the last ten years.

It would seem natural for a friend and a gentleman like yourself to ring me up at least and ask my advice instead of signing contracts behind my back.

Allow me to add, in a friendly spirit, that I don't at all like the way you exploit Russian artists discovered and trained by me. Dukelsky was not destined to write bad fox-trotts [sic] for musical comedies. When Massine dances in night-clubs and produces ballets like 'Pompeii à la Massine' he gives himself a bad name. Nor is Nemtchinova cut out for revues....

As an old friend I can't help telling you that you should create your own works with your own artists, instead of using those created by others for purposes alien to the kind of show you put on – sometimes very well.[125]

Diaghilev, either by entertaining Rothermere or by seeking advice on some subject, such as publicity, had to lure him into a position where it was possible to discuss financial backing. On 23 March Outhwaite wrote to Diaghilev, 'Lord Rothermere does not concern himself with details of the newspapers and it is a matter of complete indifference to him who is responsible for your publicity....'[126]

Nikitina recorded Rothermere's first appearance at a rehearsal of *Romeo and Juliet*.

There was a row of chairs.... Diaghilev and his suite were over-excited.... We had often had such visits, we had had the Duke of Connaught, the Kings of Spain, of Egypt, the Prince of Monaco.... We kept asking ourselves: who can it be?
He was a tall man, of modest manner, with a constant smile on his face that put everyone at their ease.... I was on my way out to change ... when I heard Diaghilev calling me; Lord R. wished to make my acquaintance. He shook my hand warmly and said, his voice ringing with sincerity: 'You're a great artist.' And turning to his secretary, Mr O., he repeated this several times.... After a short conversation he said: 'I would very much like to see you dance in London. Would you like that?'... I replied very much in the affirmative. 'Well, we'll see to it that it is done,' he concluded quickly.[127]

It was doubtless just after this that Outhwaite wrote a letter, undated, from the Hôtel de Paris: 'Lord Rothermere and party will be pleased to sup at the Carlton after the performance tomorrow. Please leave the tickets....'[128] Diaghilev told Sokolova, who had the English language in common with his potential backer, that he had already approached Lord Rothermere about a season at His Majesty's Theatre, but that nothing was settled, and he wanted her to clinch the deal at a supper party. Sokolova had already made friends with Rothermere and been to his villa La Dragonnière at Cap d'Ail, but she 'had no experience of extracting large sums of money from rich men'. She wrote,

The supper party took place at the Carlton Hotel ... and I was seated between Diaghilev and Lord Rothermere. At what he judged the right moment, the 'Old Man' whispered 'Now you must go and dance with him.' I was very nervous and it was not until we had had two dances that I summoned the courage to approach the subject. Lord Rothermere did not make it easy for me. Eventually, after a little persuasion, he said 'All right. I will do what you ask. But I want you to make it clear to Diaghilev that I am doing this for you personally.'...[129]

Nikitina recalled:

In the middle of the long horseshoe-shaped table sat Diaghilev and Lord R. surrounded by the veterans of the ballet company. I was placed at one end of the table.... This did not prevent Lord R. leaving his circle and coming to ask me to dance several times....
In spite of his tallness and corpulence, Lord R. danced with remarkable lightness and a great deal of rhythm.[130]

Lifar remembered how Diaghilev would sometimes return from his suppers for Rothermere 'full of hope'. He also remembered 'the perpetual telephonings, during which Sergei Pavlovitch, sweating profusely and quivering with nervous agitation, would call up Lord Rothermere every thirty minutes, hoping to find him in. And when at last he did succeed in speaking to him, making an appointment, ... the meeting would be either postponed or cancelled....'[131]

On 31 March Dolin wrote from London asking Diaghilev to take him back.[132] It is curious, in view of the defection of Vilzak and of the English prospects, that Diaghilev did not do so. He must have felt Lifar was not yet strong enough to hold his own against such a rival.

In the previous November Constant Lambert had told Diaghilev that Augustus John agreed to make designs for *Romeo* 'based on anonymous watercolours',[133] but Diaghilev, on a visit to John's studio in Tite Street, did not like what he saw. He liked no better the work of other English painters, such as Wyndham Lewis, to whom Sacheverell Sitwell introduced him.[134] He had, however, through the Chilean Antonio de Gandarillas, whose aunt, Mme Errazuriz, had introduced him to Picasso and had, for a time, given Stravinsky an allowance, met the pseudo-naïve painter, Christopher Wood. This young man arrived in Monte Carlo in the spring of 1926, and Diaghilev first commissioned him to design *Romeo and Juliet*, then turned him down.[135] He wrote to Lambert that, as his ballet was about a rehearsal (of a ballet based on Shakespeare's play), he intended to give it without scenery. Lambert replied indignantly that he might as well put sand on the stage in *Le Train bleu* because the scene was a beach.[136] Then, on a visit to Paris, Diaghilev saw an exhibition of Surrealist painting, became interested, bought some pictures by Ernst and Miró for Lifar, and gave the commission for *Romeo* to these two painters.[137] In London, Lambert, a close friend of Christopher Wood's, was distraught. On 14 April Max Ernst arrived in Monte Carlo. He was to paint two curtains representing Day and Night. Miró would paint a front curtain and dispose some commonplace articles around the ballet rehearsal room in which the action took place: a *barre*, two screens, a pink dressing-gown hanging on a peg.[138] In the first scene, the principal dancers who are rehearsing 'Romeo and Juliet' make love in earnest, and forget their steps. Miró's costume design for this was the mere indication of a triangular *tutu*, 'blue as in Ernst's curtain'.[139] In the second scene – the 'performance' – there are danced in Renaissance costume the episodes of the lovers' first meeting, the Nurse and Peter (Sokolova and Woizikovsky), the duel of Romeo and Tybalt (Slavinsky), the balcony scene, the *aubade* of Paris, and the death of Juliet, after which, instead of acknowledging the applause, the dancers playing Romeo and Juliet elope by aeroplane, wearing leather coats and airmen's caps with goggles.

When Lambert arrived – on leave from the Royal College of Music – his timidity battled with his intransigence. He could not agree with Diaghilev about anything, and the latter avoided him. Sokolova recalled an afternoon rehearsal, which Lambert had come to accompany, and which Diaghilev had brought Florrie Grenfell to watch. Slavinsky, who was to open the scene alone, had not turned up. Diaghilev began walking up and down, banging his stick. Grigoriev, who 'always got a red spot on his cheek when he was disturbed', knew as well as the rest of the company which lady Slavinsky, who boasted about his conquests, was probably in bed with. When the culprit had been found, he and Diaghilev nearly came to blows, and 'some of the male dancers had to pull Slavinsky away'. Constant Lambert, seated at the piano, overcome by the shouting, went deathly pale and seemed about to faint when Sokolova poured a bottle of fizzy lemonade down his throat and revived him. Diaghilev afterwards apologized to Mrs Grenfell for the squalid scene.[140]

At the last moment Diaghilev had persuaded his beloved Karsavina to play Juliet, at least in Monte Carlo. Poor Tamara, out of practice, found Lifar to be the least experienced of partners. He hardly knew how to lift her. 'She never complained. Her manners were as beautiful as her face. She would just raise her eyebrows and say, "But Serge, if you will do it this way, it will work."'[141] Nikitina had to teach the role of Juliet to Mme Karsavina, and be content with dancing it later in Paris.

Nijinska had already left Monte Carlo when Constant Lambert arrived, and he later wrote to his mother, describing his feelings.

When I arrived ... I found the 1st performance was in 2 or 3 days time and that far from doing the ballet without a décor Diaghilev had chosen two 10th-rate painters from an imbecile group called the 'Surrealistes'. I cannot tell you how monstrous the décor is.... Not only that, but Diaghilev has introduced disgraceful changes in the choreography, altering bits that Nijinska declared she would never to be induced to change. For example, at the end of the 1st tableau, instead of the dance for 3 women which Nijinska designed, the lovers (who are supposed to be dragged apart) return and do a *pas-de-deux*, with all the rest staring at them.... Of course I sent Nijinska a telegram immediately....[142]

The first scene had ended with Dubrovska, Danilova and Gevergeva doing *fouettés*. Although this was recognized as being very effective, Diaghilev had cut it because its brilliance outshone the technical capabilities of Nikitina and Lifar.[143]

'Constant Lambert came to see me,' wrote Karsavina, 'in a terrible state of agitation. Unless I could persuade Diaghilev to restore the cut, he said, he would ... remove the musicians' parts from their stands, and so prevent the performance. I rang through to Diaghilev's room.... He went to the theatre and gave orders....'[144]

Lambert's letter to his mother continued,

I was so upset by all this that I asked for and obtained an interview with Diaghilev.... He had Kochno and Grigoriev with him. To frighten me, I suppose. He started off by saying that my letter to him was so rude that he didn't wish to speak to me, but as I was so young he would pardon me. After a short pause in which I did not thank him, I asked why he had rejected Kit Wood's décor.

He became very angry and said 'I forbid you to say a word about the décor'. I then tried to speak about the choreography but he said 'I have known Madame Nijinska for 20 years and I forbid you to mention her name in my presence.' I naturally lost my temper and said I would withdraw the music entirely. I'm afraid it was rather a dreadful scene, but then it is impossible to remain calm with a man like that. The next morning I went to see a lawyer in Nice, who told me that unfortunately there was no way out of my contract. I went back to Monte-Carlo, quite calm by now, and went into the *salle d'orchestre* to listen to the only rehearsal for orchestra alone. To my surprise, they tried to stop me getting in, and when at last I 'effected an entry' I found all the orchestra waiting but no music put out. After about half an hour a sort of military funeral came in with the score and parts, and all during the rehearsal there were 2 concierges on each side of me to see I did not tear the work to pieces. After the rehearsal the parts were collected, carefully corded and sealed and taken up in a strong room. . . . Now Diaghilev has spread the report that I went quite insane at Monte-Carlo and had to be watched by 2 detectives. . . .[145]

Where Lifar was concerned, Diaghilev could even be jealous of Karsavina. Tamara Platonovna sent Lifar a bunch of roses on the opening night of *Romeo and Juliet* on 4 May. After the performance he took them to his room at the Hôtel de Paris and returned to collect Karsavina for supper. Later, when he went back to bed, he found the roses had been flung out of the window into the courtyard. Diaghilev burst in and made a furious scene. '. . . I will not permit my theatre to be turned into a den of vice. I'll turn out these women who hang round the necks of my dancers. . . .' Next morning, Lifar heard the 'faithful old friend and Nanny' Pavel Georgievitch Koribut-Kubitovitch calming Diaghilev down: 'What nonsense you're talking, Serioja: as if you didn't know our Serioja, and how utterly inaccessible Tamara Platonovna is. . . . You yourself wanted Karsavina to be kind to the boy and encourage him. . . .' At lunch, Diaghilev was in a sad but forgiving mood. 'Yes, indeed, Serioja, things have come to a pretty pass. . . . Even so good a friend as Pavel Georgievitch, who always defends you warmly, feels seriously annoyed with you this time.' Lifar burst out laughing; Diaghilev gave him 'the kindest imaginable smile, which instantly sealed our peace'.[146] Lifar's gaiety was charming: he also bubbled with enthusiasm about everything – which can be an attractive characteristic.

At the Easter celebrations held at Matilda Kchessinskaya's villa at Cap d'Ail, there was more floral trouble. Rather tight, Lifar got up from the table to present his hostess with one of her own roses. He was her partner in the traditional polonaise which opened the ball. Then he signed his name across Karsavina's in Kchessinskaya's 'golden book'. Diaghilev said, 'You seem much too gay, young man,' and took him home.[147]

Kochno was sent to ask Lambert if he had any music for an entracte, as Diaghilev thought it would be more lively if there was a transit of dancers from classroom to theatre. Lambert said he would give him some music, on the condition that none of it was danced. His offer was rejected and Diaghilev asked Balanchine to arrange what Lambert described as 'a sort of comic march-past of the characters (without music) in very dubious taste and in a style which is the complete opposite of Nijinska's....'[148] This was performed with the curtain lowered half-way, so that only the dancers' legs were visible.

The other novelties for Paris would be Auric's *Pastorale*, and *Jack-in-the-Box*, a short piece which had been found among Satie's papers after his death a few months before, and orchestrated by Milhaud. *Barabau*, too, though seen in London, would be new to Paris.

Diaghilev planned to revive *The Firebird* later in the year. The old Golovine scenery had grown shabby, and he ordered new designs from Gontcharova. Vera Sudeikina was to make the costumes, and on 26 April she telegraphed to Diaghilev, asking for an advance of four thousand francs, as she had no ready cash.[149]

The scene of this Paris season, and three of Diaghilev's remaining four, was the Théâtre Sarah Bernhardt (now Le Théâtre de la Ville), which stood facing the Châtelet near the Pont au Change. It was a barn of a place. Danilova found dusty old contracts of Bernhardt's in her dressing-room;[150] and Sokolova's was haunted by the ghost of a young actress whom the jealousy of the divine Sarah had driven to suicide.[151]

The Surrealists were the anarchists of art. Because they resented the alliance of two of their number with the 'bourgeois capitalist' Diaghilev, they prepared to attack. Even Picasso had been assaulted by them during a performance of Beaumont's 'Soirées de Paris'. The police warned Diaghilev that they expected a demonstration from the Surrealists and Communists, and offered a bodyguard. Diaghilev said he had entire confidence in any measures the police thought fit to take, but would be grateful if no uniformed men were visible in the theatre.[152]

On the night of 18 May the first ballet, *Pulcinella*, passed without incident. When the curtain rose on Miró's curtain, and this in turn rose to reveal the company in working clothes, taking a class at the *barre*, 'such a din of howls and whistling was heard that not one note of the music could pierce through.' While a battle raged in the stalls – and Lady Abdy had her dress torn off her back – leaflets showered from the gallery.[153]

It is inadmissible that thought should be at the beck and call of money.... It may have seemed to Ernst and Miro that their collaboration with M. de Diaghilew, legitimized by the example of Picasso, would not have such serious consequences. However, it forces us whose main concern is to keep the outposts of the intellect beyond the grasp of slave-traders ... [and so on]

Louis Aragon, André Breton[154]

The curtain was lowered. The demonstrators were ejected. The conductor, Desormière, resumed the ballet from the beginning. The scandal helped to fill the huge house to its maximum capacity on subsequent nights.[155]

The score of Lambert, who was still, after all, a student, showed derivations from Stravinsky and the fashionable Paris school – whose work the English composer, as critic, was later to deride so mercilessly. But there was also a breezy element in it, reminiscent of Walton's *Portsmouth Point*. Messager thought Lambert's music full of promise and dexterity, but lacking in individual character.

Auric's third ballet for Diaghilev, *Pastorale*, given on 29 May, was about the making of a film in a rustic setting. A young postman or telegraph boy with a bicycle (Lifar) is attracted to the Star (Dubrovska). In the second scene the villagers attack the film-makers, and the boy returns to his sweetheart (Danilova). There was at least one original movement which has been copied since: in their *pas de deux* Lifar knelt, and turned Dubrovska in *arabesque*, holding her by the knee.[156] Most people considered *Pastorale* the weakest of Diaghilev's later ballets. Balanchine himself thought that, in spite of a 'messy' libretto, it was 'rather nice'.[157]

The three gently melodious little pieces by Satie which make up *Jack-in-the-Box* provided dances for Idzikovsky, in a multi-coloured costume outlined in white fur, and for Danilova, Dubrovska and Tchernicheva as particoloured Golliwogs, with wigs blue on one side and white on the other. This lasted only a few minutes. Its *première* was on 3 June.

During the final years of the Ballet, although Diaghilev was already ably represented in London by Eric Wollheim, he made use of Lady Juliet Duff as a social ambassador, to whom big business, in the form of Rothermere, must defer, and whose sex, giving her immunity from insult, formed a kind of inner defence. On Sunday, 6 June, Boris telegraphed to her on behalf of Diaghilev, 'Have you received Rothermere's cheque?'[158]

Diaghilev, who in Paris had returned to the Grand Hôtel, made a change in his London arrangements for the summer of 1926. He took for Kochno, Lifar and himself a flat in a house run as 'bachelor chambers': Albemarle Court, 27 Albemarle Street, off Piccadilly. The chambers had a 'queer' reputation – Osbert Sitwell told his brother – so it may have been he who recommended them. Nevertheless, Sacheverell, who was now married to Georgia Doble and living at 16 Tite Street, next to Oscar Wilde's old house, emerged from his visits to Albemarle Court 'unscathed'.[159] As His Majesty's was almost the westernmost West End theatre, the flat had the added advantage of being nearer to it than was the Savoy.

The programmes of that season, which opened on 14 June and ended on 23 July, were exceptionally rich. Apart from the three new ballets, London was to be shown *Les Noces* for the first time; and Diaghilev had persuaded Karsavina, Lopukhova and Trefilova to take part. It was so long since London had been able to enjoy a full evening of ballet.

The *Daily Mirror* and other newspapers reported the presence on the first night of the Duchess of Rutland and her daughter, Lady Diana Cooper, who wore a pale-gold sequin dress, of Miss Viola Tree, Lord Cholmondeley, Lord Balfour (with his niece the Hon. Mrs Edward Lascelles), Mr H. G. Wells, Miss Poppy Baring, Mr Noël Coward, the Hon. Stephen Tennant, Mr Augustus John, Sir John and Lady Lavery, Lord Lathom with Miss Olga Lynn, and Anthony Asquith (whose mother had asked Diaghilev to change the programme in 1919, so that he could see *Le Tricorne* during his half-term break from Winchester).[160] Unrecorded were Marie Rambert and a young pupil she had brought, Frederick Ashton. Nigel Playfair's revue, *Riverside Nights*, was to open at the Lyric, Hammersmith, on the following day, and Ashton's first ballet, *A Tragedy of Fashion*, would be in it. Dolin sent Diaghilev a telegram of good wishes.[161] At a company party in Sir Herbert Beerbohm-Tree's old flat in the dome above the theatre, Ninette Devalois was rash enough to ask for Diaghilev's autograph on her programme. He gave her a disapproving look and wrote instead the name of Youmans's musical comedy *No, no, Nanette*.[162]

Les Noces was conducted by Eugene Goossens, and the pianists were Auric, Poulenc, Rieti and Dukelsky. (Rieti thought it was an unsuccessful 'gimmick' of Diaghilev's to employ four composers instead of four professional pianists, and noticed that Stravinsky was 'far from happy about it'.)[163] As so often, the critics were much slower to appreciate *Les Noces* than the public.[164] H. G. Wells, who loved the ballet–cantata, was moved (at Diaghilev's suggestion, perhaps) to write a 'letter' which was later printed and handed out with the theatre programmes.

Writing as an old-fashioned popular writer, not at all of the highbrow sect ... I do not know of any other ballet so interesting, so amusing, so fresh or nearly so exciting as *Les Noces*. I want to see it again and again.... How wilful the stupidity is, the efforts of one of our professional guides of taste to consider the four grand pianos on the stage as part of the scene, bear witness. Another of these guardians of culture treats the amusing plainness of the backcloth, with its single window to indicate one house and its two windows for the other, as imaginative poverty ... and they all cling to the suggestion that Stravinsky has tried to make marriage 'attractive' and failed in the attempt. Of course, they make jokes about the mother-in-law; that was unavoidable....[165]

Ernest Newman wrote of Stravinsky, 'Everyone now sees him for just what he is and always was – a Little Master who flamed up to genius for a brief year or two of his life, then declined into a talent, then into a mediocrity, and is now a nonentity....'[166]

Among the musical *entr'actes* played was Walton's *Portsmouth Point*; and on 19 June Diaghilev telegraphed to Berners in Paris, 'Shall play your magnificent fugue Wednesday. Hope you will be present.'[167]

Romeo and Juliet was given on 21 June. Constant Lambert had evidently not neglected to have a word with the critics. *The Times* understood that Lambert's music had been written to 'express something entirely foreign from the Romeo and Juliet ballet' and was used to accompany action that 'probably surprised nobody more than the young composer himself'.[168] The *Daily Telegraph* 'would not be surprised to learn that to Mr Lambert the whole setting was antipathetic. . . .'[169] The *Yorkshire Post* noted that 'it was from "Standing Room Only" that he came after repeated calls for the composer to take his share of the applause.'[170] The *Daily Express* wrote that 'he blushed like a schoolboy.'[171]

There was a little booing after *Pastorale* on 28 June and Ernest Newman was 'not surprised'.[172] Lady Cunard wrote to Diaghilev:

Thomas Beecham did *not* like *Pastorale* and thought it unworthy of your genius as a whole. There is much that is fine and interesting in it & *very new* too, but as a whole it lacks beauty & interest I feel. But I know your mind is different. . . .

Will you come & lunch with me on *Monday* at 1.30. I do so hope you can come.[173]

On 5 July there was a 'Festival Erik Satie', with *Jack-in-the-Box*, *Parade* and piano music which Marcelle Meyer had come from Paris to play. Diaghilev had taken her, Lifar and Cecil Lewis, a young friend of Charles Ricketts, to Hampton Court on the day before (a Sunday).[174] On 7 July Stravinsky telegraphed that he was arriving by air on the following day.[175] Ernest Newman had been rung up and told he would be sent no more tickets for the Russian Ballet. On 11 July Newman reported his own banishment (and he never wrote another notice of the Diaghilev Ballet).[176] On 19 July Trefilova appeared in *Aurora's Wedding*. Sokolova had to have an operation five days before the end of the season, and Lord Rothermere not only paid for this but sent enough flowers for the whole hospital.[177] Nikitina, on the other hand, had been enjoying the use of one of Rothermere's five Rolls Royces. At the final party he asked her to let him pay for her holiday at Dax, where she could have treatment for her weak foot. As she had just allowed herself the luxury of a squirrel coat, this cheque, 'fallen from Heaven', was very welcome.[178]

The Russian Ballet had paid its way at His Majesty's (without counting the cost of the new ballets, no doubt), so Diaghilev was able to repay Rothermere his advance, thus making certain of a second London season in the winter.[179] The company gave two performances at Ostend before spending a month at Le Touquet under the eye of Nuvel, while Grigoriev had a rest.[180]

It seems probable that Diaghilev visited Avignon (and perhaps Mantua) on the way to Venice. He may have been motoring with the Serts.[181]

His preoccupations during the summer were: the restoration of *The Fire-bird*; a possible revival of *The Sleeping Princess*; the composition of his company; and the new 'English' ballet, *The Triumph of Neptune*, which he was concocting with Sacheverell Sitwell, Gerald Berners and Balanchine. Sitwell's father, Sir George, had a castle, Montegufoni, near Florence; while Berners had a flat overlooking the Forum in Rome. Balanchine was summoned from France for talks.

On 7 August 1926 Diaghilev wrote to Kochno from the Lido. Asking him to call on Gontcharova and Larionov at Juan-les-Pins on his way to Venice, he laid down clearly his idea of what the two *Firebird* décors (for the magic orchard and for the final wedding) should be: 'First scene: A dark night, with phosphorescent apples. The stage is full of apples – not just one tree; the orchard is dark brown. The décor must be painted in minute detail – like Mantegna's Hunt in Mantua, or like the Avignon frescoes. Then, for the second scene the backcloth is changed: the garden is transformed into the Holy City, the apples become the gilded onion domes of churches, a countless swarm of churches crowded together.'[182]

Gontcharova obeyed Diaghilev's instructions exactly, only omitting the phosphorescence with his consent.[183]

In the same letter Diaghilev continued somewhat bitchily about Boris's friend Cole Porter:

We have stopped at the Hôtel des Bains because the din at the Excelsior makes life impossible. The whole of Venice is up in arms against Cole Porter because of his jazz and his Negroes. He has started an idiotic nightclub on a boat moored opposite the Salute, and now the Grand Canal is swarming with the very same Negroes who have made us all flee from London and Paris. They are teaching the 'Charleston' on the Lido beach! It's dreadful. The gondoliers are threatening to massacre all the elderly American women here. The very fact of their [Linda and Cole Porter's] renting the Palazzo Rezzonico is considered typically *nouveau riche*. Cole is greatly changed since his operation; he is thinner and appreciably older-looking.[184]

The following day, Sunday, 8 August, Diaghilev wrote to Grigoriev, who was on holiday in Monte Carlo:

You can congratulate me on having definitely disposed of Gulbenkian (you know who I mean, don't you? – our Monegasque and Parisian adversary who gave us so much trouble!) as well as of Stoll, from whom I have acquired the complete production of *The Sleeping Princess*. It's cold and wet here, just as it was at Ostend. Pay my respects to Lubov Pavlovna and your family, and kiss Pavka's venerable beard.

If Gontcharova asks you to show her the *Firebird* costumes [stored at Monte Carlo] let her see them. But it would be better to have them cleaned first little by little as far as you can....[185]

In fact, Vera Sudeikina, who was not only making new costumes but converting old ones, found Gontcharova, when it was a question of saving money, extremely adaptable and undemanding. Vera bought yards of common old lace curtains, painted them gold and cut them out into patterns to stick on top of Golovine's old costumes for the boyars in the wedding scene.[186]

On 18 August Diaghilev wrote to Grigoriev:

As regards Nikitina you did well to sign a contract with her. Don't take any of her parts away from her.... I never ... promised *anything*. It's sad about Gevergeva, but I don't particularly value her, and will not enter into any special conditions.... There's nothing to be done about Dubrovska now. But next autumn, when Vladimirov is in America, I shall talk to her.... If we have to part with her it will be a pity, but we can't listen to silly caprices.

In general, to give *The Sleeping Princess* and *L'Oiseau de feu* we must have a company of *at least* twenty-four women and twenty-two men dancers. Think this over carefully. Can it really be true that Balanchine cannot get us anyone from Russia? What about Woizikovsky and Warsaw? Where is he? Has he found anyone? ...

What do you mean by saying that many of the *Sleeping Princess* costumes no longer exist? What has happened to them? ...[187]

On 25 August, the day after Rudolf Valentino's death, Diaghilev was telegraphing and writing to Mestres in Barcelona.[188] *The Sleeping Princess* would never be revived by Diaghilev – though most of the costumes survived, to be sold by Sotheby in 1968 and 1969.

Boris arrived in Venice in time for a big fancy-dress charity ball given by Catherine d'Erlanger and Lady Colebrooke at the Fenice Theatre on 27 August. Crown Prince Umberto attended, as did Lady Cunard, Lady Wimborne, Lady Diana Cooper, Lady Abdy, Princess Thurn und Taxis, Princesse Baba de Faucigny-Lucinge (Baroness d'Erlanger's daughter), the Duke of Verdura, Lord Berners, Maurice Baring and Harold Acton. A young Englishman, who had borrowed twenty pounds from his father, in order to waylay Diaghilev in Venice and show him his designs, was also present. Four days later this designer, who also took photographs, and was called Cecil Beaton, hung about desperately at Florian's in the Piazza San Marco with an American lady journalist who had promised to introduce him to Diaghilev. They waited and waited; and Miss Gibson gave up. Beaton sat on for dear life.

Oh God, there he was with Lifar! I catapulted forward and spoke in English: 'Miss Gibson was to have introduced us but she's gone and may not be back and mayn't I show you my portfolio?'

Diaghilev stared at me in surprise. In spite of his colossal stature and dignified mien he reminded me of a pale and fat baby. He was impeccably dressed in white flannel trousers and a blue, double-breasted coat with a tuberose in the buttonhole. He wore a formal panama hat with an Edwardian flourish to the brim. Lifar was identically garbed, but somehow, in spite of the natty armour, continued to look like a street urchin.

They sat down at my table. D. held himself very erect, speaking meekly in pidgin English. I couldn't think what animal he reminded me of – perhaps a mole or a very nice monkey.

I fumbled with the knotted strings of my portfolio. Diaghilev pompously, yet carefully, studied the sketches I brought forth, making no remarks but nodding like a mandarin and showing definite interest.... He looked carefully at every-thing. I asked his advice on one or two designs, and with astonishing sensitivity, he quickly indicated what was lacking or where each had failed. Some he said 'nice' to, others 'original'.

I gushed; I stammered and overdid the politeness. I spilled an avalanche of sketches and photographs I had never intended to show from the portfolio. Diag-hilev bent down with difficulty, taking up in his ringed fingers my picture of a double-reflected N and B [Nancy and Baba, his two sisters]. 'You take photo-graphs, too? I like this. It is very curious.' He smiled and went through the photo-graphs.

The waiter appeared. No, the gentlemen wouldn't have anything, as they must be going. Bows and exchanges of compliments. I thanked D. for seeing my things. He thanked *me* profusely.... Then they walked away.[189]

Diaghilev stayed about ten days in Florence, talking to Sitwell and lunch-ing at Montegufoni. They also lunched once or twice at Fiesole and Sit-well took him to see the gardens of the Villa Gamberaia.[190] Diaghilev, Kochno, Lifar and Berners went out to lunch with Contessa (Mimi) Pecci-Blunt at Marlia near Lucca,[191] where photographs were taken among the statues on the stage of the open-air theatre.[192] Balanchine and Dukelsky arrived together on 14 September.[193] The old Palace Hotel had a big room on the top floor, known as the Sala de Sta Caterina, with a piano, which was ideal for work and discussions, and there[194] Diaghilev, Berners, Sitwell and Balanchine worked on *Neptune*. Walking with Diaghilev one day through scented hedges of myrtle (perhaps in the Boboli Gardens), Balan-chine heard him exclaim, 'How delicious! Like pussy's piss!'[195] Berners did not really understand what was needed in the length and proportion of danced variations, so Diaghilev gave him the score of Tchaikovsky's *The Sleeping Beauty* as a model to study.[196] Balanchine remained working with Berners in Rome, while Diaghilev, Kochno and Lifar went on to Naples.

On 25 September Diaghilev was cabling Wollheim from the Hotel Quisi-sana, Capri.[197] On the twenty-eighth he was at Naples.[198] Between 2 and 12 October he was back in Rome, working, doubtless, with Berners and Balanchine;[199] on the fifteenth he was at the Grand Hôtel, Paris. He was in Milan on the twentieth, for Toscanini was conducting there the nine sym-phonies of Beethoven; and Kenneth Clark, who met him at the Cavour Hotel, was struck by his 'physical potency'.[200] On 22 October he was again in Paris, and Outhwaite summoned him to see Rothermere that evening.[201]

Rothermere insisted that London's Lyceum Theatre was ideal for a 'popular season'.[202]

The company began rehearsals in Paris on 1 November. There were fourteen new dancers, of whom Vera Petrova from Warsaw was the most important. Karsavina was there to teach the secrets of *The Firebird* to the younger generation, but the long, strenuous dance of the Firebird was too much for Nikitina and she could not carry on.[203] The Lyceum season, in which she was to have been given her biggest chances, would take place without her. Dubrovska and Danilova learned the Firebird's role instead. Nikitina always insisted that her relationship with the 'great and good' Lord Rothermere was purely platonic, in which case the wages of virtue were considerable – five-litre bottles of Chanel No. 5, a beige and blue Panhard car with a chauffeur to match, Chanel dresses which cost twenty thousand francs each[204] (the price Nijinska had asked for arranging *Romeo and Juliet*).

Now that Sokolova was the company's chief character dancer, she thought it beneath her dignity to be one of the twelve captive princesses in *The Firebird*. She also thought, having recently recovered from an operation, that she would do best to conserve her strength for leading roles; and she told Diaghilev so at a rehearsal.

He was outwardly calm but inwardly furious. In front of everybody he told me I should consider it an honour to dance in his corps de ballet, which was only good because principal dancers took their turn to dance in it. He reminded me how Dubrovska danced with twenty-three others in *Le Lac des Cygnes*, and how Tchernicheva was one of the Nurses in *Petrushka*. It was his right, he said, to decide which ballets I should dance, not mine; and there was a clause in the new contract I had signed the day before to that effect. I said that if I had known this I should not have signed it, and that in the next contract I would make a list of ballets I wished to dance. He told me in that case we should part company for ever. By this time tears were pouring down my cheeks.[205]

The Lyceum, sacred to Henry Irving, held nearly three thousand. It was possible to charge as little as seventeen shillings for the best seat. The front row of the gallery was bookable at 2s 4d, and there were unreserved seats at 2s and 1s. This was Lord Rothermere's idea of a 'popular season': it was a sign of the times. The Ballet opened on Saturday, 13 November. Woizikovsky was the first Faun the English had seen since Nijinsky, and, of course, many had never seen the ballet at all. Diaghilev had failed to extract from Picasso a new setting that pleased him, and the minimal anonymous décor was a mere sky and a rock.[206]

On 25 November the new *Firebird* was shown, and Lopukhova danced it. She had grown plump and Diaghilev made her wear gauze trousers.[207] *The Times* thought Gontcharova's setting (suggested by Diaghilev) for the final wedding, showing a hundred pink, red and gold domed churches piled one upon the other, was 'one of the most beautiful spectacles which this company has provided'.[208]

Sokolova had danced the Ballerina in *Petrushka* on the opening night. When it came to being one of the twelve princesses in *The Firebird*, the idea of which she had so much resented, she found she enjoyed it as much as ever. A huge bouquet of white flowers had arrived for her and she asked Grigoriev to have it handed to her after *Les Biches*. Grigoriev pointed out that the envelope was inscribed 'after *L'Oiseau de feu*', and that she would get it then or not at all. During the curtain calls, as she stood in line behind Lopukhova, Lifar and Tchernicheva, she felt self-conscious to be singled out by this enormous bouquet. It was her inscrutable employer's way of thanking and recompensing her; for the visiting-card inside the envelope bore Diaghilev's name.[209]

At last, on 12 December, came *The Triumph of Neptune*, and a triumph it was. The title has a baroque ring – Sacheverell Sitwell had published his *Southern Baroque Art* in 1924 – but the story was a mixture of naïve Victorian pantomime, Jules Verne and modern satire. On London Bridge a magic telescope has been set up, through which Fairyland can be seen. A journalist (M. Fedorov) and a gallant sailor (Lifar) determine to undertake the journey of exploration. Scene 2 is Cloudland, a classical interlude, with two Sylphs (Tchernicheva and Petrova). In Scene 3 the adventurers are seen bidding farewell – and as soon as the Sailor leaves on a bus, a Dandy (Tcherkass) sets about the seduction of his wife. Next the explorers are shipwrecked and saved by the Goddess (Sokolova). In Fleet Street, rival newspapers, *The Evening Telescope* and *The Evening Microscope*, compete for the latest news of the expedition. The Frozen Wood features Danilova as the Fairy Queen. The Dandy dances a polka with the Sailor's wife, and, when their shadows are seen on the blind, they are joined by that of the Sailor – with raised dagger. Policemen rush to arrest the murderer, but he vanishes to Fairyland. Ogres saw the Journalist in half; a drunken Negro, Snowball (Balanchine), upsets the telescope, the Sailor decides to marry Neptune's daughter (Danilova) and in the Apotheosis they dance a hornpipe together.

Sitwell had taken Diaghilev to visit two old shops dealing in toy theatres: Benjamin Pollock's in Hoxton and H. J. Webb's in Old Street. ('The two rivals expressed assumed surprise on hearing of the existence of the other.') 'Thus Pollock,' wrote Cyril Beaumont (quoting the account he had from Sitwell), 'who had once been visited by Robert Louis Stevenson, now received a call from Diaghilev.' The latter was delighted by the shop and the coloured sheets of scenes and characters. When he was invited into the inner sanctum, where the hand-colouring was done, he could only exclaim, 'C'est inouï!'[210] It was probably Diaghilev's and Sitwell's gluttony for these popular prints, an English equivalent of the *images d'Epinal*, that led them to include rather too many changes of scene in the production. One scene, containing a suicide by hanging, was suppressed in deference to the sensitivity of the Monte Carlo Casino management,[211] and two or three others were cut after the first night.

The music of Berners rose to the occasion. In the Schottische there was an imitation of bagpipes, and the wild yelping of Highlanders. The 'Waltz of Cloudland' seemed to be by an English member of 'Les Six' but had some Ravellian overtones. The interruption of the polka of the Sailor's Wife and the Dandy by a drunken voice singing 'The Last Rose of Summer' from Flotow's *Martha* was a funny surprise. The musical numbers for four Harlequins, for the Hornpipe and for the Apotheosis were smash hits.

During the final rehearsals the English Lydia Sokolova was sad to find she had no outstanding part in this English ballet, and she plucked up courage to tell Diaghilev so. This time 'He was not a bit angry. Perhaps for once he recognized that I was right, and that he had been careless to overlook me.... He said, "You must speak to Lord Berners."' Diaghilev and his court departed, with Berners, for lunch. 'When they came back Lord Berners told me that a perfect place for my appearance had been found. A gay hornpipe tune [it was the Schottische] was played during one of the scene changes [after the Shipwreck], and I was to dance this in front of the drop curtain....'

'Go and get a dance fixed up,' he said. George Balanchine had the quickest invention of any choreographer I ever knew. We went under the stage together and I showed him a few steps from the Scottish reel – one of which Ninette had taught me some time before. We hummed, sang and got the hornpipe organized in no time, without a pianist. Meanwhile the orchestra had continued rehearsing, as the ballet was to be run through again with the scenery. When my time came, George pushed me out on the stage on my correct beat, and I rattled through that dance without a mistake. To my amazement I had a round of tapping on the music-stands from the orchestra ... they knew that an hour before there had been no dance at all.[212]

Pruna made sketches for most of the costumes from the old twopence-coloured prints (though he received no acknowledgement for this).[213] Diaghilev delighted in mystifying journalists with the names of the Victorian designers, George and Robert Cruikshank, Tofts, Honigold and Webb.[214] Shervashidze executed the many scenes. Sacheverell Sitwell took 'dear old Mr Pollock' to see *Neptune* and always remembered 'how pleased he was to see the scenes he had known for a lifetime on an actual stage'. Pollock was the only man Sitwell had ever met who spoke with the Cockney accent of Dickens's day: like Sam Weller, he pronounced his 'v's as 'w's.[215]

Beaumont thought the three outstanding numbers were Sokolova's Schottische, Balanchine's solo as Snowball and the Hornpipe of Danilova and Lifar. Balanchine's drunken Negro dance was 'full of subtly contrasted rhythms, strutting walks, mincing steps, and surging backward bendings of the body borrowed from the cake-walk ... a paradoxical blend of pretended nervous apprehension and blustering confidence.'[216] Beaumont also admired the dance of the Harlequins. Balanchine, who already had one weak leg, was prodigious as the leading Harlequin, but after *Neptune* he gave up virtuoso dancing for good.[217]

Danilova's final costume oddly comprised a boater hat and trousers worn under her long ballet skirt. Bernard Shaw told her that she looked – in face – just like the young Queen Victoria.[218]

Massine's contract with Cochran had expired; and one evening, towards the end of the London season, Diaghilev came to Grigoriev, as he stood at the prompt corner during a performance, sat down on a chair and announced that Massine had again asked to return. 'I don't think we really need him. Besides, he'd be expensive and upset our budget.' Grigoriev suggested trying him at a figure so low that Diaghilev thought Massine would never agree to it. But he did.[219] Since he had become the owner of his Siren Islands, Massine was so intent on cultivating and beautifying them that he was afraid to be out of work.

After the London season ended on 11 December, the Russian Ballet passed through Paris, where Diaghilev was successful in engaging Spessivtseva at last, and went on to dance in Turin between 24 December and 6 January. Massine was waiting for them in Turin, where he quietly attended Tchernicheva's daily class along with everybody else.[220]

CHAPTER 17

1927–8

Fantastic experiments – Bibliomania – First
Collaboration of Stravinsky and Balanchine – Ida
Rubinstein in Competition

O N SPESSIVTSEVA'S FIRST PERFORMANCE after her return to the company, which was on the opening night in Turin, 2 January 1927, there took place an appalling drama – for in the world of ballet a wrong tempo takes on the proportions of an international incident. According to Grigoriev, the conductor Inghelbrecht, who had not worked with the Ballet since 1912, had a row about tempo with Diaghilev at a rehearsal of *L'Après-midi d'un faune*, and, although Diaghilev got his way, Inghelbrecht refused to speak to him again. It was therefore Massine whom Inghelbrecht asked about the tempo of the *adage* and Odette's *variation* in *Le Lac des Cygnes*; and Massine told him wrong.[1] Lifar wrote, 'The *pas de deux* was played at about half the speed we had got used to, which meant almost slow motion dancing.... The whole company, with bated breath, waited to see how we should acquit ourselves....'[2] 'Serge was used to Danilova', Sokolova commented, 'and was terrified of partnering anyone new (in the previous season at Monte Carlo he had almost dropped Dubrovska over the footlights).'[3] When the time came for Spessivtseva's *variation*, Kochno noted, 'Several times Spessivtseva extended one leg in a great *développé* and remained motionless on point, waiting seconds on end – they seemed interminable – for the measure that would allow her to change her position. Upright and unfaltering, she held herself on the point of one foot as if she were being sustained by a partner, and smiled at the marvelling audience.'[4] It should be remarked here, for the record, that Spessivtseva was the most unmusical of ballerinas.[5] Lifar claimed, 'I got the company together and we worked out a petition asking for Inghelbrecht's removal....'[6] Kochno recalled, 'No stationery was at hand in the theatre at midnight, and their petition was written out on a roll of lavatory paper.'[7] Whether Diaghilev was annoyed at the joint action of the company, or because he had some reason for pinning the blame on Lifar, he got Grigoriev out of bed (according to the latter) to witness his rebuke of the unfortunate *premier danseur*. ' "What do you say to tonight's *Lac des Cygnes* as danced by our principals?" "Not very good." "Not very *good*! It was shameful. However badly a ballet may be conducted, it can always be danced in *time*. But Mlle Spessivtseva, if you please, contrived to finish her *variation* no less than *two bars late*. As for M. Lifar, I *died* of shame. . . . During the whole existence of our Ballet, never have people danced in such a fashion. . . ." and so on for about forty minutes.' Then he added 'in the most amiable tone: "Thank you. Now you must please go to bed. I'm sorry to have disturbed you at such an hour." '[8] Massine, the real culprit – if such he was – had forgotten, when he wrote his memoirs, that he was even in Turin at the time.[9] Inghelbrecht, in *his* memoirs, kept quiet about the episode.

Diaghilev's company had danced only once before at La Scala, Milan, and never would again. The few performances there in January 1927 meant much to him. He had made the mistake, however, probably on the advice of Cecchetti, of giving a predominantly classical repertoire – *Le Lac des Cygnes*, *Aurora's Wedding* and *Cimarosiana*, with *The Firebird* as a mild sample of Stravinsky and Fokine. The Milanese had expected more colourful Russian barbarities, and the Ballet's reception was lukewarm.[10]

Once the company were installed at Monte Carlo on 17 January, Diaghilev was badgered, as usual, for help with charity galas. He provided dancers for one in which Grand Duke Michael was interested. The Grand Duke had been expelled from Russia for marrying a commoner, although his wife, Countess Torby, was a granddaughter of Pushkin. After holding court for years at the fine mansion of Kenwood, between Hampstead and Highgate, north of London, they had found their funds cut off by the Revolution, and lived on a reduced scale in Cambridge Gate, Regent's Park. Sophie Torby possessed certain letters of Pushkin to his wife, Natalia, and she had been highly indignant that the Grand Duke Konstantin Konstantinovitch, when President of the Imperial Academy of Arts and Sciences before the war, had told her it was her duty to return these to Russia. Diaghilev had made no secret of the fact that he coveted the letters, and she promised to leave him one in her will. Naturally he was anxious to oblige her husband. In fact, Countess Torby died in September 1927, and Diaghilev duly received his Pushkin letter. He was subsequently able to buy the remaining eleven from the Grand Duke Michael, who was ill and hard-up, for about thirty thousand francs.[11]

The first job given to Massine was to make a new version of *Les Fâcheux*. Diaghilev's anxiety not to waste Braque's scenery and costumes, even if he considered Nijinska's version unsatisfactory, was understandable. Massine, devoted as ever to the old choreographic manuals of Feuillet and Rameau, tried to introduce an authentic eighteenth-century note into his dances. When the ballet was revived he danced Eraste himself.[12]

In the early 1930s the few people in England who wrote books about the dance (I exclude Cyril Beaumont), and who were then 'coming into power' on the emergence of an English ballet, tended to denigrate the latter-day creations of what I have called Diaghilev's Kochno period. Constant Lambert wrote sarcastically of Diaghilev's and Stravinsky's 'time travelling';[13] Haskell in his life of Diaghilev headed the 1922–9 section 'In Search of Lost Youth';[14] de Valois deplored the precarious nature of Diaghilev's company and his lack of understudies.[15] The young generation were therefore brought up to believe that the Russian Ballet fell into decline. In the 1940s Ninette de Valois told me that *Les Noces* was Diaghilev's only work of the twenties worth reviving. If she had said 'the greatest work of the twenties' I could raise no objection. Revivability, however, is a doubtful criterion of excellence in ballet, which, of all the theatrical arts, most aspires to perfection in the *here and now*. The Kochno period engendered many wonderful works, whether they have been deemed fit for revival in our day or not. Some, even in the late 1970s, might be considered too 'advanced'. Nevertheless, it is true that the elements of certain late Diaghilev ballets were incongruously mixed, and that one element, music or décor, was sometimes far superior to the others. It is also true that music and décor often had to cover up the deficiences of an inadequate troupe. We have seen that *Zéphyr et Flore* and *Romeo and Juliet* were awkwardly concocted: *Pastorale* was perhaps too clever by half. *Les Biches*, *Les Matelots* and *The Triumph of Neptune*, on the other hand, were just right, even without great designers.

In 1927 Diaghilev was to produce two new works of extreme interest. In *Le Pas d'acier* (which I should translate as 'The Steel Dance'), music and décor were planned together by Prokofiev and Yakulov, and were perfectly matched. Not so the music and décor of *La Chatte*, by Sauguet and Gabo.

Diaghilev had first heard Sauguet's music when his comic opera, *Le Plumet du Colonel*, was given at the Champs-Elysées in 1924. Roger Desormière, who had graduated from flautist to conductor for the Russian Ballet in 1925, was also a great admirer of the young Sauguet: they were both Satie's followers, members of the so-called 'School of Arcueil'. Sauguet had thought of asking first Paul Eluard, then René Crevel, for a scenario:[16] but Diaghilev, who wanted merely a pretext for Spessivtseva to dance, found all that was necessary in a simple adaptation by Kochno of an Aesop fable. Sauguet was probably quite right in thinking the little-known Christian Bérard to be the designer who would best match his mysterious score, which was not free of Gounod's influence. Kochno relates how and why Bérard was rejected:

I had met Bérard at the home of my friend Pavel Tchelitchev, but ... it was Jean Cocteau who first spoke of him to Diaghilev as the coming great painter and stage designer. Unhappily, Cocteau, wishing to rival Diaghilev's gifts as a 'discoverer', insisted too emphatically on the fact that Bérard was 'his discovery'. This only irritated Diaghilev and made him hostile to Bérard even before they met.

The meeting was uncomfortable and disappointing. Sauguet took us to the eminently bourgeois town house of the painter's father, which in no way resembled the setting in which Diaghilev's imagination placed every young, unknown artist. He had never forgotten his first visit to Picasso's studio – ramshackle and freezing cold, with a window overlooking the Montparnasse cemetery – and from that day forth Diaghilev appeared to believe that wretched quarters guaranteed their inhabitant's genius. Walking with me through the streets of Paris after a performance, Diaghilev, when he noticed a lighted dormer window, would say, 'Who knows, perhaps a great artist is working up there whom we shall never meet!' ... Bérard was intimidated by our visit and was in an indescribable state of nerves. ... It was only when Diaghilev lost patience and got up to leave that Bérard brought himself to fetch a few small canvases to the conservatory where he was receiving us. Apparently unfinished, they represented some melancholy characters – street acrobats in dirty tights, youths on crutches lounging in front of brick walls, and so on. Not one of these sombre, austere paintings gave any hint of Bérard's genius as a designer or corresponded in the slightest to Diaghilev's theatrical concepts.

Diaghilev told Sauguet that he did not want the setting for this ballet to be 'like some concierge's hovel'.[17] Nevertheless, the young composer was thrilled to be writing a ballet for Diaghilev. He went to Monte Carlo in January, stayed in an hotel on the rock and delivered his numbers one by one, playing the piano at rehearsals himself. Rieti gave him some help with the orchestration.[18]

The story of Diaghilev's acquaintance with Naum Gabo went back to the latter's Paris Exhibition of 1924. The Jewish Gabo (whose real name was Naum Pevsner) and Anton Pevsner were brothers who had experienced all the ferment of revolutionary art, and known Tatlin and Malevitch before leaving Russia in 1922: but while Gabo was a sculptor of some renown in Berlin, Pevsner was a painter without a public in Paris. When Diaghilev had had further talks with Gabo at his flat in Lichterfelde in Berlin during autumn 1924 and winter 1925–6, the subject of Gabo's designing a ballet had been broached. Gabo was warned by his Dadaist friends Duchamp and Tzara to beware of Diaghilev. They, anyway, thought 'art' was finished. But Gabo did not. In 1926 Gabo signed a contract with Diaghilev, which was to come into force when he had produced a model and it had been approved. One reason he undertook the work was to help his brother Anton financially, for he insisted that the décor should be attributed to them both.

During the summer of 1926 Gabo stayed at his brother's flat near the Gare du Nord, and spent a week in a little dark, disused room making his model. He had brought his materials, including a non-inflammable plastic called Celon, from Berlin. Diaghilev climbed the stairs to examine the gleaming construction of transparent planes and curves against a curtain of shining black 'American cloth'. It took him no time at all to pass judgement. Looking up at the sculptor, he exclaimed, 'That's a real temple!'

Diaghilev said there must be a statue of a goddess. Gabo had turned so violently against representation in art that he gave this job to his brother, who had done no sculpture before. The rhomboidal Goddess was Pevsner's sole contribution, for Gabo designed the costumes as well as the set. The cat (into which the heroine was turned) was a big toy bought at a department store. The mouse was clockwork.

Gabo told me, 'Spessivtseva made difficulties about dancing on oil-cloth (which, in fact, was not slippery) and about wearing a mica head-dress with two horns. Shervashidze asked me to go and be nice to her. Diaghilev told her that I was trying to make her into a work of art. This made her indignant as she thought she was one already.' Rehearsals proceeded at Monte Carlo.

Diaghilev was afraid the setting would fall victim to the fire regulations, but Gabo was able to assure him that Celon was not inflammable. One day Gabo left the scenic studio where he worked, and where Massine had asked if he might sometimes come and practise in solitude, to visit the rehearsal room upstairs. He found Diaghilev, Sauguet and Balanchine at a loss how to arrrange the final *marche funèbre*. Gabo suggested that the six men should walk, rather than dance, to the music. He had wanted to introduce a kinetic element, and he offered to make out of wood geometrical objects for the men to carry – a square, a circle, perhaps an ellipse and a trapeze, which would be painted black on one side, white on the other. As they walked, they would rotate these rapidly in time with their steps, so that, when the black side was turned towards the public, the objects would become invisible. At the end, when the 'dead' body of Lifar was lifted, he was to be simultaneously encased in these geometrical shapes, which would form a monument around him as he was carried off.[19]

The male corps de ballet of six had pale-yellow tops and light-grey shorts: all wore mica helmets and metallic belts. Spessivtseva had a cone of mica over her white *tutu* and tights; Lifar, a semi-breastplate in mica, hung from his left shoulder, like the tunic of Daphnis.

Because his name appeared as author of so many ballets, Boris used the pseudonym 'Sobeka', which arcanely included Sauguet and Balanchine. The story of the man who prayed to Aphrodite that his beloved cat might be turned into a woman, only to find, when his prayer was granted, that she reverted to her former habits when a mouse appeared, and his consequent death through grief, was only a pretext for dancing. The ballet, planned as a 'vehicle' for Spessivtseva, became a milestone in the process of deifying Lifar. Diaghilev had given him a new nose and some education: Balanchine created for him a style, a neoclassic style, which became Lifar's own. After Diaghilev's death this Lifar style would degenerate into empty posturings, but from 1927 to 1929 it was breath-taking. All dancers are to some extent artificial products: but since Lifar lacked the weapon of effortless technique to win his magic battles, his beauty of face and figure had to be exploited to the full and his deficiencies concealed. Alexandra Danilova, now living with Balanchine since Tamara Gevergeva had left him, witnessed the process of Lifar becoming LIFAR, the Rudolph Valentino of the ballet. She had no doubt that Balanchine created him.[20]

He did wonders for his ballerina, too. Brought up in the strict classical style of Petipa, Olga Spessivtseva had never adapted herself successfully to the Fokine style – as Columbine, for instance – and she was hopeless in the modern ballets of Massine and Nijinska.[21] Yet Diaghilev had ordered Balanchine to make *La Chatte* expressly for her, sensing perhaps that the young choreographer was Petipa's heir and would bring out her essential quality. He warned Balanchine that she had no taste at all, saying that if she disliked the ballet it must be good, but if she liked it it would be awful. When rehearsals were well advanced, he came to the choreographer and murmured, 'Congratulations!'[22] Olga may have disliked the ballet, but she was wonderful in it, and Balanchine could indeed congratulate himself. Sauguet (a keen cat-lover) watched with fascination what he called the 'feminizing' of the cat, then the 'felinizing' of the woman. After Olga's sinister pursuit of the mouse into the wings, Lifar performed corkscrew turns in the air and fell dead.[23]

Gabo's structures of transparent material, both vertical and curved, 'rising against hangings of black "American oil-cloth", flashed, as they caught the light, their message of an amazing new plastic age to the incredulous and blinking public. ... The shining transparent armour worn by the dancers gave [the ballet] a heroic, interplanetary quality, as if the little tragedy ... was taking place in a society of godlike pioneers on a newly subjugated star. ... There have been few ballets in which the beauty of young people's bodies in motion was shown to better effect.'[24]

Just as in 1913 *The Rite of Spring* ought to have been designed not by Roerich, but by Picasso, so should Gabo's setting in 1927 have been matched with music by Webern. Yet Diaghilev's incongruously potent cocktail worked.[25] Once more his instinct was justified.

Before the opening night of the ballet at Monte Carlo on 30 April, Diaghilev ran into Gabo outside the Casino. The sculptor was wearing his day clothes, and Diaghilev pounced on him like a hawk, seized him by the coat and exclaimed, 'What is this? This is no way to dress for the theatre!' Gabo went away, changed into a dinner-jacket and returned. He missed the end of his ballet because he was sent for to be presented to the Princesse Héritière in the interval (as Diaghilev had known he would be, but had refrained from warning him). She raved about *La Chatte*, saying how much she disliked *terre-à-terre* ballets – but this was so different. *La Chatte* was an immediate success. To the composer, after the performance, Diaghilev said, with a slightly surprised smile, 'Well, it works!'[26] Sauguet would write twenty-six ballets in his life, but he was never treated so well as Diaghilev treated him when he was working on his first. He never forgot the quizzical way this man, more than twice his age, called him 'cher maître', or how tactfully Diaghilev led the conversation to the question of cuts (which Sauguet violently resisted) by referring to the advice he had given Rimsky-Korsakov and Stravinsky.[27]

Meanwhile Massine had been working on *Le Pas d'acier*, the conception of which, by Prokofiev and Yakulov, has been described above, and which was a ballet well suited to his choreographic imagination. 'In my own role as the young worker,' wrote Massine, 'I used strenuous character movements to suggest the Slav temperament and the conflict in the mind of a young man torn between his personal life and his national loyalty.'[28] The members of the corps de ballet had one bare and one booted foot, and Markova remembered, when they had to move mechanically up and down ladders, how hard it was.[29]

Massine complained to Diaghilev that Balanchine stole his ideas. He grumbled about Spessivtseva's supported *pirouette* in *La Chatte*, in which she slowly went down to the floor. 'I always wanted to do that,' he protested. Diaghilev replied, 'If it is so easy to steal your thoughts, please do not think.'[30]

When one considers the extraordinary constructions of Gabo for *La Chatte* and of Yakulov for *Le Pas d'acier*, the question looms: did Lord Rothermere know what was going on? On 14 March Wollheim had telegraphed, 'Rothermere wants to know which ballets to be given. No eccentric ones.'[31] A letter from Rothermere to Diaghilev survives in which he admits having written to Lady Cunard that he had heard some of the new works were 'ugly', and stresses his opinion that 'beauty' was important.[32]

Prokofiev was at Monte Carlo for the rehearsals of his ballet, and Stravinsky was at Nice. Igor had written nothing for the company since *Les Noces*, but he had prepared a surprise for Diaghilev's twentieth Paris season. Diaghilev hoped it was a new ballet. On the day he set off to get his surprise, Kochno saw Diaghilev 'leave Monte Carlo ... radiant and smiling, and return from Nice in the evening troubled and perplexed'. The surprise was *Oedipus Rex*.[33] Igor had insisted that the production of this opera-oratorio, with its text by Cocteau translated into Latin by Abbé Jean Daniélou, should be designed by his son Théodore, who had already made sketches. Diaghilev scribbled for Kochno the conventional Greek temple-palace he had been shown, and which he did not like.[34] He decided that, if the curtain rose on a décor, the audience would look forward to dancing, and Igor had emphasized his wish for a static, oratorio-like production of what was nevertheless an opera. Diaghilev may have been right in giving *Oedipus* as a concert work, but he disappointed his audience, just the same.

On 10 April Diaghilev cabled Ansermet at Geneva, 'Can you conduct Paris season 27 May till 10 June? Create Oedipus. Probably leave South America August till November including voyage. Come with us. Try come here before 15 April see me and Igor.'[35] On 13 April Stravinsky telegraphed that Ansermet had arrived and that they expected Diaghilev that afternoon:[36] but it was, in fact, the composer who conducted *Oedipus* in Paris – and the South American tour never came off.

The Ballet were again going to the Liceo at Barcelona (with a stop at Marseilles en route) in mid-May; their Paris season was to be again at the Sarah Bernhardt: but there was confusion over London. His Majesty's broke an undertaking and there was no choice but the Prince's.

Diaghilev was only in Barcelona for the week beginning Sunday, 8 May. It was here that he heard that the company were planning some celebration in Paris for his twentieth anniversary, and, detesting anniversaries as he did, he made a little speech on stage, begging them not to. 'A jubilee', he said, 'is the beginning of the end; something that rounds off a career. But I am not ready to give up. ... I wish to remain always young.'[37] Diaghilev hated to acknowledge that he was ageing and resisted the importunities of painters – Picasso, Delaunay, Gris and Pruna – who wanted to make portraits in which he might be forced to face the ravages of time. Only exceptionally did he allow Boris to photograph him.[38]

Diaghilev realized that Kochno's mother often thought, as mothers do, that her 'heartless son' neglected her. Unknown to Boris, he wrote to her on 26 May, telling her how busy her son was, and inviting her to come 'at any time of the day' to watch a rehearsal at the Théâtre Sarah Bernhardt, where he would always be delighted to welcome her.[39]

To herald the appearance in Paris of the Russian Ballet's new star, whom he planned to call 'Spessiva', as he had in London, Diaghilev wrote an article, headed 'Olga Spessivtseva', for *Le Figaro*. This appeared on 26 May 1927, on the day before the opening of the Paris season and the revelation of *La Chatte*.

The first night of the Russian Ballet tomorrow will see the début of a new dancer, Olga Spessiva. Admittedly a ballerina of almost the same name has been dancing for two seasons at the Opéra, but for one reason or another the Mdlle Spessivtseva of the Opéra was not appreciated by the most sensitive audience in the world, the Paris public.

I have always thought that there is a limit to the joy a man can experience in his lifetime; that only one Taglioni or one Patti appears in a generation. Having seen Pavlova in my youth, and in hers, I was certain that she was 'the Taglioni of my time'. I was therefore amazed to recognize in Spessiva a nobler and purer artist even than Pavlova. That is saying a great deal.

Our great ballet master Cecchetti, who created Nijinsky, Karsavina and so many more, was saying only this winter, during a lesson at La Scala in Milan: 'An apple came into the world; and when it was cut in two, one half became Pavlova, the other Spessiva.' And I would add that, to me, Spessiva is the half which has been exposed to the sun.

I hope I may be allowed to say this after twenty years of work in the theatre. I am happy to find that, after all this time, during which hundreds of dancers have passed before me, I can still present such artists as Massine, Balanchine, Woizikovsky, Danilova, Tchernicheva and Sokolova in Paris. My joy is all the greater when remembering how I began twenty years ago with Pavlova and Nijinsky, I come to Spessiva and Lifar. The former pair have become legendary. The latter, very different from their predecessors, stand before you, waiting their turn to pass into legend – that fair, too flattering legend of the Russian Ballet's fame.[40]

This was going a bit far, and Nemesis did not delay. That very morning, during a class with Egorova, Spessiva hurt her foot, and her doctor said there was no question of her dancing on the following night.

Some people concerned, including Gabo, thought this was a diplomatic accident. So did Sauguet, to whom, when he called despairingly at her flat, Olga opened the door, showing no sign of a limp or a bandage.[41] It is true that Spessivtseva, who was always under the influence of some Svengali or other, had been assured by the diehard classicist Sergeyev that, if she persisted in dancing Diaghilev's awful modern ballets, she was certain to do herself an injury: so she had been prepared to hurt herself.[42] (A fortnight later, in London, Diaghilev received telegrams from his own Paris physician, Dr Dalimier, stating that Spessiva 'would be able to dance';[43] and from Spessivtseva, saying, 'I have pain in my foot when I dance although doctor permission – verry unhappy.'[44]) Was *La Chatte* to be postponed; and, if not, who could learn Spessiva's role in one day? Balanchine insisted that Danilova knew it already.

That afternoon, at her hotel, Nikitina received an urgent message from Pavka that Diaghilev wanted to see her. She was not, of course, for the moment a member of the company, but she had been taking class and gathering strength; and she went to the theatre. Diaghilev, she related, made her promise to say 'Yes' to anything he asked. 'Even if you asked me to marry you?' she asked. 'Yes, even to that,' he replied. After a long duel she agreed. Then Diaghilev said, 'Alice, you are dancing *La Chatte* tonight.' At the Mogador, where she went to rehearse with Lifar, Balanchine put up some resistance, as he wanted Danilova to dance: but there, and back on the set at the Sarah Bernhardt, Nikitina learned the outlines of the cat role in under two hours. Spessivtseva's costume was taken in for her during the first ballet of the evening. She appeared on stage, to find a pale, thin young man, walking up and down nervously: this was Sauguet.[45] Nikitina got through her ordeal successfully. Her streamlined modern chic suited the choreography and the designs of Gabo. She and Lifar enjoyed a greater acclaim than ever before. Paris had had its 'frisson nouveau'.

488

On 30 May, Stravinsky conducted *Oedipus Rex*. Princesse Edmond de Polignac had paid for the singers and the rehearsals: but, as Stravinsky wrote, 'Once more I had to suffer [as with *Mavra*] from the conditions under which my work was presented: an oratorio sandwiched between two ballets!' The ballet audience could not concentrate on 'something purely auditive'; and the composer would be much happier when the work was later staged in Berlin as an opera by Klemperer, or even by mere concert performances. *Oedipus* was given twice again in Paris.[46]

Diaghilev's old friends from Imperial Russia were disgusted that he should dally with the USSR. Although Benois no longer saw Diaghilev daily, he still went to the ballet, and the episode in the first scene of *Le Pas d'acier*, in which hungry noblewomen exchanged their possessions for food, struck him as a shameful mocking of the old régime, whose traditions were dear to him. Perhaps Diaghilev had reservations about this scene, too, but, having given Yakulov a free hand (after failing to engage as director either Tairov or Meyerhold, both of whom had refused to leave Russia), he may not have wished to tamper.[47] He had foretold the new régime and he was fascinated by the revolutionary art-forms it had produced. Although he had lost members of his family in the Revolution, he responded, as Isadora had when she accepted Lunatcharsky's invitation to open a school in Moscow, to the idea of a new world based on the liberty, equality and brotherhood of man. Benois, who had gone hungry in the new Russia, and had received a tirade from Malevitch,[48] did not see any point even in Russia's revolutionary art. Lifar noticed that when Yakulov arrived with Ilya Ehrenburg, neither Nuvel nor Koribut-Kubitovitch, whom Diaghilev sometimes allowed to go hungry in the capitalist West, would have anything to do with them, and 'ostentatiously refused to carry out their secretarial duties'. This made Diaghilev kinder and politer than ever.[49] He expected a White Russian demonstration at the first night of the ballet on 8 June – even attempts at assassination – and when *Le Pas d'acier* was greeted with applause, relieved by only a few cat-calls, he was rather disappointed and thought the public 'spineless'.[50] So wrote Lifar, but Kochno thought *Le Pas d'acier* 'a unanimous success'.[51] In the last three numbers of the ballet, 'The Factory', with its thunderous monotony, 'The Hammers', *moderato pesantissimo*, and the thumping, clanging 'Finale', with its trombones and trumpets, the flashing lights, the whirring wheels and the wielding of huge hammers contributed to a thrilling apotheosis of the machine age.[52]

Fritz Lang's famous film *Metropolis*, based on Ernst Toller's play and made in Ufa Studios near Berlin, came out in the following year. This masterpiece of the Expressionist cinema also had as its subject the machine age, but, instead of glorifying the worker, it showed prophetically how the State, symbolized by the City – Metropolis – reduced men to machines in its service. Perhaps the film, which has become a 'classic', owed something to the ballet, which has been forgotten.

The only real row that took place was between Cocteau and Dukelsky in the wings, and, as with many 'rows', it is hard to understand exactly how and why it happened. Cocteau, who, as a poet, saw the glorious possibilities of the new Russia, thought Massine had made a merely frivolous variation on the Soviet theme. 'Dukelsky', wrote Kochno, 'overheard Cocteau criticizing the choreography' and, 'mistaking the target of his attacks ... interrupted with some impertinence and insulted Cocteau, who lost his habitual restraint and slapped him. This scene took place in semi-darkness backstage, and for the moment passed unnoticed. ...'[53] Whatever the composer misunderstood, he was a flashy dresser, and the superimposition in the poet's mind of the image of this well-fed amateur-dandy on that of the hungry, struggling, idealistic masses of the new Republic must have produced the spark which caused the explosion. According to Dukelsky, who had sat through the ballet in Diaghilev's box with Prokofiev, he took the older composer, whom he greatly admired, into the corridor 'for a smoke', and told him that his 'massive, sinewy music' would 'deliver a crushing blow to the decadent Parisian *musiquette*'. They spoke in Russian, but Cocteau caught the last word; he screamed, 'Dima, les Parisiens t'envoyent de la merde!' and struck Dukelsky. Then (still according to the latter) Diaghilev begged him not to start a fight – 'I've enough trouble with the authorities already – we could be deported'; and Cocteau reappeared with a crowd of disciples, crying, 'Hit me back, Dima!' Dukelsky challenged him to a duel, and, after more encounters and harangues, left the theatre with Mme Paitchadze, wife of the music publisher, Stravinsky's agent.[54] Next day Kochno received a letter from Cocteau:

I very much regret having caused a disturbance on Serge's stage, but in view of Dima's mug, his rose, top hat and Louis xv cane, his denunciation of Parisian frivolity was hard to take. ... He shielded himself at the stage door by offering his arm to a lady. ... Do tell Serge how much I regret this incident. ... My views were of an aesthetic as well as of a moral order. I do reproach Massine for having turned something as great as the Russian revolution into a cotillion-like spectacle within the intellectual grasp of ladies who pay six thousand francs for a box. I was not attacking the composer or the stage designer.[55]

No duel was fought.

Diaghilev's belief in Prokofiev's talent was in no way diminished by this work, which was rougher in its harmonies than *Chout*. He asked him for another ballet: but neither of them could think of a subject on the spur of the moment.[56]

As often before, the Paris season closed on a Saturday and the London season – this time at the Prince's – opened on the Monday following – this year, on 14 June. Diaghilev, Kochno and Lifar were staying again at Albemarle Court. Nikitina was more luxuriously accommodated. Now that 'my position as star dancer had become established Lord R. considered it a good reason to make me lead an increasingly comfortable life, insisting that I should live in the best hotels. The apartment he had reserved for me in London seemed to me paradise in comparison with what my salary would have allowed me.' Some of the scenery for *La Chatte* had not arrived in time for the Monday performance, and Diaghilev sent Nikitina out in front of the curtain to make a speech which Wollheim had written for her. Wearing 'a black dress from Chanel', she said, 'Ladies and Gentlemen. I have a sad announcement to make. The Southern Railway has not yet delivered a large part of the scenery for *La Chatte*. Therefore I will be unable to dance for you tonight. But my colleagues will dance for you *Carnaval* instead. But please come tomorrow, when you will see my performance. Thank you.'[57] Rothermere sent Diaghilev good wishes from the Lido.[58]

By the next evening, the missing parts of what a stage-hand called 'the fucking greenhouse' were assembled, and Cyril Beaumont watched Lifar glueing a silver sequin to each eyelid.[59] Even Beaumont, although his taste was growing conservative in middle age, found something 'intensely refreshing and exhilarating' in *La Chatte*, and thought it had 'power to convey much more forcefully than ballets directly inspired by classical mythology, something of that ideal of physical beauty which was the dominant motive in the dance festivals of the ancient Greeks'.[60] It became and remained a favourite work

There was much correspondence that June about a German and East-European tour which Nuvel was arranging for the autumn.[61] The Prince's Theatre complained on 20 June that money owed them by Diaghilev was overdue, and held him responsible if the Lord Chamberlain closed the theatre because some of his scenery was inflammable.[62] The sets of *Le Pas d'acier* and *Prince Igor* should, according to Nuvel, arrive on the twenty-first or twenty-second.[63] Miss Wiborg was At Home for Manuel de Falla, who was in London to conduct his *Retablo* and play his Concerto, on 22 June at 10.30, and there would be music.[64] Mrs Rose Morley had a supper-party on the twenty-seventh, the night of a Stravinsky programme, and her sister [Comtesse Louis Gautier-Vignal] said she should ask Stravinsky, but as she did not know him, would Diaghilev bring him?[65] There was a new dance for Idzikovsky as Cupid in *Neptune*, which *The Times* thought was 'a burlesque, all the funnier for being carried out with the utmost gravity, of the old school of male dancer'.[66] Diaghilev laughed at this till the tears ran down his face.[67] Diaghilev must have missed Falla, for on 24 June he telegraphed to Nuvel in Paris, 'Falla arrives Paris 6.15 from London. Ask if he can play concerto and conduct *Tricorne* next week or Monday 4th. Go up to 50 pounds including fare.'[68] Nuvel replied that Falla regretted he had absolutely to return to Spain the next day.[69] On 27 June there was a Stravinsky evening, with the composer conducting *Petrushka*, *Pulcinella* and *Firebird* in the presence of King Alfonso. On the same day Geoffrey Keynes, brother of Maynard, wrote to Diaghilev proposing his ballet *Job*, with music by Ralph Vaughan Williams and décor by Gwen Raverat after William Blake. His sister-in-law, Lydia Lopukhova, had already spoken to Diaghilev about this, and he enclosed a volume of Blake's engravings and tickets for a Blake exhibition in Savile Row.[70] (Writing to Gwen Raverat, Vaughan Williams professed to be 'glad on the whole' that Diaghilev rejected this. 'Can you imagine *Job* sandwiched between *Les Biches* and *Cimarosiana* – and that dreadful pseudo-cultured audience saying to each other "My dear, have you seen God at the Russian Ballet?" ')[71] Diaghilev was in correspondence with Kurt Weill about a ballet which his old friend Harry von Kessler had proposed to him, and which came to nothing.[72] To celebrate the revival of *Les Matelots*, some of the 'Bright Young Things' gave a 'Matelots Party', to which Lytton Strachey went as an admiral and Tallulah Bankhead as a little boy in his first white sailor suit.[73] When *Le Pas d'acier* was given on 4 July, Diaghilev was prepared for trouble, as London was extremely anti-Bolshevik; and he decided to sit in the orchestra pit, next to the first flautist. 'I'm carrying my revolver,' he said, 'and at the first signs of any demonstration I shall fire it in the air.' The ballet was not interrupted, however; and, at the end, when the audience looked anxiously at the Duke of Connaught's box, the Tzaritsa's first cousin once removed led the applause, which turned into a 'stupendous ovation'. 'Diaghilev made his way out of the orchestra, more than ever perplexed by the unpredictable English.'[74] On 7 July there was a Gala for King Fuad of Egypt, which boasted three *chefs d'orchestre*; Beecham conducted *Carnaval*, Goossens *Neptune* and Malcolm Sargent *Aurora's Wedding*. Goossens was taken ill a few days afterwards and replaced at the shortest notice by young Sargent, who conducted on 11 July the first of two performances of *Mercure*. On the same afternoon Nicolas Kopeikin played Rimsky-Korsakov's Piano Concerto. Desormière arrived to replace Goossens (at the same fee and on condition he stayed at least twelve days).[75] Diaghilev suddenly decided to give Balanchine's *Chant du rossignol*, but he lacked the orchestral parts, which were in Paris. On the 'Quatorze Juillet' Nuvel telegraphed: 'Today everything shut. Paitchadze will send Rossignol tomorrow air.'[76] On 13 July Diaghilev and Lifar lunched with the Saxton Nobles at Kent House, Knightsbridge,[77] and heard his old acquaintance Vladimir Tchernikov play at the house of Lady Hawtrey (widow of the actor Charles) at 37 Hereford Street, Park Lane.[78] Two days later there was another Gala for King Alfonso, for which Lopukhova made a come-back. When the King asked her, 'How is your husband?', she replied, 'Very well, thank you. How is your wife?'[79] *Le Chant du rossignol*, in Balanchine's version, was given for the first time in England on the seventeenth. Markova was considered too young to wear in London the revealing all-over tights, and some transparent white pyjamas were made for her.[80] On 18 July Kettner's, a favourite Soho restaurant of Diaghilev's, wrote pointing out that he had not replied to their letter, and asked for a settlement of their account.[81] There had been some dodgy dealing by Zenon, a mysterious old Russian to whom Diaghilev entrusted large sums of money,[82] and who had helped with the negotiations between Diaghilev and Stoll in 1918,[83] and Wollheim took action against him, with the result that on 20 July Diaghilev was summoned by an order of court to give evidence at the chambers of Mr Francis Watt, 1a Middle Temple Lane.[84] Diaghilev and Lifar spent a sunny Sunday with Eric and Dorothy Wollheim and their children at their house at Walton-on-Thames.[85]

Lady Hawtrey asked if she might come to Diaghilev's box on the last night of the season, 23 July, when an unprecedented ceremony took place. 'A real friendship' had grown up between Diaghilev and Eugene Goossens, and the conductor thought his employer was so thorough a musician that he could have conducted the orchestra himself 'without a qualm'. They had lunched together that day at the Carlton Grill, along with 'the ever-present Kochno and Lifar'. After the performance, wrote Goossens, 'Diaghilev ... appeared on the stage while I was taking a call. With no attempt at a speech, he smilingly handed me a small package, and walked quickly off again without waiting to acknowledge the outburst which greeted him. The package contained an engraved gold fountain-pen ... with which ... I wrote two operas.'[86] Mr A. Eumorfopoulos had written from Winchester a week before to ask if the season could not be extended by one week so that he could see *Petrushka*,[87] but his wish was not granted, and Diaghilev left impatiently for Venice, arriving at the Grand Hôtel des Bains before the end of the month.[88]

Diaghilev's thoughts were on his book collection. On 8 August he sent Kochno in Paris 1,800 francs to pay a bookseller, with the warning, 'Don't buy incomplete copies.'[89] By the eleventh he had moved to the Albergo Luna on the Grand Canal.[90] The American impresario Ray Goetz came to see him in Venice, and began negotiations for an American tour which would be continued by Massine after Diaghilev's death and only broken off because of the Depression of 1930.[91] But Diaghilev was longing to get to Poland to buy books. Between two visits to Milan, where he stayed at the Cavour Hotel and negotiated with Giovanna of the Geneva theatre for a visit to Switzerland, he made a trip with Boris to Rome to get his Polish visa.[92] Rome, too, was a good hunting-ground for Russian books, as so many Russians had lived there in the nineteenth century. There was one famous collector Diaghilev was anxious to meet. His collection, it turned out, consisted of twelve books – including such things as Shakespeare's First Folio. From him Diaghilev bought one of the only seven known copies of the first

Russian grammar, from the press of Ivan Fedorov, and, from the same press, a 'Book of Hours', dated 1564, of which only two other copies were known.[93] Diaghilev and Boris spent a night or two in Florence on their way back to Milan,[94] where Lifar was working with Cecchetti.[95]

On 30 September Diaghilev was in Monte Carlo, renewing his contract and enjoying his books. Then – joy of joys! – Stravinsky had a new ballet for him. He wrote to Lifar:

Here I am, sorting out books, covered with sweat, dust and cockroaches, the place full of an uncanny silence, no one about. ...

My dear, arriving here I found a note from Stravinsky, in which he says he came round, intending to ask me to dinner, but was told I was not yet back. As next day he was leaving for London I went over to Nice in the morning, not having seen anyone in Monte Carlo, to catch Igor before he left. I spent the whole day with him, and at five saw him off at the station. It was an immensely satisfactory meeting. He himself had only got back from the mountains the day before I returned. ... I went to see him *alone*. After lunch he played me the first half of the new ballet. It is, of course, an amazing work, extraordinarily calm, and with a greater clarity than anything he has so far done; a filigree counterpoint round transparent, clear-cut themes, all in the major key; somehow music not of this world, but from somewhere above. ...[96]

This ballet was *Apollon Musagète*, commissioned by the American, Mrs Elizabeth Sprague Coolidge. Its first performance, with choreography by Adolf Bolm, was to take place in the Library of Congress in April 1928, but Stravinsky had reserved the European rights for Diaghilev.

On the whole [continued Diaghilev], one feels it is part Glinka and part sixteenth-century Italian, though without any intentional Russianizing. He played it over to me three times running, so that I have the clearest idea of it now. The Adagio *pas d'action* has a broad theme very germane to us today; it runs concurrently in four different tempi, and yet, generally speaking, the harmony is most satisfactory. I embraced him and he said: 'It's for you to produce it properly for me: I want Lifar to have all sorts of flourishes. ...'

When the train was already moving out, he shouted to me, 'Find a good title!'[97]

Having signed his contract with the Casino satisfactorily, Diaghilev had nothing to keep him in Monte Carlo, and he set off, book-hunting.[98] He did not however, get to Warsaw that year.

Diaghilev travelled with the company during part of their long German tour. Nikitina only joined them in Budapest, where they danced from 19 November until 17 December, and in her absence Markova danced *La Chatte*.[99] The Russian Ballet performed three times at the Vienna Opera, which gave Diaghilev particular pleasure. In the theatre where he had heard his first opera, his ballet danced *his* creations: *Le Tricorne*, *La Boutique fantasque*, *Les Biches* and *La Chatte*. But there was a drama one night at the

Hotel Bristol. A German girl had been following Lifar around, as Romola de Pulszky had followed Nijinsky. One night Lifar woke up to find her in his bed. He disposed of her, but when Diaghilev came in could only explain the smell of scent by breaking a large bottle of the ubiquitous Chanel No. 5 in the bath.[100]

Diaghilev's real passion in winter 1927 was not for Lifar so much as for his Russian library, and he only made jealous scenes out of habit. After four performances in Geneva the company were back in Paris to give two galas at the Opéra on 27 and 29 December.

Lydia Sokolova had been left behind, ill, in London and had thus missed the long tour. She rejoined the company in Paris and was about to begin rehearsing again, in the last week of the year, when she was stricken with a sharp pain in her right side and continual sickness. Diaghilev was kindness itself. He sent her a celebrated surgeon, who arrived at the hotel in the rue de Moscou, in a white coat, straight from an operation. She was moved to a clinic at Neuilly, and given a lumbar puncture. When Diaghilev visited her, she was too weak, after constant haemorrhage, to talk. When the Ballet stopped to perform at Lyon and Marseille on their way back to Monte Carlo, Diaghilev telephoned at each town to enquire after her; and his affectionate messages cheered her up.[101]

Would Lord Rothermere continue to finance the Russian Ballet? Could the London season take place at Covent Garden? These were two all-important questions in Diaghilev's mind while the company ran in their normal groove of classes, rehearsals, rest and sunshine at Monte Carlo during the first months of 1928. In a series of letters and telegrams we can read of the negotiations, the anxiety, the increasing part played by Lady Juliet Duff on the English side of Diaghilev's affairs, and of how the answer to both questions was eventually No.[102] The season would be at His Majesty's, and Juliet formed a committee of patronage whose members subscribed a few hundred pounds each.[103]

Stravinsky and Balanchine were about to embark on the first of their collaborations, neither guessing that the most blessed partnership in the history of ballet was being established. On 22 January Stravinsky telegraphed from Nice to Diaghilev at Monte Carlo, 'Come with Balanchine tomorrow 4. Am free till 7. Be punctual because very busy before departure.'[104]

There was a long rehearsal period, while the dancers took part in operas; their Monte Carlo season did not open till 4 April. One night, when Kochno and Lifar were bored, they summoned Dubrovska and Danilova to play cards at the Hôtel de Paris. While this secret debauch was going on, the door half opened, and an extended arm was seen, holding a bottle of lemonade. This was Diaghilev's way of miming the fears of an innocent youth who finds himself in a gaming hell.[105]

It is doubtful whether Diaghilev kept his private expenditure separate from that of the Russian Ballet. He paid himself no salary, but he stayed at the best hotels and lived well. Though Lifar was paid, Kochno was not. Diaghilev paid for both their clothes and lodging. Doubtless some of what might be considered the Ballet's money went towards his collection of books, which perhaps, as Lifar wrote, 'endangered the very future of the Ballet',[106] but which was designed to enrich the world. Early in 1928 Diaghilev decided to raise money, needed as much for the Ballet as for his library, by selling, with Picasso's consent, the curtain of *Le Tricorne*, and two of the 'boxes' and the 'still-life' from *Cuadro Flamenco*, which had been painted largely by Picasso himself; and he approached Rosenberg, one of Picasso's two dealers. With his own hands Diaghilev cut up the precious canvas.[107] On 5 May Rosenberg telegraphed that the deal was clinched.[108] Diaghilev would receive what he had named as his bottom price, 175,000 francs, for the curtain, which had been bought by a German, Dr Reber.[109] On that day Diaghilev had only 16,700 francs in his bank.[110] Diaghilev was surprisingly vague over this – perhaps he was incredulous of the acceptance of his high price – for, before the sale was concluded, he telegraphed to ask Nuvel whether it was the curtain for *Parade* or that for *Le Tricorne* which Rosenberg was selling.[111] The former had an immense painted area, and, though more precious because earlier and largely painted by Picasso, would have been much harder to place.[112] The pictorial centre of the latter, showing a box at a bull-ring, was a square brush-drawing. Diaghilev had cut off the two blank sides, which made it more manageable.[113]

Diaghilev's two new ballets for 1928 had in common that they both aimed at the sublime. *Ode* gave endless trouble. The realization of *Apollon Musagète* was simplicity itself.

The makers of *Ode* were as follows: Nicolas Nabokov, who, in spring 1927, had played Diaghilev part of an unfinished cantata based on an ode in honour of the Empress Elizabeth Petrovna by her court poet Lomonossov – 'An evening meditation on the Majesty of God on observing the Aurora Borealis' (the Empress Elizabeth being equated with that northern phenomenon); Diaghilev, who became enthusiastic about presenting this as an eighteenth-century spectacle based on engravings of court balls and of the coronation festivities of the Empress;[114] Boris Kochno, who prepared a scenario along these lines; Pavel Tchelitchev, who, after agreeing to make designs which would realize this concept, got carried away by his longing to do something totally new in the theatre; Pierre Charbonnier, a filmmaker, whom Tchelitchev asked to devise projections and neon lighting effects; and Massine, who was expected to fuse all these ideas by his choreography.

Tchelitchev, a witty, sensitive and intelligent man, was a mixture of the wordly and the other-worldly. He wanted to shine in society, to be acknowledged as the greatest painter of the day: but he believed in magic, horoscopes and Tarot cards, and was always in search of the secret of the universe. He had not designed for the theatre for five years: his colourful Berlin productions he dismissed as youthful peccadilloes. He was eager to show how much he was superior not only to the other neo-Romantics, Bérard, Eugène Berman and Berman's brother Leonid, with whom he had exhibited at the Druet Gallery in 1926, but to Picasso himself. Incidentally, he drew very well; he had a soaring imagination which made his paintings too literary for admirers of the school of Paris; and he would become before his death (in 1956) the supreme technician of the age. The Empress Elizabeth was thrown overboard, and, as Kochno wrote, 'When Diaghilev saw that Tchelitchev was moving away from the initial concept of the production he lost interest and asked me to take over the supervision of the assorted work in progress for *Ode*.'[115]

Allen Tanner was present when Tchelitchev expounded *his* scenario (with which Kochno was by then presumably in agreement) to Diaghilev:

With luminous diadem and in phosphorescent white a female figure, Nature (Isis), looks like a great Doric column as she stands on a pedestal of slowly moving clouds being projected photographically from behind. ... Awaiting her stands the Student (Initiate or Disciple of Isis), holding a large open book. He wears a costume imitating that of a French cleric of the time of Louis XV, tight, semi-transparent, emphasizing his limbs.... The blue gauze curtain has separated ... disclosing a large circle of transparent white gauze shaded to look like a sphere, the Earth. Visible behind it a large circular platform on which are dancers in pale blue leotards, without faces, but with their costumes marked by luminous geometrical figures, the Constellations. ...

'There are to be pin wheels of neon light,' explained Tchelitchev, 'representing distant nebulae and spirals representing comets: a galaxy of celestial manifestations. ...' Diaghilev exclaimed, 'Incendiary! Poisonous! Are you mad? Forbidden!' Tchelitchev continued, 'Wait! On backdrops motion pictures will be projected. The Moon will sail past, then nature will grow before the eyes, flowers and fruit, geometrical forms like natural phenomena. ... Five projection machines will be necessary, perhaps to be placed on a bridge near the ceiling of the theatre....' 'You are insane and your ideas are terrible!' said Diaghilev. Then, to Kochno, 'All right, it is your child, Boris, go ahead! But if you give birth to a monster, I'll disown you.'[116]

When young Nabokov arrived in April at Monte Carlo, full of anticipation, he found Diaghilev on the stage, watching a rehearsal of *Apollon*, and he was disappointed by his greeting. 'Ah, Nika, why are you so late? Everybody has been waiting for you to start working.' Walking back with him to the Hôtel de Paris, Diaghilev warned Nabokov, 'Boris doesn't know what he wants to do with *Ode*, and Massine knows even less. As for Tchelitchev,

497

I can't make head or tail of his experiments. . . .' As he talked, he grew 'more and more irritated and the adjectives he used became more abusive'. 'If all of you finally decide to start working, don't pull the cart in three directions!'[117] Through no fault of Nabokov's, that is what happened. The composer had supper with Boris and Alexandrina Trussevitch; and they tried to cheer him up. When Nabokov saw some of Massine's dance arrangements – and he worked with him daily from ten to one – he felt 'an inherent anomaly' in their collaboration. The only hint he received in Monte Carlo of Tchelitchev's plans was when he was needed to time some film sequences of 'young men wearing fencing masks and tights diving in slow motion', which Kochno told him represented 'the element of water'.[118]

In comparison with *Ode*, *Apollon Musagète* was plain sailing. There were two scenes. The first, called 'The Birth of Apollo', was very short and consisted of mime only. The second had eight dances and an Apotheosis. Thus, while Stravinsky turned in his string orchestra towards classical models, so did his ballet shape itself as a series of clearly defined dance numbers, such as Petipa might have laid down. Balanchine and he saw eye to eye from the start.

While these rehearsals were in progress during April, Prokofiev and Dukelsky arrived in Monte Carlo from a gastronomic tour – Dukelsky with an attack of liver. Prokofiev encouraged the younger composer to play Diaghilev his First Symphony, which he did, Kochno and Nabokov also being present. 'Diaghilev was on his best diplomatic behaviour and all he said was, "A very good symphony, but I like *Zéphyr* better." '[119]

Diaghilev had asked Boris to think of a subject for Prokofiev's next ballet – 'something simple which would not need to have a long scenario printed on the programme, as had *Chout* and *Le Pas d'acier*, and something which would be familiar to everyone'. Boris thought of the Parable of the Prodigal Son from St Luke's Gospel. The composer liked the idea at once.[120]

As a compliment to England, to please Beecham and in doing so to show gratitude for her help to Lady Cunard, who adored Sir Thomas, Diaghilev decided to arrange another new ballet, which should have its first performance in London. He knew that Handel was one of the English maestro's favourite composers; and he asked for a selection of music from operas and *concerti grossi* from which a ballet could be put together. On 30 April, just before the Ballet left for Antwerp, Beecham cabled, 'Handel music dispatched today.'[121] Kochno was again asked to devise a simple story. There was no time to rehearse anything until the company reached England.

In Brussels the Ballet danced both in the new Palais des Beaux Arts, where they could use no scenery, and at the Théâtre de la Monnaie, which was as bad, because the flies were so crammed with flown sets that Grigoriev was obliged to lower the house curtain after each of the nine scenes of *Neptune*, so that it lasted an hour and a half.[122] Since Sokolova was absent, Danilova was cast for the role of Chosen Virgin in *The Rite*, but, as no one could tell her how to count the music, she 'just plunged in and hoped for the best'. She was only the third woman to dance Massine's version, Nijinska having performed it in Paris in 1923.[123]

In Paris on 29 May, Dukelsky took Diaghilev and Prokofiev to hear Dmitri Tiomkin play Gershwin's Piano Concerto at a concert at the Opéra. Diaghilev shook his head and said something about 'good jazz and bad Liszt'. Prokofiev was more enthusiastic. A short piece by the young Aaron Copland, then studying under Nadia Boulanger, was on the programme. On 14 June Kussevitzky conducted the suite from Prokofiev's opera *The Angel of Fire*, and Dukelsky's First Symphony.[124]

With a few days to go before the opening of the season at the Sarah Bernhardt, Nabokov resumed his rehearsals with Massine, and the choreography of *Ode* was completed. The composer also had a glimpse of Tchelitchev's model, 'all in blue tulle, which when lit by a tiny flashlight became strangely alive and acquired an extraordinary mysterious and ephemeral beauty'. Until four days before the *première*, Diaghilev appeared 'completely indifferent' to the fate of his new presentation.

On the morning of 2 June, 1928 [wrote Nabokov], the telephone rang very early, despite the warning I had left ... not to disturb me until 10. ... To my utter surprise I heard the voice of Diaghilev shouting at me. 'Why don't you answer your telephone? Why are you sleeping when you should be at the theatre? ... This mess can't go on any longer. I have ordered a full stage rehearsal at ten, a full orchestra rehearsal at two, a full chorus rehearsal at five, and all evening we will rehearse the lights.'

From that moment on, and for the next three days ... I lived in a state of frenzy. Diaghilev had taken over in the fullest sense. ...[125]

Kochno's account differs:

Tchelitchev was extremely highly strung and quite incompetent in the matter of film techniques, so that the atmosphere of our collaboration was dramatic. The indescribable chaos of the dress rehearsal – the first and only rehearsal in which the various elements ... were brought together – justified my fear of a disastrous première. ...

The rehearsal had begun on the evening of 5 June: it ended at noon on the next day, which enabled us to correct the sets and lighting. We worked right up to the moment when the theatre doors were open to the audience. And it was then that the Prefecture of Police forbade the use of neon lights as fire hazards.

Throughout these hours of anguish, only Diaghilev remained imperturbable; he never interfered in our discussions, as if he wanted to test my abilities as leader of the team.[126]

On the day of the opening, 6 June, Nabokov was 'exhausted, stunned and shaking...'.

I had seen Diaghilev leave the theatre an hour before the performance.... He looked worn, grey and sallow as he crossed the stage covered with a two-day growth of beard. ... Fifteen minutes before the curtain went up, I saw Diaghilev come in through this backstage door in full evening dress. ... Calm, confident and resplendent.... I mumbled that I hoped all would go well. ... 'Well,' said Diaghilev nonchalantly, his face changing to a charming, affectionate smile, 'it's up to you,' and he opened his arms and moved them backward in the suave and deliberate gesture of a virtuoso conductor, by which in apparent modesty he raises the orchestra musicians to their feet and makes them acknowledge the public's applause.[127]

Like a wise general, Diaghilev had taken care of the staff work, brought his troops into position, fed them, kept his lines of communication open, foreseen every emergency: when there was nothing more to be done, it only remained to enjoy the battle.

Nemtchinova had felt naked when she danced without a *tutu* in *Les Biches*: but at least she had worn a little blue jacket. In *Ode*, the dancers were astounded to find themselves wearing unadorned white all-over tights, such as little Markova had worn as the Nightingale.[128] There were few in the company, apart from Danilova, Dubrovska and Nikitina, who danced the principal roles, whose figures would pass the test. It was the first time that this basic uniform, which Bérard, Jean Hugo and so many other designers were later to impose, was seen *en masse* on the stage. In this matter Tchelitchev was a pioneer – but how much more so in his lighting, his gauze transparencies, his projections and patterns of white rope, with which the dancers created alone and between each other geometrical diagrams in space!

There was a dance of masked women in inky transparent tarlatan crinolines, sewn with stars: two lines of dolls of diminishing size, similarly dressed and suspended on wires, gave the illusion of continuing the *défilé* of this court into the remote distance. Lifar had a dance with a moving (projected) ray of light. In another elegiac duet, two dancers held a pole from which lengths of gauze were suspended, leaving a gap in the middle. When one dancer was behind the gauze, he had 'an ectoplasmic quality' as he danced with the 'solid form' visible in the gap. 'Sometimes their arms alone curved and crossed in the intervening space.'[129] There was an extraordinarily difficult and intricate *pas de deux* for Dubrovska and Massine.

Tchelitchev's programme cover, based on Leonardo's illustration of the proportions of Vitruvian man, was a nude youth, with four arms and five legs enclosed in a hoop. This, the artist insisted, had to be pricked out with a pin, like a nineteenth-century transparency intended to be held up to the light. 'Contrary to my fears,' wrote Kochno, 'the première of *Ode* went off without the slightest mishap.'[130] After the ballet Diaghilev embraced him and said, 'Thank-you.'[131]

Diaghilev's passion for *Les Noces* was undiminished. He gave it as the third ballet on the opening night, following *Le Pas d'acier*, with its complicated set, and the difficult *Ode*. To stage *Les Noces* at all was an arduous – and expensive – undertaking. The four pianos were played this time by Auric, Poulenc, Rieti and Marcelle Meyer. With scores by Prokofiev, Nabokov and Stravinsky, and settings by Yakulov, Tchelitchev and Gontcharova, it was a Russian evening.

The great ballet *Apollon Musagète* was given on 12 June 1928 and Stravinsky conducted it. (The American *première* had taken place on 27 April.) Diaghilev had had the curious notion of matching the crystal purity, the 'neoclassicism', of Stravinsky's score for string orchestra with the décor of a naïve 'Sunday painter'. André Bauchant, a more intimate Douanier Rousseau, was a gardener on weekdays, and his flower paintings had an individual perfection of observation and tone. His figures left more to be desired, and Diaghilev cut four from the design for the front curtain of *Apollon*, leaving only a vase of spring flowers, which loomed large in the foreground of a paradisal landscape with meandering streams. Once the young god Apollo – whose birth took place before this curtain in the brief first scene – had been unwrapped from his caul of bandages, he was revealed in a short Greek tunic, vermilion and crimson, with a gold wreath, belt and sandals. Although Stravinsky had hoped for short *tutus*, the three Muses wore long white ballet skirts of different lengths:[132] Tchernicheva's was the longest – to hide her ugly legs, her friends told her –[133] Dubrovska's was a little shorter, and Danilova's (or Nikitina's) was shorter still.

The second scene was a bare stage, with a rock in the right background against a blue sky. Apollo's first dance begins as a violin solo, developing into 'a rather hesitant duet for two solo violins, with pizzicato accompaniment'.[134] There follows a *pas d'action*, at the end of which Apollo gives each Muse the attribute of her art – a scroll, a tragic mask, a lyre. The variation of Calliope, the Muse of Lyric Poetry, is based by Stravinsky on the couplet in which Boileau laid down the rule of the caesura in Alexandrine verses:

> Que toujours dans vos vers, le sens coupant les mots,
> Suspende l'hémistiche et marque le repos.

Polyhymnia dances to rapid semiquavers, and at the end, breaking the rule of the art of Mime, which she represents, opens her mouth to emit a cry, then guiltily suppresses it with her hand. (This had to be done subtly, to avoid getting a laugh. Diaghilev subsequently had cause to tell Dubrovska, rather unfairly, 'that she was not in a music-hall'.)[135] Terpsichore's allegretto is punctuated by pauses which allow its interpreter to strike four different classical *attitudes*. (Diaghilev professed to find the music of her lovely number too similar to Calliope's, and, either for this or for other reasons – such as Nikitina's weakness – cut it at the second and third performances.)[136] Apollo's second *variation* is a slow movement for the full string orchestra. There is a vigorous coda for Apollo and the Three, in which he seems to drive them, with building excitement, like a team of horses. To the calm but vibrant music of the Apotheosis, the god leads the procession of Muses, augmented by his mother Leto and her two attendants (from the first scene), up the slope of the rocky hill towards Parnassus, and a chariot drawn by horses descends through the air to meet them.

Balanchine's choreography, basically as classical as Petipa's, had some quirkish but telling inventions. When Apollo stood alone in the fourth position, one arm behind his waist, the other upheld, the fingers of alternate hands opened and closed to flash bursts of divine semaphore. At one moment he knelt to support all three Muses, like a troika, in *arabesque penchée*. The simple climb upwards was as solemn and moving as the close of *The Firebird*.

Gordon Craig, never one of Diaghilev's most constant admirers, found the ballet so beautiful that he left the theatre immediately afterwards, unwilling to cloud his glimpse of heaven.[137]

Diaghilev, Kochno and Lifar returned to Albemarle Court, London, on Sunday, 24 June; so did Stravinsky and Vera Sudeikina. Igor was to conduct the first English performance of *Apollon Musagète* on the season's opening night at His Majesty's on the following day, while Malcolm Sargent would conduct *Cimarosiana* and *The Firebird*.

Diaghilev asked Danilova whether she would mind if Nikitina danced Terpsichore on the first night in London. 'Otherwise it will cost me Lord Rothermere's £3,000,' he admitted. Danilova said, 'He was always quite frank about such things.' Frank, perhaps, but not scrupulously accurate, if Danilova's memory of the sum is correct: for £3,000 would have sufficed for the season's whole guarantee, and we know that this year Rothermere was only one of several guarantors on the committee organized by Juliet Duff. Danilova agreed readily.[138]

One might have expected the music critic of London's leading serious daily newspaper, *The Times*, to find something to admire in Stravinsky's score, which heralded a new 'classical' period. But no: 'It used to be said that the Russian Ballet would not be much without Stravinsky; his latest production makes us fear that soon it will not be much with him ... the work was applauded doggedly by a large audience, whose faithfulness was to be rewarded later with the popular *Firebird*. ...' The choreographer got it in the neck, too. '*Apollon Musagètes* [sic] is a very solemn matter. It is not meant to please, like *Cimarosiana*, or to be exciting, like the *Firebird*. ...'[139] Balanchine remarked in 1977, 'I could not read English in those days,

Lydia Lopukhova (Mrs Keynes) in a box at His Majesty's.
Drawing by Cecil Beaton, from *Vogue*, 1928.

so I never knew or cared what the critics wrote. If I *had* been able to read them I should have committed suicide.'[140]

Diaghilev asked his old friend Diana Cooper, who had appeared as the Madonna in Reinhardt's *Miracle* in America, and who was shortly to do so in London, to mime the part of the Goddess (or Nature) in *Ode*. She wrote back, refusing (in pencil, undated), 'All my advisers say that the first time I appear in London must be in the Miracle, which they hope to do this autumn. It is quite true, as they tell me – that I might have been very

503

bad in Ode. . . . You will hate me, & I want you to love me – but don't forget I might have spoilt your ballet. Try Viola Tree she has marvellous gestures. . . .'[141] The Goddess was mimed by a favourite model of Epstein's, the actress Oriel Ross.

For the visit of King Alfonso and his Queen on 2 July, Diaghilev put on *Las Meninas*, which he had, in fact, been giving in Brussels, but which London had not seen, and their Most Catholic Majesties not since the war.

Juliet Duff knew how rigorously Diaghilev excluded outsiders from his rehearsals, so, towards the end of the second week in London, she was surprised one afternoon to notice a small crowd assembled at the back of the stalls in the darkened theatre. She pointed them out to Diaghilev, who remarked casually, 'Oh, that is the chorus I have brought over from Paris for *Les Noces*.' As Juliet was keeping an eye on expenditure, hoping to return her friends' money at the end of the season, she was horrified.[142] The lavish Diaghilev had, however, been careful to concentrate all the works which needed singers into the week beginning Monday, 9 July, when *Ode* was given. Apart from *Les Noces* and *Ode*, the choral works were *Barabau*, *Pulcinella* and *Midnight Sun* (which had often been performed without its final song).

Even the Ballet's faithful old supporter, Richard Capell of the *Daily Mail*, thought *Ode* could 'only be compared to a nightmare – but one of the incongruous, not the horrible sort. The subject has a classic simplicity. . . . Only the interpretation is odd, – very.'[143] Cyril Beaumont was more enthusiastic:

> It is not easy to convey the strange character, the celestial beauty, and the intellectual appeal of *Ode*. Those extraordinary designs, formed of ever-changing lines and triangles of cord, suggested animations of the diagrams illustrating Euclid's propositions; and yet always in and out of those corded mazes moved, crouched, leaped, and glided those beautiful unknown forms. To me they suggested a kind of visual 'laying bare' of the intelligence at work.
>
> *Ode* could never have become a popular ballet. . . . Yet this stark conception attempted the boldest flight of all – to attain the infinite, and, more wonderful still, seemed at times to reach it.[144]

Beaumont planned a book of drawings of Serge Lifar in his various roles. These were to be done by Eileen Mayo, one of his artist friends, who, it must be admitted, were mostly less than second-rate.

> When we arrived [at His Majesty's Theatre] we found not only Lifar, in high good humour and eager to pose, but also the omnipotent Diaghilev and the cynical Kochno. This was an unexpected audience, not calculated to help our enterprise. Eileen Mayo asked if she might remove her cloak, to which Diaghilev replied 'Please take off everything if you wish.' . . . At subsequent sittings we were left to ourselves. . . . Now and again, when I was kneeling on the floor supporting Lifar's raised leg, the door of the room would silently open a few inches and Diag-

hilev's great head would peer in. Sometimes the director looked startled at the unorthodox proceedings, but, apparently reassured, he withdrew his head and softly closed the door.[145]

Boris wrote the text for this book, which was translated into English by Sacheverell Sitwell.

Each of the first four Mondays in that season had its first night. On 16 July was given the Handel ballet, *The Gods go a-begging*. Diaghilev expected so little of this that he ordered no new designs, but used Bakst's pastoral décor for *Daphnis* and the costumes of Gris for *Les Tentations de la bergère*. Kochno's *fête champêtre*, an aristocratic picnic, at which a shepherd whom the ladies find attractive causes indignation by preferring the serving-maid who lays the cloth, ends with the revelation of the two humble lovers as gods in disguise. This was so well suited to Handel's simple airs, and Balanchine, who, like the Neapolitan painter Luca Giordano, deserved the nickname 'Fa presto', produced in no time such enchanting dances that even the critics had to admit Sir Thomas Beecham's and the Russian Ballet's 'ovation' was deserved. Danilova and Woizikovsky surpassed themselves. Beaumont thought their gavotte 'one of the most poetic' of Balanchine's creations.[146] The popularity of *The Gods go a-begging*, known elsewhere as *Les Dieux mendiants*, was not confined to England. 'It became our bread and butter,' said Danilova.[147]

Marie Rambert invited Diaghilev to visit her studio in Ladbroke Road. Here he saw Diana Gould and Frederick Ashton dance a *pas de deux* arranged by the latter, 'Leda and the Swan'.[148] He admired the handsome, long-necked Diana, and promised to take her into his company in a year's time.

On 25 July, when he had luncheon with the Samuel Courtaulds[149] at their splendid Robert Adam house at the corner of Portman Square, Diaghilev would have been able to renew acquaintance, among their newly acquired Impressionist paintings, with Renoir's *La Loge*, which he and Princess Tenishev had exhibited in St Petersburg thirty years before.

Massine again parted company, quite amicably, with the Ballet, when the season ended on 28 July.[150] There were two performances to be given at Ostend, on 29 and 30 July, before the holidays, but Diaghilev made straight for Venice.

After a few days, during which time Diaghilev spent some hours, at Kochno's request, jotting down reminiscences of musical life in Russia in his youth, to be read to Boris and Serge when they came back from bathing,[151] the three set off in a hired car on a tour of north-east Italian cities to look at works of art: Padua for Giotto and for Donatello's Gattamelata and altar in Sant 'Antonio, Mantua for Mantegna, Ferrara for Tura, Ravenna for Byzantine mosaics, Perugia for Perugino, Assisi for Giotto, Arezzo for Piero della Francesca, Siena for its primitives and for Pinturicchio, and

finally Florence. There was talk of a journey to Greece; but Lifar thought
Diaghilev less eager to see the Parthenon than to hunt for Slavonic books
on Mount Athos. An epidemic in Greece put an end to this plan.[152]

Back on the Lido, Diaghilev was soon worrying again about visas for Warsaw, telegraphing his old colleague Trubecki and pestering the Polish Consul
in Rome.[153] By the end of September he and Boris were off to Poland in
search of books, and Lifar was telegraphing from the Hotel Cavour at Milan,
where he was to work with Cecchetti as usual, to the Hotel Polonia, Warsaw:
'Health good. Start with Maestro today. We embrace you.'[154] The next
day, 3 October, he heard from Diaghilev:

My dear, the landscape as one nears Warsaw, with its little copses, its women
with kerchiefs round their heads, reminds one of our little mother Russia, but
Warsaw itself is a not too bad little German town, which I cannot explore properly
because of the awful cold. It's cold in the streets, and not too warm in the rooms.
I, of course, began by starting a cold in the head, which, however, is very much
better. In addition, the swelling in my armpit proved to be neither more nor less
than a painless boil, which burst last night. All this is of no importance, rather
boring in fact.... I visited the principal *theatre* ... but the really serious performances only begin on Saturday ... and *Giselle* on Sunday. I've already seen a number
of people; they all recommend the same three ballerinas and three male dancers,
and say they're quite good. Mme Nijinska [who was now Ida Rubinstein's ballet-
mistress] has taken on four men ... but they tell me not the best. I see a great
deal of Trubecki [his former secretary], Novak [a former dancer in the Russian
Ballet] and Kurillo [unknown], who are very helpful. ... Tell Pavka I am seeing
Dima [Filosofov] and shall tell him in detail all about it. My arrival passed unnoticed to begin with, but now the whole ant-heap is beginning to sit up. I've
visited the smaller theatres....

As to books, nothing out of the way. ... No one here handles Russian books.
Levin is in London, but his brother sold me some good stuff, useful for the library.
What is really amazing here is the *food*, absolutely first class, though expensive.
Everywhere you find Russian cooking. ...

I am thinking of going for a day to Vilna ... one can return the same day. ...
On the whole it is a far cry from the Warsaw of the eighteenth century, in which
Cimarosa, Casanova and Canaletto [the younger, i.e. Bellotto] stayed. You have
to stay in a place like this to realize what a metropolis Berlin is. Nevertheless,
everyone's exceedingly civil. ...

One doesn't feel the vicinity of Russia in the least. ... Yesterday I heard a
talented *chansonette* singer in a cabaret singing a Russian song called 'Sunflower-
seed'. ... She was more genuine, more touching and pitiful than the whole of
Tairov's troupe put together. ... I had quite a lump in my throat, and for a long
time couldn't get off to sleep.

God keep you both: I embrace you, my dear.[155]

Boris was with Diaghilev when he ran into Dima Filosofov in the street.
He saw a very correctly dressed but colourless individual; and, in spite of

the joy shown by the two cousins on meeting again after more than twenty years, Boris thought they had nothing to say to each other.[156]

Diaghilev did not neglect business on this holiday. He engaged six dancers, including Petrova and Lipkovska. He was afraid Rubinstein might have lured away some of his own, and he was in doubt as to whether Sokolova's health made it worthwhile to re-engage her.[157]

By 10 October Diaghilev was at the Eden Hotel in Berlin, telegraphing to Grigoriev, 'Send Balanchine 4,000.'[158] He must have had a sudden apprehension that Prokofiev might return to Russia without finishing *Le Fils prodigue*, and telegraphed to know his movements. The composer cabled Diaghilev, 'Trip Russia put off till December. Staying Paris.'[159] On the twelfth Diaghilev cabled to Wollheim about posters for the forthcoming tour of the English and Scottish provincial cities: 'Maître de ballet Balanchine. Don't put any other artists' names on poster. How are bookings?'[160]

On 18 October Lifar was awaiting Diaghilev in Milan,[161] but the latter stayed in Italy only a few days before returning to Paris.[162] On the thirty-first Lifar had his last lesson from Cecchetti before joining Diaghilev.[163]

The British tour was a daring experiment. Diaghilev travelled with the company to Manchester, where he stayed at the Midland Hotel.[164] Grigoriev went ahead, to spy out stages further north.[165] Manchester may have been expected to take to *Cimarosiana* and *Le Tricorne*, but how would it receive *La Chatte*? 'When the lover falls sorrowing to the earth at the death [i.e. transformation into a cat] of his beloved,' wrote the *Manchester Guardian*, 'there is a cortège of squares and circles.'[166] Nikitina's poor health prevented her from joining the tour, and Markova danced *La Chatte* throughout.[167] On Tuesday, the thirteenth, news came of the death of Cecchetti. What a world of dancers would mourn him, the original Blue Bird and Carabosse of 1889, who had seen the birth of the Diaghilev Ballet and bullied all its stars! In darkest Manchester Diaghilev could look back on twenty years of classes – in St Petersburg, Paris, Monte Carlo, London, Rome and Milan. Lifar wore a black – instead of a white – scarf in *Les Sylphides* that night.[168]

Diaghilev returned with Kochno to the Grand Hôtel, Paris, before the company moved to Birmingham.[169] Grigoriev sent him a daily telegram about the box-office receipts. On Wednesday, 21 November: 'Matinée 306, evening 337.'[170] On 26 November the Russian Ballet opened at the Queen's, Glasgow,[171] while, with Boris, Diaghilev attended the opening of Ida Rubinstein's season at the Opéra, which he described to Lifar in a letter the following day:

> Paris is an awful town, impossible to find five minutes even for a couple of words. . . . Everyone seems to have gathered here. . . . Let me begin with Ida. The house was full, but there was a good deal of paper [people with free seats] about, mostly her friends. Not one of us, however, were given seats, neither myself, Boris,

Nuvel, Sert or Picasso.... We only just, just managed to get in. *All our people were there*, Misia, Juliet, Beaumont, Polignac, Igor and other musicians, not to mention Mayakovsky. The whole thing was astonishingly provincial, boring and long-drawn-out, even the Ravel [*Bolero*], which took fourteen minutes. It's a big company, but totally lacking in experience: they just made mistake after mistake, and seemed not to have the slightest notion of ensemble. And the hosts of solo dancers! Schollar was supposed to be representing a baby in the heart of a cabbage [in *Les Noces de Psyché et de l'Amour*, the ballet with music by Bach, designed by Benois] but looked more like an old woman in the green rags she was wearing. Nicolaeva [Legat] had her hair sweeping the ground, wore a slime-yellow dress, and pranced about in a classico-bacchanalian manner on her toes. The best dancer turned out to be Rupert Doone, the little Englishman we both know. And then, in the middle of the ballet, something really wonderful happened, for a certain gent in an open pink shirt with blue trimmings and a short red velvet cloak, wearing a red wig and a bright green wreath on top of it, made up to look like the worst sort of old queen, suddenly appeared borne triumphantly on his colleagues' arms, and began dancing *something that vaguely resembled a classical variation*: it was Unger, yes, Unger!

Benois seems to have lost every atom of colour and taste. He seems exactly where he was thirty years ago. But now much, much worse!

Singayevsky also came on, naked, in a grey beard and property helmet. But neither he nor the show as a whole had any success. The press is pretty luke-warm.... Stravinsky was seen in Ida's dressing-room.... Argutinsky himself told me.... But the morning after Stravinsky rang up to say how disappointed he had been, how indignant the whole thing had made him....

All this you can read during supper to the principal dancers. I've exaggerated nothing. . . . It is very useful to look at *rubbish*: it makes one think.[172]

Diaghilev was in love again. During the summer his secretary, the part-time dancer Alexandrina Trussevitch, had met, in a *pension* at Glyon-sur-Montreux in Switzerland, a fellow-exile, Mme Markevitch, with her children. The sixteen-year-old Igor Markevitch studied music under Nadia Boulanger and aspired to be a composer. Trussevitch was struck by his resemblance to the young Massine and she told Diaghilev about him. In November the youth came, satchel under arm, to call on Sergei Pavlovitch at the Grand Hôtel. At first, Diaghilev did not like what he heard, but, when Igor played the last movement of his symphony, he sat up and took notice. Igor was enraptured at the time by Ravel's *Daphnis*, and Diaghilev asked him, 'Why get so excited about yesterday?' Cheekily the student replied, 'I'm not interested in yesterday or today, but in what is forever.' Diaghilev was impressed.[173] Igor, so unsophisticated and unsure of himself, appeared unusually self-confident for his age and gave the illusion of being completely formed. He had a child's mixture of ingenuousness and cruelty; and his piercing look, which seemed to read your thoughts, was disconcerting.[174] Always on the scent of genius, Diaghilev was naturally more prone to detect it in the young and handsome. He was soon committed – to instruct, to reveal; to encourage scepticism, to invite wonder. Commitment to the fanning of Markevitch's spark of talent soon turned to adoration of his person. Diaghilev exerted himself to be amusing, and Igor laughed so much and so enjoyed his company that he sometimes broke into a run on his way to the Grand Hôtel, so as to get there sooner.[175]

As if partly conscious that this was his last great love, Diaghilev abandoned himself to it heart and soul. 'He wanted to give me the world: there was no end to his unique generosity,' said Markevitch. How can a boy of sixteen respond to such a cannonade of passion from a man of fifty-six? Boys are naturally flattered when someone is interested in them: but Igor was not homosexual. He responded as best he could. 'Diaghilev was not perverse: sentimental, rather. The physical side of his love, which certainly existed, was perhaps a necessity for him.' (Without physical consummation, however elementary, how can the fire be damped down?) Misia observed the immense burden her beloved Serge was placing on young Igor's shoulders and wondered whether it might not break his back.[176]

The Diaghilev–Kochno Russian library now contained not only the rare early books, but first and complete editions of all the classics: it was enormous, and some books had never even been unpacked. In order to house it and Lifar's growing collection of pictures, Diaghilev took a flat in his own name and in Kochno's in the Boulevard Garibaldi, behind the Invalides. He never had any intention of living in this obscure quarter. Was it with the idea of documenting his own part in the history of Russian art that Diaghilev had hoarded such quantities of letters, telegrams and hotel bills – which, though divided now between several collections in Europe and America, have proved indispensable material for the present book? (This question I asked Kochno.) Certainly not. Diaghilev had a horror of the idea of a Diaghilev Museum, in which would be displayed, as he said, 'my pince-nez and my old bedroom slippers'.[177]

Diaghilev had seen both Rieti and Prokofiev. The former played over his new ballet, *Le Bal*, which Diaghilev thought improved since he had last heard it. Prokofiev had written half of *Le Fils prodigue*.[178] 'What, already?' exclaimed Diaghilev. 'If you have written it so quickly it must be bad.' But he liked what he heard, except for some of the scene with the seductress, which Prokofiev was ready to change.[179]

On Tuesday, 27 November, Diaghilev had Rieti and Meyerhold to lunch.[180] He evolved a scheme with the Russian director of giving a joint Paris season in the spring, the Moscow Arts Theatre and the Russian Ballet performing on alternate nights. 'This is just the moment. Tomorrow may be too late.'[181] Nuvel and Koribut-Kubitovitch objected strongly to this Soviet collaboration. 'But if one took their advice,' Diaghilev wrote to Lifar, 'one might as well go straight to the cemetery. That's why Ida's performances turn out like "charity bazaars", as Tchelitchev says. . . .'[182]

The last performance in Birmingham took £473, the first in Glasgow £469.[183]

After Rubinstein's second night on 27 November Diaghilev went back to the Grand Hôtel and wrote again to Lifar. He had seen the first performance of Nijinska's ballet to Stravinsky's *Baiser de la fée* and allowances must be made for his jealousy of Igor's working for Ida.

I'm just back from the theatre with a fearful headache as a result of all the horrible things I've been seeing. Stravinsky's was the only new ballet, the other promised novelties not being ready. . . . In the first ballet, the *Bach*, I noticed this evening a little *pas de deux* which I missed the first time, danced by Nicolaeva and Unger, and which is well worth seeing. After which came Igor's ballet. It's difficult to say what it was meant to represent – tiresome, lachrymose, ill-chosen Tchaikovsky, supposedly orchestrated by Igor in masterly fashion . . . the whole arrangement lacked vitality. The *pas de deux*, however, was quite well done to a beautiful theme from Tchaikovsky, based on the song 'None but the lonely heart'. That, and the coda in the style of *Apollon* were really the only bright spots (though the latter too was somewhat melancholy). But what went on on the stage it is impossible to describe. Suffice it to say that the first scene represents the Swiss mountains, the second a Swiss village on holiday, the third a Swiss mill, and the fourth back to the mountains and glaciers. . . . Bronia showed not the least gleam of invention. As for Benois' décor, it was like the sets at the Monte Carlo Opera House. . . . The theatre was full, but as for success – it was like a drawing-room in which someone had suddenly made a bad smell. Everyone pretended not to notice, and Stravinsky took two calls. . . . All our friends shrug their shoulders, except Valetchka of course, who, when it was written, could 'find no music' in *L'Oiseau de feu*. . . .

What use is it all? No, far better let the Bolsheviks, or some Napoleon – it's all the same – blow up all their old barracks.[184]

That night in Glasgow the takings were down to £357, but on Thursday the twenty-ninth they rose to £476.[185] Diaghilev, who had intended to join the company in Edinburgh on 4 December, decided to see Rubinstein's last programme, and he telegraphed to Wollheim on the thirtieth, 'Pass through London Wednesday on way to Edinburgh. Send Nuvel photos Handel urgently.'[186]

King George of England had double-pneumonia, and Diaghilev was anxious that 'if, God forbid, the worst should happen', the tour would have to be interrupted. In spite of his scorn for Rubinstein's productions, he was also worried whether the Russian Ballet could compete in the eyes of the public with her lavish expenditure. 'Ida Rubinstein is dancing to full houses, every seat *bought and paid for*. If we're to rake in the money we need, we've really got to pull ourselves together in every way we possibly can. . . . We've got to prove to the bourgeois crowd how immeasurably superior we are, in spite of the fact that our sets weren't painted yesterday, and that our costumes aren't quite fresh....'[187]

Diaghilev thought Rubinstein's programme on 29 November began better, with an arrangement of Borodin's 'Serenade'. But 'what finished it off completely was the appearance of Ida, with her interminable classical *pas de deux*. It's impossible to describe such dancing, or her tousled red hair blown in every direction. As for Tcherepnine's arrangement, it's simply shocking. Imagine getting a tenor to sing the cello part in that famous quartet!....' *Tsar Saltan* [the ballet from Rimsky's opera was called *La Princesse Cygne*] was like 'a bad sort of *Oiseau de feu*.... Why the Smolny convent should rise from the bottom of the sea passes understanding.' Rubinstein 'appeared dressed like a Pavlova swan, specially got up for some Moulin Rouge performance (her bodice one mass of false diamonds ...). In both ballets the curtain came down too soon....'[188]

Diaghilev signed his contract with Giorgio di Chirico, whom the Surrealists claimed as one of themselves, to design Rieti's ballet, stipulating that the sketches should be done in oils, with the intention of adding them to Lifar's collection.[189] He heard again Prokofiev's *Le Fils prodigue*: 'Much of it is very good. The last scene, the prodigal's return, is beautiful. Your [Lifar's] *variation*, the awakening after the orgy ["Réveil et remords"], is, for Prokofiev, quite new. A sort of profound and majestic nocturne. Good, too, is the tender theme of the sisters, and very good, in the Prokofiev manner, the pilfering scene ["Pillage"]: three clarinets performing miracles of agility.'[190]

Diaghilev and Kochno joined Lifar at the Caledonian Hotel, Edinburgh (rooms 89, 90, 91) on 6 December.[191] Desormière was conducting the tour, but Sir Thomas Beecham appeared from London on certain nights, to conduct *The Gods go a-begging*. He had been unwell and had not conducted the Monday performance in Edinburgh, but he conducted on Friday the seventh, and the fact that he was to appear on the first two nights in Liverpool may have decided Diaghilev to travel there with the Ballet and see the opening night.[192] In Diaghilev's absence some of the company's principals, including Markova – with her mother – had been photographed outside Holyroodhouse.[193] On arrival at Liverpool on Sunday, 9 December, Diaghilev posed with Desormière, Lifar (holding a coconut), Kochno, Danilova, Tchernicheva and Dubrovska on the station platform.[194]

While the dancers read their good notice in the *Liverpool Echo* – it was 'Danilova's evening', for she danced in the Handel, in *Aurora's Wedding* and in *La Boutique*[195] – Diaghilev travelled back to Paris and to Markevitch, and sketched out a telegram to Lord Rothermere on Adelphi Hotel writing-paper: 'Many thanks for your most valuable help launching our provincial tour which has been successful for a first effort. I am organizing several performances at Paris Grand Opera commencing December 20th. Sir Thomas

Beecham conducting English ballet. May I ask you to help me in Paris and London Daily Mail these performances?'[196] Tuesday's receipts in Liverpool were £418. On Friday they had risen to £469.[197]

At the first of his four performances at the Opéra on 20 December Diaghilev gave his Handel ballet, called *Les Dieux mendiants*, for the first time in France. The second, on 24 December, was a Stravinsky evening: *The Firebird*, *Apollon*, *Petrushka*, for the last of which Karsavina had been engaged. Beecham came over to conduct the Handel at the third performance on 27 December. Tamara coached Dubrovska and Danilova in the role of the Firebird. Although Dubrovska had danced it before in Monte Carlo, she found it almost impossible to cover the vast stage of the Opéra with her jumps. Diaghilev sent Boris round during the first interval on the twenty-fourth, to ask, 'What is the matter? Why are you dancing so badly?'[198]

Diaghilev decided to bring the sick Nijinsky to see the Stravinsky performance. Romola Nijinsky had tried every kind of cure for her husband's mental disorder, long ago diagnosed as schizophrenia. She was at this time in America. Lifar wrote that Diaghilev pretended, in a cynical way, that all he wanted was to have Nijinsky photographed with his dancers; but he believed Diaghilev's real hope was that the shock of seeing *Petrushka* again, with Karsavina, might produce an improvement in his condition – a miracle. They went together to the flat in Passy, where they found Vaslav reclining on a mattress, sometimes 'affectedly playing with his wrists'. Lifar observed him growing more and more conscious of Diaghilev's presence; and when the latter explained, in Russian, that Lifar was a dancer, too, who 'loved him', Vaslav said abruptly, 'Loves me?', also in Russian. Otherwise, he spoke in French. 'Yes, Vatza, he loves you, and so do I, and all of us, as ever.' Nijinsky began laughing and exclaimed, 'C'est adorable.' Diaghilev measured the two men: Lifar was half a head taller. Nijinsky was shaved and dressed; and Lifar returned later to take him and his sister-in-law, Tessa Schmedes de Pulszky, to the theatre.[199]

Diaghilev sat with Nijinsky in his box at the Opéra. It was their last 'public appearance' together. Diaghilev had unconsciously begun to say his final good-byes. Sokolova, who was not yet dancing again, came to the box;[200] and there were other visitors. Before *Petrushka*, which was the last ballet, Nijinsky was led on the stage to be photographed. A group was formed: on the left, Kremnev, Benois, Grigoriev, Karsavina, in costume as the Ballerina, with her arm through Nijinsky's; Diaghilev behind him, smiling down benignly, with a hand on his shoulder; on the right, the smiling Lifar, dressed as the Moor, looking at Vaslav. Karsavina said that as they posed she became conscious that Nijinsky was looking sideways at her, recognition dawning; then the flash went off and Vaslav was caught with a mechanical smile.[201] Igor Markevitch, who was one day to marry Nijinsky's daughter Kyra, was standing beside the photographer.[202]

After the ballet Nijinsky did not want to leave, and when his coat was produced, cried out, 'Je ne veux pas.'[203] He was helped down the long flight of stairs to the stage-door by Diaghilev and Count Harry Kessler. Diaghilev kissed him on the forehead and he was driven away. Kessler wrote, 'We went to eat in the Restaurant de la Paix and sat until late with Karsavina, Misia Sert, Craig and Alfred Savoir. But I did not take much part in the talk; I was haunted by this meeting with Nijinsky. A human being who is burnt out.'[204] Less than a fortnight later the London *Daily Express* published an interview with Diaghilev, in which he spoke about Nijinsky's sad condition; and he received a number of letters recommending cures. Some correspondents suggested Christian Science; and one long, earnest letter guaranteed a cure which was infallible: 'Apply a cup of barley meal to the chest....'[205]

On the day after Nijinsky's visit Diaghilev heard from Dolin, who had been touring in his own ballet company with Nemtchinova and wanted a change. From the Hôtel Astor in Paris Dolin wrote:

With very great sincerity I write this letter to you.

First please do not misunderstand ... nothing I want more in life, shall always want, but realize now it is impossible would be once again to be guided in my career by you and to dance under your leadership. I am not too proud to admit this.... I beg you to receive me alone where surely we can talk ... & shake hands.

This letter is so difficult to write. I am afraid to make it too impressive, yet I want you to know how much it would mean to me to once again have the pleasure & honour to say *friend*. Please do not refuse.

Patrick[206]

Diaghilev looked upon this application favourably, as both he and Boris thought Dolin would be ideal for the hero of *Le Bal*. This was not, of course, the first time that Pat had asked to be taken back.[207]

CHAPTER 18

1929

Last Ballets and Last Love – Mozart and Wagner – Curtain

AS THE LAST YEAR of Diaghilev's life began, it was clear that his health was deteriorating. He got tired more easily and was prone to suppurating boils. His illness (only diagnosed in the spring) and the diet he observed very intermittently caused him to lose weight.[1] The last time he had spoken to Stravinsky and Vera – before they were ostracized on account of *Le Baiser de la fée* – he had opened his coat to show how thin he was.[2] This was *coquetterie*: he did not wish to acknowledge that he was ill. He took less and less trouble over dyeing his hair.[3] Although his energy was less than it had been, by the amount of work he got through and the projects he started we might think he still had the strength of three ordinary men.

Had the loneliness of old age begun to close in? As a man grows older he finds more and more friends and relations carried away by distance or death. But, though he clung to links with the past, Diaghilev disliked to speak about it, preferred to look forward, and treasured a new friendship, bright with dawning possibilities, more than all the old ones put together. Markevitch brought him a burst of renewed enthusiasm. Naturally, he wanted to show the young musician the wonders of the world and to see them again through the boy's sixteen-year-old eyes. From those old friends that remained Diaghilev felt separated by divergent views and different ways of life. Dima Filosofov might be living on another planet. Of Benois he saw little. The only other links with his childhood and youth were Koribut-Kubitovitch and Nuvel. Diaghilev enjoyed teasing Pavka, whom he called 'Red Riding Hood' because of his old-fashioned delicacy of speech – he used to say 'favourite' instead of 'mistress' – and he bullied him at meals, ordering plain spaghetti for him when he wanted the special *plat du jour*.[4] Nuvel, the cynical critic, was an infallible stand-by in his business affairs, but Diaghilev had lost faith in his artistic judgement. Of younger men, Stravinsky and Picasso were the two nearest his own age whom he most liked and respected for their genius and with whom he most loved to work: but Stravinsky was a 'traitor' and had gone over to Rubinstein – Diaghilev could never understand the need for a man to earn his living – and Picasso dwelt apart in his own titanic world. The uncouth, enthusiastic Larionov was as loyal as ever; Gontcharova had always been more solitary and with-drawn. Misia, the capricious sphinx, was as devoted as a wife, but she was married to another man. So was Karsavina, whom he loved but seldom saw. Among the young, Lifar was a cheerful, decorative boy to face across the dinner-table, if vain and empty-headed. Boris, however, understood his thoughts before they were spoken, and anticipated his wishes; and it was with him that Diaghilev could enjoy the planning and realization of new masterpieces.

Grigoriev was only a sergeant-major, rarely admitted to the officers' mess: but he had been around for so long and undergone so much, knew so many secrets and obeyed so meticulously his master's instructions, that he had become a friend. While Diaghilev maintained his company, he could never suffer the total loneliness of old age, for, with Grigoriev and the old-stagers, Kremnev (who had been one of the jesters in *Armide* in 1909), Tchernicheva (who had danced in the original *Prince Igor*) and Sokolova (who would have been the Virgin Mary in Massine's first ballet, *Liturgie*, if it had not been scrapped), he had a world of experience in common; while, with the youngsters, Danilova (so charming and well brought up, and who represented for him the new generation of Mariinsky dancers),[5] Dubrovska (a classical dancer, remodelled by Balanchine and Massine, who perfectly fulfilled those choreographers' intentions in the last Diaghilev ballets),[6] Markova (such a dear, serious little girl), Tcherkass (so cute) and Balanchine (so easy-going, yet so deep), there was the fun of seeing what they became.

It was work that made it possible for Diaghilev to 'banish age and care'; and those he worked with saw his best side. 'Diaghilev had not been in such good spirits for some time,' wrote Grigoriev about the company party on New Year's Eve. 'I wished him well of the New Year, reminding him, despite his shyness of jubilees, that with 1929 now upon us, it was twenty years since he had begun his ballet career.'[7] Lifar took a gloomier view of Diaghi-lev's predicament, but, as we shall see, he had reason to feel slighted.

Diaghilev and Dolin met in Paris, either at the New Year's Eve party or at the Ballet's fourth (and last ever) performance at the Opéra on Thurs-day, 3 January 1929. That night *The Firebird*, whose first performance had taken place at the Opéra in 1910, was given, along with *Apollon Musagète* and *La Chatte*, and Beecham once more conducted *The Gods go a-begging*. On the fifth Dolin wrote again to Diaghilev:

I take this opportunity, having had the pleasure & occasion to meet you again, in writing to you. My reason being to ask you if there is the possibility of again entering your company. I feel that maybe there is at this moment a chance that this could be realized as Massine having again left the company, there are surely certain roles I could dance, as I have of course no desire to intrude on the position of Lifar who I admire intensely & hav[e] a sincere feeling of friendship.

The conditions are not a factor that need be discussed or that difficulties need arise.[8]

Lifar, too, admired Dolin, as well he might, and had 'a sincere feeling of friendship' for him:[9] but the situation had changed since 1925. He was prepared to take it as a personal slight, and as a sign of Diaghilev's diminished regard for him, if his position as the company's star was challenged by Dolin's engagement. We have seen from Diaghilev's long letters to Lifar, about Ida Rubinstein's performances, how his friendly feelings for the young dancer were unchanged, even if passionate love had not survived. Now it was Lifar who was jealous. When Lifar left for Bordeaux with the company on 7 January, Diaghilev and Kochno remained at the Grand Hôtel in Paris, and Lifar stayed at the Grand Hôtel d'Orsay alone.[10] The Ballet had next to dance at Pau for two or three performances during the week beginning 14 January – which was a nightmare, as there were rats in the dressing-rooms and lions from a travelling circus under the stage[11] – but when they returned to Monte Carlo, Lifar lingered sulking on the west coast.

Dolin still had a few engagements to fulfil with Nemtchinova and their company, but after a fortnight at the London Palladium, ending 16 February, he would be free.

Diaghilev wanted Matisse to design *Le Fils prodigue*, and had already approached him about it in 1928. He had also asked him to design a new version of *Schéhérazade*, for the old Bakst production had grown shabby, and although Diaghilev thought Fokine's melodrama absurd, audiences clamoured for it, and he hoped that Balanchine might be able to bring it up to date. Having extracted no reply from Matisse, he employed the art critic Michel Georges-Michel as an intermediary; but on 30 January he received this telegram from Nice: 'Delighted to see you but not free today. As I cannot possibly work for you it is utterly useless for you to put yourself out with this in mind. Very sorry. Matisse. Fourth Floor.'[12]

Matisse was disillusioned by the theatre. Even in winter 1923, when Diaghilev had sent Juan Gris to see him – perhaps to talk about *Philémon* – he had been 'very cold'.[13] Boris suggested employing Georges Rouault, who was really a better choice as designer for the Old Testament subject of *Le Fils prodigue*, who had never before worked for the theatre, and who surprisingly accepted the commission at once.[14]

Diaghilev had commissioned a ballet from Paul Hindemith, to be called 'No. 27' and with a libretto by Kochno inspired by the popular Paris bicycle races known as 'Les Six Jours':[15] but Hindemith wrote on 2 January to say that for the time being he had written himself out. If Diaghilev had to have a new ballet early in 1929, Hindemith recommended Bohuslav Martinu.[16] Production of Hindemith's ballet was postponed, but Diaghilev did not relax his grip. During January, by means of telegrams, he pursued Hindemith, who had concerts in Switzerland during the latter part of the month, but who, according to his wife Gertrude, was to be in Berlin between 11 and 17 February.[17]

Diaghilev made such a nuisance of himself suggesting changes, improvements and cuts in Rieti's score for *Le Bal*, that on 27 February the composer sent him the following letter with his finished work: 'Here is *Le Bal*. It is dedicated to you. Do what you like with it, but don't expect me to do work on it any more!'[18]

As far as bookings were concerned, Diaghilev was to give twenty-eight or thirty evening performances and thirty-one matinées in Monte Carlo during February or March, showing three ballets not seen there before (*The Gods go a-begging, Apollon* and *Pastorale*) and, as a fourth *première* was contracted for, *Le Bal*. (In fact, it was not shown till May.) Mestres could not fit in the Ballet in Barcelona in May, but Wollheim had arranged a visit to the Staatsoper, Berlin, on 14 June for one week, followed by a short visit to Cologne.[19] The Paris season was no problem, as the huge Sarah Bernhardt was again available, and, if nearly full, could cover costs. After the holidays Barcelona wanted the Russian Ballet either in October or in January 1930,[20] and there was the possibility of Goetz's tour in the United States or one which the impresario Prince Zeretelli was proposing for South America. Covent Garden had agreed to a season in July, if the Lord Chamberlain gave his assent.[21]

On 13 February Lifar wrote from self-imposed exile in Bordeaux to his 'old and only remaining friend', Koribut-Kubitovitch:

That depression about which I wrote to you ... that vague discomfort which seems to have dogged me of late, turns out to have been a premonition. That subconscious inner-self of mine, which has never deceived me, that secret and greater self, greater than my I, greater than my conscious understanding, seems to have been living in hourly expectation of bitterness and scorn, and now both have descended on me, and it is as though I had died, as though all that was deepest and most sacred in me has been murdered, and as though the faith I had built up through so many years, had at one moment been scattered to the winds. My friends are gone, and now I realize they were never mine....[22]

What on earth was the matter? Dolin had signed his contract.

It is not my pride that is hurt [wrote Lifar], nor my self-love, but something deeper has been cruelly, painfully wounded by the engagement of this Englishman ... something of which I might be justly proud ... all my heroic effort in the arts, that urge which inspired me with the strength to sustain the whole ballet with my feeble forces, when every one of our principal dancers had left us. As witness the season when neither Massine, Idzikovsky, Slavinsky, Dolin or Wilzak were with us.... They cannot ignore the fact that, though I had broken both my ankles [that is, sprained one], still I went on in *Flore et Zéphyr*....²³

No doubt these outpourings of *l'âme slave* were passed on to Diaghilev, who spent the whole of February in Paris. He was standing no nonsense. He needed Lifar for *Le Fils prodigue*, just as he needed Dolin for *Le Bal* (and each would play a subsidiary part in the other's ballet). Within a few days of this last letter Lifar was in Paris; and, to keep him quiet, Diaghilev gave him another chance of becoming a choreographer. He was to try a new version of *Renard*, and good old Larionov would help him. A studio was hired at the Salle Pleyel.²⁴ To cover up any possible deficiencies in Lifar's invention, Diaghilev made the ingenious suggestion that the cast of four dancers should be 'doubled' by four acrobats. When a dancer left the stage, an acrobat, identically dressed and masked by Larionov, would take his place and perform unexpected prodigies. Lifar resisted this idea with all his might.²⁵ He did not know how lucky he was. Diaghilev's 'gimmick' would give him the reputation of originality as a choreographer, just as Balanchine's illness, after Diaghilev's death, would give him the chance, which he grabbed, to enthrone himself at the Opéra. On 24 February, according to Lifar (who later wrote that the idea of the acrobats was his own), Diaghilev saw the first sketches of movement. The next day he looked in again. On 1 March he agreed that Lifar should go ahead.²⁶ Diaghilev wrote to Grigoriev on 7 March, telling him to start rehearsing *Les Noces*, which he intended to give in Berlin. (This did not happen.) 'As for Cléopâtre, I wish her to be buried for good.'²⁷ He had to make a decision about his contribution to a gala on 18 March, and he sent Grigoriev two alternatives, with the instructions that, 'if Lifar didn't come,' Tcherkass was to dance the Hornpipe in *Neptune*.²⁸ On the fifteenth Diaghilev telegraphed Grigoriev to ask where the cimbalom previously played in *Renard* was, and heard that Grigoriev had it safely at his flat.²⁹ On the twentieth Diaghilev, Kochno and Lifar went to Monte Carlo.³⁰ Larionov found some good acrobats – a troupe of four jumping Arabs –³¹ and Nuvel was told to sign a contract with them.³² Ansermet was summoned and told to bring the address of the man (Aladar Racz) who had played the cimbalom in 1922.³³

Diaghilev's thoughts had been dwelling, as so often when he was planning new ballets, in the eighteenth century. He remembered Sacheverell Sitwell speaking to him of a mad Irishman, a friend of Scarlatti's, who wrote strange fugues. On 1 March Sitwell, who was working with his brother at the Albergo Capuccini-Convento at Amalfi, answered his letter of enquiry. Unfortunately for Diaghilev, his bête noire, Constant Lambert (who had sued in 1928 through the Society of Authors, Playwrights and Composers for non-payment of 1,050 francs, being royalties on seven performances of *Romeo and Juliet* in Germany),³⁴ was the authority on the composer in question.

Cher Maître,
   I received your letter this morning and have already written to Lambert. I think your composer was a certain Rosingrave or Roseingrave. He was Irish and a pupil of Domenico Scarlatti. Lambert has indeed copied some of his compositions, which are without exception in manuscript. I'm afraid that you'll find there is not enough music [for a ballet]. He wrote for the harpsichord and rather more for the organ, being organist at the church in Hanover Square in London. It is his extraordinary fugues – rather mad, as you say – that Lambert has copied.
   Do you know the music of Maurice Green? He was the master of Boyce, and much less provincial. . . .
I must tell you that there is a twenty-two-year-old artist called *Rex Whistler*, who is extremely talented. He is an exceptionally clever *pasticheur*. Don't go to see his frescoes in the Tate Gallery. He has done much better things since. All good wishes to Boris Kochno.³⁵

On 4 March a postcard, also in French, arrived from Lambert, who promised to send everything he had by Rosingrave within a few days.³⁶
   Another eighteenth-century composer in whom Diaghilev suddenly became interested was Floquet, and he tried, with the aid of Henry Prunières, Editor of *La Revue musicale*, to trace a ballet he had written, but without success.³⁷
   While thinking up possible new ballets to eighteenth-century music, Diaghilev was rediscovering the greatness of Wagner; and he took Boris several times to hear *Parsifal* at the Casino.³⁸ It is odd that he never, after 1914, contemplated making ballets to music either of the early or late Romantic period.
   During April, while Lifar rehearsed Woizikovsky as the Fox and Efimov as the Cock in *Renard*, and himself danced *L'Après-midi d'un faune* for the first time (with one bare foot and one sandal, as in the design of Bakst),³⁹ while Dolin danced *Le Spectre de la rose* at the request of the Duke of Connaught,⁴⁰ while Sokolova began to work again with the company,⁴¹ and while Balanchine rehearsed *Le Bal* and *Le Fils prodigue*, the question of Nikitina and Lord Rothermere raised its Janus head. On 4 April Alice was well again, wanting to rejoin the Ballet, but Rothermere was ill – though his son Esmond promised to help.⁴² On 29 April Wollheim telegraphed that Rothermere would give money and publicity if Nikitina danced.⁴³
   Chirico supervised the painting of his setting for *Le Bal* at Monte Carlo, and Diaghilev invited Rouault to visit the principality and work out his designs with Prokofiev, Balanchine and himself. The odd little man arrived in April without any sketches, but said he had brought his painting materials.

Rouault spent the mornings watching rehearsals, lunched daily with Diaghilev, then retired to his hotel room – where he was supposed to be at work.[44] Balanchine thought him a bit mad, for he used to balance chairs on his nose at rehearsals:[45] but the painter was enraptured. He wrote to a friend, 'I, who, according to some, am supposed to be a painter of horrors, hesitate to say how enchanted I was with the rhythms and movement patterns of the girl dancers. . . . I saw the entire ballet perform: friezes, bas-reliefs, pediments, compositions of every sort were formulated in space. Indeed the mind was carried far away from mere sensual spectacle.'[46]

Kochno found the lunches with Rouault 'a great bore', because the painter was obsessed by the idea that his dealer Vollard favoured his 'rival', Marc Chagall, and talked of nothing else. When the ballet was mentioned, he fell silent.[47] Boris, who gave him the idea for the tent in the middle scene,[48] wrote:

One day, Diaghilev . . . at the end of his patience, resolved to get hold of the sketches which Rouault kept saying had been finished long since. He persuaded Rouault to take a long drive along the Grande Corniche . . . and, in his absence, had his room unlocked.

Diaghilev returned from this trespass empty-handed and wild-eyed. He had searched everywhere, turned the room upside down, and had discovered not one ballet sketch. . . . He had not even found drawing paper, brushes or paints.

That evening Diaghilev announced to Rouault that a reservation had been made for him on the Paris train the next day. He said nothing about *Le Fils prodigue*. Although Rouault had arrived with a single piece of luggage, he now seemed anxious to go up to his room to pack his bags, and he disappeared for the entire evening. The following morning, before boarding the train, Rouault brought Diaghilev a stack of sketches – admirable gouaches and pastels which he had executed in one night.[49]

Diaghilev and Kochno were in Paris at the Grand Hôtel at the end of April.[50] One night Dukelsky went to see *Blackbirds*, the Negro revue from America, which, after captivating London, was on its second visit to Paris, at the Moulin Rouge, though without the famous Florence Mills (adored by Constant Lambert), who had died in November 1927. There were no seats to be had, and Dukelsky bought a ticket for the *promenoir*. As he elbowed his way through the crowd at the back of the stalls, he bumped into 'a large man in an unseasonable beaver-fur coat'.

He turned round to reprimand me haughtily for 'pushing him about' when we both stopped dead in our tracks – the large man was Diaghilev. His mustache was carefully trimmed, the monocle shone as disdainfully as ever . . . but, in spite of the determinedly youthful pose, there was something . . . that I didn't recognise and that tightened my throat. Diaghilev was accompanied by a slim, wolf-faced youth who disappeared before I had a chance of being introduced; he was Igor Markevitch, Diaghilev's official 'fourth son' and my successor in his musical affections. . . . 'It's good to see you, Dima,' he said. 'You at least didn't desert me for that ogress Ida Rubinstein – she has already annexed Sauguet, Auric and Stravinsky. . . . Rieti tells me that you played your *Mistress into Maid* for him; he liked it enormously. I'm so glad. I always adored the tale [by Pushkin].' I told Diaghilev I was sailing for the States a week later. . . . 'Not for long, I hope; I want you to come to Venice in September and play your opera for me. If I staged it I'd have arias, duets and trios sung and danced at the same time. What fun!' I stammered something about being thrilled . . . and took my departure after the traditional Diaghilev kiss on both cheeks.[51]

Markevitch remembers meeting Cocteau for the first time at a performance of *Blackbirds*, which Diaghilev so much enjoyed; so their encounter may have taken place on this same night.[52]

On 1 May, since rail transport had to be booked, Grigoriev telegraphed to Diaghilev to ask when the company were to leave Monte Carlo, their last night being the twelfth. The answer came: 'First train on the 13th.'[53] Nuvel had taken Diaghilev's place in Monte Carlo, but on 7 May Diaghilev was present at the 'try-out' *première* of *Le Bal*. It was a success. By the tenth he was back in Paris. Grigoriev sent him the unwelcome news that the Casino authorities wanted his scenery moved out. It cost 6,000 francs a year in storage charges and they demanded 3,600 before they would release it.[54] The last programme at Monte Carlo, which Diaghilev did not see, was *Cléopâtre*, *Le Tricorne* and *Schéhérazade*. On 13 May the company arrived in Paris. Juliet Duff had been at work and Wollheim telegraphed to the Hôtel Scribe, 'Lady Juliet paying you £500 today.'[55] On the fifteenth an application from Diaghilev for publicity in the Continental edition of the *Daily Mail* received this brusque reply from Mr Warden, the editor: 'If Mr Diaghilev wishes to advertise his forthcoming Paris season he must see Mr J. Luntley . . . and he will be treated as any other advertiser.'[56] Diaghilev had words with Rothermere's henchman, Outhwaite, who on 18 May wrote as follows:

After my conversation with you yesterday Lord Rothermere has given instructions to the Paris Daily Mail to give you publicity in Paris & you will also have publicity in London during your London season. He will also send £500 (five hundred pounds) to Lady Juliet Duff as a contribution towards the expenses of the Russian Ballet in London.

This of course is dependent upon Miss Nikitina joining the Ballet June 5th & continuing work with it through the London season, receiving a salary equal to that of the Premier Ballerina & being given every possible opportunity in the principal parts. . . .

Please get in touch with Miss Nikitina at the earliest possible opportunity at the Hotel Majestic, Paris.[57]

From 3 Belgrave Square Juliet had been writing: 'What is happening with Rothermere? . . . His money will be essential. I've had a lot of promises. The

Courtaulds are giving £300, but she's ill.... She's a scatterbrain and, my God, what a bore. Hardly anyone in London now because of the election. Emerald [Cunard] very sweet and well disposed to you. She's booking seats and giving money and much goodwill besides....'⁵⁸ Then again: 'Do what you can with Rothermere, I beg you. I've had a few promises, but now people think of nothing but the election.... I spent several days with Diana [Cooper] in Manchester – what a town! She's there electioneering with her husband....'⁵⁹

The costumes for *Le Fils prodigue* were made by Vera Sudeikina. Rouault gave her bits of coloured paper, and, although Kochno had drawn some indications of what was necessary, like many *artistes-peintres* without experience of dressmaking, Rouault left much to his interpreter. Vera bought forty metres of a cheap white cotton velvet, borrowed a spray-gun from a friend and sprayed patterns of red, black and ochre dye on the material before cutting it up. The painter soon became an active nuisance: he kept appearing at the theatre or in Diaghilev's room at the Grand Hôtel 'with terrible pieces of blue ribbon', saying the colours were all wrong.⁶⁰

Grigoriev thought Prokofiev's passionate music needed Fokine's style of choreography;⁶¹ Prokofiev had perhaps hoped for a big spectacle and was dissatisfied with Balanchine's staging of his ballet;⁶² Rouault complained that he had wanted the tent for the middle orgy scene to be 'like a bird descending from heaven' instead of another painted décor – 'As it is, it hides my setting [of the landscape with a minaret-like tower] for the greater part of the performance.... I had to spend three nights repainting it, so that it would not be too frightful looking ...';⁶³ Diaghilev kept urging Lifar to let himself go emotionally, which was the opposite of his usual advice.⁶⁴

On 21 May 1929 the Russian Ballet was to open its last Paris season at the Théâtre Sarah Bernhardt, opposite the Châtelet, where Diaghilev's opera and ballet company had appeared on 18 May 1909. The programme was *Les Fâcheux, Renard, Le Fils prodigue* and *Prince Igor*.

Lifar went to bed on the afternoon of the *première* and announced that he could not dance. 'Some force ... seemed to be pinning me down.' The long-suffering Koribut, an easy prey, was 'dumb with terror'. Then suddenly Lifar leapt from his bed. 'Let's go off to the theatre,' he cried. 'I have created the Prodigal Son.... It is myself.'⁶⁵

After *Renard* Lifar was supposed to take a call with Stravinsky, but, disregarding the composer's pleas and Grigoriev's order, he clung to an iron bar and refused. This he relates as though it were the result of another supernatural 'force', but it seems possible that he was already dressed and made up for *Le Fils prodigue*, which followed, and did not wish to spoil his entry in that ballet by showing himself in the Rouault costume before it began.⁶⁶ Kochno had reduced the parable of the Prodigal Son to the simplest of stories: a leave-taking, an orgy, the destitution of the Prodigal, his return and welcome home. The point of Our Lord's parable, which consisted in the jealousy of the righteous elder brother and the killing of the fatted calf for the one who 'was lost, and is found', was omitted. Just as Salome's dance could be made the centre-piece of a play or opera about the martyrdom of St John the Baptist, so had the younger son's 'wasting his substance on riotous living' with a gang of sinister Egyptian boon companions – the 'harlots' being reduced to one – become the big scene of the ballet. The powerful episode of the Prodigal's homecoming was all mime.

If Balanchine's originality and economy of means went unappreciated by Prokofiev, they had a telling effect on the public. In the orgy scene, where the Prodigal is made drunk, submits to the Siren, and is robbed by her and her gang, Diaghilev had, in fact, been given a new and up-to-date *Schéhéra-zade*, which he had not bargained for. Although the tall, frigid Dubrovska, goose-stepping on point, was comparable in her menace and pride to the Zobéïda created by Rubinstein for Fokine twenty years before, there were no voluptuous caresses in Balanchine's ballet: the sexual act was symbolized by the Siren's forming herself into a ring round the Prodigal's waist, hand grasping ankle, and being allowed to slide thus, gently, to the ground. Balanchine complained that in Kochno's librettos there always occurred the word 'promenade'. In *Le Fils prodigue* this came after the Prodigal passed out, drunk,[67] and it gave rise to some of Balanchine's most fantastic inventions – the dividing of the spoils; the insect-like pattering around of the exultant robbers, back to back, arms interlocked, knees bent; and the upturning of the long table, which became a boat, with the men's arms for oars, the Siren as figure-head and her long crimson cloak for a sail. Everyone agreed that Lifar's final return home, in black rags, haggard, dirty and dishevelled, as he dragged himself across the floor, holding on to a stout stick, to be lifted like a child and enfolded in his father's cloak, was wonderful. This emotional display, the opposite of what Diaghilev usually admired or allowed, aroused enthusiasm in the audience. (According to Lifar, 'Pandemonium broke loose. Numbers of people were crying.'[68]) It was 'Lifar, on his knees, that made the ballet,' said Balanchine generously.[69] But, according to Danilova, Balanchine had 'made' Lifar, whose Prodigal she thought 'very good'.[70]

There was a party afterwards at the Restaurant des Capucines, and Serge Lifar sat between Misia and Coco Chanel, and opposite Diaghilev, who was pleased with the way the evening had gone.[71]

Boris Kochno had taken his ideas for *Le Bal* from a Hoffmannesque story by the Romantic writer Count Vladimir Sologub[72] (whose daughter Diaghilev used to see at concerts when he was young).[73] But the ballet was little more than a *divertissement* with set dances – an Italian one for Lifar and Lipkovska, and a Spanish *pas de trois* for Dubrovska, Balanchine and Woizikovsky: and yet it *was* something more than a *divertissement*. In that 'something' lay Kochno's skill as a librettist. In his own words, 'It was a poetic episode set in the Romantic period, having a mysterious and unearthly character which few people appreciated at the time.'[74] Before the strange, striking front curtain – the exterior wall of a house, with three doors and the incised letters B A L on high, and with two gigantic naked male figures in relief, one playing cymbals, the other dancing – the guests arrive. The main décor is the interior of an empty, commonplace room in which classical props have been placed for the ball. A young officer, Dolin, comes alone to the fancy-dress ball and is attracted by a mysterious beauty, Danilova. When he pursues her, she removes her mask, to reveal the face of a wrinkled hag; then, as he flees, she pursues him. In the end, as she leaves on the arm of her Astrologer, she removes her second mask to disclose the features which are truly fair, and the young man falls senseless at her feet. Chirico's costumes were *appliqués* with architectural motives – scrolls, triumphal arches, Ionic capitals – and clouds.

On 2 June Massine telegraphed from the Roxy Theatre in New York to know whether he might dance in the London season, offering to pay for his own journey.[75] In his special roles, however, the Can-can Dancer, the Miller and Petrushka, Woizikovsky was more than adequate, and Diaghilev refused his offer.

The English elections were over and Ramsay MacDonald was for the second time Labour Prime Minister. Juliet Duff was exhausted by her fund-raising for Diaghilev; and it worried her that he demanded the money as soon as she received it, instead of letting it accumulate undisturbed until the end of the London season. On 12 June she wrote:

> I've just had a cheque from Lord Rothermere for the London season. Wollheim tells me you need this at once, but to what purpose? Money given me by other people for the London season is a great responsibility for me, and Wollheim must explain to me why he needs the money now.
>
> Cher chéri, even for you I couldn't go through this again next year. One writes 100 letters to people who don't answer for weeks, then one has to write another 100 to get the money they have promised. When all the money comes in I shall have £2,000. I think that should be enough for Covent Garden, seeing the theatre is so big. It should bring in much more than His Majesty's.[76]

But Diaghilev got his way, and on 13 June Wollheim telegraphed that the cheque had been paid in. What is more, seventeen books had arrived for Diaghilev and he had them in his safe.[77]

Before leaving Paris, Diaghilev visited Dr Dalimier, for he was covered in running sores. The doctor told him he had diabetes, put him on a strict diet and ordered him to eat saccharine instead of sugar. He spoke of a new miracle drug which was available in Switzerland, although there was none in France. This was insulin. He issued a grave warning.[78]

Rouault attended the last night of Diaghilev's ballet in Paris. With painters and poets there is often trouble about 'the right clothes'. Years before, Misia had brought Renoir to the Opéra in his paint-spotted working clothes.[79] Rouault had invited the poet André Suarès and he wrote to reassure him: 'About the dress suit I want you to know that I myself went once in street clothes although, true enough, I had on a white collar and a black bow tie. In any case, should you have any difficulty, ask for M. Diaghilev in my name, and don't walk out with your ticket the way you did the other time.'[80]

The Diaghilev Ballet danced for the last time in Paris on 12 June, the programme being *Le Bal, Le Fils prodigue, Renard* and *Prince Igor*. Chanel gave a great party afterwards. The garden of her house in rue du Faubourg Saint-Honoré was lit up; and a cabaret was provided by Snakehips Johnson, with other Blackbirds. Igor Markevitch was dazzled by the splendour of the scene;[81] and Sauguet noticed that caviare was served from soup tureens.[82]

The Berlin season, with Ansermet conducting, was surprisingly successful, in view of the Ballet's cool reception in 1926.[83] On the last night, after *Le Bal* and *Le Fils prodigue*, Dolin joined friends in their box; and he thought that in *The Rite* Sokolova, who, after her long illness, had dreaded the ordeal of the Chosen Virgin's dance, received 'one of the greatest receptions given to a dancer that he had ever witnessed'. There was a party for the company at the flat of Catherine Devillier (an ex-member) and the Princesse de Rohan. When Dolin came in, Sokolova greeted him with the words, 'Heavens, Pat, you didn't half clap. What a night! Good for old England I say!'[84]

In Cologne, where the Ballet gave two performances on their way to England, it was *Les Fâcheux* which was acclaimed. Here Dolin danced for the first time the *pas de trois* in *Le Lac des Cygnes*.[85]

In Berlin, Diaghilev had received at the Hotel Bristol a telegram from his Paris bank telling him that he was overdrawn 75,000 francs, that cheques to the amount of 20,000 francs had been returned, and that cover was essential.[86] From London, where he went ahead of the company on 23 June, he sent them £400.[87]

Diaghilev, Kochno and Lifar were once more and for the last time at Albemarle Court, and Stravinsky and Vera Sudeikina were in the apartment next door, so that they could hear the voices of Diaghilev and his friends through the wall – but Serge and Igor were not on speaking terms.[88] Stravinsky was to conduct *Apollon* and *Le Baiser de la fée* with the BBC Orchestra at the Kingsway Hall on Thursday, 27 June.

The first calls Diaghilev had to make were at the St Martin's Lane office of the faithful Wollheim (who had become almost as much part of his life as Nuvel), on Colonel Blois (the Managing Director of Covent Garden) and on Juliet Duff, who had worked so hard to raise the guarantee for his season, at 3 Belgrave Square. People used rather to laugh at Lady Juliet, who was so tall and no beauty, and there was a saying that Lady Ripon had had her excessively well educated in the hopes that people would overlook her other deficiencies. She had made Diaghilev's last London season possible, however, as her mother had made his first, and she would be part of history.

English friends who had not seen Diaghilev for months were shocked by his appearance; but he, who had always made such a fuss about the slightest indisposition, spoke lightly of his increasing weakness.

Diaghilev's usual *Observer* interview appeared on 30 June, the day before the opening:

I return to Covent Garden with the sentiment of great emotion, for it was here, at the Command Performance in the year of King George's Coronation, that my Russian Ballet made its first appearance in London. When I came into the theatre the spirit of the Marchioness of Ripon seemed to pervade the place. She was the great friend of the Ballet, the first person in England to love and appreciate our work, and the tradition is still in the family. I am happy to say that her daughter, Lady Juliet Duff, is the principal patron of our present season, which I hope will be no less brilliant than the ones patronized by her mother.[89]

On 1 July the season opened. 'Youth came back that night to Diaghilev,' wrote Dolin. 'Dressed perfectly, with a white carnation in his buttonhole, opera hat and stick, he came and spoke to us all on stage and gave us his blessing as he always did before the beginning of an important season.'[90]

The Prodigal Son (*Le Fils prodigue*) was sandwiched between two favourites, *The Gods go a-begging*, in which Danilova and Woizikovsky were always acclaimed, and *Aurora's Wedding*, with Lifar as the Prince, supporting Danilova's Aurora, and Tchernicheva, Sokolova, Dubrovska and Nikitina among the other fairies. Markova and Dolin danced the Blue Bird *pas de deux* for the first time together. *The Times* thought Lifar had turned into a 'first-class mime'. 'He gave to the first and last scenes [of *Le Fils prodigue*] a Blake-like intensity of texture and expression.... The moment when the Prodigal crept into the bosom of his father was genuinely moving....'[91] Richard Capell, one of the Russians' earliest admirers, and still writing for the *Daily Mail*, wrote,

Among the impressions brought away was that made by Mme Dubrovska, who played the part of the courtesan.... Was there ever woman more strangely serpentine? There was not a hint of voluptuousness in the scene.... The prodigal was fascinated by the siren's inhuman contortions, and he joined her in those strained acrobatical feats which characterize M. Balanchine's choreography. Another impression is that of the returned prodigal, mimed with peculiar intensity, and as though in torture, by young M. Serge Lifar.... One feels that Balanchine is a serious artist, striving with much intelligence to make new expressive forms....[92]

When Capell wrote his first ballet notice (of *Carnaval* in 1911) the word 'choreography' had not been in common use.

Tuesday's programme contained outstanding works by three very different 'choreographers', whom Diaghilev had brought to the eyes of the Western world and whose names will live as long as the art of ballet survives: Fokine's *Les Sylphides*, Balanchine's *Apollon Musagète* and Massine's *La Boutique fantasque*. On Wednesday, 3 July, at the matinée, Tamara Karsavina danced the Ballerina in *Petrushka*, in which London had first seen her at the same theatre in spring 1913. Now Woizikovsky had taken the place of Nijinsky as her Petrushka. She was to dance this undemanding role, 'in which', according to Richard Capell, 'she had never been surpassed,' five times during July, thus lending lustre to the season and establishing the feeling of historic continuity that Diaghilev prized.

It may have been of this performance or of a later one that Karsavina wrote:

> The last picture of Diaghilev in my mind is that of a friend faithful in heart.... I ran to meet him as he walked slowly behind the backcloth, leaning on the cane that he used to whirl around in such a debonair way. Arm-in-arm we came to my dressing-room. He leaned back in an armchair, huddled and heavy. Gone was all the buoyancy, the peculiar lazy grace. He said, 'I left my bed to come and see you. Judge of my love.' But his face was not worried: he talked of Venice and of some young composers in whose future he believed.[93]

Capell's notice of this performance, published on Thursday the fourth, was his last piece on the Russian Ballet. (He was evidently going on holiday.) 'She played the part (for she is not merely a dancer, but also an actress),' he wrote of Karsavina, as she first played it seventeen years before – with 'a touch of pathos, and (yes! although she is but a doll) of dignity all her own. This was a doll from a princess's nursery. The whole ballet – which

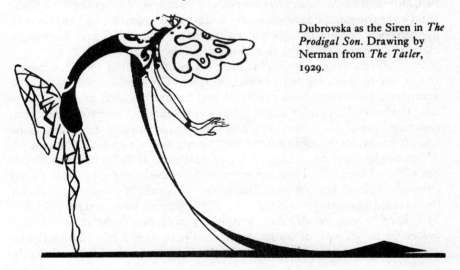

Dubrovska as the Siren in *The Prodigal Son*. Drawing by Nerman from *The Tatler*, 1929.

is Stravinsky's masterpiece and perhaps the high-water mark of the vast Diaghilev repertory – went well under the conductorship of M. Roger Desormière.'[94] In the evening, *Pastorale*, of which Diaghilev was evidently not ashamed, took its place in the repertoire.

Diaghilev's health was getting steadily worse, and his London doctor, Talariko, recommended that he should have a nurse to dress his sores. This he absolutely refused, and Boris had daily to squeeze the pus out of every abscess on his body, of which, at one time, there were sixteen. He had kept strictly to his diet; then, one day, Boris noticed him feasting on forbidden dishes. When he remonstrated, Diaghilev looked surprised. 'But it's Sunday!' he protested. He took to staying in bed most of the day and entrusted Kochno with the lighting at Covent Garden.[95]

On Monday, 8 July, London saw *Le Bal* (*The Ball*). It was a huge hit, particularly for Chirico and Dolin. The *Morning Post* reported that 'it pleased everybody of every section of opinion. It was certainly the most successful novelty of the last few years.'[96] In the left-wing intellectual weekly, *Nation and Athenaeum*, the reviewer was none other than Lydia Lopukhova, Mrs Keynes. She was not on the whole an admirer of Balanchine's choreography, which she found lacking in heart or soul. 'After the throbbing *Prodigal Son*, M. Diaghilev has presented us with a sort of *pâtisserie* in a lighter vein. . . . The choreography was lively, muscular and pretty, but not inspiring; though the *pas de deux* of Dolin and Danilova, who danced very well indeed, and the tarantella of Lipkowska and Lifar were excellent set pieces. . . . The joy and beauty of this ballet is [*sic*] to be found in Chirico's décor. . . . This is the smartest ballet we have seen for many seasons.'[97] No one commented on the mystery which was a special characteristic of this ball, although the *Saturday Review* allowed a glimpse of it between the lines: 'And after the guests have gone, sylphides, archaeologists and all, the two door-keepers, in beautiful white tights, upon which figleaves have been modestly woven, sweep the floor with delicious grace.'[98]

Pat Dolin had taken a studio in Glebe Place, off the King's Road, Chelsea. It was one of those big high rooms, with a kitchen leading off it, and the bedroom on a screened-off gallery,[99] and he had decided to give a party after the ballet. 'Diaghilev's appearances at rehearsals,' he wrote, 'had been fewer and fewer. . . . I asked Kochno if he was coming to my party as he had promised, but he could not tell me. "Sergei Pavlovitch is ill," he said. . . . About two hundred turned up. . . . By 12.30 the whole Ballet had assembled; but still no Diaghilev. Then the curtains drew aside and Lady Juliet Duff entered – behind her followed Diaghilev. . . . Astafieva greeted him as she had greeted him many years before. . . .'[100] Nikitina wore 'a tight gold turban'. Rieti, whose 'Noah's Ark' had been played that night as an *entr'acte* before his ballet, was, of course, present. There were Lady Hadfield, who had often entertained Dolin in the South of France, and Anthony Asquith,

Lady Oxford's son,[101] who was to become a famous film director. Dorothy Dickson, the ravishing musical-comedy star from Chicago (then appearing in *Hold Everything!* at the Palace) asked Diaghilev why someone did not make a ballet about his life and work. '*You* tell them,' he said.[102] Tallulah Bankhead and Beatrice Lillie were also there. Sokolova observed her beloved tyrant. 'His face was ashen, the flesh was loose round his cheeks, his eyes were sunken and his grey hair showed through the dye. He sat down on a chair near the door and folded his hands on top of his cane, just as I remembered him doing when I went for my first audition at Covent Garden sixteen years before....'[103] Douglas Byng and Misha de la Motte sang their witty numbers and did impersonations. 'Diaghilev smiled benignly.'[104] He stayed nearly an hour.[105]

On 9 July *Le Tricorne* was danced by Woizikovsky and Tchernicheva. Dolin appeared in *Les Matelots* for the first time on the tenth. Igor Markevitch arrived from Paris to rehearse his Piano Concerto, which was to be performed at Covent Garden. On the twelfth Diaghilev was invited to lunch with the Samuel Courtaulds.[106] On the thirteenth Misia arrived from Paris with Lady Abdy, having telegraphed before to ask Diaghilev to book her two rooms at the Savoy 'with baths'.[107] For the great events – Lifar's first ballet and Markevitch's Piano Concerto, which Rieti had helped him orchestrate – were to take place on Monday, 15 July. Invitations to an unprecedented midday party for the Press and friends, to herald the evening's *première*, were sent out.

Two days before, Diaghilev had given a boost to his young pioneers in a letter to *The Times*. He had not lost his old Wildean touch.

The longer the globe revolves, the less movement we find on it! Peoples may fight world wars, empires may tumble, a colossal Utopia may be given birth to, but the inborn traditions of humanity remain the same.

Our century interests itself with *Mouvements mécaniques*, but whenever new *Mouvements artistiques* occur people seem to be more frightened of being run over by them than by a motor-car in the street. For 25 years I have endeavoured to find a new *Mouvement* in the theatre. Society will have to recognize that my experiments, which appear dangerous today, become indispensable tomorrow. The misfortune of art is that everyone thinks he is entitled to his own judgement. When a scientist invents an electrical machine it is only experts who assume the right to be competent to criticize, but when I invent my artistic machine, everybody, without ceremony, puts his finger into the most delicate parts of the engine and likes to run it his own way....

The appreciation of my 'spectacles' of today is a series of exclamations: What an 'Etrange', 'Extravagant', 'Repellent' show, and the new definitions of the choreography are 'Athletics' and 'Acrobatics'. I can picture to myself the bewilderment of the people who saw the first electric lamp, who heard the first word on the telephone.

Royal Opera House

COVENT GARDEN

Mr. Serge Diaghileff

requests the honour of the Company of

to assist at the Final Rehearsal on

MONDAY, JULY. 15th, at noon

at the

ROYAL OPERA HOUSE. COVENT GARDEN

of

IGOR STRAVINSKY'S Music

for the

"RENARD"

Previous to its first presentation in England

and the

CONCERTO for Piano

by

IGOR MARKEVITCH

Played by the Composer and the
COVENT GARDEN ORCHESTRA

12 Noon, Monday, July 15th   Cocktails 1 p.m.

There followed a whopping lie: 'My first electric bell for the British public was the *Polovtsian Dances* from *Prince Igor*. The small audience could not then tolerate this eccentric and acrobatic savagery, and they fled. And this only happened in 1911, at Covent Garden.' He defended Balanchine at the expense of Petipa: 'The classical dance has never been and is not today The Russian Ballet. Its birthplace was France; it grew up in Italy, and has been conserved in Russia.... The coarsest acrobatic tricks are the toe-dancing, the "doubles tours en l'air", next to the "Pirouettes en dehors", and the hateful "32 fouettés".... In the plastic efforts of Balanchine in *The Prodigal Son*, there are far less acrobatics than in the final classical *pas de deux* of *Aurora's Wedding*.'

Then he concluded with a reference to Lifar and Markevitch: 'The public and the critics will probably be annoyed with my two young friends, but they are both "débutants", and they are not afraid of it.'[108]

Of course Igor Markevitch was writing a ballet for the company, and naturally Boris Kochno had thought of a subject. It was taken from Hans Andersen's story 'The Emperor's New Clothes', and the ballet was to be called *L'Habit du roi*. It was agreed, after much discussion, that at the moment of climax, when the King appeared in procession in the beflagged street, the Child should actually call out in a high, piping voice, 'But the King is naked!' Following this, Markevitch wanted the orchestra to go mad: to illustrate the shock on the King's court and the crowd, each instrument was to improvise a few bars at random; and the resulting cacophony would bring the ballet to an end. Diaghilev was delighted with this idea, which, if the ballet had seen the light of day, would have been the first aleatory music in history, a quarter of a century before Stockhausen. Boris urged during lunch at the Savoy that the setting for *L'Habit* should be as bare and simple as possible – something like *Les Noces*, with its grand pianos. Diaghilev had more flamboyant plans – a décor by Picasso, at least – and he burst out, 'We've had all that. You can fuck yourself with your grand pianos!'[109] Although Diaghilev 'always wanted Picasso for everything', he felt that *L'Habit du roi* was entitled to a designer as young and new as its composer.[110] He might well have decided to give it a kinetic décor, for he had already discussed with Gabo the possibility of mobile scenery.[111]

In Paris Diaghilev had made Markevitch play his concerto privately, both to Misia and to Princesse Edmond de Polignac. On Sunday, 14 July, on the eve of Igor's début before the world, Diaghilev hired a car and took him to Hampton Court. He loved the old brick palace on the banks of the unpretentious Thames. It was a sunny afternoon. During lunch under a leafy arbour at a restaurant by the river Sergei Pavlovitch impressed upon Igor the importance of his first concert on the following day, and warned him not to expect the public to appreciate his music.[112]

Before the Monday midday party the principal female dancers were assembled in the bar at Covent Garden and told to act as hostesses. Diaghilev asked Sokolova, as she spoke English, to tell the critics what a brilliant composer Markevitch was.[113]

After the cocktail party there were six for lunch at the Savoy. This summer Diaghilev was always given table 23.[114] The concerto was received by public and critics without rapture, as Diaghilev had predicted. Once again he was ahead of his time, and the truffle of talent he had sniffed out would be exposed in *Icare* and *Paradis perdu* only after his death. That evening Markevitch insisted on bringing Desormière, for whose good work he was grateful, back to supper at the Savoy. He himself was staying at the hotel, though Diaghilev was at Albemarle Court. Markevitch returned to Paris next day.[115] It had been arranged that Diaghilev should take him to Baden-Baden, Munich and Salzburg when the season was over.

Stravinsky's *Renard* had not been heard before in England. The four singers had come from France just for the final ten days of the season. 'A high-class circus ... a grotesque entertainment,' wrote the critic of *The Times*.[116] *Renard* was given five times in all, the last performance being on 25 July, the penultimate night.

In the same economical way, Olga Spessivtseva's four guest appearances in *Le Lac des Cygnes* all took place between the sixteenth and the twenty-second. Those who saw Spessivtseva as Odette that season never forgot the experience. Her visit not only gave Diaghilev the gratification (to the extent that he was still capable of pleasure) of presenting the one he believed to be the purest living exponent of classical dancing, but enabled him to enlarge the range of his repertoire to show the choreography of Ivanov as well as that of Petipa – but Ivanov was given no credit.

After the ballet on the seventeenth Mrs Grenfell – 'la fidèle amie', as she signed herself – gave a party for Diaghilev and the company at 4 Cavendish Square.[117] It was the first big party Markova had attended.[118] Spessivtseva always wore her hair plastered close to her head, with a centre parting. That night, when Dolin arrived to take her to the party, he was horrified to find she had a mass of curls and looked like 'an exaggerated golliwog'. Even Diaghilev for a moment failed to recognize 'his beloved Olga'. It was Dubrovska who put Spessivtseva's head in a bucket of water later that night, to straighten out 'those terrible curls'.[119] Just as well, for Olga was dancing *Le Lac des Cygnes* again on the eighteenth. Lady Colefax invited Diaghilev to cocktails at Argyll House, Chelsea, on that day.[120]

On the nineteenth Lifar danced *L'Après-midi d'un faune* for the first time in London and Diaghilev was asked to dine in South Street with Christabel McLaren (later Lady Aberconway).[121] On 20 July, when *Baba-Yaga* (without the other 'Children's Tales') was included in the programme, Juliet Duff sent round a message to Diaghilev: 'The Prince [of Wales] is miserable but he has not got a free evening next week. He told me to tell you how disappointed he is and hopes to have the pleasure next year. I must go to the country tomorrow ... but I'll come on Wednesday, Thursday and Friday. Please ask the Booking Office to leave me 2 Stalls (on the right as usual). ...'[122]

The twenty-second was not only the night of the fourth and last *Lac des Cygnes* but of the first *Rite of Spring*, which had last been seen in London on the restricted stage of the Prince's, in 1921. The *Daily Express* had a headline: 'LYDIA SOKOLOVA TRIUMPH', and described how she 'received an ovation quite as tremendous as that accorded, two months ago, to Mlle Rosa Ponselle, the singer. People nearly fell out of their seats and boxes to cheer her back after her long illness.'[123] The gossip columnist in the *Evening News* wrote that his companion whispered, ' "She's like Lillian Gish". He meant it for high praise.'[124]

That day the faithful Nuvel had cabled for 522 francs to pay the Customs; and on the twenty-third he begged Wollheim: 'Tell Diaghilev impossible leave Paris [for Ostend] Friday if I don't receive Wednesday 2,000 for myself and 4,500 for tickets Vichy which I must buy before leaving for Ostend.'[125]

Nikitina's foot had given way again and after 10 July she appeared no more that season.[126] Markova therefore danced the other performances of *La Chatte*, and Sauguet was in London to see her.[127] The matinée of Wednesday the twenty-fourth was her third and last. She was not in the fourth ballet, and Grigoriev told her Diaghilev wanted to see her after she had changed. Standing in the wings, to the sound of the music for *Baba-Yaga*, he told Alicia that she had now established her position in the company and would one day be its ballerina. Next season Spessivtseva was going to make guest appearances in *Giselle*; Markova must study the role.[128] This was a moment of happiness and fulfilment for her.

That night there was a gala for King Fuad; the programme had to be changed because the King wanted to see *Le Fils prodigue*;[129] and Diaghilev saw his company dance for the last time. In *Petrushka*, there were Woizikovsky, Karsavina and Lifar. Lifar and Dubrovska danced in *Le Fils prodigue*. Before the décor of Bakst and in costumes of Benois, Danilova and Lifar performed the *Grand pas de deux*, Markova and Dolin the Blue Bird dances, from *Aurora's Wedding*.

The young writer Harold Acton was with Lady Cunard in the Royal box.

His Majesty of Egypt was a robust man with tyrannical eyes and a rasping voice which frequently broke into a yelping cough – the result of having been shot in the throat by one of his relatives. But he talked vivaciously in spite of this: Lord Lloyd's resignation [from the post of High Commissioner to Egypt and the Sudan] had put him in an excellent humour. ... King Fuad shifted uneasily during *The Prodigal Son* and expressed disapproval in a series of violent yelps. King George had told him [doubtless because he had heard of the British dancers, such as

Lifar as the Prodigal in *The Prodigal Son*. Drawing by Nerman from *The Tatler*, 1929.

Sokolova and Dolin] the ballet was really English, he said, not Russian at all. 'Mais je me demande si c'est possible. Pour un ballet britannique ça me paraît bien bizarre.'[130]

Diaghilev went back-stage to say goodbye to the company. He told them that he had excellent bookings for them after the holidays. He said, 'I cannot kiss you all, but' – to Danilova – 'I must kiss you, Shura.'[131] He shook hands with the others, saying a few words to some, according to Sokolova, 'in the manner of Royalty'.[132] Lifar wrote of 'how tenderly and at length he took leave of all the veterans of the company, particularly Kremnev and the faithful Vassili'.[133] Grigoriev wrote, 'He and I embraced.'[134] Tchernicheva was retiring and the company had clubbed together to give her a topaz ring 'the colour of her eyes'.[135]

After the performance [wrote Harold Acton] I accompanied Lady Cunard to sup with Diaghilev at the Savoy. The ageing magician was feverishly gay, but

534

at moments I detected a resemblance to King Fuad: he had the same tyrannical eyes, the same air of Oriental opulence. Lifar, having danced in every ballet that evening and in a previous matinée, showed no symptoms of fatigue. He seemed a schoolboy abashed in Diaghilev's presence, devoured a great many sweets and smoked a cigarette as soon as his back was turned. As he puffed, quickly and guiltily, at this forbidden luxury, he looked like a marmoset on a spree, and nothing could have been more mischievous than his eyes twinkling over the disposal of the cigarette-butt, which was fizzling innocently in my coffee-cup when Diaghilev reminded him of bedtime.[136]

Sir Harold remembered that when Lifar 'longed to light a cigarette Kochno prevented him from doing so and kept him in order like a prefect'. Lady Juliet Duff, too, was at this supper, her farewell to Diaghilev.[137]

Diaghilev spent his last night in England at Albemarle Court: and on Thursday, 25 July, set off with Boris for France. Nuvel met him at the station and noticed that he looked 'years older and dragged his feet as he walked'. From the hotel he telephoned to make an appointment with his doctor.[138]

Dalimier (of whose children Diaghilev had once commissioned a portrait group by Pruna as a present) was seriously distressed by Diaghilev's condition – the open sores left by boils did not heal – and he issued a warning. Since the Ballet were going to Vichy, he must take a cure there. It was the ideal place, and he must stay there, resting and dieting throughout the summer. But when Diaghilev left the doctor, he went directly to order his tickets for the musical tour with Markevitch.[139] Since the doctor had recommended fresh air, he dined with Nuvel in the Bois.[140]

Nuvel had to leave for Ostend on the Friday morning and he visited Diaghilev in his bedroom at the Grand Hôtel to say good-bye before he left. 'When shall we meet again?' asked Serioja. His old friend was looking forward to a holiday undisturbed by telegrams. 'Never!' was Valetchka's flippant reply.[141]

On Thursday the twenty-fifth, in London, the Ballet gave *The Rite*, *L'Après-midi d'un faune*, *Renard* and *The Gods go a-begging*. On Friday, 26 July, their last night, the programme was *The Ball*, *The Prodigal Son* and *Aurora's Wedding*. Wollheim telegraphed news of the takings, £850; and added that the Prime Minister had been present.[142] The Ballet left for Ostend, where they gave two performances; Boris joined them on their way through Paris, and travelled with them to Vichy in central France, where they gave four more. Chaliapine was there, drinking the waters; he sent Markova chocolates.[143] Dolin and Lifar rowed together on the lake.[144] The final performance of the Diaghilev Ballet was on 4 August 1929: *Cimarosiana*, *Le Tricorne*, *La Boutique fantasque* – a Massine programme of which Woizikovsky may be said to have been the star, dancing the Miller with Sokolova, and the Can-can with Danilova. Dolin had had to leave before the last night.

Balanchine was the Corregidor in *Le Tricorne*. Lifar had never given up his role of the Shop Assistant in *La Boutique* because it was such a good one, and he loved playing the fool in it.[145]

Lifar had evidently telegraphed to Diaghilev about the ovation after the last night in London. At Vichy he had found a letter waiting for him. Before leaving Paris, Diaghilev wrote:

Dearest, my congratulations on the end of your brilliant season in London. I am overjoyed with the success of *Le Fils prodigue* – what flowers and bays! Who can possibly have sent them?

I am leaving today at two. My health is better, but the wound not yet healed. Dalimier was dumbfounded at the sight, and says I have had a lucky escape. Yesterday I signed for Spain, i.e. Barcelona. I think that ought to please you. Write to me at Munich, Regina Palace.

Embraces and blessings.

Your friend S. D. [with a sketch of a cat]

Be a good boy now you're turning six.[146]

Diaghilev set off on his journey to the Rhine. Markevitch, who was in Switzerland with his mother, was to meet him at Basel. They spent the night there at the famous old hotel, *Die drei Königen*. Next day they travelled on to Baden-Baden for the music festival, and stayed at the Hôtel Stéphanie on the hill among the pine-woods, where Diaghilev had planned the Bach ballet with Benois, Nuvel and Nijinsky in 1913. Sergei Pavlovitch said it was his favourite hotel in the world. God knows, he had stayed in many. He told Igor that the three previous great loves in his life had been his cousin Dima, Nijinsky and Massine.[147]

The main object of the visit to Baden-Baden was a discussion with Hindemith, whose work was being played at the festival, about the ballet he was going to write for Diaghilev. Hardly anything had been put on paper, but, as Hindemith was such an extraordinary craftsman and fast worker, Diaghilev was not worried. He intended that Alexandre Cassandre, whose posters he admired, should design this ballet.[148]

On 28 July Diaghilev and Markevitch heard Hindemith's *Lehrstück*, which had words by Berthold Brecht.[149] Princesse Edmond de Polignac was at the festival, and Nicolas Nabokov ran into her with Diaghilev and Markevitch at a concert. He walked with the two friends back to their hotel. 'His face was puffy,' he wrote of Diaghilev, 'with the glazed yellow quality of diabetics during or after an attack. ... Despite his appearance, his mood seemed happy. He talked gaily about his plans for the rest of the summer and for the autumn season. "Why don't you come with us?" ' He was interested to hear Nabokov was writing his first symphony, and wanted to know all about it. Would it be 'romantic and lyrical', like *Ode*? Diaghilev went to the station to see Nabokov off, and the latter took a photograph of him.[150]

536

Milhaud, too, was in Baden-Baden, and he made a short film of Diaghilev and Markevitch with his cine-camera.[151]

On 30 July the two companions were at the Regina Palast Hotel in Munich. This was a royal progress and it was natural that luncheon on the following day should be with Richard Strauss. The elder composer was polite to Markevitch. 'Don't fight against tradition,' Strauss told him. 'Follow it.' Diaghilev received an inscribed copy of *Elektra* for his library. Later that afternoon he and Igor heard Dr Strauss conduct a performance of *Die Zauberflöte* at the Residenz-Theater. It was the first opera Igor had ever heard.[152]

Next day, at four o'clock, Diaghilev took Igor to a performance of *Tristan* at the Prinz-Regenten-Theater. It was sung by Otto Wolf and Elisabeth Ohms and conducted by Karl Elmendorff. In the interval Diaghilev made for a shady corner of the garden, and Markevitch noticed that he was weeping. 'What is the matter?' he asked. Diaghilev murmured that it was 'the same thing as with his cousin Dima'.[153] He meant that he was forty years older than when he first heard the opera with Filosofov, and that he was now hearing it with another young man: but love was always love, and Wagner was eternal. That afternoon's music made a profound impression on both men, though the one to whom it was new had longer to remember it in. Diaghilev wrote to Lifar:

Dearest, your telegram made me feel easier in my mind. I haven't, however, had the tiniest little note from you. Why didn't you write? Forgot Kotja? Did you get my letter from Paris?

The Hindemiths are very nice, but so far he has done nothing. But he's full of goodwill and hope. His Cantata is a strange piece of work, but you can see it was rushed, and the show that goes with it is pretty poor. I've seen masses of friends from Paris, not to mention Mme de Polignac. . . . etc. My sustenance here is Wagner and Mozart. What geniuses, and how well performed here! Today, at *Tristan*, I shed bitter tears. Books take up a lot of my attention. Thank Boris for his first letter. It was alarming, but, from the telegrams, everything seems to be all right now.

Don't forget your 'cat' who embraces and blesses you. [Drawing of a cat with its tail in the air].[154]

On the second the two companions heard *Così fan tutte*, and on the fourth *Die Meistersinger*.

Of course, Diaghilev took Igor to see the Rembrandts and Rubens in the picture gallery and the sculpture in the Glyptothek, as he had taken Lifar four years before. They drove to Nymphenburg, and in the blue-and-silver rococo décor of Amalienburg Diaghilev explained about Cuvilliès, who had come from France to create that pavilion and the Residenz-Theater, his two masterpieces.[155]

At Salzburg, where they heard *Don Giovanni*, Diaghilev continued irrepressibly happy and gay, and Igor sometimes laughed till he cried. He could not believe, when he read about Diaghilev's illness after his death, that it had not come upon him suddenly in Venice, or that Sergei Pavlovitch had been suffering when they were together.[156] To appear carefree and young, however, was Diaghilev's final *coquetterie*, and the effort must have accelerated the course of his disease,[157] which at this time there was no available insulin to cure.

Before leaving Salzburg, Diaghilev wrote to Koribut-Kubitovitch about business, but invited him to come to Venice and keep him company, and to bring a large bottle of Guerlain's scent 'Mitsouko', and a precious parcel from Levin, the Warsaw bookseller.

I have sent you a telegram asking you to join me in Venice. I want very much to see you, particularly as I am ill, and it would be a great boon for me to have you recuperating here also. The wound has healed, but I'm now full of that beastly rheumatism, and it gives me a great deal of pain.

Impatiently expecting you. ....[158]

On Wednesday, 7 August, Diaghilev saw Igor off to Vevey, walking alongside the train, clasping his hand, crying a little and making the sign of the cross over him.[159] He travelled alone to Venice and arrived at the Grand Hôtel des Bains de Mer on the Lido on the evening of Thursday the eighth. On the same day Kochno left Paris for Toulon, with his step-nephew,[160] and Lifar travelled to Venice, arriving in the evening. He was surprised that Diaghilev was not at the station to meet him, but, when he reached the Grand Hôtel, he saw him waving from a window.

Diaghilev was worn out, had a pain in his back, complained of not being able to sleep, eat or move. He had swallowed a tooth and was afraid it would give him appendicitis. The German doctors had told him he was merely suffering from rheumatism, but he thought it was something much more serious.

During the following days, while Lifar nursed Diaghilev, he felt (as he admitted) a repulsion for, and an estrangement from, the sick man. Nevertheless, on that first evening he took him to see a doctor, who tended to make light of Diaghilev's condition, attributing it to 'rheumatism', as the Germans had done, to overwork and the after-effect of boils. Diaghilev and Lifar spent the evening in the Piazza San Marco, where the former sat quietly, in a 'beatific mood', only complaining constantly of fatigue. At the Grand Hôtel des Bains he took a large room on the fifth floor for Lifar and himself, room 518. It was low-ceilinged for its size and faced the sea.

During the next week Diaghilev grew steadily weaker, but he sometimes got up and, with Lifar's help, put on his clothes and sat in a chair. Lifar gave him medicine and massaged his legs. Diaghilev spoke of the company and its future, of his childhood in Russia, of the Volga and the landscapes of Levitan, of Tchaikovsky and his Sixth Symphony. On the morning of 10 August, after a sleepless night, Diaghilev lay singing snatches of *Tristan* in his 'unattractive, inflexible' voice. He also spoke of death, which he dreaded.

On 12 August Diaghilev took to his bed for good, and his temperature began to rise. On the fourteenth it was over 38° Centigrade (101° Fahrenheit). Two doctors, Vittoli and Bidali, visited him constantly, but were puzzled by his condition.[161] Diaghilev telegraphed to Boris, 'The weather is beautiful. Do not forget me.' His temperature rose to 39° (103°). On the fifteenth he telegraphed to Boris again, 'Health not very good. When do you expect to come?' That same evening Kochno received the message, 'Am ill. Come at once.'

Kochno[162] was at Toulon station at 10 p.m. and had to sleep on a bench till he could catch the connection for Vintimille at three in the morning. A porter woke him to say the train would be late. On the evening of Friday the sixteenth, as he approached Venice, he hoped that all might still be well, that life would go on as before, that new ballets would be planned and made, and that Diaghilev would be waiting at the station, fanning himself with his white panama hat. But there was no Diaghilev. Boris was the last to leave the station, and then he met a man from the Grand Hôtel, who took him by motor-boat to the Lido. Lifar was on the landing-stage to meet him.

Boris had had his head shaved in Toulon, so that people asked him, 'When did you get out of prison?'; and as he came into Diaghilev's bedroom, the latter, who was deep in conversation with the Italian doctor, seemed not to recognize him. Sergei Pavlovitch lay still after the doctor had gone, and though he asked Boris various questions, seemed indifferent to the answers. He was in despair at the state of his health and the incompetence of the Venetian physician, who had no idea what was the matter with him, and returned from time to time merely to observe the successive stages of his deterioration.

On the morning of the seventeenth Boris found Diaghilev smiling and gay in his sunny room. He said, 'Now you are here all will be well,' then, afraid of having made a painful impression, hastened to joke. He talked a lot, obviously trying to forget his pain and anxiety, and described his journey with Markevitch. Whenever Lifar was out of the room – for Boris was his confidant over the love affair with Igor, which Serge greatly resented – he spoke of the stay in Salzburg, and kept interrupting himself to exclaim, 'I have so much to tell you.' Boris understood that Diaghilev's escape from his usual duties and preoccupations, his walks in streets and in a countryside where no one recognized him, had made him feel young. He had found again the rapture of first love, with its 'triumphant mornings'. He was thunderstruck by the greatness of Wagner. He, who had instructed so many young people, had given his last lesson to Markevitch and in doing so had found confirmation in his mind of what he felt he had known all along.

From memories Diaghilev turned to plans for the future. Boris was to continue work on *L'Habit du roi* without delay. It was to be quite unlike any other ballet. '*L'Habit* must inaugurate the new art form of which we spoke in London.' The room was full of sunshine, and it was a day of possibilities – as if the dawn of a new life in art and love. In the evening Diaghilev said, 'I have deposited 60,000 lire in the safe downstairs. It is the money for our summer holiday. Bring it to me. Here is the receipt.' Boris fetched the money and placed it on the bed. Diaghilev said, 'Now go down and deposit it in your name. God knows what may happen to me.'

While Boris was absent, Misia and Coco Chanel came to see Diaghilev. They had been cruising on the Duke of Westminster's yacht, which had put in at Venice. Diaghilev was much struck by their appearance in his sickroom. 'They looked so young,' he told Boris. 'They were all in white. They were *so white*!' Boris decided to spend the night in a big armchair in Diaghilev's room, to give Lifar a rest. But Sergei Pavlovitch did not sleep. He was in a state of extreme agitation, alternately hot and cold, and complained so often of draughts, asking for the door to be shut or the window opened, or vice versa, that Boris got cross. At dawn on the eighteenth, as Boris was dropping off to sleep, Diaghilev said, 'Sorry!'

After some hours of sleep Diaghilev woke calmer, and talked again of the future. He was weaker than on the previous day, however, and his plans were for rest, not work. 'We'll go to Sicily. Next week I'll be better and we'll go south.' In the afternoon Boris went to the beach. On his return he met Cathérine d'Erlanger leaving Diaghilev's room, and her words gave him a shock. 'He could still recognize me. We mustn't give up hope.' A nurse was engaged, and as she unpacked and stuck a temperature chart on the wall by the bed, Boris looked with horror at this *dame blanche*, who appeared to him like the figure of death: but Diaghilev ignored her. He was exhausted and sent Kochno and Lifar off to dine. They had hardly sat down in the restaurant when a waiter brought a scribbled message. Diaghilev was nervous; he wanted to consult the doctor; he asked them to come back. Boris and Serge both decided to sleep in the sick man's room: but Boris, seeing Diaghilev grow calm and fall asleep, returned to his own. He was soon woken by Lifar. Diaghilev's fever was mounting. He breathed with difficulty, and he murmured unintelligible words in French and English. The nurse said he would last till dawn. The doctor came and took his temperature, which continued to rise. Boris telephoned to Misia, who had been sitting fully dressed in the drawing-room of her hotel waiting for – she knew not what. Diaghilev was burning up; his breath whistled and sweat poured from his forehead as he appeared to be struggling with a giant seated on his chest. After his temperature reached 41° (105°) it was taken no more. Misia came and summoned a Catholic priest. He was asked to pray quickly, for fear his appearance might alarm Diaghilev and make him worse. Gradually the dying man's breath grew calm, and he ceased to struggle. The nurse was packing. In the silent room Diaghilev's friends heard him breathing gently – too gently, too lightly, then not at all. As Sunday's sun shone through the window on to the head of Diaghilev, that heavy head fell sideways towards his shoulder and a big tear rolled down his cheek.

It had been in the ballroom downstairs that Stravinsky played the beginnings of *The Rite of Spring* to Diaghilev in September 1912. That was seventeen years, a war, a revolution, and forty-eight ballets ago.

At the turn of the century there lived a Venetian sea-captain whose steamboat made a daily tour of the islands. Returning at evening, he set his course by the Campanile of St Mark's, which, even when the city was a mere smudge on the horizon, rose above the lagoon. At dusk on 14 July 1902, this man turned his boat as usual towards Venice, but the bell-tower was no longer there; and he went mad. Diaghilev loved this story.[163] His own disappearance caused no less a sensation throughout Europe than that of the Campanile. People ran from room to room to announce the news, or shouted from windows that Diaghilev was dead. Lying on a beach in the South of France, Sokolova looked up from the newspaper Woizikovsky had handed her to observe him walking along the edge of the sea, kicking the water with his foot.[164] Lopukhova, Dolin and Balanchine read the obituary in a film studio near London.[165] When Grigoriev, in Monte Carlo, received a telegram from Lifar, he fainted.[166] That night, as Dubrovska and Vladimirov stood on the steps of the Hôtel de Paris, on their way to a party of Pavlova's, they saw Grigoriev and Tchernicheva approaching from the town, making desperate gestures.[167]

At the end of *Le Bal*, as the hero lay thunderstruck on the ground, a group of Sylphides came in by the doors and windows to surround his body.[168] Rieti allowed just four bars for this. Let us borrow Kochno's pretty conceit to begin our new ballet, and let us carry it further, for I am sure our opening tableau will arouse the expectation of the audience. It will not only be Sylphs who slide down the sunbeam to keep watch over the mortal remains of Diaghilev: we shall bring on high-cheekboned Fauns, the bland shepherds of Beoetia, malodorous Polovtsi, the harem of the Persian king, characters of the *commedia dell' arte*, finger to lips – as in the drawing of Beardsley – the merrymakers of St Petersburg's Butter Week Fair, stamping peasants from Spain, high-kicking Parisian can-can dancers, the good-humoured ladies of Venice, Apollo and his muses, the court of Armida, the ghost of a rose.

The music strikes up; there are distant horn-calls; and the long afternoon of Diaghilev begins.

Source Notes

My sources are (1) printed books and articles in learned journals, (2) newspapers, (3) theatre programmes, (4) documents in Libraries or Foundations available to the public, (5) unpublished manuscripts, (6) correspondence or conversations with people who knew Diaghilev.

In the list of books in the Bibliography, the date of their first publication in English is given, or, if they have not been published in English, their first appearance in French or another language. But the page references in my Notes are, for the sake of the student's convenience, given not to the first edition of a book, but to the latest and most available edition – perhaps paperback – published in England or America. Thus, in the Bibliography will be found: 'Karsavina, Tamara, *Theatre Street*, Heinemann, London, 1930; Revised edition, Constable, London, 1948; [Notes refer to] Dutton (paperback), New York, 1961.' (I have made an exception to this rule in the case of the series of Stravinsky-Craft books. Since only two of these have been reprinted as one paperback, I have referred in all cases to the original editions.) Some books referred to have not, of course, been reprinted.

Translations from French, German, Italian and Spanish newspapers are by the author, and can safely be assumed to be the first ever made into English.

The principal collections of documents available to the public are: (a) In the New York Public Library's theatre collections lodged in the Museum and Library of Performing Arts, Lincoln Center. These are always attributed simply to 'Lincoln Center', with the additional specification 'Astruc papers' when applicable. (b) In the Stravinsky–Diaghilev Foundation at 525 East 85th Street, New York, N.Y., referred to as 'Stravinsky–Diaghilev'. (c) Stravinsky Archives in the possession of Trapezoid Inc. and referred to as Stravinsky Archives. (d) In that part of the collection of the Bibliothèque

Nationale, Paris, which is lodged in the Musée de l'Opéra, and, as they are all from Boris Kochno's papers sold to the French State in 1975, they are referred to as 'Bibliothèque Nationale, Kochno collection'. (e) In the Dans-museet, Stockholm. (f) In the British Museum.

Unpublished sources include: Diaghilev's Memoirs which Boris Kochno, who owns the manuscript, translated from Russian into French, and which the present author rendered from French into English; an essay by Lady Juliet Duff; the albums of the late Lady St Just (compiled when she was Florence Henderson); the Romola Nijinsky–Lincoln Kirstein draft of the first part of Mme Nijinsky's life of her husband, partly in typescript, partly in Mr Kirstein's hand, given to the present author by the latter; typescripts of broadcasts by, letters to and manuscripts of Valentine Gross, given to the author by M. Jean Hugo, and now mostly in the Theatre Museum, London.

Indications such as 'Rieti correspondence' or 'Balanchine conversations' are self-explanatory.

PART I
CHAPTER I 1872–90

1 This book of Leskov's had appeared (1878, 1879, 1880) during his life. When the Complete Works were published (1888–9), the volume which contained this story was seized and destroyed by the police. In the posthumous Moscow edition of the Complete Works (1956–8) it was restored. The critic Yuri Slonimsky drew the attention of Ivor Guest to Leskov's connection with Diaghilev's grandfather, and the information arrived *via* Mary Clarke with me. Boris Kochno later told me that Diaghilev's father had known Leskov. Mr Igor Vinogradoff and Mrs Larissa Haskell helped me verify quotations.

2 Leskov, *Anecdotes of Archiepiscopal Life*, while Leskov's Bishop is sympathetic character, the *nouveau riche* religious fanatic – who sleeps in a coffin with holy relics – is shown in a ridiculous light. Lifar, in his biography, takes Diaghilev's grandfather more seriously.

3 Exact figures are hard to come by, but in 1889, for instance, the State revenue from the tax on vodka was 275 million roubles.

4 Ikonnikov. It was Mr Igor Vinogradoff, son-in-law of Diaghilev's friend, Lady Ottoline Morrell, who disclosed the information about Diaghilev's ancestry, in the course of helping me over a number of Russian problems. It must be pointed out, however, that Ikonnikov may be wrong about Pavel

Dmitrievitch belonging to the Chevaliers Gardes, for the usually accurate *Dictionary of the Chevaliers Gardes* does not include the name of P. P. Diaghilev.

5 Lifar, p. 8. When Lifar wrote his life of Diaghilev, published 1940, he had the help of Diaghilev's first cousin Pavel Georgievitch Koribut-Kubitovitch, who assembled various family papers and set down his own memories for him.

6 Leskov, Complete Works, Vol. VI, *Anecdotes of Archiepiscopal Life*, pp. 465, 480.

7 Anna Pavlovna Filosofov, MS, quoted Lifar, p. 50.

8 *Dictionary of the Chevaliers Gardes*. There is no doubt about Pavel Pavlovitch having served in the exclusive regiment, whether his father did or not.

9 Elena (Panaev) Diaghilev, MS, quoted Lifar, p. 6.

10 There is an unsolved mystery about the family name of Diaghilev's mother, which the *Dictionary of the Chevaliers Gardes* gives as Essipov, as I have done, but which Diaghilev gave on his passport (reproduced Kochno, p. 284), and which Lifar gives, as Evreinov. A *Necrology of St Petersburg* (cited in Ikonnikov, F.I. no. 482, 2nd ed., Paris, 1958) lists an Evgenia Nikolaevna Diaghilev, née Essipov, buried with members of the Khitrovo family. Now, Lifar knew from Diaghilev or his cousin Koribut-Kubito-

vitch, who helped him (p. 3, footnote), that Diaghilev's maternal grandmother was a Khitrovo; and it was through the Khitrovos and their Rumiantsev ancestors that Diaghilev liked to believe that he was descended (on the wrong side of the blanket) from Catherine the Great. In the tree of the Diaghilev family in Ikonnikov the first wife of Pavel Pavlovitch Diaghilev (1849–1914), General ADC, is Evgenia Nikolaevna Essipov. It is possible that Evgenia changed her name to Evreinov because of adoption or an inheritance.

11 Lifar, pp. 12, 13. J. P. Parensov's account quoted.
12 Pavel G. Koribut-Kubitovitch, MS, quoted Lifar, p. 13.
13 Dobujinsky, p. 34.
14 Lifar, p. 14 et seq.
15 Elena Valerianovna Panaev's father-in-law, General Pavel Petrovitch Kartsov (1821–96), married Alexandra Petrovna Tchaikovsky (1835–99).
16. D. V. Filosofov, MS, quoted Lifar, pp. 16, 17.
17 Diaghilev, Memoirs.
18 This description of St Petersburg sights and sounds is taken from Dobujinsky, pp. 30, 31, but the phrase describing the sound of ice

floes brushing against each other is prompted by the author's experience in Montreal.
19 Lifar, p. 19.
20 Igor Vinogradoff's information.
21 Koribut-Kubitovitch, MS, quoted Lifar, p. 18.
22 Photographs deriving from a cousin of Diaghilev's, reproduced in Roslavleva, *Era of the Russian Ballet*, facing pp. 160 and 161.
23 Koribut-Kubitovitch, MS, quoted Lifar, p. 20.
24 E. V. Diaghilev, MS, quoted Lifar, pp. 21, 22.
25 O. Vassiliev, MS, quoted Lifar, p. 27 et seq.
26 Benois, *Memoirs*, I, p. 260 et seq.
27 Ibid., II, p. 61 et seq.
28 Ibid., pp. 74, 75.
29 Ibid., pp. 75, 76.
30 Lifar, pp. 37, 38.
31 Diaghilev, Memoirs.
32 Ibid.
33 Neither Benois in his *Memoirs* nor Lifar in his *Life* states definitely that Filosofov and Diaghilev had a love affair. It was Igor Markevitch who told the present author this in Feb. 1978.
34 Kchessinskaya, *St Petersburg*, pp. 28, 29.
35 Ibid., p. 32 et seq.

CHAPTER 2   1890–8

1 Benois, *Reminiscences*, p. 119. Haskell, p. 48.
2 Olive Stevens's opinion.
3 Grabar, p. 73, specially translated by Larissa Haskell.
4 Lifar, p. 3.
5 Benois, *Memoirs*, II, pp. 77, 78, 83, 84. Also Benois, *Reminiscences*, p. 163.
6 Lifar, pp. 66, 67.
7 Grabar, p. 155.
8 Rubinstein, p. 89.
9 Diaghilev, Memoirs. A similar story is told by the author of the Supplement to Rubinstein's brief *Memoirs* (Rubinstein, p. 171) about the pianist's final concert in Moscow in Jan. 1889.
10 Ibid.
11 Alhambra Theatre programme, *The Sleeping Princess*, 1921, Bakst's essay 'Tchaikovsky at the Russian Ballet'.
12 Benois, *Memoirs*, II, p. 59.
13 Ibid., p. 58 et seq. It is hard to reconcile Benois' statement that 'the Tchaikovsky cult was only at its beginning' with Diaghilev's that Tchaikovsky was the 'idol of musical St Petersburg'.
14 Ibid., p. 86 et seq.
15 Diaghilev, Memoirs.
16 Melba, pp. 53–7, 70 et seq.

17 Diaghilev, Memoirs.
18 Ibid.
19 Kchessinskaya, p. 37.
20 Ibid., p. 43.
21 Diaghilev, Memoirs.
22 Ibid.
23 Benois, *Memoirs*, II, pp. 78, 79.
24 Ibid., p. 80.
25 Ibid., p. 105 et seq.
26 Dubrovska, conversations.
27 Diaghilev, Memoirs.
28 Lifar, pp. 51, 52.
29 Kchessinskaya, p. 49 et seq.
30 Benois, *Memoirs*, II, pp. 114, 115.
31 Ibid., p. 122 et seq.
32 Lifar, p. 47.
33 Kochno, conversations.
34 Haskell, p. 58.
35 Benois, *Reminiscences*, p. 190.
36 Karsavina, conversations.
37 Benois, *Memoirs*, II, pp. 126, 127.
38 Larissa Haskell, information.
39 Benois, *Memoirs*, II, pp. 126, 127.
40 Benois, *Reminiscences*, p. 177 et seq.; Diaghilev always wrote his name with a German 'w'.
41 Benois, *Memoirs*, II, pp. 129, 130, 83, 84.
42 Ibid., pp. 127–30.

43 Ibid., pp. 131, 132.
44 Kchessinskaya, pp. 57, 58.
45 Ibid., pp. 58, 59.
46 Benois, *Memoirs*, II, p. 145.
47 Ibid., p. 148.
48 Ibid., p. 152.
49 Ibid., p. 154.
50 Kchessinskaya, pp. 63, 64.
51 Benois, *Memoirs*, II, pp. 158, 159.
52 Ibid., p. 159.
53 Ibid., p. 156.
54 Ibid., p. 158.

55 Ibid., p. 206.
56 Nicolas II gave only three new titles, those of Counts Solsky, Witte and Kokovtsov. His father had been almost as sparing.
57 When Princess Peter Lieven rang up Countess Kleinmichel on my behalf to ask if she thought Diaghilev would have been received at Court ('*à la cour*'), the disdainful reply was: 'Certainly not, *dans la cour* [in the courtyard] perhaps.'
58 Mossolov, pp. 192–8.
59 Benois, *Memoirs*, II, p. 157.

PART II

CHAPTER 3   1898–1900

1 Haskell, p. 108. Prospectus for *Mir Iskusstva*: 'Zincography by Meizenbach and Riffart of Berlin, and phototype by Albert Fischer of Berlin. Chromo-Zincography by A. I. Mamontov in Moscow and J. Verne in Paris. Chromo-lithography by I. Kulushina in Petersburg.'
2 *M.I.*, Vol. IV, Nos 15,16; Diaghilev's article on Levitan.
3 Hart–Davis, *Wilde Letters*, letter to Leonard Smithers, p. 734.
4 Ibid., letter to Robert Ross, p. 748.
5 Kochno, conversations. It sounds as if Diaghilev made rather too much of this story to Kochno.
6 Letter from D. to Benois, 2.6.1898, quoted Lifar, p. 63.
7 *M.I.*, Vol. I, No. 1.
8 *Catalogue, Impressionist and Post-Impressionist Pictures from the USSR*, lent by the Hermitage Museum, Leningrad, and the Pushkin Museum, Moscow. Knoedler, 1973. Introduction by John Richardson.
9 Tenishev, p. 265.
10 Ibid., pp. 266, 270.
11 Ibid., p. 272.
12 Ibid., p. 270.
13 *M.I.*, Prospectus.
14 Bakst's eagle is familiar in the West, as Haskell reproduced it on the title-page of his *Diaghileff*, and Prince Peter Lieven had it on

the binding of his *The Birth of the Ballets Russes*.
15 *M.I.*, Vol. I, No. 1, Diaghilev, manifesto.
16 Ibid.
17 Benois, *Memoirs*, II, pp. 167, 168.
18 Tenishev, p. 273.
19 Benois, *Memoirs*, II, p. 169.
20 Tenishev, p. 277.
21 Benois, *Reminiscences*, p. 184 et seq. Also Benois, *Memoirs*, II, pp. 172, 173. Also Kochno, conversations: Diaghilev told him about Bakst retouching the photographs.
22 Benois, *Memoirs*, II, pp. 172, 173.
23 *M.I.*, Vol. I, Nos 7–8, 'Chronicle'.
24 Tenishev, pp. 273–5.
25 Kochno, conversations.
26 *M.I.*, Vol. I, Nos 7–8.
27 Kchessinskaya, p. 78.
28 Rzwesky, p. 188.
29 Rimsky-Korsakov, p. 378.
30 The 'shameful' pictures included Aivazovsky's *Flood*, Makovsky's *Study of a Man's Head*, Moller's *St John on Patmos*, Sedov's *Vasilisa Melentseva* and Ritzioni's *Jewish Smugglers*.
31 In view of an article Repine had written in Oct. 1897 in *Books of the Week*.
32 Wolkonsky, Vol. II, p. 72.
33 Ibid., p. 77–81.
34 Benois, *Memoirs*, II, pp. 181, 182.
35 Diaghilev, Memoirs.

CHAPTER 4   1900–1902

1 Kchessinskaya, pp. 72, 73.
2 Benois, *Memoirs*, II, p. 194.
3 Ibid., pp. 185–8.
4 Wolkonsky, p. 71.
5 Kochno, conversations.
6 Karsavina, conversations. 'I was virtuous,' she told me.
7 Wolkonsky, p. 72.

8 *M.I.*, Vol. I, Nos 11–12.
9 Tenishev, p. 278.
10 Haskell, p. 121. Nuvel's information.
11 Ibid., pp. 123, 124.
12 Dobujinsky, p. 321.
13 Tenishev, p. 279.
14 *M.I.*, Vol. IX, No. 4.
15 Tenishev, p. 280. Dobujinsky wrote (p.

321), 'The Princess was wrong. The journal continued for another two years,' but he had got his dates mixed up. He brought in the story of the Tsar and Serov's portrait at this point: but it is clear that (a) the Princess's imposition of Roerich took place in 1904, and (b) the Tsar's portrait referred to was painted before Jan. 1901, when it was exhibited in the *World of Art* Exhibition at the Academy. Benois, in his *Memoirs*, II, p. 216, suppresses the fact that his own retirement from the board was a condition of the Princess's financial support in 1904. In fact, he writes, 'Tenisheva insisted that we should accept a third editor in addition to Diaghilev and myself.'

16 Diaghilev, Memoirs.
17 Reproduced *M.I.*, Vol. VIII, No. 12.
18 Haskell, p. 124.
19 Reproduced in a book I have mislaid.
20 Haskell, p. 124.
21 Shown in the exhibition from Soviet Metropolitan Museum, New York, 1977.
22 *M.I.*, Vol. III, Nos 3, 4.
23 Ibid., Nos 5, 6.
24 Haskell, pp. 98, 99.
25 Benois, *Memoirs*, II, p. 193.
26 *M.I.* Vol. IV, Nos 21, 22.
27 The judges included Repine, who sent a report to *M.I.*, Vol. IV, Nos 17, 18.
28 Benois, *Reminiscences*, p. 187. But Benois does not mention the Engineering Castle or the Shuvalov Palace. New editorial address announced, *M.I.*, Vol. IV, Nos 17, 18.
29 Engineering Castle: Vol. III, Nos 3, 4.
30 Toboggan Pavilion: Vol. III, Nos 7, 8.
31 Yusupov pictures: Vol. IV, Nos 23, 24.
32 An exaggeration. Tchekhov, for instance, admired him greatly.

33 *M.I.*, Vol. IV, Nos 15, 16.
34 Reproduced *M.I.*, Vol. VIII, No. 12.
35 Diaghilev, Memoirs.
36 *M.I.*, Vol. V, No. 2.
37 Haskell, p. 146.
38 *M.I.*, Vol. V, No. 6. From 1901 the idea of fortnightly numbers was given up, and twelve numbers a year was the limit.
39 Wolkonsky, p. 73.
40 Benois, *Reminiscences*, p. 213 et seq.
41 Haskell, p. 141.
42 Wolkonsky, p. 74.
43 Benois, *Memoirs*, II, pp. 197, 198; also *Reminiscences*, p. 217.
44 It seems likely that the thick coloured paper covers of *Mir Iskusstva* were ordered for the year *en bloc*. In 1901 they all had the same design by Lancerey, but No. 1 was dark blue-grey printed in gold, Nos 2–3 (double) was brown, No. 4 was light terra-cotta, No. 5 was to have been dull purple, and No. 6 was pale grey-green. In the bound volumes in the British Museum, the purple cover of No. 5 is bound in at the back of Vol. V with the other covers, but there is no No. 5. The pagination carries straight on from No. 4 to No. 6.
45 Kchessinskaya, pp. 81, 82.
46 Wolkonsky, Vol. II, p. 100 et seq.
47 Now in the Tate Gallery, London.
48 *M.I.*, Vol. V, No. 6.
49 Ibid., Vol. VI, No. 7.
50 Ibid., Nos 8–9.
51 Ibid., No. 10.
52 Grabar, p. 153 et seq.
53 *M.I.*, Vol. VII, No. 2.
54 Benois, *Reminiscences*, p. 220 et seq.
55 Kchessinskaya, pp. 87, 88.
56 *M.I.*, Vol. VII, No. 2.

CHAPTER 5   1902–5

1 *M.I.*, Vol. VIII, Nos 9–10.
2 Dobujinsky, p. 20.
3 Ibid., pp. 20, 21.
4 Tchekhov letters: Diaghilev's letter quoted p. 434.
5 Ibid., letter from Tchekhov to D., 30.12.1902, p. 434.
6 *M.I.*, Vol. VIII, No. 11.
7 Ibid., Vol. VII, No. 3.
8 Ibid., No. 4.
9 Ibid., Vol. IX, Nos 1–2.
10 Ibid., Vol. X, Nos 7–8.
11 Tchekhov letters: Diaghilev's letter quoted p. 453.
12 Ibid., letter from Tchekhov to D., 12.7.1903, p. 453.
13 Benois, *Memoirs*, II, p. 207 et seq.

14 *M.I.*, Vol. XI, No. 1.
15 Ibid., Vol. IX, Nos 1–2.
16 The portrait of Benois (Vol. VI, No. 12), *Countess Keller* (Vol. VIII, No. 12), *Siamese Dancers* (Vol. VIII, No. 12) and *Catherine the Great in Hunting Costume* (Vol. X, Nos 7–8).
17 Four letters of Bakst to his wife, dated 20.4.1904, 4, 7, 8. 6.1904. G.T.G. Manuscript Department, 111/148, 152, 156, 157, quoted E. N. Prujan, *Bakst*, 1975.
18 *M.I.*, Vol. X, Nos 10–12.
19 Ibid., Nos 7–8.
20 Dobujinsky, pp. 309, 310.
21 I have mislaid the evidence for this.
22 It is rather confusing because Vols XI and XII are intermingled. The Diaghilev-edited numbers are here referred to as belonging

to Vol. XI, the Benois-edited numbers to Vol. XII.
23 Haskell, p. 170.
24 *M.I.*, Vol. XI, No. 1.
25 Duncan, p. 119.
26 Ibid., p. 119.
27 *M.I.*, Vol. XI, No. 1.
28 Benois, *Memoirs*, II, p. 217.
29 Duncan, p. 120.
30 One full-length drawing is in the Ashmolean Museum, Oxford, Braikevitch Bequest (reproduced Buckle, *In Search*, plate 2); the head is reproduced by Haskell, facing p. 186.
31 Benois, *Memoirs*, II, pp. 217, 218.
32 Karsavina, pp. 158–62.
33 Romola Nijinsky, p. 41.
34 Benois, *Memoirs*, II, pp. 221, 222.
35 Haskell, p. 148. Told to Haskell by Nuvel.
36 Grabar, p. 156.
37 Catalogue of the Exhibition of Historical Russian Portraits, ed. Diaghilev (St Petersburg 1905).
38 Told to the author by Mme Braikevitch, who gave her husband's collection to the Ashmolean Museum, Oxford.
39 Stravinsky, *Memories*, p. 44, footnote.
40 The architecture of the Tavrichevsky Palace is described and illustrated in Audrey and Victor Kennett, *Palaces of Leningrad*, pp. 79–82.

41 Letter quoted Lifar, pp. 157, 158.
42 Kochno, conversations.
43 Benois, *Memoirs*, II, pp. 223, 224.
44 Catalogue of the Exhibition of Historical Russian Portraits, ed. Diaghilev (St Petersburg 1905).
45 Sitwell, conversations.
46 Benois, *Memoirs*, II, p. 224.
47 Lifar, p. 158. Letter quoted.
48 Ibid. p. 158.
49 Grabar, p. 156.
50 Haskell, pp. 160, 161. All the documents provided by Nuvel for Haskell were destroyed in the 1939–45 war. Nuvel could not have memorized this speech, nor is it likely that he would have kept a press cutting. He evidently had access to a report of Diaghilev's speech in some journal that I have been unable to find. Only in 1978 did I learn that this speech was delivered in Moscow. In the Haskell/Nuvel translation Diaghilev is made to say 'with fear and misgiving'. I feel that 'without' makes more sense, and have changed it.
51 Lifar, p. 161.
52 Ibid., pp. 159, 160.
53 I was able to examine one set (the only one I know of in England) in the collection of Mr E. Mollo.
54 Lifar, p. 160.

PART III

CHAPTER 6   1906–7

1 Lifar, p. 161. Haskell, p. 166 (Nuvel's information). But I have no evidence – from Kochno, for instance – of any impression made on Diaghilev by Greece.
2 Vera Stravinsky, conversations.
3 Larionov, conversations. In 1954, when I was organizing the Diaghilev Exhibition, Larionov never ceased extolling the genius of Diaghilev.
4 Visible in a photograph in *M.I.*, Vol. IV, Nos 21–2.
5 Among the Russian members of the Committee, most of whose names are familiar from association with *The World of Art* and its exhibitions, Hirschmann, a businessman who lived in Paris, and his wife, were mentioned by Benois as being 'our Maecenas' (Benois, *Memoirs*, II, p. 232, footnote). Serov's portrait of Hirschmann (pronounced in Russian 'Girschmann') was on show in the Exhibition of Paintings from the USSR at the Metropolitan Museum, New York, in spring 1977. I admired it a few days before being entertained by Hirsch-

mann's son, Mr André Harley. In Plate 1, both W. Hirschmann, standing on the right, and his wife, in a white dress seated centre, can be seen.
6 All but one of the ikons were from the renowned Likhatchev collection.
7 Translated by the present author.
8 Benois, *Memoirs*, II, p. 231.
9 Inghelbrecht, p. 170.
10 Comtesse Greffulhe was the daughter of Prince Caraman-Chimay, Belgian Foreign Minister. Her mother was a Montesquiou.
11 Lifar, pp. 167, 168.
12 According to Diaghilev himself (Memoirs), we know that Tchaikovsky was far from ideal as a conductor; and Nuvel told Haskell (p. 173, footnote), 'Tchaikovsky, Glazunov and Rimsky-Korsakov had amongst us the reputation of being mediocre conductors.'
13 Haskell, p. 172.
14 Ibid., p. 170.
15 Ibid., p. 171.
16 Lincoln Center, Astruc papers, letter from D. to A., 18.1.1907.

17 Ibid., telegram, D. to A., 7.3.1907.
18 Ibid., telegram, Nuvel to A., 2 Mar. 1907.
19 Haskell, p. 174, footnote.
20 Lincoln Center, Astruc papers. Telegram, 29.3.1907.
21 Ibid., telegram, D. to A., 30.3.1907.
22 Diaghilev, Memoirs.
23 Rimsky-Korsakov, p. 433.
24 Diaghilev, Memoirs.
25 Lincoln Center, Astruc papers, telegram, 14.4.1907.
26 Ibid., 29.4.1907.
27 Diaghilev, Memoirs. Another story is that Strauss said, 'We are no longer children,' and that this was repeated to the composer (Rimsky-Korsakov, p. 434).
28 *Le Figaro*, 17.5.1907.
29 Ibid., 17.5.1907.
30 Haskell, p. 174.
31 Diaghilev, Memoirs.
32 *Le Figaro*, 17.5.1907.
33 Diaghilev, Memoirs.
34 Ibid. Stravinsky tells a similar story of Rimsky (*Chronicle*, p. 35). Whether Diag-

hilev heard the story from Stravinsky and included it in his brief (unpublished) Memoirs, written in 1928, or whether Stravinsky heard it from Diaghilev and put it in his *Chronicle*, published (in English) in 1936, is a moot point.
35 Haskell, p. 176.
36 Rimsky-Korsakov, p. 434.
37 Calvocoressi and Abraham, p. 481 (Abraham's chapter).
38 *Le Figaro*, 20.5.1907.
39 Ibid., 24.5.1907.
40 Haskell, pp. 176, 177. Nuvel's story.
41 Rimsky-Korsakov, p. 435. Readers of the 1974 edition of Rimsky-Korsakov's *My Musical Life* (Eulenburg Books, London) will be confused, because, although New Style dates are said to be given in brackets after Old Style dates, those of Rimsky's return to Russia from Paris are given in reverse order.
42 *Le Figaro*, 27.5.1907.
43 Ibid., 31.5.1907.
44 Calvocoressi, p. 177.

CHAPTER 7 1908

1 Rimsky-Korsakov, p. 436.
2 Ibid., p. 436.
3 Ibid., p. 437.
4 Ibid., Judah A. Joffe's comment on Sobinov's voice, footnote, pp. 436, 437.
5 Ibid., p. 437.
6 Ibid., p. 437.
7 Ibid., p. 437.
8 Ibid., p. 438.
9 Ibid., p. 438.
10 Ibid., pp. 438, 439.
11 Ibid., p. 443, letter from Mamontov to Rimsky-Korsakov.
12 Calvocoressi, pp. 177, 178.
13 Calvocoressi and Abraham, p. 213. Diaghilev in his Memoirs stated that he had studied Mussorgsky's manuscript, and that after the death of Boris the composer wrote 'End of the Opera'. He appears to have been unaware that the Revolution Scene was an afterthought, not in the original score rejected by the Mariinsky in 1870. Diaghilev's notes on *Boris*, along with the other fragmentary autobiographical sketches, were written in Venice in the summer of 1928, the year that the first complete edition of Mussorgsky's version of the opera was at last published. He bought a copy of this, probably after writing his notes. A letter exists at Lincoln Center from Edwin Evans to D. (29.11.1928), asking for the return of a Rimsky edition which Diaghilev had

borrowed to compare with his own and the new publication.
14 Diaghilev, Memoirs.
15 Calvocoressi and Abraham, p. 246 (Abraham's chapter).
16 Diaghilev, Memoirs. How Diaghilev, who was *mal vu* at Court, found himself talking to the Empress, who was such a recluse, is not clear.
17 Benois, *Reminiscences*, p. 268, also footnote. See also *Memoirs*, II, p. 246.
18 Diaghilev, Memoirs.
19 Rimsky-Korsakov, p. 437.
20 Ibid., pp. 451, 452.
21 Ibid., p. 450.
22 Ibid., p. 453.
23 *Le Gaulois*, 9.5.1908.
24 Diaghilev, Memoirs.
25 Calvocoressi, pp. 184, 185.
26 Ibid., pp. 185, 186.
27 *Le Gaulois*, 13.5.1908.
28 *Le Figaro*, 16.5.1908.
29 Benois, *Memoirs*, II, p. 249. Benois writes 'Petroman' for 'Pétrémand'.
30 Ibid., p. 250.
31 Benois, *Memoirs*, II, p. 250.
32 Diaghilev, Memoirs. But I have inserted Sanin, whom Diaghilev does not name.
33 Chaliapine, pp. 179–81.
34 Benois, *Memoirs*, II, p. 250.
35 Diaghilev, Memoirs.
36 Ibid.

37 Calvocoressi, pp. 187–9.
38 Ibid.
39 Chaliapine, p. 128.
40 Ibid., p. 129.
41 Diaghilev, Memoirs.
42 Ibid.
43 Benois, *Memoirs*, II, p. 251.
44 Diaghilev, Memoirs.
45 *Le Figaro*, 18.5.1908.
46 Diaghilev, Memoirs.
47 Benois, *Memoirs*, II, pp. 252, 253. Benois wrote 'Hôtel Mirabeau' for 'Hôtel de Hollande'.
48 *Le Gaulois*, 20.5.1908.
49 *Le Théâtre*.
50 Diaghilev, Memoirs.
51 *Le Figaro*, 25.5.1908.
52 Diaghilev, Memoirs.

53 Ibid.
54 Misia Sert, pp. 111, 112. According to Benois, it was after the first night of *Boris* that 'We' – which I take to mean Diaghilev, possibly Chaliapine, Diaghilev's cousin Pavel Koribut-Kubitovitch and Benois himself – 'celebrated our success quite intimately with Misia Edwards and Mme Benardaky in the Café de la Paix' (*Memoirs*, II, p. 252). Yet it would seem that Misia had heard *Boris* a day or two before meeting Diaghilev. They may, of course, have just 'met' after the first night, and 'celebrated' together after the subsequent six.
55 Diaghilev, Memoirs.
56 Calvocoressi, p. 192.
57 Diaghilev, Memoirs.
58 Ibid.

PART IV

CHAPTER 8   1908–9

1 *La Revue Musicale*, Dec. 1930, Brussel's article 'Avant la Féerie', pp. 39, 40. It was at the cabaret Yar, in Moscow, where gypsies sang, that Diaghilev announced to Brussel during the winter of 1906–7 his intention of showing the Russian Ballet in Paris.
2 Dandré, p. 206.
3 Fokine, p. 138.
4 Romola Nijinsky, p. 64.
5 *La Revue Musicale*, Dec. 1930, Astruc's article 'Le Premier Feu d'artifice', pp. 43–5. Astruc wrote 'Théâtre Michel', but I have changed this to 'Mariinsky'.
6 Lincoln Center, Astruc papers.
7 I had evidence for this statement but mislaid it long ago. The reference given in *Nijinsky* (Astruc's article in *La Revue Musicale*) is wrong.
8 The contract is summarized in Astruc's report to the Tsar, Nov. 1909. Lincoln Center, Astruc Papers.
9 Fokine, pp. 87–90.
10 Ibid., p. 89.
11 Karsavina, speech at the Diaghilev Exhibition, Forbes House, London, 1954. Quoted Buckle, *In Search*, pp. 28, 37. 'We spoke of art – mostly.'
12 Lopukhova, conversations. Mme Lopukhova (Lady Keynes) told me she had 'dared' to ask Mme Karsavina why she had not married Fokine. 'My mother did not think it would be a good idea,' was the reply.
13 Suvtchinsky, conversation. In Feb. 1977 Mme René Mayer introduced me in Paris to the musicologist Pierre Suvtchinsky, and it

turned out that his wife, also present, was Mme Karsavina's niece. He knew Mukhin.
14 Fokine, pp. 93–6.
15 Nijinska, conversations.
16 Fokine, pp. 94–6.
17 Ibid., pp. 99–103.
18 Benois, *Reminiscences*, pp. 225–7, 240–43. Fokine, pp. 106–7.
19 Bourman, p. 104.
20 Fokine, pp. 110. 111.
21 Benois, *Reminiscences*, pp. 249–51.
22 Ibid., pp. 247, 256–8.
23 Ibid., p. 265.
24 Ibid., p. 266.
25 Fokine, p. 121.
26 Nijinska, conversations.
27 Bourman, p. 140. He called Alexandrov 'Vassilev'.
28 Baroness Budberg, conversations.
29 Nijinska, conversations.
30 Nijinsky, p. 59.
31 Nijinska, conversations.
32 Bourman, pp. 151, 152.
33 Grigoriev, p. 15. It is not clear exactly when Grigoriev paid his first visit to Diaghilev and was ordered to start signing contracts.
34 Nijinsky, p. 49. The English editor of the Diary misread 'Lvov' as 'Ivor'.
35 It is merely my assumption that Nijinsky was not much good as a lover. Lvov did not mind passing him on to Diaghilev. My instinct tells me that the physical side of Nijinsky's relationships with Diaghilev and his wife did not last very long. Mme Bronislava Nijinska told me, laughing, and pointing to the appropriate place, 'Vaslav very

small here!' There are few partners who would not be put off by such an inadequate provision of nature.

36 Grigoriev, pp. 14, 15.
37 Fokine, pp. 140–42.
38 Grigoriev, pp. 14, 15.
39 Karsavina, conversations.
40 Ibid.
41 Grigoriev, pp. 15, 16.
42 Fokine, p. 144.
43 Grigoriev, pp. 17–19.
44 Ibid., p. 19.
45 Fokine, p. 129.
46 Stravinsky, letter to the *Observer*, 27.11.1961, quoted *Dialogues*, p. 132.
47 Benois, *Reminiscences*, p. 280. This is the only mention of the sum the Tsar had promised.
48 Grigoriev, pp. 19, 20.
49 Ibid., p. 20.
50 Karsavina, pp. 190–92.
51 Grigoriev, p. 22.
52 Diaghilev, Memoirs.
53 Maurice Denis, II, pp. 104–6. The painter was in Russia in Jan., although I have been obliged to refer to his visit after the Grand Duke's death in Feb.
54 Karsavina, conversations.
55 Kchessinskaya, p. 111.
56 Benois, *Reminiscences*, pp. 279, 280. Also Haskell (Nuvel's evidence), p. 206. But Nuvel told Haskell that the scheme for ennobling 'Mr K' 'went through' as a result of 'other influences'.
57 Grigoriev, p. 23.
58 For instance, Grigoriev gives no sign in his chronicle of knowing what a financial disaster the 1909 season was; and Massine said Diaghilev never discussed business with him (Massine).
59 Lincoln Center, Astruc papers, Astruc's report to the Tsar.
60 Ibid., pro forma drawn up for the prospective guarantors.
61 Grigoriev, p. 24. Karsavina, p. 193. She only mentions Mme Edwards.
62 Grigoriev, pp. 23, 24.
63 Lincoln Center, Astruc papers, telegram, 12.3.1909.
64 Letter quoted Lifar, pp. 181, 182. Presumably obtained from Kchessinskaya.
65 Lincoln Center, Astruc papers, telegram, 12.3.1909.
66 Ibid., telegram, 14.3.1909.
67 Benois, *Reminiscences*, p. 281.
68 Grigoriev, p. 25.
69 Grigoriev, correspondence.
70 Grigoriev, pp. 25, 26.
71 Ibid., p. 26.
72 Fokine, pp. 149, 150.

73 Grigoriev, p. 26.
74 Benois, *Reminiscences*, p. 283.
75 Ibid., p. 288.
76 Svetlov, pp. 85–6. Benois, *Reminiscences*, p. 300. Lincoln Center, Astruc papers; correspondence with Fontanes and Belsacq; telegrams from D. to A., 29.3.1909 and 3.4.1909.
77 Benois, *Reminiscences*, p. 283.
78 Lincoln Center, Astruc papers, telegram to A., 31.3.1909.
79 Ibid.
80 Ibid., telegram, 6.4.1909.
81 Ibid., telegram, 7.4.1909.
82 Ibid., telegrams, 20, 21, 23, 26, 27, 28, 29.4.1909.
83 Grigoriev, p. 27.
84 Karsavina, p. 193.
85 Grigoriev, p. 27.
86 Nijinska, conversations.
87 Contract between Diaghilev and Nijinsky dated 10.10.1908, sold Sotheby, London, 15.10.1963. This was the one and only contract he signed with Diaghilev.
88 Lincoln Center, Astruc papers, report to the Tsar.
89 Benois, pp. 285, 286.
90 Grigoriev, p. 27.
91 Karsavina, pp. 193, 194.
92 Karsavina, conversations.
93 Lincoln Center, Astruc papers, report to the Tsar. Also letters from D. to A. on Hôtel de Hollande writing-paper. That Mavrine was also staying there is only my assumption.
94 Benois, *Reminiscences*, p. 287, also footnote.
95 *Le Figaro*, 3.5.1909.
96 Ibid., 10.5.1909.
97 Ibid., 11.5.1909.
98 Ibid., 14.5.1909.
99 Benois, *Reminiscences*, p. 288.
100 Karsavina, pp. 194–6.
101 *Le Figaro*, 17.5.1909.
102 Ibid., 18.5.1909.
103 Ibid., 19.5.1909, and other newspapers.
104 *La Revue Musicale*, Dec. 1930, Astruc's article 'Le Premier Feu d'artifice'.
105 Benois, *Reminiscences*, p. 292.
106 Ibid., p. 291.
107 Karsavina, conversations.
108 Benois, *Reminiscences*, pp. 291, 292.
109 Ibid., p. 292.
110 Ibid., p. 244. I have changed the tense.
111 Karsavina, conversations.
112 Benois, *Reminiscences*, p. 291.
113 Karsavina, conversations.
114 Karsavina, p. 197.
115 Henri Gauthier-Villars wrote in *Commedia* (20.5.1909), 'An incredulous *Ah*! burst from the ladies. It was truly le Bond des Soupirs.'

(A pun on *Le Pont des Soupirs*, the Bridge of Sighs in Venice.)

116 Karsavina, p. 197.
117 As in Adolphe de Meyer's photograph.
118 Whitworth, pp. 41, 42.
119 Romola Nijinsky, p. 73. 'From what Vaslav told me later ... a murmur went through the public which almost terrified him.'
120 Mme Karsavina 'danced' this for me, seated in a chair. There are photographs by Bert and Hoppé. In *Theatre Street* (p. 198) she only wrote, 'The orchestra stopped after my solo.'
121 Fokine, p. 107.
122 Grigoriev describes Chaliapine singing in *Prince Igor*, which he did not do in the West till 1914.
123 Beaumont, *Complete Book*, p. 685.
124 Karsavina, p. 198.
125 Fokine, p. 145.
126 Karsavina, p. 198.
127 Ibid., p. 199.
128 *Le Figaro*, 18.5.1909.
129 Many of these were given by M. Jean Hugo to the Theatre Museum, London.
130 *Le Figaro*, 19.5.1909.
131 *Commedia*, 20.5.1909, etc.
132 *Le Figaro*, 21.5.1909.
133 Karsavina, conversations.
134 Benois, *Reminiscences*, p. 287.
135 *Le Figaro*, 26.5.1909.
136 Rimsky-Korsakov, p. 376.
137 *Le Figaro*, 27.5.1909.
138 Unidentified press cutting.
139 Ibid.
140 *Le Figaro*, 27.5.1909.
141 Karsavina, p. 200.
142 Lieven, p. 104.
143 Haskell, p. 217. Nuvel's information. Diaghilev's Black Notebook, Lincoln Center. In this, which was begun in 1910, *Daphnis* is first mentioned on p. 5. Fokine (p. 195) mistakenly gives 1910 as the year in which he gave Diaghilev the scenario of his *Daphnis*.
144 Grigoriev, p. 34.
145 Lieven, p. 98.
146 Well, nearly everyone. Robert Brussel, Maxime Dethomas, Chaliapine, the Aga Khan, for a start. And see note 150.
147 Karsavina, conversations.
148 Told to the author by M. Jean Hugo.
149 Karsavina, pp. 282, 283.
150 Ibid., p. 200.
151 Karsavina, conversations. Mme Romola Nijinsky (p. 135) wrongly stated that Eleonora Nijinska left Russia for the first time with the Ballet in 1912. Mme Bronislava Nijinska told me that her mother always travelled with her.
152 *Le Figaro*, 28.5.1909.

153 Benois, *Reminiscences*, p. 295.
154 *Le Figaro*, 5.6.1909.
155 Benois, *Reminiscences*, p. 294.
156 Svetlov, *Le Ballet*, pp. 98, 99.
157 Karsavina, conversations.
158 Fokine, p. 130.
159 Johnson, pp. 81, 82.
160 Benois, *Reminiscences*, pp. 295-7.
161 Ibid., p. 298.
162 Ibid., p. 296.
163 *L'Intransigeant*. Undated press cutting.
164 Karsavina, conversations. In *Theatre Street* Mme Karsavina wrongly stated that 'Pavlova made but a fleeting appearance and left us after a couple of performances.'
165 Calvocoressi, pp. 216, 217.
166 *Le Figaro*, 19.6.1909.
167 *Le Gaulois*, 19.6.1909 and 20.6.1909.
168 Ibid., 20.6.1909.
169 Grigoriev, p. 35. Karsavina, conversations. Grigoriev omitted the name of Karsavina. Hers and, later, Sokolova's were the two which occurred in his chronicle less often than might be expected. His wife danced some of their roles.
170 Karsavina, conversations.
171 Romola Nijinsky, p. 80. Romola Nijinsky, conversations.
172 Lincoln Center, Astruc papers, letter from A. to D., 15.6.1909.
173 Ibid., report to the Tsar.
174 Ibid., report to the Tsar. Also the bill promising to repay on 7.10.1909, which was not honoured.
175 Ibid., list of payments and receipts, with deficit. The deficit of 68,000 francs (before 30,000 was repaid) revealed by the Astruc papers is a figure which tallies roughly with the '60,000 francs' which Nuvel remembered in 1934 and told Haskell about (Haskell, p. 215). It is curious to read in the long inventory, for instance, a summary of the items in Nijinsky's *Armide* costume: '1 tunique drap d'argent/1 tunique de dessous en cachemir orange/1 culotte en satin merveilleux blanc/1 paire souliers de danse peau dorée/1 turban avec plumes d'autruche/1 petit collier drap or avec pierreries.' The correspondence with Monte Carlo also survives at Lincoln Center.
176 Ibid., various documents.
177 Karsavina, p. 202.
178 Calvocoressi, p. 217.
179 *Le Figaro*, 20.6.1909.
180 *La Vie Parisienne*, 3.7.1909. The article is obviously inspired by Diaghilev, Astruc, Brussel or Calvocoressi.
181 Calvocoressi, p. 217.
182 See note 143.
183 Calvocoressi, p. 136.

184 Romola Nijinsky, p. 80. Also conversations.
185 Lincoln Center, Astruc papers, letter, 19.7.1909.
186 Letters from Debussy to Laloy quoted in *La Revue de Musicologie*, Jul.–Dec. 1962, p. 34; and in Lockspeiser, Vol. II, p. 169.
187 Lincoln Center, Astruc papers, letter, 6.8.1909.
188 Romola Nijinsky, p. 81.

CHAPTER 9 1910

1 Benois, *Reminiscences*, p. 303.
2 Lincoln Center. Diaghilev's Black Notebook, started in 1910, often referred to by Grigoriev and bought by the New York Public Library at Sotheby, is an important document for the study of Diaghilev's thinking in pre-war years. It was analysed by Dr Brian Blackwood, whose findings were published in the *Journal* of the Museum and Library of Performing Arts, Lincoln Center. I have followed him in most instances, and have used his numbering of the (unnumbered) pages.
3 *The Firebird* is first mentioned (with *Le Lac des Cygnes* and *Daphnis et Chloë*) on p. 5, *Les Orientales* on p. 27, *Giselle* on p. 38, *Schéhérazade* on p. 74, *Carnaval* on p. 83.
4 Benois, *Reminiscences*, pp. 303, 304.
5 Lieven, pp. 106, 107. Benois was his source of information.
6 Fokine, p. 158.
7 Benois, *Reminiscences*, p. 304.
8 Kochno, conversations. So Diaghilev told him.
9 Benois, *Reminiscences*, p. 304.
10 Licven, p. 107. He was, as ever, quoting Benois.
11 Fokine, pp. 158, 159.
12 Grigoriev, p. 38.
13 Benois, *Reminiscences*, p. 304.
14 Lieven, p. 106.
15 Fokine, pp. 159, 160.
16 Stravinsky, *Expositions*, p. 127.
17 Ibid., p. 128.
18 Ibid., p. 129.
19 Ibid., pp. 128, 129.
20 Stravinsky, *Memories*, p. 32. Pavlova did not like Stravinsky's music, anyway.
21 Fokine, p. 159.
22 Ibid., p. 159.
23 Petipa's scenarios, quoted Yuri Slonimsky, *Petipa*, trans. A. Chujoy, *Dance Index*, Vol. VI, nos 5, 6, p. 133.
24 Kirstein, p. 39.
25 Stravinsky, *Expositions*, p. 129.
26 Karsavina, pp. 212, 213.
27 See conversation with Astruc, p. 120.
28 Grigoriev, pp. 38–40.

189 Painting in Museum of Modern Art, New York.
190 Lincoln Center, Astruc papers.
191 Ibid., draft of letter to Chaliapine, 9.10.1909.
192 Ibid., report to the Tsar.
193 Ibid.
194 Ibid., draft of letter to Brussel, 23.12.1909.
195 Ibid., telegrams between Brussel, A. and others from 8.1.1910 to 15.1.1910.

29 Lincoln Center, Astruc papers, telegram, 10.2.1910.
30 Lincoln Center, Black Notebook, p. 61. On pp. 67 and 68 the list of the proposed repertoire includes *The Sleeping Beauty* and *Coppelia* (another of Kchessinskaya's ballets). On p. 60 Diaghilev wrote '1910', which led Brian Blackwood to guess that this page was inscribed on 1 Jan.
31 Kochno, conversations. So Diaghilev told him.
32 Benois, *Reminiscences*, pp. 309, 310.
33 Ibid., p. 310.
34 Ibid., p. 310, also footnote.
35 Fokine, p. 151. So did Nuvel, apparently (Haskell, p. 222).
36 Grigoriev, p. 38.
37 Ibid., p. 152.
38 Grigoriev, p. 42.
39 Rimsky-Korsakov, pp. 446, 447.
40 Ibid., pp. 292, 293.
41 Lincoln Center, Astruc papers, telegram, 2.2.1910.
42 Ibid., telegram, 8.2.1910.
43 Ibid., telegram, 10.2.1910.
44 Ibid., telegram, 11.2.1910.
45 Ibid., letter from Schidlovsky to A., 11.2.1910.
46 Ibid., telegram, 15.2.1910.
47 Ibid., telegram, 16.2.1910. The dates given were 22 and 24 May.
48 Ibid., telegrams 12, 13.1.1910.
49 Ibid. Receipts exist.
50 Ibid., telegram, 10.4.1910.
51 Ibid., telegram from Gunsburg to A., 23.4.1910.
52 Haskell, p. 217.
53 Benois, *Reminiscences*, p. 312.
54 Lincoln Center, Astruc papers, notes by A.
55 Fokine, p. 134.
56 There were differences of opinion between Mme Karsavina, Mme Bronislava Nijinska, the English edition of Fokine's *Memoirs* and Beaumont's *Complete Book*, about this cast, which I hope I have now given correctly, with the aid of Mr Vitale Fokine's Russian researchers.
57 Grigoriev, p. 40.

58 Ibid., p. 40.
59 Lincoln Center, Black Notebook, pp. 29, 85 et al.
60 Ibid., p. 15.
61 Benois, *Reminiscences*, p. 313.
62 Karsavina, pp. 213, 214.
63 Ibid., p. 215.
64 Ibid., pp. 214, 215.
65 Karsavina, conversations.
66 Lieven, pp. 115, 116.
67 Benois, *Reminiscences*, pp. 313, 314.
68 Grigoriev, p. 44.
69 Ibid., p. 44. One's faith in Grigoriev is somewhat diminished when one reads of Karsavina being 'much appreciated' in Berlin, when she was in London, and of her brilliance and Nijinsky's in *Carnaval* in Paris, when neither danced it.
70 Vaudoyer, p. 26.
71 Kochno, conversations.
72 Karsavina, p. 219. Bakst told Mme Karsavina this.
73 *Le Gaulois*. The dress rehearsal announced on 1.6.1910 was cancelled on 2.6.1910.
74 Ibid., 5.6.1910.
75 Grigoriev, p. 46.
76 Benois, *Reminiscences*, p. 316.
77 Fokine, p. 155.
78 Ibid., pp. 155, 156.
79 Such as: Whitworth, p. 57; Benois, *Reminiscences*, p. 316; Nijinska, conversations, quoted Buckle, *Nijinsky*, p. 160; Guerra, in an interview with Françoise Reiss, Reiss, p. 78; Cocteau, *La Difficulté d'être*, p. 70.
80 See page 300.
81 Grigoriev, p. 43.
82 Proust, p. 188.
83 Calvocoressi, pp. 218, 219.
84 Benois, *Reminiscences*, pp. 310, 311.
85 Ibid., p. 311.
86 Stravinsky Archives, Stravinsky, letter to Roerich finished after 30.6.1910, doubtless during July.
87 Quoted Benois, *Reminiscences*, pp. 314–16.
88 Karsavina, p. 218.
89 Karsavina, conversations. 'Not her!' she told me.
90 Karsavina, p. 220.
91 Benois, *Reminiscences*, pp. 289, 337, 338.
92 Whitworth, p. 57.
93 Svetlov, *Karsavina*, p. 97.
94 Benois, *Reminiscences*, p. 313.

95 *Le Gaulois*, 19.6.1910.
96 Karsavina, p. 220.
97 Painter, II, p. 164.
98 Karsavina, conversations.
99 Benois, *Reminiscences*, pp. 304, 305.
100 Stravinsky, *Expositions*, p. 128. 'Descriptive music of a kind I did not want to write.'
101 Stravinsky, *Conversations*, p. 96. Stravinsky wrote, 'Vrubel was dying or going mad.'
102 Benois, *Reminiscences*, pp. 306, 307.
103 Ibid., p. 307.
104 Stravinsky, *Expositions*, p. 129.
105 Ibid., pp. 130, 131.
106 Photographed by Drian and de Meyer; painted by Blanche, Barbier; drawn by Cocteau.
107 Stravinsky, *Expositions*, p. 140.
108 Stravinsky Archives, letter from Stravinsky to Roerich. The date has been interpreted by Robert Craft as 19.6.1910, but, even allowing for the Julian Calendar, this seems unlikely.
109 Benois, *Reminiscences*, p. 308.
110 Karsavina, p. 285.
111 Karsavina, conversations.
112 Karsavina, p. 221.
113 Ibid., p. 284.
114 Ibid., p. 286.
115 Calvocoressi, p. 221. It is not clear what 'terms' Diaghilev had not 'adhered to'.
116 Grigoriev, p. 52.
117 Benois, *Reminiscences*, p. 323.
118 Stravinsky Archives, letters to Roerich, 19 and 27.6.1910, Stravinsky, *Expositions*, p. 67.
119 Ibid., p. 134.
120 Benois, *Reminiscences*, pp. 324, 325. Lieven, pp. 135, 136.
121 Stravinsky, *Expositions*, p. 134.
122 Benois, *Reminiscences*, pp. 324, 325.
123 Lincoln Center, Astruc papers, telegrams from D. in Venice to A. in Paris, 1.9.1910 to 10.10.1910.
124 Ibid., telegram from D. in London to A. in Paris, 10.10.1910.
125 Lucienne Astruc collection, letter card, 27.10.1910, quoted Buckle, *In Search*, p. 95.
126 Benois, *Reminiscences*, p. 327.
127 Ibid., p. 326.
128 Ibid., p. 327.
129 Stravinsky, *Expositions*, p. 134.
130 Benois, *Reminiscences*, p. 328, footnote.

CHAPTER 10   1911–12

1 Grigoriev, p. 54.
2 Ibid., p. 58.
3 Lincoln Center, Astruc papers, telegram from D. to A. Grigoriev, p. 58.
4 Karsavina, p. 286: 'Diaghilev ... regarded the choreography of Fokine as belonging to the past.' Morrell, p. 227: 'Such ballets as [*Le Spectre de la rose*] did not interest [Nijinsky]. He said it was "*trop joli*". ...'
5 Rambert, conversations.

6 Reiss, p. 102. Her interview with Larionov.
7 Lincoln Center, Black Notebook, p. 123.
8 Nijinska, conversations.
9 Ibid.
10 Ibid.
11 Lincoln Center, Astruc papers, telegram from D. to A., 10.2.1911.
12 *La Revue de Paris*, 15.7.1910, quoted 'Variations sur les Ballets russes', p. 17.
13 Lifar, pp. 252, 253. He quotes what Vaudoyer told him.
14 Fokine, p. 180.
15 Lincoln Center, Astruc papers, letter from D. to A., 22.5.1911.
16 Sold at Sotheby, London, 13.6.1967.
17 Benois, *Reminiscences*, p. 318.
18 Ibid., p. 318; Romola Nijinsky, p. 102; Haskell, pp. 234–5. According to Romola Nijinsky and Nuvel, (1) Nijinsky left off his jock-strap, and (2) Teliakovsky was present. Mme Nijinsky confused the issue by writing about 'a black velvet gilet', but this was the second-act costume, which *did* have puffed trunks. In Haskell, Nuvel quotes a correspondence of 1934 between Svetlov and Krupensky on the subject.
19 Karsavina, p. 226. (Lady Ripon had taken her photographs to show the Empress at Sandringham.)
20 Nijinska, conversations.
21 Articles in *Novoye Vremya* and *Le Journal de St Pétersbourg*, 3.2.1911.
22 Sotheby catalogues.
23 Lincoln Center, Astruc papers, telegram from D. to A., 10.2.1911.
24 Ibid., telegram from Gunsburg to A.
25 Romola Nijinsky, p. 102. This may be quite untrue.
26 Lincoln Center, Astruc papers, telegram from D. to A., 13.3.1911.
27 Ibid., telegram from D. to A., 14.2.1911.
28 Ibid., another telegram, 14.2.1911.
29 Ibid., letter from A. to D., 14.2.1911.
30 Bennett, p. 4.
31 Lincoln Center, Astruc papers, telegram from D. to A., 2.3.1911.
32 Ibid., telegram from D. to A., 18.2.1911.
33 Ibid., another telegram, 18.2.1911.
34 Ibid. But apparently first mentioned to A. in a telegram from D. in Rome, 26.5.1911.
35 It was Serov's only work for the Russian Ballet, and he died soon afterwards. The curtain was sold at Sotheby on 17.7.1968 and returned to the USSR.
36 Lincoln Center, Astruc papers, telegrams from D. to A., 3, 15.3.1911.
37 Ibid., telegram from D. to A., 12.3.1911: 'Bakst arrive demain.'
38 Ibid., telegram from D. to A., 15.3.1911.
39 Ibid. I guess that *La Péri* was first discussed

during D.'s brief visit to Paris, because the first surviving reference to it is in a telegram from D. in Beaulieu to A. in Paris, 23.3.1911, two days after he left. In *Nijinsky* I wrote mistakenly, I now think, that Diaghilev and Nijinsky spent only two days in Paris.
40 Ibid. D's telegrams to A. between 23 and 25.3.1911 are from Beaulieu.
41 Ibid., telegram from D. to A., 30.3.1911: 'Suis définitivement Riviera Palace.' He may have stayed elsewhere between 25 and 30.3.1911. Grigoriev, p. 59.
42 Grigoriev, p. 60. But Grigoriev states the opening was on 6 Apr.
43 Programmes provide evidence of the company's elements, and suggest that the Molodzov troupe were inadequate, as they were got rid of between Jul. and Oct.
44 Grigoriev, p. 55.
45 Karsavina, conversations, and Nijinska, conversations.
46 Grigoriev, p. 55.
47 Fokine, p. 134. 'I created *Les Sylphides* in three days ... that which was so hastily conceived was never changed by me.'
48 Lincoln Center, Astruc papers, telegrams from D. to A., 23 and 25.3.1911, 3.4.1911.
49 Koribut-Kubitovitch is in a photograph taken by Bezobrazov of Diaghilev, Benois, Stravinsky, Nijinsky, Karsavina and the Botkine sisters, reproduced in Stravinsky, *Memories*, facing p. 29 (wrongly listed under 'Illustrations'), and Buckle, *Nijinsky* (paperback), plate 12a. The evidence of his perfect manners comes from several sources, Mme Karsavina among them.
50 Photograph, previous note. Stravinsky saw his first aeroplane during a visit to Monte Carlo from Beaulieu (*Expositions*, p. 136), and when he exclaimed in wonder Diaghilev remarked sarcastically, 'I expect that tomorrow you will gaze in amazement at a taxi.'
51 Ibid.
52 Karsavina, conversations. Aga Khan, p. 109.
53 Lincoln Center, Astruc papers, telegram from D. to A., 5.4.1911.
54 Lincoln Center, Astruc papers, telegram from D. to A., 21.4.1911, quoting telegram received from Rubinstein: 'Regrette mais nécessité de mon travail m'empêche venir dimanche. Pouvez absolument compter sur moi le vingt-trois.'
55 Karsavina, p. 223.
56 Kchessinskaya, p. 125.
57 *Le Monte Carlo*.
58 Ibid.
59 Nijinska, conversations.
60 Ibid.
61 Describing this, Fokine (p. 182) appears to

555

be taking the credit for the unusual *port de bras*. Mme Bronislava may have exaggerated the inventive part her brother played.

62 Romola Nijinsky, pp. 114, 115.
63 Nijinska, conversations.
64 Benois, *Reminiscences*, p. 340.
65 Karsavina, p. 240.
66 Unidentified press cuttings. Grigoriev, p. 60.
67 Lincoln Center, Diaghilev's Black Notebook, p. 141.
68 Lincoln Center, Astruc papers, letter from D. to A., 27.5.1911. 'Quand Rubinstein a voulu monter une série de danses sur la musique compliquée de St Sébastien elle est venue a Monte Carlo pour 5 jours. Et tout a été fait quoiqu'elle fût tombée en plein dans la période si difficile de la création de Narcisse.'
69 Benois, *Reminiscences*, p. 340. Because of Benois' words – 'After his trip to Greece, where he had visited Athens and Crete in company with Serov, Bakst demanded ... the opportunity of expressing all his knowledge of ancient Hellas' – I assumed that the journey had taken place in summer 1910, shortly before Serov's death, and stated this wrongly in my *Nijinsky*. In the little Russian book commemorating the journey, there is not a single date. Larissa Haskell tells me the journey took place in 1903.
70 Ibid., p. 342.
71 Ibid., pp. 341, 342.
72 Karsavina, p. 212.
73 Beaumont, p. 38.
74 Sokolova, conversations.
75 Lincoln Center, Astruc papers, telegram from D. to A., 5.5.1911.
76 Grigoriev, p. 62.
77 Ibid.
78 Benois, *Reminiscences*, p. 332.
79 Diaghilev drawing reproduced in Benois, *Reminiscences*, facing p. 319, and Lieven, facing p. 160. Stravinsky drawing, Lieven, facing p. 142.
80 Benois, *Reminiscences*, pp. 330, 331.
81 Karsavina, conversations.
82 Karsavina, p. 231.
83 Lincoln Center, Astruc papers, telegram from D. to A., 15.5.1911.
84 Benois, *Reminiscences*, pp. 331, 332.
85 Lincoln Center, Astruc papers, letter from D. to A., 22.5.1911.
86 Ibid., telegram from Bakst to A., 24.5.1911.
87 Ibid., telegram from D. to A., 26.5.1911.
88 Ibid., letter from D. to A., 27.5.1911.
89 Ibid., telegram from D. to A., 31.5.1911.
90 Juliet Duff, conversations.
91 *Le Gaulois*, 6.6.1911.
92 Buckle collection, programme of 8.6.1911.

93 *Comoedia Illustré*, 15.6.1911, Cocteau's article.
94 *Le Gaulois*, 7.6.1911.
95 *Commedia*, 7.6.1911.
96 Lieven, pp. 142, 143.
97 Ibid., p. 143.
98 Fokine, p. 190. An existing photograph shows the extras staring at the camera.
99 Kochno, p. 68.
100 Benois, *Reminiscences*, pp. 333–5.
101 Fokine, pp. 191, 193, 194.
102 Benois, *Reminiscences*, pp. 337, 338.
103 Juliet Duff, conversations. Diaghilev acknowledged Lady Ripon's patronage in an interview with the *Observer*, 30.6.1929.
104 Benson, p. 180 et seq.
105 Pavlova at the Palace; Gelzer and Tikhomirov at the Alhambra; Kyaksht (now spelt Kyasht) in a version of *Sylvia* at the Empire; and a Mme Sobinoff at the Hippodrome.
106 Grigoriev, p. 66. Covent Garden Market moved in 1974 south of the Thames.
107 *Daily Mail*, 21.6.1911.
108 Diaghilev Memoirs. Diaghilev also forgot that the Coronation gala was not his first performance in England.
109 *The Times*, 22.6.1911.
110 *Daily Mail*, 23.6.1911.
111 *Daily News*, 22.6.1911.
112 *Morning Post*, 23.6.1911.
113 Lincoln Center, Astruc papers, telegram from D. to A., 23.6.1911.
114 *Daily Mail*, 26.6.1911.
115 *Observer*, 25.6.1911.
116 *The Times*, 24.6.1911.
117 Bedells, pp. 51, 52.
118 Diana Cooper, conversation and letter.
119 St Just albums.
120 Covent Garden archives.
121 *The Times*, 27.6.1911.
122 Diaghilev, Memoirs.
123 *Daily Mail*, 27.6.1911.
124 Ibid.
125 Royal Archives.
126 Diaghilev, Memoirs.
127 *Daily Telegraph*, 28.6.1911.
128 *Daily Mail*, 28.6.1911.
129 Karsavina, conversations.
130 St Just albums.
131 Ibid.
132 Grigoriev, p. 68.
133 Lincoln Center, Astruc papers, telegram from D. to A., 1.9.1911.
134 Ibid., telegram from D. to A., 25.9.1911.
135 Ibid., telegrams from D. to A., 13.10.1911, 10.10.1911.
136 Ibid., telegram from D. to A., 15.10.1911.
137 Grigoriev, p. 68.
138 Karsavina, conversations.

139 *Observer*, 15.10.1911.
140 Rosenthal, p. 359.
141 *The Times*, 17.10.1911.
142 *Daily Mail*, 17.10.1911.
143 *Observer*, 22.10.1911.
144 *Daily Mail*, 17.10.1911.
145 *Sunday Times*, 22.10.1911.
146 *The Times*, 30.10.1911.
147 *Daily News*, 30.10.1911.
148 *Daily Mail*, 30.10.1911.
149 St Just albums.
150 Kchessinskaya, pp, 132, 133.
151 *Daily Telegraph*, 15.11.1911.
152 Kchessinskaya, p. 133.
153 Respectively, *Daily News*, 15.11.1911; *Daily Mirror*, 16.11.1911; *Daily Telegraph*, 15.11.1911.
154 Juliet Duff, conversations.
155 St Just albums.
156 Lincoln Center, Astruc papers, telegram from D. to A., 15.11.1911.
157 *Lady*, 7.12.1911.
158 Kchessinskaya, p. 134.
159 Ibid.
160 *The Times*, 1.12.1911.
161 *Daily Mail*, 1.12.1911.
162 *Morning Post*, 1.12.1911.
163 *The Times*, 1.12.1911.
164 Kchessinskaya, p. 134.
165 Collection of the Revd Gerald Carnes, Lady Juliet Duff's Birthday Book.
166 Ricketts, p. 195.
167 *Daily Mail*, 11.12.1911.
168 Lincoln Center, Astruc papers, telegram from D. to A., 9.12.1911.
169 Ibid., telegram from D. to Keynote (agency), 11.12.1911.
170 Ibid., telegram from D. to A., 12.12.1911.
171 Ibid., telegram from D. to A., 15.12.1911.
172 Karsavina, pp. 240, 241. Also Bourman, p. 212, for a more lurid account.
173 Lincoln Center, Astruc papers, telegram from D. in Berlin to Kchessinskaya in St Petersburg, 4.1.1912.
174 Ibid., document.
175 Ibid., telegram from D. to A., 8.1.1912, and another with indecipherable date.
176 Ibid., draft of contract.
177 Stravinsky, *Expositions*, p. 142.
178 Nijinska, conversations.
179 Grigoriev got the date of the theatre's burning wrong, and even described Diaghilev as being 'dejected' about it in Paris in Dec., nearly a month before it happened.
180 Lincoln Center, Astruc papers, telegram from D. to A., 9.2.1912.
181 Karsavina conversations.
182 Karsavina, pp. 225, 226.
183 Grigoriev, pp. 72, 73.
184 Benois, *Reminiscences*, pp. 343, 344.
185 Ibid., pp. 344, 345.
186 Hofmannsthal-Strauss, pp. 121, 122.
187 Stravinsky, *Expositions*, p. 260; Grigoriev, p. 74.
188 Lincoln Center, Astruc papers, telegram from D. to A., 6.3.1912.
189 Romola Nijinsky, conversations.
190 Romola Nijinsky, p. 12.
191 Romola Nijinsky, conversations.
192 Romola Nijinsky, p. 13.
193 Lincoln Center, Astruc papers. The telegrams to A. from D. at Beausoleil begin on 19.3.1912.
194 Grigoriev, pp. 75, 76.
195 Rambert, conversations.
196 Stravinsky Archives, letter of 19.4.1912 quoted by Robert Craft in a review, *New York Review*, 21.2.1974.
197 Grigoriev, pp. 76, 77.
198 Kchessinskaya, pp. 138, 139.
199 *Le Monte Carlo*, 14.4.1912.
200 Monte Carlo programmes.
201 Lincoln Center, Astruc papers, telegram from D. to A., 2.5.1912. Grigoriev wrote that they left on 5.5.1912.
202 Grigoriev, p. 77.
203 Karsavina, conversations.
204 Evidence in Astruc papers, Lincoln Center.
205 V. Svetlow, *Le Ballet contemporain, ouvrage édité avec la collaboration de L. Bakst. Traduction française de M. D. Calvocoressi* (St Petersburg, Société R. Golicke et A. Willborg, 1912). M. de Brunoff, Paris. 520 numbered copies.
206 The photographs of Bert and the drawings of Valentine Gross show that Nijinsky had slightly elongated and padded slippers, and stood on the tips of them.
207 *Le Figaro*, 14.5.1912.
208 Many of these were reproduced in *Comoedia Illustré*, but I also studied them from life when I catalogued them for the sale at Sotheby, London, on 17.7.1968, and was enabled to buy some for the Theatre Museum, London.
209 Sokolova, pp. 36, 37.
210 Beaumont, p. 59.
211 Calvocoressi, pp. 170, 171.
212 Karsavina, p. 212.
213 Benois, *Reminiscences*, pp. 348, 351.
214 Stravinsky, *Memories*, p. 36.
215 Fokine, p. 205.
216 A musical score, inscribed by Nijinsky with indications of staging and with his choreographic notation, is in the British Museum.
217 Romola Nijinsky, p. 141.
218 Nijinska, conversations.
219 Buckle, *Nijinsky*, p. 280.
220 Grigoriev, p. 79.

221 Ibid., p. 79.
222 It seems reasonable to assume that Diaghilev's subsequent pride in the acclaim won by Nijinsky's first ballet, of which various telegrams to Astruc and interviews with the Press bear witness, sprang from genuine admiration for the work's quality.
223 *Commedia*, 30.5.1912.
224 *Le Figaro*, 30.5.1912.
225 Ibid., 31.5.1912.
226 Ibid., 3.6.1912.
227 Programme of the season announced in *Comoedia Illustré*.
228 Fokine, pp. 209–11.
229 Ibid., p. 211. Fokine also wrote, which was clearly untrue, that the house was empty for *Schéhérazade*.
230 Ibid., p. 212.
231 *Le Figaro*, 9.6.1912.
232 Fokine, p. 215.
233 Ricketts, pp. 176, 177.
234 *Daily Mail*, 13.6.1912.
235 *Daily News*, 13.6.1912.
236 *The Times*, 13.6.1912.
237 *Pall Mall Gazette*, 13.6.1912.
238 Beaumont, pp. 9, 10.
239 Ibid., pp. 16, 17.
240 St Just albums.
241 Beaumont, p. 20.
242 Hofmannsthal-Strauss, pp. 133, 134.
243 Ibid., p. 136, letter, 28.6.1912.
244 Ibid., p. 139, letter, 21.7.1912.
245 *The Times*, 10.7.1912.
246 *Morning Post*, 10.7.1912.
247 *Daily Express*, 10.7.1912.
248 *Daily Mail*, 10.7.1912.
249 *Sunday Times*, 14.7.1912.
250 Ricketts, p. 179.
251 Morrell, pp. 226, 227.
252 Ibid., pp. 227, 228.
253 Duncan Grant, letter to the author.
254 Lady Ottoline Morrell's Visitors' Book, the property of Mrs Igor Vinogradoff. The next names on the page were Frederick Etchells, a member of the Vorticist group formed in the following year, and Jacob Epstein, whose Oscar Wilde monument had just been on show at his Cheyne Walk studio before being shipped to Paris: so they may have been there at the same time.
255 Morrell, p. 228.
256 Nijinska, conversations.
257 Lady Ottoline Morrell's Visitors' Book.
258 Blanche, *Portraits*, II, pp. 257, 258.
259 Ibid., p. 258.
260 Lady Juliet Duff, essay.
261 Ibid.
262 *Sunday Times*, 23.6.1912.
263 *Daily News*, 3.7.1912.
264 *The Times*, 9.7.1912.
265 Lady Juliet Duff, essay; also *Lady*, 4.7.1912.
266 *Lady*, 4.7.1912.
267 *Sketch*, 10.7.1912.
268 *The Times*, 18.7.1912.
269 *Lady*, 1.8.1912.
270 Told the author by Mr Hoppé.
271 Sir Geoffrey Keynes, letter to the author.
272 Cathleen Nesbitt, conversation.
273 Marsh, p. 75. Letter quoted.
274 So it appears to me, for I think he visited Strauss (at Garmisch, near Munich) at the end of the month when he went to see Benois at Lugano – and heard *Parsifal* at Bayreuth, presumably. We know from Benois (*Reminiscences*, pp. 346–8) that Diaghilev, Nijinsky and Stravinsky visited Lugano; a photograph taken on the Stresa-Isola Bella steamer survives, dated by Stravinsky 25.8.1912; and Stravinsky remembered hearing *Parsifal*, performed for the last time at Bayreuth that summer on 20.8.1912, with Diaghilev. (It was also given on 23 Jul., and 1, 4, 7, 8, and 11 Aug.) In view of the Deauville dates and Diaghilev's telegram to Astruc from London on 30.8.1912, Robert Craft and I were long perplexed about the events of Aug. The finding at Lincoln Center of a telegram from Diaghilev at Lugano to Astruc dated 25.8.1912 helped to make the picture clearer.
275 Lincoln Center, Astruc papers.
276 See note 274.
277 Benois, *Reminiscences*, pp. 343–8.
278 Lincoln Center, Astruc papers, telegram from D. to Bessel, 27.8.1912.
279 Ibid., telegram from D. to A., 30.8.1912.
280 When Mr and Mrs Stravinsky visited Venice in 1951, Robert Craft noticed that 'he seemed more excited in pointing out the room in the Grand Hotel in which he had played *Le Sacre* for Nijinsky and Diaghilev than by anything else in Venice.' Of course, he had played parts of it to Diaghilev before in other places.
281 Stravinsky Archives. Diaghilev's telegrams to Stravinsky at Ustilug begin on 6.9.1912. He urges him on 22.9.1912 to return for discussions with Maeterlinck in Paris 'on Monday'.
282 Lincoln Center, Astruc papers, telegram from D. to A., 24.10.1912.
283 Debussy, *Lettres à son éditeur*, pp. 110, 111.
284 Stravinsky, *Expositions*, pp. 141, 142.
285 Stravinsky, *Conversations*, p. 69.
286 Ibid., p. 69.
287 Lincoln Center, Astruc papers, telegram from D. to A., 12.12.1912.
288 Hofmannsthal-Strauss, p. 150.
289 *Ballet*, Vol. X, No. 2, de Zoete, 'The

1,000,000 mile Journey': [Part] V; Jaques-Dalcroze.

290 Rambert, correspondence.
291 Rambert, p. 51.
292 Rambert, conversations.
293 From her memory of the programme, her

CHAPTER II 1913–14

1 Lincoln Center, Astruc papers, telegram from D. to A., 2.1.1913.
2 At this performance of *Petrushka* Stravinsky remembered the Arch-Duke Franz Ferdinand being present. (*Expositions*, p. 80.)
3 Romola Nijinsky, p. 19.
4 Grigoriev, p. 88.
5 Karsavina, conversations.
6 Grigoriev, p. 88.
7 Stravinsky Archives. Correspondence confirms this.
8 Romola Nijinsky, pp. 15, 16.
9 Romola Nijinsky, conversations.
10 Romola Nijinsky, pp. 20–22.
11 Nijinska, conversations.
12 Romola Nijinsky, conversation. It was at Boulestin's Restaurant in Southampton Street. My question was sudden: I was sure her answer was frank. I always had the impression that she had long since forgotten what she had written in her biography. Editions subsequent to 1933 contained no emendations or changes.
13 Stravinsky Archives, telegram from D. to Stravinsky, 17.1.1913.
14 Lincoln Center, Astruc papers, telegram from D. to A., 31(?).1.1913.
15 Ibid., telegram from Nijinsky to A., 27.1.1913.
16 Grigoriev, p. 89. Grigoriev wrote, 'We arrived in London six weeks before we were due to start performing.' It was about six days.
17 Rambert, pp. 58, 59.
18 Valentine Gross, typescript in possession of the Theatre Museum, London.
19 Stravinsky Archives, telegram from D. to Stravinsky, 2.2.1913.
20 Beaumont, p. 42.
21 *The Times*, 5.2.1913.
22 *Daily Mail*, 6.2.1913.
23 *Lady*, 13.2.1913.
24 Beaumont, pp. 43–5.
25 O. Sitwell, *Great Morning*, pp. 242, 241.
26 *Daily Mirror*, 17.2.1913.
27 *Daily Mail*, 18.2.1913.
28 *The Times*, 18.2.1913.
29 *Daily Mail*, 20, 21.2.1913.
30 Ibid., 21.2.1913.
31 Lincoln Center, Astruc papers, copy of a letter from Gunsburg to Bewicke, 15.12.1912.

first sight of the ballet could only have been on the last night of the season.

294 Rambert, p. 54.
295 Ibid.
296 Romola Nijinsky, p. 14. Romola Nijinsky, conversations.

32 Sokolova, p. 31.
33 *Daily Mail*, 8.3.1913.
34 Ursula Vaughan Williams, pp. 93, 94.
35 *Daily Mail*, 8.3.1913.
36 Grigoriev, p. 90.
37 Karsavina, pp. 587, 588.
38 Rambert, p. 57.
39 Ibid., p. 58.
40 Rambert, conversations.
41 Ibid.
42 Ibid.
43 Romola Nijinsky: Kirstein MS.
44 Nijinska, conversations.
45 Rambert, conversations.
46 Romola Nijinsky, conversations.
47 Karsavina, pp. 293, 294.
48 E. W. White, letter from Ravel to Stravinsky, Monday (probably 21 or 28.4.1913), quoted in Appendix B, p. 548.
49 Nijinska, conversations.
50 Rambert, conversations.
51 E. W. White, letter from Ravel to Stravinsky, 5.5.1913, quoted in Appendix B, p. 549.
52 Astruc, p. 287.
53 Grigoriev, p. 91.
54 Rambert, p. 70.
55 Kochno, conversations.
56 Nijinska, conversations.
57 Ansermet, conversation.
58 Debussy, *Lettres* (1913). Letter to Robert Godet, 9.6.1913.
59 Brian Blackwood's analysis in Buckle, *Nijinsky*, p. 342.
60 *Le Figaro*, 17.5.1913.
61 *Gil Blas*, 30.5.1913.
62 Lockspeiser, Vol. II, p. 172.
63 Fokine, p. 209.
64 E. W. White, letter from Ravel to Stravinsky, Apr. 1913, quoted in Appendix B, p. 548.
65 Photograph reproduced Buckle, *Nijinsky*, plate 13b.
66 *Le Figaro*, 24.5.1913.
67 *La Nouvelle Revue Française*, Nov. 1913.
68 Stravinsky, *Expositions*, p. 142.
69 *Gil Blas*, Apr. 1913, article by Georges Pioch.
70 On the second (dress-circle) level there were boxes with their own drawing-rooms all round the back; to the left and right, in front

of these, were two rows of *fauteuils de corbeille* and in the centre ten *loges de corbeille*, each containing eight chairs, the best seats in the house. From the seating plan of the theatre, unchanged to this day.

71 Cocteau, *Cock*, pp. 48, 49.

72 Valentine Gross, typescript of a broadcast, Theatre Museum, London. Fifty pastels of the Ballet by Gross were on show in the foyer.

73 Stravinsky, *Conversations*, p. 46.

74 Rambert, conversations.

75 Romola Nijinsky, p. 166. She calls Mme de Pourtalès 'Princesse de P.'

76 Manuel, p. 74.

77 Romola Nijinsky, pp. 165, 166.

78 Astruc, p. 286.

79 Rambert, conversations.

80 Stravinsky, *Conversations*, pp. 46, 47. See Chapter 10, note 274. This playing of *The Rite* on the Lido was certainly not the first time Diaghilev heard any of the score.

81 *Commedia*, 31.5.1913.

82 *Le Gaulois*, 1.6.1913.

83 *Le Monde Musical*, Apr. 1913.

84 Louis Laloy in *La Revue Française de la Musique*, Apr. 1913. Henry Postel du Mas in an unattributed cutting in the Arsenale.

85 *Le Figaro*, 31.5.1913.

86 *Le Gaulois*, 30.5.1913.

87 E. W. White, letter from Delius to Stravinsky, 27.5.1913, in Appendix B, p. 550.

88 Ibid., letter from Debussy, 31.5.1913, and *pneumatique* from Emma Debussy, 4.7.1913 (presumably), pp. 550 and 551 and note.

89 Ibid., letter from Ravel to Stravinsky, 5.6.1913, p. 551.

90 Stravinsky, *Chronicle*, p. 85.

91 *Le Gaulois*, 7.6.1913.

92 Johnson, pp. 216–21; Svetlov, *Karsavina*, p. 62.

93 Karsavina, conversations.

94 Grigoriev, p. 94.

95 Valentine Gross, MS article, Theatre Museum, London.

96 Romola Nijinsky, pp. 169, 170.

97 Ibid., p. 171.

98 Romola Nijinsky, conversations.

99 Romola Nijinsky, p. 172.

100 *Boris Godunov*: 24, 26.6.1913. *Khovanshchina*: 1, 10.7.1913. *Ivan the Terrible*: 8, 15.7.1913. *Jeux*: 25, 27.6.1913; 2, 7, 25.7.1913. (*Jeux* was called *Playtime* in London.) *La Tragédie de Salomé*: 30.6.1913; 4, 9, 25.7.1913. *Le Sacre*: 11, 14, 18, 23.7.1913.

101 Buckle collection, letter from Bakst to Astruc.

102 *Daily Mail*, 26.6.1913.

103 *The Times* and the *Morning Post*, 12.7.1913.

104 Stravinsky, archives: letter from Misia Sert to Stravinsky, 10.7.1913; cable from her to Stravinsky, 12.7.1913; letter from her to Stravinsky, 15.7.1913. Quoted in *Ballet Review*, Vol. 6, no. 4, Robert Craft's article, 'Stravinsky, Diaghilev and Misia Sert', pp. 63–70.

105 Romola Nijinsky, p. 177.

106 Benois, *Reminiscences*, p. 349.

107 This assumption is based on Ravel's letter of 28.8.1913 to Stravinsky, quoted in E. W. White, Appendix B, p. 552: 'Je dois écrire à Diaghilew qu'il ne compte pas sur moi pour le ballet Scarlatti. J'ai vraiment mieux à faire.'

108 This is my assumption. It is possible that Diaghilev intended to make a Scarlatti *and* a Bach ballet, but I doubt if he would have put on both in the same season.

109 Benois, *Reminiscences*, pp. 350, 351.

110 The list of compositions is in the Musée et Bibliothèque de l'Opéra, Paris. I devised a ballet to it called *Garden Party*, orchestrated by Richard Stoker, with décor by Andy Warhol and choreography by Peter Darrell. This was performed at a charity gala at the London Coliseum on 23.4.1971. Margot Fonteyn danced Prelude 1 from the First Book of Preludes and Fugues.

111 Benois, *Reminiscences*, pp. 350, 351. But in the list of places visited, it seems Benois wrote 'Einsiedeln' (which is in Switzerland) for 'Vierzehnheiligen'. Sir Sacheverell Sitwell pointed this out after the first edition of *Nijinsky* had appeared. I corrected the mistake in the English paperback edition.

112 If my assumption in note 107 above is correct, Benois expected Diaghilev to bring Ravel to him at Lugano soon afterwards. See note 129 below.

113 Benois' letter to Stravinsky, quoted below (see note 130).

114 Records of the Royal Mail Steam Packet Company, now Royal Mail Lines Ltd. Romola Nijinsky, p. 178.

115 See letter from Benois to Stravinsky, also note 129.

116 Benois, *Reminiscences*, p. 353.

117 Romola Nijinsky, p. 179 et seq. Her account has been checked against the ship's log of SS *Avon*, through courtesy of Royal Mail Lines Ltd. See also Buckle, *Nijinsky*, pp. 372–82.

118 Rambert, conversations.

119 Romola Nijinsky, p. 195.

120 I presume it was Zuikov who telegraphed to Diaghilev.

121 Romola Nijinsky, pp. 196, 197.

122 See plate 74 in first (hardback) edition of Buckle, *Nijinsky*.

123 Supposition arrived at after discussion with Mme Lydia Sokolova.

124 Benois, *Reminiscences*, p. 352.

125 Sert, pp. 120, 121. *SS Avon* docked in Buenos Aires on 6.9.1913 and Nijinsky was married on 10.9.1913. When Misia Sert wrote to Stravinsky in Russia on 6.9.1913 (letter in Stravinsky archives), she did not mention the marriage, so the news of the engagement or wedding (in the form, presumably, of a telegram from Vassili Zuikov or Grigoriev) may have arrived in Venice any day after that.

126 Hofmannsthal-Strauss, p. 176.

127 Buckle collection, letter from de Brunoff to Gross, 14.9.1913.

128 Boris Kochno thought it possible.

129 Stravinsky, *Memories*, letter, Sept. 1913, quoted p. 134.

130 Ibid., letter, 28.9.1913, quoted p. 135. According to evidence in the Stravinsky archives, quoted by Robert Craft in *Ballet Review*, Vol. 6, no. 4, Diaghilev visited Stravinsky at Lausanne on 1.10.1913 and stayed two days.

131 Romola Nijinsky, p. 207.

132 Grigoriev, pp. 100, 101.

133 Romola Nijinsky, conversations.

134 Romola Nijinsky, p. 210.

135 Lincoln Center, Astruc papers, telegram from Nijinsky to A., 5.12.1913.

136 Stravinsky, *Memories*, letter, 9.12.1913, quoted pp. 38–40.

137 Nekludov, pp. 236–9.

138 Countess Shuvalov gave two balls, one in black-and-white, the other with wigs. A photograph of the former is in Marvin Lyons, *Russia in Original Photographs, 1860–1920*, pp. 36, 37.

139 A photograph of this is reproduced in Meriel Buchanan, facing p. 144.

140 Nekludov, pp. 236–8.

141 Grigoriev, pp. 102, 103.

142 Fokine, p. 224.

143 Grigoriev, p. 93.

144 This happened, so I imagine it was one of the conditions. The agreement between Diaghilev and Fokine must have been reached before 27.12.1913, when Misia Edwards telegraphed to Stravinsky about it (Stravinsky Archives, telegram).

145 Benois, *Reminiscences*, p. 360.

146 Stravinsky, *Conversations*, p. 57, footnote. But it appears that Stravinsky was wrong in writing that Diaghilev went to Leysin to discuss *Le Rossignol* with him.

147 Benois, *Reminiscences*, pp. 354–6.

148 Ibid., p. 356.

149 Fokine, p. 226.

150 Ibid., p. 227.

151 Stravinsky Archives, telegram from D. and Misia in Paris to Stravinsky in Switzerland, 15.1.1914.

152 Ibid., letter to Catherine Stravinsky. Also Stravinsky, *Conversations*, p. 57, footnote; but this is not wholly accurate. See note 146. After D. had departed for Russia on 21.1.1914, Stravinsky played *The Nightingale* to Rivière, Cocteau, Ravel, Delage, Monteux and others at *La Nouvelle Revue Française*. On 4.2.1914 Rivière wrote to Stravinsky, saying he was 'rather late' in thanking him (letter printed in *Conversations*, p. 57).

153 Hofmannsthal-Strauss, p. 189.

154 Massine, conversations. Also Massine, pp. 40–42.

155 Massine, p. 37.

156 Massine, conversations.

157 The phrase used by Ninette de Valois after first seeing the young Robert Helpmann.

158 Massine, pp. 41, 42.

159 Ibid., pp. 43, 44.

160 Ibid., pp. 44, 45.

161 Ibid., pp. 45, 56. When we were discussing this, Mr Massine remembered, 'Giulio Romano was a painter Diaghilev loathed.'

162 Ibid., pp. 46–8.

163 Ibid., pp. 48, 49.

164 Grigoriev, p. 106.

165 Massine, pp. 51, 52.

166 Sokolova, p. 61.

167 Ibid. Sokolova wrote that she and Kremnev looked after Massine from his first arrival in Cologne, but, as Massine (in spite of a poor memory for trivialities) would hardly be wrong about his first stay in a 'grand hotel', I have followed his account, and assumed that he did not stay with Sokolova and Kremnev until after Diaghilev went away.

168 Grigoriev, p. 107.

169 Romola Nijinsky, p. 214.

170 Ibid., pp. 213, 214.

171 Beaumont, pp. 79, 80.

172 Romola Nijinsky, p. 214. To read her account one would think that Nijinsky's appearances at the Palace covered two days only. Also Romola Nijinsky, conversations; *Daily Telegraph*, 17.3.1914; Beaumont, p. 83.

173 Romola Nijinsky, p. 215.

174 Romola Nijinsky, conversations.

175 Romola Nijinsky, p. 213.

176 This fact only emerges later in Romola Nijinsky's story (p. 252), but she mentions that it was Sir George Lewis who made the financial arrangements with Nijinsky's troupe (p. 215).

177 Benois, *Reminiscences*, p. 360.

178 Kochno, conversations.

SOURCE NOTES

179 Rambert, conversations.
180 Benois, *Reminiscences*, p. 361.
181 Grigoriev, p. 99.
182 Karsavina, conversations.
183 Benois, *Reminiscences*, p. 363.
184 Bibliothèque de l'Arsenale, Paris, unattributed press cutting.
185 Romola Nijinsky, p. 218.
186 Massine, conversations.
187 Misia Sert, p. 122. Lady Ripon's letter quoted.
188 Buckle collection, letter from de Brunoff to Gross.
189 Beecham, pp. 183, 184.
190 *The Times*, 9.6.1914.
191 Ibid., 10.6.1914.
192 Ricketts, p. 199.
193 Sitwell, *Great Morning*, p. 245.
194 Stravinsky, *Conversations*, p. 47.
195 Ricketts, p. 236.
196 Karsavina, p. 245.
197 Massine, p. 61.
198 Ricketts, pp. 233–7.

199 Ibid., p. 205.
200 Serov, pp. 96–100.
201 He omitted the 'sh'.
202 Romola Nijinsky, pp. 220, 221.
203 Fokine, p. 224. Vitale Fokine wrote that his father's contract 'contained a clause specifically excluding Nijinsky's participation'.
204 *Standard*, 7.7.1914.
205 Balanchine, conversations. Diaghilev told him this.
206 Karsavina. But I have mislaid my printed source.
207 Karsavina, conversations.
208 Grigoriev, p. 111.
209 Romola Nijinsky, pp. 222, 223.
210 Morand, *Journal*, pp. 74, 75. Looking back, a year or two later, Morand wrongly wrote, 'Friday, 30 July.' The scene is rather fanciful, but it must be nearly true. Edward Horner in fact joined the army and was killed in 1917.
211 Karsavina, pp. 251, 252.

PART V

CHAPTER 12   1914–AUG 1918

1 Massine, conversations.
2 Massine, p. 65. In his book Massine seemed to imply that he had travelled to Italy on his own and only joined Diaghilev in Viareggio. This, as he admitted in conversation, was not the case.
3 Ibid., p. 66.
4 Massine's letter to Bolshakov (pp. 71, 72) gives his itinerary from Viareggio to Florence, which I have not hesitated to insert in what I believe to be its proper place, although in the body of his text Massine implies that the visits to Pisa etc. followed his arrival in Florence. His vagueness about dates is always misleading. No reader of his book could guess that nearly a year elapsed between the outbreak of war and his settling with Diaghilev in Switzerland. We have the Florence address from Diaghilev's letters to Stravinsky, which survive among the composer's papers.
5 Massine, pp. 68, 69. In the previous paragraph Massine stated that 'Although Diaghilev was busy reassembling his company, he found time to show me round Florence.' There is no evidence that Diaghilev took steps to reassemble his company until 1915, although he tried to get in touch with Nijinsky before then.
6 Massine, pp. 19, 20.
7 Ibid., p. 69.

8 Ibid., p. 70. Massine describes visiting Ravenna and other cities 'with the Serts' – i.e. with Sert and Misia Edwards, but Misia was with her ambulance unit on the Marne, and did not come back to Italy till 1916. I have left the first visit to Ravenna in 1914, because it seems to have had an influence on Massine's first (unrealized) ballet, *Liturgie*, made in 1915. No doubt he and Diaghilev revisited Ravenna with Sert and Misia later.
9 Massine, p. 70.
10 Mestrovic had shown work in London in 1913, where perhaps Diaghilev saw it. Some of his large works were 'smuggled' out of Italy and exhibited at the Victoria and Albert Museum in Jul. 1915, to arouse sympathy for Serbia.
11 Stravinsky Archives, telegrams.
12 Stravinsky Archives, letter from D. to Stravinsky, 1.11.1914, quoted Stravinsky, *Memories*, p. 48.
13 Some of Cocteau's experiences when he was a member of Misia Edwards's ambulance unit, along with Sert, Paul Iribe, François le Gouy and Louis Gautier-Vignal are described in his novel *Thomas l'Imposteur*.
14 Massine, p. 71.
15 Stravinsky Archives, letter from D. to Stravinsky, 25.11.1914, quoted *Memories*, pp. 48, 49.
16 Ibid., pp. 49–51.

17 Stravinsky Archives. Evidence from un-identified Press cuttings in Stravinsky's albums.
18 Ibid.
19 Kochno, conversations. Mme Khvotchinsky appears in a photograph taken at Bellerive, reproduced Lifar, facing p. 424, and Kochno, *Le Ballet*, p. 190.
20 Serov, p. 103.
21 Ibid., p. 104.
22 Stravinsky Archives, letter from D. to Stravinsky, 3.3.1915, quoted Stravinsky, *Memories*, p. 51.
23 Serov, p. 104.
24 Ibid., pp. 82, 83. Glazunov had disliked Prokofiev's youthful work, as he had Stravinsky's. He had also discouraged the young Rachmaninov.
25 Massine, p. 171.
26 Stravinsky Archives, letter of 3.3.1915. Quoted *Memories*, pp. 51, 52.
27 Stravinsky Archives, letter of 8.3.1915, quoted Stravinsky, *Memories*, pp. 101, 102. In this interesting letter Diaghilev wrote, 'After having thirty-two rehearsals of *Liturgie*, we have decided that absolute silence is death, and that absolute silence in air-space does not and cannot exist. The action must be supported not by music but by sounds ... the source of which is un-known. There should be no rhythm at all, since neither the beginning nor the end of the sounds should be perceptible. The in-struments that we have in mind are the *gusli*, the aeolian harp, and bells (the tongues of which can be wrapped in felt).... Marinetti has suggested that we meet in Milan, if only for one day, and listen to the different possi-bilities of a "noise" orchestra....' (Quoted from Robert Craft's second trans. in *Ballet Review*, Vol. VI, No. 4, p. 72.)
28 Serov, p. 104.
29 Stravinsky, *Memories*, p. 48, footnote.
30 Serov, p. 105.
31 Ibid., p. 106.
32 Grigoriev, pp. 113, 114.
33 Massine, pp. 65, 66.
34 Grigoriev, p. 113.
35 Ibid., p. 113.
36 Sandoz, p. 60.
37 Stravinsky, *Expositions*, pp. 67–69.
38 Ibid., p. 118.
39 Ramuz, p. 11. But Stravinsky claimed that Ramuz introduced himself in a Lausanne restaurant (*Expositions*, p. 95).
40 Their courtship is described in H. J. Bruce's *Silken Dalliance*.
41 Grigoriev, pp. 114, 115.
42 Nemtchinova, correspondence. The Poles were: Bonietska, Klementovitch, Potapo-

vitch, Slavitska, Vassilievska, Zalevska, Karnetsky, Kegler, Kostecki, Novak, Okhimovsky and Woizikovsky.
43 Ibid. The others from St Petersburg were: Antonova, Shabelska I and II, de Galanta and Khokhlova.
44 Ibid. The new dancers from Moscow were: Katchuba, Kostrovsky, Kurtner, Nemt-chinova I and II, Sumorokova I and II and Zamukhovska.
45 Sokolova, p. 69.
46 Ibid., p. 67.
47 Nemtchinova, conversations.
48 Sokolova, pp. 68, 69.
49 Ibid., p. 69.
50 Sandoz, pp. 50–56. I have not quoted some of Sandoz's more colourful anecdotes, as they strike me as later inventions. The account he gives of Diaghilev's views on Fokine's choreography is taken straight (with a few words changed) from Grigoriev, *The Diaghilev Ballet*, published a few months before his own book.
51 Romola Nijinsky, conversations.
52 Stravinsky–Diaghilev, telegrams. But most of these are dated Sept. and Oct. 1915.
53 Beaumont, who later made friends with Barocchi, wrote that he had a marble statuary business. Massine told me he knew nothing about this. If it is not true (and Barocchi may have boasted to Beaumont), my idea that he put up money for Diaghilev is probably wrong.
54 Sokolova, pp. 70, 71.
55 There are several photographs taken at Villa Bellerive showing Diaghilev, Bakst, Stra-vinsky, Massine, Gontcharova and Larionov in various combinations, indoors and out. (In one Mme Khvotchinsky appears. See note 19.)
56 Massine, p. 73. Grigoriev wrote (p. 114) that his wife Tchernicheva was to have been the Virgin, but a photograph of Massine rehearsing with Sokolova exists (reproduced Massine, between pp. 136 and 137).
57 Ibid., p. 74.
58 Ibid.
59 Hindemith's *Nobilissima Visione*, 1938; *Laudes Evangeli*, 1952.
60 Massine, pp. 74, 75.
61 Lincoln Center, Astruc papers, telegram from Gatti-Casazza to A., 14.12.1915.
62 *New York Times*, 9.1.1916.
63 Ibid.
64 Sotheby (London) catalogue, sale, 7.7.1971. The *Christ in the House of Mary and Martha* was wrongly catalogued as *Marie Madeleine*. Massine told me that the Futurist pictures were the first Diaghilev bought him.
65 Announced in American publicity.

66 Ansermet, conversations.
67 Sokolova, pp. 71, 72.
68 Massine, p. 76. In his book Massine – or his 'ghost', who clearly knew little about ballet – described Lopukhova dancing at Geneva, when, of course, she was in America.
69 Ibid., p. 77.
70 *Journal de Genève*, 22.12.1915.
71 Blanche, *Cahiers*, IV, p. 60.
72 Ibid., pp. 55–7. In his more or less factual war diaries Blanche calls Misia 'Sonia'. No key or prompting was needed to see who Sonia was. Blanche, perhaps for some reason of mystication, does not say Diaghilev was present, but it is inconceivable that he was not, as he undoubtedly arranged the session. I have substituted the name 'Misia' for 'Sonia'.
73 Ibid., pp. 60–63.
74 Grigoriev, p. 118.
75 Massine, p. 78.
76 Sokolova, pp. 72, 73.
77 Kramer, *Heywood Broun*, pp. 70, 71.
78 Sokolova, p. 73.
79 *New York Times*, 19.1.1916. (*Prince Igor* had had its first American performance on 30.12.1915.)
80 *New York Times*, 23.1.1916, and *Boston Post* (signed Olin Downes). Diaghilev obviously spoke in French, and the two versions differ slightly. I have mainly followed the text of the latter, but a few additional passages or an alternative phrase in translation, *as printed in the New York Times*, are given in brackets.
81 Wilde, *Impressions of America*, p. 24.
82 *New York Times*, 18.1.1916.
83 Massine, p. 80.
84 *New York American*, 18.1.1916.
85 *New York Globe*, 18.1.1916.
86 *New York Tribune*, 18.1.1916.
87 *New York Sun*, 18.1.1916.
88 *New York Journal of Commerce*, 19.1.1916.
89 *New York Tribune*, 18.1.1916.
90 American press.
91 *New York Tribune*, 19,1.1916.
92 *New York Morning Sun*, 20.1.1916.
93 *New York Post*, 24.1.1916.
94 *New York Times*, 25.1.1916; *New York Sun*, 25.1.1916; *New York Tribune*, 26.1.1916.
95 *New York Tribune*, 27.1.1916.
96 *New York Times*, 26.1.1916.
97 Ibid.
98 *New York Tribune*, 27.1.1916.
99 Ibid., 3.2.1916.
100 *Boston Evening Transcript*, 3.2.1916.
101 *Chicago Daily Tribune*, 16.2.1916.
102 Ibid.
103 *Chicago Sunday Tribune*, 20.2.1916.
104 *Chicago Post*, 24.2.1916.

105 *Milwaukee News*, 28.2.1916.
106 Ansermet, p. 20. The conductor wrote 'Minneapolis' for 'Milwaukee'. St Paul and Minneapolis are, of course, adjacent. It is possible that a taxi drive to the theatre which he describes was from St Paul to Minneapolis.
107 Ibid.
108 *Kansas City Star*, 4.3.1916.
109 Armitage, pp. 91, 92.
110 *Kansas City Star*, 5.3.1916.
111 *Kansas City Times*, 6.3.1916.
112 *Kansas City Star*, 5.3.1916.
113 *St Louis Globe*, 8.3.1916.
114 *Indianapolis News*, 10.3.1916.
115 *Cincinnati Times-Star*, 13.3.1916.
116 *Cleveland Plain Dealer*, 17.3.1916.
117 *Pittsburgh Gazette Times*, 21.3.1916.
118 *Pittsburgh Post*, 23.3.1916.
119 Sokolova, p. 75. Mme Sokolova does not name Tchernicheva in the book as the lady who attracted Massine, although she identified her to me. Massine himself told me he had forgotten the episode.
120 *New York Telegraph*, 24.3.1916.
121 Ibid.
122 Sokolova, pp. 75, 76.
123 *New York American*, 4.4.1916.
124 Romola Nijinsky, pp. 223–52.
125 Ibid., pp. 252–5. Nijinsky, *Diary*, pp. 39, 40.
126 Romola Nijinsky, p. 255.
127 Romola Nijinsky wrote that the ship was the *Rochambeau* (p. 255).
128 Romola Nijinsky, p. 258.
129 *New York Evening World*, 5.4.1916; *New York Times*, 6.4.1916.
130 *New York Tribune*, 8.4.1916; *New York Times*, 8.4.1916.
131 *New York Times*, 8.4.1916.
132 *New York Globe*, 8.4.1916.
133 *New York Times*, 8.4.1916.
134 *New York Tribune*, 8.4.1916.
135 Ibid., 10.4.1916.
136 *New York Telegraph*, 10.4.1916.
137 Romola Nijinsky, p. 260.
138 *New York Herald*, 13.4.1916.
139 *New York Times*, 13.4.1916.
140 *New York Evening Post*, quoted in *Musical America*, 22.4.1916.
141 *New York Tribune*, 13.4.1916.
142 *Dance Index*, Vol. I, Nos 9, 10, 11. The Dance Criticisms of Carl Van Vechten, p. 171.
143 *Musical America*, 22.4.1916; Grigoriev wrote (p. 120) that Nijinsky's dancing 'was by no means what it had been'.
144 Ibid.
145 Massine, pp. 86, 87.
146 *New York Tribune*, 23.4.1916.
147 Matinée, 25.4.1916, and evening perform-

ance, 26.4.1916. *New York Tribune* announcement, 23.4.1916.
148 *New York Tribune*, 23.4.1916.
149 Massine, p. 88.
150 Romola Nijinsky, conversations.
151 *New York Graphic*, 20.7.1929; Romola Nijinsky, p. 265; Grigoriev, p. 121.
152 Sokolova, p. 86. Massine merely wrote, 'with about sixteen dancers.' I make it eleven, including Grigoriev, but, according to Grigoriev (p. 125), Cecchetti later brought from Milan a girl called Ladetta; and other dancers were engaged in Italy.
153 Grigoriev, p. 121.
154 Ibid., p. 122.
155 *New York Times*, 29.4.1916.
156 *New York Times*, 30.4.1916. It was announced that Nijinsky, Revalles and Bolm were not sailing with the company. (But Bolm did.) Massine told me Otto Kahn admired Revalles.
157 Ansermet, p. 21. But Massine told me he thought it improbable that Diaghilev would have kissed the ground. 'He was not sentimental.'
158 Grigoriev, p. 122.
159 Sokolova, p. 81.
160 See Cooper, p. 20, note 20, for the reason why Cooper assumed 'Diaghilew must ... have come to Paris in May 1916.' We can further narrow down the dates between which his visit must have taken place. The *Dante Alighieri*'s voyage from New York to Cadiz took 'ten days' (Sokolova, p. 80). She therefore docked at Cadiz about 16 May. Diaghilev must have travelled with the company to Madrid to see the theatre, to wait upon the King and to see his dancers started on rehearsals. If he was quick, he might have left Madrid for Paris on the 19th or 20th. The Madrid ballet season opened on 26 May. Diaghilev would surely have been back for a dress rehearsal at least a day before. I surmise he was in Paris and met Picasso between the 21st and 24th. The 22nd and 23rd are the most likely dates.
161 Cocteau, *Du*. See Cooper, p. 16, note 6: 'Varèse sailed for New York on 18 December 1915.'
162 Cooper, p. 18, note 12. He cites a letter shown him by Valentine Gross, in which Satie on 15.10.1915 anticipates the dinner. Astruc was also a guest.
163 Misia Sert, p. 139. If she is telling the truth.
164 Cooper, pp. 18, 19, also note 14. He cites letters of Cocteau to Valentine Gross and of Satie to Cocteau, lent him by Mme Gross (Hugo) and M. Edouard Dermit.
165 The fact that Diaghilev told Kochno that his first meeting with Picasso took place in a 'sinister' room, overlooking a cemetery, provides further evidence of the meeting taking place in May, for Picasso left rue Schoelcher, as Cooper points out (p. 20, note 20), in summer 1916. There is some doubt as to whether Cocteau was present. Kochno told me that Mme Errazuriz introduced Diaghilev to Picasso.
166 Kochno, conversations.
167 *La Epoca*, 27.5.1916.
168 Sokolova, p. 82.
169 Grigoriev, p. 123.
170 On the 27th, 29th and 31st, for instance, all thirty lines.
171 *La Epoca*, 27.5.1916.
172 *La Epoca*, 30.5.1916, 1.6.1916.
173 Ansermet, p. 23.
174 Sokolova, conversations.
175 Stravinsky Archives. Robert Craft has no doubt from the evidence of various papers that Stravinsky arrived just in time for the performance, but did not conduct it.
176 Morand, p. 28.
177 *La Epoca*, 31.5.1916.
178 Vera Stravinsky, conversations.
179 Ibid.
180 Telegram quoted in *New York Telegraph*, 19.6.1916, and possibly in other papers.
181 Massine, pp. 89, 90.
182 Castillo, *Sert*. These decorations were done during the years 1916 and 1917, which leads me to guess that Sert and Misia were in Sitges in June and that this was the reason Diaghilev decided to spend his holiday there. Massine does not remember. But, after all, Sert designed the dresses for *Las Meninas*, which was given in San Sebastian in Aug.
183 *Ballet*, Vol. VIII, No. 3, Gontcharova's article in *Les Noces*, p. 20: 'We found ourselves ... at San Sebastian.'
184 As Balanchine firmly stated to me at dinner in Paris on 20.2.1975. He may have been echoing Diaghilev: but we know Diaghilev and Stravinsky adored Flamenco – as opposed to 'sophisticated' Spanish music.
185 Massine, p. 90.
186 Morand, p. 84.
187 Massine, p. 91.
188 Grigoriev, p. 123.
189 Ibid.
190 Massine, conversations.
191 Sokolova, pp. 83, 84.
192 Ansermet, pp. 22, 23.
193 Sokolova, pp. 84, 85.
194 Stravinsky, *Memories*, p. 109. But he gives the year wrongly as 1915. The visa stamp on Stravinsky's passport shows that he arrived in San Sebastian on 2 September (Stravinsky Archives). The following characters

invented by Massine reveal the influence of Chaplin: Niccolo the waiter (among others) in *The Good-humoured Ladies*; the Little American Girl in *Parade*; the male Can-can Dancer in *La Boutique fantasque*; the Barman in *Union Pacific*; the Peruvian in *Gaieté Parisienne*.

195 Guard arrived back from Russia to travel with the company. Spessivtseva and Frohman arrived in New York on 24.10.1916.

196 Grigoriev, p. 124. There are photographs of Diaghilev and Stravinsky at Bordeaux dated 8 September.

197 Sokolova, p. 86.

198 Romola Nijinsky, p. 266 et seq., 274.

199 *New York Times*, 27.9.1916; Romola Nijinsky, p. 274.

200 *Dance Index*, Vol. IV, No. 4, p. 52, R. E. Jones's article, 'Nijinsky and Till Eulenspiegel'.

201 *New York Tribune*, 6.10.1916, announcement of postponement in theatre column. Sokolova wrote (p. 90) that at the time the company thought Nijinsky's sprained ankle was only 'a delaying tactic', 'since the ballet was quite incomplete'.

202 *Musical America*, 19.10.1916.

203 Sokolova, pp. 89, 90.

204 *New York Tribune*, 24.10.1916.

205 Dansmuseet, Stockholm, Grigoriev's Notebook.

206 *Boston Evening Transcript*, 7.11.1916. For that matter, *Musical America* (2.11.1916) called *Till* 'a distinct masterpiece'.

207 Romola Nijinsky, conversations.

208 *New York Telegraph*, 25.10.1916.

209 The innumerable telegrams are in the Stravinsky–Diaghilev Foundation.

210 *Boston Evening Transcript*, 7.11.1916. 'A return that much excels the first visit.' *Chicago Journal*, 29.1.1917: 'With Nijinsky the company was complete.'

211 *Fort Worth Record*, 9.12.1916. 'The most appreciative and enthusiastic ... audience of the season. ...'

212 *Rocky Mountain News*, Denver, Colorado, 19.12.1916. The headlines were: 'Ballet Russe Is Gorgeous in Its Grace. ... Music Is Most Unusual and Faultless. ... Trappings Wonderful, Nijinski and Lopokova Entrance Audience With Dancing.'

213 San Francisco paper 3.1.1917. The lighting among other things. Ernest J. Hopkins called the Ballet the 'Greatest show on Earth'.

214 Romola Nijinsky, p. 287.

215 Stravinsky–Diaghilev, telegram to Grigoriev in Rome, 27.1.1917.

216 In Morand, *Journal*, p. 97 (4.11.1916), we read that 'Misia ... revient d'Italie et

d'Espagne,' where she had been with Diaghilev; in Misia Sert, pp. 106–10, that Sert and Misia motored about Italy, and in Massine, p. 70, that he and Diaghilev visited these cities with them (but he gives the wrong year). I therefore deduce that they all motored together from Spain.

217 Massine, pp. 91, 92.

218 Ibid., p. 92. Massine wrote, 'At one time I had a room in the Corso': but his intermittent attempts to suggest that he lived apart from Diaghilev do not deceive. On p. 106 he wrote, 'In Diaghilev's flat in the Corso Umberto.'

219 Ibid., pp. 92–4.

220 Cooper, p. 20. He quoted a joint letter Cocteau and Satie wrote to Valentine Gross (which she presumably showed him): 'Picasso is joining us in Parade.'

221 Ibid., p. 20. 'On 14 September Satie wrote again to Valentine Gross. . . . "*Parade* is changing, for the *better*, *behind* Cocteau's back. . . ." '

222 Morand, pp. 27, 28.

223 At Providence, Rhode Island, 30.10.1916; New Haven, Conn., 31.10.1916 and 1.11.1916; Brooklyn, NY, 2.11.1916; Springfield, Mass., 3, 4.11.1916; Boston, Mass., 6–11.11.1916; Worcester, Mass., 13.11.1916; Hartford, Conn., 14.11.1916; Bridgeport, Conn., 15.11.1916.

224 For Atlantic City, N.J., 16.11.1916; Baltimore, Md, 17–20.11.1916; Washington, DC, 21, 22.11.1916; Philadelphia, Pa, 23–5.11.1916; Richmond, Va, 27.11.1916; Columbia, SC, 28.11.1916; Atlanta, Ga, 29.11.1916; and New Orleans, La, 30.11.1916–2.12.1916.

225 Massine, pp. 95, 96.

226 Ibid., pp. 96–8.

227 Bakst had been given a visa by Morand at the Quai d'Orsay on 8.11.1916, but was still in Paris, dining with Princesse Eugène Murat – and hearing Stravinsky play *Petrushka* and Darius Milhaud play Satie's 'Cinq Morceaux en forme de poire' – on 17.11.1914. (Morand, p. 78).

228 A large sketch for this first version of the set is in the collection of Lady Daubeny, London.

229 Morand, p. 98.

230 Morand, pp. 126, 127. Cocteau and Morand were at dinner with Misia, and Morand wrote that he and Misia went on to the music-hall. I cannot prove that Cocteau went too, but, if he did not go that night, I am sure he went on another – and got his idea for the Manager with the Megaphone in *Parade*.

231 Houston, Texas, 5.12.1916; Austin, Texas,

6.12.1916; Dallas, Texas, 7.12.1916; Fort Worth, Texas, 8.12.1916; Tulsa, Okla., 11.12.1916; Kansas City, Missouri, 13, 14.12.1916; Des Moines, Iowa, 15.12.1916; Omaha, Neb., 16.12.1916; Denver, Colorado, 18, 19, 20.12.1916; Salt Lake City, Utah, 22, 23.12.1916; Los Angeles, Calif., 25–30.12.1916; San Francisco, Calif., 2–8.1.1917.

232 Romola Nijinsky, p. 286. Chaplin, pp. 205–7. His description, which includes a conversation with Diaghilev (then in Europe), is fantastic.

233 Ibid., p. 287.

234 Sokolova, p. 94.

235 Massine, p. 98.

236 Ibid., pp. 98–101.

237 Ibid., pp. 99, 100.

238 Letter of 11.1.1917 in Lifar collection, quoted Buckle, *In Search*, p. 94.

239 Letter of 12.1.1917 in Lifar collection, quoted Buckle, *In Search*, p. 93. The 3,000 francs advance, payable in two parts, was to go to Satie; then Cocteau was to receive the performance rights (100 francs a performance in countries not covered by the Société des Auteurs) until they had equalled the advance, after which composer and librettist were to share equally.

240 Stravinsky Archives, letter from D. to Stravinsky.

241 *Horizon*, Vol. XII, No. 68.

242 As E.W.White points out (p. 203, note 2), Stravinsky's arrangement with the Princess must have been made in Jan. 1916, just after the Ballet sailed for the USA for the first time, not, as he wrote in *Expositions* (p. 121), in Apr. 1915.

243 Stravinsky archives, letters from Ansermet to Stravinsky.

244 So quotes E. Walter White in his *Stravinsky* (p. 193), but attributing the quotation to Stravinsky's *Chronicle*. But in his *Chronicle* Stravinsky wrote (p. 134) that he had already written his *Chant du rossignol* as a symphonic poem destined for the concert platform, and thought a 'choreographic rendering' unnecessary. It was given at a concert at Geneva on 6 December 1919. I cannot trace the source of E.W.W.'s quotation elsewhere.

245 E. W. White, p. 215.

246 Lincoln Center, Dance Collection, 'Stravinsky and the Dance', a survey of ballet productions, 1910–62.

247 After San Francisco the Ballet danced at Oakland, Calif., 9, 10.1.1917; Portland, Oregon, 12, 13.1.1917; Vancouver, BC, 15.1.1917; Seattle, Washington, 16, 17.1.1917; Tacoma, Washington,

18.1.1917; Spokane, Washington, 20.1.1917; Minneapolis, Minnesota, 21.1.1917; St Paul, Minnesota, 23, 24, 25.1.1917; Milwaukee, Wisconsin, 27.1.1917; Chicago, Ill., 28.1.1917. It seems extraordinary that after two Sunday performances in Spokane the company should have crossed the great plain in time to perform in Minnesota on the following day, but they did.

248 Romola Nijinsky, pp. 289, 290. She calls Zverev 'H'.

249 Dolin, conversations. Zverev told Dolin this.

250 *Pittsburgh Post*, 22.2.1917. Zverev was reported as dancing *Le Spectre* with Lopukhova at the evening performance.

251 Sokolova, p. 92. Also Nemtchinova, conversations. Nijinsky had noticed Nemtchinova in New York and given her chocolates. He promoted her to dance the mazurka in *Les Sylphides*. She observed that, when he ran to take his famous jump in *Le Spectre*, he compressed his lips to keep in the breath In a group photograph of the company taken at Denver, she is sitting next to him.

252 Romola Nijinsky, conversations.

253 Romola Nijinsky, pp. 289, 290.

254 After Chicago the Ballet danced at Indianapolis, Indiana, 29.1.1917; St Louis, Missouri, 30.1.1917; Memphis, Tennessee, 31.1.1917; Birmingham, Alabama, 1.2.1917; Knoxville, Kentucky, 2.2.1917; Nashville, Tennessee, 3.2.1917; Louisville, Kentucky, 4.2.1917; Cincinnati, Ohio, 6, 7.2.1917; Dayton, Ohio, 8.2.1917; Detroit, Michigan, 9, 10.2.1917; Toledo, Ohio, 12.2.1917; Grand Rapids, Michigan, 13.2.1917; Chicago, Ill., 15.2.1917; Cleveland, Ohio, 16, 17.2.1917; Pittsburgh, Pa, 19, 20, 21.2.1917; Syracuse, NY, 23.2.1917; Albany, NY, 24.2.1917.

255 Programme of Harmanus Bleecker Hall, Albany, NY, 24.2.1917, reproduced Macdonald, pp. 212, 213.

256 Cooper, p. 21, note 28. He quotes a letter of Satie to Valentine Gross, written on 18.2.1917, saying, 'Jean et Picasso sont partis hier. ...'

257 Yale University Library, Stein Bequest, letter from Picasso to Gertrude Stein, quoted Cooper, p. 24.

258 Cocteau, *Picasso*, quoted Cooper, p. 24.

259 Notebook in the collection of M. Edouard Dermit. It is inscribed by Massine to Cocteau: 'A mon cher Jean Cocteau – premier jour à Rome, Massine.'

260 Cooper, p. 23, note 40. Ansermet's expression in a conversation with the author was 'du genre "populaire savante"'

261 Cocteau, *Nord-Sud*, quoted Cooper, pp. 20, 21.
262 From the vellum notebook, Collection Edouard Dermit; quoted Cooper, p. 23.
263 Cocteau, *Nord-Sud*, quoted Cooper, p. 21.
264 Ansermet, p. 26. Ansermet also placed Satie and Sert at the table, but Satie never went to Rome, and Sert was not, I think, there at this time.
265 Massine, p. 106.
266 Drawings reproduced Cooper, plates 65–70, 76.
267 Cocteau, *Picasso*, quoted Cooper, p. 24.
268 Stravinsky–Diaghilev. Telegrams from D. in Rome to Grigoriev c/o the Russian Embassy, Madrid, survive. Not all dates are decipherable, but Grigoriev was in Madrid at least till 24.3.1917, when he conducted the company to Italy.
269 Drawing reproduced Cooper, plate 75. Cooper dates the drawing 'April 17'. If we could be sure of this, it would prove Picasso made a second trip to Naples with the company, as Massine states (p. 108): but we know that Cocteau, whom Massine includes in this journey to Naples following the Roman season, did not. I would call it 'March' for safety. It seems certain the sight-seeing excursion to Naples was about the second week in Mar.
270 Morand, p. 206.
271 Stravinsky–Diaghilev, telegram from D. to Grigoriev in Madrid, 19.3.1916. 'Drobecki telegraphs décors will arrive only end of March so too late for Italian season. Try arrange Spain beginning April till 15 June with interval three weeks for Paris.'
272 Ibid. There are telegrams from D. in Paris to Grigoriev in Madrid on those dates, but other dates are indecipherable.
273 Ibid. Telegram date illegible. 'Serano's offer absurd.'
274 In fact, I cannot be sure of the date the company arrived in Rome, and I only assume from Sokolova's memoirs (p. 96) that Diaghilev was in Rome.
275 Yale University Library, Stein Bequest, Picasso letter to Gertrude Stein, quoted Cooper, p. 24.
276 Ansermet, pp. 25, 26.
277 Notebook in collection of E. Dermit.
278 Told the author by Jean Hugo.
279 Stravinsky–Diaghilev, telegram from D. to Soloviev, the Councillor at the Russian Embassy in Madrid, for Grigoriev, date indecipherable (Mar., obviously). In another telegram he specified ballets to be given in Italy, and wrote, 'If he does not come replace Faune by Sylphides.'
280 Sokolova, p. 96.

281 Vera Stravinsky, conversations.
282 Stravinsky, *Chronicle*, pp. 112, 113. The orchestration, dictated to Ansermet in Gerald Tyrwhitt's apartment, was dated 8.4.1917.
283 Morand, p. 228.
284 The dating of the Roman newspaper *Giornale d'Italia* and its indiscriminate use of 'today' and 'tomorrow' had baffled me. 'Tonight's gala' is announced and 'Yesterday's triumph' is described in two copies of the paper dated 10 April. The gala could have taken place on the 9th.
285 *La Tribuna*, 12.4.1917.
286 This second gala was announced for Thursday the 12th, and certainly took place on Thursday the 12th, but it is also reported at length in a newspaper dated Thursday the 12th! *Giornale d'Italia*, 12.4.1917.
287 Or Monday afternoon. *Giornale d'Italia*, Sunday, 15.4.1917, announces, 'Domani di giorno al Costanzi, si darà l'ultima dei balletti russi a prezzi popolari. . . .' A Sunday matinée at popular prices seems more likely.
288 Both *Feu d'artifice* and the Scarlatti ballet were first performed at the second gala on 12.4.1917.
289 As stated in note 269, Massine telescopes the two Naples visits together. Cocteau was not present during the second. Paul Morand met Cocteau at the Ritz in Paris on 22.4.1917 (*Journal*, p. 239), and Picasso wrote to him on 24.4.1917 from Rome. Picasso may or may not have returned to Naples.
290 Sokolova, p. 101.
291 *Il Giorno*, 19, 22.4.1917.
292 Massine, pp. 108, 109.
293 Morand, *Journal*, pp. 258, 259. Morand is more reliable as a chronicler of the audience than as a historian of the ballet. He seems to think Nijinsky had danced in *The Firebird*.
294 Lifar, pp. 301, 302. Letter quoted.
295 *Le Figaro*, 14.5.1917.
296 At least, that is my guess. See note 230.
297 Cocteau, *Cock and Harlequin*, p. 56. For drawings on Horseback, see Cooper, plates 90, 91, 92, 96.
298 Ibid. The varied nature of her pantomime recalls that of the first American dance ever recorded by a French poet, that of the Indian girl Chateaubriand watched near Niagara, who mimicked a prisoner tortured and burnt at the stake, died, swam a river, canoed down rapids, climbed a mountain and defended her baby from the enemy. I think Cocteau must have read this.
299 Massine, p. 105.
300 Cocteau, conversations, reported Buckle, *In Search*, p. 93.

301 Ibid.
302 Cooper, p. 27, Note 63.
303 Morand, p. 266.
304 Programme of Ballets Russes, May 1917, article by Apollinaire.
305 *Le Figaro*, 20.5.1917.
306 Morand, p. 266.
307 Ibid., p. 277.
308 Romola Nijinsky, p. 294.
309 Ibid., pp. 295, 296.
310 Ibid., p. 296.
311 *La Epoca*, 3.6.1917.
312 Romola Nijinsky, p. 298. Mme Nijinsky does not name the Duquesa in her book, but she told me who she was; and Sir Sacheverell Sitwell knew her well.
313 *La Epoca*, 4.6.1917.
314 Ibid., 7.6.1917.
315 Grigoriev, p. 132.
316 *La Epoca*, 7.6.1917, and subsequent issues.
317 Idzikovsky, conversations.
318 Massine, p. 113.
319 Ibid., p. 113.
320 Sokolova, p. 105.
321 Romola Nijinsky, pp. 299–301.
322 Ibid., pp. 298–301.
323 Sokolova, p. 106.
324 Romola Nijinsky, pp. 298–301.
325 *La Epoca*, 11.6.1917.
326 Romola Nijinsky, p. 300.
327 Ansermet, pp. 22, 23.
328 *La Epoca*, 14.6.1917.
329 Romola Nijinsky, p. 302.
330 Ibid., p. 302.
331 Grigoriev, pp. 133, 134.
332 Bibliothèque Nationale, Opéra, Kochno collection, telegram to Darosa and Mocchi, Teatro Colon, Buenos Aires: 'Chers amis. Nijinsky a fait énormes troubles. Police hier dut l'arrêter empêchant s'enfuir. Donc son arrivée Argentine improbable. . . .'
333 Romola Nijinsky, p. 303.
334 Dansmuseet, Stockholm, Grigoriev's Notebook. The performances at Barcelona were on 23, 24, 26, 28, 29, 30.6.1917.
335 Grigoriev, pp. 134, 135.
336 Stravinsky, *Memories*, p. 80.
337 Massine, pp. 115, 116.
338 Ibid., p. 115.
339 Ibid., pp. 114, 115.
340 Stravinsky Archives, letter from Stravinsky to Ansermet, 26.5.1919: 'In the train in which Diaghilev was going to Italy ... we reached an agreement ... we separated at Aigle....' Presumably Diaghilev returned to Spain *via* Italy.
341 Massine, p. 116.
342 Ibid., pp. 116–18. I have rearranged Massine's order of the cities visited to suggest a more likely itinerary.

343 Ibid., pp. 118, 119.
344 Romola Nijinsky, p. 307. Milhaud, pp. 67, 68.
345 Milhaud, p. 67.
346 Romola Nijinsky, p. 311.
347 Grigoriev, pp. 140, 141; Sokolova, p. 110.
348 Romola Nijinsky, conversations.
349 Grigoriev, p. 137.
350 Sokolova, p. 109.
351 Romola Nijinsky, p. 311.
352 Grigoriev, p. 140.
353 Romola Nijinsky, p. 313. She writes that Rubinstein accompanied Nijinsky, but, in fact, the great pianist *alternated* with the great dancer, and Domingo Dente accompanied the latter (André de Badet, quoted Reiss, pp. 172, 173).
354 British Library, Bloomsbury, Manuscript Room, Ricketts, *Journals*, entry for Monday, 8.10.1917.
355 Ricketts, p. 283, letter to Thomas Lowinsky, Oct. 1917.
356 Winterthur. The date is on the last page of the score.
357 Stravinsky, *Memories*, pp. 43, 44. Stravinsky relates how 'in the early 1920s, he [Diaghilev] suddenly decided to stage it. . . . The dancers were to go about wearing advertisements, American sidewalk walking-advertisements, "sandwich men" ...' But we may be fairly certain that Diaghilev, if he had gone ahead with the production, would have discarded any incongruous elements.
358 Cooper, p. 34, note 86.
359 Grigoriev, pp. 141, 142.
360 Sokolova, p. 113.
361 The Madrid season lasted from about 20.11.1917 till 26.11.1917 – at least, I have newspapers (*La Epoca*) of the 23rd and 27th describing the second and last nights of the season.
362 Grigoriev, p. 142.
363 Massine, pp. 120, 121.
364 Sokolova, pp. 114, 115.
365 Ibid., p. 116.
366 Massine, p. 121.
367 Grigoriev, p. 144.
368 Ibid.
369 Sokolova, pp. 116, 117.
370 Ibid., p. 117.
371 Dansmuseet, Stockholm, Grigoriev's Notebook.
372 Grigoriev, p. 145.
373 Ibid.
374 Sokolova, pp. 121, 122.
375 Massine, conversations.
376 Sokolova, p. 122.
377 Massine, conversations.
378 Massine, p. 122. Massine, who gets confused over dates, describes Diaghilev, Picasso and

himself listening together to Falla playing *Le Tricorne*, so this may have happened in Barcelona in the previous autumn, before Lisbon and the long tour.

379 Nekludov, p. 520.
380 Ibid., p. 521.
381 Bibliothèque Nationale, Opéra, Kochno collection, telegram from Torres to D. at Barcelona.
382 Ibid., telegram from Meyendorff in Madrid to D. in Barcelona, 30.6.1918.

383 Ibid., letter from Torres to D., 4.7.1918.
384 Stravinsky–Diaghilev, telegram from Stoll in London to D. in Madrid, 16.7.1918.
385 Ibid., telegram from Cook, Barcelona, to Cook, London, 16.7.1918.
386 Ibid., telegram from Grigoriev in Barcelona to D. in Madrid, 17.7.1918.
387 Sokolova, pp. 123–5.
388 Grigoriev, p. 148.
389 Massine, pp. 127, 128.
390 Sokolova, p. 125.

CHAPTER 13   AUG 1918–JAN 1921

1 Beaumont, p. 105, and other sources.
2 Sokolova, p. 131. Also Sokolova, conversations.
3 Ibid., pp. 127, 128.
4 Polunin, pp. 37, 38.
5 Ibid., p. 39.
6 Sokolova, p. 127.
7 Although I believe Tchernicheva had danced one of these roles once in London before the war, she would hardly have been remembered.
8 Polunin, pp. 39, 40.
9 Ibid., pp. 40, 41.
10 *The Times*, 6.9.1918.
11 Beaumont, p. 110.
12 Sokolova, p. 129.
13 Massine, p. 129.
14 *Dancing Times*, November 1918.
15 Massine, p. 129.
16 Ricketts, pp. 301, 302.
17 *Observer*, 11.9.1912.
18 Grigoriev, p. 150.
19 Beaumont, pp. 108, 109.
20 Polunin, pp. 42–7.
21 Beaumont, p. 126.
22 *The Times*, 4.11.1918.
23 *Lady*, 7.11.1918.
24 O. Sitwell, *Laughter*, pp. 9, 10.
25 Ibid., pp. 16, 1, 2.
26 Ibid., pp. 17–22.
27 Beaumont, p. 233.
28 Dr Wendy Baron's information about the Ethel Sands–Nan Hunter correspondence.
29 O. Sitwell, *Laughter*, p. 16. Massine refers to Lady Ottoline's 'flat in Suffolk Street' (p. 134).
30 Massine, p. 131.
31 Grigoriev, p. 137; Polunin, p. 47.
32 Polunin, pp. 47–9.
33 Beaumont, p. 125.
34 British Library, Bloomsbury, Manuscript Room, letter from D. to Ricketts, 6.1.1918.
35 Lincoln Center, letter from Ricketts to D., undated.
36 Beaumont, p. 114 et seq.

37 Ibid., pp. 117–19.
38 Bibliothèque Nationale, Opéra, Paris, Kochno collection, letter from Bakst to D., 24.3.1919, quoted Kochno, p. 129.
39 Massine, p. 132.
40 Perhaps Bakst, with his 'Naples, 1832', had misunderstood Diaghilev's and Massine's intentions. There would hardly have been an American family in Naples in 1832. But the surviving sketches of Bakst seem to veer between 1830 and 1860.
41 Massine, p. 133.
42 Ibid.
43 Massine, conversations.
44 Rambert, conversations.
45 Stravinsky Archives, correspondence between S. and Ansermet.
46 Massine, p. 134.
47 Massine, conversations.
48 Sokolova, pp. 134, 135.
49 Karsavina, p. 245.
50 Ibid., p. 245.
51 Beaumont, pp. 134–6. The 'well-known painters' included Picasso, who had arrived with Olga on 25 May.
52 Ibid., p. 136.
53 My own opinion was arrived at years before I read in Polunin's book, 'The chief difficulty in planning the scene arose from the fact that the back-cloth was not sufficiently visible through the enormous windows' (p. 57). Grigoriev, whose taste I belittle, had enough to think that the blue curtains 'ruined the design' (p. 155).
54 Polunin, p. 58.
55 Grigoriev, pp. 154, 145.
56 Drawings reproduced Cooper, plates 140, 141, 148–57.
57 Polunin, p. 53.
58 Ibid., p. 55.
59 Collection Mrs Whorwell (Polunin's daughter), reproduced Buckle, *In Search*, plate 169.
60 Buckle collection, Sokolova, unpublished papers.

61 Juliet Duff, conversations.
62 Sokolova, conversations. Also Sokolova, p. 157.
63 Sokolova, p. 140, but see also p. 139. Barocchi was so humiliated by his wife's elopement that he fled to Italy. There is a letter of his to Diaghilev about it in the Bibliothèque Nationale, Opéra, Kochno collection. He returned later and briefly resumed some kind of relations with Lydia.
64 Stravinsky Archives, letter from Ansermet to S., 18.7.1919: 'Diaghilev returned from Paris Saturday evening.'
65 Sokolova, p. 140.
66 Massine, p. 139.
67 Massine, pp. 141, 142.
68 Letter from the hospital authorities to Mme Sokolova, quoted by her in 'A pair of castanets', *Ballet*, Vol. 9, No. 6. In the letter Felix was referred to as 'Fernando', and Mme Sokolova copies them in her article.
69 Massine, conversations.
70 Lincoln Center, letter from Mrs Asquith to D., 23.7.1919.
71 *Sunday Times*, 27.7.1919. 'M. Serge de Diaghilev wears to the last moment [of the season] his mantle of triumph. His latest triumph. . . .'
72 *Observer*, 27.7.1919.
73 Bibliothèque Nationale, Opéra, Paris, Kochno collection, draft of undated telegram.
74 Collection Mrs Igor Vinogradoff, Lady Ottoline Morrell's Visitors' Book.
75 Kochno, conversations.
76 Massine, p. 144.
77 Ibid., p. 145, 146.
78 Ibid., p. 146. Massine wrote, 'fifteen hitherto unpublished instrumental pieces', but there were eighteen numbers, and, as E.W. White points out, although 'it is possible that the material handed over [to Stravinsky] contained a small proportion of unknown unpublished work, the music actually chosen by Stravinsky comes entirely from published sources of Pergolesi's music, particularly the Trio Sonatas, various other instrumental works, and three operas. . . .' (E. W. White, p. 245).
79 Stravinsky Archives, letter from Ansermet to Stravinsky, 10.6.1919.
80 Massine, p. 147.
81 On 14.11.1919.
82 Lady Kennet (K. Scott), p. 178. This was on 1.11.1919.
83 Lincoln Center, Dance Collection, letter (undated) from Mrs Asquith to D., Oct. 1919.
84 Polunin, p. 61.
85 Massine, p. 147.
86 Sokolova, pp. 146–8; Massine, p. 147.
87 Polunin, p. 62.
88 Grigoriev, p. 159.
89 Ibid.
90 Stravinsky, *Chronicle*, p. 139; *Memories*, p. 42.
91 Stravinsky, *Expositions*, pp. 111–14.
92 Cooper, pp. 46, 47. He reports a conversation with Picasso. He reproduces many projects for *Pulcinella* (plates 248–54, 257–70).
93 Stravinsky, *Conversations*, p. 108; but Kochno told me that Diaghilev said it was Picasso who had lost his temper and stamped on the designs. Picasso told me (probably untruthfully) that Diaghilev had liked the designs so much he did not know which to choose.
94 *La Vie Parisienne*, 2.2.1920.
95 Kochno, p. 138. He quoted Diaghilev.
96 Sokolova, p. 149.
97 Grigoriev, p. 162.
98 Ibid., p. 161. Massine, pp. 148, 149.
99 Photograph reproduced Kochno, p. 159.
100 Grigoriev, p. 163.
101 Ibid.
102 Hugo, p. 57 et seq.
103 Sokolova, p. 151.
104 Buckle collection, Sokolova, papers.
105 S. Sitwell, correspondence.
106 Ibid.
107 Ibid.
108 Hugo, p. 67. Hugo told me that Comte Anne d'Orgel was based by Radiguet on Etienne de Beaumont. The social-climbing Paul was Georges Auric – with the appearance of Paul Morand. La Princesse d'Austerlitz was Princesse Eugène (Violette) Murat, descended from Marshal Ney and married to a descendant of Marshal Murat. The pathetic Russian exile, Prince Naroumoff, was Diaghilev's old friend and enemy Sergei Volkonsky.
109 Serov, pp. 134, 135.
110 *Observer*, 20.6.1920.
111 Milhaud, p. 93.
112 Haskell, pp. 307, 308.
113 From which most of his telegrams quoted in subsequent chapters were sent.
114 Grigoriev, p. 165.
115 Sokolova, pp. 154–6.
116 Grigoriev, pp. 165, 166.
117 Morand, p. 277.
118 Chanel would design the costumes for Cocteau's *Antigone* in Dec. 1922.
119 Morand, *L'Allure de Chanel*, p. 63 et seq.
120 So Edmonde Charles-Roux writes in her *Chanel*, p. 196 but she does not give her source.
121 Massine, pp. 151, 152.
122 Kochno, p. 89. Kochno does not mention

the sum, but Chanel apparently did to
Morand (*L'Allure de Chanel*): 'I don't regret
the 300,000 francs it cost me.'
123 Grigoriev, p. 166.
124 Sokolova, pp. 157–8.
125 Ibid., pp. 159–61.
126 Ibid., p. 162.
127 Ibid., p. 163.
128 Ibid., pp. 163, 164.
129 Ibid., pp. 166, 167.
130 Ibid., pp. 167, 164.
131 Ibid., pp. 167, 168.
132 Massine, conversations.
133 Sokolova, pp. 168, 169.
134 Grigoriev, pp. 167, 168.

135 Sokolova, p. 170.
136 Stravinsky–Diaghilev, hotel bill.
137 Sokolova, pp. 170, 171. Also Sokolova, conversations.
138 Beaumont, pp. 167, 168.
139 This story I heard both from Mme Sokolova and Mme Vera Stravinsky. Beaumont, whose story differs, gives the date of the crisis as 30.1.1920.
140 Sokolova, p. 171.
141 Ibid. Compare Grigoriev, p. 169.
142 Haskell, p. 312.
143 Sokolova, conversations.
144 Grigoriev, pp. 171, 172.
145 Sokolova, p. 173.

PART VI

CHAPTER 14   FEB 1921–FEB 1922

1 Kochno, conversations. Szymanovsky's family estate was near Elizabetgrad. The other pianist (Kochno learned later) was Genrikh Gustafovitch Neuhaus, professor of the Moscow Conservatoire, whose first wife married *en seconde noce* the poet Boris Pasternak.
2 Dukelsky, pp. 74, 78.
3 Vera Stravinsky, conversations.
4 Kochno, conversations. Some of the story told in the preceding paragraphs is summarized in Kochno, pp. 152–5.
5 Bibliothèque Nationale, Opéra, Kochno collection, contract signed 15.3.1921, quoted Kochno, p. 159.
6 Ibid., letter, 24.3.1921, from Larionov to D. in Madrid, quoted Kochno, pp. 159, 160.
7 Diaghilev Exhibition Catalogue, 1954. Also Kochno, conversations. Kochno's description of the picture gallery in Seville sounds very much like the Museo Provincial as I remember it in 1952, but he thinks he saw the picture which was evidently *St Hugh and the Miracle of the Holy Vow* by Zurbaran in the deserted Carthusian monastery before it was moved to the gallery.
8 Kochno, conversations.
9 Kochno, p. 164.
10 Cochran, p. 367.
11 Ibid.
12 Ibid.
13 Grigoriev, p. 173.
14 Kochno, p. 165.
15 Vera Stravinsky, conversations.
16 Kochno, conversations.
17 Dolin, conversations.
18 Serov, p. 137.
19 Kochno, conversations.
20 Kochno, p. 166.

21 Kahnweiler, p. 30. Telegrams quoted in letter of 14.4.1921 to Kahnweiler.
22 Kochno, p. 166.
23 Bibliothèque Nationale, Opéra, Kochno collection, telegrams, 27.4.1921–10.5.1921, quoted Kochno, pp. 165, 166.
24 Kochno, conversations.
25 Ibid. According to Kochno, the large Matisse drawing, after being reproduced, was rolled up, left in an hotel drawer and lost.
26 Kahnweiler, p. 38, letter to Kahnweiler, 26.4.1921.
27 Serov, pp. 137, 138.
28 Kochno, conversations.
29 *Le Gaulois*, 20.5.1921.
30 Kochno, conversations. The *Spectacle Bouffe* had been advertised by a leaflet inserted in the Russian Ballet's programmes. I have one.
31 Hugo, p. 117.
32 Kochno, p. 200.
33 Sleeve of record album, *Cinq Musiciens Français des Ballets Russes*, La Guide Internationale du Disque, SMS 5227–5228.
34 Sokolova, p. 182.
35 *The Times*, 1.6.1921.
36 Beaumont, pp. 186, 187.
37 Kochno, pp. 166, 167. There is a letter in the Bibliothèque Nationale, Opéra, Kochno collection, from Merry del Val to Diaghilev asking for Dalbaicin and two guitarists to appear at the embassy, but this is dated 20.6.1921.
38 Sokolova, p. 176.
39 Goossens, p. 161. Goossens describes the three late arrivals as 'a trio of weary travellers'. Because Stravinsky had been expected from France, the interval had been pro-

longed; but, of course, Diaghilev and Massine had been in London for ten days. The programme also contained Berners's *Spanish Fantasy*, Ireland's *Forgotten Rite* and Ravel's *La Valse*. Lord Howard de Walden had put up £500 to make the concert possible.

40 Ibid., p. 161; *Observer*, 12.6.1921; *Sunday Times*, 12.6.1921.

41 Stravinsky–Diaghilev, telegram, 6.5.1921, from D. to de Blasio, Rome.

42 *Observer*, 5.6.1921.

43 Serov, pp. 138, 139.

44 Kochno, p. 160.

45 *Daily Mail*, 10.6.1921.

46 *Sunday Times*, 12.6.1921.

47 *Pall Mall and Globe*, 10.6.1921.

48 *The Times*, 10.6.1921.

49 Cochran, p. 372.

50 *Sunday Times*, 3.7.1921.

51 *Observer*, 3.7.1921.

52 Stravinsky–Diaghilev, hotel bill.

53 Ibid.

54 Lopukhova said that Diaghilev changed the title of the ballet because of her unclassical nose (Lopukhova, conversations).

55 Bibliothèque Nationale, Opéra, Kochno collection, telegram from Nuvel to D., London, 8.7.1921: 'Argoutinsk[y] reçoit lettre de Choura. . . .'

56 Kochno, conversations.

57 Goossens, p. 178.

58 Lincoln Center, receipt.

59 My deduction. The receipt of £1 advance, paid by Barocchi for a room booked for the end of Sept. 1921, implies that an abortion was contemplated, but proved unnecessary.

60 *Sunday Times*, 31.7.1921.

61 *Dancing Times*, Oct. 1921.

62 Stravinsky–Diaghilev, telegram, 20.7.1921, from Nuvel in Paris to D. at Monte Carlo.

63 Kochno, conversations.

64 Bibliothèque Nationale, Opéra, Kochno collection, letter from Nuvel to D., quoted Kochno, p. 171.

65 *Apollo*, April 1970, Vol. 91, No. 98, pp. 300–308 Deborah Howard, 'A Sumptuous Revival'. (This was a brief extract from her Cambridge thesis.) Bakst's wedding-dress design for Aurora is in the Fitzwilliam Museum, Cambridge.

66 *Ballet Review*, Vol. 3, No. 2, article by David Vaughan.

67 Diaghilev Memoirs. Diaghilev presumably meant 'the orchestral score as used by the Mariinsky Theatre'.

68 Bibliothèque Nationale, Opéra, Kochno collection, letter, quoted Kochno, p. 171.

69 Polunin, p. 67.

70 Kochno, conversations.

71 Kochno, p. 171.

72 Kochno, conversations.

73 Beaumont, pp. 193, 194.

74 Kochno, conversations.

75 Beaumont, pp. 195, 196.

76 Ibid., p. 197.

77 Dubrovska, conversations.

78 Kochno, conversations.

79 Beaumont, p. 199, footnote. 'A former member of Diaghilev's company' told Beaumont this.

80 Vera Stravinsky, conversations. She remembered the arrival of one critic: late for lunch with Diaghilev at the Savoy, he asked for 'just a little cold chicken and some champagne'.

81 Sokolova, p. 190.

82 Beaumont, pp. 200, 201.

83 Ibid., pp. 201, 202.

84 S. Sitwell, correspondence.

85 *Daily Mail*, 3.11.1921.

86 *Daily Express*, 3.11.1921.

87 *The Times*, 3.11.1921.

88 *Observer*, 6.11.1921.

89 *Sunday Times*, 6.11.1921.

90 Beaumont, conversations.

91 I have mislaid my source.

92 Diaghilev, Memoirs, quoted (in a different translation) Kochno, p. 172.

93 Kochno, conversations.

94 Lincoln Center, bill, 3.12.1921.

95 Kochno, conversations.

96 Dubrovska, conversations.

97 Bibliothèque Nationale, Opéra, Kochno collection, letter from Bakst to D., 12.12.1921, quoted Kochno, p. 174.

98 Vera Stravinsky, conversations.

99 Bibliothèque Nationale, Opéra, Kochno collection, telegram, 19.11.1921, from Sudeikine to D.

100 Vera Stravinsky, conversations.

101 Alhambra programmes.

102 Dolin, *Spessivtseva*, p. 29.

103 Dubrovska, conversations.

104 Kochno, p. 172.

105 Haskell, *Balletomania*, pp. 60, 61.

106 Dubrovska, conversations.

107 Dolin, *Spessivtseva*, p. 27.

108 Kochno, conversations. Lifar told the author that Gulbenkian paid for the whole production, that the theatre was sold out nightly and that Gulbenkian terminated the season out of spite because Spessivtseva would not sleep with him. Lifar was not in London in 1921, so his story was not accepted as evidence. Nevertheless, Gulbenkian did something to justify Diaghilev referring to him as 'our old enemy'. See Chapter 16, p. 473.

109 Nemtchinova, conversation.

110 Dubrovska, conversations.
111 Beaumont, p. 209 et seq.
112 Ibid., p. 213.
113 There survive telegrams they exchanged in later years (Stravinsky–Diaghilev).
114 Grigoriev, pp. 131, 132.
115 Rambert, conversations. See Chapter 16, note 112.
116 Haskell, *Diaghilev*, p. 322.
117 Kochno, p. 173. Kochno was not present.

Beaumont, who was, described (p. 214) 'some comical noises' introduced by 'a member of the orchestra', and wrote, 'I saw Diaghilev flush with indignation.' But Diaghilev was not present.
118 Spessivtseva later telegraphed that she would rejoin Diaghilev if he paid her what he owed her. See Chapter 15, p. 402, note 18.
119 Kochno, conversations.

CHAPTER 15   1922–4

1 Their first Paris season opened 24.10.1920.
2 Sokolova, pp. 197, 198.
3 Ibid., p. 198. Lopukhova, too, joined the group. The show, *You'd be surprised*, was 'a disaster' (Sokolova, p. 198).
4 *La Vie Parisienne*, 18.2.1922.
5 Grigoriev, pp. 183, 184.
6 Ibid., p. 184.
7 Stravinsky, *Expositions*, p. 118.
8 *Ballet*, Vol. 8, No. 3, 'The Creation of *Les Noces* by Gontcharova': 'I produced several sets of designs.... I was very pleased by the last but one of these ... in pastel colours ... embroidered with silver, pale gold, white and grey pearls and red silk.'
9 Bibliothèque Nationale, Opéra, Kochno collection, telegram from Nijinska in Vienna to D. in Paris, 5.4.1922: 'Will leave at once on receiving money straight to Monte Carlo.'
10 Loguine, article by Nijinska, p. 117 et seq. Gontcharova's account differs. See note 8.
11 Bibliothèque Nationale, Opéra, Kochno collection, telegram from Stravinsky to D., 24.4.1922.
12 E.W. White, p. 216.
13 Haskell, *Diaghilev*, p. 322. Nuvel's information. Stravinsky, *Chronicle*, p. 168.
14 Kochno, conversations. See also Kochno, p. 176.
15 Ibid. Other writers, such as Macdonald (p. 271), have wrongly stated that the cause of the quarrel was that Bakst was *not* paid for *The Sleeping Princess*.
16 Loguine, article by Survage, p. 133 et seq.
17 Bibliothèque Nationale, Opéra, Kochno collection, draft of letter to Poincaré.
18 Ibid., telegram from Spessivtseva in Berlin to Bakst in Paris, 4.4.1922.
19 Grigoriev, p. 184.
20 Bibliothèque Nationale, Opéra, Kochno collection, letter from Rouché to D., 26.4.1922, quoted Kochno, p. 180. According to Erté (Roman de Tirtoff), who was introduced at this time to Diaghilev by Princess Tenishev (then living in Monte Carlo), Diaghilev commissioned *him* to redesign the short ver-

sion of *The Sleeping Princess*; but, when he had made only two sketches, he was offered a lucrative job designing an American revue and had to turn D. down. The latter 'was very understanding; in fact, he said he would have done exactly the same in my position.' (Erté, *Things I Remember*, p. 48.)
21 Grigoriev, p. 185. He gives no date for Diaghilev's letter, which was obviously written during the second week in May.
22 Kochno, conversations.
23 French press.
24 Stravinsky, *Memories*, p. 40. .
25 *Le Gaulois*, 20.5.1922. *Le Gaulois*, 21.5.1922: 'Stravinsky's music makes one wonder where the line can be drawn between music and mere noise.'
26 *Commedia*, 20.5.1922.
27 Kochno, conversations. Kochno thought Diaghilev always referred to the '42 *fouettés*' instead of 'the 32' out of contempt.
28 Painter, pp. 340, 341. But Painter's source for the story about Stravinsky is not given.
29 Sokolova, pp. 178, 225, 264.
30 Loguine, article by Survage, p. 134.
31 *Le Gaulois*, 26.5.1922.
32 Kochno, pp. 184, 185.
33 Kochno, conversations.
34 Grigoriev, p. 186.
35 Dubrovska, conversations. It may have been during this season that the following incident, described by Karsavina, took place. 'When on one occasion my name appeared [on the playbill] beneath that of a minor member of the company, I drew Diaghilev's attention to it.... Without a word to me, he called my dresser and sent her to fetch the man responsible for billing, incidentally the minor lady's husband. When the poor little culprit appeared, Diaghilev rose up. Showing him the bill, he said in a strangled voice, "If that ever happens again ...", seized the man by the collar, shook him savagely and with all his might hurled the poor wretch against the wall. The man staggered out. I sat petrified. Diaghilev, with an "Excuse me, Tata," left the room.' I take

this to refer to Grigoriev and Tchernicheva, although Grigoriev was not 'little'. It may have been Barocchi and Lopukhova.

36 Ibid.
37 Kochno, conversations.
38 Grigoriev, pp. 187, 188.
39 Ibid., pp. 188, 189.
40 Kochno, conversations.
41 Ibid. Whether Stravinsky sent Diaghilev to the Trianon Lyrique or vice-versa is uncertain. Kochno thought he had gone there with Diaghilev in the summer of 1922. Stravinsky wrote (*Chronicle*, pp. 181–2): 'In the winter of 1922–1923 I often went to the small Trianon–Lyrique Theatre ... Louis Masson, its director, was an excellent conductor.... I took great pleasure in ... Cimarosa's *Le Secret Mariage* and Gounod's *Philémon et Baucis* ... Diaghilev was as much in love with it as I was....'
42 Kochno, p. 195. When Kochno sold his papers to the French State, he retained Diaghilev's letters to himself.
43 Ibid., pp. 195, 197.
44 Kochno, p. 284. A page from Diaghilev's notebook is reproduced alongside the text.
45 Ibid., p. 262. Kochno, conversations. Kochno denies that Diaghilev attended Proust's funeral, as Painter states (Vol. 2, p. 363).
46 Stravinsky–Diaghilev, telegram from Mayakovsky in Berlin to D. in Paris, 17.11.1922: 'Visa reçu. Paris vendredi. 2 heures 30.'
47 Stravinsky–Diaghilev, telegram, 1.1.1923.
48 Stravinsky–Diaghilev, a series of telegrams between Trubecki and Hoyer in Warsaw and D. in Paris, 9–29.12.1922.
49 Kochno, conversations.
50 Lifar, p. 347 et seq.
51 Kochno, conversations.
52 Lifar, p. 352.
53 Lifar, *Ma Vie* (English edition, in spite of the title), p. 122. 'I was sought after by people of both sexes.... I have always been a poor lover.... A stranger to the pleasures of the bed....'
54 Lifar, p. 355 et seq.
55 Lifar, pp. 359, 360.
56 Loguine, article by Nijinska, p. 119. Nijinska wrote, 'We were sitting in my little drawing-room.' Kochno told me he remembered the conversation at the Hôtel de Paris.
57 Kochno, p. 189.
58 See Loguine, article by Nijinska, p. 121. But Kochno attributed the final idea for the costumes to Diaghilev (p. 189) and Gontcharova claimed it was hers (*Ballet*, Vol. 8, No. 3, pp. 25, 26.)
59 Kochno, p. 189, and Kochno, conversations.

60 Stravinsky, *Expositions*, p. 115.
61 Loguine, article by Nijinska, p. 121.
62 Lifar, p. 362.
63 Vera Stravinsky, conversations. In Morand's *L'Allure de Chanel*, the great dressmaker was bitchy, by implication, about Princess 'Winnie' too.
64 *Le Gaulois*, 14.6.1923.
65 Ibid., 17.6.1923.
66 Lifar, pp. 363, 364.
67 Ibid., p. 364.
68 Kochno, conversations.
69 Milhaud, p. 132.
70 Ibid., p. 133.
71 Kochno, conversations.
72 Grigoriev, pp. 194, 195; Sokolova, p. 209.
73 Lifar, pp. 364, 365.
74 Bibliothèque Nationale, Opéra, Kochno collection, letter from Benois to D., quoted Kochno, p. 198.
75 Poulenc, *Entretiens*, p. 53.
76 Bibliothèque Nationale, Opéra, Kochno collection, letter from Poulenc to D., 24.9.1922.
77 De Valois, *Invitation*, pp. 35, 36.
78 Dolin, *Divertissement*, p. 49.
79 Ibid., p. 50.
80 Kochno, p. 222.
81 Vera Stravinsky, conversations.
82 Kochno, conversations.
83 Kahnweiler, pp. 50, 51.
84 Dolin, conversations.
85 Kochno, conversations.
86 Ibid.
87 Ibid.
88 Kochno, p. 192.
89 Kochno, p. 206. Kochno gives no date for the letter, but as Diaghilev concludes, 'Tomorrow is a holiday.... Monte Carlo is hung with splendid flags,' we can place it as the eve of Ste Dévote, the local saint celebrated on 18 Nov.
90 Kochno, pp. 206, 207.
91 De Valois, conversations.
92 Vera Stravinsky, conversations. See also a letter from Laurencin to Diaghilev in the Bibliothèque Nationale, Opéra, Kochno collection: 'Le décor vert me dégoûte.... Je préfère revenir au blanc peint avec une fenêtre....'
93 Dolin, conversations.
94 Ibid.
95 Ibid. The Gris design for Dolin is in the Theatre Museum, London.
96 Kochno, conversations.
97 Stravinsky–Diaghilev, telegram from Cocteau to D., 12.12.1923.
98 Kochno, conversations.
99 Kahnweiler, p. 52.
100 Vera Stravinsky, conversations.

101 Nemtchinova, conversations.
102 Kochno, conversations.
103 *Commedia*, 11.1.1924.
104 Nemtchinova, conversations.
105 Sokolova, p. 216.
106 Dolin, conversations.
107 Stravinsky–Diaghilev, telegram from Nuvel to D., 3.1.1924.
108 Myers, conversation.
109 Stravinsky–Diaghilev, telegram, 3.1.1924.
110 Bibliothèque Nationale, Opéra, Kochno collection, letter from Cocteau to D., 28.12.1923.
111 Poulenc, p. 60.
112 Ibid., p. 61.
113 Dolin, conversations.
114 Lifar, *Ma Vie*, pp. 33, 34.
115 Kochno, p. 213.
116 Kahnweiler, p. 52.
117 Sokolova, p. 217.
118 Polunin, pp. 69, 70.
119 Kochno, p. 210. Lifar wrote (p. 370) that Diaghilev dismissed Maikherska on this account.
120 Kochno, p. 211.
121 Sokolova, p. 219 (but Mrs Fellowes's name was not given). À propos cocaine, Lifar boasted (p. 432) that he cured Diaghilev of this habit. I asked Kochno about this. Dr Dalimier had prescribed some drops for Diaghilev when he had a cold and a blocked nose. When Kochno asked about them, Diaghilev said, 'It's quite a nice feeling. There's cocaine in them.' There was no question of curing a bad habit, as none was ever formed. (Kochno, conversations.)
122 Grigoriev, pp. 200, 201.
123 Kochno, conversations.
124 Stravinsky–Diaghilev, telegram from Dolin in London to D. in Paris, 4.2.1924.
125 Vera Stravinsky, conversations.
126 Kochno, conversations.
127 Kochno, p. 257.
128 Ibid., p. 215.
129 Kochno, conversations.
130 Milhaud, p. 135; but I have retranslated a few words.
131 Bibliothèque Nationale, Opéra, Kochno collection, letter from Braque to D., quoted Kochno, p. 257.
132 Ibid., quoted Kochno, p. 257.
133 Ibid., quoted Kochno, p. 216.
134 Sokolova, pp. 218, 219.
135 Kochno, p. 216.
136 Dolin, pp. 67, 68.
137 Ibid., p. 74.
138 Kochno, pp. 216, 217, 215.
139 Stravinsky–Diaghilev, telegram from Wollheim in London to D. in Barcelona, Apr. 1924 (exact date indecipherable).
140 De Valois, *Invitation*, pp. 46, 47.
141 Kochno, p. 216.
142 Sokolova, p. 218.
143 Grigoriev wrote (p. 196) that this was the only season when Diaghilev called his company 'Les Ballets Russes de Monte Carlo'. Kochno, reading my typescript, commented that Diaghilev hated doing this, but that he himself had suggested it out of gratitude to the Principality. But I found that the Paris programme bore the usual inscription, 'Ballets Russes de Serge de Diaghilew'.
144 *Le Gaulois*, 25.5.1924.
145 *Commedia*, 25.5.1924.
146 Ibid.
147 Kochno, p. 219. Kochno implies and Grigoriev states that the Picasso curtain was intended solely for *Le Train bleu*, but Dolin told me – and the newspapers confirm – that it was a front curtain for the Olympic season. Later, in London, Diaghilev gave it to *Le Train bleu*.
148 It is now in the Theatre Museum, London.
149 Sélysette in a Press cutting I have mislaid (6?.6.1924).
150 *Commedia*, 6.6.1924.
151 *Le Gaulois*, 6.6.1924.
152 *Le Figaro*, 13.6.1924. Stravinsky, *Chronicle*, p. 183. 'It was nauseating,' wrote Stravinsky, and turned his vilification of the largely foreign audience into an attack on Wagner, whom he scorned them for pretending to admire.
153 Serov, pp. 148, 149.
154 Tyler, p. 229.
155 Dukelsky, pp. 116, 117.
156 Kochno, p. 228.
157 Nabokov, pp. 146, 147.
158 Sokolova, p. 222.
159 De Valois, *Invitation*, pp. 48, 49.
160 Kochno, p. 219.
161 Dolin, *Divertissement*, p. 83.
162 Sokolova, p. 222.
163 The passages in quotes are from the libretto prefacing the piano score of *Le Train bleu*. Publishers (Heugel), 1924.
164 Lifar, pp. 376, 377.
165 Ibid., p. 380.
166 Sokolova, p. 213.
167 Lifar, pp. 380–83.
168 Ibid., pp. 383–7.
169 Ibid., p. 391.
170 Ibid., p. 389.
171 Ibid., p. 392. Authors mentioned in following letter.
172 Dolin, conversations.
173 Lifar, p. 392.
174 Kochno, conversations.
175 Letter quoted Kochno, p. 223.
176 Kochno, p. 222.

177 Ibid., pp. 223, 224.
178 Ibid., p. 224.
179 Ibid., pp. 224, 226. It is hard to tell whether 'Aeolus ... heading for the police station' is a reference to Lifar or even Dolin in private life. Lifar was to play 'Aeolus', i.e. Boreas, but it was Dolin whom Diaghilev saw before him under turquoise Adriatic skies.
180 Dolin, *Divertissement*, p. 85. In this first of his autobiographies (pub. 1931) Dolin naively concealed the fact that he was staying with Diaghilev on the Lido.
181 Dolin, conversations.
182 Lifar, p. 392.
183 Ibid., pp. 393–6.
184 Stravinsky–Diaghilev, telegram, 2.8.1924.
185 Stravinsky–Diaghilev, hotel bill.
186 Dolin, conversations.
187 Lifar, pp. 397, 399.
188 Stravinsky–Diaghilev, telegram from Nuvel in Paris to D. at Monte Carlo, 7.8.1924.
189 Ibid., telegram from Kochno in Paris to D. at Monte Carlo, 7.8.1924.
190 Ibid., draft of telegram written on previous one from Kochno.
191 Ibid., telegram from D. to Nuvel, 9.8.1924.
192 Ibid., telegram from D. to Kochno, 9.8.1924.
193 Ibid. On the 14th and 18th, at least.
194 Lifar, pp. 398, 399. Telegram and letter quoted.
195 Stravinsky–Diaghilev, telegram from D. to Nuvel, received 20.8.1924.
196 Lifar, p. 399.
197 Ibid., pp. 399, 400.
198 Stravinsky–Diaghilev, telegram, 23.8.1924.
199 Lifar, pp. 400, 401.
200 Stravinsky–Diaghilev, telegram, 26.8.1924. On the 29th Nuvel cabled D., 'Munich money arrrived.'
201 Dolin, conversations.
202 Lifar, p. 102.
203 Dolin, *Divertissement*, pp. 88, 89.
204 Lifar, p. 402.
205 Ibid., p. 403.
206 Grigoriev, p. 199.
207 De Valois, *Invitation*, p. 53.

208 Lifar wrote (p. 403) that Diaghilev did not join the company till the 21st. I assume that he went to London to negotiate with Stoll.
209 Letter from Stoll to D., 23.9.1924, reproduced Macdonald, p. 293.
210 Dolin, pp. 89, 90.
211 Dolin, conversations.
212 Lifar, p. 404.
213 Dolin, *Divertissement*, p. 94.
214 Balanchine, Danilova and Geva, conversations.
215 *Dancing Times*, November 1924.
216 Balanchine, Danilova and Geva, conversations.
217 Mayakovsky letters quoted in English language Soviet cultural publication.
218 Kochno, conversations.
219 *Observer*, 23.11.1924.
220 Stravinsky–Diaghilev, telegram from Balantchivadze in Paris to D. in London, 23.11.1924.
221 Balanchine, conversations.
222 Danilova, conversations.
223 *Daily Mirror*, 25.11.1924.
224 *Morning Post*, 25.11.1924.
225 *Daily Herald*, 25.11.1924.
226 *Daily Mail*, 25.11.1924.
227 *Daily Express*, 25.11.1924.
228 *The Times*, 25.11.1924.
229 *Daily Telegraph*, 25.11.1924.
230 Told by Henry Moore to Lord Goodman on the afternoon of 17.7.1968, and repeated by the latter to the present author the same evening, when he gave him instructions to buy the Picasso curtain in the Sotheby sale that night. It was the sculptor's birthday.
231 Balanchine, conversations.
232 Dolin, *Markova*, pp. 81–83.
233 Balanchine, conversations.
234 Kochno, conversations.
235 Ibid. Lifar's account (p. 405) differs.
236 Massine, p. 162. Lifar claims that he persuaded Diaghilev to re-engage Massine.
237 Massine, conversations.
238 Massine, pp. 162, 163.
239 Dolin's notes for a lecture at the Diaghilev Exhibition, 1954, 1955.

CHAPTER 16   1925–6

1 *Observer*, 11.1.1925.
2 *People*, 11.1.1925.
3 Ticker-tape in Dolin's album.
4 Dolin, p. 102.
5 Stravinsky–Diaghilev, telegram from D. in Paris to Grigoriev in Monte Carlo, 13.1.1925.
6 Markova, conversations.
7 Grigoriev, pp. 208, 209.
8 Lifar, p. 407.

9 Sokolova, p. 228.
10 Dolin, p. 104.
11 Geva, conversation.
12 Danilova, conversations.
13 Sokolova, p. 233.
14 Stravinsky–Diaghilev, telegrams from D. to Nuvel, 3.2.1925, and to Auric the same day.
15 Ibid., telegram from Auric to D., 5.2.1925: 'Shall arrive Tuesday with score.'

16 Ibid., telegram from D. to Wollheim, 6.3.1925.
17 Ibid., seven telegrams between Diaghilev and Nuvel, from 10.2.1925 to 13.4.1925.
18 Ibid., telegram from Nuvel to D., 5.2.1925.
19 Ibid., telegram from Nuvel to D., 6.2.1925.
20 Ibid., telegram from Nuvel to D., 7.2.1925.
21 Ibid., telegram from Nuvel to D., 3.3.1925.
22 Ibid., telegram from D. to Pruna, 3.3.1925.
23 Ibid., telegram from D. to Nuvel, 25.3.1925.
24 Ibid., telegram from Wollheim to D., 25.3.1925.
25 Ibid., telegram from Kochno to D., 8.4.1925.
26 Kochno, conversations.
27 Dubrovska, conversations.
28 Danilova, conversations.
29 Dukelsky, p. 145.
30 Ibid., pp. 137, 138. Confirmed by Dame Alicia Markova, who danced her Rubinstein waltz, improved by Balanchine. See also Grigoriev, pp. 209, 210.
31 Ibid., pp. 138–40.
32 Grigoriev, p. 210.
33 Markova, conversations.
34 Balanchine, Danilova and Geva, conversations.
35 Markova, conversations.
36 Danilova, conversations.
37 Balanchine, conversations.
38 Sokolova, pp. 231, 232.
39 Stravinsky–Diaghilev, telegram from Nuvel to D., 9.4.1925.
40 Ibid., telegram from Kochno to D., 8.4.1925: 'We leave Thursday.'
41 Ibid., telegram from Nuvel to D., 27.4.1925.
42 A photograph including Evans is reproduced in Dolin, Divertissement, facing p. 104.
43 Stravinsky–Diaghilev, draft of telegram from D. to Cocteau, 25.4.1925, signed 'Serge and Boris'.
44 Kochno, conversations. The six little jokes, mounted together, hang on Kochno's wall.
45 Lifar, p. 409.
46 Dukelsky, p. 144.
47 See photographs, Dolin, Divertissement, facing p. 108, and Sokolova, facing p. 246.
48 Lifar, p. 410. Dolin, pp. 114, 115.
49 Stravinsky–Diaghilev, telegram from Poulenc to D., 7.5.1925.
50 Ibid., telegram from Koribut-Kubitovitch at Monte Carlo to D. in Barcelona, 11.5.1925.
51 Ibid., telegram from Wollheim to D., 12.2.1925.
52 Ibid., telegram from D. to Wollheim, 6.5.1925.
53 Ibid., telegram from D. to Nuvel, 12.5.1925.
54 Lincoln Center, restaurant bills, 1, 4, 9.1.25, kept by Diaghilev.
55 Ibid., letter from Manager, Café Parisien, to D. at Monte Carlo, 15.1.1925.
56 Ibid., letter from H. W. Graedel, General Manager, Savoy, to Wollheim, 7.5.1925.
57 Stravinsky–Diaghilev, telegram from D'Oyly Carte in London to Goossens in Barcelona, 12.5.1925.
58 Dolin, pp. 116–18.
59 Stravinsky–Diaghilev, telegram from Wollheim to D. in Paris, 22.5.1925.
60 Sunday Express, 5.7.1925.
61 Unidentified Press cutting in Dolin's album. The paragraph is headed 'Ballet of Degenerates'.
62 Unidentified Press cutting in Dolin's album.
63 Stravinsky–Diaghilev, telegram from Wollheim to D. in Paris, 11.6.1925.
64 Ibid., telegram from D. in Paris to Grigoriev in London, 11.6.1925.
65 Serov, pp. 154–6.
66 Dolin, p. 121.
67 Dolin, pp. 122–4.
68 Markova, conversations.
69 Dolin, p. 125.
70 Lifar, p. 413. Sokolova, pp. 234, 235.
71 Lifar, p. 214.
72 Hamnett, pp. 274, 275.
73 Stravinsky–Diaghilev, telegram from Kochno in Paris to Massine in London, 18.6.1925.
74 Massine, conversations.
75 Dolin, p. 125.
76 Dolin, conversations.
77 Dolin, p. 126.
78 Lifar, p. 411.
79 Dolin, conversations.
80 Dukelsky, pp. 155–7. One does not have to take Dukelsky's 'colourful' descriptions too literally.
81 Observer, 28.6.1925.
82 Queen, 8.7.1925.
83 Lifar, pp. 414, 415.
84 Lincoln Center, bill, 12, 13.7.1925. A 'jacket suit'; also accounts for Lifar and Kochno. 'Please pay cash on delivery.'
85 Stravinsky–Diaghilev, hotel bill, 12, 13, Jul. Appartements 59/62.
86 Dukelsky, p. 160.
87 Stravinsky–Diaghilev, letter of 23.6.1925, enclosing an old bill.
88 Told the author by Mrs Arne Ekstrom.
89 Stravinsky–Diaghilev, bill, Hôtel Vouillement, 24–30.7.1925.
90 Kochno, conversations.
91 Dubrovska, conversations.
92 Lifar, p. 416 et seq. Also Lifar, Ma Vie, pp. 49, 50 (where the Countess's name is given).

93 Lifar, p. 421.
94 Danilova, conversations.
95 Stravinsky–Diaghilev. Nuvel telegraphed there, 17.8.1925.
96 Kochno, p. 230.
97 Rieti, correspondence. The session took place at the Liceo Musicale Benedetto Marcello.
98 Sokolova, p. 236 et seq.
99 Kochno, conversations.
100 Lifar, p. 428.
101 Sokolova, p. 238.
102 Kochno, conversations.
103 Lifar, pp. 428, 429. Lifar does not mention the presence of Kochno in Venice, Florence, Rome or Naples.
104 Rieti, correspondence.
105 Lifar, p. 429.
106 Ibid.
107 Kochno, p. 233.
108 *Daily News*, 27.10.1925.
109 *The Times*, 13.11.1925.
110 Dukelsky, pp. 172–3. Dukelsky does not mention the invitation to *Ruslan* at the RCM (an interpolation by me into his account), but Lambert's letter to Diaghilev is at Lincoln Center.
111 Ibid., p. 175.
112 Ibid.
113 Stravinsky–Diaghilev, letter from Le Brasseur and Oakley to E. Wollheim, 21.11.1925.
114 Sokolova, p. 240.
115 Ibid., p. 240.
116 Grigoriev, p. 219.
117 Kochno, conversations.
118 Lincoln Center, letter, 1.3.1926. Beaverbrook refuses an invitation (or an interview), as he is leaving for Canada.
119 Kochno, conversations.
120 Stravinsky–Diaghilev, telegram from Nuvel in Paris to D. at Monte Carlo, 6.2.1926.
121 Ibid., telegram, 17.2.1926.
122 Ibid., telegram from Wollheim in London to D. at Monte Carlo, 18.2.1926.
123 Nemtchinova, conversations. In 1977 she told me, 'Massine made me lie to Diaghilev. I was so sad.'
124 Lifar, p. 431.
125 Bibliothèque Nationale, Opéra, Kochno collection, draft of letter from D. to Cochran, 30.3.1926.
126 Lincoln Center, letter from Outhwaite to D., 23.3.1926.
127 Nikitina, pp. 61, 62.
128 Lincoln Center, letter from Outhwaite to D., undated.
129 Sokolova, p. 245 et seq.
130 Nikitina, p. 62.
131 Lifar, p. 432.
132 Bibliothèque Nationale, Opéra, Kochno collection, letter from Dolin to D., 31.3.1926. Dolin writes with touching eagerness in fluent, misspelt French.
133 Bibliothèque Nationale, Opéra, Kochno collection, letter, 20.11.1925.
134 S. Sitwell, correspondence.
135 Kochno, p. 236.
136 Bibliothèque Nationale, Opéra, Kochno collection, letter, 7.4.1926.
137 Lifar, p. 433.
138 Bibliothèque Nationale, Opéra, Kochno collection, design by Miró, reproduced Buckle, *In Search*, p. 108.
139 Ibid., reproduced Buckle, *In Search*, p. 108.
140 Sokolova, pp. 243, 244.
141 Ibid., p. 244.
142 Shead, p. 56. Letter quoted.
143 Danilova, conversations.
144 *Dancing Times*, Mar. 1967, article by Mme Karsavina.
145 Shead, p. 57. Letter quoted.
146 Lifar, pp. 435-7.
147 Ibid., pp. 437, 438.
148 Shead, p. 59. Letter quoted.
149 Stravinsky–Diaghilev, telegram from Sudeikina in Paris to D. in Monte Carlo, 26.4.1926.
150 Danilova, conversations.
151 Sokolova, p. 247.
152 Lifar, p. 439.
153 Ibid.
154 Kochno, p. 237. Manifesto reproduced in full.
155 Lifar, p. 440.
156 Dubrovska, conversations.
157 Balanchine, conversations.
158 Stravinsky–Diaghilev, draft of telegram in Kochno's hand, 6.6.1926.
159 S. Sitwell, correspondence.
160 *Daily Mirror*, 15.6.1926; *Daily Chronicle*, etc.
161 Stravinsky–Diaghilev, telegram, 13.11.1926.
162 De Valois, *Step by Step*, pp. 173, 174.
163 Rieti, correspondence.
164 Hannen Swaffer in *Daily Express*, 16.2.1926: '*Les Noces* filled my cup of bitterness to overflowing'; *The Times*, 15.6.1926: 'If that was the way Russian peasants got married . . . no wonder things have happened as they have'; *Daily News*, 15.6.1926: 'Nothing but ugliness and aimless noise.' The *Daily Mail* and the *Daily Sketch* were more appreciative.
165 Leaflet, text in Macdonald, p. 327. Beaumont states incorrectly that the letter was printed in *The Times*.
166 *Sunday Times*, 20.6.1926.
167 Stravinsky–Diaghilev, telegram, 19.6.1926.
168 *The Times*, 22.6.1926. It is hard to see why Lambert's Sinfonia, Siciliana, Fugue and so

on should be right for Adam and Eve, but not for Romeo and Juliet.

169 *Daily Telegraph*, 22.6.1926.
170 *Yorkshire Post*, 22.6.1926.
171 *Daily Express*, 22.6.1926.
172 *Sunday Times*, 4.7.1926.
173 Lincoln Center, letter from Lady Cunard to D., undated.
174 Cecil Lewis, correspondence. Mr Lewis was the editor of *Self Portrait: Letters and Journals of Charles Ricketts*, which has provided me with such riches. I also studied the Ricketts Mss in the British Library, but Mr Lewis had missed few passages of interest to the historian of ballet.
175 Stravinsky–Diaghilev, telegram, 7.7.1926.
176 *Sunday Times*, 11.7.1926.
177 Sokolova, p. 250.
178 Nikitina, p. 67.
179 Grigoriev, p. 229.
180 Ibid., pp. 229, 230. Telegrams from Nuvel, now in the Stravinsky–Diaghilev Foundation, confirm his presence in Ostend and Le Touquet. It seems Lifar did not dance in these places (Lifar, p. 441).
181 In view of references in his letter to Kochno, quoted below, to the frescoes in the Palais des Papes and in the Ducal Palace of Mantua, Kochno thinks this likely.
182 Kochno, p. 54. Letter quoted.
183 Ibid., p. 54.
184 Ibid., p. 222.
185 Letter (formerly belonging to Grigoriev), quoted Buckle, *In Search*, p. 43.
186 Vera Stravinsky, conversations.
187 Letter (formerly belonging to Grigoriev), quoted Buckle, *In Search*, pp. 43, 44.
188 Stravinsky–Diaghilev, draft telegram, 25.8.1926.
189 Beaton, pp. 127, 128.
190 S. Sitwell, correspondence.
191 Kochno, conversations.
192 Photograph of Diaghilev reproduced Kochno, p. 242.
193 Stravinsky–Diaghilev, telegram from Nuvel in Paris to D. in Florence, 7.9.1926: 'Balanchine expects leave for Florence Thursday.' Dukelsky wrote: 'I left Villennes for Paris on September 8th, picked up Balanchine ...'.
194 S. Sitwell, correspondence.
195 Balanchine, conversations.
196 Ibid.
197 Stravinsky–Diaghilev, telegram, 25.9.1926. (Kochno wrote to his mother from Capri.)
198 Ibid., telegram, 28.9.1926.
199 Ibid., telegrams, 2, 12.10.1926.
200 Clark, p. 158.
201 Lincoln Center, letter from Outhwaite to D., 22.10.1926.
202 Stravinsky–Diaghilev, telegram from Wollheim in Paris to D. in Naples, 1.10.1926.
203 Nikitina, p. 70.
204 Ibid., pp. 69, 70, 71.
205 Sokolova, p. 255.
206 Or did he use what Kochno calls the 'simple backdrop of a washed-out grey' and merely omit Picasso's name from the programme? (Kochno, p. 81).
207 Kochno, conversations.
208 *The Times*, 26.11.1926.
209 Sokolova, p. 256.
210 Beaumont, pp. 263, 264.
211 Kochno, conversations.
212 Sokolova, pp. 251, 252.
213 Designs reproduced Kochno, p. 245.
214 Beaumont, p. 264.
215 S. Sitwell, correspondence.
216 Beaumont, pp. 269, 270.
217 Kochno, conversations.
218 Danilova, conversations.
219 Grigoriev, p. 233.
220 Ibid., p. 234.

CHAPTER 17 1927–8

1 Grigoriev, pp. 234, 235.
2 Lifar, p. 443.
3 Sokolova, p. 257.
4 Kochno, p. 73.
5 Grigoriev, p. 235.
6 Lifar, pp. 443, 444.
7 Kochno, p. 73.
8 Grigoriev, pp. 235, 236. One would have thought that if the music were so slow the ballerina would have finished too soon rather than too late.
9 Massine, p. 170. He speaks of joining the Ballet at Monte Carlo.
10 Grigoriev, p. 236.
11 Lifar tells the story of Diaghilev's acquisition of the letters (pp. 464, 465), but describes talking to Countess Torby in 1928, whereas she died in Sept. 1927. He placed the gala in the wrong year. Grigoriev (pp. 246, 247) copies him. The Grand Duke telegraphed to Diaghilev on 8.10.1927 (Bibliothèque Nationale, Opéra, Kochno collection) thanking him for his 'touchante lettre', presumably on his wife's death. The daughters of Grand Duke Michael and Countess Torby married Sir Harold Wernher and Lord Milford-Haven, so there are British descendants of Pushkin.
12 Massine, pp. 170, 171.
13 Lambert, *Music Ho!*, Part II, Chapter (b) was entitled 'Diaghileff and Stravinsky as Time Travellers'.

14 Haskell, *Diaghilev*, p. 324.
15 De Valois, conversations.
16 Bibliothèque Nationale, Opéra, Kochno collection, letter from Sauguet to D., 12.11.1926: 'Abandonnant la trop dangereuse idée d'une collaboration avec Paul Eluard, qu'il êut certainement refusé, c'est à René Crevel que j'ai parlé de notre projet....' Referred to in Kochno, p. 248.
17 Kochno, pp. 252, 253.
18 Sauguet, conversation.
19 Gabo, conversation.
20 Danilova, conversations.
21 Kochno, conversations.
22 Balanchine, conversations.
23 Sauguet, conversation.
24 Sokolova, p. 259. Much of Sokolova's *Dancing for Diaghilev* was in her own words. Lady Juliet Duff was quick to comment that the passage quoted here had been reworked by her editor.
25 Sauguet, conversation. He liked the mixture.
26 Gabo, conversation.
27 Sauguet, conversation.
28 Massine, p. 172.
29 Markova, conversations.
30 Balanchine, conversations.
31 Stravinsky–Diaghilev, telegram from Wollheim to D., 14.3.1927.
32 Bibliothèque Nationale, Opéra, Kochno collection, letter from Rothermere to D., undated.
33 Kochno, p. 254.
34 Kochno, conversations.
35 Stravinsky–Diaghilev, telegram from D. to Ansermet at Geneva, 10.4.1927.
36 Ibid., telegram, 13.4.1927.
37 Grigoriev, p. 240.
38 Kochno, conversations.
39 Kochno was touched to find this letter among his mother's papers in Apr. 1978, and wrote to me about it.
40 *Le Figaro*, 26.5.1927. Quoting this letter, Lifar (p. 448) inserted the name of Idzikovsky in the list of dancers Diaghilev was so proud of presenting.
41 Gabo, conversation. Also Sauguet, conversation. But Sauguet seemed to think (surely wrongly, in view of the *Figaro* article) that Spessivtseva had 'hurt' herself a week before.
42 Dubrovska, conversations.
43 Stravinsky–Diaghilev, telegram from Dalimier to D., 8.7.1927.
44 Bibliothèque Nationale, Opéra, Kochno collection, telegram from Spessivtseva to D., 10.7.1927.
45 Nikitina, p. 74 et seq.
46 Stravinsky, *Chronicle*, p. 217. *Oedipus Rex* was performed as an opera in Vienna on 23.2.1928 before being performed under Klemperer at the Krolloper, Berlin, two days later (when Schönberg was present and disliked it). Stravinsky hated the staging of Klemperer's production, while admiring its musical side.
47 Benois, *Reminiscences*, p. 382. Kochno, p. 264. Kochno writes that Diaghilev also tried to lure the choreographer Goleizovsky out of the USSR.
48 Malevitch, *Ecrits*, L'Age d'Homme, Lausanne, 1971. Malevitch reacted against Benois' criticism of his *Black Square on a white ground*.
49 Lifar, p. 449 et seq. Sotheby catalogue, 21.6.1973, Lot 44. In one of over 20 letters from Koribut-Kubitovitch to Diaghilev sold in this lot, Diaghilev's cousin wrote (2.12.1924): 'You gave me 200 francs at the station... I have 20 francs in my pocket and live on sandwiches and coffee....'
50 Ibid., pp. 450, 451.
51 Kochno, p. 265.
52 My old friend, the expatriate Russian photographer Cyril Arapoff, always spoke to me of *Le Pas d'acier* as the finest of all Diaghilev's ballets.
53 Kochno, p. 265.
54 Dukelsky, pp. 195–7.
55 Bibliothèque Nationale, Opéra, Kochno collection, quoted Kochno, p. 265.
56 Kochno, p. 272.
57 Nikitina, pp. 79, 80.
58 Stravinsky–Diaghilev, telegram, 14.6.1927.
59 Beaumont, p. 273. As he left a blank for the adjective, it was presumably not 'bloody'.
60 Ibid., p. 274.
61 Stravinsky–Diaghilev, telegrams, June and Jul. 1927.
62 Lincoln Center, letter, 20.6.1927.
63 Stravinsky–Diaghilev, telegram, 20.6.1927.
64 Lincoln Center, invitation.
65 Lincoln Center, letter, 23.6.1927.
66 *The Times*, 21.6.1927.
67 S. Sitwell, correspondence.
68 Stravinsky–Diaghilev, telegram, 24.6.1927.
69 Ibid., telegram 25.6.1927.
70 Lincoln Center, letter, 27.6.1927.
71 Letter from Vaughan Williams to Gwen Raverat, quoted Macdonald, p. 353.
72 Bibliothèque Nationale, Opéra, Kochno collection, letter from Weill to D., 1.7.1927.
73 *Lady*, 28.7.1927.
74 Goossens, pp. 246, 247. Lifar, p. 451.
75 Stravinsky–Diaghilev, telegram, 13.7.1927.
76 Ibid., telegrams, 13, 14.7.1927.
77 Lincoln Center, letter from Sir Saxton Noble to D., 11.7.1927.

78 Ibid., letter from British Brunswick (agency), 13.7.1927.
79 Kochno, conversations.
80 Markova, conversations.
81 Lincoln Center, letter, 18.7.1927.
82 Sokolova, unpublished Mss.
83 Beaumont, pp. 102, 103.
84 Lincoln Center, letter from Burton and Ramsden, solicitors, 20.7.1927.
85 Photograph reproduced *Dance and Dancers*, Jan. 1951.
86 Goossens, pp. 247, 248. The reference for Lady Hawtrey's request is: Stravinsky–Diaghilev, telegram 22.7.1927.
87 Lincoln Center, letter, 15.7.1927.
88 Stravinsky–Diaghilev, bill, Grand Hôtel des Bains, Lido, 30.7.1927–10.8.1927.
89 Ibid., telegram, 8.8.1927.
90 Ibid., hotel bill, Albergo Luna, 10–19.8.1927.
91 Ibid., telegrams, Aug. 1927.
92 Ibid., telegram, 17.9.1927, and others.
93 Kochno, conversations.
94 Lifar, p. 458. He received a letter from Florence written in Sept.
95 Ibid., p. 452.
96 Ibid., pp. 452, 453.
97 Ibid., p. 453.
98 Ibid., p. 459.
99 Nikitina, p. 83.
100 Lifar, pp. 461–3.
101 Sokolova, p. 262 et seq.
102 Lincoln Center, letters; Stravinsky–Diaghilev, telegrams.
103 The known subscribers in 1928 and/or 1929 were Lady Juliet Duff, Mrs Samuel Courtauld, Lady Cunard, Lord Rothermere (Lincoln Center, Juliet Duff letters). Boris Kochno thinks also Sir Saxton Noble.
104 Stravinsky–Diaghilev, telegram from Stravinsky to D., 22.1.1928.
105 Dubrovska, conversations.
106 Lifar, p. 455.
107 Kochno, conversations. Grigoriev wrongly places the cutting up and sale of curtains in 1926 (p. 224).
108 Stravinsky–Diaghilev, telegram from Rosenberg in Paris to D. at Monte Carlo, 4.5.1928.
109 Ibid., telegrams from D. to Rosenberg, 3.5.1928, and from Reber to D., 7.5.1928.
110 Ibid., telegram from Nuvel to D., 5.5.1928.
111 Ibid., telegram from D. to Nuvel, date indecipherable.
112 It is now in the Musée d'Art Moderne, Paris.
113 It is now in the lobby outside the Four Seasons Restaurant in the Seagram Building, New York. It can be seen from Park Avenue.
114 Kochno, pp. 269, 260.
115 Ibid., p. 260.
116 Tyler, pp. 329 et seq. Tyler's evidence of Diaghilev's interjections, with which he has broken up Tchelitchev's surviving scenario (dictated apparently to Charbonnier), are no doubt hearsay: but I have followed him, while making many cuts.
117 Nabokov, p. 151 et seq.
118 Ibid., p. 156.
119 Dukelsky, pp. 208, 209.
120 Kochno, conversations.
121 Stravinsky–Diaghilev, telegram from Beecham to D., 30.4.1928.
122 Grigoriev, p. 249.
123 Danilova, conversations.
124 Dukelsky, p. 210.
125 Nabokov, pp. 156, 157.
126 Kochno, p. 260.
127 Nabokov, pp. 158, 159.
128 Dubrovska, conversations.
129 Beaumont, pp. 287, 288.
130 Kochno, p. 260.
131 Kochno, conversations.
132 Stravinsky, *Chronicle*, p. 234. Kochno conversations.
133 Dubrovska, conversations. But Dubrovska said Tchernicheva's was longer in front than at the back, and her own shorter in front. This Kochno denies.
134 E. W. White, p. 304.
135 Dubrovska, conversations.
136 Balanchine, conversations.
137 *The Mask*, Vol. XV, No. 2. Reprinted Rood, 'Gordon Craig on Movement and Dance', *Dance Horizons*, 1977.
138 Danilova, conversations.
139 *The Times*, 26.6.1928.
140 Balanchine, conversations.
141 Lincoln Center, letter from Lady Diana Cooper to D., undated.
142 Juliet Duff, conversations.
143 *Daily Mail*, 10.7.1928.
144 Beaumont, p. 288.
145 Ibid., pp. 288, 289.
146 Ibid., p. 291.
147 Danilova, conversations.
148 Rambert, p. 128.
149 Stravinsky–Diaghilev, letter from Mrs Courtauld to D., 20.7.1928.
150 Grigoriev, p. 252.
151 Kochno, conversations. Of course, Kochno hoped that Diaghilev would write a complete autobiography.
152 Lifar, p. 469.
153 Stravinsky–Diaghilev, telegrams, 3, 5.9.1928.
154 Ibid., telegram, 2.10.1928.
155 Lifar, pp. 470–73.
156 Kochno, conversations.
157 Stravinsky–Diaghilev, telegrams, 5.10.1928.
158 Ibid., telegram, 10.10.1928.

159 Ibid., telegram from Prokofiev to D., 11.10.1928.
160 Ibid., telegram from D. to Grigoriev, 12.10.1928.
161 Ibid., telegram from Lifar in Milan to D. in Berlin: 'Nous attendons.' 18.10.1928.
162 Lifar, p. 473.
163 Ibid.
164 Stravinsky–Diaghilev, bill, Midland Hotel. Also telegram from Barocchi.
165 Ibid., telegram from Grigoriev in Glasgow to D. in Birmingham, 11.11.1928.
166 *Manchester Guardian*, 13.11.1928.
167 Markova, conversations. But Lifar describes Diaghilev snubbing Nikitina on the English tour (p. 481).
168 Lifar, p. 473.
169 Grigoriev writes of visiting 'four of the largest towns' and only names Manchester and Edinburgh. Macdonald, who also quotes Glasgow and Liverpool papers, takes him at his word and omits Birmingham from her list. She makes the ballet spend from 12 till 24.12.1928 at Manchester.
170 Stravinsky–Diaghilev, telegram, 21.11.1928.
171 Ibid., telegram, 26.11.1928.
172 Letter quoted Lifar, pp. 474, 475.
173 Markevitch, conversations.
174 Sauguet, conversation.
175 Markevitch, conversations.
176 Ibid.
177 Kochno, conversations.
178 Lifar, p. 475. 'Prokofiev had already composed a good half of his ballet,' Diaghilev wrote to Lifar. See next note.
179 Serov, p. 173: 'He had already completed the rough draft of the piano score.'
180 Lifar, p. 475. Rieti does not remember meeting Meyerhold.
181 Ibid., pp. 475, 476. 'How very typical of Diaghilev the last remark is!' Lifar rightly commented.
182 Ibid., p. 476. Tchelitchev did a drawing of the bony, beaky Rubinstein with knobbly knees, on point, as an ostrich.
183 Stravinsky–Diaghilev, telegrams, 25,

27.11.1928. Grigoriev's statement (p. 253) that 'though we usually had good houses on our first nights, our other performances were extremely ill attended' appears not to be true.
184 Letter quoted Lifar, pp. 476, 477.
185 Stravinsky–Diaghilev, telegrams, 27, 29.11.1928.
186 Ibid., telegram, 30.11.1928.
187 Lifar, p. 478. Letter quoted.
188 Lifar, pp. 479, 480. Letter quoted.
189 Ibid., p. 480. Chirico was to receive 15,000 francs, half payable on receipt of the sketches, the other half on the day after the *première*. He was to supervise the execution of the décor. The draft agreement in Diaghilev's hand was exchanged with a letter from Chirico, dated 29.11.1928. At the foot of the agreement Chirico later wrote that he had been paid in full, Monte Carlo, 9.5.1929. Bibliothèque Nationale, Opéra, Kochno collection.
190 Ibid., p. 480.
191 Stravinsky–Diaghilev, hotel bill.
192 Ibid., telegrams from Wollheim to D., 30.11.1928, 3.12.1928.
193 Photograph exhibited Diaghilev Exhibition, 1954.
194 Ibid. In 1954 Grigoriev told me this photograph was taken in Edinburgh.
195 *Liverpool Echo*, 12.12.1928.
196 Stravinsky–Diaghilev, draft of Diaghilev's telegram to Rothermere.
197 Ibid., telegrams, 11, 14.12.1928.
198 Dubrovska, conversations.
199 Lifar, pp. 485–7.
200 Sokolova, p. 269.
201 Karsavina, conversations.
202 Markevitch, conversations.
203 Lifar, p. 489.
204 Kessler, pp. 580, 581.
205 Lincoln Center, letters.
206 Ibid., letter from Dolin to D. (in English), 25.12.1928.
207 Dolin had written to Diaghilev on 31.3.1926, asking if he might rejoin the Ballet. Bibliothèque Nationale, Opéra, Kochno collection.

CHAPTER 18 1929

1 Kochno, correspondence. Kochno corrected an impression which Mme Stravinsky had given me – that Diaghilev deliberately tried to lose weight.
2 Vera Stravinsky, conversations. The last letter D. wrote to Stravinsky was from Venice on 8.8.1928. He told him *Apollo* had been given five times in London; asked jealously if it was true Rubinstein wanted to perform it; expressed the opinion that Beecham

would conduct *Le Sacre* very well; said he was hoping to go to Mount Athos; and announced the gift of a Russian typewriter he had found for Igor. In reply, Stravinsky expressed doubts about Beecham and asked for oleographic reproductions of ikons and a wooden cross blessed on Mount Athos. (Stravinsky Archives.)
3 Kochno, conversations. With the result, Kochno wrote to me, that 'l'artifice était

visible.' See also Dolin, *Divertissement*, p. 197.

4 Ibid.

5 I had written 'so chic and witty', both of which Mme Danilova *is*. But Kochno corrected me, writing 'she was neither at that time', and made me substitute the phrase in the text.

6 Kochno, correspondence.

7 Grigoriev, p. 256.

8 Lincoln Center, letter from Dolin to D., 5.1.1929.

9 Lifar, p. 414.

10 Stravinsky–Diaghilev, bills for Diaghilev, Kochno and Lifar at Grand Hôtel, Paris, 1–7.1.1929, for Diaghilev and Kochno at the same hotel, 7–13.1.1929, and for Lifar at the Grand Hôtel d'Orsay, Bordeaux, 7–13.1.1929.

11 Markova, conversations.

12 Stravinsky–Diaghilev, telegram from Matisse to D., 30.1.1929. The telegraphic correspondence with Michel Georges-Michel is in the same collection.

13 Bibliothèque Nationale, Opéra, Kochno collection, letter, undated, from Gris to D. The implication was that Matisse had lost money by working for *Le Chant du rossignol*.

14 Kochno, p. 274.

15 Kochno, correspondence.

16 Hindemith Archives, letter from Hindemith to D., 2.1.1929.

17 Stravinsky–Diaghilev, telegrams from Frau Hindemith. Also Hindemith Archives, letters.

18 Bibliothèque Nationale, Opéra, Kochno collection, letter from Rieti to D., 27.2.1929, quoted Kochno, p. 270.

19 Stravinsky–Diaghilev, telegrams, Jan.–Apr. 1929.

20 Ibid., telegram from Nuvel to D., 22.3.1929.

21 Ibid., telegram from Wollheim to D., 11.4.1929.

22 Lifar, p. 491. Letter quoted.

23 Ibid.

24 Ibid., pp. 492, 494.

25 Kochno, conversations.

26 Lifar, pp. 494, 495.

27 Letter formerly belonging to Grigoriev, reproduced Buckle, *In Search*, p. 44.

28 Stravinsky–Diaghilev, telegram, 11.3.1929.

29 Ibid., telegram from Grigoriev to D., 15.3.1929.

30 Ibid., bill, Hôtel de Paris. Diaghilev arrived on 21.3.1929.

31 Kochno, conversations.

32 Stravinsky–Diaghilev, telegram, date indecipherable.

33 Ibid., telegram from D. to Ansermet. Date indecipherable, but it must have been just

before one of Diaghilev's departures to Paris: 'Shall be at Grand Hôtel tomorrow.'

34 Lincoln Center, letter from Incorporated Society of Authors, Playwrights and Composers to Nuvel, 20.4.1928.

35 Ibid., letter from S. Sitwell in Amalfi to D., 1.3.1929, in French.

36 Ibid., postcard from Lambert to D., 4.3.1929.

37 Ibid., letter from Prunières to D., undated.

38 Kochno, conversations.

39 Ibid.

40 Dolin, *Divertissement*, p. 199.

41 Sokolova, p. 272. On 8.4.1929.

42 Stravinsky–Diaghilev, telegrams, 4.4.1929 and 28.3.1929.

43 Ibid., telegram from Wollheim to D., 29.4.1929.

44 Kochno, p. 275.

45 Balanchine, conversations.

46 Courthion, p. 204.

47 Kochno, p. 275.

48 Kochno, correspondence.

49 Kochno, p. 275.

50 Stravinsky–Diaghilev, bill, Grand Hôtel, Paris. Diaghilev arrived 27.4.1929.

51 Dukelsky, pp. 216, 217.

52 Markevitch, conversations.

53 Stravinsky–Diaghilev, telegrams, 1, 2.5.1929.

54 Ibid., telegram from Grigoriev at Monte Carlo to D. in Paris, 10.5.1929.

55 Ibid., telegram, 13.5.1929.

56 Lincoln Center, letter from W. Warden to D., 15.5.1929.

57 Ibid., letter from Outhwaite to D., 18.5.1929.

58 Ibid., letter from Lady Juliet Duff to D., undated.

59 Ibid., letter from Lady Juliet Duff to D., undated.

60 Vera Stravinsky, conversations.

61 Grigoriev, p. 260.

62 Serov, p. 175.

63 Courthion, p. 206. In the same letter Rouault wrote, 'In my opinion, the man who writes the libretto should be the choreographer and the set decorator as well.' This indeed would be an ideal solution.

64 Grigoriev, pp. 260, 261. Also Lifar, p. 499.

65 Lifar, pp. 500, 501.

66 Ibid., pp. 501, 502.

67 Balanchine, conversations. The table was not only turned upside down to become a ship, but, in the final scene, was the gate in an imaginary fence round the Father's house. This last use for it was Kochno's idea.

68 Lifar, p. 502.

69 Balanchine, conversations.

70 Danilova, conversation.

71 Lifar, pp. 504, 505. Lifar, in fact, wrote, 'Sergei Pavlovitch raised his glass, gazed at me for some time and then his eyes dimmed with tears.... "Thank you, thank you, Seriozha. You are a great, a true artist. There is nothing more I can teach you.... I can only learn from you now...."' It had been a remarkable evening apart from Lifar, for Stravinsky had conducted *Renard* and Prokofiev *Le Fils prodigue*.
72 Kochno, p. 270.
73 Diaghilev, Memoirs.
74 Kochno, correspondence.
75 Stravinsky–Diaghilev, telegram, 2.6.1929.
76 Lincoln Center, letter from Lady Juliet Duff, 12.6.1929.
77 Stravinsky–Diaghilev, telegram from Wollheim to D., 13.6.1929.
78 Kochno, conversations.
79 Jean Renoir, pp. 359, 360. This could have been 1910, 1911, 1912, 1913 or 1914. Jean Renoir writes of Edwards carrying the crippled Renoir up a big staircase, which sounds like the Opéra, but his whole account (particularly the description of Misia's life) is fantastic. Apparently Renoir saw the ballet more than once, and was 'carried away' by it. Kochno thinks Diaghilev never met Renoir, for Diaghilev often exclaimed, 'What a décor Renoir might have made for me!'
80 Courthion, p. 204.
81 Markevitch, conversations.
82 Sauguet, conversation.
83 Grigoriev, pp. 261, 262.
84 Dolin, *Divertissement*, pp. 202, 203. It had been quite a Berlin season for Stravinsky too, for he had played his Piano Concerto under Klemperer in a programme which included *Apollo* and *Les Noces* on 17.7.1929.
85 Ibid., p. 203.
86 Stravinsky–Diaghilev, telegram from Comptoir d'Escompte to D. in Berlin, 21.6.1929.
87 Ibid., telegram from D. to Comptoir d'Escompte, 28.6.1929. Diaghilev and Kochno travelled on the same train as Stravinsky and Vera without speaking.
88 Vera Stravinsky, conversations. On 19.6.1929 Stravinsky had written to Ansermet in Berlin: 'Let Diaghilev know that I will be in London at the same time he is there, and living at Albemarle Court.... Since he has avoided any encounter with me for some time ... I think he should be informed of my plans.' (Stravinsky Archives, letter quoted by Robert Craft, *Ballet Review*, Vol. VI, No. 4, p. 77).
89 *Observer*, 30.6.1929.
90 Dolin, p. 205.
91 *The Times*, 2.7.1929.
92 *Daily Mail*, 2.7.1929.
93 Karsavina, p. 295.
94 *Daily Mail*, 4.7.1929.
95 Kochno, conversations.
96 *Morning Post*, 9.7.1929.
97 *Nation and Athenaeum*, 13.7.1929.
98 *Saturday Review*, 17.7.1929.
99 Personal reminiscence of the author's.
100 Dolin, p. 207.
101 *Sunday Dispatch*, 14.7.1929, and *New York Times*, 14.7.1929.
102 Dorothy Dickson, conversations.
103 Sokolova, pp. 278, 279.
104 *New York Times*, 14.7.1929.
105 Dolin, p. 207.
106 Lincoln Center, letter from Mrs Courtauld to D., 4.7.1929.
107 Stravinsky–Diaghilev, telegram, 11.7.1929. Misia Sert telegraphed, 'avec une amie.' Markevitch said this was Iya Abdy.
108 *The Times*, 13.7.1929.
109 Markevitch, conversations. The French for 'grand piano' is '*piano à queue*', and, as '*une queue*' is slang for a penis, there is a pun which is untranslatable.
110 Kochno, conversations.
111 Gabo, conversation.
112 Markevitch, conversations.
113 Sokolova, p. 277.
114 Stravinsky–Diaghilev, restaurant bill for £3 19s 9d, signed (as usual) by Diaghilev. We can guess that Diaghilev's guests were Misia Sert, Lady Abdy, Kochno, Lifar and Markevitch.
115 Markevitch, conversations.
116 *The Times*, 15.7.1929.
117 Lincoln Center, letter, 2.7.1929. Mrs Grenfell had also, in the same invitation, asked Diaghilev and Lifar to lunch on the 9th.
118 Markova, conversations.
119 Dolin, p. 209.
120 Lincoln Center, invitation. Lifar was included in the invitation.
121 Ibid., letter, 15.7.1929. The 'dinner' was at 6.30 p.m. 'Bring anyone.'
122 Ibid., letter from Lady Juliet Duff to D., 20.7.1929.
123 *Daily Express*, 23.7.1929.
124 *Evening News*, 23.7.1929.
125 Stravinsky–Diaghilev, telegram from Nuvel to Wollheim, 23.7.1929.
126 Nikitina, p. 94.
127 Sauguet, conversations.
128 Markova, conversations. Dame Alicia thought the musical background of her talk with Diaghilev was *Prince Igor*, but the programme states otherwise. Kochno does not think Diaghilev really intended to revive *Giselle*.

129 Covent Garden programme.
130 Acton, pp. 221, 222.
131 Danilova, conversation.
132 Sokolova, p. 279.
133 Lifar, p. 508. Lifar wrote, 'With Grigoriev ...[Diaghilev] had fallen out. ...' This may be just as untrue as Lifar's statement that Diaghilev intended to get rid of Balanchine. If Diaghilev planned to part with Balanchine or Grigoriev, he was a bigger fool than I think.
134 But Grigoriev wrote that this farewell took place after the last night of the season, which was untrue.
135 Sokolova, p. 275.
136 Acton, p. 222.
137 Acton, correspondence.
138 Haskell, p. 340.
139 Kochno, conversations.
140 Haskell, p. 341.
141 Ibid.
142 Stravinsky–Diaghilev, telegram from Wollheim in London to D. in Paris, 26.7.1929.
143 Markova, conversations.
144 Dolin, p. 210.
145 Dubrovska, conversations.
146 Letter, evidently written on Saturday, 27.7.1929, quoted Lifar, p. 509.
147 Markevitch, conversations.
148 Kochno, conversations. Cassandre designed a number of ballets after Diaghilev's death.
149 Baden-Baden Festival programme, looked up for me by Peter Heyworth. He also pointed out to me that Diaghilev and Markevitch had missed the Hindemith-Weill-Brecht collaboration, *Lindberghsflug*, on 27.7.1929.
150 Nabokov, p. 159.
151 Markevitch, conversations. I wrote to Mme Milhaud about this, but she told me that all her husband's possessions, including the film, were looted or destroyed in her Paris flat during the war.
152 Ibid.
153 Ibid.
154 Lifar, p. 511. Letter quoted.
155 Markevitch, conversations.
156 Ibid.
157 Kochno, conversations.
158 Lifar, p. 510.
159 Markevitch, conversations.
160 Kochno, conversations.
161 Lifar, pp. 511–17.
162 Kochno, conversations. Some of the account that follows appeared in Kochno, pp. 278, 279. On the afternoon of 12.2.1978 Boris Kochno read me his description of Diaghilev's last days, written immediately after his friend's death. I took down a breathless abbreviation of his words, in a mixture of French and English. (With this, a few observations of my own – such as the sentence with the quotation from Victor Hugo – are interspersed.) I was late for a rendezvous with Markevitch, who had come from the South of France to spend a few hours with me. (We were to meet at the Diaghilev Exhibition at Le Centre Culturel du Marais.) It was snowing outside. Then Kochno, after a number of telephone calls, succeeded in ordering me a taxi. He had spent many hours working with me during the past week, as he had done in the course of my four-day visit to Paris a year before. I owed so much of my book to him. I was only half-an-hour late for Markevitch, who, at dinner that evening, told me his side of the Diaghilev story, never before recorded. Of course, both Kochno and Markevitch read through this final chapter when I had rewritten it to incorporate the new information they had given me.
163 Kochno, conversations.
164 Sokolova, p. 280.
165 Dolin, *Divertissement*, p. 214.
166 Grigoriev, p. 265.
167 Dubrovska, conversations.
168 Kochno's libretto in the score of *Le Bal*, Universal Editions.

Bibliography

ABRAHAM, GERALD, and CALVOCORESSI, M. D., *Masters of Russian Music*, Duckworth, London, 1936.

ACTON, HAROLD, *Memoirs of an Aesthete*, Methuen, London, 1948.

ANSERMET, ERNEST, *Ecrits sur la musique*, à la Baconnière, Neufchâtel, 1971.

ARMITAGE, MERLE, *Accent on Life*, Iowa State University, 1965.

ASTRUC, GABRIEL, *Le Pavillon des fantômes*, Grasset, Paris, 1929.

'Le Premier Feu d'Artifice' in *La Revue Musicale*, 1 December 1930 (Paris).

BALLET (magazine), ed. Richard Buckle, 1939–53.

BARBIER, GEORGE, and MIOMANDRE, FRANCIS DE, *Nijinsky*, Bernouard, Paris, 1912.

BARON, WENDY, *Miss Ethel Sands and Her Circle*, Peter Owen, London, 1977.

BEATON, CECIL, *Diaries 1922–1939: The Wandering Years*, Weidenfeld, London; Brown & Co., Boston, 1961.

BEAUMONT, CYRIL, *The Complete Book of Ballets*, Putnam, London, 1937; Revised 1949, 1951.

The Diaghilev Ballet in London, Putnam, London, 1940.

Michel Fokine and his Ballets, Beaumont, London, 1935.

Vaslav Nijinsky, Beaumont, London, 1932.

BEDELLS, PHYLLIS, *My Dancing Days*, Phoenix House, London, 1954.

BEECHAM, THOMAS, *A Mingled Chime: Leaves from an Autobiography*, White Lion, London, 1973.

BENNETT, ARNOLD, *The Journals of Arnold Bennett, 1911–1921*, edited by Newman Flower, Cassell, London, 1932.

BENOIS, ALEXANDRE, *Early Memories of Diaghilev*, introduction to the catalogue of the Diaghilev Exhibition, 1954.

Memoirs, Vol. I, translated by Moura Budberg, Chatto, London, 1964.

Memoirs, Vol. II, translated by Moura Budberg, Chatto, London, 1964.

Reminiscences of the Russian Ballet, translated by Mary Britnieva, Putnam, London, 1941.

BENSON, E. F., *As We Were*, Longmans. London, 1930; Penguin, Harmondsworth, 1938.

BLANCHE, JACQUES-EMILE, *Portraits* II, trans. and ed. Walter Clement, Dent, London, 1939.
   Cahiers d'un artiste, 6 vols, Paris, 1915–20.
BOURMAN, ANATOLE (with D. Lyman), *The Tragedy of Nijinsky*, Hale, London, 1937.
BRAUN, EDWARD, *Meyerhold on Theatre*, Methuen, London, 1969.
BUCHANAN, MERIEL, *Ambassador's Daughter*, Cassell, London, 1958.
BUCKLE, RICHARD, *In Search of Diaghilev*, Sidgwick, London, 1955.
   Nijinsky, Weidenfeld, London, 1971; Avon, New York, 1975; Penguin, London, 1975.
CALVOCORESSI, M. D., *Musicians Gallery*, Faber, London, 1933; Reissued 1934.
CALVOCORESSI, M. D., and ABRAHAM, G., *Music and Ballet*, Faber, London, 1938.
CASTILLO, ALBERTO DEL, *José Maria Sert, su vida y su obra*, Argos, Barcelona, 1947.
CHALIAPIN, FEODOR, *Man and Mask*, Gollancz, London, 1932.
CHAPLIN, CHARLES, *My Autobiography*, Bodley Head, London, 1964.
CHUJOY, ANATOLE, 'Russian Balletomania' in *Dance Index*, Vol. VII, no. 3, March 1948 (New York).
CLARK, KENNETH, *Another Part of the Wood*, Murray, London, 1974.
CLARKE, MARY, *Dancers of Mercury*, A. & C. Black, London, 1962.
COCHRAN, C. B., *The Secrets of a Showman*, Heinemann, London, 1925.
COCTEAU, JEAN, *Cock and Harlequin*, translated by Rollo H. Myers, Egoist Press, London, 1921.
   La Difficulté d'Etre, Paul Morihien, Paris, 1947.
   Thomas L'Imposteur, Nouvelle Revue Française, Paris, 1923.
   Journals, Museum Press, London, 1957.
   Entre Picasso et Radiguet, ed. André Fermigler, Series *Miroirs de l'Art*, Paris, 1967.
COOPER, DOUGLAS, *The Courtauld Collection*, University of London–Courtauld Institute, London, 1954.
   Picasso Theatre, Weidenfeld, London, 1968.
COURTHION, PIERRE, *Georges Rouault*, Thames & Hudson, London, 1962.
COSSART, MICHAEL DE, *The Food of Love*, Princesse Edmond de Polignac (1865–1943) and her Salon, Hamish Hamilton, London, 1978.
CRAFT, ROBERT, see STRAVINSKY.
CRAIG, GORDON, *Gordon Craig on Movement and Dance*, Dance Horizons, New York, 1977.
DANDRÉ, V., *Anna Pavlova*, Cassell, London, 1932.
DEBUSSY, CLAUDE, *Lettres de Claude Debussy à son editeur*, Durand, Paris, 1927.
DENIS, MAURICE, *Journal*, Tome II (1905–20), La Colombe, Paris, 1957.
DE VALOIS, NINETTE, *Step by Step*, W. H. Allen, London, 1977.
   Invitation to the Ballet, John Lane/Bodley Head, London, 1937.
DIAGHILEV, S. P., *D. E. Levitsky, 1735–1822*, St Petersburg, 1901.
DOBUJINSKY, M. V., *Memoirs* (Vospominania), Vol. I, New York, 1976.
DOLIN, ANTON, *Divertissement*, Sampson Low, Marston & Co., London, 1930.

588

The Sleeping Ballerina: The Story of Olga Spessivtseva, Muller, London, 1966.
Markova, W. H. Allen, London, 1953.
DUKELSKY, VLADIMIR, *Passport to Paris*, Little Brown, Boston, 1955.
DUNCAN, ISADORA, *My Life*, Gollancz, London, 1928; Sphere, London, 1968.
ERTE (Roman de Tirtoff), *Things I Remember*, Owen, London, 1975.
FOKINE, MICHEL, *Against the Tide*, Leningrad and Moscow, 1962.
Memoirs of a Ballet Master, translated by Vitale Fokine; edited by Anatole Chujoy, Little Brown, Boston, 1961; Constable, London, 1961.
GEVA, TAMARA, *Split Seconds*, Harper & Row, New York and London, 1972.
GOOSSENS, EUGENE, *Overture and Beginners*, Methuen, London, 1951.
GRABAR, J. E., *My Life*, Iskusskvo, Moscow–Leningrad, 1937.
GRIGORIEV, S. L., *The Diaghilev Ballet 1909–1929*, Constable, London, 1953; Penguin, London, 1960.
GUEST, IVOR, *Adeline Genée*, A. & C. Black, London, 1958.
HAHN, REYNALDO, *Notes: Journal d'un musicien*, Plon, Paris, 1933.
HAMNETT, NINA, *Laughing Torso*, Constable, London, 1932.
HASKELL, ARNOLD, *Balletomania*, Gollancz, London, 1934.
Diaghileff, Gollancz, London, 1935.
HOFMANNSTHAL, HUGO VON, and STRAUSS, RICHARD, *Correspondence between Richard Strauss and Hugo von Hofmannsthal*, Collins, London, 1961.
HUGO, JEAN, *Avant d'oublier*, Fayard, Paris, 1976.
HUGO, VICTOR, *A life related by one who has witnessed it*, Vol. II, W. H. Allen, London, 1863.
IKONNIKOV, *Noblesse Russe*, Paris, 1957.
IMPERIAL THEATRES, Annual of
INGHELBRECHT, D. E., *The Conductor's World*, translated by G. Prerauer and S. Malcolm Kirk, P. Nevill, London and New York, 1953.
JANKELEVITCH, VLADMIR, *Ravel*, Grove Press, New York; and Calder, London, 1959 (paperback).
JOHNSON, A. E., *The Russian Ballet*, Constable, London, 1913.
JONES, ROBERT EDMOND, 'Nijinsky and Til Eulenspiegel' in *Dance Index*, Vol. IV, no. 4, April 1945 (New York).
KAHNWEILER, DANIEL, *Juan Gris: His Life and Work*, translated by D. Cooper, Lund Humphries, London, 1947.
KARSAVINA, TAMARA, *Theatre Street*, Heinemann, London, 1930; Revised edition, Constable, London, 1948; Dutton (paperback), New York, 1961.
KCHESSINSKAYA, M. F., *Dancing in St Petersburg*, Gollancz, London, 1960.
KENNET, LADY (KATHLEEN SCOTT), *Self-portrait of an Artist*, Murray, London, 1949.
KESSLER, COUNT HARRY, *The Diaries of a Cosmopolitan*, translated and edited by Charles Kessler, Weidenfeld, London, 1971.
KHAN, AGA, *The Memoirs of Aga Khan*, Cassell/Constable, London, 1954.
KIRSTEIN, LINCOLN, *Fokine*, British-Continental Press, London, 1934.
Three Pamphlets Collected, Dance Horizons, New York, 1967.
KOCHNO, BORIS, *Diaghilev and the Ballets Russes*, translated by Adrienne Foulke, Harper & Row, New York, 1970; Allen Lane/Penguin Press, London, 1971.
Le Ballet, Hachette, Paris, 1954.

KRAMER, DALE, *Heywood Broun*, Current Books, A. A. Wyn, New York, 1949.

KYASHT, LYDIA, *Romantic Recollections*, edited by Erica Beale, Brentano, London, 1929.

LAMBERT, CONSTANT, *Music Ho!*, Faber, London, 1934.

LEGAT, NICOLAS, *Ballets Russes*, Methuen, London, 1939.

LESKOV, NICOLAI, *Anecdotes of Archiepiscopal Life*, Vol. VI of *Complete Works*, Moscow, 1956–8.

LIEVEN, PRINCE PETER, *The Birth of Ballets Russes*, translated by L. Zarine, Allen & Unwin, London, 1936.

LIFAR, SERGE, *Serge Diaghilev*, Putnam, London, 1940.
Ma Vie, Hutchinson, London, 1970.

LOCKSPEISER, EDWARD, *Debussy*, Dent, London, 1936; Revised 1951, 1963.
Debussy, His Life and Mind, Vol. II, Cassell, London, 1965.

LOGUINE, TATIANA (ed.), *Gontcharova et Larionov*, Klincksieck, Paris, 1971.

LYONS, MARVIN, *Russia in original photographs, 1860–1920*, edited by Andrew Wheatcroft, Routledge, London, 1977.

MACDONALD, NESTA, *Diaghilev Observed*, Dance Horizons, New York, and Dance Books, London, 1975.

MALEVITCH, KASIMIR, *Ecrits*.

MANUEL, ROLAND, *Maurice Ravel*, translated by Cynthia Jolly, Dobson, London, 1947.

MARSH, EDWARD, *A Number of People*, Heinemann/Hamish Hamilton, London, 1939.
Rupert Brooke: A Memoir, Sidgwick and Jackson, London, 1918.

MASSINE, LEONIDE, *My Life in Ballet*, edited by Phyllis Hartnoll and Robert Rubens, Macmillan, London, 1968.

MAYAKOVSKY, VLADIMIR, *Life and Works*, translated and edited by Herbert Marshall, Dobson, London, 1965.

MELBA, NELLIE, *Melodies and Memories*, Butterworth, London, 1925.

MILHAUD, DARIUS, *Notes Without Music*, Dobson, London, 1952.

MIR ISSKUTSVA, 12 volumes, St Petersburg, 1899–1904.

MORAND, PAUL, *Journal d'un attaché d'ambassade, 1916–17*, Table Ronde, Paris, 1949.
L'Allure de Chanel, Hermann, Paris, 1976.

MORRELL, LADY OTTOLINE, *Ottoline*, edited by Robert Gathorne-Hardy, Faber, London, 1963.

MOSSOLOV, A. A., *At the Court of the Last Tsar*, translated by E. W. Dickes, edited by A. A. Pilenco, Methuen, London, 1935.

NABOKOV, NICOLAS, *Bagazh*, Atheneum, New York, 1975.

NEKLUDOV, ANATOLY, *Diplomatic Reminiscences*, Murray, London, 1920.

NIJINSKA, BRONISLAVA, 'Création des "Noces"' in *Gontcharova et Larionov*, edited by Tatiana Loguine, Klincksieck, Paris, 1971.

NIJINSKY, ROMOLA, *The Last Days of Nijinsky*, Gollancz, London, 1952.
Nijinsky, Gollancz, London, 1933; Penguin, London, 1960; Sphere, London, 1970.

NIJINSKY, VASLAV, *The Diary of Vaslav Nijinsky*, translated and edited by Romola Nijinsky, Gollancz, London, 1937; Panther, London, 1962.

NIKITINA, ALICE, *Nikitina*, translated by Moura Budberg, Allan Wingate, London, 1959.

PAINTER, G. D., *Marcel Proust*, Vol. II, Chatto, London, 1965.

POLIGNAC, PRINCESSE EDMOND DE, 'Memoirs' in *Horizon*, Vol. XII, No. 68, August 1945.

POLUNIN, VLADIMIR, *The Continental Method of Scenepainting*, Beaumont, London, 1927.

POULENC, FRANCIS, *Correspondance, 1915–1963*, edited by Hélène de Wendel, Preface D. Milhaud, Editions du Seuil, Paris, 1967.

PROPERT, W. A., *The Russian Ballet in Western Europe, 1909–1920*, Bodley Head, London, 1921.

The Russian Ballet, 1921–1929, Bodley Head, London, 1931.

PROUST, MARCEL, *Lettres à Reynaldo Hahn*, edited by Philippe Kolb, Paris, 1956.

RAMBERT, MARIE, *Quicksilver*, Macmillan, London, 1972.

RAMUZ, C. F., *Souvenirs sur I. Strawinsky*, Gallimard, Paris, 1929.

REISS, FRANÇOISE, *Nijinsky*, A. & C. Black, London, 1960.

RENOIR, JEAN, *Renoir, My Father*, Collins, London, 1962.

RICKETTS, CHARLES, *Self Portrait*, edited by Cecil Lewis, Peter Davies, London, 1939.

RIMSKY-KORSAKOV, N. A., *My Musical Life*, translated by J. A. Joffé, edited by Carl van Vechten, Secker, London, 1924; Eulenburg Books, London, 1974.

RIVIÈRE, JACQUES, 'Le Sacre du Printemps' in *Nouvelle Revue Française*, Paris, November 1913.

ROSENTHAL, HAROLD, *Two Centuries of Opera at Covent Garden*, Putnam, London, 1958.

ROUX, CHARLES-EDMONDE, *L'Irrégulière*, Grasset, Paris, 1974; *Chanel*, translated by Nancy Amphoux, Cape, London, 1976.

RZWESKY, FR. O. P., *A travers l'invisible cristal*, Plon, Paris, 1976.

SANDOZ, MAURICE, *The Crystal Salt Cellar*, Guildford Press, London, 1954.

SEROV, VICTOR, *Sergei Prokofiev*, Leslie Frewin, London, 1969; Readers Digest, New York, 1968.

SERT, MISIA, *Two or Three Muses*, Museum Press, London, 1953.

SETON-WATSON, HUGH, *The Decline of Imperial Russia, 1855–1914*, Methuen, London, 1952.

SHEAD, RICHARD, *Constant Lambert*, with a Memoir by Anthony Powell, Simon Publications, London, 1973.

SITWELL, OSBERT, *Great Morning*, Macmillan, London, 1948.

Laughter in the Next Room, Macmillan, London, 1949.

SLONIMSKY, YURI, 'Marius Petipa', edited by Anatole Chujoy, in *Dance Index*, Vol. VI, Nos 5 and 6, May–June 1947 (New York).

SOKOLOVA, LYDIA, *Dancing for Diaghilev*, edited by Richard Buckle, Murray, London, 1960.

SOTHEBY PARKE-BERNET, Catalogues of sales of material relating to the Diaghilev Ballet: 15 October 1963; 27 May 1964; 13 June 1967; 16, 17 and 18 July 1968; 9 and 10 July 1969; 15, 16 and 19 December 1969.

STEEGMULLER, FRANCIS, *Cocteau*, Macmillan, London, 1970.

STRAVINSKY, IGOR, *Chroniques de ma vie*, Denoël et Steele, Paris, 1935; *Chronicle of My life*, Gollancz, London, 1936.
The Rite of Spring, Sketches 1911–1913, Boosey and Hawkes, London, 1969.
(with Robert Craft), *Conversations*, Faber, London, 1959.
(with Robert Craft), *Expositions and Developments*, Faber, London, 1962.
(with Robert Craft), *Memories and Commentaries*, Faber, London, 1962.

SURVAGE, LÉOPOLD, 'Larionov, Homme Actif; Gontcharova, Femme Douce et Discrète' in *Gontcharova et Larionov*, edited by Tatiana Loguine, Klincksieck, Paris, 1971.

SVETLOV, VALERIEN, *Le Ballet contemporain*, designed by Leon Bakst, Golicke & Willborg, St Petersburg; translated by M. D. Calvocoressi, Brunoff, Paris, 1912.
Tamara Karsavina, translated by H. de Vere Beauclerk and Nadia Evrenov, edited by Cyril Beaumont, Beaumont, London, 1922.

TCHEKHOV, ANTON, *Letters*, translated by Heim, Bodley Head, London, 1973.

TENISHEV, PRINCESS, *Impressions of My Life* (in Russian), Paris, 1933.

TERRY, ELLEN, *The Russian Ballet*, Sidgwick, London, 1913.

TYLER, PARKER, *The Divine Comedy of Pavel Tchelitchew*, Fleet Publishing, New York, 1967.

VAN VECHTEN, CARL, 'Vaslav Nijinsky' in *Interpreters*, Knopf, New York, 1917; Reprinted in *Dance Index*, Vol. I, Nos 9–11, September–November 1942 (New York); and in Paul Magriel, *Nijinsky*, Holt, New York, 1946.

VAUDOYER, JEAN-LOUIS, 'Variations sur les Ballets Russes' in *La Revue de Paris*, July 1910 (Paris).

VAUGHAN, DAVID, 'Pavlova's American "Beauty"' in *Ballet Review*, Vol. 3, No. 2, 1969 (New York).

VAUGHAN WILLIAMS, URSULA, *R.V.W.: A Biography of Ralph Vaughan Williams*, O.U.P., London, 1964.

WHITE, E. WALTER, *Stravinsky: The Composer and His Works*, Faber, London, 1966.

WHITWORTH, GEOFFREY, *The Art of Nijinsky*, Chatto, London 1913.

WILDE, OSCAR, *The Letters of Oscar Wilde*, edited by Rupert Hart-Davis, Hart-Davis, London, 1962.
Impressions of America, edited by Stuart Mason, Keystone Press, Sunderland, 1906.

WOLKONSKY, PRINCE SERGE, *My Reminiscences*, translated by A. E. Charnot, 2 vols, Hutchinson, London, 1925.

WORLD OF ART, see *MIR ISSKUTSVA*.

Index

Abbreviations: D=Sergei Pavlovitch Diaghilev; RB=Russian Ballet.
Figures in italic refer to line illustrations in the text.
References to notes are indicated thus: 11/n60 (i.e. chapter 11, note 60).